D1165554

Handbook of Probability

Handbook of Probability

Theory and Applications

Tamás Rudas Editor

Eötvös Loránd University, Budapest

SAGE Publications
Los Angeles • London • New Delhi • Singapore

For information:

Sage Publications, Inc.
2455 Teller Road
Thousand Oaks, California 91320
E-mail: order@sagepub.com

Sage Publications Ltd.
1 Oliver's Yard
55 City Road
London EC1Y 1SP
United Kingdom

Sage Publications India Pvt. Ltd.
B 1/I 1 Mohan Cooperative Industrial Area
Mathura Road, New Delhi 110 044
India

Sage Publications Asia-Pacific Pte. Ltd.
33 Pekin Street #02-01
Far East Square
Singapore 048763

Printed in the United States of America

Library of Congress Cataloging-in-Publication Data

Rudas, Tamás.
Handbook of probability: Theory and applications / Tamás Rudas.
p. cm.
Includes bibliographical references and index.
ISBN 978-1-4129-2714-7 (cloth)
1. Probabilities. I. Title.
QA273.R8814 2008
519.2–dc22

2007036434

This book is printed on acid-free paper.

08 09 10 11 12 10 9 8 7 6 5 4 3 2 1

Acquisitions Editor: Vicki Knight
Associate Editor: Sean Connelly
Editorial Assistant: Lauren Habib
Production Editor: Melanie Birdsall
Copy Editor: QuADS Prepress (P) Ltd.
Typesetter: QuADS Prepress (P) Ltd.
Proofreader: Dennis W. Webb
Indexer: Sheila Bodell
Cover Designer: Bryan Fishman
Marketing Manager: Stephanie Adams

CONTENTS

PART II: Probability Theory in Research Methodology 67

PREFACE

There exists no scientific knowledge without some degree of uncertainty concerning its validity, reliability, or precision. Probability is our most important construct to deal with this uncertainty. Although uncertainty exists in all fields of scientific activity, the standard of dealing with it varies from subject to subject, depending mostly on the particular way in which scientific knowledge is obtained and formulated, but also on traditions. This *Handbook* sets the ambitious goal of presenting the fundamentals and several applications of probabilistic thinking in the social and behavioral sciences, economics, and law. Elements of probability are included in most relevant university curricula, but very often probability is discussed as background material for statistics only, generating the impression that statistics itself is nothing else than the application of existing statistical methods. Just like the role of careful statistical modeling, as opposed to routine application of statistical tools, is often suppressed, the presentation of probabilistic thinking is also often reduced to the static presentation of simple rules of the calculus of probability.

In fact, probability is a lively subject that develops very fast, and some understanding of it is necessary for the correct interpretation of any scientific finding. The chapters of the *Handbook* cover different aspects of probability. Some are philosophical, some are mathematical, and some are statistical in their nature. The diversity of the approaches to probabilistic thinking is well represented by the diverging views of what is probability and how it is related to reality. The authors of Chapters 2 and 3 agree that probability is a construction that helps us conceptualize uncertainty, but Chapter 2 takes the view that observable events occur with a certain probability that may be revealed by repeated observations (the so-called frequentist definition of probability), while Chapter 3 discusses probability related to subjective judgment and expectation (the so-called subjective probability). On the other hand, Chapter 4 illustrates that not all subjective interpretations of probability are consistent. Closely related to probability is the concept of randomness: An event is random if the observer has uncertainty with respect to it. The observer may choose a deterministic or a stochastic model to describe the behavior of the possible observations, and the choice is often dictated by the available knowledge and other resources, but very often it also has an element of free choice (Chapter 2). On the other hand, Chapter 9 attributes "real" randomness to certain physical processes and takes the perhaps surprising but very useful position that processes that cannot be distinguished from a real random process with a reasonable amount of effort may be considered random. Furthermore, Chapter 6 distinguishes between aleatory and epistemic uncertainty (to refer to a kind of impossibility to remove uncertainty and to the actual lack of knowledge to do so). These issues are also related to the debate between the frequentist and the Bayesian views on statistical analysis (discussed in Chapters 5 and 6). Yet another possibility of handling uncertainty by using fuzzy sets is mentioned (in a particular context) in Chapter 20. A related topic that has attracted significant scientific interest recently and is taken up in more than one chapter is the definition and analysis of causality in stochastic models—that is, when causal relationships have to be identified in the presence of uncertainty. Chapters 8 and 23 discuss the most important approaches, one through the definition of individual causal effects and the other by the application of graphical models. There are several other topics discussed in more than one chapter, including time-dependent observations, measurement of and protection from investment risk, and DNA evidence.

While some of the chapters cover standard textbook material in a concise way and some others tend to describe cutting-edge developments, the presentation is intuitive throughout and the mathematical details are suppressed, so that all chapters are accessible with good high school or first-year college mathematics. The *Handbook* largely neglects the calculus of probability: Such details are left to specialized textbooks, and it concentrates mostly on the conceptual development of probabilistic thinking and on many of its applications. Most of the chapters are self-contained, which implies that some material is discussed in more than one chapter, perhaps from a different perspective, as was illustrated above. The references given at the end of each chapter vary from mentioning the few most fundamental sources to listing a complete collection of research papers, depending on the material covered in the chapter.

The *Handbook* is divided into three parts. The first part covers the theory of probability and gives an introduction to its mathematical and philosophical aspects in a fairly nontechnical way but well beyond the level at which most social or behavioral scientists study this topic at university. Chapter 1, written by Peter Lee, presents the most important developments in the history of probability theory. Many of these results are discussed and explained in detail in later chapters. Chapter 2, written by Herwig Friedl and Siegfried Hörmann, summarizes the main results of probability theory, as a mathematical subject. They give an intuitive but precise description of some of the more involved theorems, including the law of large numbers and the central limit theorem. Chapter 3, written by Igor Kopylov, gives an overview of the subjective definition and interpretation of probability. The chapter shows that many of the fundamental properties of probability, which were derived in the previous chapter in a frequentist setting (as this leads most easily to these results), may also be obtained from a different approach to the relationship between reality and probabilistic thinking. Chapter 4, written by Nicholas Shackel, takes a critical view on assumptions and beliefs often associated with probability and shows many of these to be untenable. These paradoxes occur, of course, not within the mathematical theory of probability but rather in our thinking when we try to formulate probabilistic models to describe reality.

The second part extends the theory given in the first part and discusses the general ways in which probabilistic approaches are used in research. The coverage here concentrates on applied probability and theoretical statistics. Chapter 5 is an account of the standard (frequentist) way in which probability theory is applied in statistics. Probability theory tells us how random observations from a population ("the reality") tend to behave, depending on the characteristics of this population and the sampling procedure, and statistics uses this knowledge to infer from observations to the characteristics of the population whence they were selected. Chapter 6, written by Tony O'Hagan, gives an account of Bayesian statistics and compares it with the frequentist approach. The main difference is that in frequentist statistics the characteristics of the population from which the observations came are assumed to be fixed but unknown, while in Bayesian statistics uncertainty regarding population characteristics is allowed (and is described probabilistically). However modest this difference appears to be, it leads to wide-ranging deviations in terms of the questions that may be asked and also in the ways in which those questions are answered. Chapter 7, written by Mauro Gasparini and Maria Piera Rogantin, describes experiments—one of the most important ways in which researchers collect information with respect to reality. The design of experiments is fundamental in technical applications of statistical analysis, but the chapter, in addition to defining the general concepts of main effect and interaction, emphasizes conceptual aspects and applicability to human populations. Chapter 8, written by Michael Sobel, gives an account of one of the most exciting areas of probabilistic thinking these days: how causal effects may be defined, observed, and tested in the presence of uncertainty. The chapter summarizes the ongoing scientific debate on this topic and also gives practical illustrations of the most important analyses. Chapter 9, written by Oded Goldreich, presents yet another approach to defining and handling randomness through computational complexity. This approach proves very useful not only in apparently theoretical efforts, such as algorithmic theorem verification, but also in related practical applications, such as cryptography.

The third part considers several applications of probabilistic modeling. Much of the content of the third part describes methods and uses concepts from statistics, but the focus here is not on estimation or testing, although these aspects are also discussed, but rather on model building with the aim of incorporating uncertainty. Chapter 10, written by Michael Lewis, describes the fundamentals of time-series analysis. This approach is used when one has reason to believe that phenomena observed over time are governed not only by the actual status of the population where the observations came from but also by earlier statuses of the same population. Chapter 11, written by Nancy Brandon Tuma, discusses another aspect of the temporal nature of observations, when the information recorded describes the occurrence of certain events of interest. This approach, survival analysis, also referred to as event history analysis, deals with modeling the factors that influence the probability of a certain event occurring within a specific period of time. Chapter 12, written by Jeffrey Wooldridge, deals with sampling and the implications of the sampling procedure for estimation and testing. The discussion goes way beyond elementary simple random sampling and, among other topics, proposes methods for modeling nonresponse. Chapter 13, written by Edward Frees and Jee-Seon Kim, presents another approach to modeling observations over an extended period of time. Particular attention is paid to the advantages and disadvantages of data arising from repeated observations of the same sample (the panel) and to temporal aspects that may be relevant to explain cross-sectional associations. Chapter 14, written by Vasja Vehovar, Metka Zalatel, and Rudi Seljak, deals with probabilistic methods in official statistics. Official statistics has played and continues to play an important role in the development of probabilistic methods for surveys, and the chapter describes the designs of the most frequently carried out surveys by national statistical offices and discusses related issues such as small-area estimation, data fusion, and seam effects. Chapter 15, written by Nick Longford, discusses probabilistic models for measurement error and misclassification. The proposed method of inference considers the true value as a latent variable, and a general solution based on imputation is suggested. Chapter 16, written by Klaas Sijtsma and Wilco Emons, considers a very important case when inference is to be based on imprecise observations: probabilistic developments of tests, in particular for educational purposes, using item response theory. The chapter describes several models and illustrates their applications to real data. Chapter 17, written by Klaus Troitzsch, shows how probabilistic simulation methods may be used to model societal phenomena such as demographic processes or opinion formation. The discussion covers approaches of different complexity, including microsimulation and multi-agent models. Chapter 18, written by Philippa Pattison and Garry Robins, is about the rapidly developing topic of probabilistic network analysis. Probabilistic models are discussed for the evolution of social networks, and several ways for the probabilistic analysis of such networks are described, including simulation methods based on Markov Chain Monte Carlo. Chapter 19, written by Chas Friedman, gives insight into the topic of probabilistic analysis of gambling, a topic that played a very important role in the historic development of probability theory. Several games are investigated, and strategies that are optimal on the average are developed for these. Chapter 20, written by Richard Derrig and Krzysztof Ostaszewski, describes how probabilistic approaches are applied in insurance. In addition to discussing the most important theoretical aspects of actuarial science, the chapter expands on several theoretical and practical problems of the insurance business. Chapter 21, written by Ad Feelders, discusses probabilistic methods for another financial problem, the scoring of credit applicants. Several models for determining the probability that someone will not pay back a loan are described, and special attention is given to the difficulties arising from the fact that observations are available only for those who were actually given a loan, leading to a special incomplete data problem. Chapter 22, written by Craig Rennie, shows how optimal investment portfolios are designed from risky securities, where risk is measured by the standard deviation of the return of the investment. Among other theories, the famous Black-Sholes option-pricing model is described. Chapter 23, written by George Luger and Chayan Chakrabarti, describes how probabilistic reasoning may be used in achieving automatic decisions. The chapter discusses expert systems and belief networks based on graphical models, showing how the Bayesian approach may lead to simplified and efficient decisions. Chapter 24, written by Julia Mortera and Philip Dawid, discusses how uncertainty related to evidence should be correctly interpreted in criminal investigations. In addition to discussing common mistakes and misinterpretations, they also show how Bayesian networks may be used to interpret complex evidence, including DNA data. Chapter 25, written by Basil C. Bitas, describes practical aspects of the presentation of probabilistic arguments in the courtroom. Science should be interpreted so that it becomes relevant for the law, and in addition to the main aspect of this integration, the prevailing practice in several countries from all over the world is discussed.

An edited volume, like this one, is always the result of the effort of several contributors. First and foremost, I am indebted to all the authors for their contributions and also for their willingness to subject their manuscripts to the several rounds of the review procedure. Perhaps no editor could be equally well qualified in all the fields covered in the *Handbook*, and I learned a lot while working with the authors. I am also indebted to the members of the Advisory Board, who helped me through several stages of this project. Very special thanks go to Lisa Cuevas Shaw, former Acquisitions Editor at Sage, who first proposed the idea of such a *Handbook* and applied successful tactics to convince me that I should try to put it together. She also provided me with constant moral support throughout the two years of actual editorial work. I feel fortunate to have been able to work with Sage's production team and, in particular, with Melanie Birdsall and Shankaran Srinivasan, who not only masterly handled the technical aspects of book production but were also very accommodating when it came to consolidating the individual chapters into one volume.

Paul Barrett (Auckland, New Zealand) made a very special contribution to the *Handbook* by trying to write a chapter on probabilistic profiling in psychology (criminal profiling, executive recruitment, etc). After much effort, he came to the conclusion that very little probability was being actually used in these activities and suggested that we drop the chapter. I thank him for his effort, and perhaps, this could be a new and fruitful field for the application of probabilistic thinking.

My very sad duty is to let the readers of the *Handbook* know that Professor Chas Friedman (Austin, Texas), author of the chapter on gambling, passed away shortly after completing the manuscript of his contribution, at the age of sixty. Although I have never had a chance to meet Professor Friedman personally, during our collaboration I learned to appreciate his disciplined thinking and wide-ranging scientific interests. This chapter is likely to be his last publication.

The hope, shared, I am sure, by all contributors, that such a *Handbook* may not only serve as a source of reference but also influence the way scientific research is conducted by some of its readers helped us overcome many difficulties while working on the manuscript. When the work is close to coming to an end, the editor may only wish that many readers will find the effort worthwhile.

—Tamás Rudas
Budapest, May 2007

ACKNOWLEDGMENTS

The publisher and the editor wish to express their indebtedness for the unusually helpful, constructive, and encouraging comments from the following reviewers during the planning phase of the book: Michael A. Clump, Marymount University; Robert P. Dobrow, Carleton College; Jeffrey C. Fox, Fort Lewis College; Kosuke Imai, Princeton University; Peter M. Lee, Wentworth College, University of York; Leland G. Neuberg, Boston University; and Timo Seppäläinen, University of Wisconsin–Madison.

Advisory Board

PART I

BACKGROUND AND THEORY OF PROBABILITY

1

History of Probability Theory

Peter M. Lee

Preliminary Remarks

The mathematical study of probability and statistics began comparatively late, and there is little trace of it before the late middle ages. It eventually grew from three rather disparate sources between which connections were gradually discovered and exploited. The sources are as follows:

1. The study of games of chance, beginning with Cardano and Tartaglia and, somewhat later but more widely known, with Pascal and Fermat.
2. The study of demography and the study of the state (which etymologically is where the word "statistics" originated), beginning with Graunt and Petty.
3. The study of the theory of errors of observation and their treatment, which, while it can be traced back to contemporaries of Newton, came to prominence through the work of Mayer and Bošcović and to fruition with the work of Legendre, Gauss, and Laplace.

In the course of this chapter, we will endeavor to show how these three sources intertwined and led to the modern developments of probability and statistics. In a short account, selectivity is inevitable, and so we will concentrate on a number of the most important workers in the field, and even in these cases look at only one or two of the topics that they concerned themselves with. This will, however, allow us to give a fairly full account of the limited number of topics that we *do* deal with and to show the ways in which the original development of the subject was similar to that to be found in modern textbooks and the ways in which it differed.

It is convenient for the English-speaking world that a large number of the sources for the history of statistics is available in English (which is not the case in many other branches of mathematics).

It has been remarked by a number of authors that, while the Greeks made serious contributions to many aspects of mathematics, they never concerned themselves with the mathematics of chance. The usual explanation given for this is that they were unfamiliar with the sorts of apparatus (e.g., coins and dice) that give rise to a stable system of relative frequencies. Whatever the reason, the first writings of any significance on the subject came in 16th-century Italy.

It should be borne in mind that the history of mathematics is arguably the last redoubt of the Whig interpretation of history, and there is a tendency to treat the study as if everything was a steady upward climb and to ignore anything which did not lead toward our present knowledge and interpretations. While this can be highly misleading, it is difficult to avoid.

THE 16TH AND 17TH CENTURIES

Girolamo Cardano (1501–1576) is best known among mathematicians as one of those involved in the solution of the cubic equation. He was, however, a man of very wide interests, and about 1565 he wrote a book called *Liber de Ludo Aleae* (*The Book of the Games of Chance*), which unfortunately was not published until the appearance of a 10-volume edition of his works in 1663. While some of his enumerations are correct, he has to resort to approximations such as, in effect, saying that if you try a chance of $1/c$ on n occasions then the chance it happens at least once is n/c. He and his contemporary *Niccolò Tartaglia* (1506?–1559) (also involved in the controversies surrounding the solution of the cubic equation) were both responsible for contributions to combinatorial theory,

Galileo Galilei (1564–1642) also wrote a fragment on the theory of dice, explaining why, while there are as many ways of scoring 9 as 10 with three dice (six each), the latter is more probable than the former.

It is generally held that the real beginnings of probability theory lie in a correspondence between *Blaise Pascal* (1623–1662) and *Pierre de Fermat* (1601–1665). Their correspondence originated because the Chevalier de Méré, an inveterate gambler about whom Pascal wrote *Il est tres bon ésprit mais quel dommage, il n'est pas géomètre (c'est, comme vous savez, un grand défaut)* ("He is very able, but he is not a geometrician (this, as you know, is a great defect)") (although Maistrov points out that he was not in fact a complete mathematical ignoramus), asked Pascal a question. It was usual among gamblers to bet even money that among four throws of a true die the six would appear at least once, and he had concluded that the same even chance should hold for "double six" in 24 throws (since 6 times 6 is 36 and 4 times 6 is 24), and yet his experiences with the second type of bet compared unfavorably with those in the first case (or so he claimed). *Un problème relatif aux jeux de hasard, proposé à un austère Janséniste par un homme du monde a été l'origine du calcul des probabilités* ("A problem in games of chance, proposed to an austere Jansenist by a man of the world was the origin of the calculus of probability") writes S. D. Poisson in his *Recherches sur la probabilité des jugements*... (1837).

They had no difficulty in dealing with this problem and went on to discuss a number of others, of which the most important was the *problem of points*. This problem arises when two players A and B agree to play a series of fair games until one of them has won a specified number of games, s, say. For some accidental reason, play is stopped when A has won s_1 and B has won s_2 games. How should the stakes be divided? Their work led to the publication in 1656 by *Christiaan Huygens* (1629–1695) of *Van Rekeningh in Spelen van Geluck* (*The Value of all Chances in Games of Fortune*), the first book on probability theory, subsequently translated into Latin and English.

Pascal in particular was fascinated by the properties of the arithmetical triangle

$$\begin{array}{llllll} 1 & 1 & 1 & 1 & 1 & 1 \quad \ldots \\ 1 & 2 & 3 & 4 & 5 & \ldots \\ 1 & 3 & 6 & 10 & \ldots & \\ 1 & 4 & 10 & \ldots & & \\ 1 & 5 & \ldots & & & \\ 1 & \ldots & & & & \end{array}$$

about which he wrote a *Traité du triangle arithmétique* published posthumously in 1653 (there is a little-known English translation in *Pascal: Encyclopedia Britannica Great Books of the World*, Vol. 33).

John Graunt (1620–1674) published the first edition of *Natural and Political Observations mentioned in a following Index and made upon the Bills of Mortality* in 1662. In it he studied the recorded causes of death in the City of London, pointing out the way in which corrections could be made to the statistics to allow for the reluctance of relatives to report deaths from plague, syphilis, and so on. He also attempted (not very successfully) to make a life table. His work was followed up by *Sir William Petty* (1623–1687).

The correct pricing of annuities on lives was poorly understood until surprisingly late, but a very good attempt at solving the problem was made by *Jan de Witt* (1625–1672), in letters dated 1674 to the States General under the title *Waardye van lyf-renten naer proportie van Losrenten* (*Treatise on Life Annuities*).

While well known for many other things, notably studies of his comet, *Edmund Halley* (1656–1742) enters into this chapter because he published a paper in the *Philosophical Transactions of the Royal Society*, Vol. 17 (1693), which contained the first reasonable life table, based on real data from Breslau [Wrocław].

James Bernoulli (1654–1704) (sometimes known as James I because there were other James Bernoullis) wrote the first substantial treatise on probability, the *Ars Conjectandi* (a translation of which by Edith Sylla has very recently been published under the title *The Art of Conjecturing*), which was published posthumously in 1713. This book contains many remarkable combinatorial and other results, for example, formulas for sums of powers of integers and results on games of chance which extend those of Pascal, Fermat, and Huygens. The really important result he proves (rigorously) is what is now known as the Weak Law of Large Numbers for Bernoulli trials (i.e, independent trials with two possible outcomes, "success" and "failure" with probabilities p and q, respectively, where $p+q=1$). In modern notation, he shows that if n independent trials with probability of success p and failure $1-p$ result in X successes, then for any fixed ε

$$\mathsf{P}\left(\left|\frac{X-np}{n}\right| > \varepsilon\right) \to 0 \quad \text{as} \quad n \to \infty.$$

In many contexts, what one would like to be able to do is to make statements about the value of p for given X and n rather than (as the Weak Law does) about the value of X for given p and n. It has been argued that awareness of this was one reason why Bernoulli did not publish his treatise in his lifetime.

THE 18TH CENTURY

John Arbuthnot (1667–1735) published a paper titled "An Argument for Divine Providence, taken from the constant Regularity observed in the Births of both Sexes" in the *Philosophical Transactions of the Royal Society*, Vol. 27 (1710). He quoted the number of yearly christenings for males and females for the period 1629–1710, noting that there are more males then females every year, and saying that if the chances were equal this would only happen with a probability of $1/2^{82}$. From this he concluded "that it is Art, not Chance, that governs." This is often said to constitute the first published test of statistical significance.

The most important publication of *Pierre Rémond de Montmort* (1678–1719) was his *Essay d'Analyse sur les Jeux de Hazard* (1708 and 1713) (*Essay on the Analysis of Games of Chance*), the title of which is more or less self-explanatory (most of the games in question being card or dice games).

Nicholas Bernoulli (1687–1759) who had been responsible for the posthumous publication of his uncle's *Ars Conjectandi* produced some useful extensions of his work in *De Usu Artis Conjectandi in Jure* (*On the Use of the Art of Conjecture in Law*), which not merely dealt with applications in law but also with various games of chance. He also introduced the "Petersburg problem," which was an impetus towards the development of "moral expectation" or utility.

The magnum opus of *Abraham De Moivre* (1667–1754) was his book *The Doctrine of Chances* (1718, 1738, and 1756), and most of his important results were in due course incorporated into that book. He did basic work on the "gambler's ruin" problem in which a gambler with a finite fortune x plays successive (independent) games in each of which he has a probability p of winning until his fortune drops to 0 and he is bankrupt or he reaches a fortune of a with which he will be satisfied. Clearly, he would like to know the chance that the outcome is in his favor. A more difficult problem which he also dealt with is the "duration of play," that is, finding the expected time until the gambler's fortune reaches 0 or a, whichever happens sooner.

His most important result amounted to finding an approximation to the symmetric binomial, which we would now think of as an approximation by the normal distribution. If we write

$$b(x) = \binom{n}{x}\left(\frac{1}{2}\right)^x\left(\frac{1}{2}\right)^{n-x},$$

he shows with a little help from *James Stirling* (1692–1770) that

$$b(\tfrac{1}{2}n) = \frac{2e}{\sqrt{2\pi}}\frac{(1-\frac{1}{n})^n}{\sqrt{n-1}}.$$

He went on to show that $\ln\{b(\frac{1}{2}n)/b(\frac{1}{2}n+l)\} = 2l^2/n$ plus terms of order $1/n^2$, which are negligible by comparison, so that

$$b(\tfrac{1}{2}n+l) = \frac{2}{\sqrt{2\pi n}}\exp\left\{-\frac{2l^2}{n}\right\},$$

which amounts in modern terminology to a proof that the symmetric binomial distribution can be approximated by the normal distribution. Strictly speaking, he has no notion of a normal distribution and thinks of this as merely a useful formula. Subsequently, he extended his result to the general binomial.

It commonly occurs in astronomy that one observes a large number of quantities that are linearly dependent on a smaller number of unknown parameters, the observations being subject to error. One of the first to attempt to deal with this problem was *Tobias Mayer* (1723–1762). In the problem he was dealing with, he had 27 observations dependent on 3 parameters, and his method was to divide the equations into 3 groups of 9, add the equations in each group, and thus end up with 3 linear equations in 3 unknowns, which he could solve.

Subsequently, *Rudjer Josip Bošković, S. J.* (1711–1787) (or Ruggiero Giuseppe Boscovich or Roger Joseph Boscovich) attempted to deal with a similar problem by seeking a solution that minimized the sum of absolute deviations. He discovered that while this method has considerable intuitive appeal, it presents formidable computational difficulties, and substantial progress in this area had to await the development of the theory of least squares.

Leonhard Euler (1701–1783) made significant contributions to probability, many of them based on a study of the Genoise lottery. In particular he dealt with the problem of rencontres, showing that if two people each of whom has a shuffled pack of cards numbered 1, 2, ..., n show their cards to one another one at a time, the probability of a match is approximated by 1/e for large values of n.

Thomas Simpson (1710–1761) attempted to show that "the taking of the mean of a number of observations, greatly diminishes the chances for all the smaller errors, and cuts off almost all possibilities of any great ones.... And the more observations or experiments that are made, the less will the conclusion be liable to err...," which would constitute some form of law of large numbers. Unsurprisingly, he did not succeed in proving more than a special case of his assertion, but in the course of his researches he did introduce the *continuous* distribution of error, in fact a triangular distribution, in his book *Miscellaneous Tracts on Some Curious, and Very Interesting Subjects* (1757).

In accordance with Stigler's Law of Eponymy, *Thomas Bayes* (1702–1761), whose key paper was submitted posthumously by his literary executor *Richard Price* (1723–1791) to *Philosophical Transactions of the Royal Society*, Vol. 53 (1763), did not prove anything close to the result we now know as Bayes's theorem (which first appeared in the second edition of Laplace's *Théorie Analytique*). He was, however, the first person to introduce what used to be known as inverse probability and is now regarded as a form of Bayesian inference. He gave his problem in the form: *Given* the number of times in which an unknown event has happened and has failed, *required* the chance that the probability of its happening in a single trial lies somewhere between any two degrees of probability that can be named. In effect, he adopted a uniform prior for the unknown probability, that is, a prior density

$$p(\theta) = 1 \qquad (0 < \theta < 1),$$

and used a Bayesian argument. A modern follower of Bayes's ideas would reason that if the unknown chance is θ and x successes have been observed in n trials, then the posterior density of θ is given by

$$\text{posterior} \propto \text{prior} \times \text{likelihood},$$

which in this case takes the form

$$\begin{aligned} f(\theta|x) &\propto f(\theta)f(x|\theta) \\ &\propto 1.\binom{n}{n-x}\theta^x(1-\theta)^{n-x} \\ &\propto \theta^x(1-\theta)^{n-x} \qquad (0<\theta<1). \end{aligned}$$

Normalizing to produce a density which integrates to 1, we find that

$$f(\theta|x) = \frac{\theta^x(1-\theta)^{n-x}}{B(x+1,n-x+1)},$$

where

$$\begin{aligned} B(x+1,n-x+1) &= \frac{\Gamma(x+1)\Gamma(n-x+1)}{\Gamma(n+2)} \\ &= \frac{x!(n-x)!}{(n+1)!} \end{aligned}$$

is a beta function, so that the posterior is a beta distribution. Bayes (and Price) gave very crude approximations to probabilities given by this distribution. His treatment of the foundations of probability was much more careful than that of other writers of his time (he did not, for example, regard it as self-evident that the formula for $\mathsf{P}(A|B)$ would be the same when the event B preceded the event A as when it followed it). It is worth noting that he defined "the *probability of any event* as the ratio between the value at which an expectation depending on the happening of the event ought to be computed, and the chance of the thing expected upon its happening," stating that "By *chance* I mean the same as probability."

Bayes's grounds for the use of a uniform prior appear to depend on assuming that this leads to a uniform distribution for the number of successes, that is (in modern notation),

$$\begin{aligned} \mathsf{P}(X=x) &= \int_0^1 \binom{n}{x}\theta^x(1-\theta)^{n-x}\,d\theta \\ &= 1/(n+1) \quad \text{for all } 0 \leqslant x \leqslant n. \end{aligned}$$

Note that this argument is unaffected by taking any monotonic transformation of X. It does not appear that Bayes supported the "principle of indifference" introduced by Laplace (as discussed later in this chapter).

The 19th Century

Adrien-Marie Legendre (1752–1835) was the first person to publish the method of least squares, which he did in *Nouvelles Méthodes pour la détermination des orbites des comètes* (1805). He gave no argument for it other than that it was convenient and easy to use.

Pierre Simon, Marquis de Laplace (1749–1827) is the towering genius of the history of probability. Todhunter's *A History of the Mathematical Theory of Probability From the Time of Pascal to That of Laplace* devotes a quarter of the book to the work of Laplace. Much of his work eventually found its way into his book *Théorie Analytique des Probabilités* (*Analytical Theory of Probability*) (1812, 1814, and 1820). He also wrote a more popular account, the *Essai Philosphique sur les Probabilités* (1814), which was incorporated into the second edition of the *Théorie Analytique* and which has subsequently been translated into English. He made many other contributions to mathematics, notably to celestial mechanics and was also a figure of some political significance.

He gave what was for a long time the standard definition of probability, namely, the number of cases favorable to an event divided by the number of all equally likely cases. (A version of this had been used before Laplace but not as a basic definition.) The "equally likely cases" are *les cas également possibles, c'est à dire tels que nous soyons également indécis sur leur éxistence* (*Essai philosophique*), that is, "equally possible, that is to say, to such as we may be equally undecided about in regard to their existence." This definition is associated with what he referred to as the "principle of indifference," which in modern terms means the adoption of uniform priors in Bayesian inference. This is of course subject to criticism because a uniform prior for a parameter θ implies a *non*uniform prior for most functions of the parameter, for example, θ^3, and therefore the choice of scale of measurement in such an inference is of considerable importance.

Laplace developed the methods of inverse probability (Bayesian inference with a uniform prior) beginning with his "Mémoire sur la probabilité des causes par les évenments" ("Memoir on the probability of the causes of events") in 1774.

His most infamous conclusion was "Laplace's Rule of Succession." In the situation treated by Bayes, if no failures have been observed and n successes, then the (posterior) distribution for the unknown probability of success is $\theta^n/B(n,0) = (n+1)\theta^n$. He wanted to find the unknown probability θ of success and reasoned that, since θ was itself unknown but he had this probability density function over possible values that it might take, then he could find a value for the probability of success by taking the expected value of θ over this density, that is, as

$$\begin{aligned} \mathsf{P}(\text{success}) &= \int \theta f(\theta)\, d\theta \\ &= \int_0^1 \theta\,(n+1)\theta^n\, d\theta \\ &= (n+1)/(n+2). \end{aligned}$$

This gave rise to understandable controversy when it was applied to deduce that if the sun had been observed to rise n times, there was a probability $(n+1)/(n+2)$ that it would rise tomorrow. In general, Laplace's work on inference for the binomial distribution was more successful than Bayes's although he was less careful about the foundations, but more successful about the evaluation of beta probabilities, which he was able to approximate in terms of the normal density. In the course of his investigation of approximations to binomial probabilities (following De Moivre), he gave the first evaluation of the probability integral $\int_0^\infty \exp\left(-\frac{1}{2}x^2\right)\, dx$.

It turned out to be easier to work with random distributions of errors. He reasoned on the following lines. If ε is the error, O the observation, and T the true value he wished to know about, then $O = T + \varepsilon$ is equivalent to $T = O - e$. If it is assumed that ε has a symmetric distribution, then supposing T fixed gives a distribution for O and conversely supposing O fixed gives a distribution for T. This symmetry, which hangs on what was later called the *pivotal quantity* $\varepsilon = O - T$, makes inversion natural. Later (in the 20th century) Fisher called this a *fiducial* argument. He went on to give an independent proof of the same special case of Bayes's theorem as Bayes himself.

He attempted to decide on a suitable distribution for errors of observation, proposing the double-exponential or Laplace distribution with density $(m/2)\exp(-m|x|)$ $(-\infty < x < \infty)$, although he discovered that this was in fact very difficult to deal with, and later he suggested another density, $(1/2a)\log(a/|x|)$ $(-a \leqslant x \leqslant a)$, only to discover that this was even more difficult to deal with.

The probability generating function of a random variable X, that is, the mean or expected value of t^X where t is a "dummy" real variable, had been used (without being named) by De Moivre in the *Doctrine of Chances* and by various others. However, it is Laplace's extensive discussion of generating functions as incorporated in the *Théorie Analytique* and applied to games of chance and other matters. It is his use of them that is the source of their widespread use in probability, combinatorics, and the solution of finite difference equations and recurrence formulae. He also invented, though he did not name, the characteristic function of a random variable X, namely, $\phi(t) = \mathsf{E}\exp(itX)$, which is a variant of the moment-generating function with the advantage that it is finite for all t.

Laplace was also the man who established the preeminence of the normal distribution in probability and discovered its major properties, although we have seen that in some sense it grew out of De Moivre's work. He was able to show that in reasonably general circumstances a sum of independently identically distributed random variables was well approximated by a normal distribution (the "central limit theorem").

Carl Friedrich Gauss (1777–1855) was the first person to propose the use of the normal distribution as a "law of error." He did this in his book *Teoria Motus Coporum Coelestium...* (which has been translated as *The Theory of Motion of Heavenly Bodies...*), which appeared in 1809. His justification for it is somewhat suspect from a modern standpoint, being (in Stigler's words) "both circular and *non sequitur*." Like Laplace he employed the methods of inverse probability. He assumed that when a single unknown was observed on several occasions with equal care, the posterior probability was maximized by the arithmetic mean of the observations and shows that this assumption implied that the only symmetric error density with a maximum at 0 took the form

$$\varphi(\Delta) = \frac{h}{\sqrt{\pi}} e^{-h^2\Delta^2},$$

where h was some sort of measure of precision. Having thus deduced the normal law of errors, he concluded that the principle of least squares was justified in essence because in the situation of the general linear model $\boldsymbol{Y} = \boldsymbol{A}\boldsymbol{\beta} + \boldsymbol{\varepsilon}$ it led to estimates which maximized the posterior probability (which with a uniform prior coincide with maximum likelihood estimates, although the notion of maximum likelihood was introduced much later by Fisher). Thus he deduced least squares by assuming a special case of it! Gauss was very clear that it was his principle rather than Legendre's, and he probably did think of it before Legendre's publication, but he certainly did not publish before Legendre.

While his reasoning was suspect, its importance lay in the fact that it caused Laplace to think of the normal density as a possible error curve, something which does not appear to have occurred to him before he became aware of Gauss's work. Once he had seen that, he adopted the normal distribution as an error law and was able to use his central limit theorem in justification of it. It should be noted that a number of error curves had been tried and the choice of the normal distribution was far from obvious.

(Lambert) Adolphe (Jacques) Quetelet (1796–1874) was a man of enormous influence during his lifetime who is almost forgotten today. One of his principal ideas was that of the "average man." He distinguished between a *mean*, such as one obtains by measuring the same building 20 times to estimate the true height of the building and an *arithmetical mean* such as one would find by measuring the heights of 20 buildings in a street to give a measure applicable to the street.

In roughly this way, he passed from a real physical unknown, the height of one person, to a postulated reality, an objective property of a population at a time, its mean height or longevity or whatever. This postulated true unknown value of the mean was thought of not as an arithmetical abstract of real heights, but as itself a number that objectively describes the population.

Quetelet was able to obtain the height and chest measurements (in inches) of more than 5,000 Scottish soldiers classified by regiment for 11 regiments and on examining them found that the results really occurred as though the chests that have been measured had been modeled from the same type from the same individual—an ideal one, if you will, but one whose proportions we ascertain by a sufficiently long trial. In effect, he estimates a mean and a probable error for the data and then compares his data with data distributed with the "law of error" which has the same mean and probable error. The modern statistician would expect the law of error to be normal, but in fact, though it makes little difference, Quetelet's is of the form $m + kX$, where X is binomial of large index (sample size) m and parameter $\frac{1}{2}$, so is symmetric. He did *not* use formal tests of goodness of fit; he just looked to see whether the fit appeared to him to be sufficiently good.

His real importance lay in his using methods and distributions that had been used for measurement errors and other physical quantities in analyzing human populations and, while the way he went about this has been superseded, he led the way to the wide application of probabilistic methods that we find today.

His best-known work is *Sur l'homme et le développement de ses facultés* (translated as *A Treatise on Man, and the Developement of His Faculties*) (1835).

Siméon Denis Poisson (1781–1840) is of course famous for the Poisson distribution

$$\mathsf{P}(X = k) = \frac{\lambda^k}{k!} e^{-\lambda} \qquad k = 0, 1, \ldots,$$

which appears as an approximation to the binomial distribution of large index n and small parameter p when $\lambda = np$, which he did derive, although he gave no special emphasis to it (as a matter of fact, De Moivre had got close to this result in Problem III I of the *Doctrine of Chances*). He built on work by Laplace and Quetelet in applying probabilistic models to the verdicts given by juries, considering that the verdicts of jurors constitute Bernoulli trials. He was the first to cite the density

$$f(x) = \frac{1}{\pi} \frac{1}{1 + x^2}$$

(now known as the Cauchy distribution) as a case where the central limit theorem does not apply.

Unlike Laplace, he made a clear distinction between "subjective" and "objective" probability, calling the latter "chance" and the former "probability."

Friedrich Robert (1843–1917) derived the chi-squared distribution as the distribution of sums of squares of errors in a normal linear model, using the so-called Helmert transformation,

$$\boldsymbol{H} = \begin{pmatrix} \frac{1}{\sqrt{n}} & \frac{1}{\sqrt{n}} & \frac{1}{\sqrt{n}} & \frac{1}{\sqrt{n}} & \cdots & \frac{1}{\sqrt{n}} \\ \frac{1}{1.2} & \frac{-1}{1.2} & 0 & 0 & \cdots & 0 \\ \frac{1}{2.3} & \frac{1}{2.3} & \frac{-2}{2.3} & 0 & \cdots & 0 \\ \vdots & \vdots & \vdots & \vdots & \ddots & \vdots \\ \frac{1}{\sqrt{(n-1)n}} & \frac{1}{\sqrt{(n-1)n}} & \frac{1}{\sqrt{(n-1)n}} & \frac{1}{\sqrt{(n-1)n}} & \cdots & \frac{-(n-1)}{\sqrt{(n-1)n}} \end{pmatrix}$$

introduced in *Zeitschrift für Mathematik und Physik*, Vol. 21 (1876). In essence, his argument consists in taking a set of random variables X_i with a normal distribution of mean μ and variance σ^2, which can be reduced to standard normal variables $Y_i = (X_i - \mu)/\sigma$. Applying the Helmert transformation to these produces a set of variables Z_i which (since $\boldsymbol{H}$ is orthogonal, i.e., $\boldsymbol{H}\boldsymbol{H}^{\mathrm{T}} = \boldsymbol{I}$ where $\boldsymbol{I}$ is the identity matrix, so that the inverse of $\boldsymbol{H}$ is equal to its transpose) are also of mean 0 and variance 1 and are uncorrelated and so (because jointly normal) independent. It is then easily checked that $Z_1 = \sqrt{n}\overline{Y} = (\overline{X} - \mu)/\sigma$ while $(n-1)s^2 = \sum_{i=1}^{n} Y_i^2 - n\overline{Y}^2 = \sum_{i=2}^{n} Z_i^2$ from which it follows that $\overline{X}$ and s^2 are independent, $\overline{X}$ is normally distributed and s^2 is distributed as a multiple of a sum of squares of $n-1$ squared normal variates, that is, as a multiple of a chi-squared variate on $n-1$ degrees of freedom.

Wilhelm Lexis (1837–1914) is best known for investigations of binomial models for time series such as the number X_i of male births from a total number of n births for a number of years. Supposing this number to have a binomial distribution of index n and parameter p_i for $i = 1, 2, \ldots, N$, he wished to investigate evidence as to whether $p_1 = p_2 = \cdots = p$. His method amounted to computing the estimated variance of the X_i by

$$R^2 = \sum (X_i - \bar{X})^2$$

and comparing this with the value

$$r^2 = \bar{X}(1 - \bar{X})/N.$$

Sir Francis Galton (1822–1911) was a man of extraordinarily wide interests (he coined the term "anti-cyclone" and persuaded the Metropolitan Police to use fingerprints) whose first work in probability and statistics was very much in the footsteps of Quetelet. He developed the notion of a *statistical scale* by which individuals were ranked and the results fitted to a normal distribution. Insofar as this refers to data such as chest measurements, this is effectively what Quetelet did. His first extension of Quetelet's methodology, which he termed "statistics by intercomparison" and which became the method of "scaling" for psychological tests, considered in applying similar methodology for qualities such as "talent" or "genius," which were at most susceptible to a simple ordering. If a hundred individuals' talents were ordered, each could be assigned the numerical value corresponding to its percentile in the curve of "deviations from the average." The midpoint (or median talent) had value 0, an individual in the upper quartile was assigned the value 1 (representing one probable error above mediocrity; on a modern scale in terms of standard deviations and assuming, as Galton did, an underlying normal distribution this would be 0.6745), and so on. The argument for such a procedure was, and remains, weak; it rests solely on analogy.

Galton was then faced with a problem, in that he could see the normal curve arising in quantitative data but could not connect that curve with the transmission of quantities such as the weight of seeds from generation to generation. He found a solution by supposing that the weights of the seeds were normally distributed with variance σ^2. The key idea was *reversion*, whereby the weights of the progeny were normally distributed, *not* about the weights of their parents, but rather about a value which reverted by being (linearly) closer to the population average. This train of ideas led to the introduction of regression theory, which is, of course, a very widely used technique to this day. His work on correlation appeared in the *Journal of the Anthropological Institute*, Vol. 15 (1886).

He went on to invent the notion of correlation. As an example, he supposed, "Two clerks leave their office together and travel homewards in the same and somewhat unpunctual omnibus every day. They both get out of the omnibus at the same halting-place, and thence walk by their several ways to their respective homes.... The upshot is that when either clerk arrives at his home later than his average time, there is some reason to expect that the other clerk will be late also...." Note that such a situation will always lead to *positive* correlation, and it appears that Galton never conceived of negative correlation. He was not very distinguished as a mathematician, but he had good intuition, which led to very important ideas. This work appeared in *Proceedings of the Royal Society*, Vol. 45 (1888).

Late in the 19th century *Pavnutii Lvovich Chebyshev* (or Čebyšev or Tchebycheff) (1821–1894) founded the Russian school of probabilists, which has been of considerable importance ever since. He is widely known nowadays for the famous inequality $\mathsf{P}(|X - \mathsf{E}X| \geqslant k) \leqslant \operatorname{Var} X/k^2$ for a random variable X with expectation $\mathsf{E}X$ and variance $\operatorname{Var} X$, his proof of which appeared in *Journal de Mathématiques Pures et Appliquées* (sér. 2), Vol. 12 (1866). Although he did not know it, his derivation of this inequality had been anticipated in a paper in *Comptes Rendus*, Vol. 31 (1853) by *Irénée-Jules Bienaymée* (1796–1878).

After him, *Andrei Andreevich Markov* (1856–1922) among many other things started the theory of "Markov chains," that is, processes that move through a number of states through time in such a way that the probability distribution of its next state depends only on its present state, and not at all on its past history, which he first wrote about in *Izvestiya Fiziko-matematicheskogo obshchestva pri Kazanskom universitete* (Ser. 2) 8 (1898). Interestingly, he set a precedent for mathematical study of literature in that one of his first examples concerned the succession of vowels and consonants in Pushkin's *Evgeniĭ Onegin*.

The 20th Century

Geometric probability had been a subject of wide interest at least from the time that *George Louis Leclerc, Comte de Buffon* (1707–1788) introduced his famous needle, but the subject was considerably developed in an article by *Morgan William Crofton* (1826–1915) in an article on "Probability" appearing in 1885 in the famous ninth edition of the *Encyclopedia Britannica*.

Karl Pearson (1857–1936) is probably best remembered nowadays for the further development of correlation leading on from Galton's work, which led to the product moment coefficient of correlation, and for his introduction of the chi-squared test, which provided the first formal method of testing the goodness of fit of a proposed distribution. He was in fact an extremely prolific author and was responsible for many other innovations, notably the study of skew curves, which could be used for modeling situations for which the normal distribution was manifestly unsuitable. Much of his work appeared in a series of works entitled (somewhat misleadingly) "Mathematical contributions to the theory of evolution," which appeared in *Proceedings of the Royal Society*. He was also responsible for founding the influential journal *Biometrika*.

"Student" (*William Sealy Gosset*, 1876–1937) (who used a pseudonym at the request of Guiness, his employers) published a paper in *Biometrika*, Vol. 6 (1908), which made plausible the distribution of (something equivalent to) what is now known as Student's t.

Sir Ronald Aylmer Fisher (1890–1962) (better known as R. A. Fisher), who was the most distinguished statistician of the 20th century, gave a rigorous integrated treatment of the sampling distributions of the χ^2, t and F distributions, which commonly occur in problems of inference concerned with the normal distribution.

The beginning of the century brought considerable advances in applied probability. The Borel-Cantelli lemmas appeared in the work of *Émile Félix-Edouard-Justin Borel* (1871–1956) and *Francesco Paolo Cantelli* (1875–1966). They state that an infinite sequence of events A_i with probabilities p_i is such that if the series $\sum p_i$ converges, then the probability that infinitely many of the A_i occur is 0. Conversely, if the series diverges *and the events are independent* then the probability that infinitely many of them occur is 1.

We recall that Bernoulli had proved the Weak Law of Large Numbers for so-called Bernoulli trials, namely, that (for any $\varepsilon > 0$) if X is the number of successes observed after n trials, then

$$\mathsf{P}\left(\left|\frac{X-np}{n}\right| \geqslant \varepsilon\right) \to 0.$$

Early in the century, Borel proved the Strong Law of Large Numbers, that is,

$$\mathsf{P}\left(\lim_{n\to\infty} \frac{X-np}{n} = 0\right) = 1.$$

This result is stronger because it concerns probabilities for a whole sequence of trials rather than probabilities for fixed values of n.

The theory of stochastic processes developed rapidly in the 20th century. Five years before the 1905 article in *Annalen der Physik*, Vol. 17 by *Albert Einstein* (1879–1955) on Brownian Motion, in which Einstein derived the equation (the partial differential heat-diffusion equation of Fourier) governing Brownian motion and made an estimate for the size of molecules, *Louis Bachelier* (1870–1946) had worked out the distribution function for what is now known as the Wiener stochastic process in honor of *Norbert Wiener* (1894–1964) (the stochastic process that underlies Brownian motion) linking it mathematically with the diffusion equation. It appears that Einstein in 1905 was ignorant of the work of Bachelier.

At roughly the same time, *Agnar Krarup Erlang* (1878–1929) laid the foundations of queuing theory (see E. Brockmeyer, *The Life and Works of A. K. Erlang*).

Slightly later in the century, *Aleksandr Mikhailovich Lyapunov* (or Liapounov) (1857–1918) and *Jarl Waldemar Lindeberg* (1876–1932) extended the work of Laplace and others on the central limit theorem, finally showing that sums $S_n = \sum_r X_{rn}$ of independent random variables are approximately normal not merely when the summands are identically distributed but also when they are "uniformly asymptotically negligible," which really means that no small proportion of them is at all likely to dominate the rest. Since many of the random variables we observe, such as errors of observation, are likely to be the result of a large number of small contributions, although the contributions will not necessarily have the same distribution, this is of help in understanding the predominance of the normal distribution (despite the remark of *Henri Poincaré* (1854–1912) that "Everybody firmly believes in it because the mathematicians imagine it is a fact of observation, and observers that it is a theory of mathematics"). Lindeberg's work was continued and extended by *Boris Vladimirovich Gnedenko* (1912–1995).

The mathematical foundations of probability were somewhat murky until *Andrei Nikolaevich Kolmogorov* (1903–1987) showed in his 1933 article titled "Grundbegriffe der Wahrscheinlichkeitsrechnung" (translated as *Foundations of the Theory of Probability*) how to establish probability theory in the context of measure theory.

We have an underlying set Ω, a σ-algebra $\mathcal{F}$ of subsets of Ω, and a function P assigning real numbers to members of $\mathcal{F}$. The members of $\mathcal{F}$ are those subsets of Ω that are called "events."

1. For any set, that is, for any event, $0 \leqslant \mathsf{P}(E)$. That is, the probability of an event is a nonnegative real number.
2. $\mathsf{P}(\Omega) = 1$. That is, the probability that one of the elementary events in the entire sample set will occur is 1.
3. Any countable sequence of pairwise disjoint events E_1, E_2, ..., satisfies $\mathsf{P}(E_1 \cup E_2 \cup \cdots) = \sum \mathsf{P}(E_i)$. That is, the probability of an event set which is a (possibly countably infinite) union of other disjoint subsets is the sum of the probabilities of those subsets. This is called σ-additivity. If there is any overlap among the subsets, this relation does not hold.

Random variables are then defined as (measurable) real-valued functions defined on the space Ω.

Kolmogorov was also responsible for important developments in stochastic processes, including his famous "forward" and "backward" differential equations.

Partly because of their generality and the fact that they are not attached in any way to the applications commonly made of probability theory, not everyone has agreed that Kolmogorov said all that needed to be said about the foundations of probability. *Richard von Mises* (1883–1953), building on earlier work by *John Venn* (1824–1923), *Charles Sanders Peirce* (1839–1914), and others, tried to define probability in terms of "collectives."

In effect, he tried to formalize an old idea by which probabilities are to be identified with limiting relative frequencies of events or attributes therein. Thus, we require an infinite sequence of trials to define such probabilities. There are obvious problems with such a formulation since what if the actual world may not provide an infinite sequence of trials of a given experiment. Indeed, that appears to be the norm, and perhaps even the rule. In that case, we are to identify probability with a hypothetical or counterfactual limiting relative frequency. We are to imagine hypothetical infinite extensions of an actual sequence of trials; probabilities are then what the limiting relative frequencies would be if the sequence were so extended. While he appears to have few followers left, his work was useful in exposing the strengths and limitations of such a theory.

More influential nowadays are subjective theories of probability (often called "Bayesian" although it appears unlikely that Bayes himself would have subscribed to such a point of view). In modern terms, such theories have been developed by *Frank Plumpton Ramsey* (1903–1930) and *Leonard Jimmie Savage* (1917–1971) and perfected by *Bruno de Finetti* (1906–1985) (which is not to say that they have been accepted by all or even most workers in the field). The study of "objective" prior distributions was, however, continued by various workers, notably *Sir Harold Jeffreys* (1891–1989) in his influential book *Theory of Probability* (1939).

Of more recent developments in probability, the idea of a martingale, which generalizes the notion of a sum of independent random variables of mean zero to a sequence of random variables S_n such that the expectation of S_{n+1} given all past values $S_1, S_2, \ldots$, is equal to its present value S_n. It can be thought of as a model for your winnings or losses in successive plays of a fair game. S_n is just equal to the value of the most recent variable S_n. *Paul Georges Victor Lévy* (1886–1971) and *Joseph Leo Doob* (1910–2004) (see especially the latter's 1953 book *Stochastic Processes*) were able to make useful generalizations of results about sums of independent random variables to martingales, which have wide applications. A notable example is the Martingale convergence theorem, which states that if $\{S_n\}$ is a martingale such that for some c the condition $\mathsf{E}S_n^2 \leqslant c < \infty$ holds for all n, then there exists a random variable S_∞ such that $S_n \to S_\infty$ on a set of probability one. Defining $X_n = S_n - S_{n-1}$ and applying this result to the martingale $S_n = X_1 + X_2 + \cdots + X_n$, where the X_i are independently identically distributed random variables, the Strong Law of Large Numbers follows on using "Kronecker's lemma," but the Martingale convergence theorem has many other applications. Results about martingales have proved to be of very wide application.

Lévy was also responsible for the development of "stable" distributions, which are like the normal distribution in that a sum S_n of independently identically distributed random variables with such a distribution have the same distribution as the summands up to location and scale. Any such distribution other than the normal distribution necessarily has an infinite variance. A related concept is that of an "infinitely divisible" distribution, which is one such that it can occur as the distribution of a sum S_n of independently identically distributed random variables. Examples include the normal and Poisson distributions (and there are others, but there is a sense in which these are the most important). This notion was originated by de Finetti who also invented the fruitful concept of "exchangeable" random variables, which would take too long to explain in detail.

It might have been thought that with both Laws of Large Numbers and the De Moivre-Laplace limit theorem by which $(x - np)/\sqrt{n}$ has an approximate normal distribution, everything about the asymptotic behavior of Bernoulli trials had been established. However, *Aleksandr Yakovlevich Khinchin* (or Hinčin) (1894–1959), building on the work of various others, established the Law of the Iterated Logarithm by which

$$\mathsf{P}\left(\limsup_{n\to\infty} \frac{|X - np|}{\sqrt{2npq \ln\ln n}} = 1\right) = 1$$

so that the random variable $|X - np|$ is as large as $\sqrt{2npq \ln\ln n}$ infinitely often but gets larger than that only finitely often.

In the second half of the 20th century, many areas closely related to probability theory developed apace. To mention but two, the theory of games developed from the work of *John von Neumann* (1903–1957) and *Oskar Morgenstern* (1902–1977), which appeared in their book *The Theory of Games and Economic Behavior* in 1944, and information theory developed largely out of the 1948 book *The Mathematical Theory of Communication* by *Claude Elwood Shannon* (1916–2001).

REFERENCES

A good simple account of the early history is to be found in David (1952), with further information in Maistrov (1967/1974), Adams (1974), and Hacking (1973, 1990). Todhunter (1865) is the classic account which (in David's words) "will always be read but for profit rather than for pleasure." More recent, fuller, accounts are given by Stigler (1986) and Hald (1990, 1998). Krüger, Daston, and Heidelberger (1989a, 1989b) is good on the background in society and the sciences, particularly in the 19th century. Pearson and Kendall (1970) and Kendall and Plackett (1977) contain a large number of essays on various topics. Jordan (1972) and Feller (1950/1957/1968, 1966/1971) are recent books on probability (Jordan's with an old-fashioned feel to it) that give useful historical references.

Adams, W. J. (1974). *The life and times of the central limit theorem.* New York: Kaedmon.

David, F. N. (1952). *Games, gods and gambling*. London: Griffin.

Feller, W. (1968). *An introduction to probability theory and its applications* (Vol. 1, 3rd ed.). New York: Wiley. (First edition published 1950, second edition published 1957)

Feller, W. (1971). *An introduction to probability theory and its applications* (Vol. 2, 2nd ed.). New York: Wiley. (First edition published 1966)

Hacking, I. (1973). *The emergence of probability.* Cambridge, UK: Cambridge University Press.

Hacking, I. (1990). *The taming of chance*. Cambridge, UK: Cambridge University Press.

Hald, A. (1990). *A history of probability and statistics and their applications before 1750.* New York: Wiley.

Hald, A. (1998). *A history of mathematical statistics from 1750 to 1930.* New York: Wiley.

Jordan, K. (1972). *Chapters on the classical calculus of probability.* Budapest, Hungary: Akadémiaio Kiadó.

Kendall, M. G., & Plackett, R. L. (Eds.). (1977). *Studies in the history of probability and statistics* (Vol. 2). London: Griffin.

Krüger, L., Daston, L. J., & Heidelberger, M. (Eds.). (1989a). *The probabilistic revolution: Vol. 1. Ideas in history.* Cambridge, MA: MIT Press.

Krüger, L., Daston, L. J., & Heidelberger, M. (Eds.). (1989b). *The probabilistic revolution: Vol. 2. Ideas in the sciences.* Cambridge, MA: MIT Press.

Maistrov, L. E. (1974). *Probability theory: A historical sketch* (S. Kotz, Trans. and Ed.). New York: Academic Press. (Original work published 1967. Moscow: Izdatel'stvo Nauka)

Pearson, E. S., & Kendall, M. G. (Eds.). (1970). *Studies in the history of statistics and probability.* London: Griffin.

Stigler, S. M. (1986). *The history of statistics: The measurement of uncertainty before 1900.* Cambridge, MA: Belknap Press of Harvard University Press.

Todhunter, I. (1865). *A history of the mathematical theory of probability from the time of Pascal to that of Laplace.* London: Macmillan. (Reprinted 1949, New York, NY: Chelsea)

Web Sites

http://www-groups.dcs.st-and.ac.uk/~history/index.html

http://www.york.ac.uk/depts/maths/histstat/welcome.htm

2

FREQUENTIST PROBABILITY THEORY

HERWIG FRIEDL AND SIEGFRIED HÖRMANN

INTRODUCTION AND BASIC CONCEPTS

The purpose of the following discussion is to give a brief introduction to probabilistic concepts, which will be elaborated and extended in the course of this chapter. We will introduce some important ideas and some results and examples. For the reader who is interested in more details and examples, we especially recommend the following literature. The book by Gordon (1997) is nicely written and gives a basic introduction to discrete probability theory with many exercises. A classical higher level introduction, which also contains measure theoretic aspects of probability theory is the book by Billingsley (1995). Due to the lack of space, we will not give any proofs here. The interested reader will find these proofs, for example, in Durrett (1994), a book on an intermediate level between Gordon (1997) and Billingsley (1995). It contains many examples and exercises, and the main ideas of some advanced topics are described in an elementary way. Rudas (2004) gives an elementary introduction to probability theory and explains many of the concepts used here intuitively.

Deterministic and Probabilistic

The objective target of natural sciences is to describe laws of nature by means of formulas and mathematical models. Starting from axioms based on fundamental observations we try to gain new expertise by combining such formulas and models. A model is said to be "good" if it describes the reality well. The quality check a mathematical model has to pass in order to match with reality is its ability to predict the future. If a physicist wants to model the stopping distance of a car with respect to the velocity and weight of the car, the model is found to work well if the calculated stopping distance is close to the measurements carried out after each experiment. This is an example of a deterministic model, that is, a model which allows prediction of the outcome of an experiment via the initial condition. For example, Galileo was able to compute the time a stone needs to fall to the ground based on the height (the initial condition) from which it starts to fall. Newton was able to make precise predictions of the planetary configuration by knowing the interaction of gravities, and more refined models allowed us to put satellites into orbit and to make use of modern global positioning systems.

Many natural phenomena, however, cannot be described through deterministic models. Even in alleged simple experiments a deterministic description is impossible. For example, we cannot predict the outcome when we toss a coin or throw a die. In our everyday life, we frequently encounter events with uncertain outcomes, such as the outcome of an election, the fluctuation of the oil price, the government fiscal deficit, and so on. We describe such events by using the terms probability, likelihood, or chance. We make statements such as (1) tomorrow there is a 30% chance of rain, (2) it is more likely to have a car accident than to be a victim of a plane crash, (3) the odds of winning a coin-tossing game is 50%, and (4) the probability of getting 6 on throwing a die is $1/6$. A common mathematical term for random is *stochastic*. For example, we say that the oil price forms a stochastic process.

We make decisions based on these "virtual" concepts. Although we do not know in advance if our decisions will be correct, we (perhaps unconsciously) make use of probabilities. Phrases such as "the risk is too high..." actually contain the concept of probabilistic thinking. But what do we mean when we say that something occurs with 50% probability or with a probability of 0.5?

Probabilities and Relative Frequencies

The term *probability* is related to phenomena with uncertain outcomes. In the following, we will talk about the "outcome of an experiment," where the notion "experiment" is used in its broadest sense. A suggestive way to explain the concept of probability is by means of *relative frequencies*. If we think of any experiment, we can always distinguish between two complementary outcomes: something either happens or does not happen (e.g., coin tossing, head/no head; throwing a die, 6/not 6; playing darts, hit the bull/do not hit the bull; the weather on March 19, rain/no rain). One of the two outcomes we call *success*. Now we repeat an experiment under the same conditions for several times and look at the ratio r_N between the number of successes S_N and the total number of trials N:

$$r_N = \frac{S_N}{N}. \tag{2.1}$$

The ratio r_N is called *relative frequency of successes*. Note that r_N is in any case a real number between 0 and 1. According to an intuitive meaning one should expect that r_N "converges" in some sense to a fixed number in the interval $[0,1]$. If we set S_N the number of "heads" out of N trials in the coin-tossing game, it seems plausible that r_N will approach $1/2$ if N is large, since $100 \cdot r_N$ is the percentage of successes (number of heads). When rolling a die, we may define S_N as the number of "6"s out of N trials and expect that r_N should be approximately $1/6$ for sufficiently large N. Indeed, experience shows that if we repeat some experiment sufficiently often, then the relative frequency of the number of successes will level off to a real number p in the interval $[0,1]$. Thus, if we perform an experiment and want to assign a probability p for the event "success," then p should be the limit of r_N for $N \to \infty$. This is the so-called *statistical or frequentist definition* of probability. Of course, up to now we do not have any prior mathematical concept which proves that this limit will exist and therefore this definition is unsatisfactory from a mathematical point of view. In modern probability theory, one goes the other way round. The basic idea is to develop a concept that allows to prove that r_N converges to p, whenever we assign p as the probability of success. For example, experience shows that in the coin-tossing game r_N, the relative frequency of heads, say, approaches $1/2$ if N is large. Hence we set $p_{\mathrm{H}} = 1/2$ if p_{H} is the probability of heads. Our mathematical model should be conceived now in such a way that r_N converges to the defined probability p_{H}. Indeed, we will achieve this target. It is possible to construct a mathematical model that allows to prove that if S_N is the number of successes and we assign p to the probability for success, then r_N converges to p. This follows from the so-called *law of large numbers*, which we will discuss later. It is crucial to note that we define probabilities ourselves, mostly based on empirical observations.

Events and Their Probabilities

In any experiment, we have a set of different outcomes. For example, the set $\{\text{head}, \text{tail}\}$ when tossing a coin, $\{1,\ldots,6\}$ when throwing a die, $\{0,\ldots,N\}$ for the number of people out of N who smoke, the set of sections on a dart disk, or the positive reals in some interval $[0,t]$ for the time one waits in front of a traffic light. If we perform some experiment, we will denote by Ω the set of all possible outcomes and by $\omega \in \Omega$ some special possible outcome (e.g., "head" or "6," etc.). The set Ω is called *sample space* and $\omega \in \Omega$ is an *elementary event* or *outcome*. A subset A of Ω is called *event* (e.g., the even numbers on the die or the bull's-eye on the dart disk). To depict it, we can think of an experiment as "randomly" drawing an element from the set Ω. We say that the event A occurs if we draw an element in A. Hence, if B is another subset of Ω, we say that A and B occur when we pick some ω that is an element of A and of B, that is, $\omega \in A \cap B$. Similarly, A or B occurs if we pick some ω that is either in A or in B, that is, $\omega \in A \cup B$. If A does not occur, this means that we choose an element in the complement of A, shortly, $\omega \in A^{\mathrm{c}}$. We might also be interested in the event "A occurs and B does not." Formally we write $\omega \in A \cap B^{\mathrm{c}}$ or shorter $\omega \in A \backslash B$. Note that Ω and $\emptyset$ (the empty set) are also events. Of course, we can augment the number of events we want to combine. We leave it to the reader to interpret events like $A \cup B \cup C \cup D$ or $(A \cup B) \backslash C \cap D$.

The set-theoretical operations allow us to create events by making intersections, unions, or complements. For the poll example, let $A = \{a, \ldots, N\}$ and $B = \{1, \ldots, b\}$, $0 \leqslant a \leqslant b \leqslant N$. Then the event A is given as follows: a or more people smoke; $A \cap B = \{a, \ldots, b\}$: the number of people smoking is between a and b; and $A^{\mathrm{c}} = \{0, \ldots, a-1\}$: less than a people smoke.

Our main goal is to assign a probability to each event, that is, we want to find a mapping P from the set of events that assigns every event a real number

$$A \mapsto P(A).$$

We say that $P(A)$ is the probability that A occurs. Again we point out that *we* define the probability of some event. But clearly we should make some restrictions. For example, we should assume that

$$0 \leqslant P(A) \leqslant 1$$

for any event A. Of course, otherwise we cannot hope to achieve that the relative frequency of the occurrence of A in a series of experiments approaches $P(A)$. Furthermore, it is quite natural to set

$$P(\Omega) = 1, \qquad (2.2)$$

that is, the probability that anything possible happens should be 1. Another condition we will pose on P is *additivity*. (Actually we need the so-called σ-additivity, which will be introduced later.) Additivity of P amounts to

$$P(A \cup B) = P(A) + P(B) \quad \text{if} \quad A \cap B = \emptyset. \qquad (2.3)$$

If $A \cap B = \emptyset$ we say that A and B are *disjoint events*. This means that they cannot happen at the same time. For example, if we roll a die and A is the event that the die shows an even number and B is the event that the die shows an odd number, then A and B are disjoint, because the outcome is either even or odd, and there is no number having both properties. Additivity is quite an intuitive property if you compare P with a measure of length or area. We learn in school that the combined length of two disjoint intervals can be calculated from the sum of the individual lengths. Furthermore, if we weigh several different weights, then we know that the total weight is the sum of the individual weights. It is an easy exercise to show that for a sequence $A_1, \ldots, A_n$ of disjoint events, property (2.3) generalizes to

$$P(A_1 \cup \cdots \cup A_n) = \sum_{i=1}^{n} P(A_i). \qquad (2.4)$$

If Ω is a finite set, then a mapping $P : \mathcal{P}(\Omega) \to [0,1]$ satisfying (2.2) and (2.3) is called *probability measure*. Here $\mathcal{P}(\Omega)$ denotes the power set of Ω, which is the set of all subsets, that is, all possible events. An immediate consequence of (2.3) is

$$P(\Omega) = P(\Omega \cup \emptyset) = P(\Omega) + P(\emptyset),$$

showing that $P(\emptyset) = 0$. This should of course be fulfilled in every feasible model: The probability for something impossible is zero. Below we cite two important calculation rules that arise directly from (2.2) and (2.3), namely,

$$\begin{aligned} P(A^{\mathrm{c}}) &= 1 - P(A), \\ P(A \cup B) &= P(A) + P(B) - P(A \cap B). \end{aligned}$$

Note that the last identity implies $P(A \cup B) \leqslant P(A) + P(B)$, where equality holds if and only if the probability that A and B both occur is zero. Furthermore, if $A \subset B$ we have $B = A \cup (B \backslash A)$ and hence

$$P(A) \leqslant P(B) \quad \text{if} \quad A \subset B. \qquad (2.5)$$

Conditions (2.2) and (2.3) are technical restrictions for the mapping P. Another restriction on P is due to its modeling character. If we toss a coin, we can define $P(\text{head}) = p$, with $p \in [0,1]$. If S_N is the number of heads in N trials, then the law of large numbers will show that r_N, the relative frequency of heads, converges to p in our model. Our experience shows that r_N will converge to $1/2$. Thus, we will define $p = 1/2$ and not 0.67, say. On the other hand, if we replace the coin by a thumbtack, then one side is probably favored. Suppose that we made 1 billion trials and found that the beaked part shows in about 67% of the trials, then it will be a better choice to set $p = 0.67$.

The Die and Laplace Experiments

A die is to be thrown. Then $\Omega = \{1,\ldots,6\}$ and the set of all possible events is $\mathcal{P}(\Omega)$, the powerset of Ω. For example, $\{1,4,5\}$, $\{2\}$, Ω, $\emptyset$ are events. We need a mapping $P : \mathcal{P}(\Omega) \to [0,1]$, such that (2.2) and (2.3) hold, and propose P as

$$P(A) = \frac{|A|}{|\Omega|} = \frac{|A|}{6},$$

where $|A|$ denotes the cardinality of some set A, that is, the number of elements included in A. Clearly, $|A| \in \{0,\ldots,6\}$ ($|\emptyset| = 0$), which shows that $P(A) \in [0,1]$. Furthermore, we have $P(\{i\}) = 1/6$ for any $i \in \{1,\ldots,6\}$. Hence, the elementary events were all given the customary probabilities and since $|\Omega| = 6$, we see that (2.2) holds. To show that (2.3) holds, we assume that $A \subset \{1,\ldots,6\}$ and $B \subset \{1,\ldots,6\}$. It is easy to verify that if $A \cap B = \emptyset$, then $|A \cup B| = |A| + |B|$. Hence,

$$P(A \cup B) = \frac{|A \cup B|}{6} = \frac{|A| + |B|}{6} = P(A) + P(B).$$

Now we try to generalize this very simple example. Think of a die with n faces. We have $\Omega = \{1,\ldots,n\}$ and set

$$P(A) = \frac{|A|}{|\Omega|}. \qquad (2.6)$$

By the same arguments, one can also show that P satisfies (2.2) and (2.3). It follows that $P(\{i\}) = 1/n$ for every $i \in \{1,\ldots,n\}$, that is, every elementary event has the same probability. On the other hand, if every elementary event has probability $1/n$, it is easy to see that (2.6) holds.

Hence, the probability measure P defined in (2.6) is the only one which assigns the same probability to every element ω in a finite sample space Ω. An experiment where we assume that every elementary event is equally likely is called a *Laplace experiment*. Besides tossing of a coin and rolling of a die, a further simple example is the roulette game. Here we have 18 black and 18 red numbers ranging from 1 to 36, and also a green, which has a value zero. Since every number is assumed to be equally likely, we have $P(\text{black}) = 18/37$.

Considering (2.6), it seems rather simple to calculate probabilities in Laplace experiments. However, in general this is not true as the following example shows. Assume that we play roulette n times and at each trial we bet a fixed amount of money on "black." We ask for $P(\text{have a gain after } n \text{ trials})$. A possible outcome ω will look like $\omega = (\text{black, black, not black}, \ldots, \text{black, not black})$, a sequence of length n. Hence, we might set

$$\Omega = \{(\varepsilon_1,\ldots,\varepsilon_n) | \varepsilon_i \in \{\text{black, not black}\}\}.$$

Because of the green zero, "not black" is more likely than "black." Thus, it is not plausible that every $\omega \in \Omega$ occurs with the same probability. The more "blacks" are contained in ω, the less likely it should occur. But if we set

$$\Omega = \{(\varepsilon_1,\ldots,\varepsilon_n) | \varepsilon_i \in \{0,\ldots,36\}\},$$

then ω represents the exact sequence of numbers obtained in n trials, for example, $\omega = (8,32,\ldots,22)$, and as a result of symmetry we assume that every such sequence has the same probability. For every coordinate of $(\varepsilon_1,\ldots,\varepsilon_n)$ there are 37 possibilities, hence $|\Omega| = 37^n$. To get $P(\text{have a gain after } n \text{ trials})$ we count the number of ωs that show more often a black number than a number which is not black. To get this count is not quite simple. In general, it might be a combinatorial challenge to calculate the number of ωs satisfying a certain restriction. This example follows a *binomial distribution*, which is treated in the section about discrete distributions.

Conditional Probabilities and Independence

Assume we want to calculate the probability of some event A if we know already that some other event B has occurred. For example, if we know that the die shows an even number then the probability of "2" is $1/3$ whereas the outcome "3" has probability zero. For some event B, we can define a new probability measure as follows.

Definition 2.1. *Let B be an event such that $P(B) > 0$. For any event A define the* conditional probability of A given B, *$P(A|B)$ in short, by*

$$P(A|B) = \frac{P(A \cap B)}{P(B)}. \tag{2.7}$$

The idea behind this definition for the conditional probability with a fixed B is rather simple. Since B already happened, we can only observe events of the form $A \cap B$. To get (2.2) we just have to rescale the probability measure with $P(B)$. We leave it to the reader to prove (2.2) and (2.3).

If we think of some experiment where B has no influence on A, then we expect

$$P(A|B) = P(A). \tag{2.8}$$

For example, if we roll a die twice and if we know the outcome of the first game then this has no influence on the second game. This gives rise to the following important definition.

Definition 2.2 (Independence). *If (2.8) holds, then we say that A and B are* independent. *Equivalently, (2.8) may be written as*

$$P(A \cap B) = P(A)P(B). \tag{2.9}$$

Often it is difficult to compute the probability of some event A directly, whereas it is simple to compute $P(A|B)$. The next theorem allows us to get $P(A)$ by means of some conditional probabilities $P(A|B)$.

Theorem 2.1. *Let $B_1, B_2, \ldots$ be events such that $B_i \cap B_j = \emptyset$, if $i \neq j$, and $\cup_{i \geqslant 1} B_i = \Omega$. Then, for any event A, we have*

$$P(A) = \sum_{i \geqslant 1} P(B_i)P(A|B_i).$$

A sequence $B_1, B_2, \ldots$ of events satisfying the conditions of the last theorem is called a *partition* of Ω. Note that in many examples the partition is finite, that is, $B_1 \cup \cdots \cup B_n = \Omega$, but since this restriction is not necessary we omit it.

To underline the usefulness of Theorem 2.1, we give a simple example. Assume that a fingerprint access control system identifies a registered person with probability 0.95 at the first try. If the person is not identified, it has a second try, where it is checked more thoroughly; it is identified with probability 0.98, given it is registered. On the other hand, an unregistered person is falsely identified with probability 0.07 at the first try and with probability 0.01 at the second try. Finally, we assume that 8% of the people trying to get access are not registered. We ask for the probability that some person is misclassified, that is, it is accepted without being registered or the other way round.

We define the events $M = \{\text{misclassified}\}$, $R = \{\text{registered}\}$, and $R^c = \{\text{unregistered}\}$. Clearly, R and R^c define a partition of Ω. Thus by Theorem 2.1 we have $P(M) = P(R)P(M|R) + P(R^c)P(M|R^c)$. The probability $P(M|R)$ that a registered person is misclassified is the probability that it is rejected twice. We assume that the first rejection of a registered person has no influence on the second trial, that is, the tries are independent. Then $P(M|R) = 0.05 \times 0.01$. Similarly, an unregistered person can be either directly accepted with probability 0.07, or first rejected and then accepted with probability 0.93×0.01, giving $P(M|R^c) = 0.07 + 0.93 \times 0.01$. Together this results in $P(M) = 0.007$, that is, $P(M) < 1\%$.

What about the probability that a person who has been accepted is registered? Thus, we ask for $P(R|A)$, where $A = \{\text{accepted}\}$. From Definition 2.1 and Theorem 2.1, we get

$$\begin{aligned} P(R|A) &= \frac{P(A \cap R)}{P(A)} \\ &= \frac{P(A \cap R)}{P(R)P(A|R) + P(R^c)P(A|R^c)}. \end{aligned} \tag{2.10}$$

Using the probability tree, it is again easy to compute $P(A \cap R)$, $P(A|R)$, and $P(A|R^c)$. From Figure 2.1 we read, for example,

$$\begin{aligned} P(A|R) &= P(A_1|R) + P(A_1^c|R)P(A_2|R \cap A_1^c) \\ &= 0.95 + 0.05 \times 0.98. \end{aligned}$$

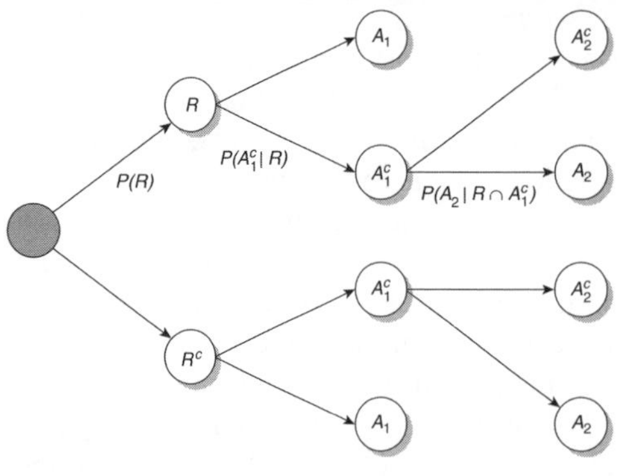

Figure 2.1 The access control can be visualized by a *probability tree*. Each person will take one of the paths from the root (full circle) to an endpoint of the tree. Here A_i denotes the event $\{\text{access at trial } i\}$. For example, the probability of the path $R - A_1^c - A_2$ is $P(R \cap A_1^c \cap A_2) = P(R)P(A_1^c|R)P(A_2|R \cap A_1^c)$.

Relation (2.10) is a special case of the following.

Theorem 2.2 (Bayes's Theorem). *Let $B_1, B_2, \ldots$ be a partition of Ω. Then, for any event A with $P(A) > 0$, we have*

$$P(B_j|A) = \frac{P(A \cap B_j)}{\sum\limits_{i \geqslant 1} P(B_i)P(A|B_i)}.$$

The Probability Space

So far the formalism is relatively simple since we only deal with experiments with a finite sample space. In this context, it is easy to give the definition of a probability space. Let $\mathcal{P}(\Omega)$ be again the power-set of Ω. For example if $\Omega = \{a, b, c\}$, then

$$\mathcal{P}(\Omega) = \{\emptyset, \{a\}, \{b\}, \{c\}, \{a,b\}, \{b,c\}, \{a,c\}, \{a,b,c\}\}.$$

If P is a probability measure, the triple $(\Omega, \mathcal{P}(\Omega), P)$ is called *probability space*. However, in many situations it is not natural to assume $|\Omega| < \infty$. If we agree upon tossing the coin until we observe "head" for the first time, then we might set

$$\Omega = \{1, 2, 3, \ldots\}, \tag{2.11}$$

that is, $|\Omega| = \infty$. Clearly, experience tells us that the number of trials will not be very large. However, it is mathematically unsatisfactory to assume a fixed number of trials that will not be exceeded. Although Ω in (2.11) contains infinitely many elements, it is still "handsome" since it is *denumerable* (countable). A set Ω is denumerable if we can write Ω as an ordered sequence $\Omega = \{\omega_1, \omega_2, \ldots\}$. In this case, we say that Ω is a *discrete* sample space. But Ω can be a really "large" set, for example, if Ω is an interval on the real line, $[0, 1]$ say. Then Ω has infinitely many elements and it is no longer denumerable. If $A = [a, b]$ is a subinterval of $\Omega = [0, 1]$, we may define $P(A) = \text{length}(A) = b - a$. Since $\text{length}([0, 1]) = 1$ we have (2.2) and (2.3) as already discussed. It may appear satisfactory to consider as events only the class of intervals contained in Ω, but we will go further and take only classes $\mathcal{A}$ that are "closed" under countable set operations. That is, if $A_1, A_2, \ldots$ are elements of $\mathcal{A}$, then we want, for example, that $A_1 \cup A_2 \cup \cdots \in \mathcal{A}$, $A_1 \cap A_2 \cap \cdots \in \mathcal{A}$, $A_1^c \in \mathcal{A}$, or $A_n \backslash A_m \in \mathcal{A}$. For example, let A_i denote the event $\{i\text{th coin tossing shows head}\}$. If A denotes the event that "head" will show ultimately then $A = \cup_{i=1}^{\infty} A_i$, which is clearly also of interest. A class of events that is closed under countable set operations is called *σ-algebra*. For example, $\mathcal{P}(\Omega)$ always defines a σ-algebra. Note that any σ-algebra contains the sets Ω and $\emptyset$. To see this, take some set $A \in \mathcal{A}$. Since $\mathcal{A}$ is a σ-algebra, it is obviously closed under finite set operations and we have $A^c \in \mathcal{A}$, $\Omega = A \cup A^c \in \mathcal{A}$, and $\emptyset = A \cap A^c \in \mathcal{A}$. In our former example, the set of intervals defines no σ-algebra. The smallest σ-algebra containing all the intervals in $[0, 1]$ (or more generally in $\mathbb{R}$) is called the *Borel σ-algebra* on $[0, 1]$ (in short $\mathcal{B}([0, 1])$) or *Borel σ-algebra* on $\mathbb{R}$ (in short $\mathcal{B}(\mathbb{R})$). We say that the Borel σ-algebra is *generated* by the intervals.

Definition 2.3. *Let Ω be a set and $\mathcal{A} \subset \mathcal{P}(\Omega)$ be a σ-algebra. A mapping*

$$P : \mathcal{A} \to [0, 1]$$

is called probability measure, *if*

(M1) $P(\Omega) = 1$,

and if for any sequence (A_i) of pairwise disjoint sets in $\mathcal{A}$

(M2) $P(A_1 \cup A_2 \cup \cdots) = P(A_1) + P(A_2) + \cdots$.

The triple $(\Omega, \mathcal{A}, P)$ is called probability space.

The difference between (2.3) and (M2) is that the latter requests countable additivity (σ-*additivity*), which is of course more restrictive. In the case where Ω has only finitely many elements, they are equivalent since as a matter of fact we have only finitely many disjoint events. For a detailed discussion on the meaning of the assumptions (M1) and (M2), we refer to Rudas (2004).

One important example is the discrete probability space. Here, $\Omega = \{\omega_1, \omega_2, \ldots\}$ is a countable set. To define a probability measure, we need a sequence $p_1, p_2, \ldots$ of nonnegative numbers with $\sum_{i=1}^{\infty} p_i = 1$. If A is some subset of Ω, then A is again a countable set, i.e. a countable union of elementary events. Now we define

$$P(A) = \sum_{\omega_i \in A} p_i.$$

It follows that $(\Omega, \mathcal{P}(\Omega), P)$ is a probability space.

Another important example is $\Omega = \mathbb{R}^n$. Here, we will endow the sample space with the Borel σ-algebra on $\mathbb{R}^n$ ($\mathcal{B}(\mathbb{R}^n)$), this is the smallest σ-algebra containing the rectangles $(a_1, b_1] \times (a_2, b_2] \times \cdots \times (a_n, b_n]$ where $a_i \leqslant b_i$. We would like to allude to the fact that $\mathcal{B}(\mathbb{R}^n)$ contains actually all sets of interest. For example, it is not hard to see that any circular area may be written as a (countable) disjoint union of rectangles. Indeed there exist no examples of intuitive meaningful sets that are not contained in the Borel σ-algebra. However, there are sets not contained in $\mathcal{B}(\mathbb{R}^n)$ and *one can in general not define a measure on* $\mathcal{P}(\mathbb{R}^n)$. In the next section, we will give examples for probability measures on $\mathcal{B}(\mathbb{R}^2)$.

Continuous Distributions and Modeling

Assume that we are playing darts. We can describe the dart disk by the set of points (x, y) in plane with $x^2 + y^2 \leqslant r^2$, where r is the radius of the disk. Hence

$$\Omega = \{(x, y) \in \mathbb{R}^2 | x^2 + y^2 \leqslant r^2\}.$$

Assume that we are throwing darts at random, without aiming, and for simplicity we also assume that we never miss the disk. That is, we assume that different sections of the disk that have the same "size" (area) are hit with the same probability and the probability of hitting the disk is 1. A promising way to generalize the Laplace model for this experiment is to define

$$P(A) = \frac{\text{area}(A)}{\text{area}(\Omega)}, \tag{2.12}$$

that is, the probability of A is proportional to its size. If A_1 and A_2 are disjoint sections, then $\text{area}(A_1 \cup A_2)$ is $\text{area}(A_1) + \text{area}(A_2)$. Hence, it is clear that (2.2) and (2.3) both hold. This is an example of how one can define probabilities for a continuous experiment. In contrast to a discrete experiment, our probability space (the circle with radius r) contains infinitely many elements, which cannot be counted. Since Ω is not countable, we usually cannot represent some event A as a countable union of elementary events. Consequently, it is not possible to proceed in the same fashion as in the discrete case, where it is enough to define only the probabilities of elementary events and to deduce $P(A)$ from (M2).

Note that we can also interpret $P(A)$ in (2.12) as the volume of a right prism with base A and height $1/\text{area}(\Omega)$ (see left side of Figure 2.2). This approach enables us to describe a more realistic version of the last game. Suppose that the player aims to hit the bull's-eye. Then it will be more likely that he or she scores a hit closer to the center than near the margin. The idea is to define some body B with base Ω and volume equal to 1. Then we define $P(A)$ as the volume of the perpendicular body that is trapped between the base A and the surface of B (see right picture in Figure 2.2). A nonnegative function f that encloses some area (body) with measure 1 is called *density function*. Since we can set $f(x, y) = 0$ if $x^2 + y^2 > r^2$, we can assume without loss of generality that $\Omega = \mathbb{R}^2$. Hence, $(\Omega, \mathcal{B}(\mathbb{R}^2), P)$ defines a probability space. The concept of modeling random experiments with the help of density functions proves rather useful and is discussed next.

Random Variables and Distributions

To define random variables, we imagine the following gambling variants. We throw a coin twice. The bet, which is one u, charges the bank.

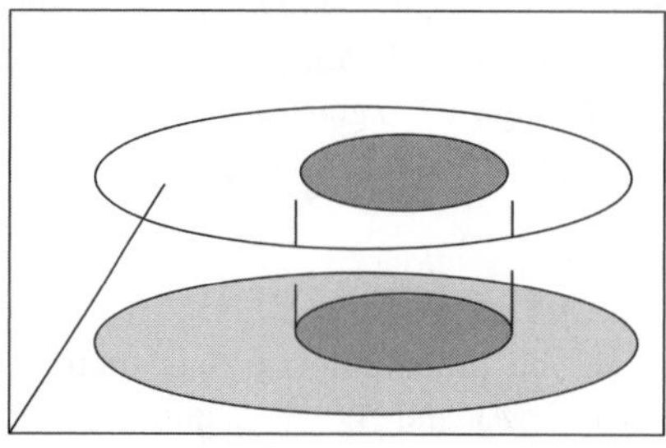

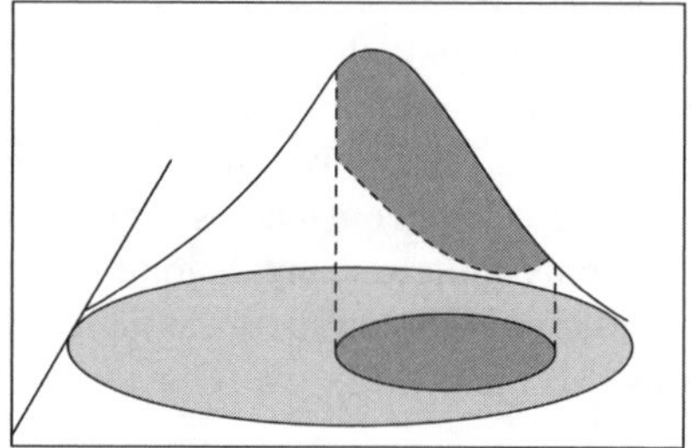

Figure 2.2 $P(A)$ is the volume enclosed by $\Omega \cap A$ and some *density function*, which describes the surface of the body B. See text for explanation.

a. If {head, head} occurs we get $2u$, otherwise we lose.

b. If {head, head} occurs we get $4u$, otherwise we lose.

c. If head occurs at least once, we get $2u$, otherwise we lose.

Each of these variants is described by the simple probability space $(\Omega, \mathcal{A}, P)$ where $\Omega = \{$(tail, tail), (tail, head), (head, tail), (head, head)$\}$, $\mathcal{A} = \mathcal{P}(\Omega)$, and $P(\omega) = 1/4$. But we are not interested in describing the elementary events from the sample space Ω but rather to discuss the gain. In many situations, it is more convenient to work with a chosen summary variable instead of concentrating on the original probability structure. In the above example, we assigned real numbers to every elementary event in Ω, according to our variant of the game. For example, if X describes the gain in game (a), then we have X(head, head) $= u$, X(head, tail) $= -u$, and so on. Assume now that we flip a coin n times. Then we are usually not that much interested in which of the possible 2^n different n-tuples ω in Ω has exactly occurred but rather in the number of heads in the n tosses. Defining X as the number of heads out of n will exactly capture the essence of our interest. The outcome of X depends on which event ω occurred in the experiment, hence the outcome of X is random. A *random variable* X is a function that maps elements from Ω onto a new sample space S, that is,

$$X : \Omega \to S.$$

If $S \subseteq \mathbb{R}$, then S is called the *range* of X. For example, if X describes the loss or gain in game (b), then X maps from Ω to $\{-u, 3u\}$. As another example, let X describe the number of heads out of n coin tosses, then X maps each possible sequence of heads and tails onto $S = \{0, 1, \ldots, n\}$. To give a more practical example, we may define Ω as a certain population. In this case, each $\omega \subset \Omega$ is some person in the population and X may assign age, sex, confession, and so on. Note that the outcomes of sex and confession are no real numbers. As a final example, consider some medical treatment where X assigns the labels "no success," "success" (0, 1 say) to each patient ω in the set of patients Ω.

Sometimes it is useful to consider probability spaces that are defined by a random variable. The following example illustrates the simple idea for the construction of this space. Consider game variant (c). If X describes the gain or loss, then $X : \Omega \to \{-u, u\}$, that is, $S = \{-u, u\}$. We set $\mathcal{A} = \mathcal{P}(S) = \{\{\emptyset\}, \{u\}, \{-u\}, S\}$ and define

$$\begin{aligned} P_X(\pm u) &:= P(X = \pm u) \\ &= P(\{\omega | X(\omega) = \pm u\}). \end{aligned}$$

For example, we get $P_X(-u) = P(\{\text{tail, tail}\}) = 1/4$. Here it is an easy exercise to show that P_X defines a measure on $\mathcal{A}$. Hence $(S, \mathcal{A}, P_X)$ is a probability space.

Another version of the above coin-tossing experiment consists of $n = 3$ trials. Thus, we have $\Omega = \{$HHH, HHT, HTH, THH, HTT, THT, TTH, TTT$\}$. To count the number of heads, we simply consider the random variable X with

ω	$X(\omega)$	ω	$X(\omega)$
HHH	3	HTT	1
HHT	2	THT	1
HTH	2	TTH	1
THH	2	TTT	0

Thus, the range of X is the set of counts $S = \{0,1,2,3\}$. Since for a fair coin each elementary event ω has associated probability $1/8$, we get as induced probability

x	0	1	2	3
P(X=x)	1/8	3/8	3/8	1/8

To see this, consider

$$\begin{aligned} P(X=1) &= P(\{\omega | X(\omega)=1\}) \\ &= P(\{\text{HTT}, \text{THT}, \text{TTH}\}) \\ &= P(\{\text{HTT}\}) + P(\{\text{HTT}\}) \\ &\quad + P(\{\text{HTT}\}) \\ &= 3/8. \end{aligned}$$

More generally, let X be a random variable having range $S = \{x_1, x_2, \ldots\}$, that is, X has a countable range. We say in this case that X is a *discrete* random variable and define P_X on $\mathcal{P}(S)$ as

$$\begin{aligned} P_X(x_i) &:= P(X = x_i) \\ &= P(\{\omega \in \Omega | X(\omega) = x_i\}). \end{aligned} \tag{2.13}$$

For a discrete random variable X, the function P_X is called *probability mass function* (PMF). It is not hard to show that P_X is a probability measure on $\mathcal{P}(S)$ satisfying the constraints in (M1) and (M2). In short, one can say that the measure properties of P are inherited by P_X. We note that it is common to use uppercase letters (such as X, Y, Z) to denote random variables and the respective lowercase versions (such as x, y, z) for their possible values.

The derivation of the induced probability was pretty easy for discrete random variables, and it is also not difficult in the general setting. Assume now that X is a random variable that may not only have a countable but also an uncountable range. We define the induced probability function for any (Borel)-set $B \subset \mathcal{B}$ as

$$\begin{aligned} P_X(B) &:= P(X \in B) \\ &= P(\{\omega \in \Omega | X(\omega) \in B\}). \end{aligned} \tag{2.14}$$

The advertent reader may ask if it is a priori clear that $\{\omega \in \Omega | X(\omega) \in B\}$ is an element of $\mathcal{A}$, which is necessary to determine the probability of this set. This property, which is called *measurability*, is not automatic but rather needs to be assumed. This aspect will not be discussed here.

Definition 2.4. *The cumulative distribution function (CDF) $F_X(x)$ associated with the random variable X is defined as*

$$F_X(x) = P(X \leqslant x), \qquad x \in \mathbb{R}.$$

A CDF $F(x)$ induced by a probability measure and a random variable is growing monotonously, right continuous, tends to 1 if $x \to \infty$ and to 0 if $x \to -\infty$ (see Theorem 2.3 later). On the other hand, given a function F having these properties we get a probability measure on $(\mathbb{R}, \mathcal{B}(\mathbb{R}))$ by defining $P((a,b]) = F(b) - F(a)$. In many situations, we may argue that X has a specific distribution function by means of combinatorial (as in the foregoing examples) or physical considerations. For example, it is usual to describe survival or waiting times by the *exponential distribution* function

$$F(x) = \begin{cases} 1 - e^{-\lambda x} & \text{if } x \geqslant 0,\ \lambda > 0 \\ 0 & \text{otherwise.} \end{cases}$$

Assume that X is the lifetime of a bulb. Then the assumption that X has an exponential distribution implies that the probability that the bulb lives longer than $t+s$ time units, knowing that it is still working after t units, equals $P(X > s)$. This means if it has survived a certain time, then this should have no influence on its future expected lifetime. That is, $P(X > t+s | X > t) = P(X > s)$ holds, and the exponential distribution function is the only continuous CDF having this property.

For the coin-tossing example, we define again X as the number of heads observed when tossing the coin three times. Using the PMF derived before (see left part of Figure 2.3) yields the CDF

$$F_X(x) = P(X \leqslant x) = \begin{cases} 0 & \text{if } -\infty < x < 0 \\ 1/8 & \text{if } 0 \leqslant x < 1 \\ 1/2 & \text{if } 1 \leqslant x < 2 \\ 7/8 & \text{if } 2 \leqslant x < 3 \\ 1 & \text{if } 3 \leqslant x < \infty. \end{cases}$$

Here, F_X defines a *step function* (compare with right part of Figure 2.3). For example, if we

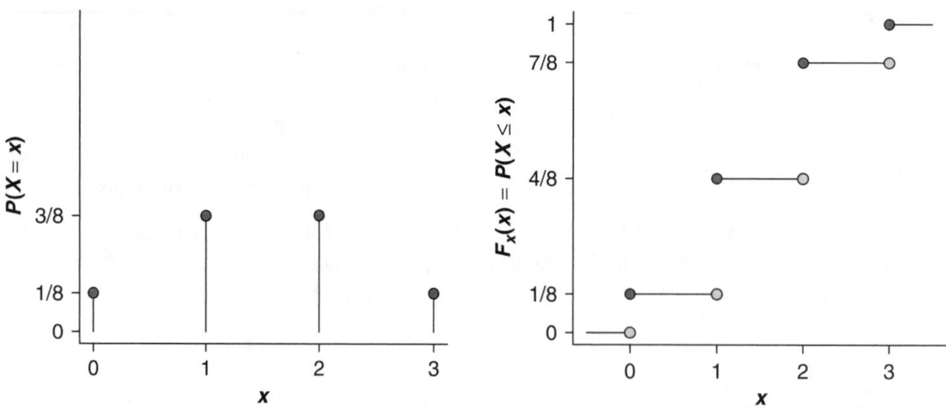

Figure 2.3 Probability mass function (left) and cumulative distribution function (right) of X, the number of heads when tossing a coin three times.

evaluate F_X at $x = 2.5$ we get

$$\begin{aligned} F_X(2.5) &= P(X \leqslant 2.5) \\ &= P(X \in \{0,1,2\}) = 7/8. \end{aligned}$$

The jumps are all in $x_i \in S$. Moreover, the height of the jump at x_i is exactly $P(X = x_i)$. For any $x < 0$, we have $F_X(x) = 0$ since X cannot be negative. Furthermore, for any $x \geqslant 3$ we get $F_X(x) = 1$. Generally, for discrete distributions we derive the CDF in terms of the respective PMF. Let $p_X(y) = P(X = y)$, then

$$\begin{aligned} F_X(x) &= \sum_{y \leqslant x} P(X = y) \\ &= \sum_{y \leqslant x} p_X(y), \qquad x \in \mathbb{R}. \end{aligned}$$

In contrast to this situation where the CDF is a step function and thus of discrete type, we say a random variable X is *continuous* if the associated CDF $F_X(x)$ is a continuous function of x. There are examples where the CDF is a piecewise continuous function, that is, neither discrete nor continuous. This issue is not treated here. In many important examples, the distribution function $F_X(z)$ can be obtained by calculating the area that a nonnegative function $f_X(t)$ encloses with the x-axis in the interval $(-\infty, z]$. The mathematical tool for calculating areas is *integration*. Instead of saying "area below $f_X(t)$ on the interval $(-\infty, z]$," we write

$$F_X(z) = \int_{-\infty}^{z} f_X(t)\,dt. \qquad (2.15)$$

The right-hand side of (2.15) displays the integral of the function $f_X(t)$ over the interval $(-\infty, z]$. Although integration is one of the most important concepts in mathematical analysis and in probability theory, we will not have an in-depth discussion here. For the less conversant reader, it suffices to have the concept of area in mind.

Definition 2.5. *Assume that $f_X(x)$ is a nonnegative function such that the integral $\int_{-\infty}^{\infty} f_X(x)dx$ (the area below f_X) exists and equals 1. Then $f_X(x)$ is called the* probability density function *(PDF) of a random variable X.*

A typical example is the density function of a triangle distribution, which can be used to model the behavior of measurement errors. We define the PDF as

$$f_X(x) = \begin{cases} x+1 & \text{if } -1 < x \leqslant 0 \\ 1-x & \text{if } 0 < x \leqslant 1 \\ 0 & \text{otherwise.} \end{cases}$$

Integrating this over x yields the corresponding distribution function

$$F_X(x) = \begin{cases} 0 & \text{if } -\infty < x < -1 \\ \frac{(x+1)^2}{2} & \text{if } -1 < x \leqslant 0 \\ \frac{1}{2} - \frac{x^2}{2} + x & \text{if } 0 < x \leqslant 1 \\ 1 & \text{if } 1 < x < \infty. \end{cases}$$

Both functions are displayed in Figure 2.4. The interpretation is that the measurement error is

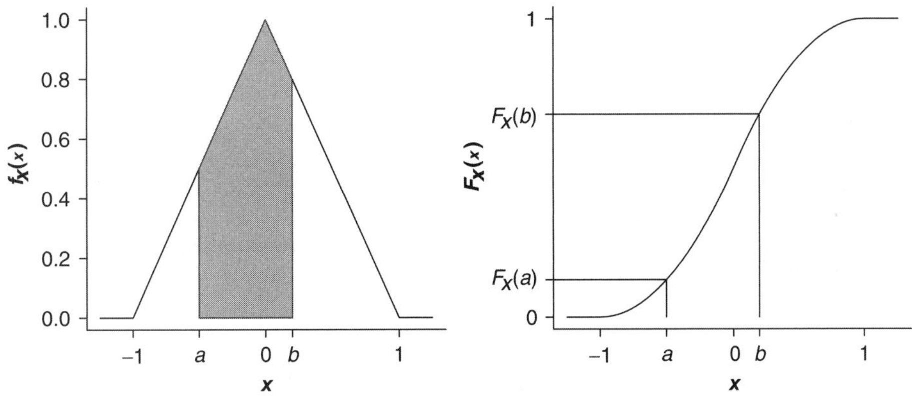

Figure 2.4 Probability density function (left) and cumulative distribution function (right) of a random variable X from a triangular distribution.

between -1 and $+1$ and symmetric around zero. The probability of a small error is higher than the probability of a larger error, since the PDF decreases when moving away from zero.

The following theorem summarizes some important properties of a CDF.

Theorem 2.3. *Any CDF $F_X(x)$ has the following properties:*

(1a) for x sufficiently small $F_X(x)$ has to become arbitrarily close to 0, that is, $\lim_{x \to -\infty} F_X(x) = 0$,

(1b) for x sufficiently large $F_X(x)$ has to become arbitrarily close to 1, that is, $\lim_{x \to +\infty} F_X(x) = 1$,

(2) $F_X(x)$ is a nondecreasing function of x,

(3) $F_X(x)$ is a right continuous function. That means, if we approach some value x_0 from the right, that is, $x > x_0$, then we will end in $F(x_0)$. In other words, we have $\lim_{x \to x_0, x > x_0} F(x) = F(x_0)$.

Clearly, all the characteristics of any random variable are fully described either through its associated CDF or by its PMF or PDF, depending on whether it is of discrete or continuous type, respectively. A PMF $p_X(x)$ has the advantage that it has an interpretation as a probability mass at any point x, that is, $p_X(x) = P(X = x)$. We have to be very careful with such an interpretation if X is continuous. Here, we get $\{X = x\} \subset \{x - \varepsilon < X \leqslant x\}$ for any $\varepsilon > 0$. Therefore, we infer from (2.5) that $P(X = x) \leqslant P(x - \varepsilon < X \leqslant x) = F_X(x) - F_X(x - \varepsilon)$. But because of the continuity of F_X we further get

$$0 \leqslant P(X = x) \leqslant \lim_{\varepsilon \to 0} \Big(F_X(x) - F_X(x - \varepsilon) \Big) = 0.$$

Thus, any point mass has to be zero for a continuous random variable X. Because of this, interval probabilities have the following property:

$$\begin{aligned} P(a < X < b) &= P(a \leqslant X < b) \\ &= P(a \leqslant X \leqslant b) \\ &= P(a < X \leqslant b). \end{aligned}$$

Also shown in Figure 2.4 is how we can calculate the probability that a continuous random error X stemming from a triangular distribution is observed within the interval (a, b). By means of the PDF, it is the probability mass (shown as shaded area) above this interval. But such an area is exactly described by the respective CDF. Using the CDF, it is thus just the difference

$$P(a < X \leqslant b) = F_X(b) - F_X(a).$$

Expected Value and Variance

An important characteristic of a random variable is its *expected value*, sometimes also called *expectation* or the *mean*. The expected value describes the average of all possible outcomes, weighted according to the probability of their occurrence. If X has a density, it is the area enclosed between the positive part of $xf_X(x)$ and the x-axis minus the area enclosed between the negative part of $xf_X(x)$ and the x-axis. If one of these areas is infinite, we say that the expected value of X does not exist. Below we give the formal definition.

Definition 2.6. *Let X be a discrete (continuous) random variable with PMF (PDF) $p_X(x)$ ($f_X(x)$). The expected value of X is*

$$\mathrm{E}(X) = \sum_{x \in S} x p_X(x) \qquad \left(= \int_{-\infty}^{\infty} x f_X(x)\, dx \right),$$

provided the sum (the integral) exists. It is common to write $\mu := \mathrm{E}(X)$.

Before we discuss some important calculation rules and the interpretation of the expected value, we consider two examples. Assume we are tossing a coin three times and let X denote the number of heads. Then we have

$$\begin{aligned}\mathrm{E}(X) &= \sum_{x=0}^{3} x P(X=x) \\ &= 0 \cdot \frac{1}{8} + 1 \cdot \frac{3}{8} + 2 \cdot \frac{3}{8} + 3 \cdot \frac{1}{8} = \frac{3}{2}.\end{aligned}$$

Thus, the mean is $\mu = 3/2$, which is exactly the horizontal center of the masspoints (compare with the PMF in Figure 2.3).

If X denotes the waiting time for the first occurrence of "head," then we have $P(X = x) = 1/2^x, x = 1, 2, \ldots$, and thus

$$\mathrm{E}(X) = \sum_{x=1}^{\infty} x 2^{-x} = 2.$$

Assume that X has the triangular distribution then $xf_X(x) = 0$ if x is outside the interval $[-1, 1]$ and hence it follows that

$$\mathrm{E}(X) = \int_{-1}^{0} x \cdot (1+x)\, dx + \int_{0}^{1} x \cdot (1-x)\, dx = 0.$$

This can be also seen in Figure 2.4, which shows the symmetrical behavior of the PDF around $\mu = 0$, the associated center of gravity.

An important property of the expected value is its linearity. Let X and Y be random variables and a some constant. We have

$$\mathrm{E}(aX + Y) = a\mathrm{E}(X) + \mathrm{E}(Y). \qquad (2.16)$$

The expected value is a so-called location parameter. It can be seen as the best guess for the outcome of some random experiment if we have no further information. If we repeat the same experiment independently under the same conditions, then the observations will vary around the expected value. The so-called *variance* measures the magnitude of this variation.

Definition 2.7. *The* variance *of a random variable X, short* $\mathrm{var}(X)$, *is defined as*

$$\mathrm{var}(X) = \mathrm{E}(X - \mu)^2.$$

The standard deviation *of X, short* $\mathrm{sd}(X)$, *is defined as* $\mathrm{sd}(X) = (\mathrm{var}(X))^{1/2}$.

If X has a large variance, then its realizations will probably deviate much from the expectation whereas if the variance is small the opposite holds. The following theorem is useful to determine the expectation of some functional $g(X)$ of X.

Theorem 2.4. *Assume that $g(\cdot)$ is a real function. Let X be a discrete (continuous) random variable with PMF (PDF) $p_X(x)$ ($f_X(x)$). Then*

$$\mathrm{E}(g(X)) = \sum_{x \in S} g(x) p_X(x) \qquad \left(= \int_{-\infty}^{\infty} g(x) f_X(x)\, dx \right),$$

provided the sum (integral) exists.

Here, we discuss only one important choice of $g(\cdot)$, namely $g(X) = (X - \mu)^2$, giving the variance. First, we calculate the variance of the random variable X describing the number of heads in the coin-tossing game.

$$\begin{aligned}\mathrm{var}(X) &= \sum_{x=0}^{3} (x-\mu)^2 P(X=x) \\ &= \left(\frac{3}{2}\right)^2 \times \frac{1}{8} + \left(\frac{1}{2}\right)^2 \times \frac{3}{8} + \left(\frac{1}{2}\right)^2 \\ &\quad \times \frac{3}{8} + \left(\frac{3}{2}\right)^2 \times \frac{1}{8} \\ &= \frac{3}{4}.\end{aligned}$$

Since the variance is measured on a quadratic scale, it is more convenient to consider its positive square root, that is, the standard deviation of X. For the example, we get $\mathrm{sd}(X) = \sqrt{3/4} \approx 0.866$. In case of the triangular distribution, we get

$$\begin{aligned}\mathrm{var}(X) &= \int_{-1}^{0} x^2 \cdot (x+1)dx + \int_{0}^{1} x^2 \cdot (1-x)dx \\ &= \frac{1}{6}.\end{aligned}$$

So we have $\mathrm{sd}(X) = \sqrt{1/6} \approx 0.408$. We finally summarize some important facts.

Theorem 2.5. *Let X be a random variable with $\mathrm{E}(X) = \mu$ and let a, b be some constants. Then we have*

$$\mathrm{var}(X) = \mathrm{E}(X^2) - \mu^2, \tag{2.17}$$

$$\mathrm{var}(aX+b) = a^2\mathrm{var}(X). \tag{2.18}$$

Furthermore, we have $0 \leqslant \mathrm{E}(|X-\mu|) \leqslant \mathrm{sd}(X)$.

Some Discrete Distributions

Now we provide a short discussion of some important discrete distributions. Besides mentioning typical applications we state their PDFs together with their means and their respective variances.

Discrete Uniform Distribution

If a and b ($a < b$) are integers, we say that a random variable X is *discrete uniform on* $\{a,\ldots,b\}$ ($X \sim \mathrm{Uniform_d}(a,b)$), if

$$P(X=k) = \frac{1}{b-a+1}, \qquad k \in \{a,\ldots,b\}.$$

Expected value and variance:

$$\mathrm{E}(X) = \frac{a+b}{2}, \qquad \mathrm{var}(X) = \frac{(b-a)^2-1}{12}.$$

Applications: We already mentioned some examples. If X denotes the outcome of a die, then $X \sim \mathrm{Uniform_d}(1,6)$. To describe the roulette game, we use $X \sim \mathrm{Uniform_d}(0,36)$. The discrete uniform distribution models *Laplace experiments.*

Binomial Distribution

Consider an urn with w white and b black balls, that is, a total of $N = w+b$ balls. Hence, the probability to draw a black ball is $p := b/N$. Now draw n times with replacement and let X denote the random number of black balls contained within the n balls. Then some combinatorics shows

$$P(X=k) = \binom{n}{k} p^k (1-p)^{n-k}, \qquad k = 0,1,\ldots,n,$$

where

$$\binom{n}{k} = \frac{n(n-1)\cdots(n-k+1)}{(n-k)(n-k-1)\cdots 2\cdot 1}$$

is a so-called *binomial coefficient.* We say that X is *binomially distributed,* $X \sim \mathrm{Binomial}(n,p)$. If $n=3$ and $k=2$, then the event $\{X=2\}$ is the union of $A_1 = \{\mathrm{bbw}\}$, $A_2 = \{\mathrm{bwb}\}$, and $A_3 = \{\mathrm{wbb}\}$. Since the drawings are with replacement, they are independent and we have $P(A_i) = p^2(1-p)$, $i \in \{1,2,3\}$. The binomial coefficient counts the number of different possibilities to get k black balls in n drawings. Here it is 3.

Expected value and variance:

$$\mathrm{E}(X) = np, \qquad \mathrm{var}(X) = np(1-p).$$

Application: Whenever we repeat a Laplace experiment with two different outcomes like success/no success n times, then the random frequency of successes $X \sim \mathrm{Binomial}(n,p)$, where p denotes the success probability of each experiment.

Geometric Distribution

Assume that we perform a Laplace experiment that allows for two different outcomes like success/no success with success probability p. Let X denote the number of trials we need till we observe a success for the first time. Then

$$P(X=k) = (1-p)^{k-1}p, \qquad k = 1,2,\ldots.$$

We say that X is *geometrically distributed,* $X \sim \mathrm{Geometric}(p)$. To observe $X=k$ we need $k-1$ times "no success" followed by a "success" in the

kth trial. The difference to the binomial distribution is that the order of failures is important; hence, the binomial coefficient is not needed here.

Expected value and variance:

$$\mathrm{E}(X) = \frac{1}{1-p}, \qquad \mathrm{var}(X) = \frac{1-p}{p^2}.$$

Application: How often do we have to throw a die until we get a "6"?

Hypergeometric Distribution

As with the binomial model, assume that we have an urn with w white, b black, and thus a total of $N = w + b$ balls. Now we draw n balls without replacement and define X as the number of black balls drawn. Then some combinatorics yields

$$P(X = k) = \frac{\binom{b}{k}\binom{N-b}{n-k}}{\binom{N}{n}}, k = 0, \ldots, b, \text{ and } n = 1, \ldots, N.$$

We say that X is *hypergeometrically distributed*, $X \sim \text{Hypergeometric}(n, N, b)$. Here we have $\binom{b}{k}$ possibilities to choose k blacks out of b black balls, $\binom{N-b}{n-k}$ possibilities to choose $n-k$ white balls out of their total number $N - b$, and $\binom{N}{n}$ is the total number of possibilities.

Expected value and variance:

$$\mathrm{E}(X) = \frac{bn}{N},$$
$$\mathrm{var}(X) = \frac{bn(1 - b/N)(N-n)}{N(N-1)}.$$

Application: Take $n = 13$ playing cards out of all $N = 52$. What is the probability to have a pair of aces (i.e., $k = 2$ out of all $b = 4$)? Here we get $P(X = 2) \approx 21.3\%$.

If n is much smaller than N, the binomial distribution can be used to approximate hypergeometric probabilities. For a poll (success="in favor"/no success="against"), we usually do not interview a person twice. In terms of the urn model, we draw without replacement, where the urn is the population and the black balls are the people voting "against," say. However, the population is usually huge compared with the number of people interviewed. Thus, eliminating one voter who is "against," will only negligibly change the ratio of "against" voters.

Poisson Distribution

Assume that we draw from an urn with replacement. Let p be the probability of drawing a black ball, set $\lambda := np$, and let X denote the number of black balls in n trials. If p is "small" and n is "large," one can show that

$$P(X = k) = \binom{n}{k} p^k (1-p)^{n-k}$$
$$\approx \frac{\exp(-\lambda)\lambda^k}{k!}, \qquad k = 0, 1, \ldots,$$

where $k! = k(k-1)\cdots 1$. A random variable with PMF

$$P(X = k) = \frac{\exp(-\lambda)\lambda^k}{k!}, \qquad k = 0, 1, \ldots$$

is called *Poisson distributed* and we write $X \sim \text{Poisson}(\lambda)$. Some simple analysis shows that $\sum_{k=0}^{\infty} P(X = k) = 1$ is fulfilled. A rule of thumb is to use the Poisson approximation for binomial variables only if $n \geqslant 30$ and $p \leqslant 1/10$.

Expected value and variance:

$$\mathrm{E}(X) = \lambda, \qquad \mathrm{var}(X) = \lambda.$$

Applications: Usually, we model counts by Poisson variables. Especially when counting rare events such as the number of typos on book pages, a Poisson model fits well. Alternatively, this model is often applied when sampling is done without specifying the sample size beforehand, such as for an exit poll where every third person leaving the polling station is to be interviewed.

Some Continuous Distributions

Here we give a brief survey of three important families of continuous distributions. For this, it is convenient to define the *indicator function* of the set A as

$$1_A(x) = \begin{cases} 1 & \text{if } x \in A \\ 0 & \text{otherwise.} \end{cases}$$

Continuous Uniform Distribution

We say that X is *uniformly distributed* on the interval (a, b) and write $X \sim \text{Uniform}(a, b)$, if X has PDF

$$f_X(x) = \frac{1}{b-a} 1_{(a,b)}(x), \qquad x \in \mathbb{R}.$$

The respective CDF thus is

$$F_X(x) = \begin{cases} 0 & \text{if } x \leqslant a \\ (x-a)/(b-a) & \text{if } a < x \leqslant b \\ 1 & \text{otherwise.} \end{cases}$$

It is the continuous extension of the discrete uniform distribution.

Expected value and variance:

$$\mathrm{E}(X) = \frac{a+b}{2}, \qquad \mathrm{var}(X) = \frac{(b-a)^2}{12}.$$

Application: X has range (a,b). For $A \subset (a,b)$ the probability of the event $\{X \in A\}$ depends solely on the length of A. If there is a bus every 10 minutes and we arrive at the station at any time, then the waiting time is uniformly distributed on $(0,10)$.

Exponential Distribution

Let $\lambda > 0$. We say that a random variable X is *exponentially distributed* with parameter λ, $X \sim$ Exponential(λ), if X has PDF

$$f_X(x) = \exp(-\lambda x) 1_{[0,\infty)}(x), \qquad x \in \mathbb{R}.$$

For this, we get

$$F_X(x) = [1 - \exp(-\lambda x)] 1_{[0,\infty)}(x), \qquad x \in \mathbb{R}.$$

Expected value and variance:

$$\mathrm{E}(X) = \frac{1}{\lambda}, \qquad \mathrm{var}(X) = \frac{1}{\lambda^2}.$$

Application: A typical application has already been given in the section Random Variables and Distributions. It is the continuous analogue of the geometric distribution.

Normal Distribution

Let $\mu \in \mathbb{R}$ and $\sigma^2 > 0$. We say a random variable X is *normally distributed* with mean μ and variance σ^2, $X \sim \mathrm{N}(\mu, \sigma^2)$, if X has PDF

$$f_X(x) = \frac{1}{\sqrt{2\pi\sigma^2}} \exp\left(-\frac{(x-\mu)^2}{2\sigma^2}\right), \quad x \in \mathbb{R}.$$

This function is bell shaped and puts probability mass symmetrically around μ. If $\mu = 0$ and $\sigma^2 = 1$ we call it the standard normal distribution and write $F_X(x) = \Phi(x)$ for its CDF evaluated at some x. However, $\Phi(x)$ cannot be calculated explicitly in closed form. Instead it is given in *normal distribution tables.*

Expected value and variance:

$$\mathrm{E}(X) = \mu, \qquad \mathrm{var}(X) = \sigma^2.$$

Application: The normal distribution arises as limiting distribution in the *central limit theorem* (see section The Central Limit Theorem). In many statistical models, the assumption of a normal distribution plays a central role. A combination of usefulness and simplicity in applications implies that this distribution is of utmost importance. Although the assumption of normality is attractive, it is not always justified.

Sequences of Independent Random Variables

Assume that X and Y are both random variables and that we know the distribution of X and the distribution of Y. That means we know $F_X(x) = P(X \leqslant x)$ and $F_Y(y) = P(Y \leqslant y)$. What can we say about their joint distribution

$$P(X \leqslant x \text{ and } Y \leqslant y)?$$

We know nothing about this probability if we do not know how X and Y depend on each other. For example, let X and Y be the outcomes of a coin-tossing game. We recode {head, tail} to $\{-1,1\}$ and consider two extremes. First, we assume that X and Y are both outcomes of the same game, that is, $X = Y$. Then we assume that X and Y are the outcomes of two subsequent games. In both cases, X and Y have the same (marginal) distribution: $P(X = \pm 1) = P(Y = \pm 1) = 1/2$. However, in the first case we have $P((X,Y) = (1,-1)) = 0$, whereas in the second $P((X,Y) = (1,-1)) = 1/4$. In the first case, X and Y completely depend on each other, whereas in the second, X and Y behave independently. We clearly see that to analyze a collection of random variables we need to know their dependence structure. In general, it is very difficult to cope with dependent variables and thus we will concentrate here on random variables that are *independent*. So far we did not give a precise definition of independence of random variables. We only introduced independence of events in the section Conditional Probabilities and Independence. Since the concept of independence is extremely important in classical probability, we will lay additional emphasis on it apart from providing the mathematical definition.

Independence

Consider the special situation when every X_i is the outcome of the ith Laplace experiment out of a series of n unrelated experiments, that is, assume that $X_i \in \Omega_i$ with $|\Omega_i| = N_i < \infty$ and $P(X_i \in A_i) = |A_i|/N_i$. We further assume that one experiment has no influence on the other. The number of possible outcomes of the experiment described by $X_1, \ldots, X_n$ is $N_1 \cdot \cdots \cdot N_n$ and there are $|A_1| \cdot \cdots \cdot |A_n|$ possibilities for the event $\{X_1 \in A_1, X_2 \in A_2, \ldots, X_n \in A_n\}$. Hence

$$\begin{aligned} P(X_1 \in A_1, X_2 \in A_2, \ldots, X_n \in A_n) \\ = \frac{|A_1| \cdot \cdots \cdot |A_n|}{N_1 \cdot \cdots \cdot N_n} \\ = \prod_{i=1}^{n} P(X_i \in A_i). \end{aligned}$$

This leads to the following.

Definition 2.8. *A sequence of random variables $X_1, X_2, \ldots, X_n$ is said to be independent if for all $A_i \in \mathcal{B}$*

$$\begin{aligned} P(X_1 \in A_1, X_2 \in A_2, \ldots, X_n \in A_n) \\ = \prod_{i=1}^{n} P(X_i \in A_i). \end{aligned}$$

When we consider a random sequence $X_1, \ldots, X_n$ we usually do not try to prove independence but we demand that the random variables are independent by our model assumption. If a statistician analyzes an experiment that was carried out independently n times, then he or she will say that $X_1, \ldots, X_n$ are independent random variables where X_i represents the outcome of the ith trial. If all the X_is are from the same distribution, then $X_1, \ldots, X_n$ is called an independent and identically distributed sequence, in short *iid*. Hence if we know the distribution of each individual X_i, we can obtain the distribution of the whole sequence.

For any two random variables X and Y, we have $\mathrm{E}(X+Y) = \mathrm{E}(X) + \mathrm{E}(Y)$ by (2.16). For the product XY we generally cannot split up its expectation. However, if X and Y are independent random variables this is possible, that is, $\mathrm{E}(XY) = \mathrm{E}(X)\mathrm{E}(Y)$. The next theorem is an immediate consequence of this.

Theorem 2.6 (Bienaymé). *Let $X_1, \ldots, X_n$ be a sequence of independent random variables. Then*

$$\operatorname{var}(X_1 + \cdots + X_n) = \sum_{i=1}^{n} \operatorname{var}(X_i).$$

In principle it is very difficult to obtain the distribution of a sum of random variables, even if they are independent. However, if $X_1, \ldots, X_n$ are independent and if $X_k \sim \mathrm{N}(\mu_k, \sigma_k^2)$, then we obtain the following *convolution property*:

$$X_1 + \cdots + X_n \sim \mathrm{N}(\mu_1 + \cdots + \mu_n, \sigma_1^2 + \cdots + \sigma_n^2). \tag{2.19}$$

Especially, if the X_k are iid $\mathrm{N}(\mu, \sigma^2)$ we have $X_1 + \cdots + X_n \sim \mathrm{N}(n\mu, n\sigma^2)$.

Concepts of Convergence

Assume that $X_1, X_2, \ldots$ is a sequence of random variables. If there is another random variable X such that for large n the random variable X_n "behaves" like X, we would like to develop a concept of convergence of X_n to X, that is, $X_n \to X$. Since X_n and X are random, we have to ask what does it really mean when we say X_n behaves like X. In the sequel, we will discuss two types of convergence $X_n \to X$, the *weak convergence* and the *convergence in probability*.

Definition 2.9. *Let $X, X_1, X_2, \ldots$ be a sequence of random variables with respective CDFs $F, F_1, F_2, \ldots$. We say that X_n converges weakly to X (and write $X_n \xrightarrow{\mathcal{L}} X$) if $F_n(x) \to F(x)$ in any point of continuity x of F. This is also called convergence in distribution.*

First of all we owe an explanation of "in any point of continuity x of F." For that purpose, we define $X_n = 2^{-n}\varepsilon_n$, where $\varepsilon_n = \pm 1$ each with probability $1/2$ and $X = 0$, that is, a constant random variable. Clearly, whatever ε_n is, we have $|X - X_n| = 2^{-n}$. Thus, the difference tends to zero very quickly. The distribution function of

X is $F(x) = P(X \leqslant x) = 0$ if $x < 0$ and 1 if $x \geqslant 0$. Hence $F(x)$ is not continuous in 0. A moment's reflection shows that if $x \neq 0$ we have $P(X_n \leqslant x) = P(X \leqslant x)$ whenever $2^{-n} < |x|$. However, $P(X_n \leqslant 0) = 1/2$ for all $n \geqslant 0$ and $P(X \leqslant 0) = 1$. Therefore, $P(X_n \leqslant 0) \not\to P(X \leqslant 0)$. To dispose of such disagreeable situations, it makes sense to require only convergence in points of continuity.

Weak convergence of X_n to X does not imply that $|X_n - X|$ is becoming small. For example, let $X, X_1, X_2, \ldots$ be iid such that $P(X = \pm 1000) = 1/2$. The difference $|X - X_n|$ is either 2000 or 0, each with probability $1/2$. Nevertheless, since X has the same distribution as X_n we have $P(X_n \leqslant x) = P(X \leqslant x)$, which shows that $X_n \xrightarrow{\mathcal{L}} X$. In general, if two random variables X and X_1 have the same distribution, this does not imply that they are close.

The second type of convergence discussed here is the so-called *convergence in probability*. If X_n converges to X in probability this means that X_n is near X in distance with high probability.

Definition 2.10. *Let $X, X_1, X_2, \ldots$ be a sequence of random variables. We say that X_n converges in probability to X and write $X_n \xrightarrow{P} X$, if for every $\varepsilon > 0$*

$$P(|X_n - X| > \varepsilon) \to 0, \qquad n \to \infty.$$

What is the difference between weak convergence and convergence in probability? We already pointed out that if two CDFs are close, it no way implies that the associated random variables are close. However, the other direction holds. That is, if $X_n \xrightarrow{P} X$ then $X_n \xrightarrow{\mathcal{L}} X$. The theorem below states some important facts in this regard.

Theorem 2.7. *Let $X, X_1, X_2, \ldots$ and $Y_1, Y_2, \ldots$ be two sequences of random variables and c a constant. The following assertions hold:*

- *$X_n \xrightarrow{P} X$ implies $X_n \xrightarrow{\mathcal{L}} X$,*
- *$X_n \xrightarrow{\mathcal{L}} c$ implies $X_n \xrightarrow{P} c$,*
- *(Slutzky's Theorem) $X_n \xrightarrow{\mathcal{L}} X$ and $Y_n \xrightarrow{P} c$ implies $X_n + Y_n \xrightarrow{\mathcal{L}} X + c$ and $X_n Y_n \xrightarrow{\mathcal{L}} c \cdot X$.*

In our next example, we assume that $Y_1, Y_2, \ldots$ are iid normally distributed random variables with mean μ and variance σ^2. We set $X_n = (Y_1 + \cdots + Y_n)/n$. From (2.19) we know that $X_n - \mu \sim \mathrm{N}(0, \sigma^2/n)$. Hence some analysis shows that

$$\begin{aligned} &P(|X_n - \mu| > \varepsilon) \\ &= \frac{2\sqrt{n}}{\sqrt{2\pi\sigma^2}} \int_{\varepsilon}^{\infty} \exp(-nx^2/2\sigma^2)\, dx \to 0. \end{aligned}$$

This illustrates that the arithmetic mean of iid normally distributed random variables converges in probability to its expected value. This is a special case of the (weak) law of large numbers, which we will formulate in the next section.

The Law of Large Numbers

We have already emphasized that a mathematical model that describes random experiments should provide the relation $S_N/N \to p$, if p is the success probability and S_N counts the number of successes out of N trials (in the sense of (2.1)). But we have not specifically defined what "$\to$" means. From the law of large numbers below we obtain that this relation holds in probability.

Theorem 2.8 (Law of Large Numbers). *Let $X_1, X_2, \ldots$ be iid random variables with mean μ. Set $S_n = X_1 + \cdots + X_n$. If $\mathrm{E}|X_1| < \infty$, then*

$$S_n/n \xrightarrow{P} \mu\,, \qquad \textit{for } n \to \infty.$$

Assume that we repeat some experiment independently. We consider the events {success}, {no success}, where success can be any specific outcome of interest. Now set $X_i = I\{\text{success at trial } i\}$. We have

$$\begin{aligned} \mathrm{E}(X_i) &= 0 \cdot P(X_i = 0) + 1 \cdot P(X_i = 1) \\ &= P(X_i = 1) \\ &= P(\{\text{success at } i\text{th trial}\}). \end{aligned}$$

Since $X_1 + \cdots + X_n$ is the number of successes in n trials, we see that the law of large numbers implies relation (2.1). Theorem 2.8 is one of the most important theorems in probability theory. To illustrate its usefulness, we provide a common application, the so-called *Monte Carlo integration*. This technique is used to numerically approximate complicated integrals that cannot be calculated explicitly. The idea behind this is best described by a simple example in two dimensions

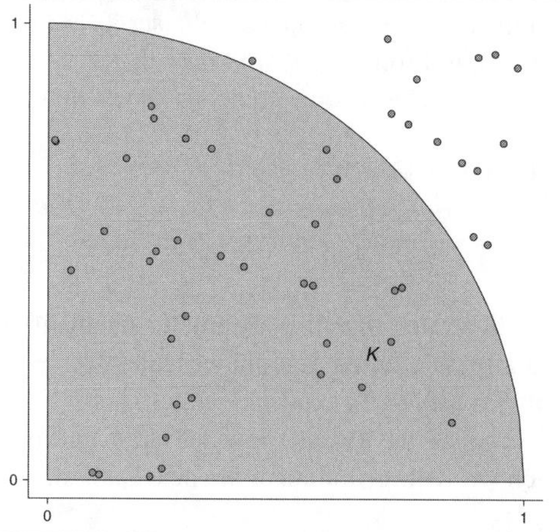

Figure 2.5 In this example, 36 out of 50 points are inside K.

although it also proves useful in higher dimensions. In the following example, we want to calculate the area of the unit circle, that is, a circle with radius 1. We know that the area is π, and thus a Monte Carlo approach will yield a probabilistic method to approximate the numerical value of π. We take only one quarter K of the circle, which is contained in the set $T = [0,1] \times [0,1]$ and we are interested in $4 \cdot \text{area}(K)$. The idea is the following. We pick out points of T randomly and check whether they are inside K or not.

Intuitively, the relative number of points inside K should be close to $\text{area}(K)/\text{area}(T) = \text{area}(K)$. Formally, we assume that Y is uniformly distributed and that Z is an independent copy of Y. Then $(Y,Z) \subset T$ and $P((Y,Z) \in K) = \text{area}(K)$. Let $X = I_K(Y,Z)$ and finally let $X_1, X_2, \ldots$ be a sequence of independent copies of X. Since $\text{E}(X) = P((Y,Z) \in K) = \text{area}(K)$, we get by the law of large numbers that

$$(X_1 + \cdots + X_n)/n \xrightarrow{P} \text{area}(K),$$

that is, the relative frequency of observations within K tends to $\pi/4$, if n becomes large.

The Central Limit Theorem

In many important examples, the mean of a random variable determines its distribution. Examples are $X \sim \text{Binomial}(1,p)$, $X \sim \text{Exponential}(\lambda)$, or $X \sim \text{N}(\mu,1)$. Often, a statistician knows the family of CDFs that X belongs to, but does not know the specific value of the parameter, say θ. Assume the parameter is a function of the mean, that is, $\theta = g(\mu)$. If $S_n = X_1 + \cdots + X_n$ the law of large numbers tells us that S_n/n is close to μ and thus if $g(\cdot)$ is "smooth," then $\hat{\theta} = g(S_n/n)$ will be close to θ. For example, in the Monte Carlo integration example before, we had $X_n \sim \text{Binomial}(1, \pi/4)$. More generally, if we choose some area $A \in [0,1] \times [0,1]$ with $\text{area}(A) = p$, then a corresponding definition of X_n will give $X_n \sim \text{Binomial}(1,p)$. We can again estimate the unknown parameter p by Monte Carlo integration and have $S_n/n \xrightarrow{P} p$. From a statistical point of view, however, the limiting behavior $S_n/n \xrightarrow{P} p$ alone is not satisfactory. It does not say anything about the probability that S_n/n is in some specified neighborhood of p for a sample of size n. Often it is important to know how we have to choose n to ensure, for example, $P(|S_n/n - p| \leqslant 0.01) \geqslant 0.95$? We could take the direct approach, that is, to find the distribution of S_n. This is in general very hard or even impossible. However, if $X_n \sim \text{Binomial}(1,p)$ we have $S_n \sim \text{Binomial}(n,p)$ and thus

$$\begin{aligned} P(|S_n/n - p| \leqslant 0.01) &= P(-0.01n + np \leqslant S_n \leqslant 0.01n + np) \\ &= \sum_{k=-0.01n+np}^{0.01n+np} \binom{n}{k} p^k (1-p)^{n-k}. \end{aligned} \tag{2.20}$$

To get a sufficiently large n that fulfills our requirements, we have to assure that (2.20) is greater than or equal to 0.95. The further procedure might be as follows. We choose a fixed value for p and calculate the sum for different values of n. Then we choose the smallest n such that (2.20) is greater than or equal to 0.95. Now we repeat this procedure for different values of p. Since we do not know p, we have to look for its worst choice, that is, the value p that needs the largest n such that (2.20) is greater or equal to 0.95. It will turn out that the worst choice is $p = 1/2$. Of course, this procedure causes considerable numerical costs. We now state the *central limit theorem* (CLT), which allows us to overcome these obstacles. The CLT plays a fundamental role in probability theory and statistics.

Theorem 2.9 (Central Limit Theorem)**.** *Let* $X_1, X_2, \ldots$ *be iid random variables with* $\text{E}(X_1) = \mu$ *and* $\text{var}(X_1) = \sigma^2 < \infty$ *and let*

$S_n = X_1 + \cdots + X_n$. *Then*

$$\frac{S_n - n\mu}{\sigma\sqrt{n}} \xrightarrow{\mathcal{L}} N(0,1).$$

The CLT states that if S_n is appropriately normalized, then it behaves probabilistically like a standard normal random variable, that is,

$$P\left(\frac{S_n - n\mu}{\sigma\sqrt{n}} \leqslant x\right) \approx \Phi(x).$$

When and how do we use the CLT in practice? Often, we use the CLT if we want to approximate the distribution of the partial sums S_n of any iid random variables. In general, it is very difficult to get the exact distribution of S_n, and even if it is possible it may involve extensive numerical costs. The important case we consider now is the normal approximation of the binomial distribution, that is, we concentrate on $X_i \sim$ Binomial$(1,p)$ with $S_n \sim$ Binomial(n,p). Here we get

$$P(a \leqslant S_n \leqslant b) = \sum_{a \leqslant k \leqslant b} \binom{n}{k} p^k (1-p)^{n-k}. \tag{2.21}$$

Although the explicit formula (2.21) is available, the exact calculation of the probabilities $\binom{n}{k} p^k (1-p)^{n-k}$ is numerically not quite simple and one may soon overstrain the pocket calculator. If n is large, we have huge values from the binomial coefficient and very small values arising from $p^k(1-p)^{n-k}$. Hence, we should use the CLT to approximate the distribution of S_n when n is sufficiently "large." A rough rule of thumb states that in case of a binomial variable S_n we should ensure that $n\min\{p,(1-p)\} > 5$ to get a satisfactory approximation. The procedure in practice looks as follows. We have

$$\begin{aligned} &P(a \leqslant S_n \leqslant b) \\ &\quad = P\left(\frac{a-np}{\sqrt{npq}} \leqslant \frac{S_n - np}{\sqrt{npq}} \leqslant \frac{b-np}{\sqrt{npq}}\right), \end{aligned}$$

where we write q instead of $1-p$ in sequel. Since by Theorem 2.9 the term $(S_n - np)/\sqrt{npq}$ is approximately normally distributed, we further have

$$P(a \leqslant S_n \leqslant b) \approx \Phi\left(\frac{b-np}{\sqrt{npq}}\right) - \Phi\left(\frac{a-np}{\sqrt{npq}}\right). \tag{2.22}$$

Note that if a and b are integers, then we have

$$P(a \leqslant S_n \leqslant b) = P(a - \varepsilon_1 \leqslant S_n \leqslant b + \varepsilon_2)$$

for any $0 \leqslant \varepsilon_1, \varepsilon_2 < 1$ because S_n is in any case an integer as well. From a numerical point of view, it is advisable to choose $\varepsilon_1 = \varepsilon_2 = 1/2$ giving

$$\begin{aligned} P(a \leqslant S_n \leqslant b) &= P\left(a - \frac{1}{2} \leqslant S_n \leqslant b + \frac{1}{2}\right) \\ &\approx \Phi\left(\frac{b + \frac{1}{2} - np}{\sqrt{npq}}\right) \\ &\quad - \Phi\left(\frac{a - \frac{1}{2} - np}{\sqrt{npq}}\right). \end{aligned} \tag{2.23}$$

The replacement of a by $a - 1/2$ and b by $b + 1/2$ is often called *continuity correction* and yields a better approximation than (2.22). After inserting the specific values of a, b, p, and n, one can get the values of $\Phi(\cdot)$ either from tables or by some computer software.

We shall now treat the Monte Carlo integration problem from above with the help of the CLT and approximate (2.20) by

$$\begin{aligned} &P(|S_n/n - p| \leqslant 0.01) \\ &\quad \approx \Phi\left(0.01\sqrt{\frac{n}{p(1-p)}}\right) \\ &\quad\quad - \Phi\left(-0.01\sqrt{\frac{n}{p(1-p)}}\right). \end{aligned}$$

Using $\Phi(-x) = 1 - \Phi(x)$ and observing that $1/p(1-p)$ has its minimum at $p = 1/2$, we infer

$$\begin{aligned} &P(|S_n/n - p| \leqslant 0.01) \\ &\quad \approx 2\Phi\left(0.01\sqrt{\frac{n}{p(1-p)}}\right) - 1 \\ &\quad \geqslant 2\Phi\left(0.02\sqrt{n}\right) - 1. \end{aligned}$$

Thus we need $n \approx 9600$ to have a 95% guarantee that the error is less than 0.01.

In a next example, we want to find out if our die is a "fulham." Assume that in a casino we roll this die 60 times and observe "6" only five times although the expected number of "6"s is 10. Let $X_n = 1$ if the nth die shows "6" and zero otherwise. Then $S_{60} = \sum_{i=1}^{60} X_i \sim$ Binomial

$(60, 1/6)$ and we are interested in $P(S_{60} \leqslant 5)$. Of course, it can happen that the "6" shows rarely although the die is fair. However, we are suspicious of the die and we shall stop the game if $P(S_{60} \leqslant 5) \leqslant 0.05$. This can be calculated directly by applying the exact distribution of S_{60}, that is, the binomial distribution. We obtain $P(S_{60} \leqslant 5) = \sum_{i=0}^{5} \binom{60}{i} (1/6)^i (5/6)^{60-i} \approx 0.051$. On the other hand, we can use (2.23) to get $P(S_{60} \leqslant 5) \approx 0.06$.

REFERENCES

Billingsley, P. (1995). *Probability and measure* (3rd ed.). New York: Wiley.

Durrett, R. (1994). *The essentials of probability*. Belmont, CA: Duxbury Press.

Gordon, H. (1997). *Discrete probability*. New York: Springer.

Rudas, T. (2004). *Probability theory: A primer*. Thousand Oaks, CA: Sage.

3

SUBJECTIVE PROBABILITY

IGOR KOPYLOV

Personalistic views hold that probability measures the confidence that a particular individual has in the truth of a particular proposition.

—Savage (1972, p. 3)

INTRODUCTION

Historically, the term *probability* has been associated with a number of different concepts. The standard mathematical definition due to Kolmogorov (1933/1950) identifies probability with a countably additive measure on a σ-algebra.[1] This definition underlies a powerful theory that includes the law of large numbers and the central limit theorem. Yet in the applications of this theory, probability has different extramathematical interpretations.

Since its inception by Bernoulli (1713), de Moivre (1756), and Laplace (1814/1917), the calculus of probability has been applied to—or even designed for—repetitive experiments with gambling apparatus, such as coins, cards, dice, roulette wheels, and so on. Each of these devices has a natural symmetry that is commonly known a priori. This symmetry determines an exhaustive collection of equally possible states and motivates the *classical* interpretation of probability as "the fraction whose numerator is the number of favorable cases and the denominator is the number of all the cases possible" (Laplace, 1917, pp. 6–7).

More broadly, probability theory has been used to analyze repetitive observations of various physical, biological, and social systems for which one cannot find any compelling symmetry a priori. Motivated by such applications, Ellis (1863) and Venn (1866/1962) proposed to identify probability of any observed attribute with the limit of the relative *frequency* of this attribute in a long, ideally infinite, series of trials. Venn (1866/1962) writes,

> The run must be supposed to be very long indeed, in fact never to stop. As we keep on taking more terms of the series, we shall find this proportion [i.e. the relative frequency] still fluctuating a little, but its fluctuations will grow less. The proportion, in fact, will gradually approach toward some numerical value, ... its limit. (p. 164)

Note that the classical and the frequentist interpretations of probability complement rather than contradict each other. For example, the statistics of Bose-Einstein and Fermi-Dirac are both

[1] A σ-algebra is a class of events that is closed under taking complements and countable unions. See Billingsley (1995) for an excellent modern introduction to probability theory.

derived from a priori symmetry considerations but then matched with real physical particles (photons and electrons, respectively) via observed frequencies.

Another application for mathematical probability has been to quantify human *beliefs*. In this area, neither the classical nor the frequentist interpretation of probability seems satisfactory. Indeed, beliefs need not be based on a priori symmetry or observed relative frequencies. For example, I think that in 20 years (1) the U.S. income tax rates are more likely to go up than down and (2) the global climate is more likely to get warmer than colder. However, I derive these beliefs from articles in *Wall Street Journal* and *National Geographic* and from superficial and vague perception of recent budget deficits and unusual weather conditions. Is it meaningful to describe my (or anybody else's) beliefs in terms of mathematical probability?

Keynes (1921) and Carnap (1950) propose to answer this question on the premise that beliefs are derived from the available *evidence* via universally acceptable principles. In their interpretation, probability is an objective relation between propositions—a relation that by logical necessity describes all reasonable beliefs. This *logical* approach suffers from two serious practical limitations. First, the available evidence can be informal, vague, and voluminous (think about a transcript of a court trial!). Second, there are hardly any undisputable principles that translate such evidence into beliefs. Instead, most beliefs appear to come from an impenetrable mix of instincts, intuition, experience, analogy—a mix that defies a satisfactory logical analysis. As a result, beliefs are often idiosyncratic, even if their owners share the same meticulously controlled evidence (think about a jury in a court trial!). In the words of Savage (1972),

> there is no fundamental objection to the possibility of constructing a necessary [i.e. logical] view, but it is my impression that the possibility has not yet been realized, and though unable to verbalize the reasons, I conjecture that the possibility is not real. (p. 61)

To break through this impasse, Ramsey (1931) proposes to associate beliefs with *decisions* rather than with the underlying evidence: "... the degree of a belief is a causal property of it, which we can express vaguely as the extent to which we are prepared to act on it" (p. 170). Indeed, beliefs do affect choices that people actually make, or plan to make, in suitable circumstances. For example, subjective judgments about the future income tax rates and global warming effects can influence how much a person chooses to save and what car he chooses to drive. In general, it seems that almost any human belief should manifest itself in some material choice behavior, which, at least in principle, can be observed by a modeler.

Building on the seminal contributions of Ramsey (1931), de Finetti (1937), and Savage (1972), the theory of *subjective* probability seeks to describe choice under uncertainty in terms of probabilistic beliefs. In particular, this theory seeks a probability measure p to represent a *betting preference* $\succeq_0$ so that for all events A and B,

$$A \succeq_0 B \quad \Leftrightarrow \quad p(A) \geqslant p(B). \qquad (3.1)$$

Here the decision maker exhibits the preference $A \succeq_0 B$ if, ceteris paribus, he or she chooses to bet on the event A rather than on the event B. Intuitively, this choice manifests his or her belief that A is at least as likely as B. Thus, the sought-after probability measure p should reflect exclusively personal beliefs rather than any objective characteristics of the physical world.

Representation (3.1) interprets subjective probability in terms of choice among bets that have dichotomous (i.e., the good and the bad) outcomes. However, uncertain prospects that people face in everyday life—as well as in models of game theory, finance, economics, and other sciences—usually have three or more possible outcomes. Does it make sense to use subjective probability to evaluate such prospects? What sort of evaluation is reasonable? These questions are addressed by Savage's theory of *subjective expected utility*, which is distinguished by Kreps (1988) as "the crowning glory of choice theory." This theory portrays a person who (1) assigns subjective probabilities $p(\cdot)$ to relevant events, (2) assigns a utility index $u(\cdot)$ to relevant outcomes, and (3) evaluates every uncertain prospect f via the expected utility

$$U(f) = \sum_{\text{outcomes } x} u(x) \cdot p(\{f \text{ yields } x\}). \qquad (3.2)$$

Here, in contrast with the classic treatments of expected utility by Bernoulli (1713) and by von Neumann and Morgenstern (1944), the probability measure p is not given exogenously but derived from personal choice. In particular, decision makers may differ not only in their tastes over possible outcomes but also in their assessment of probabilities.

An important special case of subjective expected utility obtains when the outcomes x are monetary and the decision maker is risk neutral with the utility index $u(x) = x$. Then, the decision maker's subjective probability $p(A)$ equals the price at which he or she is willing to buy or sell a ticket that pays a unit of money if A occurs and nothing otherwise. Following de Finetti, some authors have used this equality as the basic definition of subjective probability. In this way, one can derive probabilities directly from pricing decisions that are well understood by most people. Moreover, if probabilities are identified with prices, then it is straightforward to argue that they must be additive because the decision maker must avoid *Dutch books*, that is, losing money for sure. Unfortunately, the assumptions that outcomes are monetary and people are risk neutral are too restrictive for many applications. Thus, to construct subjective probabilities $p(\cdot)$ in the general representations (3.1) and (3.2), one needs devices more subtle than monetary prices.

The mathematical definition alone is a rather minimalist constraint for subjective probability. It does not exclude unrealistic beliefs that do not correlate with experience. Thus, it may be desirable to derive additional structure for subjective probability in applications. For example, it is intuitive that personal beliefs should converge to empirical frequencies in the long run. Formally, this property can be obtained by *de Finetti's theorem* or by the *market selection* argument.

The general theory of subjective probability is *normative*: it seeks to explain why an idealized rational person should use a probabilistic belief to make hypothetical decisions under uncertainty. Thus, it is neither very surprising nor completely disappointing that the findings of this theory have little empirical support. One problem is that abstract decision frameworks where subjective probability is derived do not fit empirical settings very well. For example, a person who moves to work in another city faces an uncertain prospect that is not easily represented as a Savage-style function that maps states of the world into outcomes. Even if the person himself or herself were able to write such a representation, this task may be still problematic for the modeler. On the other hand, the construction of subjective probability requires so many hypothetical decision problems that one could not possibly observe a personal response in each of them. In fact, a large portion of these problems are so unrealistic and complex that they cannot be a part of any experiment.

Moreover, there is a lot of direct empirical evidence that violates the representations (3.1) and (3.2). Such violations have been reported by Allais (1953), Ellsberg (1961), Kahneman and Tversky (1979), and many others. Do these departures refute the theory of subjective probability? Put differently, is it possible to modify this theory to accommodate the observed patterns of choice behavior? The discussion of these questions will conclude this chapter.

SUBJECTIVE PROBABILITY AND BETTING PREFERENCES

Following Savage (1972), consider a set S of *states* of the world and a person who knows that there exists a unique *true* state in S, but does not know the identity of the true state with certainty. In other words, assume that the person (also known as the subject or the decision maker) views the state space S as an exhaustive list of mutually exclusive descriptions of the world.[2]

Uncertainty in this framework is atemporal and may relate to the past, present, and future of the universe, as well as to the abstract realm of human cognition. For example, a state $s \in S$ may specify

- the number that will be hit by the next spin of a roulette wheel,

[2]The specification of the state space is further discussed by Savage (1972, pp. 8–17, 82–91), Kreps (1988, pp. 34–37), Machina (2003), and others. Dekel, Lipman, and Rustichini (2001) derive a unique state space from preferences. Karni (2006) models subjective probabilities without a state space altogether.

- the next winner of the FIFA World Cup,
- the spot where the next hurricane will strike the American shore,
- the decimal expansion of the number π, and
- whether Abraham Lincoln was the 16th president of the USA.

To incorporate all of these different aspects of the world into one state space, it is natural to use a product structure and take $S = S_1 \times S_2 \times S_3 \times S_4 \times S_5$ with

- $S_1 = \{0, 00, 1, 2, \ldots, 36\}$ (allowing for a double zero),
- S_2 the set of all FIFA members,
- S_3 the set of all geodesic points along the American shore,
- $S_4 = [3, 4]$,
- $S_5 = \{\text{yes, no}\}$.

Note that the source of uncertainty can be purely cognitive: for example, the fact that Lincoln was the 16th president is known to many people but may still appear uncertain to a participant in a quiz or a student at a closed-book exam.

Assume that S is a separable metric space. In particular, it can be a finite set, a subset of a Euclidean space, or a finite or countable product of such sets because all the corresponding topologies—discrete, Euclidean, and product—are separable and metrizable.

Let Σ be the Borel σ-algebra on S, and call its elements $A \in \Sigma$ *events*.[3] Say that an event $A \in \Sigma$ *occurs* if it contains the true state of the world. Note that S is the universal event that occurs with certainty, and $\emptyset$ is the vacuous event that never occurs.

Adopt Kolmogorov's definition and say that a real function $p : \Sigma \to \mathbb{R}$ is a *probability measure* if it obeys the following properties for all $A, B, A_i \in \Sigma$:

(K1) $p(A) \geqslant 0$,

(K2) $p(S) = 1$,

(K3) if $A \cap B = \emptyset$, then $p(A \cup B) = p(A) + p(B)$,

(K4) if $A_i \downarrow A$, then $p(A) = \lim_{i \to \infty} p(A_i)$,

where the convergence $A_i \downarrow A$ means that $A_1 \supseteq A_2 \supseteq \cdots$ and $A = \cap_{i=1}^{\infty} A_i$.

Let a binary relation $\succeq_0$ on Σ be the subject's *betting preference*. Formally, for any event A, let t_A be a ticket that yields a unit of money—say \$1—if A occurs, and nothing otherwise. Write $A \succeq_0 B$ if the subject accepts the ticket t_A when t_B is a feasible alternative. Note that $A \succeq_0 B$ and $B \succeq_0 A$ may hold together, which means that the subject is indifferent between the tickets t_A and t_B. Let the indifference $\sim_0$ and the strict preference $\succ_0$ denote the symmetric and asymmetric parts of $\succeq_0$, respectively.

Intuitively, a preference $A \succeq_0 B$ to bet on an event A rather than on B manifests the decision maker's implicit belief that the event A is at least as likely as the event B. Therefore, to quantify such beliefs by probabilities, one may seek a probability measure p such that for all events A and B,

$$A \succeq_0 B \quad \Leftrightarrow \quad p(A) \geqslant p(B). \qquad (3.3)$$

In other words, the sought-after probability p is a *utility* representation for the personal ranking of bets. When does such p exist? When is it unique? These questions have been addressed by de Finetti (1937), Koopman (1940), Savage (1972), Scott (1964), Luce (1967), Villegas (1964), Wakker (1981), and others.

Any binary relation $\succeq_0$ that complies with representation (3.3) must satisfy the following list of conditions for all events $A, A_i, B, C \in \Sigma$. (This list is a compilation from de Finetti, 1937, and Villegas, 1964.)

(L1) *Completeness:* $A \succeq_0 B$, or $B \succeq_0 A$ (or both).

[3] In other words, Σ is the minimal σ-algebra that contains all open sets in S. Note that the explicit description of some Borel sets in Σ may be very complex (Billingsley, 1995, pp. 31–32). To avoid this complexity, probability theorists describe the measure explicitly on "simple" events and then apply a measure extension theorem (recall the construction of the Lebesgue measure). The same approach works for subjective probability: one can first derive it on a "small" domain, and then extend it to the Borel σ-algebra (see Kopylov, 2007, for details).

(L2) *Transitivity:* If $A \succeq_0 B \succeq_0 C$, then $A \succeq_0 C$.

(L3) *Monotonicity:* $A \succeq_0 \emptyset$.

(L4) *Nondegeneracy:* $S \succ_0 \emptyset$.

(L5) *Additivity:* If $A \cap C = B \cap C = \emptyset$, then $A \succeq_0 B$ is equivalent to $A \cup C \succeq_0 B \cup C$.

(L6) *Continuity:* If $A_i \downarrow A$ and $A_i \succeq_0 B$, then $A \succeq_0 B$.

Here completeness and transitivity are well-known general postulates of rational choice, while the conditions of monotonicity, nondegeneracy, additivity, and continuity are more specific for the choice among bets. In particular, additivity asserts that the preference to bet on the events A and B should be unaffected by whether a monetary prize is paid contingent on an event C that is *disjoint* from both A and B. Continuity requires roughly that bets on events A and A_i in a converging sequence $A_i \downarrow A$ are almost imperceptible for sufficiently large i.

Despite having a direct analogy with Kolmogorov's definition, the list (L1) to (L6) does not guarantee that representation (3.3) exists. Kraft, Pratt, and Seidenberg (1959) formulate a counterexample on a five-element state space $S = \{1,2,3,4,5\}$. They show that conditions (L1) to (L6) are consistent with the rankings

$$
\begin{aligned}
A_1 &= \{4\} \succ_0 \{1,3\} = B_1, \\
A_2 &= \{2,3\} \succ_0 \{1,4\} = B_2, \\
A_3 &= \{1,5\} \succ_0 \{3,4\} = B_3, \\
A_4 &= \{1,3,4\} \succ_0 \{2,5\} = B_4.
\end{aligned}
$$

By definition, any probability measure p satisfies

$$
\begin{aligned}
\sum_{i=1}^{4} p(A_i) &= 2p(\{1\}) + p(\{2\}) + 2p(\{3\}) \\
&\quad + 2p(\{4\}) + p(\{5\}) \\
&= \sum_{i=1}^{4} p(B_i),
\end{aligned}
$$

and hence, $p(B_i) \geqslant p(A_i)$ for some i. Thus p does not represent $\succeq$.

Moreover, even if representation (3.3) does exist, it need not be unique. For example, the ranking $S = \{a,b\} \succ_0 \{a\} \succ_0 \{b\} \succ_0 \emptyset$ can be quantified by any probability measure p such that $1 > p(\{a\}) > \frac{1}{2}$.

To guarantee existence and uniqueness of representation 3.3, impose an extra condition on the preference $\succeq_0$.

(L7) *Nondiscreteness:* For every $s \in S$, $\{s\} \sim_0 \emptyset$.

This condition asserts that the subject should view any single state $s \in S$ as practically impossible, and the corresponding ticket $t_{\{s\}}$ as worthless. For example, nondiscreteness seems intuitive if every state $s \in S$ specifies an *infinite* sequence of coin flips or similar independent random experiments. Unfortunately, nondiscreteness must be violated if S is finite.

Now the sought-after representation (3.3) can be derived from the results of Savage (1972) and Villegas (1964).

Theorem 3.1. *$\succeq_0$ satisfies (L1) to (L7) if and only if $\succeq_0$ can be represented by a probability measure p such that $p(\{s\}) = 0$ for all $s \in S$. This representation is unique.*

One can view this theorem as a foundation for the use of subjective probabilities in decision making. Here, probabilities are (a) consistent with Kolmogorov's definition and (b) purely subjective because they are derived exclusively from personal choice behavior rather than from any exogenous numerical representation of uncertainty. In particular, two people may both comply with the conditions of Theorem 3.1 but differ in their assignments of probabilities.

The construction of the probabilities $p(\cdot)$ in Theorem 3.1 can be done via an elegant formula, which reveals another connection between betting preferences and the underlying beliefs. Call any partition of the universal event S into disjoint events $S_1, \ldots, S_m$ a *grand partition*. Say that a grand partition is *finer* than an event A if $A \succ_0 S_i$ for all i, that is, if all events S_i are subjectively less likely than A. Among all grand partitions finer than A, take one with a minimal number of elements. Let $\nu(A)$ be this minimal number; let $\nu(A) = +\infty$ if there is no partition finer than A. Then the unique probabilities $p(A)$ for all events

A are given by the formula

$$p(A) = \sup\left\{\sum_{i=1}^{n} \frac{1}{v(A_i)}\right\}, \tag{3.4}$$

where the supremum is taken across all partitions of A into disjoint events $A_1, \ldots, A_n$. (See Kopylov, 2007 for details.)

Note that the original results of Savage and de Finetti derive a *finitely additive* subjective probability measure, which satisfies (K1) to (K3) but may violate (K4). The restriction to countable additivity in Theorem 3.1 has two advantages. First, it permits the use of subjective probability in the law of large numbers, the central limit theorem, and other standard results that require countable additivity. Second, the "technical" conditions L6 and L7 in Theorem 3.1 appear more transparent than their counterparts, such as Savage's fineness and tightness, in the finitely additive model.

Unfortunately, Theorem 3.1 fails when S is finite and hence, $\succeq_0$ violates nondiscreteness. To accommodate this case, Scott (1964) strengthens additivity. He postulates that if every state $s \in S$ belongs to as many events in a list $A_1, \ldots, A_n$ as in another list $B_1, \ldots, B_n$, and if $A_i \succeq_0 B_i$ for all $i < n$, then $B_n \succeq_0 A_n$. Obviously, this postulate rules out the counterexample of Kraft et al. (1959). Scott shows that this stronger form of additivity, together with (L1) to (L4), is necessary and sufficient for the preference $\succeq_0$ to have representation (3.3). As mentioned above, this representation need not be unique.

Alternatively, one can follow Luce (1967) and obtain subjective probabilities via the theory of extensive measurement. This approach applies to both finite and infinite settings, but in the finite case it requires essentially that all states are equally likely.

Instead of confronting a person with monetary bets, one can simply ask him or her which of two events A or B he or she views as more probable. By this kind of interrogation, one can also derive a subjective ranking $\succeq_0$ of likelihoods of events and then seek a probability measure p to represent this ranking. This intuition-oriented approach is adopted by Koopman (1940) and in part, by de Finetti (1937).

Of course, the formal statements and proofs of Theorem 3.1 and similar representation results are unaffected by the extramathematical interpretation that one adopts for the ranking $\succeq_0$. However, the intuition- and decision-oriented interpretations do have some practical distinctions. First, most people find material decisions more important and more suitable for scientific analysis than intuitive judgments. This point is emphasized by Savage (1972):

> Many doubt that the concept "more probable to me than" is an intuitive one, open to no ambiguity and yet admitting further analysis. Even if the concept were so completely intuitive, which might justify direct interrogation as a subject worthy of some psychological study, what could such interrogation have to do with the behavior of a person in the face of uncertainty, except of course for his verbal behavior under interrogation? If the state of mind in question is not capable of manifesting itself in some sort of extraverbal behavior, then it is extraneous to our main interest. If, on the other hand, it does manifest itself through more material behavior, that should, in principle, imply the possibility of testing whether a person holds one event more probable than another, by some behavior expressing, and giving meaning to, his judgement. (p. 27)

Moreover, in some settings betting preferences may differ persistently from the intuitive perception of probabilities. For example, a person may believe that she is more likely to retire rich rather than poor, but still prefer to bet on the latter event. In this case, the personal value of a monetary payoff clearly depends on the event where this payoff is obtained. See Karni (1993) for a model of subjective probability with state-dependent preferences.

Subjective Expected Utility

Subjective probability in Theorem 3.1 represents personal choices among bets—uncertain prospects that have only *two* possible outcomes, such as \$1 and \$0. However, people often face more complex decision problems where more than just two outcomes appear possible. For example, potential consequences of economic or financial decisions may include a whole range of monetary payments or consumption bundles, which can be written as real numbers or vectors, respectively. Any game between a player with m

strategies and a player with n strategies has up to mn distinct outcomes, which may have a purely verbal description (think about various trips to ballet and boxing in the battle of the sexes). Is it still meaningful to apply subjective probabilities in these more complex settings?

To address this question formally, let X be the set of all *outcomes* (payoffs, prizes) that the subject may obtain after his or her decisions are made, and the true state of the world is revealed. Assume that each of these outcomes can be potentially experienced in any state of the world.[4] Interpret any function $f: S \to X$ as an uncertain prospect that yields the outcome $f(s)$ when s is the true state of the world; call this function an *act*. Formally, require that each act f is a Borel function that has a finite range in X. Given any event A and acts f, g, let fAg be a *composite* act that yields $f(s)$ if $s \in A$ and $g(s)$ if $s \notin A$.

For example, a constant act x represents an action that yields the same payoff x in any state of the world, and a binary act $t_A = \$1\ A\ \$0$ represents a bet that yields \$1 if the event A occurs and \$0 otherwise. To illustrate the use of more complex acts, Savage portrays an omelette maker who has broken five eggs into a bowl and needs to decide what to do with the remaining sixth one. This subject contemplates an event $E = \{\text{the sixth egg is rotten}\}$ in a suitable state space, and then identifies three different actions "to break the egg in the bowl," "to throw the egg away," and "to break the egg in a separate saucer for inspection" with the following acts f, g, and h:

	f	g	h
$s \in E$	No omelette	Five-egg omelette	Five-egg omelette
$s \notin E$	Six-egg omelette	Five-egg omelette	Six-egg omelette

Here, the acts f, g, h map states of the world into the set of outcomes

$$X = \{\text{no omelette, five-egg omelette, six-egg omelette}\}.$$

[4]Nau (2001) reviews the critique of Savage's concept of outcomes. Skiadas (1997) formulates a model of subjective probability that does not take outcomes as given.

Note that even in this simplistic world, some acts have little practical meaning. For example, consider f' that yields a six-egg omelette if E occurs and no omelette otherwise. While it is not hard to imagine f' as a hypothetical uncertain prospect, it is doubtful that such a strange bet has ever been proposed to any omelette maker.

Let a binary relation $\succeq$ describe the personal preference over acts. More precisely, the comparison $f \succeq g$ means that the person accepts the act f when g is a feasible alternative. Write the indifference and strict preference as $\sim$ and $\succ$, respectively.

There are two broad venues for studying preferences over acts. First, one may collect empirical data about choice behavior from surveys or laboratory experiments and then design models to fit this data well. Alternatively, one may search for *normative* principles that reasonable people—including the modeler—would want to obey both in real and in hypothetical decision problems. In Savage's words, the primary goal of such conditions is "to police ... decisions for consistency and, where possible, to make complicated decisions depend on simpler ones"(Savage, 1972, p. 20).

From the normative standpoint, the following conditions on the preference $\succeq$ may be reasonable for all events A, B, A_i, outcomes x, x', z, z', and acts f, g, h, h':

(P1) *Order:* $\succeq$ is complete and transitive.

(P2) *Sure-thing principle:* If $fAh \succeq gAh$, then $fAh' \succeq gAh'$.

(P3) *Monotonicity:* If $x \succeq x'$, then $xAh \succeq x'Ah$.

(P4) *Comparative probability:* If $x \succ x'$, $z \succ z'$, and $xAx' \succeq xBx'$, then $zAz' \succeq zBz'$.

(P5) *Nondegeneracy:* $\succ$ is not empty.

(P6) *Nondiscreteness:* $x\{s\}f \sim f$.

(P7) *Continuity:* If $A_i \downarrow A$ and $h \succeq xA_i f \succeq g$, then $h \succeq xAf \succeq g$.

The sure-thing principle asserts that the ranking of acts f and g that are *conditioned* on an event A is independent of the outcomes that are obtained if A does not occur. Monotonicity requires roughly that the ranking of outcomes in X is invariant of the event where these outcomes are obtained. Comparative probability states that the preference to bet on an event A rather than on B should be unaffected by the stakes that are involved in these bets. The other axioms in the above list are similar to their counterparts for the betting preferences.

While axioms P1 to P7 are compelling in some settings, they may be problematic in others. First, if events have a direct effect on the value of outcomes, then monotonicity may fail: for example, a person who prefers "six-egg omelette" with certainty to "no omelette" with certainty may reverse his or her preference if these outcomes are conditioned on the event "his or her cholesterol level is high". Second, if acts affect the relative likelihoods of events (i.e., there is a moral hazard), then comparative probability may be violated: for example, a student may prefer to bet a million dollars on his passing an exam rather than on a coin flip, but reverse his or her preference if the monetary stake is just \$1. Third, if the state space is finite, then nondiscreteness does not hold. Last but not the least, the axioms of order and sure-thing principle can be problematic for several other reasons as well, which we discuss later.

The following theorem is another nontrivial corollary to Savage's results (see also Fishburn, 1970).

Theorem 3.2. *The relation $\succeq$ satisfies conditions (P1) to (P7) if and only if $\succeq$ can be represented by expected utility*

$$U(f) = \int_S u(f(s))\,dp = \sum_{x \in X} u(x) \cdot p(\{s : f(s) = x\}), \tag{3.5}$$

where u is a nonconstant utility index on X, and p is a probability measure such that $p(\{s\}) = 0$ for all $s \in S$. This representation is unique up to a positive linear transformation of the index u.

The decision maker portrayed by (3.5) assigns probabilities $p(\cdot)$ to all events A, attaches utilities $u(\cdot)$ to all outcomes x, and then ranks all uncertain prospects f via expected utility. Thus Theorem 3.2 provides foundations for the use of subjective probability in a wide class of decision problems, not necessarily restricted to the ranking of bets. Moreover, it advocates the use of subjective probability as a component of the well-known expected utility functional form.

The expected utility criterion was originally proposed by Bernoulli (1713) as an ad hoc solution to the St. Petersburg paradox, and was characterized axiomatically by von Neumann and Morgenstern (1944). These authors assume that probabilities are objective and exogenous to decision making. Accordingly, one can view Theorem 3.2 as an extension of the expected utility theory to subjective probabilities. (In fact, Theorem 3.2 invokes von Neumann and Morgenstern's result to obtain the utility index after deriving the probability measure p from preference.) Such an extension provides a useful flexibility in economic applications. For example, many people buy insurance even though they expect that by doing so, they will lose money on average. This phenomenon can be explained by a difference in attitudes toward risk: individuals are usually risk averse and hence, have a *concave* index u_1, while insurance companies are risk neutral (or almost so) and have a linear index u_2.[5] On the other hand, even risk-averse people with certain endowments may choose to bet against each other. Such betting can be explained within the expected utility paradigm but only if there is a difference in subjective beliefs.

The expected utility representation (3.5) allows different interpretations for the subjective probabilities $p(\cdot)$. First, one can define a betting preference $\succeq_0$ by

$$A \succeq_0 B \quad \Leftrightarrow \quad xAx' \succeq xBx' \quad \text{for all } x \succ x',$$

and then check that $\succeq_0$ complies with conditions (L1) to (L7). Obviously, the measure p represents $\succeq_0$, and hence, can be computed via formula (3.4). This approach is used in the formal proof of Theorem 3.2.

Alternatively, a probability $p(A)$ can be interpreted as a rate at which the decision maker evaluates the outcomes that are obtained contingent on the event A. This interpretation appears in the famous essay of Bayes (1763): "The probability of any event is the ratio between the value

[5]Pratt (1964) formulates the standard measurements of risk aversion in the expected utility model.

at which an expectation depending on the happening of the event ought to be computed, and the value of the thing expected upon its happening."

To make this interpretation formal, one needs to determine the utility index u prior to computing subjective probabilities. The easiest way to do so is to assume that outcomes are monetary and the utility over money is linear $u(x) = x$. In other words, the person is assumed to be *risk neutral*, that is, indifferent between taking a monetary gamble and getting the mathematical expectation of this gamble for sure. Then the subjective probability $p(A)$ equals the *price* at which he or she is willing to buy or sell the ticket t_A that yields a unit of money if A occurs and nothing otherwise. Indeed, it is easy to check that either of these transactions leaves his or her subjective expected utility unchanged. Thus under the assumption of risk neutrality, subjective probabilities $p(\cdot)$ can be computed as prices. This method is clearly more practical than formula (3.4): throughout the history of civilization, people have set monetary odds to express their beliefs in a credible, transparent, and numerically precise way.

Moreover, the identity between probabilities and prices permits a straightforward argument for additivity. This argument, due to Ramsey and de Finetti, asserts that a rational person should not accept a *Dutch book*, that is, a portfolio of bets that produces a sure loss in any state of the world. To avoid Dutch books, a person must set additive prices for tickets like t_A. Indeed, if $p(A) + p(B) < p(A \cup B)$ for some events A and B, then the person will lose money for sure after selling t_A and t_B and buying $t_{A \cup B}$. Similarly, if $p(A) + p(B) > p(A \cup B)$, a person will end up with a Dutch book after buying t_A and t_B and selling $t_{A \cup B}$.

Note that pricing the ticket t_A is not the only way for a risk-neutral person to manifest his or her subjective probability $p(A)$. For example, consider a *quadratic scoring rule*, which Brier (1950) proposed for evaluating the accuracy of probabilistic weather forecasts. According to this procedure, the decision maker is asked to choose a number π and then he or she is paid $-(\pi - 1)^2$ if A occurs and $-\pi^2$ otherwise. To maximize his or her expected utility,

$$p(A)\left[-(\pi - 1)^2\right] + (1 - p(A))\left[-\pi^2\right],$$

the person should choose the number π that satisfies the first-order condition

$$2p(A)(\pi - 1) + (1 - p(A))\pi = 0,$$

that is, $\pi = p(A)$. It follows that this procedure provides incentives for the risk-neutral person to reveal his or her subjective probabilities truthfully.

Unfortunately, the assumptions that outcomes are monetary and people are risk neutral are too restrictive for many natural applications of subjective expected utility. For example, outcomes in game theory may have a purely verbal description; financial decisions, such as buying insurance or lottery tickets, are often incompatible with risk neutrality. Yet it can still make sense to derive any subjective probability $p(A)$ as a suitable rate of substitution. To do so, Anscombe and Aumann (1963) assume that outcomes of acts are objective probability distributions, called *lotteries*, ranked by von Neumann and Morgenstern's expected utility measured in *utils*. Then the subjective probability $p(A)$ equals the price (specified in utils) that the decision maker is willing to pay to receive an extra util contingent on the event A. Thus, it is much simpler to construct subjective probability in Anscombe and Aumann's framework than in Savage's more general counterpart. However, Anscombe and Aumann's approach is not innocuous: it takes objective probabilities for granted and requires a more complex structure for objects of choice. Thus, Savage's theory is commonly viewed as a more solid foundation for subjective probability.[6]

Refining Subjective Probabilities: de Finetti's Theorem, Bayes's Law, Market Selection

Both Theorems 3.1 and 3.2 above seek to explain why a rational person should have a probabilistic belief and how he or she should use it in decision

[6]Ghirardato, Maccheroni, Marinacci, and Siniscalchi (2003) show that, in principle, one can reformulate any model in Anscombe and Aumann's framework without the use of objective randomization.

making. These models put absolutely no restrictions on what personal beliefs should be, as long as they comply with the mathematical definition of probability. Thus, in applications it may be desirable to derive additional structure for subjective probability.

Consider first a setting where uncertainty is resolved in a state space

$$S = \{0,1\}^{\mathbb{N}} = \{0,1\} \times \{0,1\} \times \cdots$$

via a sequence of identical experiments. For example, let this sequence be produced by flipping a coin, by shooting basketball free throws, or by screening random votes at a poll. Objective statisticians commonly model such experiments as independent with unknown probability of success π in each trial. Yet for the decision maker in Theorems 3.1 and 3.2, statistical independence may be counterintuitive. For instance, he or she may strongly prefer to bet on a free throw after 10 have been made rather than after 10 have been missed. Thus, the decision maker may adjust his or her beliefs to experience in a way that violates independence.

Yet a weaker condition called *exchangeability* (or *symmetric dependence*) is still intuitive for subjective probabilities $p(\cdot)$ in this setting. This condition requires that beliefs are unaffected by the labeling of experiments. Formally, for any fixed sequence or zeros and ones $a_1, \ldots, a_n$ and for any permutation θ of the set $\{1, \ldots, n\}$,

$$p(\{s : s_1 = a_1, \ldots, s_n = a_n\}) \\ = p(\{s : s_1 = a_{\theta(1)}, \ldots, s_n = a_{\theta(n)}\}).$$

For example, the events "tails, then heads twice" and "heads, tails, heads again" in three initial coin tosses should have the same probabilities (not necessarily equal to $\frac{1}{8}$). Despite its innocuous appearance, exchangeability has some striking implications established by de Finetti.

Theorem 3.3. *If p is exchangeable, then there is a unique probability measure μ on $[0,1]$ such that for any sequence $a_1, \ldots, a_n$ that has k ones and $n-k$ zeros,*

$$p(\{s : s_1 = a_1, \ldots, s_n = a_n\}) \\ = \int_0^1 \pi^k (1-\pi)^{n-k} \, d\mu(\pi).$$

This result asserts that the decision maker with exchangeable beliefs behaves as if he or she integrates binomial distributions with respect to some prior distribution on the parameter space $[0,1]$. De Finetti's theorem has another important lesson. For each $s \in S$ and n, let $\xi_n(s) = \frac{s_1 + \cdots + s_n}{n}$ be the empirical frequency of successes in the first n trials, and let $\pi_n(s)$ be the subjective probability of success in nth trial conditional on the observation of $s_1, \ldots, s_{n-1}$. Then for an exchangeable p,

$$p(\{s : \lim \pi_n(s) = \lim \xi_n(s)\}) = 1.$$

Thus, the decision maker believes that with probability one (1) the empirical frequencies $\xi_n(s)$ converge, (2) the subjective conditional beliefs $\pi_n(s)$ are well defined and converge, and (3) $\xi_n(s)$ and $\pi_n(s)$ have the same limits. In other words, the decision maker believes that asymptotically his or her beliefs will coincide with empirical frequencies. Generalizations of de Finetti's theorem are obtained by Hewitt and Savage (1956) and Diaconis (1977).

Subjective probability in Theorems 3.1 and 3.2, as well as in de Finetti's theorem, is static. Accordingly, these results say nothing about how personal beliefs should evolve over time as new information becomes available. The standard updating procedure in statistics is Bayes's law, which asserts that the posterior probability of an event A after an event B has been observed is the ratio of the prior probabilities $p(A \cap B)/p(B)$. To derive this law for subjective probability in a temporal setting, one needs to impose the principle of *dynamic consistency*. In Savage's framework, this principle asserts that the decision maker who has ex ante preference $fAg \succeq g$ should still prefer f to g after observing A (see Ghirardato, 2002). However, people may violate Bayes's law and the associated dynamic consistency because of deeper introspection, surprise, or cognitive dissonance. See Epstein (2006) for a model of non-Bayesian updating.

Alternatively, one can use evolutionary arguments to show that eventually people with the most accurate beliefs will dominate the population. For instance, if evolution is performed by markets, asset prices should eventually reflect rational beliefs. This *market selection hypothesis*, due to Alchian (1950) and Freedman (1953), has been recently confirmed theoretically by Sandroni (2000). In a complete market setting with a common discount factor, Sandroni shows that if there are agents who eventually make accurate predictions, then these agents are exactly those who survive in the long run, and the market prices eventually reflect true objective probabilities.

EMPIRICAL CONTENT OF SUBJECTIVE PROBABILITY

Normative models of subjective probability, such as Theorems 3.1 and 3.2, have many practical limitations. First, it may be hard to establish a one-to-one correspondence between physical actions and Savage-style abstract acts. Indeed, many decisions that people make under uncertainty are not easily formulated in terms of states of the world and outcomes. For example, consider a person who has a choice between jobs in two different cities, say New York and Los Angeles. It is easy to write a long list of uncertainties—such as salary growth, professional satisfaction, colleagues, housing, neighbors, commute, nightlife, weather—that may be relevant for this choice. Yet it is not clear how to specify a state space S and a set of outcomes X. The decision maker himself or herself may fail to identify S and X which are exhaustive, sufficiently detailed, and independent of each other. Indeed, it seems quite reasonable for the decision maker to admit that he or she cannot foresee all contingencies that may occur in New York or Los Angeles. Even if the decision maker does have some particular S and X in mind, then how can the modeler learn about them? In principle, the modeler could take universal $\hat{S}$ and $\hat{X}$ that include all states of the world and outcomes that people might possibly have in mind. But then what is the act that describes a particular job for a particular person in the universal framework?

On the other hand, there are many choice problems that can be embedded naturally in some Savage-style framework. For example, a number of hypothetical and real experiments in decision theory involve bets on the color of a ball drawn randomly from an urn. In this context, states are colors and outcomes are monetary. Then there is a concern that some acts are pure abstractions that do not correspond to any natural physical actions. This concern is especially grave in Theorems 3.1 and 3.2, where S must be infinite. Many acts and events in this setting are too complex to have any practical meaning. It is clearly impossible to observe preferences over such acts with any reasonable degree of approximation.

The inherent complexity of the construction of subjective probability in Savage's framework is a normative concern as well. The reliance on purely abstract objects that cannot be used in any physical or mental experiment weakens the normative power of Savage's theory. Instead, one might derive subjective probability on a finite state space, as in Anscombe and Aumann (1963), Gul (1993), or Abdellaoui and Wakker (2005). However, the gain in simplicity is illusory because these models impose an additional structure on the set of outcomes and less transparent axioms on preference.

Indecision, Framing, and Regret

The first postulate of the theory of subjective probability is that preferences are complete and transitive. These assumptions are often violated by experimental evidence. One explanation is that people often fail to produce a compelling argument in favor of any of the available alternatives. If they are forced to make a choice while being in this state of *indecision*, the response may be random and easily manipulated by the experimenter's presentation of different alternatives. For example, consider a hypothetical situation when an outbreak of a rare Asian disease may kill up to 600 victims and there are several programs to combat the disease:

- program f will save 200 victims;
- program g with probability $\frac{1}{3}$, will save all victims and with probability $\frac{2}{3}$, will save none of them;
- if program f' is adopted, then 400 victims will die;
- if program g' is adopted, then with probability $\frac{1}{3}$, none of the victims will die and with probability $\frac{2}{3}$, all victims will die.

Kahneman and Tversky (1983) report an experiment where 72% of decision makers prefer f to g, and 78% prefer g' to f'. Yet in real terms, programs f and g are indistinguishable from f' and g', respectively.

Indecision may also lead to *intransitivity* of preference. For example, given a slightly bent coin and three events

$A =$ {The next 101 flips will give at least 40 heads},

$B =$ {The next 100 flips will give at least 41 heads}, and

$C =$ {The next 1,000 flips will give at least 460 heads},

a person may have betting preferences $A \sim_0 C$ and $B \sim_0 C$ due to indecision but firmly prefer to bet on A rather than on B. Another possible explanation for intransitivity among acts is *regret.* Loomes, Starmer, and Sugden (1991) support this explanation with experimental evidence.

Allais's Paradox

In settings originally studied by Allais (1953), all events have explicit numerical probabilities, but preferences cannot be represented by expected utility. For example, Kahneman and Tversky (1979) report that a majority of subjects in their experiments prefer to get \$3,000 for sure rather than \$4,000 with probability 0.8, but also prefer to get \$4,000 with probability 0.2 rather than \$3,000 with probability 0.25. These choices constitute a violation of expected utility for any index u: $u(3000) > 0.8u(4000)$ but $0.25u(3000) < 0.2u(4000)$. Thus, it is hard to believe that expected utility holds in more general settings where objective probabilities are not given. Is it possible to separate subjective probability from the expected utility criterion?

Machina and Schmeidler (1992) propose an elegant solution. Their model of *probabilistic sophistication* portrays a person who ranks acts in two stages: first, the person uses subjective probabilities to translate each act into a lottery—a distribution over outcomes—and then he or she ranks the induced lotteries via a *risk preference*, which need not be represented by expected utility. Formally, a probabilistically sophisticated person, who has a belief p, reduces every act f to a distribution $l_p(f)$ assigning a probability $p(\{s : f(s) = x\})$ to each outcome x. Then he or she evaluates the act f via a utility function

$$U(f) = V(l_p(f)),$$

where V represents the risk preference over all relevant lotteries. To accommodate probabilistic sophistication, Machina and Schmeidler (1992) relax the sure-thing principle and require roughly that only the betting preference can be conditioned on any event A independently of outcomes that are obtained if A does not occur. This separability of preference need not hold when acts more complex than bets are conditioned on A.

Ellsberg's Paradox

Another famous paradox, due to Ellsberg (1961), illustrates the empirical importance of the Knightian distinction between *risk*, which can be represented by numerical probabilities, and *ambiguity*, which cannot.[7] In particular, this paradox arises when a person is told that (1) a ball will be drawn randomly from an urn that contains balls of three possible colors (red, green, and blue), and (2) the probability of drawing a red ball is $\frac{1}{3}$. Then the typical preference is to bet on the event $\{R\}$ rather than on the event $\{B\}$ because the probability of $\{R\}$ is known to be $\frac{1}{3}$, while the probability of $\{B\}$ is not known precisely and lies between 0 and $\frac{2}{3}$. Analogously, it is typical to bet on $\{B, G\}$ rather than on $\{R, G\}$. This betting preference cannot be represented by any subjective probability measure p because the inequalities $p(\{R\}) > p(\{B\})$ and $p(\{B\}) + p(\{G\}) > p(\{R\}) + p(\{G\})$ are inconsistent with the additivity of p. What could be the meaning of subjective probability in this case?

To accommodate Ellsberg-type behavior, one can use a utility representation called *epsilon contamination*:

$$U(f) = \varepsilon \min_{q \in \Delta} \int_S u(f(s))\,dq + (1-\varepsilon) \int_S u(f(s))\,dp. \qquad (3.6)$$

[7]Knight (1921) refers to *uncertainty* rather than *ambiguity*. Modern literature widely uses Ellsberg's terminology, where uncertainty is comprehensive and includes both risk and ambiguity.

Here, the set Δ is given exogenously: it consists of all probabilistic scenarios on S that are consistent with the available objective evidence. For example, in the Ellsberg paradox $\Delta = \{q : q(\{R\}) = \frac{1}{3}\}$. The decision maker, as portrayed by (3.6), evaluates every act f via an ε-mixture of the most unfavorable scenario in Δ and the subjective probability p. Note that the weight $1-\varepsilon$ can be interpreted as a degree of confidence that the decision maker has in his or her belief p. Kopylov (2006) characterizes epsilon contamination by relaxing Anscombe and Aumann's postulates of the subjective expected utility theory. Note also that representation (3.6) is a special case of the multiple priors model due to Gilboa and Schmeidler (1989). However, unlike this more general model, epsilon contamination specifies a *unique* and *additive* probability measure that underlies choice among uncertain prospects. Thus it suggests that subjective probability can be meaningful even for people who distinguish between risk and ambiguity and behave accordingly.

SUMMARY

To conclude, we evaluate the concept of subjective probability via the following three criteria due to Salmon (1966): (1) *coherence* (or admissibility), so that probability should comply with Kolmogorov's definition; (2) *ascertainability*, so that at least in principle, it should be possible to find out values of probabilities; and (3) *applicability*, so that it should be clear how probability relates to the objective world and how it should be used in decision making.

Subjective probability derived in Theorems 3.1 and 3.2 is coherent but does not fully satisfy the other two criteria. First, to find out the values of subjective probability, one needs to find out a preference relation $\succeq$ that satisfies a suitable list of rationality conditions. Even in principle, such a preference is hard to come by. Next, both Theorems 3.1 and 3.2 relate subjective probabilities to decision making rather than to any observations of the physical world.

Thus, there is a growing body of literature that (1) derives subjective probability from weaker primitives and (2) relates subjective probability with objective evidence. The full impact of this literature remains to be seen.

ACKNOWLEDGMENTS

The author thanks the editor for his infinite patience and many insightful comments.

REFERENCES

Abdellaoui, M., & Wakker, P. (2005). The likelihood method for decision under uncertainty. *Theory and Decision, 58*, 3–76.

Alchian, A. (1950). Uncertainty, evolution, and economic theory. *Journal of Political Economy, 58*, 211–221.

Allais, M. (1953). La psychologie de l'home rationnel devant le risque: Critique des postulats et axiomes de l'école Américaine. *Econometrica, 21*, 503–546.

Anscombe, F., & Aumann, R. (1963). A definition of subjective probability. *Annals of Mathematical Statistics, 34*, 199–205.

Bayes, T. (1763). An essay towards solving a problem in the doctrine of chances. *Philosophical Transactions of the Royal Society London, 53*, 370–418. (Available from http://www.stat.ucla.edu/history/essay.pdf)

Bernoulli, J. (1713). *Ars Conjectandi.* Basel, Switzerland: Impenfis Thurnisiorum.

Billingsley, P. (1995). *Probability and measure* (3rd ed.). New York: Wiley.

Brier, G. (1950). Verification of forecasts expressed in terms of probability. *Monthly Weather Review, 78*, 1–3.

Carnap, R. (1950). *Logical foundations of probability.* Chicago: University of Chicago Press.

de Finetti, B. (1937). La prévision: Ses lois logiques, ses sources subjectives. *Annales de l'Institute Henri Poincare, 7*, 1–68.

Dekel, E., Lipman, B. L., & Rustichini, A. (2001). Representing preferences with a unique subjective state space. *Econometrica, 69*, 891–934.

de Moivre, A. (1756). *The doctrine of chances: A method for calculating the probabilities of events in play.* London: A. Miller. (First edition published, 1711)

Diaconis, P. (1977). Finite forms of de Finetti's theorem on exchangeability. *Synthese, 36*, 271–281.

Ellis, R. (1863). on the foundations of the theory of probabilities. In W. Walton (Ed.), *the mathematical and other writings of Robert Leslie Ellis* (pp. 295–319). Cambridge, UK: Deighton & Bell. (First published in 1844)

Ellsberg, D. (1961). Risk, ambiguity, and the Savage axioms. *Quarterly Journal of Economics*, *75*, 643–669.

Epstein, L. (2006). An axiomatic model of non-Bayesian updating. *Review of Economic Studies*, *73*, 413–436.

Fishburn, P. C. (1970). *Utility theory for decision making*. New York: Wiley.

Freedman, M. (1953). *Essays in positive economics*. Chicago: University of Chicago Press.

Ghirardato, P. (2002). Revisiting Savage in a conditional world. *Economic Theory*, *20*, 83–92.

Ghirardato, P., Maccheroni, F., Marinacci, M., & Siniscalchi, M. (2003). A subjective spin on roulette wheels. *Econometrica*, *71*, 1897–1908.

Gilboa, I., & Schmeidler, D. (1989). Maxmin expected utility with non-unique prior. *Journal of Mathematical Economics*, *18*, 141–153.

Gul, F. (1993). Savage's theorem with a finite number of states. *Journal of Economic Theory*, *61*, 99–110.

Hewitt, E., & Savage, L. J. (1956). Symmetric measures on Cartesian products. *Transactions of the American Mathematical Society*, *80*, 470–501.

Kahneman, D., & Tversky, A. (1979). Prospect theory: An analysis of decision under risk. *Econometrica*, *47*, 263–291.

Kahneman, D., & Tversky, A. (1983). Choices, values, and frames. *American Psychologist*, *39*, 341–350.

Karni, E. (1993). A definition of subjective probabilities with state-dependent preferences. *Econometrica*, *61*, 187–198.

Karni, E. (2006). *Subjective expected utility theory without states of the world* (Working Paper). Baltimore, MD: Johns Hopkins University.

Keynes, J. M. (1921). *A treatise on probability*. New York: Macmillan.

Knight, F. (1921). *Risk, uncertainty and profit*. Boston: Houghton Mifflin.

Kolmogorov, A. N. (1950). *Foundations of the theory of probability*. New York: Chelsey. (Original work published, *Grundbegriffe der Wahrscheinlichkeits Rechnung*, 1933, Berlin: Springer-Verlag)

Koopman, B. O. (1940). The axioms and algebra of intuitive probability. *Annals of Mathematics*, *41*, 269–292.

Kopylov, I. (2006). *Subjective probability under objective ambiguity* (Working Paper). Irvine, CA: University of California Irvine. Available from http://webfiles.uci.edu/ikopylov/www/files/par_hedge.pdf.

Kopylov, I. (2007). Subjective probabilities on small domains. *Journal of Economic Theory*, *133*, 236–265.

Kraft, C., Pratt, J., & Seidenberg, A. (1959). Intuitive probability on finite sets. *Annals of Mathematical Statistics*, *30*, 408–430.

Kreps, D. M. (1988). *Notes on the theory of choice*. Boulder, CO: Westview Press.

Laplace, P. S. (1917). *A philosophical essay on probabilities*. New York: Wiley. (Original work published, *Essai philosophique sur les probabilités*, 1814, Paris: Courcier)

Loomes, G., Starmer, C., & Sugden, R. (1991). Observing violations of transitivity by experimental methods. *Econometrica*, *59*, 425–439.

Luce, D. (1967). Sufficient conditions for the existence of a finitely additive probability measure. *Annals of Mathematical Statistics*, *38*, 780–786.

Machina, M. (2003). States of the world and the state of the decision theory. In D. Mayer (Ed.), *The economics of risk* (pp. 17–46). Kalamazoo, MI: W. E. Upjohn Institute for Employment Research.

Machina, M., & Schmeidler, D. (1992). A more robust definition of subjective probability. *Econometrica*, *60*, 745–780.

Nau, R. (2001). De Finetti was right: Probability does not exist. *Theory and Decision*, *51*, 89–124.

Pratt, J. W. (1964). Risk aversion in the small and in the large. *Econometrica*, *32*, 122–136.

Ramsey, F. P. (1931). Truth and probability. In R. B. Braithwaite (Ed.), *The foundations of mathematics and other logical essays* (pp. 156–198). New York: Harcourt, Brace and Company. (First published in 1926)

Salmon, F. P. (1966). *The foundations of scientific inference*. Pittsburgh, PA: University of Pittsburgh Press.

Sandroni, A. (2000). Do markets favor agents able to make accurate predictions? *Econometrica*, *68*, 1303–1342.

Savage, L. J. (1972). *The foundations of statistics* (2nd rev. ed.). New York: Dover. (First edition published, 1954)

Scott, D. (1964). Measurement structures and linear inequalities. *Journal of Mathematical Psychology*, *1*, 233–247.

Skiadas, C. (1997). Subjective probability under additive aggregation of conditional preferences. *Journal of Economic Theory*, *76*, 242–271.

Venn, J. (1962). *Logic of chance* (4th ed.). New York: Chelsey. (Original work published 1866)

Villegas, C. (1964). On qualitative probability σ-algebras. *Annals of Mathematical Statistics*, *35*, 1787–1796.

von Neumann, J., & Morgenstern, O. (1944). *Theory of games and economic behavior*. Princeton, NJ: Princeton University Press.

Wakker, P. (1981). Agreeing probability measures for comparative probability structures. *Annals of Statistics*, *9*, 658–662.

4

Paradoxes in Probability Theory

Nicholas Shackel

Introduction

We call something a paradox if it strikes us as peculiar in a certain way, if it strikes us as something that is not simply nonsense, and yet it poses some difficulty in seeing how it could be sense. When we examine paradoxes more closely, we find that for some the peculiarity is relieved and for others it intensifies. Some are peculiar because they jar with how we expect things to go, but the jarring is to do with imprecision and misunderstandings in our thought, failures to appreciate the breadth of possibility consistent with our beliefs. Other paradoxes, however, pose deep problems. Closer examination does not explain them away. Instead, they challenge the coherence of certain conceptual resources and hence challenge the significance of beliefs which deploy those resources. I shall call the former kind weak paradoxes and the latter, strong paradoxes. Whether a particular paradox is weak or strong is sometimes a matter of controversy—sometimes it has been realised that what was thought strong is in fact weak and vice versa, but the distinction between the two kinds is generally thought to be worth drawing.

The pressure of paradox has often been a spur to intellectual endeavour. Weak paradoxes have on occasion led us to greater clarity and precision in our thought. Strong paradoxes have on occasion led us to radical conceptual innovation and, indeed, have been the basis of entire research programmes. Such programmes often bifurcate. On the one hand, various means of evading the paradox are instituted, such as conceptual refinement, restriction, or substitution. On the other hand, we continue to think about the paradox and think about what status should be accorded the means that avoids the paradox. One way for a strong paradox to be resolved is for the means of evasion to be shown to be adequate to the issues raised by the paradox. For example, it is at least arguable that the mathematical resources developed by 19th-century mathematicians are adequate to the conceptual problems in understanding time and space that Zeno's paradoxes raised.

In this chapter, I shall cover both weak and strong probabilistic paradoxes. Before we turn to them, I need to mention a point about the nature of probability itself. In philosophy of probability, we standardly distinguish subjective or epistemic probability, which is regarded as a feature of persons, from objective probability, which is regarded as a feature of the objective world. Subjective probability may be taken to be a model of the degree to which a person believes something or a measure of the degree to which a person ought to believe something. Objective probability may be taken to be a model of the propensity that the world has to go in a certain way. One way in which they may be held to be related is by Lewis's (1986a) principal principle, which says, roughly, that reasonable subjective probabilities conform to known objective probabilities. By and large, what I say applies to probability as a guide to belief and so is largely concerned with subjective probability. In some cases, the point of taking probability as a guide to belief is a matter of looking at what belief is warranted by the evidence, and in others, the point is to believe in accordance with the objective probabilities. When a probability in a scenario could be an objective probability, I shall call it a chance.

WEAK PARADOXES

Probability is especially rich in weak paradoxes, since (it turns out) we are not good probabilistic thinkers but are rather prone to probabilistic fallacy, and for this reason we can find ourselves surprised by what is probabilistically correct and taken in by what is not. For example, we are prone to confusing the conditional probability of an event E given F with the probability of F given E, and this gives rise to the xenophobic paradox (see Clark, 2002), the prosecutor's fallacy (representing the probability of the evidence given innocence as if it were the probability of innocence given the evidence) and the medic's fallacy (confusing the reliability of a test with the chance of illness/health given a positive/negative test). We are also prone to ignoring prior probabilities and base rates, confusing probability with representativeness, and we are subject to framing effects with probabilistic information. Examples of these errors are addressed elsewhere in this book, and given the pressure on space, I shall mention only a few weak paradoxes before devoting most time to strong paradoxes.

Failure to Appreciate How Aggregation Can Lead to Misleading Proportional Information

Despite the conviction of generations of the innumerate, $\frac{a}{b} + \frac{c}{d}$ is not equal to $\frac{a+c}{b+d}$. A consequence of this is that aggregated proportional information such as percentages can be significantly misleading.

Simpson's Paradox

We have a new treatment for a disease, and when we compare it with the old treatment it cures 2% more people.[1] Surely that means it is a better treatment? Not necessarily. When we analyse the results by sex, we find that the new treatment cures 18% fewer men and 17% fewer women (Table 4.1).

It would be reasonable to conclude that the aggregated proportions produce an illusion that the new treatment is better. This is certainly surprising, but it is a simple consequence of the mathematics of means and what results when you aggregate or disaggregate results. This kind of problem arises more easily when there is a wide disparity in the numbers of the two groups involved, say 1,000 women versus 100 men, but does not require such a disparity. In this example, the numbers are comparable, 1,100 versus 1,050. There is no guarding against this problem, and it has nothing to do with sample sizes in general nor with problems to do with base rates. Its implication is that aggregation of groups with relevant differences may be dangerously misleading. Here is a topical example.

It is possible for every department in a university to massively discriminate against Group B in admissions, yet when looking at the figures for the university as a whole, it may look as if the university discriminates against Group A. Consider a university which has only two departments and applications and acceptances as laid out in Table 4.2.

Group A is massively preferred to Group B in both psychology and mathematics, and yet on the overall figures, it looks as if Group B is being favoured. The conclusion should be that aggregation can result in dangerously misleading data, especially when attempting to use statistical proportions as proof of discrimination.

The illusions we have just analysed arise because it is mistakenly assumed that aggregation over a conditioning variable (sex or subject) is

[1] I say "cure" on the basis of 2% more recovering. We assume here that the circumstances are such as to allow correlation licensing the inference to causation.

Table 4.1

Treatment	*Men*		*Women*		*Cured Percentages*		
	Ill	*Cured*	*Ill*	*Cured*	*Men*	*Women*	*Overall*
Old	1,000	500	100	80	50%	80%	53%
New	250	80	800	500	32%	63%	55%

Table 4.2

Group	*Psychology*		*Mathematics*		*Acceptance Proportions*		
	Applications	*Accepted*	*Applications*	*Accepted*	*Psychology*	*Maths*	*Overall*
A	1,000	500	100	80	50%	80%	53%
B	250	80	800	500	32%	63%	55%

Table 4.3

Treatment	*Feel Worse*		*Feel Better*		*Cured Percentages*		
	Ill	*Cured*	*Ill*	*Cured*	*Feel Worse*	*Feel Better*	*Overall*
Old	1,000	500	100	80	50%	80%	53%
New	250	80	800	500	32%	63%	55%

irrelevant to determining the significant correlations between the input variable (treatment or group) and the output variable (response to treatment or admission status). Historically, these are the kinds of illusions into which we have fallen. Might there be cases in which *disaggregation* is similarly misleading? Considered purely mathematically, one may take *any* arbitrary variables as input, output, and conditioning. For example, we could take feeling as a conditioning variable in the treatment case (Table 4.3). Here, it would seem implausible to conclude that the old treatment is in fact better, and so here disaggregation is misleading.

How then do we determine which disaggregations are required and which are misleading? On the one hand, it is worth noting that constructing examples of Simpson's paradox in which disaggregation is clearly misleading tends to depend on cases in which the conditioning variable is more plausibly seen as part of the output. It being part of the output tends to make the figures look gerrymandered: Could there really be 500 people who were both cured *and* felt worse? What we would really like, though, is to have criteria for correct aggregation and disaggregation. Since the general project is to find the true reasons for the variability in the output, conditioning variables are properly disaggregated into those that could be among such reasons. To be such a reason is presumably to be something on which the output depends rather than vice versa. The debate takes off from here on the basis of interpreting dependence in evidential terms or in causal terms.

A Little Knowledge of Probability Theory Is a Dangerous Thing

Monty Hall

When you were young, you probably learnt the classical basis for assigning numerical probabilities: to give equal probability to the equally possible. That is why you think the chance of getting heads is 1/2, the chance of throwing a six is 1/6, and the chance of drawing the ace of spades is 1/52. You are on TV taking part in Monty Hall's game show and have just answered the final question correctly. You are now eligible for the big prize. There are three doors in front of you, and Monty tells you that behind one is a car and behind the other two are goats. He invites you to pick a door. As he always does at this point in the show, Monty then opens one of the other doors, shows you a goat behind it, and asks you whether you want to change the door you picked. Can you improve your chance of winning by changing? "Surely not," you think, "since there are two closed doors, a car behind one of them, it is equally possible for them to be behind either, so the chance that it is behind mine is the same as the chance it is behind his, namely, 50%."

Wrong answer, but you are in good company. When this was published by Marilyn vos Savant,[2] a number of mathematicians insisted that it was the right answer, and for the very same reason. If Monty chose his door at random, you would be right, but he doesn't.

The quick way to see why it is wrong is to remember that when you first picked your door, there was a one-third chance it was behind your door and a two-thirds chance it was behind Monty's doors. That hasn't changed just because Monty opened one of his two doors, since when you first chose, you knew that Monty would open a door and show you a goat. All that has changed is that if you were wrong in the first place, the car must now be behind the door which Monty didn't open. So there is a two-thirds chance that the car is behind Monty's other door. What confuses us here is that we don't take into account that whenever the car is behind one of his doors, Monty doesn't have a free choice of doors to open. He can only open the one with the goat behind it. We fail to realise that we are not equally ignorant about which door it is behind. If that doesn't convince you, think of the case in which there are 100 doors; you pick one, and Monty opens 98 doors showing a goat in each case. Still sure you don't want to swap?

The proof is in conditional probability. You need to know the probability that the car is behind your door given that you see a goat behind one of his, $P(Y|G)$:

$$P(Y|G) = \frac{P(G|Y)P(Y)}{P(G)} = \frac{1 \times (1/3)}{1} = \frac{1}{3}.$$

But if Monty chooses his door to open at random, then instead of the probability of seeing a goat, $P(G)$, being 1, it drops to $2/3$, and then $P(Y|G) = 1/2$.

The Significance of the Distinction Between Numerical Identity and Qualitative Identity

Bertrand's Box

There are three boxes, each with two compartments. In one box there are two gold coins, in another two silver coins, and in the third one gold and one silver coin. You open one compartment and see a gold coin. What is the chance that the other coin in the box is silver? "Well," you may think, "the other coin is either silver or gold, and they are equally possible, so it must be $1/2$." Alternatively, you may think that since you have seen a gold coin, the box is either the box with two gold coins or one gold and one silver, but we don't know which so it must be $1/2$. But that is incorrect.

We must distinguish two kinds of identity, qualitative identity and numerical identity. If we say that Jack and John are the same age, we mean that there is a property that they have in common, their age. This is qualitative identity, because it is a matter of the identity of a property rather than of an object. But if we say that Jack and John are the same person, we don't mean that Jack and John are distinct objects who share the property of personhood (if we meant that, we would say that they are *both* persons) but that Jack and John are one and the same person. This is numerical identity, and it is a matter of the identity of an object.

Returning to the coins, it is true that so far as qualitative identity goes, there are only two distinguishable options for the other coin—namely, gold or silver. But the possibilities we must distinguish are distinguished in terms of numerical identity. There are in fact *three* different gold coins that you might have revealed on opening the compartment. Only one of those coins is paired with a silver coin, the other two are paired with each other. So the chance is $1/3$.

---

[2]Marilyn vos Savant "rose to fame through her listing in the Guinness Book of World Records under 'Highest IQ'. Since 1986, she has written 'Ask Marilyn,' a Sunday column in *Parade* magazine, in which she answers questions from readers on a variety of subjects" (http://www.en.wikipedia.org/wiki/Marilyn_vos_Savant).

Bose-Einstein Paradox

Suppose the boxes have not gold and silver coins but two kinds of bosons, call them yellow and blue. You open a compartment and see a yellow. What is the chance that the other particle in the box is a blue? Our earlier reasoning would imply that the answer is $1/3$, but astonishingly, both physical theory and empirical investigation show it to be $1/2$! Why is that? The physicists say bosons (and fermions) are *indistinguishable* particles, by which they seem to mean that they lack numerical identity. If that is the case, the earlier argument we gave based on numerical identity lapses, and instead, we can reason only on the basis of qualitative identity and distinction. Since the other particle is either yellow or blue, the chance is $1/2$.

The idea of particles lacking numerical identity is very difficult to understand. It might be that seeing a yellow is merely acquiring the information that *a* particle is yellow, so the possibilities consistent with that information are both yellow or one yellow and one blue, hence the chance is $1/2$. However, that can't be the whole story. In the case of indistinguishable particles, whilst they are countable, the claim is not the epistemological claim that what we know fails to distinguish them but the metaphysical claim that there is no fact of the matter about whether this particle is the same particle as that particle. That is a deeply puzzling claim, but we shall leave its further investigation to the philosophers of physics!

Strong Paradoxes

So far, we have looked at weak paradoxes, paradoxes that highlight our weaknesses in understanding probability. We now turn to strong paradoxes, paradoxes that pose challenges to probability itself, either by apparently falsifying principles or axioms of probability which we have independent reasons to think true or by threatening our confidence in the coherence and comprehensiveness of probability theory. We examine them in two areas, probability as a guide to belief and rational decision theory as a guide to action, given by defining choiceworthiness in terms of expected value. In the case of weak paradoxes, I was able to suggest the root of the problem. In the case of strong paradoxes, I can only indicate the kind of proposals that have been offered as solutions.

Trouble for Belief

Bertrand's Chord

Choose a chord of a circle at random. What is the chance that it is longer than a side of the inscribed equilateral triangle?

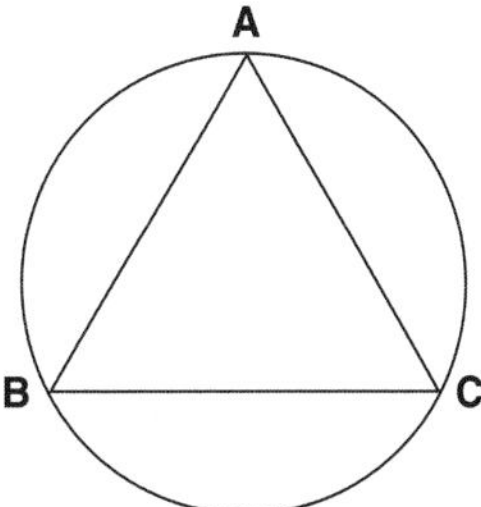

1. Consider all the chords that start at A on the circumference. Any chord whose other end is on the circumference between A and B or A and C will be shorter, whilst any chord whose other end is on the circumference between B and C will be longer. The angle subtended by the set of longer ones is therefore 60°, and hence, the chance of these being longer is $60/180 = 1/3$. By symmetry, this applies to all chords, so the chance of their being longer is $1/3$.

2. Now consider the chords with centres on the radius bisecting BC. They are perpendicular to the radius. Those whose centre is on the same side of BC as the centre are longer, and those on the other side are shorter. The distance from the centre to BC equals the distance along the radius from BC to the circumference. Therefore, the chance of these chords being longer is $1/2$, and by symmetry, this applies to all chords.

3. Now consider all the chords whose centre lies within the circle inscribed in the equilateral triangle. All these chords are longer, and the chords whose centre lies outside the inscribed circle are shorter. The area of the inscribed circle is $1/4$ that of the circumscribing circle, therefore the chance of a longer chord is $1/4$.

Hence, the chance of a longer chord is $1/3$ and $1/2$ and $1/4$. But probabilities are unique, so this is a contradiction.

To cut a long story very short, given a range of possible outcomes, mathematical probability theory *alone* does not give numerical probabilities for those possibilities.[3] What probability theory will do, given numerical probabilities for what can be regarded as, in some sense, the atomic possibilities, is tell you what the numerical probabilities for all the compound possibilities are. The right basis on which to assign probabilities to the atomic possibilities is a controversial issue in the philosophy of probability. One position in that controversy is called the principle of indifference,[4] which says that possibilities of which we have equal ignorance have equal probability. For example, given a shuffled pack of cards, I am equally ignorant with respect to the 52 possibilities for the top card and so should assign the probability of $1/52$ to each possibility. Supposing that I know that the top card is red, then I am now no longer equally ignorant over all the possibilities, but I am equally ignorant over the red cards, so I assign a probability of 0 to the top card being black and $1/26$ to each of the red cards.

Bertrand designed his paradox as a refutation of the applicability of probability to infinite sets of possibilities. In each of the calculations above, we made implicit use of the principle of indifference. For example, in the second case, we take it that we are equally ignorant with respect to the distance of the centre of the chord from the centre of the triangle and so apply a uniform distribution to that random variable. His argument is roughly that numerical probabilities can only be got by use of the principle of indifference, but there is no unique way to apply that principle to infinite sets, therefore probability does not apply to infinite sets. It has recently turned out that there is reason to reject the third calculation (see Shackel, 2007), but that is of no help. The problem is that the three cases are merely examples of the infinitely many ways there are of applying the principle of indifference to calculating the probability of a longer chord.

This paradox has sometimes been thought to be resolved (e.g., Jaynes, 1973; Marinoff, 1994). Certainly there are some empirical cases in which a particular way of calculating the probability of a longer chord both fits the features of the case and gets the right empirical answer. But the problem posed by Bertrand is quite general. Arguably (see Shackel, 2007), the current main contenders for resolution do not work, and there are good reasons for thinking that it is irresolvable. We may not wish to join Bertrand in his finitism, but whilst his paradox is unresolved, it threatens our confidence in the coherence of applying probability to infinite sets.

Sleeping Beauty

It is Sunday night, and you, sleeping beauty, go to sleep knowing the following. We will toss a fair coin. If it lands heads, we will wake you briefly on Monday and put you back to sleep with a drug which will erase your memory of that wakening, and you won't wake till Wednesday. If it lands tails, we will wake you briefly on both Monday and Tuesday, putting you back to sleep with the same drug. Before you go to sleep on Sunday, you think the probability of the coin landing heads, $P(H)$, is $1/2$. We wake you on Monday. You don't know what day it is. What now is the probability that the coin landed heads?

- It must be $1/2$, since it was a fair coin. That was your opinion of Sunday night, and you have learnt nothing new (since you knew when you went to sleep that you would wake at least once not knowing which day it was).

- It must be $1/3$. This is either a Monday wakening following a head (HM) or a Monday wakening following a tail (TM) or a Tuesday wakening following a tail (TT).

[3]Part of the long story cut short is the distinction that philosophy of probability makes between the mathematical *theory* of probability and *probability*. The mathematical theory is a part of measure theory and is not, as such, about probability, properly so-called, until we have interpreted it as a model of degrees of belief or propensities. Compare the distinction between mechanics as a piece of mathematics and interpreted in terms of particles, motions, and forces. Bertrand was one of the originators of measure theory, and one of the points he hoped to make with this paradox was that the mathematical probability theory in its full generality lacks interpretation as probability properly so-called.

[4]So named by Keynes (1921/1963). J. Bernouilli and Leibniz called an essentially similar principle the principle of insufficient reason.

> These possibilities are indistinguishable to you so equiprobable. Furthermore, by the law of large numbers, were this experiment repeated many times, the proportion of wakenings when the coin fell heads tends to $1/3$.

What we need to know here is a conditional probability—namely, the probability that the coin is heads given that you woke, $P(H|W)$. We can prove that this probability is the same as the probability that it fell heads and today is Monday, $P(\text{HM})$. Since we know that this wakening is either HM or TM or TT and that these three events are mutually exclusive and jointly exhaustive, we know that

$$P(\text{HM or TM or TT}) = P(\text{HM}) + P(\text{TM}) + P(\text{TT}) = 1.$$

So if we can determine some relations between $P(\text{HM})$, $P(\text{TM})$, and $P(\text{TT})$, we can determine $P(\text{HM})$. Elga (2000) argues that the principle of indifference gives us that $P(\text{TM}|\text{TM or TT}) = P(\text{TT}|\text{TM or TT})$ and the latter implies that $P(\text{TM}) = P(\text{TT})$. We also know that

$$P(H|M) = P(\text{HM})/(P(\text{HM}) + P(\text{TM})),$$
$$P(T|M) = P(\text{TM})/(P(\text{HM}) + P(\text{TM})) = 1 - P(H|M).$$

So far, this is compatible with either answer. Elga now argues that $P(H|M) = P(T|M)$, and this together with the last two equations means that $P(\text{HM}) = P(\text{TM})$. But since $P(\text{TM}) = P(\text{TT})$ and the three together add up to 1, $P(\text{HM}) = 1/3$.

The basis of Elga's argument that $P(H|M) = P(T|M)$ is that it doesn't really matter when we toss the coin. We could just as well toss it after the Monday wakening. In that case, you would agree that $P(H|M) = P(H) = 1/2$, and hence, $P(T|M) = 1 - P(H|M) = 1/2$.[5] So knowing that it is Monday increases the probability of heads by $1/6$: $P(H|M) - P(H|W) = P(H|M) - P(HM) = 1/2 - 1/3 = 1/6$.

Lewis (2001) rejects this argument on the ground that knowing that you are awake in one of three indistinguishable wakenings is not *relevant* evidence to the question of heads, and so $P(H|W)$ must equal $P(H) = 1/2$. Hence, although he agrees that knowing it is Monday increases the probability of heads by $1/6$, so agrees with Elga that $P(H|M) = P(H|W) + 1/6$, he thinks that $P(H|M) = 2/3$ and therefore is not equal to $P(T|M)$.

So we have two plausible thoughts which seem compatible yet which result in a contradiction. On the one hand, it seems that your ignorance means it doesn't matter when the coin is tossed, and hence, knowing it is Monday and the coin is yet to be tossed makes $P(H|M) = P(H) = 1/2$ plausible. On the other hand, knowing that you are awake in one of three indistinguishable wakenings doesn't seem relevant evidence for how the coin landed. The first implies that $P(H|W)$ is $1/3$ and the second that it is $1/2$.

Lewis discusses Elga's application of Lewis's principal principle to future chances, saying that applications to future chance events must satisfy a proviso that doesn't apply in the case to which Elga applies it, the case where you know that it is Monday and the coin has yet to be tossed. Interestingly enough, Lewis's position here might be thought to be at odds with his very own principal principle. One notion of objective probability is limiting frequency, and on that basis, the objective probability of a head given you awoke is $1/3$. According to his principle, that means that your subjective probability ought also to be $1/3$. And yet Lewis is saying that the subjective probability is $1/2$.

This paradox bears an analogy to Monty Hall and perhaps also to Bertrand's Box (compare the Tuesday wakenings with two goats or the two different gold coins in the same box). What makes it importantly different is that in those paradoxes there are no plausible arguments to be given on both sides; rather, we can explain why one of the two claims about probabilities is erroneous. In sleeping beauty, both sides have put forward plausible arguments and neither side has shown the other side's arguments to be decisively flawed. Although most of the discussion so far has inclined towards Elga's position, Lewis has a substantial band of defenders. The paradox is still a developing controversy, and recently, authors have even put forward arguments for probabilities between

[5]This amounts to an application of Lewis's principal principle to future chances: "Credences about future chance events should equal the known chances" (Lewis, 2001, p. 175).

1/3 and 1/2. (For further recent literature, see Dorr, 2002; Horgan, 2004; White, 2006.)

Doomsday Argument

As far as we can tell, even if the life of the universe is infinite, there is a finite (if very large) amount of time before all life will become impossible, and that means a finite amount of time for life to continue. There are only finitely many humans in existence. Therefore, the total number of humans there will ever be is finite. Is the end of humanity near or far?

We estimate that there have been 60 billion (60×10^9) humans so far and there are millions of years in which humans might well flourish. Consider two hypotheses:

Few:
The total number of humans will be 100 billion.

Many:
The total number of humans will be 1 million billion.

There is nothing special about you, and so you should consider yourself a typical human. But if Many is true, then you are a very untypical human. Relatively speaking, to be roughly the 60 billionth human is to be very early in the whole history of mankind if Many is true. So Many is probably false (cf. Leslie, 1996).

That seems a bit quick. Can it be right to conclude thus only on the basis of your numerical place in the birth order of humans? Well, consider an analogous argument which seems correct. Suppose you had two vases in front of you, one containing 1 million numbered balls and one containing only 10 numbered balls. You pick a ball out at random, and it has the number 7 on it. It is very unlikely you would have got such a low number from the first vase, so it looks like you picked it from the vase containing only 10 balls.

We can firm up the Doomsday argument reasoning with some probability calculus. To keep the maths simple, we'll assume that Few and Many are the only possibilities. Prior to taking into account your birth order, but given only the information about the millions of years in which humans might flourish, you might reasonably estimate $P(F) = 5\%$ and $P(M) = 95\%$. Now we consider the evidence: that you exist and are roughly the 60 billionth human. Gott (1993) proposes the Copernican anthropic principle: that you should take yourself to be a random sample from the set of all intelligent observers (which so far as we know means a random sample from all humans) and that it is equally likely for you to be any one of those observers. Applying that principle means that the conditional probabilities of you being the 60 billionth human are $P(E|F) = 1$ in 100 billion and $P(E|M) = 1$ in 1 million billion. Then,

$$P(F|E) = \frac{P(E|F)P(F)}{P(E)} = \frac{10^{-11} \times 0.05}{P(E)}$$

$$= \frac{5 \times 10^{-13}}{P(E)},$$

$$P(M|E) = \frac{P(E|M)P(M)}{P(E)} = \frac{10^{-15} \times 0.95}{P(E)}$$

$$= \frac{9.5 \times 10^{-16}}{P(E)},$$

$$\frac{P(F|E)}{P(M|E)} = \frac{5 \times 10^{-13}}{9.5 \times 10^{-16}} \approx \frac{10^3}{2}.$$

So the probability of Few given the evidence of your place in the birth order is roughly 500 times the probability of Many. If you thought I was unreasonably optimistic in setting $P(M)$ at 95% and think that Few and Many should start as equally likely, then the probability of Few given your place in the birth order is 10,000 times as likely!

There are many versions of the Doomsday argument in addition to these. For example, Gott (1993) uses his Copernican principle to work out the probability that the total number of humans born will be less than 20 times the number already born is greater than 95%.

The Doomsday argument has received much attention, and there are numerous conflicting attempts at refuting it. One interesting line proposes that your existence as an observer makes probable there being many observers in the world history, and this increased likelihood undermines the Doomsday argument (see Dieks, 1992). What is interesting about this line is that reasoning on the basis of one's own existence is used in two different ways, and it draws attention to the very feature which many people find fishy about the argument.

The Doomsday argument makes use of anthropic reasoning, reasoning which takes as a premiss one's own existence as an intelligent reasoner capable of making observations. There are many other uses of such reasoning; for example, what are called fine-tuning arguments[6] make frequent use of the premiss that if a theory implies that the existence of such reasoners is very unlikely, then that would seem to count against the theory.[7]

The status of anthropic reasoning is controversial. As Bostrom (2002) has shown, a serious problem for anthropic reasoning is its vulnerability to what he calls observation selection effects, for example:

> How big is the smallest fish in the pond? You catch one hundred fishes, all of which are greater than six inches. Does this evidence support the hypothesis that no fish in the pond is much less than six inches long? Not if your net can't catch smaller fish. (p. 1)

Bostrom (2002) proposes that we need a comprehensive theory of observation selection effects if we are to use anthropic reasoning without falling foul of various subtle fallacies. In his view, the Doomsday argument is a central case in illuminating the difficulties here, and this is the explanation for the very extensive disagreements about how best to formulate it and what might be right or wrong about it. It is one of the cases which he thinks should drive us to a principle of anthropic reasoning, which he calls the strong self-sampling assumption (SSSA): "Every observer at every moment should reason as if their present observer-moment were randomly sampled from the set of all observer-moments" (p. 162).

The Doomsday argument is a good example of the nagging power of a strong paradox. The premisses seem reasonable, and the steps in the argument appeal to principles which in other areas we think unobjectionable. By the rational principle that requires us to follow where an argument leads, we ought to accept the conclusion. Yet the argument takes us much further than we think reasonable. When we try to settle what has gone wrong, we cannot do so in a satisfactory manner. We can dispute the premisses or the steps in the argument, but the weaknesses we find are not severe enough to resolve the matter.

A good review of the literature on the Doomsday argument is Bostrom (1998). The Doomsday argument's wider significance as a paradox is grounded in the general controversy about the status of probabilistic anthropic reasoning and, most recently, its uses by proponents of intelligent design such as Dembski (1998).

Trouble for Action

St. Petersburg

In gambling, a fair price for a bet is regarded as the expected return on the bet. So if you stand to win £4 on the cut of a card and bet on hearts, the fair price is $\frac{1}{4} \times 4 = £1$. A bet cheaper than its fair price is a good bet. Casinos make very large amounts of money from taking all good bets that are only a few percent cheaper than their fair price. But let's be cautious. Perhaps as individuals we shouldn't take all good bets but only all very good bets—say, all bets that are at least 50% cheaper than their fair price.

A coin is going to be tossed until it lands heads. If it takes one toss, you will be paid £2; two tosses will pay £4; and, in general, n tosses will pay £2^n. What is the fair price?

The expected return is the sum of the products of the probability of the number of tosses until heads with the winnings on that number. The probability of the first head being on the first toss is $1/2$; on the second, it is the probability of getting first a tail and then a head, which is $\frac{1}{2} \times \frac{1}{2}$; and, in general, the probability of the first head being on the nth toss is $1/2^n$. The expected return is an infinite sum.

$$\begin{aligned}\text{Expected return} &= \frac{1}{2} \times 2 + \frac{1}{4} \times 4 \\ &\quad + \cdots + \frac{1}{2^n} \times 2^n + \cdots \\ &= 1 + 1 + \cdots + 1 + \cdots.\end{aligned}$$

[6]Fine tuning is there being only very narrow ranges within which various physical constants must lie if the possibility of life is to be permitted by the laws of nature.

[7]But see Sober (2002) for a rejection of the validity of such reasoning.

We say that this sum tends to infinity because for any finite number, add up enough terms of this infinite sum and we can exceed it.

Of course, there is the practicality of there being an upper bound on the amount of goods in the world and therefore an upper bound on the amount of money. But consider that the universe is unbounded and that were we part of an intergalactic civilisation, there might really be an infinite amount of goods in the universe. Or just consider the matter as a theoretical problem. In principle, the expected return on this game is infinite, and consequently, any finite price is massively cheaper than the fair price. So on the principle of taking all very good bets, you should play the game for any finite amount. Your entire savings is a finite amount, so you should take the bet if offered at that price. But that's mad, isn't it?

Nicholas Bernoulli posed this problem in 1713, and his cousin Daniel offered a solution. The starting point is two thoughts: that what matters about wealth, its value, is its usefulness to us and that an extra £1 to a millionaire is not as useful as an extra £1 to a tramp. In general, the usefulness of your first £100 is greater than that of your second £100 and so on. We define the measurement of usefulness to be utility. What we need in order to properly assess the value of an amount of money is to know the utility of that amount of money. In general, what we need to know is the utility function of money. It is perhaps misleading to speak of *the* utility function, since we can make inferences about a person's utility function from his or her behaviour and we find that people have differing utility functions which reflect their differing attitudes to risk. But for the sake of this argument, we will consider only utility functions that respect the point about decreasing usefulness, which, technically put, amounts to the marginal utility of wealth decreasing as wealth increases. What this means is that the gradient of the utility function decreases and looks something like this:

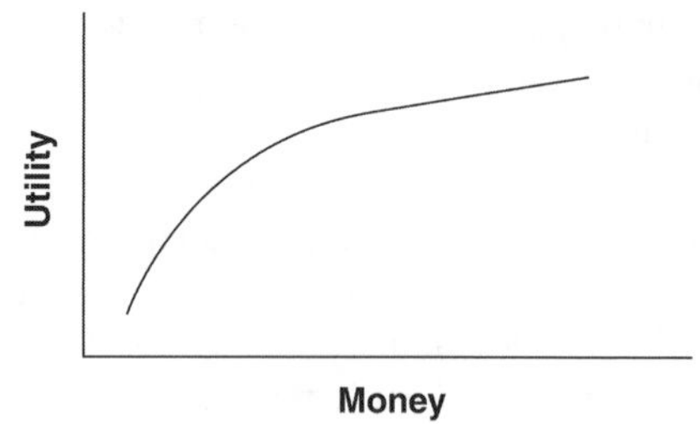

A logarithmic utility function looks roughly like this. Suppose, for the sake of illustration, we take our utility function to be U(money) = the logarithm to base two of money.[8] This would give the utility of £2 to be 1 utile,[9] the utility of £4 to be 2 utiles, and in general the utility of £2^n to be n utiles. When we now work out the expected return not in terms of money but in terms of utility, we get

$$\begin{aligned}\text{Expected utitlity} &= \frac{1}{2} \times U(2) + \frac{1}{4} \times U(4) + \cdots \\ &\quad + \frac{1}{2^n} \times U(2^n) + \cdots \\ &= \frac{1}{2} \times 1 + \frac{1}{4} \times 2 + \cdots \\ &\quad + \frac{1}{2^n} \times n + \cdots \\ &= 2.\end{aligned}$$

We say that this sum equals 2 because (roughly) adding up more and more terms of this infinite sum gets us closer and closer to 2.

Now 2 utiles is probably too cheap, but that is because we chose a utility function that would make the mathematics easy to illustrate the point. The critical point is that the decreasing utility of wealth means that the value of the bet is finite. On another utility function,[10] the bet is worth 2,884 utiles, which is £2,895.

Whether the solution succeeds can be questioned. The notion of utility is certainly correct, but then you might be offered the opportunity of playing St. Petersburg in terms of utiles rather than money, when once again it seems that you should bet your entire savings on the game. This doesn't seem rational. If that is right, then the claim that expected utility determines choiceworthiness in the case of betting is weakened. But what other basis for the rational choiceworthiness of *bets* can there be? In this way, the

[8] $U(m) = \log_2 m$.

[9] We define utiles to be the units of utility.

[10] $U(m) = m^{0.9995}$.

Table 4.4

A		*B*		*C*		*D*	
Payoff	*Chance*	*Payoff*	*Chance*	*Payoff*	*Chance*	*Payoff*	*Chance*
1,000	0.09	5,000	0.08	1,000	0.09	5,000	0.08
1,000	0.91	1,000	0.91				

St. Petersburg paradox continues to discomfort us, eroding our confidence in the applicability of probability theory exactly where it would seem to be unquestionably applicable in guiding action. Hence, it remains a strong paradox. (For more extensive discussion, see Jeffrey, 1990, 150ff.)

Allais's Paradox

You are offered a choice of

A: certainty of £1,000 or

B: 8% chance of £5,000, 91% chance of £1,000, 1% chance of nothing.

You are offered a choice of

C: 9% chance of £1,000, 91% chance of nothing or

D: 8% chance of £5,000, 92% chance of nothing.

Most people prefer A to B and prefer D to C. But choosing A over B and D over C is not consistent with determining choiceworthiness by expected utility. Let U be our utility of money function, with $U(0) = 0$. Preferring A over B on the basis of expected utilities gives

$$\mathrm{EU}(A) > \mathrm{EU}(B);$$

that is,

$$U(1000) > \frac{8}{100}U(5000) + \frac{91}{100}U(1000);$$

that is,

$$\frac{9}{100}U(1000) > \frac{8}{100}U(5000);$$

that is,

$$\mathrm{EU}(C) > \mathrm{EU}(D).$$

So if choiceworthiness is given by choosing to maximise expected utility, then if you choose A over B, you ought to choose C over D.

Allais (1953) produced his paradox in order to embarrass the independence axiom of von Neumann and Morgenstern's (1944) decision theory: For any lotteries x, y, z[11] and for any $p \in [0,1]$, you prefer x to y iff you prefer $px + (1-p)z$ to $py + (1-p)z$. The independence axiom implies that preference doesn't change if you supplement both sides of a choice with the same further benefit. Setting out our scenario by decomposing A makes this evident (Table 4.4).

Examining Table 4.4 makes it clear that the choice between A and B is the choice between C and D supplemented with the same opportunity in each case—namely, a 91% chance of winning £1,000. So independence implies that we will choose A over B iff we choose C over D.[12]

Savage's (1972) sure thing principle implies the same result: If choosing x or y produces the same result in circumstances consistent with Q, then the choice between them should depend only on the consequence of circumstances consistent with not-Q. So we suppose here that the 91% chance of £1,000 in choices A and B are circumstances consistent with Q. Then, only the other consequences should determine which way we choose between A and B. But the other consequences are the same consequences we are choosing between when choosing between C and D. Hence, the sure thing principle implies that we will choose A over B if we choose C over D.

We all feel a pressure to choose A over B and D over C, and it is rumoured that even

[11] A lottery is a probability function on a set of outcomes. So the lottery B is $\{P(0) = 0.01,\ P(1000) = 0.91,\ P(5000) = 0.08\}$.

[12] This way of presenting the paradox is sometimes known as the common consequence effect (see Kahneman & Tversky, 1979).

Savage chose this way when first presented with this paradox. If it were clear that this tendency is irrational, then the Allais paradox would amount to an illusion of choice under uncertainty. But it is controversial whether it is irrational. On the one hand, considered over many decisions for moderate amounts as above, choosing in accordance with *A* over *B* does significantly worse—on average, £310 worse per decision. That sounds like a bad policy and is arguably irrational. On the other hand, if we make it a single decision for an amount that is life changing, such as *A* being certainty of £100 million, one might think that it was a bad policy to risk getting nothing by choosing *B* over *A*. Furthermore, this is not evaded by the decreasing marginal utility of money, since one can pose the whole problem in utilities instead. The question is rather, given certainty of a great benefit, is it worth taking a small risk of having nothing for the sake of a greater, perhaps even enormous, benefit? The independence axioms and Savage's sure thing principle can commit us to saying yes, but is that really right? It depends on what our attitudes to risk should be and whether facts such as magnitude of reward and frequency of opportunity to risk something for the reward influence what those attitudes should be.

Allais himself argued that his paradox shows that choiceworthiness is not expected utility but is rather a function of both expected utility and the variance of utility. Variance of outcome is sometimes regarded as a measure of risk. So we might understand him as seeking to make some allowance for risk in assessing choiceworthiness. But the example of the Allais paradox raises the suspicion that analogous problems can be posed to any attempt at characterising choiceworthiness in these formal terms. Prima facie, for any formal specification, one can always gerrymander an example in which the certainty of a big enough bird in the hand intuitively outweighs the risk of letting it go for a chance at the many in the bush. The wider significance of Allais's paradox may be that it leads us to develop arguments for the proposition that choiceworthiness is not scale-free, and its scale dependence cannot be represented by the formal apparatus of standard decision theory—a proposition which is paradoxical for standard decision theory. (For extensive discussion, see the edited collection of papers Allais & Hagen, 1979.)

Newcomb's Problem

There is an opaque and a transparent box in front of you. You can see £1,000 in the transparent box. You know that if a reliable predictor has predicted that you will open only the opaque box, he will have put £1,000,000 in that box. Otherwise, he will leave it empty. You can either open both boxes or just the opaque box, and you get to keep whatever is in the boxes you open. What should you do?

What is the expected value of opening one box and opening two boxes? Suppose the probability that the predictor is right is *p*. Then, the expected value of opening both boxes

$$\begin{aligned} E(\text{two boxes}) &= 1000p + 1001000(1-p) \\ &= 1001000 - 1000000p \\ &\quad (= 251000 \text{ if } p = 3/4). \end{aligned}$$

The expected value of opening just the opaque box

$$\begin{aligned} E(\text{one box}) &= 1000000p + (1-p) \times 0 \\ &= 1000000p \\ &\quad (= 750000 \text{ if } p = 3/4). \end{aligned}$$

Comparing the two,

$$E(\text{two boxes}) < E(\text{one box}) \text{iff } 1000/1999 < p.$$

So as long as the chance that the predictor is right is a little bit more than 1/2, then maximising expected value means you should open only the opaque box.

Now consider what is called the dominance principle, which says that if one action is better than another in each of the possible circumstances that might obtain, then you ought to choose that action. Here, whether or not the predictor has put £1,000,000 in the opaque box, you will be £1,000 better off taking two boxes than one. So the dominance principle says to open both boxes.

This paradox has been very fruitful in the development of decision theory. The challenge it poses is twofold: on the one hand to explain which answer is correct and on the other to explain what is wrong with the other answer.

Causal decision theorists generally think that two-boxing is the right answer. When deciding what to do, you should focus on the causal powers of your actions, not their evidential aspect. For example, suppose that both smoking and cancer were caused by a gene. In that case, the correlation of smoking with cancer would not be because smoking caused cancer. Rather, the correlation would arise because smoking is evidence that you have the cancer-causing gene. But because of the correlation, smokers would still have a higher probability of getting cancer than non-smokers. Consequently, calculating the expected utility of smoking would make it look like it was a bad thing to do despite the fact it had no causal impact on your getting cancer or not.

Likewise, say causal decision theorists, what is relevant about your choice in Newcomb's problem is the expected benefit of an act as a cause of benefits, not what evidence your choice is for what the predictor did. In this case, nothing you do now can change what the predictor has already done. Consequently, two-boxing is the right answer.

What is wrong with the calculations of expected value of each act (two-boxing or one-boxing) is that it uses probabilities conditional on the act. When your act has evidential significance in addition to its causal significance, then the conditional probability will be different from the absolute probability in part because of that evidential significance. So in such cases, calculating the expected value of an act using conditional probabilities rather than absolute probabilities will amount to tainting what you want—numerical information about the expected causal benefit of that act—with quantities which arise out of the irrelevant evidential significance of that act. Hence, the proposal of causal decision theory is to reform standard decision theory by the use of absolute rather than conditional probabilities in calculating expected values, but absolute probabilities based on dependency hypotheses about causal efficacy.[13]

[13]*Dependency hypotheses* is Lewis's (1986b) term. Other explanations may be given in terms of counterfactual conditionals (e.g., see Gibbard & Harper, 1978).

Evidential decision theorists disagree, but in two different ways. There are evidential decision theorists who are two-boxers and who propose their own adjustment to standard decision theory to avoid the expected value calculation recommending one-boxing. There are others who think that standard decision theory is right. They may criticise the dominance argument on the ground that dominance reasoning assumes the truth of the general principle of acting so as to maximise value. Consequently, the dominance principle is a *subsidiary* principle to the general principle. In Newcomb's problem, the application of the dominance principle results in transgressing the general principle, since dominance reasoners don't get rich but one-boxers do (remember, the predictor is *reliable*). Consequently, because it is subsidiary, the dominance principle must give way to the more general principle.

For an edited collection on the paradox, with extensive bibliography, see Campbell and Snowden (1985). For a lucid exposition of causal decision theory covering his own and other's, see Lewis (1986b), and for an interesting argument that prisoner's dilemma is a kind of Newcomb problem see Lewis (1986c). For an evidential decision theory compatible with two-boxing, see Price (1986) and Jeffrey (1990). For some recent argument in favour of one-boxing, see Blackburn (2000, p. 189).

Two-Envelope Paradox

There are two envelopes, one of which has twice the amount of money in it as the other. You take one at random, and I take the other. I ask you whether you'd like to swap. Eager to apply your newfound knowledge of probability theory, you decide that the way to decide is to work out the expected value of my envelope. If it is higher than yours, you'll decide to swap; if lower, not; and if the same, you won't care. So let the amount in your own envelope be x; then, the amount in mine is either $(1/2)x$ or $2x$, and they are both equally likely. So the expected value of my envelope is

$$\text{Expected value} = \frac{1}{2} \times \frac{1}{2}x + \frac{1}{2} \times 2x = \frac{5}{4}x > x.$$

So the expected value of my envelope is greater than the value of your envelope, so you should swap. But just before you do, you decide to check the expected value of your own envelope. So you reason that the amount in my envelope is y and then proceed as before, finding that the expected value of your envelope is $(5/4)y$; so you conclude that the expected value of your envelope is greater than mine. So my envelope is worth more than yours, and my envelope is worth less than yours. That can't be right!

It is important to be clear about the precise nature of the problem here. It is not that there is any problem in knowing what to do. Quite obviously, you should be indifferent between your and my envelope. The problem is that an apparently correct application of rational decision theory gets the wrong answer and, worse still, gives two contradictory answers.

It has turned out that this paradox has hidden depths. First, it is devious in its exploitation of our tendency to erroneous understandings of probability theory. Second, correction of the errors eliminates the paradox as first presented but leads us on to versions for which the paradox remains. To understand it, we will have to make full use of the technical vocabulary of probability theory.

First, we must distinguish cases in which there is an upper bound on the amount of money in the envelopes from those in which there is not. We call the former finite cases and the latter infinite cases. In all cases, the calculation you applied is simply incorrect if the amount in your envelope is the minimum sum that could be in an envelope (since there is no possibility of having half that amount), and in finite cases, it is also incorrect if it is the maximum (since there is no possibility of having twice that amount).

In analysing a stochastic situation, when we say let A be the amount of money in my envelope and B the amount in yours, what we have done is specified two random variables, A and B. What you wanted to know was the expectation of each envelope—that is, $E(A)$ and $E(B)$. When you calculated what you called the expected value of my envelope, what you actually calculated was the *conditional* expectation of A given B and compared it with the conditional expectation of B given B. You took the statement $E(A|B) > E(B|B)$ either as if it were the statement $E(A) > E(B)$ or as if it implied that statement—and likewise for the statement $E(B|A) > E(A|A)$. So the first point to note is that as it stands, you either mistook conditional expectations for absolute expectations or assumed, perhaps without reason, that a statement about conditional expectations implied a statement about absolute expectations.

The second point to note is that you have been beguiled into mistaking random variables for an expectation. The term *conditional expectation* is ambiguous between being an expectation properly so-called and being a random variable. If I calculate the conditional expectation of A given that $B = 5$—that is, $E(A|B = 5)$, then I will have calculated a true expectation. But if I calculate such an expectation just given the random variable B, then the conditional expectation of A given B, $E(A|B)$, is itself a random variable and to get a true expectation we must calculate the expectation of *this* random variable—namely, $E(E(A|B))$, and a standard theorem of probability theory shows this to be equal to $E(A)$. This technique of calculating an expectation via a conditional expectation is a standard and valuable technique of problem solving, frequently applied when there is no means of calculating $E(A)$ directly.

When we calculate $E(E(A|B))$ in finite cases, the paradox vanishes entirely, so we need only consider the infinite cases. There is a substantial taxonomy of infinite cases which is too extensive to properly explain here. So I will now simply mention some of the results that are available (Clark & Shackel, 2000, 2003).

1. In the infinite cases, because there cannot be a uniform probability function over an infinite set, it is not possible that for all amounts in your envelope, the conditional probability of the other envelope being half yours is $1/2$ and the conditional probability of the other envelope being twice yours is $1/2$.

2. It is possible for $E(B|A) > E(A|A)$ and yet for $E(B) = E(A)$, and so the inference from $E(B|A) > E(A|A)$ to $E(A) > E(B)$ is invalid.

3. If $E(A)$ is finite, then no paradoxical cases arise. If $E(A)$ is not finite, then two kinds

of paradoxical cases arise. There are cases in which the expected gain on swapping envelopes $(E(E(A|B) - B))$ is infinite (so setting the paradox off again). However, in infinite cases, all the expectations are sums of infinitely many terms, and the mathematics of such sums must be respected. Saying that a sum is infinite is just shorthand for saying that it is unbounded; that is, for any finite number however large, one can add up finitely many of the infinitely many terms and exceed that number. We (Clark & Shackel, 2000, 2003) therefore call such cases "unbounded paradoxical." Because of the just explained precise meaning of "having an infinite sum," it is controversial whether having an infinite sum is a way of having a well-defined value, and some people have rejected the paradox on that ground (e.g., see Chalmers, 1996, 2002).

4. Whether those who reject unbounded paradoxical cases on those grounds are right or not, there are infinite cases for which the expected gain on swapping is finite, and hence, that rejection cannot solve the paradox in general. The latter cases we call "best paradoxical," best because the expected gain on swapping being finite is uncontroversially a way of the value of swapping being well defined, and yet from the setup of the scenario, there should not be an argument for swapping over sticking.

5. If best paradoxical cases are to be solved, then some explanation must be given for why we can rule out calculating the expected gain on swapping by the formula $E(E(A|B) - B)$ when using the technique of calculating an expectation via a conditional expectation.

6. In our published work on this paradox, we advance the proposal that applying the latter technique must be done in such a way as to respect the causal features of the situation. Applying this constraint to the two-envelope case rules out using $E(E(A|B) - B)$ because of the symmetry of the causal features but permits using $E(E(B - A|A + B)$ for the same reason, and the latter calculation gives zero expected gain on swapping. Hence, when rational decision theory is formulated in a way which respects the causal features of the situation, it can get the right answer. It is controversial whether this proposal is a solution (see Meacham & Weisberg, 2003, and our reply in Clark & Shackel, 2003).

One line of attack is based on a thought which strikes many people as appealing on first hearing the paradox: that the paradoxical outcome is foisted on us by a subtle equivocation on x and so can be solved by specifying constraints that rule out such errors. I do not think that this line can succeed and suspect that it is in part based on a failure to understand the nature of random variables and the points made above about mistaking a conditional expectation for an expectation. For publications in this line, see Jackson, Menzies, and Oppy (1994), Chihara (1995), Horgan (2000), and Schwitzgebel and Dever (2004).

There is a variant of the paradox in which you open your envelope and then decide to swap and a further variant based on the argument that since you know that you would want to swap if you opened the envelope, you should swap anyway. We say that these thoughts are simply ways to beguile you into calculating the wrong expectation again (Clark & Shackel, 2000, p. 429), but again, our solution is controversial. Smullyan (1993, pp. 189–192) puts forward an interesting non-probabilistic variant: that you will either gain x or lose $x/2$, so you will gain more than lose on swapping (or sticking when so reasoning based on the other envelope), and a good discussion of this variant is Chase (2002).

For further literature, see bibliographies of the mentioned literature. Wikipedia has a reasonable online bibliography at http://www.en.wikipedia.org/wiki/Two_envelope_problem.

Pasadena Paradox

A new paradox based on the St. Petersburg game was published by Nover and Hajek (2004), which they called the Pasadena paradox. The mathematical details of this paradox are complex, and so, whilst I am going to give the full story, I am not going to explain it in full mathematical generality. Similar to the St. Petersburg game, we toss a coin until the first head appears. The outcome of the game is given according to the instructions on a stack of cards:

Top card:
If the first head is on the first toss, we pay you £2.

Next card:
If the first head is on the second toss, you pay us £2.

Next card:
If the first head is on the third toss, we pay you £8/3.

Next card:
If the first head is on the fourth toss, you pay us £4.

⋮

nth card:
If the first head is on the nth toss, the payment is $(-1)^{n-1}2^n/n$.

⋮

Should you play the game?

Working out the expected value gives what is called an alternating series, which is an infinite sum in which the sign of the terms alternates.

$$E(\text{value of game}) = 1 - \frac{1}{2} + \frac{1}{3} - \frac{1}{4} + \cdots$$
$$= \log_e 2 \approx 0.69.$$

This is positive, so you should play. Before we play, the cards are knocked over, and when they are restored, it turns out that their order is now a positive card for you (instruction for payoff if first head on first toss), followed by the next five negative cards (instructions for payoffs if first head is on toss No. 2, 4, 6, 8, or 10), followed by the next positive card (instruction for payoff if first head on third toss), and then the next five negative cards, and so on. When we now calculate the expected value in this way, we get

$$E(\text{value of game})$$
$$= 1 - \frac{1}{2} - \frac{1}{4} - \frac{1}{6} - \frac{1}{8} - \frac{1}{10}$$
$$+ \frac{1}{3} - \frac{1}{12} - \frac{1}{14} - \frac{1}{16} - \frac{1}{18} - \frac{1}{20} - \cdots$$
$$= \log_e 2 + \frac{1}{2}\log_e \frac{1}{5} \approx -0.11.$$

This is negative, so you shouldn't play. But hang on a minute—all we've done is rearrange the instruction cards, so now we have shown both that you should and shouldn't play.

This paradox has not been much discussed in the literature yet. It exploits a well-known feature of alternating series,[14] which is that if a series is convergent (has a finite sum) but not absolutely convergent (the sum of the absolute values of their terms does not converge), then for any real number its terms can be rearranged to give a series which sums to that number; also, for any of the three ways a series can diverge, its terms can be rearranged to give a series that is divergent in that way. It may appear that the two alternating series given above are the same infinite sum just because one is the rearrangement of the other. But that is not the case. The identity of an infinite sum is defined not just by what its terms are but also by the order of those terms. In effect, the case we are considering contains a proof of that fact. Sums must have unique answers (since if they don't, we can prove that all numbers are the same number), and hence if two sums have different answers, they must be distinct sums (e.g., since $1+1=2$ and $2+3=5$, the sum $1+1$ is distinct from the sum $2+3$). The two infinite sums above have different answers, therefore the sums must be distinct.

If we are willing to accept the infinite set of instruction cards and that rearrangements of sequences of that set of cards don't change the game that is being played, then apparently the game is well specified, and yet decision theory gives contradictory advice. We might deny the existence of the infinite set of cards, and so reject the game, but the cards are merely heuristic devices. If we accept the abstract nature of ordinary mathematics and of language, there doesn't seem to be any problem with the existence of an

[14]Called the rearrangement theorem.

infinite set of instructions, nor any problem with rearrangements of sequences of those instructions. The significant question is whether a rearrangement of those instructions still constitutes the same game. On the one hand, it is not obvious that it doesn't. On the other hand, given the contradictions into which we easily fall when considering infinite sets, one might insist that our proper understanding of such sets is constituted by the conceptual resources of the mathematics of such sets. Hence, in proposing and thinking about decision cases involving infinite sets, our proposals and thoughts must respect the content of those conceptual resources. In that case, since the mathematics of infinite sets insists that sequences with the same members in different orders are *necessarily* distinct, it is not enough to appeal to the heuristic of shuffling cards to ground the claim that the same cards in a different order constitute the same game. On the contrary, some reason must be given for why, *despite* the sequences of cards being regarded as necessarily distinct sequences, the game is the same.

An answer that has some force is this. The sequence of cards is not necessary for specifying the game. All that is required to fully specify the game is that all the possible outcomes of the game be specified and the payoff for each outcome be specified. As described, for each natural number, it is specified what the payoff is if the number of throws to the first head is that number. But every possible outcome is correlated with a natural number, and hence the payoffs for any particular outcome *are* specified. Hence, it is merely the set of instructions that determines the identity of the game, not their order. If this answer is correct, then the value of the Pasadena game is indeterminate. In a recent discussion, Colyvan (2006) proposed that the Pasadena game is ill-posed just because it has no expected value, and Hajek and Nover (2006) have rebutted that proposal.

REFERENCES

Allais, M. (1953). La Psychologie de L'homme Rationnel Devant le Risque: Critique des Postulats et Axiomes de L'école Américaine. *Econometrica, 21*, 503–546.

Allais, M., & Hagen, O. (1979). *Expected utility hypotheses and the Allais paradox: Contemporary discussions of decisions under uncertainty with Allais' rejoinder.* Dordrecht, The Netherlands: D. Reidel.

Blackburn, S. (2000). *Ruling passions.* Oxford, UK: Clarendon Press.

Bostrom, N. (1998). *The Doomsday argument: A literature review.* Retrieved September 20, 2007, from http://www.anthropic-principle.com/preprints/lit/index.html.

Bostrom, N. (2002). *Anthropic bias: Observation selection effects in science and philosophy.* New York: Routledge.

Campbell, R., & Snowden, L. (1985). *Paradoxes of rationality and cooperation: Prisoner's dilemma and Newcomb's problem.* Vancouver, Canada: University of British Columbia Press.

Chalmers, D. J. (1996). *The two-envelope paradox: A complete analysis?* Retrieved September 20, 2007, from http://www.consc.net/papers/envelope.html

Chalmers, D. J. (2002). The St. Petersburg two-envelope paradox. *Analysis, 62*(2), 155–156.

Chase, J. (2002). The non-probabilistic two envelope paradox. *Analysis, 62*(2), 157–159.

Chihara, C. S. (1995). The mystery of Julius, a paradox in decision theory. *Philosophical Studies, 80*, 1–16.

Clark, M. (2002). *Paradoxes from A to Z.* London: Routledge.

Clark, M., & Shackel, N. (2000). The two-envelope paradox. *Mind, 109*, 415–442.

Clark, M., & Shackel, N. (2003). Decision theory, symmetry and causal structure: Reply to Meacham and Weisberg. *Mind, 112*, 691–701.

Colyvan, M. (2006). No expectations. *Mind, 115*, 695–702.

Dembski, W. A. (1998). *The design inference: Eliminating chance through small probabilities.* Cambridge, UK: Cambridge University Press.

Dieks, D. (1992). Doomsday—or: The dangers of statistics. *Philosophical Quarterly, 42*, 78–84.

Dorr, C. (2002). Sleeping beauty: In defence of Elga. *Analysis, 62*(4), 292–295.

Elga, A. (2000). Self-locating belief and the sleeping beauty problem. *Analysis, 60*(2), 143–146.

Gibbard, A., & Harper, W. L. (1978). Counterfactuals and two kinds of expected utility. In C. A. Hooker, J. J. Leach, & E. F. McLennen (Eds.), *Foundations and applications of decision theory* (pp. 125–162). Dordrecht, The Netherlands: D. Reidell.

Gott, J. R. (1993). Implications of the Copernican principle for our future prospects. *Nature, 363*, 315.

Hajek, A., & Nover, H. (2006). Perplexing expectations. *Mind, 115*, 703–720.

Horgan, T. (2000). The two-envelope paradox, nonstandard expected utility, and the intensionality of probability. *Nous*, *34*(4), 578–603.

Horgan, T. (2004). Sleeping beauty awakened: New odds at the dawn of the new day. *Analysis*, *64*(1), 10–21.

Jackson, F., Menzies, P., & Oppy, G. (1994). The two envelope "paradox". *Analysis*, *57*, 34–41.

Jaynes, E. T. (1973). The well posed problem. *Foundations of Physics*, *4*(3), 477–492.

Jeffrey, R. C. (1990). *The logic of decision* (2nd ed.). Chicago: University of Chicago Press.

Kahneman, D., & Tversky, A. (1979). Prospect theory: An analysis of decision under risk. *Econometrica*, *47*, 263–291.

Keynes, J. M. (1963). *A treatise on probability*. London: Macmillan. (Original work published 1921)

Leslie, J. (1996). *The end of the world: The science and ethics of human extinction* (paperback ed.). London: Routledge.

Lewis, D. (1986a). A subjectivist's guide to objective probability. In *Philosophical papers* (Vol. 2, pp. 83–132). Oxford, UK: Oxford University Press. (Reprinted from *Studies in inductive logic and probability*, Vol. 2, pp. 263–293, by R. C. Jeffrey, Ed., 1980, Berkeley: University of California Press)

Lewis, D. (1986b). Causal decision theory. In *Philosophical papers* (Vol. 2). Oxford, UK: Oxford University Press. (Reprinted from *Australasian Journal of Philosophy*, 1981, *59*, 5–30)

Lewis, D. (1986c). Prisoner's dilemma is a Newcomb problem. In *Philosophical papers* (Vol. 2). Oxford, UK: Oxford University Press. (Reprinted from *Philosophy and Public Affairs*, 1981, *8*, 235–240)

Lewis, D. (2001). Sleeping beauty: Reply to Elga. *Analysis*, *61*(271), 171–176.

Marinoff, L. (1994). A resolution of Bertrand's paradox. *Philosophy of Science*, *61*(1), 1–24.

Meacham, C. J. G., & Weisberg, J. (2003). Clark and Shackel on the two-envelope paradox. *Mind*, *112*, 685–690.

Nover, H., & Hajek, A. (2004). Vexing expectations. *Mind*, *113*(450), 237–249.

Price, H. (1986). Against causal decision theory. *Synthese*, *67*, 195–212.

Savage, L. J. (1972). *The foundations of statistics* (2nd rev. ed.). New York: Dover.

Schwitzgebel, E., & Dever, J. (2004). *Using variables within the expectation formula.* Retrieved September 20, 2007, from http://www.faculty.ucr.edu/~eschwitz/SchwitzPapers/TwoEnvelope040216.pdf.

Shackel, N. (2007). Bertrand's paradox and the principle of indifference. *Philosophy of Science*, *74*(2), 150–175.

Smullyan, R. M. (1993). *Satan, Cantor and infinity: And other mind boggling puzzles*. Oxford, UK: Oxford University Press.

Sober, E. (2002). Intelligent design and probability reasoning. *International Journal for Philosophy of Religion*, *52*(2), 65–80.

von Neumann, J., & Morgenstern, O. (1944). *Theory of games and economic behavior*. Princeton, NJ: Princeton University Press.

White, R. (2006). The generalized sleeping beauty problem: A challenge for thirders. *Analysis*, *66*(290), 114–119.

PART II

PROBABILITY THEORY IN RESEARCH METHODOLOGY

5

PROBABILITY THEORY IN STATISTICS

TAMÁS RUDAS

INTRODUCTION

This chapter gives an overview of the use of probability theory or, more generally, of probabilistic concepts in statistics. The focus is not on how statistical procedures are performed but rather on the probabilistic underpinnings of these procedures. In other words, we are interested more in "why" than "how." Statistics is understood here as inferential statistics, as opposed to official statistics. Official statistics deals with the collection and analysis of data using official records or censuses, and uncertainty in this activity is usually restricted to measurement errors, which often take the form of clerical (like administrative or reporting) errors. Inferential statistics also deals with an additional source of error—namely, that the data available to it are based on the observation of a sample and not of the entire population. The two branches of statistics, however, are not entirely distinct. Sample surveys are being used increasingly often in official statistics to complement information obtained from censuses. For example, the unemployment rate is estimated in several countries from administrative records (unemployment benefit applications) and from sample surveys (labor force surveys) too. Or, post-enumeration surveys are used routinely to assess the coverage of the census (which, of course, is hoped to be close to 100%).

Inferential statistics is often called mathematical statistics because it relies heavily on mathematical arguments in figuring out what conclusion, with respect to the underlying population, seems justified based on the information in a given sample. Obviously, such conclusions need to be made in a form that reflects the inherent uncertainty implied by sampling (as opposed to complete observations of the entire population), and the whole procedure is justified only if the sample, on which the inference is based, "represents" the population from which it was selected, in relevant ways. Good representation can be ensured by using a randomly selected sample with controlled selection probabilities. One might say that while official statistics deals only with epistemic uncertainty, inferential statistics handles both epistemic and aleatory uncertainty.

In general, the observed distributions of variables in a random sample may not be entirely identical to their population distributions, but at least, after appropriate transformations taking into account the characteristics of the sampling procedure, large deviations are unlikely to occur. This claim is an example of the kinds of statements that may be made regarding the relationship between the truth in the population and the observations in the sample when inference is based on samples. More precisely, the previous claim has two possible interpretations. The first one is that knowing the true distribution in the population, observing a distribution far from it is unlikely. The second is that the observed distribution (or the sample itself) is unlikely to have been obtained from a population where the true distribution is far from it. The first claim belongs to probability theory, the second one to statistics. Obviously, there is much more to statistics than just the reversal of probabilistic results, though this aspect is almost always present.

Inferential statistics considers the variables whose values are observed to be random variables. Sometimes the distributions of such variables are assumed to belong to some parametric family of distributions (e.g., normal or uniform or exponential), and in such cases, the parameters of those distributions need to be estimated from the data. In other settings, the distributions are not assumed to belong to any parametric family, and the main goal is to reveal certain features of the true distributions (e.g., being unimodal). Certain parameters, such as the expected value, may also be estimated in this case. An interesting and important special case is that of categorical observations when all possible distributions belong to a parametric family (specified by one probability for every category) but this family implies no restriction on the general shape or other characteristics of the distributions.

Another important group of problems in inferential statistics deals with testing assumptions regarding the characteristics of distributions in the population (e.g., that the distribution of a random variable belongs to a given parametric family or that the joint distribution of two variables is such that they are independent from each other). Such an assumption is usually called a statistical hypothesis.

This chapter reviews the basic concepts of parameter estimation and of hypothesis tests, primarily from the frequentist viewpoint, but most of the procedures discussed remain meaningful under different interpretations of the concept of probability (subjective probability) and if the role of parameters and hypotheses are defined somewhat differently (as in Bayesian statistics).

The Fundamental Theorem of Mathematical Statistics

The frequentist view of the probability of an event is that it is a number (subject to certain restrictions) that governs the relative frequencies with which this event can be observed in long sequences of independent repetitions (called replications) of an experiment. But if one reads carefully the axioms (i.e., fundamental properties) of probability, there is no reference to any relative frequencies or the stability thereof. It is our interpretation that uses these notions to develop the concept of probability. Have we succeeded in building up a probability theory that yields the fundamental property we wanted to formulate? In other words, may sequences of observations, perhaps very long ones, be used to reveal probabilities? The answer to this question is affirmative, meaning that probability theory implies the property we wanted to have, although it was not directly built into that theory. This justification of the frequentist interpretation of probability is the fundamental theorem of mathematical statistics.

Let A be an event that may occur as a result of an experiment with probability $P(A)$, and let X_A be its indicator variable—that is, a variable that takes on the value of 1 if A occurred and 0 if it did not occur. Then, $P(X_A = 1) = P(A)$, and $P(X_A = 0) = 1 - P(A)$, so that $E(X_A) = P(A)$. As discussed in Chapter 2, the law of large numbers implies that the average of several independent observations of X_A converges in probability to $E(X_A) = P(A)$. But the sum of the X_A indicators is the number of times A occurred—that is, the frequency of A, and the average of the indicators is the relative frequency of A. This proves that *the relative frequency of an event converges in probability to the probability of the event as the number of observations goes to infinity*. Note that the applicability of the law of large numbers requires that the repetitions of the experiment are independent from each other (i.e., whether or not A was observed at any earlier repetition has no influence whatsoever on whether or not A occurs this time). Also, the probability of A occurring should remain the same during the repetitions of the experiment (i.e., the same experiment is being repeated). These two conditions are often referred to as having an independent, identically distributed (iid) sample.

The fundamental theorem of mathematical statistics implies that, irrespective of the personal views taken by a scientist concerning the "right" interpretation of probability, if the experiment that may yield the event A may be replicated, at least in theory, arbitrarily many times, the frequentist interpretation (i.e., that probability governs the relative frequencies in a long series of repetitions and that the probability may be approximated by computing the relative frequencies from long sequences) is valid.

The fundamental theorem of mathematical statistics applies to situations more general than the probability of an event. Consider a random variable Y and one of its values, say y, and let A be the event that Y is less than or equal to y. The previous result readily implies that the relative frequency of A converges (in probability) to the probability that Y is less than or equal to y. The empirical cumulative distribution function of Y is defined at y as the fraction of the observation less than or equal to y—that is,

$$F_Y^e(y) = \frac{1}{n}\sum_i X_{A(i)},$$

where $A(i)$ is event A observed at the ith repetition of the experiment. Therefore, the empirical cumulative distribution function of Y converges to the cumulative distribution function of Y,

$$F_Y(y) = P(Y \leqslant y),$$

in probability, for every real y. It is also true that the empirical cumulative distribution function converges to the cumulative distribution function (though this is not immediate from the above result and rather requires a—quite involved—proof). Consequently, it is not only probabilities of events but also distributions of random variables that may be revealed through repeated observations.

Methods of Estimation

When a variable of interest has a distribution that is characterized by parameters (which is the case if it is assumed to belong to a parametric family or if it is categorical), then its cumulative distribution function may be written as $F_Y(y, \theta)$, where θ is a possibly vector-valued parameter. A standard task in statistics is to obtain an estimate of the value of the parameter that characterizes the distribution in the population, based on the data in a sample. For example, it may be known that the logarithms of incomes in the population follow (an approximate) normal distribution with a known variance and an unknown mean. This may be an appropriate approximation when the variance changes relatively slowly compared with the mean. In this case, the only parameter to estimate is the mean (expected value).

The expected value is an important example of parameters known as moments. The kth moment of a random variable Y, $M_k(Y)$, is defined as the expected value of its kth power. That is,

$$\begin{aligned} E(Y) &= M_1(Y), \\ V(Y) &= M_2(Y - M_1(Y)) \\ &= M_2(Y) - (M_1(Y))^2 . \end{aligned}$$

The kth moment of a random variable is often estimated using the kth empirical moment—that is, the average of the kth powers of the observations. This leads to the usual sample mean as an estimator of the expected value and the sample variance:

$$\frac{1}{n}\sum (Y_i - \overline{Y})^2 \tag{5.1}$$

as the estimate of the variance of Y. Note that, strictly speaking, one needs to distinguish the estimator, as given in (5.1), that is a random variable, from an estimate that is its actual value after observations were made. An estimator can be thought of as being a mathematical formula or a computer program (a function, in fact) the application of which to the sample yields the estimate. The latter would be described by the same formula but using lowercase letters for y. This distinction is fundamental in mathematical statistics, because probability theory provides one with a lot of knowledge regarding the likely behavior of estimators, but the properties of the actual estimates computed from a given sample are usually not known. For example, the density (and, consequently, the typical behavior) of the difference between the estimator and the true parameter value may be derived in several cases, but the actual difference between an estimate and the true value is never known. If it were known, then one would also know the true parameter value and there would be no need to determine an estimate at all.

When the distribution of Y is entirely parameterized by some of its moments (as in the case of a normal or uniform distribution), the estimates for the moments may be used to estimate any other characteristics of the distribution function. In particular, if a parameter is a function of some of the moments of the distribution,

$$\theta = h(M_1, \ldots, M_k)$$

for some function h, then θ may be estimated as

$$\hat{\theta} = h(M_1^e, \ldots, M_k^e),$$

where M_i^e is the ith empirical moment. This is called the method of moments estimator.

Another, and more often used, estimation procedure is based on the concept of the likelihood of the sample. The likelihood of the sample $Y_1, Y_2, \ldots, Y_n$ is defined as

$$\prod_i f_Y(Y_i, \theta), \tag{5.2}$$

where $f_Y(y, \theta)$ is the density function of Y at the value y. When Y is discrete, $f_Y(y, \theta)$ is the probability that $Y = y$. The likelihood function depends both on the observed data and on the parameter value. In probability theory, θ is assumed to be known, and the focus of the analysis is the likelihood (in the discrete case, probability) of different samples. In other words, the parameter value is fixed and known, and the observations are the variables. In statistical inference, one considers the observations to be known (from the sample), but the parameter value is unknown, and the goal is to estimate its value. The maximum likelihood principle states, *Choose, as the estimate of the parameter, the value that maximizes the likelihood of the actual sample.* This is the parameter value that, if it was the true parameter, would have produced the actual sample with a higher likelihood than any other parameter value. Instead of the likelihood function (5.2), often its logarithm is maximized. Because the logarithm is a monotone function, the same estimates are obtained, but instead of the product, the sum of the terms $\log f_Y(Y_i, \theta)$ has to be maximized, and that is often a simpler task. An additional advantage may be that for certain forms of the density function, its logarithm is a simpler function (this is the case, for example, with normal densities).

As an example of maximum likelihood estimation, assume that Y has a uniform distribution on the interval $(0, a)$ and the goal is to estimate the value of a, the only parameter. The expected value of Y is $a/2$, so

$$a = 2E(Y),$$

and therefore the method of moments estimator of a is $2\overline{Y}$. To determine the maximum likelihood estimate (MLE), consider the likelihood of the sample. The density function is $1/a$ on the interval $(0, a)$ and is 0 otherwise. Therefore, as long as $0 \leqslant Y_i \leqslant a$ for all observations, the likelihood of the sample is

$$\frac{1}{a^n},$$

but if Y_i exceeds a for any observation, the likelihood is 0. Therefore, to maximize the likelihood, one has to choose a as small as possible, subject to $\max Y_i \leq a$. This implies that the MLE of a is the maximal observed value.

Because twice the sample mean is not necessarily equal to the largest observed value, the method of moments estimate may be different from the MLE. This fact raises the issue of which one out of two competing estimators performs better, and the next section will present the criteria by which alternative estimators can be compared.

The sample mean and the sample variance (5.1) are maximum likelihood estimators of the expected value and of the variance, respectively, under the assumption of normality.

The MLE is not the most likely value of the parameter, given the sample. The parameter value is supposed to be constant (though unknown), and therefore, it does not have probabilities associated with it. The MLE is the parameter value that would have produced the sample with a higher likelihood than any other possible parameter value. The existence and uniqueness of the MLE are questions that need to be considered in any estimation problem, and they sometimes do not have easy answers.

CHARACTERIZATION AND COMPARISON OF ESTIMATORS

Estimators are random variables, and all information with respect to their behavior is summarized by their respective density functions. While the densities of estimators are well-known in several cases, little can be said about how good one particular estimate is. Rather, probabilistic statements may be made about their likely behavior. Perhaps the most important aspect is whether or not the estimates obtained from a procedure are correct on average. This property is formalized by a comparison of the true parameter value, θ, with the expected value of the estimator T. If

$$E(T) = \theta,$$

then the estimator is said to be unbiased. For example, the sample mean is an unbiased estimator of the population mean, but the sample variance (5.1) is a biased estimator of the variance. To obtain an unbiased estimator of the population variance, one has to use, instead of n, $n-1$ in the denominator:

$$\frac{1}{n-1}\sum(Y_i - \overline{Y})^2 \tag{5.3}$$

is an unbiased estimator of the variance.

Among the unbiased estimators (i.e., estimators that, on average, yield the correct estimate), one prefers the estimator with the smallest variance, because this will have, if applied repeatedly, the smallest deviations from the true parameter value. If (some of) the estimators to be compared are biased, the one with the minimum variance may not be preferable: A biased estimator with a small variance may yield estimates that are almost always far from the true value. In such cases, the comparison of estimators is based on the *mean squared error* (MSE) of the estimators, defined as the expected value of the squared deviation of the estimate from the true parameter value. If T is an estimator of θ, then

$$\text{MSE}(T) = E(T-\theta)^2 = \text{Var}(T) + (E(T) - \theta)^2;$$

that is, the mean squared error is the sum of the variance of the estimator and the square of the bias. If the estimator is unbiased, the mean squared error is its variance. A general criterion that may be applied to select estimators is to choose the one with the smallest mean squared error. This rule suggests that one should choose the estimator with the minimum variance from among the unbiased estimators and if T_1 is an unbiased estimator of θ and T_2 is a biased estimator thereof, with bias b, then T_2 is preferable to T_1 if $\text{Var}(T_2) + b^2$ is less than $\text{Var}(T_1)$.

For example, out of the two estimators obtained for the parameter of a $(0, a)$ uniform distribution, $2\overline{Y}$ is unbiased because $E(\overline{Y}) = a/2$. The MLE (the largest observed value) is biased because the expected value of the largest observation out of a sample of size n is

$$\frac{n}{n+1}a.$$

Therefore, the bias is

$$\frac{n}{n+1}a - a = -\frac{1}{n+1}a. \tag{5.4}$$

The mean squared error of the method of moments estimator is equal to its variance,

$$\frac{1}{3n}a^2,$$

and the mean squared error of the MLE is the sum of the square of its bias and of its variance:

$$\left(\frac{1}{(n+1)^2} + \frac{n}{(n+2)(n+1)^2}\right)a^2$$
$$= \frac{2a^2}{(n+1)(n+2)}.$$

As the MSE of the method of moments estimator is in the range of $1/n$ and that of the MLE is in the range of $1/n^2$, for large enough sample sizes the use of the MLE is preferable in spite of its being biased. In particular, the MLE (the maximal observed value) is a better estimator than the method of moments estimator (twice the sample mean) if $n \geqslant 3$. Note that the variance always, in general, converges to 0 if the sample size increases, and in the present case the bias (5.4) also converges to 0 if the sample size increases.

Sometimes a more general comparison pertaining to one estimator versus all other estimators in a class of estimators is possible. For example, for an arbitrary random variable X, the sample mean is a linear estimator of $E(X)$ of the form

$$\sum_{i=1}^{n} a_i, X_i, \tag{5.5}$$

with $a_i = 1/n$ for all i. It is easily seen that a linear estimator of the form (5.5) is unbiased if and only if

$$\sum_{i=1}^{n} a_i = 1,$$

which, of course, is also true for the sample mean. One may ask at this point, which unbiased linear estimator has the minimum variance. Note that asking for the minimum variance estimator only from among unbiased estimators is meaningful, because if a minimum variance estimator would be sought among, say, all estimators, a constant estimator (e.g., one that always gives the value of 0) would have the possible minimum variance—namely, 0. Obviously, such an estimator—as it does not depend on the data—would be of no use. It turns out that an unbiased linear estimator has minimum variance if all the a_i coefficients are equal, and as their sum has to be 1, they are also equal to $1/n$. This means that *the sample mean is the minimum variance unbiased estimator of the expected value from among the linear estimators*. In general, we say that an unbiased estimator with minimum variance is *efficient*.

Asymptotic Behavior of Estimators

It was noted in the previous section that for large sample sizes, the MLE is preferable to the method of moments estimator for the parameter of $U(0,a)$. The bias of the MLE was given in (5.4), and one can see that as the sample size increases, the bias converges to 0. In other words, the MLE is an *asymptotically unbiased* estimator of the parameter.

The most important asymptotic property (i.e., a characteristic of the limiting behavior for large sample sizes) of an estimator is *consistency*. An estimator T of a parameter θ is said to be consistent if it converges (when the sample size increases) to the true parameter value in probability; that is, if

$$P(|T_n - \theta| \leqslant \varepsilon) \to 1,$$

where T_n is the estimator based on n observations, for all positive ε values, when n goes to infinity. Consistency essentially means that the estimate is arbitrarily close to the true parameter value with arbitrarily large probability for a sufficiently large sample size. For example, the law of large numbers states that the sample mean is a consistent estimator of the expected value (if it exists). Most of the estimators used in practice are consistent, and this justifies the general expectation of survey researchers that larger sample sizes will, generally, lead to better estimates.

In some cases, the asymptotic distribution of some estimators may be determined. A straightforward tool to do so is the application of the central limit theorem, which essentially says that the sum of iid variables, when appropriately standardized, converges in distribution to a standard normal variable. This applies readily to the sample mean. If the random variable has expectation $E(X)$ and standard deviation $\mathrm{SD}(X)$, then

$$\frac{\overline{X}_n - E(X)}{\frac{1}{\sqrt{n}}\mathrm{SD}(X)}, \tag{5.6}$$

where $\overline{X}_n$, the sample mean based on a sample of size n, converges in distribution to a standard normal—that is, its distribution for large n becomes more and more similar to that of the standard normal. Alternatively, this can be expressed as saying that the asymptotic distribution of $\overline{X}_n$ is

$$N\left(E(X), \left(\frac{1}{\sqrt{n}}\mathrm{SD}(X)\right)^2\right), \tag{5.7}$$

and this normal distribution is used for approximate calculations. For some finite-sample settings, results are available for assessing how well the sample distribution is approximated by the relevant asymptotic distribution. These approximations are commonly used in practice, especially when the exact distribution is not tractable. For example, such approximate calculations are used when sample sizes are determined that are required to achieve a certain level of accuracy of the estimates in a survey.

Suppose that a survey is conducted to estimate the fraction of voters who support a certain candidate who is considering running for an office, and suppose that the survey is based on a simple random sample and the respondents are exactly those who were selected for the sample (no nonresponse, no substitution). These are simplifying assumptions, and for a more realistic setup, more involved calculations would be needed than those presented here. We define the outcome variable X as an indicator variable taking up the value of 1 if a respondent says yes and 0 otherwise. The sum of the observed values of these indicators is the number of those who say that they support the candidate, and the average of the indicators is the fraction of the supporters in the sample. Therefore, the law of large numbers applies readily. The expected value of the indicator variable is $E(X) = 1p + 0(1-p) = p$, where p is the population proportion (unknown to the researcher) of those supporting the candidate. The standard deviation (note that the standard deviation of a statistic computed from a sample is often called the standard error) of the indicator variable is

$$\sqrt{(1-p)^2 p + (0-p)^2(1-p)} = \sqrt{p(1-p)}.$$

Consequently (see (5.7)), the observed fraction is asymptotically normal, with mean p and standard deviation

$$\sqrt{\frac{p(1-p)}{n}}. \qquad (5.8)$$

To assess how far the observed fraction is likely to be from the true p (which is its expectation), one needs the value of the standard deviation (5.8). One can either use the estimated value of p in (5.8) or use the fact that the value of (5.8) is maximal from among all possible values of p for $p = 0.5$. In that case, the standard deviation is $0.5\sqrt{1/n}$, and as a conservative procedure, we shall use this maximal value. With this, one obtains that the error of the estimator—that is, $\overline{X}_n - E(X) = \overline{X}_n - p$—is approximately normal with standard deviations (depending on the sample size) as shown in Table 5.1.

Standard calculation using a general property of the normal distributions yields that approximately

$$P\left(p - 2\sqrt{\frac{p(1-p)}{n}} \leqslant \overline{X}_n \leqslant p + 2\sqrt{\frac{p(1-p)}{n}}\right) = 0.95; \qquad (5.9)$$

that is, with probability 0.95, the error is smaller than two standard deviations. Conservative approximations of the relevant values can be read off from Table 5.1 (or may be approximated as $0.5\sqrt{1/n}$). If the researcher wants the error to be less than, say, 0.02, with probability 0.95, then the sample size should be selected to have a standard deviation not exceeding 0.01, so $n = 2{,}500$ is a good choice.

Table 5.1 Approximate Standard Errors of the Estimate for a Fraction

Sample Size (n)	*Standard Deviation*
100	1/20 = 0.050
400	1/40 = 0.025
900	1/60 = 0.016
1,600	1/80 = 0.012
2,500	1/100 = 0.010

The standard deviation formula (5.8) applies only if a fraction of all respondents is considered. If, instead, as is done often in practice, the fraction of supporters of the candidate among those who say they intend to cast their vote is reported, the standard deviation becomes very different. This is because not only the numerator (the number of those saying they will support the candidate) but also the denominator (the number of those saying they will vote) is estimated from the data. Because both the numerator and the denominator have to be estimated, the standard deviation of this ratio is bigger than it would be if the denominator were known. While the actual standard deviation formulas are too involved to be discussed here, a good rule of thumb is that the standard deviations may be as much as twice those reported in Table 5.1. This fact is frequently overlooked by pollsters reporting overly optimistic (i.e., too small) margins of errors.

Confidence Intervals

Another characterization of the estimation procedure is obtained by a certain inversion of (5.9). By rearranging the terms in (5.9), we get

$$P\left(\overline{X}_n - 2\sqrt{\frac{p(1-p)}{n}} \leqslant p \leqslant \overline{X}_n + 2\sqrt{\frac{p(1-p)}{n}}\right) = 0.95. \qquad (5.10)$$

While (5.9) states that a random quantity (the average of the indicator variable) is within a fixed (although unknown to the researcher) interval with a given probability, (5.10) states that a random interval (the length of which is fixed and unknown but the starting and ending points are random) contains a fixed (but unknown) quantity with a given probability. This is why the rearrangement is a kind of inversion. The interval with the random location is called a *confidence interval.* Its length may be (conservatively) approximated without knowing p by assuming 0.5 as its value. From Table 5.1, one sees that—for example, with sample size 2,500—its length is not greater than 0.04.

If the sampling and estimation procedure is replicated several times, the confidence intervals will usually take on different positions, and in the long run, from among 100 confidence intervals of the form given in (5.10), about 95 will, in fact, contain the true parameter value, and the others will not contain it. Therefore, the construction of such a confidence interval is a method of estimation, called *interval estimation*. In about 95% of the times when we calculate such an interval, we are right—it does contain the true parameter, while in about 5% of the applications, we will be wrong—it does not contain the true parameter value. Note that the confidence interval given in (5.10) is random because it is based on the sample mean as a random variable. Indeed, the sample mean is a random variable before the actual sample was observed. To be able to determine the confidence interval, one needs, of course, a sample to be observed. Once the mean of the sample is determined, there remains nothing random about the actual sample mean and also nothing random about the confidence interval. It does or does not, in fact, contain the true parameter value, so one is either right or wrong when one applies the interval estimate. It is the same procedure applied repeatedly that may be characterized by probabilities—namely, that the interval estimate will be correct with probability 0.95, out of several applications of the procedure.

The same may be said about confidence intervals in general. If T is an estimator of the parameter θ such that for some c

$$P(\theta - c \leqslant T \leqslant \theta + c) = 1 - \alpha,$$

then

$$P(T - c \leqslant \theta \leqslant T + c) = 1 - \alpha$$

and $(T - c,\ T + c)$ is said to be a $(1 - \alpha)$-level confidence interval for the parameter θ.

Just like estimator and estimate, a confidence interval has two forms, a random interval (a formula) prior to data inspection and its realized version, when the relevant sample quantities are substituted in the formula. The first is a random interval, which contains the true but unknown parameter θ with probability $(1 - \alpha)$. Once the value of the statistic T is computed from the sample, the interval $(t - c,\ t + c)$ may or may not contain the parameter. This is unknown to the researcher, but there is nothing random about it. However, one knows that the procedure will lead to an interval that does cover the parameter with probability $(1 - \alpha)$. That is why we say that $(1 - \alpha)$ is our level of confidence that the actual interval contains the parameter value. The length of the confidence interval $(T - c,\ T + c)$ is $2c$, and in general, one is interested in finding the shortest confidence interval, with the given level of confidence. For example, if X is distributed as $N(E(X), \mathrm{Var}(X))$, then

$$\overline{X}_n \sim N\left(E(X), \frac{1}{n}\mathrm{Var}(X)\right)$$

and, consequently,

$$\left(\overline{X}_n - \frac{2}{\sqrt{n}}\mathrm{SD}(X), \overline{X}_n + \frac{2}{\sqrt{n}}\mathrm{SD}(X)\right)$$

is a 95% confidence interval but

$$\left(\overline{X}_n - \frac{1.65}{\sqrt{n}}\mathrm{SD}(X), \infty\right)$$

is also a 95% confidence interval. Apparently, the first one is shorter and is, therefore, preferable to the second one.

STATISTICAL HYPOTHESES

A hypothesis is an assumption regarding the true distribution in the population. Hypotheses are often formulated as restrictions on the values of some of the parameters of the distribution. For example, the assumption that the logarithms of incomes this year grew, on average, by 1% compared with last year is a hypothesis. If the income distribution this year is known (and so is the one for last year), the hypothesis can be easily decided on. But if this year's income distribution is not known (the tax returns were not yet filed and processed), the hypothesis cannot be decided for sure. One possibility is to take a statistical approach and select an appropriate sample, interview the respondents regarding their incomes this year and the previous year, and try to decide whether or not the assumption of a 1% growth is reasonable. Such a decision procedure will have to handle uncertainty with respect to how the actual respondents' incomes changed compared with the entire population's incomes. This depends on the sample selected and is, therefore, aleatory uncertainty (and we will neglect the epistemic uncertainty related to possible untruthful reporting of the incomes). As soon as the population income figures become available (e.g., from tax returns), no sampling is needed, and the aleatory uncertainty disappears.

How such a decision is reached, and what the characteristics of the procedures applied are, depends to a great extent on what additional assumptions (not to be tested) are made with respect to the true distribution in the population. For example, it may be assumed that the logarithms of the incomes are normally distributed. Such an assumption may be justified by the analysis of tax returns during several of the earlier years. Furthermore, such an investigation may also suggest that the variance of the log-income distribution changes very little between years, and therefore, it may be assumed that the variance is also known (i.e., is equal to last year's variance). Furthermore, it will make a difference, whether the hypothesis is formulated knowing a particular average log-income figure for the previous year (and in this case, the hypothesis assumes a 1% increase compared with that particular figure) or without knowing the previous year's average log-income (in which case the assumption is 1% increase compared with the previous year's average, whatever it happened to be). In general, the more information one puts into the analysis (in the form of knowledge or assumptions not to be tested), the better the decision procedure may be.

An apparently different kind of hypothesis assumes a structural property of the true population. Such assumptions often formulate some kind of simplicity. If the population had this feature, understanding of the true status of the population of interest would be simplified. For example, such a hypothesis may state that in a certain country, gender is independent of the level of education; that is, men and women have the same distribution in the categories of levels of education. If, for simplicity, we consider only three levels of education, the hypothesis of independence is formulated as follows. Let p_{ij} denote the fraction of those in the ith gender and jth educational level category ($i = 1,2; j = 1,2,3$), p_{i+} the fraction of those in the ith gender category, and p_{+j} the fraction of those in the jth educational level category. Then, independence requires that

$$p_{ij} = p_{i+}p_{+j}, \qquad \text{for all } i \text{ and } j. \qquad (5.11)$$

The six $(= 2 \times 3)$ population probabilities could—if they were known—conveniently be written into a 2×3 table (called a *contingency table*), and the observed frequencies from a sample could be written into a table of the same structure too.

A structural hypothesis, like that of independence in a 2×3 contingency table, may also be formulated as some parameters having restricted values, but this aspect will not be pursued here. In general, one may think of a hypothesis formulated under some assumptions (that are not part of the hypothesis) made with respect to the population, and these assumptions are restricting the set of possible distributions. For example, when the logarithms of the incomes are normally distributed, then the possible distributions are those that have the property that their logarithms are normal. When the variance is known, this further restricts the set of possible distributions. The hypothesis itself is a further restriction that may or may not be true in reality. It states that the true distribution belongs to a subset of the possible distributions. When this subset contains only one distribution (e.g., if the log-income distribution is believed to be normal, its variance is considered known based on previous experience, and last year's average log-income is given, then the hypothesis of 1% growth entirely specifies the distribution), the hypothesis is called *simple*. When the hypothesis contains several distributions (e.g., independence in the contingency table, 1% growth without the assumption of a constant variance), then the hypothesis is called *composite*.

In several cases, a decision is required between a so-called *null* hypothesis and an *alternative* hypothesis. Both the null and the alternative are hypotheses, they are disjoint (i.e., only one of them may be true). The null and the alternative may be the complements of each other, but it also may be the case that some possibilities are not contained in either one. For example, based on data from a national surveillance system of congenital malformations, one may wish to test the null hypothesis that the incidence rate of a certain malformation this year is the same as it has been historically against the alternative that it has grown by at least, say, 5%. When the null is rejected, some intervention (e.g., an investigation of the territorial distribution of the new cases to reveal possible environmental factors behind the increased incidence) is warranted. But if the incidence rate this year is not greater than the historical rate, no investigation is warranted and the null hypothesis is not rejected. In general, the null hypothesis is rejected only if strong evidence against it is found in the data. If, however, the evidence against the alternative is stronger than against the null, the null is not rejected even if evidence is strong against it too. In the example, if the observed incidence rate this year is 7% lower than it was last year, then this is strong evidence against the null that the incidence rate is the same but even stronger evidence against the alternative that the incidence rate grew by at least 5%. Therefore, the null is not rejected (i.e., no investigation of the causes is initiated).

Decisions About the Hypothesis

A hypothesis-testing procedure concludes with either the decision to reject or the decision to not reject the null hypothesis. Note that there are also so-called sequential procedures that may also end up deciding that more observations are needed before a decision may be reached. These procedures are very important in reducing the expected number of observations needed to reach decisions with prespecified characteristics, in particular in cases with ethical or funding constraints or when the observation is destructive and the testing procedure is being applied repeatedly, as is frequently the case in industrial quality control. Such procedures will not be discussed here.

The decision is based on the available information, that is, on the data observed in the sample, and, formally, is a function of the sample. It has to be realized early in the study of tests of hypotheses that one has to use procedures that sometimes reject and sometimes do not reject the null hypothesis. If one used a procedure that always rejects the null hypothesis (or one that never does so), then the decision would not depend on the data and the true status of the population (belonging to the null hypothesis or not) would not have a chance, not even through making certain samples more likely than others, to influence the decision.

In reality, either the null hypothesis or the alternative may be true. The decision may be to reject or not reject the null hypothesis. These options lead to four possible combinations, as illustrated in Figure 5.1. When the alternative is true and one chooses to reject the null or when the null hypothesis is true and one chooses not to reject it, the decision is correct. When the null hypothesis is true and one chooses to reject it or when the alternative is true and one chooses not to reject the null, the decision is erroneous. The first of these errors is called Type I error, and the second one is called Type II error. For a fixed sample size, a hypothesis-testing procedure is characterized by the conditional probabilities of committing the two types of errors. Type I error may be committed only when the null hypothesis is true. Type II error may be committed only if the alternative hypothesis is true.

The decision is based on the observed sample, and a testing procedure is defined if, for every possible sample, it is decided whether the observation of that sample leads to rejection or no rejection. Let S be the set of all possible samples (for a fixed sample size), and let it be divided into two subsets, C and $S \setminus C$. Suppose the hypothesis is rejected if the observed sample is in C (often called the *critical region*) and is not rejected if the sample falls into $S \setminus C$. An alternative decision procedure may be based on a proper subset of C, C'. The difference between the two procedures is that the observation of a sample in $C \setminus C'$ leads to rejection with the first procedure and to no rejection with the second procedure. This implies that

		Decision	
		Reject null	*Do not reject null*
Truth	*Null is true*	Error Type I	Correct
	Alternative is true	Correct	Error Type II

Figure 5.1 The decision table for statistical hypotheses.

the probability of Type I error (wrong rejection) for the first procedure is greater than or equal to the probability of Type I error for the second procedure. Similarly, the probability of Type II error (erroneous failure to reject) for the second procedure is greater than or equal to the probability of Type II error for the first procedure. Therefore, one cannot expect that both error probabilities may be made arbitrarily small. It is also implied that once the critical region is determined, the whole procedure is specified. We note that in practice, to decide whether a sample s belongs to a critical region C, an appropriate test statistic is defined, so that values of the test statistic either above or below certain value, called the *critical value*, are obtained for samples in the critical region.

How should the critical region be specified? Before a technical discussion is given, we note that, in general, if the sample s_1 is less likely, if the null hypothesis is true, than the sample s_2, then it is more reasonable to choose C to contain s_1 than to contain s_2, if the alternative is the complement of the null. To illustrate this simple idea, imagine that one sits in a windowless office and formulates the hypothesis that it is raining outside. Having access to population data and, consequently, being able to decide for sure would be equivalent to looking out through a window, but this is impossible. A decision about the hypothesis needs to be made as soon as possible. Information will be collected by observing whether the shoes of the first person entering the office from outside the building are wet or not. Therefore, there are only two possible samples, one with wet and one with dry shoes. One wants to reject the hypothesis having seen one of the samples and not to reject having seen the other sample, otherwise the decision would not depend on the data. So essentially, one has to decide whether rejecting rain having seen dry shoes (and not rejecting rain having seen wet shoes) or rejecting rain having seen wet shoes (and not rejecting rain having seen dry shoes) is more reasonable. Arguably, everybody finds the first procedure more acceptable than the second one. It is not because wet shoes imply rain (the person may just have stepped into a puddle that remained there from an earlier rain) and not because dry shoes imply no rain (the person may just have used a large umbrella). Rather, it is because wet shoes are more likely to occur when it rains than when it does not and dry shoes are more likely to occur if it does not rain.

The Neyman-Pearson Theory of Testing Hypotheses

As the simplest possible case, assume that both the H_0 null and the H_1 alternative hypotheses are simple. The likelihood of every sample may be determined. Let

$$L(s,H) \tag{5.12}$$

denote the likelihood of the sample s if the hypothesis H is true. Note that if the hypothesis specifies a single parameter of a parametric family, (5.12) has the form of (5.2). There may be no parameter specified by the hypothesis in the sense of (5.2), but even in this case, the likelihood in (5.12) is equal to the products of the likelihoods of the observations constituting the sample s, assuming the hypothesis is true. In the discrete case, the likelihoods are replaced by the probabilities.

Consider now

$$\frac{L(s,H_0)}{L(s,H_1)}, \tag{5.13}$$

the so-called likelihood ratio. It measures how many times the sample is more likely under the null than under the alternative. Our general idea now implies that, having observed the sample s, we want to reject the null, if the likelihood ratio, given in (5.13), is small, but we will see no reason to reject the null if that ratio is large. Now define a subset of all possible samples C as follows:

$$P(s \in C, H_0) = \alpha. \tag{5.14}$$

$$\text{If } s \in C \text{ and } \frac{L(s', H_0)}{L(s', H_1)} \leqslant \frac{L(s, H_0)}{L(s, H_1)}, \text{ then } s' \in C. \tag{5.15}$$

That is, C contains samples in such a way that the total probability, if the null hypothesis is true, of observing any sample in C is α, and samples with the smallest likelihood ratios are selected into C. In other words, C is a collection of least likely (under the null, relative to the alternative) samples, so that the probability of observing a sample from C, if the null is true, is α. Then, the testing procedure with critical region C has Type I error probability equal to α. Rejection, if the null is true, is a Type I error, and this will happen when the observed sample is in C and this has probability α in the case when the null is true. At the same time, this is the test that will commit Type II error with the smallest probability from among the tests that have Type I error probability equal to α.

The *power of a test* is defined as the complement of the probability of Type II error, and the probability of Type I error is often referred to as the *size* of the test. Using these concepts, the previous result may be formulated as follows: *The test of H_0 against H_1 using the critical region defined by (5.14) and (5.15) is the most powerful of the tests that have size α.*

The Likelihood Ratio Test

When the null and alternative hypotheses are not simple, the determination of the error probabilities and of the likelihoods of the samples under the null and the alternative is not easy. Even if any of these hypotheses is true, the true distribution on the population may be one of several, and the likelihood of the sample depends on which one out of these is the true distribution. In this case, the requirement that the Type I error probability should be equal to α is replaced by the requirement that the probability of erroneous rejection of the null does not exceed α for any distribution in H_0, and the Type II error probability is defined in a similar way.

To determine the likelihood of a sample, one considers the maximum likelihood the sample may have under any distribution in the hypotheses, and these maximized likelihoods are used in (5.13). In other words, for any possible sample, any of the hypotheses is given the best opportunity to deem the actual sample likely under this hypothesis. Rejection will occur only if no distribution in the null hypothesis would associate a high enough likelihood with the sample (relative to any distribution in the alternative). Define

$$L(s, H_i) = \sup_{F \in H_i} L(s, F), \qquad i = 0, 1, \tag{5.16}$$

where $L(s, F)$ is the likelihood of sample s if F is the true distribution in the population and sup (supremum) means the lowest upper bound. Then consider

$$\frac{L(s, H_0)}{L(s, H_1)} \tag{5.17}$$

similarly to (5.13), but now both the numerator and the denominator are supremums (see 5.16) over the respective hypotheses, as opposed to (5.13), where they were simply determined based on the single distributions in the hypotheses. Note that in some applications, the denominator of (5.17) is replaced by the maximum likelihood in the union of the null and the alternative hypotheses.

The likelihood ratio (5.17) may be used for testing the null against the alternative. Obviously, small values of the likelihood ratio suggest rejection, and large values suggest no rejection. In several setups, the distribution of the likelihood ratio (or of simple transformations of it) may be determined under the assumption of the null being true, at least asymptotically. When the distribution of the likelihood ratio is known, the critical region of the test is specified by choosing a critical value so that the probability that the likelihood ratio is less than the critical value, if the null is true, is α. This procedure is called the likelihood ratio test. Here, the likelihood ratio serves as the test statistic. The procedure discussed in the previous section is a special case of the application of the likelihood ratio as the test statistic.

In practice, it is very often more convenient to maximize, instead of the likelihood, the logarithm of the likelihood. Because the logarithm function is monotone, it will have its maximum for the same parameter value as the likelihood function, but instead of a product, one will have to maximize a sum, which is often easier. Further, additive terms in the log-likelihood that do not depend on the parameter are omitted. The remaining function is the *kernel of the log-likelihood.* Likelihood ratio tests may also be based on a comparison (difference) of the kernels of the log-likelihoods.

Some Testing Procedures

This section describes testing procedures for a number of common hypotheses. Note that the ideas behind these tests may be different from using the likelihood ratio.

When X is normally distributed with known variance $\mathrm{Var}(X)$ and the null assumes that $E(X) = \mu$ and the alternative is that $E(X) \neq \mu$, then an obvious test statistic is

$$\frac{\overline{X} - \mu}{\frac{1}{\sqrt{n}}\sqrt{\mathrm{Var}(X)}}. \tag{5.18}$$

Under the null, the above test statistic is distributed as standard normal, and the null is rejected with size α if the absolute value of this statistic exceeds the $z_{\alpha/2}$ critical value of the standard normal distribution. This procedure is called the *z test.*

If the alternative is that $E(X) > \mu$ (the so-called one-sided alternative), then one rejects the null hypothesis if the test statistic in (5.18) exceeds the z_α critical value of the standard normal distribution.

If the variance is not known, one may estimate it from the sample. To test the hypothesis that $E(X) = \mu$ against the alternative that $E(X) \neq \mu$, use the test statistic

$$\frac{\overline{X} - \mu}{\frac{1}{\sqrt{n}}\mathrm{sd}(X)}, \tag{5.19}$$

where $\mathrm{sd}(X)$ is the square root of the unbiased estimator of the variance in (5.3). The distribution of the statistic in (5.19) under the null hypothesis (if X is normal) is called *t distribution.* It is somewhat similar to the standard normal distribution, but because of the uncertainty related to using the estimated (as opposed to the known) standard deviation, it is somewhat heavier in the tails. Obviously, when the sample size increases, the estimate of the standard deviation converges in probability to the true standard deviation, and the distribution of (5.19) becomes less and less different from the standard normal. In fact, the t distribution has a parameter called the number of degrees of freedom, which is equal to the sample size minus 1. For larger sample sizes (and certainly for the sample sizes used in survey practice), the t distribution is well approximated by the standard normal distribution. In fact, for large sample sizes, the requirement that X is normally distributed may also be relaxed. Even if X is not normal, the distribution of the sample mean in (5.19) converges to that of a normal by the central limit theorem. The hypothesis of the specified expected value is rejected when the absolute value of the distribution in (5.19) exceeds the $t_{n-1,\alpha/2}$ critical value of the t distribution on $n-1$ degrees of freedom. For large sample sizes, critical values from the standard normal distribution may be used. For example, the 95th percentiles of the t distribution on 50 degrees of freedom and of the standard normal distribution are 1.675 and 1.645, respectively.

When observations are classified into a finite number of prespecified categories $c_1, \ldots, c_k$ that are mutually exclusive and exhaustive and the null hypothesis prescribes the probabilities of these categories as $p_1, \ldots, p_k$, where the probabilities sum to 1 (the alternative contains all other distributions), the following procedure is used. The data are in the form of observed frequencies $f_1, \ldots, f_k$, with the sum of these frequencies being the sample size n. Then expected frequencies (under the null hypothesis) are determined as $np_1, \ldots, np_k$. Note that these are MLEs. The meaning of these is not that one expects to observe these frequencies if the null hypothesis is true but rather that these are the expected values of the observed cell frequencies under the null. The following statistic, the *Pearson chi-squared statistic*, compares the observed and expected frequencies:

$$\sum_{i=1}^{k} \frac{(f_i - e_i)^2}{e_i}, \tag{5.20}$$

where $e_i = np_i$. Large values of the Pearson statistic (5.20) suggest rejecting the null hypothesis, because they imply that the observed frequencies differ substantially from the expected ones. The distribution in (5.20) depends on the true distribution in the population for any finite sample size, but asymptotically, it depends only on whether or not the null is true and on the number of categories. If the null hypothesis is true, the asymptotic distribution of (5.20) is chi-squared, with $k-1$ degrees of freedom. The precise meaning of this is that the random variable (5.20) converges in distribution to a random variable that is the sum of $k-1$ independent standard normal squares.

An important special case is when the probability of a certain event is prescribed by the null hypothesis as $p = p_0$. Here, there are two categories with respective probabilities p and $1-p$. If, however, the null hypothesis is

$$H_0 : p \leqslant p_0,$$

then the situation becomes much more complicated, because this is not a simple hypothesis. If the event is observed with frequency f out of n observations, the MLE of p in the model is

$$\hat{p} = \frac{f}{n},$$

the relative frequency, as long as it is not greater than p_0. If this is the case, then $e = n\hat{p} = f$, and (5.20) will take on the value of 0. Because the relative frequency converges in probability to the true probability of the event investigated, if the true p is strictly less than p_0, the relative frequency will be asymptotically less than p_0, and then for large samples, the value of the Pearson chi-squared statistic will converge to 0.

If $p = p_0$ in reality, then by the central limit theorem, the relative frequency (as the average of indicator variables) will tend to be normally distributed, so that its expected value is the true probability. By the symmetry of the normal distribution, even asymptotically, the observed relative frequency will be below $p = p_0$ with probability of 0.5 and will be above it with probability of 0.5. In the former case, the MLE is the relative frequency, and the value of the statistic in (5.20) is 0, just like in the case of $p < p_0$. In the latter case, the MLE will be equal to p_0 and asymptotically, the statistic in (5.20) is distributed as chi-squared with 1 degree of freedom. That is, if $p = p_0$, then the test statistic in (5.20), with $k = 2$, will be distributed as a mixture of chi-squared with 1 degree of freedom and of 0, each with probability of .5. Thus, to have a test of size α, one has to use the critical value $0.5\chi^2_{1,\alpha}$.

Another frequently encountered hypothesis is independence in a two-way contingency table, defined in (5.11), with the alternative that independence is not true. The MLEs of the cell expected frequencies are

$$e_{ij} = \frac{f_{i+}f_{+j}}{n}. \tag{5.21}$$

The Pearson chi-squared statistic (5.20) may be computed using (5.21), so that the summation pertains to all cells of the table. If the null hypothesis is true, it has an asymptotic chi-squared distribution with $(I-1)(J-1)$ degrees of freedom, where I is the number of rows and J is the number of columns of the table.

In this case, the likelihood ratio statistic may also be applied directly. For many sampling schemes, including multinomial sampling—that is, when a prespecified number of observations are classified into the cells, the kernel of the log-likelihood of the sample is

$$\sum f_{ij} \log p_{ij},$$

where p_{ij} is the probability in cell $(i,\ j)$. Under the null, this is maximized by

$$\sum f_{ij} \log(p_{i+}p_{+j})$$

and in the alternative hypothesis, by

$$\sum f_{ij} \log(f_{ij}/n).$$

The likelihood ratio test (a simple function of the likelihood ratio) used in this case is

$$-2\sum f_{ij} \log \frac{p_{i+}p_{+j}}{f_{ij}/n}.$$

For the test of independence, the likelihood ratio test also has an asymptotic chi-squared distribution with $(I-1)(J-1)$ degrees of freedom. The Pearson chi-squared and the likelihood ratio statistics have the same asymptotic distribution, even though they are based on apparently very different test statistics.

Some Practical Considerations

The choice of the Type I error probability is largely conventional. Only rarely can one quantify the loss incurred by committing either one of the errors. Because the power is usually implied by the size, in such cases one could look for an optimal choice of the Type I error probability. Such a situation may occur in an industrial quality control setting when the protocol prescribes sampling from the product—say, at a rate of n observations every hour. The product is characterized by certain parameters, and these should have values within prespecified limits. If the product is outside these limits, it cannot be sold. The machine used to manufacture the product requires adjustments to be made at certain times. Let the null hypothesis be the assumption that the product is correct and no adjustment is needed, with the alternative that the machine needs adjustment. In this case, Type I error is to stop production and adjust the machine, when it does not require adjustment, and its cost is the cost of the adjustment plus lost profit for the adjustment period. Type II error is failing to stop production when the machine needs adjustment, and its cost is the cost of production till the next inspection time plus lost profit for that period. If adjustment is expensive and the product is cheap, Type I error should be avoided, but Type II error does not appear to be that serious. If adjustment is cheap but the product (more precisely, the total products manufactured between two inspections) is expensive, then Type II error should be avoided.

When such an assessment is not possible, a Type I error probability of 0.05 is being used frequently, often without an explicit reference to the Type II error probability. What are the implications of this choice? Obviously, one wants to have small error probabilities, but as discussed above, when one reduces the Type I error probability, the Type II error probability increases (at least for a fixed procedure and a fixed sample size). One wants to have a small Type I error probability, but one wants it to be big enough, so that the Type II error probability is also small enough. Therefore, when the Type I error probability is determined without an explicit determination of the Type II error probability, then it should be selected to be the "largest small number"—that is, the largest of those numbers that are considered small enough so that a Type I error probability of that value is acceptable. Without such considerations, it is very often simply convention that dictates the choice of Type I error probability in practice.

Sometimes studies are designed so that a testing procedure can have a predetermined size and power. This is usually achieved by choosing the appropriate sample size: For a given size of a test, a larger sample size usually leads to increased power.

The problem of arbitrarily selected Type I error probability is often overcome by reporting the achieved probability level (also called the p-value) of a test rather than the reject/do not reject decision. The achieved probability level of a test of a hypothesis is the probability that the test statistic takes on a value more extreme than the actual value of the test statistic, assuming that the null hypothesis is true. (More extreme means larger if large values lead to rejection, and it means smaller if small values lead to rejection.) In other words, the achieved probability level is the largest Type I error probability with which the test results in no rejection. If someone has a Type I error probability in mind and the achieved probability level is smaller than this, the null hypothesis should be rejected.

When the test statistic is more extreme than the critical value (i.e., it exceeds it if large values lead to rejection), the result of the test is said to be *significant* at the appropriate level. More precisely, this is statistical significance, to be distinguished clearly from subject matter significance. Statistical significance means that the actual sample happens to belong to a small group of most unlikely samples under the null. In other words, the actual sample is extreme enough to provide the analyst with enough evidence against the null hypothesis. On the other hand, subject matter significance means deviation (from what one would expect under the null) in a magnitude large enough to be considered significant, taking into account the precision of the measurements and other circumstances.

To illustrate this difference, think of a multicampus university where the same class—say, Introduction to Statistics—is being offered on two campuses. To test the null hypothesis that the performance of the students is the same on both campuses, the same exam is given to samples selected from the students on the two campuses. Under the null, the two averages have the same expected value, and the decision about the hypothesis may be based on the difference of the two means. This difference is compared with its (known or estimated) standard deviation, and if the difference is too big compared with its standard deviation, the null hypothesis is rejected. Because the standard deviation will decrease as the sample sizes increase, any given difference in the sample means may lead to rejection if it is observed in the case of a large enough sample size. For example, consider the case when the difference in the sample means is 0.2. The standard deviation of the estimated difference may be, say, 0.5 for a certain sample but only 0.05 for a sample 100 times larger. For large enough samples, the test is essentially a z test, and it will not reject the null in the first case but will reject it in the second case. That is, the difference of 0.2 is not statistically significant in the first case, but it is statistically significant in the second case. The substantive importance of the difference of 0.2 is, of course, unaffected by the study; rather, it is related to the precision of the measurements, and so forth. The question concerning substantive significance cannot be answered by using statistical procedures. Establishing statistical significance does not imply subject matter significance. A scientifically sounder approach is to decide what is the smallest difference in the average grades that has a subject matter relevance, say r. If the difference in the population means exceeds r, one has subject matter significance. Rejecting the hypothesis that the population means are the same says nothing about the magnitude of the difference. To design a statistical test for subject matter significance, one should choose, as the null, the assumption that the population means differ by less than r, with the alternative that they differ by more than r. The difficulty of this approach is that it makes the null composite.

Further Reading

The material in this chapter is quite standard. We suggest some books that may serve as further reading to those interested. The classical text by von Mises (1981) is a very popular review of how probability and statistics are related to one another and to "truth." Giri (1993) is an easily accessible and self-contained introduction to probability, statistics, and their relationship. Suhov and Kelbert (2005) is a somewhat unusual but useful presentation of much of probability theory and statistics through worked-out examples. Kanji (1999) is a collection of several of the most important hypothesis-testing procedures.

Giri, N. C. (1993). *Introduction to probability and statistics* (2nd ed.). New York: Marcel Dekker.

Kanji, G. K. (1999). *100 Statistical tests*. Thousand Oaks, CA: Sage.

Suhov, Y., & Kelbert, M. (2005). *Probability and statistics by example*. Cambridge, UK: Cambridge University Press.

von Mises, R. (1981). *Probability, statistics and truth* (2nd ed.). New York: Dover.

6

THE BAYESIAN APPROACH TO STATISTICS

ANTHONY O'HAGAN

INTRODUCTION

By far the most widely taught and used statistical methods in practice are those of the frequentist school. The ideas of frequentist inference, as set out in Chapter 5 of this book, rest on the frequency definition of probability (Chapter 2), and were developed in the first half of the 20th century. This chapter concerns a radically different approach to statistics, the Bayesian approach, which depends instead on the subjective definition of probability (Chapter 3). In some respects, Bayesian methods are older than frequentist ones, having been the basis of very early statistical reasoning as far back as the 18th century. Bayesian statistics as it is now understood, however, dates back to the 1950s, with subsequent development in the second half of the 20th century. Over that time, the Bayesian approach has steadily gained ground, and is now recognized as a legitimate alternative to the frequentist approach.

This chapter is organized into three sections. The first gives an outline of the Bayesian method. The second section contrasts the Bayesian and frequentist schools, linking their differences to fundamental differences over the interpretation of probability, and argues that the Bayesian approach is more consistent and reflects better the true nature of scientific reasoning. The final section addresses various features of modern Bayesian methods that provide some explanation for the rapid increase in their adoption since the 1980s.

BAYESIAN INFERENCE

We first present the basic procedures of Bayesian inference.

Bayes's Theorem and the Nature of Learning

Bayesian inference is a process of learning from data. To give substance to this statement, we need to identify who is doing the learning and what they are learning about.

Terms and Notation

The person doing the learning is an individual scientist, analyst, or decision maker who wishes to learn from the data. Where we need to refer to this person explicitly, we will call him or her "You." The choice of word emphasizes the fact that Bayesian inference is concerned with the knowledge of a particular person, and so is intrinsically subjective, but the capital letter "Y" when discussing general principles distinguishes this person from "you, the reader" and shows that we are referring to an abstract or arbitrary person.

As with other approaches to statistics, the object of analyzing the data is to make inferences about some unknown parameters. It is conventional to denote parameters by Greek letters, and when discussing general principles we denote them by θ. In context, θ may represent a single parameter or more generally a collection of parameters. The data are usually denoted by Roman letters, and in general discussion we use the symbol x. In Bayesian statistics, You use the data x to learn about the parameters θ. Your beliefs and knowledge about θ are *updated* in this learning process.

We, therefore, need notation and terminology to describe Your state of knowledge before and after learning from the data. We refer to knowledge before observing the data as *prior* information, and to that obtaining after observing the data as *posterior* information. The words "prior" and "posterior" are relative to the data under consideration.

The description of prior or posterior knowledge in the Bayesian framework is a probability distribution. Your prior distribution for θ is denoted by $f(\theta)$ and Your posterior distribution by $f(\theta \mid x)$. For the purposes of this chapter, we will take these to be probability density functions, since in the great majority of applications the parameters are continuous variables.[1] Thus, the state of knowledge after observing the data is distinguished from that before observing the data simply by conditioning on x.[2]

The prior distribution is a complete description of Your prior knowledge, in the sense we can derive from it Your prior probability that θ lies in any set of interest. Similarly, $f(\theta \mid x)$ is a complete description of Your posterior information about θ. This conceptual description of the prior distribution will suffice as we explore the mechanics of Bayesian inference. We will consider the prior information in more detail in the section Prior Distributions.

Bayes's Theorem

Bayes's theorem (written "Bayes' theorem" by some and named after the 18th-century clergyman and mathematician Thomas Bayes) is the formula for deriving the posterior distribution. In the form used in Bayesian statistics, the theorem can be simply expressed as

$$f(\theta \mid x) \propto f(\theta)\, f(x \mid \theta). \qquad (6.1)$$

To understand this formula, first note that on the left-hand side of (6.1) is the posterior density $f(\theta \mid x)$, whereas on the right-hand side is the product of two terms, one of which is the prior density $f(\theta)$. The other term, $f(x \mid \theta)$, is the probability distribution for the data, conditional on the parameter θ. This distribution also appears in all other approaches to statistics, and in particular in frequentist theory. When thought of as a function of the unknown parameters θ (and for fixed data x), it is called the *likelihood function* (or simply the likelihood); see Chapter 5.

Note next that the left- and right-hand sides of (6.1) are linked by the proportionality symbol, "$\propto$." The theorem therefore says that the posterior density is *proportional to* the product of the prior density and the likelihood. We need a proportionality symbol here rather than an equals sign because the posterior density, like any density function, must have its integral (i.e., the area under the curve) equal to 1. If we simply multiply the prior density and the likelihood function, then the result will not integrate to 1 (except by some remote accident). Therefore, to obtain the posterior density function we must scale the right-hand side by multiplying it by a suitable constant to make it integrate to 1 over the full range of possible values of θ. This is the meaning of proportionality: The posterior density is the product of the prior density and likelihood *except* for a constant (in the sense of not depending on θ) scaling factor.

---

[1] It is straightforward to adapt everything to deal with discrete-valued parameters, but to do so here in any rigorous way would make the notation and discussion unnecessarily complex.

[2] Strictly, we should explicitly show Your prior information as, say, I. Then, posterior information comprises both I and the observed data x. In this more explicit notation, the prior distribution would be $f(\theta \mid I)$ and the posterior distribution $f(\theta \mid I,x)$. However, it is usual to suppress the prior information to simplify the notation.

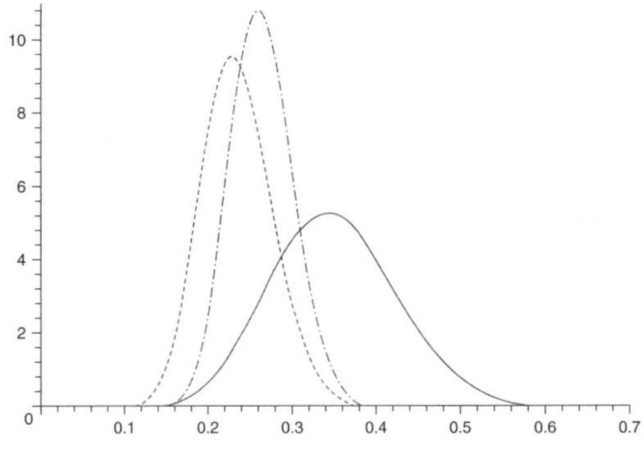

Figure 6.1 Example of mobile phone usage.

NOTE: Solid line: prior density; dashed line: likelihood; dot-dashed line: posterior density.

Learning

The way in which Bayes's theorem operates is best seen through examples. Suppose that You are interested in the proportion of people in the United Kingdom who have used a mobile phone while driving in the last year. If we denote this proportion by θ, then it can take any value in the range 0 to 1.[3] Suppose that we obtain data from a survey of 100 people in the United Kingdom, of whom 23 report having used a mobile phone while driving last year. Figure 6.1 illustrates the use of Bayes's theorem in this case. The solid line is Your prior distribution, which for this example indicates a belief that θ would most probably be in the range 0.3 to 0.4 and is unlikely to lie outside the range 0.2 to 0.5. The dashed line is the likelihood, with the data indicating θ is around the observed frequency of 0.23. The posterior distribution is the dot-dashed line.

Bayes's theorem multiplies the prior density and likelihood. Where either of these is very near zero, the product is near zero, so the posterior density is negligible for $\theta < 0.15$ (because the prior is negligible there) or $\theta > 0.4$ (because the likelihood is negligible there). It covers a narrower range, and so is more informative, than either the prior or the likelihood. The posterior reaches its maximum at $\theta = 0.264$, which represents a compromise between the prior density's maximum at $\theta = 0.35$ and the likelihood's maximum at $\theta = 0.23$. Both the data and prior information have a role in Bayesian inference, and the posterior distribution synthesizes the two sources of information. In this case, the data are more informative than the prior distribution, so this compromise yields a value closer to the data estimate than the prior maximum. We see this also in the fact that the posterior is similar to the likelihood, although the prior information has had some influence in moving the posterior toward larger θ values than the data alone suggest.

This example illustrates very typical behavior of Bayes's theorem.

- The posterior distribution combines the information in both the prior distribution and the likelihood. This typically results in the posterior representing stronger information, and supporting a narrower range of possible values for θ, than either of the separate sources of information.
- The posterior distribution centers around a value that is typically a compromise between the values that are well supported by the prior and by the data separately.
- This compromise also reflects the relative strengths of the prior information and data. The posterior is generally more similar to, and is centered nearer to the center of, the stronger information source.

Figure 6.1 is an example of a triplot, in which the prior, likelihood, and posterior are plotted together on a single graph. When there is just a single unknown parameter, it is a powerful way to see the operation of Bayes's theorem. In practice, however, statistical models nearly always have many more parameters. Bayes's theorem still operates in the same way, but it is no longer so simple to visualize graphically.

Bayes's theorem is the fundamental paradigm for learning from experience, allowing You to update Your prior information to Your posterior information via the evidence in the data. Psychologists have studied how people actually process information, and although we typically do not do so as efficiently as Bayes's theorem dictates, and

[3]Strictly, if N is the population of the United Kingdom, it takes values $0, \frac{1}{N}, \frac{2}{N}, \ldots$, but N is large!

are inclined to make some predictable kinds of judgmental errors, it is clear that people do learn from evidence in broadly this way.

Sequential Learning

We never stop learning. Learning is an ongoing process, and Bayes's theorem reflects this fact in a nice way. Remember that the words "prior" and "posterior" are relative to the data being assimilated. We can apply Bayes's theorem sequentially, to assimilate data piece by piece (or in chunks, as we wish), but then we have to recognize that at any point in this process Your prior distribution should represent the information that is available prior to the particular piece of data that You are about to observe. This, of course, is what You would have called Your posterior distribution after observing the previous piece of data. There is a nice phrase that sums up this analysis: "Today's posterior is tomorrow's prior."[4]

Bayes Estimates and Other Inferences

The basic principle of Bayesian inference is that all inferences are derived from Your posterior distribution. The posterior density $f(\theta\,|\,x)$ expresses all the information that You have about θ after observing the data, and can itself be considered an inference, in the sense of being Your answer to the question, "What do we now know about θ?" For a single parameter, simply drawing its posterior distribution, as in Figure 6.1, provides a clear visualization of that knowledge. It is usual, however, to require more quantitative inferences, such as point estimates, interval estimates, or tests of hypotheses. All of these are derived, in the Bayesian framework, from the posterior distribution.

A point estimate is a single value for θ that represents in some sense a "best guess" in the light of the data and Your prior information. There are several possible choices, depending on what kind of "best" value is required. The posterior median is one kind of Bayesian estimate. We can think of it as a central value, such that the probability that θ is higher than this value equals the probability that it is lower. Another choice is the posterior mean, which is the expected value of θ. This is widely used, and is usually understood when we talk about "Bayes estimates." Finally, the posterior mode is also commonly used, representing the most probable value.[5]

A Bayesian interval estimate is simply an interval having a specified posterior probability. For instance, a 90% interval is a range of values, say $[a,b]$, such that $P(a \le \theta \le b\,|\,x) = 0.9$. The usual term for such an interval is a *credible interval.*[6] Bayesian hypothesis testing is particularly straightforward: If You wish to decide, for example, whether to accept the hypothesis that θ is positive, You simply evaluate Your posterior probability that it is true, $P(\theta > 0\,|\,x)$.[7]

For example, in the case of the posterior distribution in Figure 6.1, the median, mean, and mode are, respectively, 0.263, 0.264, and 0.261, so the differences between them are very small and it would not matter in practice which we used. This is because the posterior density is nearly symmetric. In a skewed distribution, the differences between these point estimates will be larger. Next, suppose that You require a 75% credible interval

[4]It can be shown mathematically that Bayesian sequential updating is consistent, in the sense that You will obtain the same posterior distribution by assimilating all the data in one application of Bayes's theorem as You would obtain from applying it sequentially with the same data broken into individual items or blocks of data.

[5]Informally, it might also be called the "most likely" value, but this invites confusion with the frequentist "maximum likelihood estimator," which is quite different. Strictly, for a continuous parameter θ, there is no most probable value since the probability that θ takes any value precisely is zero. However, the mode maximizes the probability that θ will be within a small neighborhood of the estimate.

[6]Although this is a similar term to the frequentist "confidence interval," it is quite different and has a different interpretation; see section "Implications for Inference."

[7]Bayesian methods thereby separate the evaluation of how probable a hypothesis is from any decision whether to "accept" or "reject" it. The probability is a scientific judgment, but to make an accept/reject decision You should take into account the consequences of incorrect decisions. In some situations, You might be willing to accept a hypothesis if its probability is larger than 0.5, but in other situations You may require a much larger probability. For instance, in British criminal law, the accused is judged guilty only if the hypothesis of guilt is proved "beyond all reasonable doubt," whereas in civil law a judgment between two people is made "on the balance of probabilities."

for θ. There are many that we could use, ranging from $[0, 0.289]$ (which takes the 75% lowest possible values) to $[0.239, 1]$ (which uses the 75% highest values). The shortest possible 75% credible interval is, however, $[0.220, 0.305]$.[8] Finally, if You wish to decide whether to accept the hypothesis that $\theta < 0.25$, the posterior probability is $P(\theta < 0.25 \,|\, x) = 0.36$. So it is more probable, according to Your posterior distribution, that $\theta > 0.25$, but there is still substantial uncertainty about this hypothesis.[9]

Prior Distributions

The prior distribution is an intrinsic part of the Bayesian approach and the most obvious feature that distinguishes it from the frequentist approach. Much of the controversy about which inference paradigm is better has centered on the prior distribution. We will discuss the main arguments in this debate in the section Parameters as Random Variables, but first we consider how the prior distribution is specified in practice.

Elicitation

The most basic way to specify Your prior distribution for θ is a process known as *elicitation*. The word derives from the fact that elicitation usually involves an external facilitator who constructs the prior distribution to represent the knowledge of the person whose prior information is to be elicited. In practice, whereas the analysis of the data, construction of the posterior distribution, and derivation of appropriate inferences might be carried out by a statistician, the person whose prior information is to be elicited (that we have called You) will typically not be knowledgeable about statistics. We therefore consider elicitation to be a dialogue between the facilitator (someone with expertise in statistics and the elicitation of expert knowledge) and the subject-matter expert (You).[10]

In response to questions from the facilitator, You will specify particular features of Your prior knowledge. For instance, You might specify Your prior median and a prior 80% credible interval. The facilitator then constructs a prior distribution to represent Your stated beliefs. The skill of the facilitator lies in deciding which features of Your prior knowledge to ask about and how to ask those questions without biasing the answers. It is important to be aware of the considerable research in psychology concerning the ways that people respond to questions about uncertainty (see, for instance, O'Hagan et al., 2006).

Elicitation is not a precise process. First, it is difficult for You to think quantitatively about Your prior knowledge, and we cannot expect Your answers to be precise. For instance, if You are asked to specify Your prior probability that $\theta < 0.25$ in the mobile phone example, You might feel that θ is probably larger than 0.25, but how probable? You might say $P(\theta < 0.25) = 0.1$, but if pressed by the facilitator You might be perfectly happy with any value between 0.07 and 0.15 for this probability. The second source of imprecision is that You can only specify a relatively small number of features of Your prior distribution, partly because time is always limited and partly because the task becomes more complex as more questions are asked. In choosing a distribution to represent Your stated beliefs, the facilitator is making an arbitrary choice, and in reality there is a whole range of prior distributions that might fit Your statements equally well.

Because elicitation is imprecise, there is imprecision in the posterior distribution, and in inferences derived from it. It is important in practice to explore how robust any derived inferences might be to perturbing the prior distribution.

Fortunately, this prior imprecision often does not matter, because the posterior distribution is

[8]The shortest credible interval for any given probability of containing the true values is known as the *highest density interval*, because it is found by including in the interval all those values of θ having highest (posterior) density.

[9]However, Your prior probability $P(\theta < 0.25) = 0.09$ has been greatly increased by the data.

[10]The separation of roles is not always necessary, and certainly You could elicit Your prior distribution by playing both parts in the dialogue. Nevertheless, in situations where prior information is substantial and the problem of sufficient importance, the use of an experienced facilitator is advisable. In some projects, the opinions of several experts might be elicited, either individually or in a group.

almost unaffected by varying the prior distribution over quite a wide range. This is the case when the data are sufficiently strong. We have seen that Bayes's theorem synthesises the two sources of information by giving more weight to the stronger source. When the data are far more informative than the prior distribution,[11] the posterior distribution is almost entirely determined by the likelihood, and varying the prior distribution produces little effect. This is, therefore, when the posterior inferences will be robust to imprecision in the prior distribution.

Noninformative Priors

Another way to look at this is to say that we can avoid the posterior distribution being dependent on the prior if we make the prior information very weak. Prior distributions that express negligible prior knowledge have been given a huge variety of names, but we will use here the term "noninformative."[12] Several justifications have been proposed for considering such prior distributions.

1. Those who like the elegance of the Bayesian approach (with particular reference to its benefits over frequentist methods as discussed in the section Contrast With Frequentist Inference), yet are concerned about criticisms of the use of prior information, see noninformative prior distributions as a way to achieve the Bayesian benefits without the Bayesian prior.
2. To study the relationship between Bayesian and frequentist methods, it can be useful to formulate noninformative prior distributions, since this should bring the two approaches as close together as possible.
3. When prior information is genuinely weak compared with the data, so that the posterior distribution should not anyway be sensitive to the particular distribution that we use, then a noninformative prior is a convenient choice that avoids the need to go through a process of elicitation.

There has been a substantial amount of research into defining noninformative priors for various kinds of parameters in various models, but this is a contentious topic (see Berger, 2006; Goldstein, 2006; and discussions following those articles). There is no consensus over which of the competing recipes best represent prior "ignorance" in any given situation, and indeed many scholars would argue that complete ignorance never exists and there is no such thing as a totally noninformative prior. Nevertheless, in most cases the various noninformative priors that have been proposed in the literature for any given problem should lead to essentially the same posterior inferences, provided the data are not themselves weak.

The author's view is that genuine, informative prior distributions should be used wherever substantive prior information exists, but that when prior information is truly weak relative to the data then so-called noninformative prior distributions play a useful role in Bayesian inference (following the third justification above). In problems with several unknown parameters, it is rare for there to be useful prior information about all the parameters, so it is sensible to make efforts to formulate proper prior distributions for those parameters where genuine prior information exists, and to place conventional noninformative prior distributions on the others.

Data-Based Priors

Prior information often includes other data, say y, separate from the particular data x being analyzed. Then, in principle, we can say that "today's" prior distribution (before observing x) is "yesterday's" posterior distribution (after observing y). It might then be written $f(\theta \mid y)$ and could be derived using Bayes's theorem from "yesterday's" likelihood $f(y \mid \theta)$ and "yesterday's" prior $f(\theta)$.

In practice, though, it is not simple to deal with "prior data" in this way. First, the problem of specifying "today's" prior distribution has

[11] We are using the term *informative* here in the sense of the discussion of the triplot (Figure 6.1). We refer here specifically to the situation where the prior distribution is very much broader and flatter than the likelihood.

[12] Some of the other names are "weak," "reference," "default," "vague," "objective," or "ignorance" priors.

simply been deferred to that of specifying "yesterday's" prior, and it will generally be difficult to think about what prior distribution would have applied in the hypothetical state of knowledge prior to observing y. Second, y often relates only indirectly to θ. This is the case when prior information relates to knowledge of *similar* problems. For instance, if required to assess a prior distribution for the efficacy θ of some new drug, You may have prior experience of the performance of similar drugs. To use such data formally alongside x, it is necessary first to formulate its relationship to θ in the form of "yesterday's" likelihood $f(y \mid \theta)$ (e.g., by explicitly formulating some assessment of similarity between the new and old drugs). Such complications mean that it is often no easier to make explicit use of prior data than to elicit Your current prior distribution (so incorporating y implicitly).

Contrast With Frequentist Inference

Where appreciable prior information exists, perhaps the most significant difference between Bayesian and frequentist methods is the ability of the Bayesian analysis to make use of that additional information in the form of the prior distribution. As a result, Bayesian methods will typically produce stronger inferences from the same data. Furthermore, the prior information allows the Bayesian analysis to be more responsive to the context of the data. However, the prior distribution is also the focus of opposition to Bayesian methods from adherents of the frequentist philosophy. Frequentists regard its use as unscientific, so do not believe that such stronger or more responsive inferences can be obtained legitimately.

Parameters as Random Variables

Although the use of a prior distribution does distinguish Bayesian methods from frequentist methods, we have seen that some users of Bayesian ideas attempt to nullify the prior information by using noninformative priors. Even where genuine prior distributions are employed, they may have very little impact on the inferences. A better defining characteristic for the Bayesian approach is the willingness to treat unknown parameters as random variables.

The Nature of Probability and Uncertainty

We can only have a posterior distribution if θ is considered as a random variable. In frequentist statistics, parameters cannot be random variables, and it is not legitimate to make probability statements about them. This, more than whether one feels discomfort with the use of prior information, is what makes frequentist inference fundamentally different from Bayesian inference.[13]

Underlying this distinction is a still more fundamental difference over what probability means. Frequentist inference is so called because it relies on the frequency interpretation of probability, so that every probability is defined as the long run relative frequency with which events of that type occur under repeated observation. Probability statements cannot be made about parameters because they cannot meaningfully be considered as repeatable. In any statistical problem, we have data that are generally sampled from some population or data-generating process that is repeatable. We can consider drawing samples indefinitely from such a process, and so x is a random variable within the frequency formulation, and its distribution $f(x \mid \theta)$ is well defined in terms of frequency probabilities.[14] However, θ represents the unknown features of that data-generating process. They are fixed and specific to this problem. θ is unique and cannot be considered part of a repeatable sequence, so we cannot meaningfully assign frequency probabilities to it.[15]

---

[13]In some problems, frequentist statistics makes use of "random effects" formulations, in which some parameters in an analogous "fixed effects" model become random variables. However, the random effects are then not then treated as parameters, and inference cannot be made about individual random effects.

[14]Technically, in frequentist inference, because θ is not a random variable we do not formally *condition* on its value, and hence the notation $f(x \mid \theta)$ is strictly incorrect. It is usual to write it instead as $f(x; \theta)$ or $f_\theta(x)$.

[15]Even if we could conceive of a collection of data-generating processes, the one under study is not randomly sampled from that collection and inevitably has its own characteristics that make it not comparable with the others.

Philosophically, different kinds of uncertainty are associated with x and θ. The data are subject to random variability, and the associated uncertainty is termed *aleatory* (from the Latin "alea" for a die). Parameters are not random (in the everyday sense of this word), but they are uncertain. The uncertainty in this case arises from a lack of knowledge and is termed *epistemic* (from the Greek "episteme" for science or knowledge).[16] Frequency probability is only applicable to quantify aleatory uncertainties. In contrast, the subjective or personal interpretation of probability defines Your probability for an event as a measure of Your degree of belief in the assertion that the event will occur. This definition clearly applies to any uncertain event, whether the uncertainty is epistemic or aleatory.[17]

The willingness to express uncertainty about θ through probabilities, and to assign a probability distribution to θ either before or after observing x, means that Bayesian inference is intrinsically based on the subjective formulation of probability.

Implications for Inference

Frequentist inference cannot make probability statements about parameters, yet it often appears to do just that.

Consider a hypothesis testing problem, where the inference question is to decide whether to accept the hypothesis H. We have seen that the Bayesian approach to this is very simple: We report the posterior probability that H is true. This probability is meaningless in the frequency framework, and the frequentist approach to hypothesis testing is more convoluted. First, it is necessary to choose a *rule* for testing, which determines for any given data x whether to accept or reject H. Next, the behavior of this rule must be evaluated in repeated sampling, to find out the probability α that H would be rejected if it is actually true (the probability of "first kind of error"). Finally, if x does indeed lead to rejection of H then we report that H is "rejected at the $100\alpha\%$ level of significance." Otherwise it is "not rejected at the $100\alpha\%$ level of significance."[18]

Notice that the extra complexity of the frequentist approach is necessary because we can only talk of probabilities when they are associated with aleatory uncertainty. Hence, it is necessary to consider all frequentist inferences as instances of inference rules, whose properties are determined by imagining them to be applied in repeated sampling.

One problem with the frequentist formulation is that it is rarely fully understood (even by many practising statisticians, let alone by their clients). When told that H is rejected at the 5% level, this is almost universally interpreted as saying that there is only a 5% chance that H is true. Of course, this cannot be the correct interpretation because it makes a probability statement about the hypothesis (and hence about θ). Only a Bayesian analysis can make such a statement. Yet frequentist inferences are invariably misinterpreted in this way because they seem to make a much simpler and more useful statement ("the probability that H is true is 0.05") than they really do ("if H were true, then the probability that the data would fall in the prespecified region in which they have been observed to fall on this occasion is 0.05").

Similarly, a frequentist confidence interval is nearly always interpreted as a Bayesian credible interval. Thus, the statement that $[1.2, 4.7]$ is a 95% confidence interval for some parameter θ is almost invariably understood as saying that there is a 95% chance that θ lies between 1.2 and 4.7. This cannot be correct because it is a probability statement about θ. The correct interpretation is: that a rule of inference has been applied which yields an interval estimate for θ, that in repeated sampling the intervals constructed by

[16] The distinction between aleatory and epistemic uncertainty is not always clearly delineated in practice. It is even arguable that at a fundamental level true randomness does not exist. Nevertheless, the distinction is useful in discussing the difference between Bayesian and frequentist approaches.

[17] In fact, Your uncertainty about the data x is both aleatory and epistemic. Since the parameters of the data-generating process have epistemic uncertainty, the uncertainty in x is more than just the aleatory uncertainty induced by randomness.

[18] There are actually two different versions of the frequentist hypothesis test. This is the Neyman–Pearson form of significance test. The Fisherian p-value requires a nested set of rejection regions to be defined, and then p is the α value of the region for which the observed data x lie on the boundary.

this rule contain θ with probability 0.95, and that when applied to the particular data x this rule has produced the interval $[1.2, 4.7]$. The confidence interval is generally interpreted as a credible interval because the Bayesian statement is simpler and more natural.

The Bayesian methods answer inference questions in direct and simple ways. The frequentist inferences have more indirect and easily misunderstood interpretations.

Paradoxes in Frequentist Inference

There is much abstract and theoretical debate about the merits of Bayesian versus frequentist methods. In general, the Bayesian approach is seen to be more philosophically consistent, whereas the frequentist approach gives rise to quite paradoxical properties. Rather than dwell in detail on these, we present here just two related instances where frequentist and Bayesian methods behave quite differently, and try to present both sides of the argument in each case.

The Likelihood Principle

To illustrate the difference between Bayesian and frequentist methods, consider again the example of mobile phone usage while driving. We supposed that the data comprised a survey of 100 people, in which 23 admitted to using the phone while driving. The usual frequentist estimate of θ in this situation is $\hat{\theta} = 23/100 = 0.23$. However, this presupposes that the survey size $n = 100$ was fixed and the observation is $r = 23$. If we took repeated samples of 100 people and calculated $\hat{\theta} = r/100$ every time, then on average these estimates would equal the true value of θ; this is the frequentist estimation property known as *unbiasedness*. Suppose, however, that the survey was conducted differently, so that we kept sampling until we obtained 23 people who claimed to have used a mobile phone while driving in the last year. Now $r = 23$ is fixed, and it is $n = 100$ that is random. If we repeatedly took samples, in each case sampling until $r = 23$, and calculated $\hat{\theta} = 23/n$ in each case, then the values we got would not average to θ. In this different kind of sampling, the appropriate frequentist unbiased estimator is $\theta^* = 22/(n-1)$, which in the particular case that we observed of $n = 100$ yields $\theta^* = 22/99 = 0.2222$.

A Bayesian analysis of this problem would be quite different. The posterior distribution would be the same in both cases, so You would obtain the same Bayesian inferences, including estimates, no matter which sampling method was used.

Both frequentists and Bayesians regard this example as favoring their approach. Frequentists assert that if the data are obtained from different sampling methods, then it is obvious that they have different meaning and we should make different inferences. The Bayesian argument is that in both cases we have observed 23 people out of 100 who have used their mobile phones while driving, and knowing whether we fixed 23 or fixed 100 is irrelevant because this knowledge in itself obviously conveys no information about θ.

To add a further twist to this example, suppose that the experiment were conducted in yet another way, with the survey being continued until we ran out of time, money, or energy to continue.[19] Now neither r nor n is fixed. The frequentist theory can have enormous trouble with such a situation, because it may be almost impossible to determine what repeated samples, conducted under the same conditions, would look like. The Bayesian theory has no such difficulty. It is obvious that the mechanism for determining the sample size is not itself informative about θ, and the inference is again the same as if n were fixed at 100, or r at 23.

Formally, Bayesian inference adheres to the Likelihood Principle, which in simple terms says that inference should depend on the data but not on what data we might have obtained; see Berger and Wolpert (1988) for a much more detailed explanation. Different sampling mechanisms lead to different alternative samples. For instance, $r = 23, n = 101$ is possible if r is fixed (or if neither is fixed) but not if n is fixed at 100. Because frequentist methods are evaluated in terms of repeated sampling, they do depend on the

[19]Many actual surveys are in reality conducted like this, even though the scientists may subsequently report them as if the sample size was predetermined!

sampling mechanism. To adherents of the frequentist philosophy, this is natural and unexceptional. To Bayesians, the frequentist approach is illogical in giving inferences that depend on features of the experiment (such as whether $n = 100$ or $r = 23$ was predetermined) that do not in themselves convey any information about the unknown parameters.

Applying Inferences to Particular Data

In a similar way, frequentist inference depends on the rule of inference having been prespecified. Suppose in the mobile phone use example (with fixed $n = 100$), we consider the estimation rule $\theta^+ = r/100$ if r is an odd number and $\theta^+ = r/101$ if r is an even number. Now this rule is not unbiased, and indeed is biased downwards (tending to give estimates that are too low). Given our actual observation, both rules give the same estimate, $23/100 = 0.23$. In one case, however, the estimate results from applying an unbiased estimation rule, while in the other it comes from a biased rule. So is the actual estimate, 0.23, biased or unbiased? Unbiasedness or biasedness is a property of the rule, and in frequentist terms it does not make sense to ask whether an estimate obtained from a particular set of data is unbiased.

Perhaps a more convincing example can be given in the case of a confidence interval. If we are told that $[1.2, 4.7]$ is a 95% confidence interval for θ, then we know that on 95% of the occasions that this rule is used the calculated interval will contain θ. It is now particularly compelling to say that we should give a probability of 0.95 to the interval containing θ on *this* occasion. Admittedly, this is a Bayesian statement, but what is wrong with this very natural transfer of the 95% property from the rule to the instance? The answer is that $[1.2, 4.7]$ could easily also be obtained by applying some other interval estimation rule that is, for instance, a 90% confidence interval. So is the probability 95% or 90% that $[1.2, 4.7]$ contains θ?

From the frequentist perspective, the answer depends again on what might have been obtained but was not, since different rules that give the same inferences on the actual data x would give different inferences on other data. Bayesian inferences apply unambiguously to the particular data that have been observed.

Subjectivity and Science

The most persistent criticism that is made of Bayesian inference is that it is subjective. This is undeniably true, since Bayesian methods are based on the subjective formulation of probability; the posterior distribution represents the beliefs of a particular person (You) about θ. To people who were trained to think that statistical analysis of data must be based on scientific principles, and that science is above all objective, this seems to provide a compelling reason to reject the Bayesian approach. However, closer examination shows—in the author's opinion, at least—that the criticism is vacuous because neither frequentist methods nor science itself is objective.

It is certainly true that science aspires to be objective, and avoids subjective judgments wherever possible. But in every field of science we find controversy and differences of opinion over topics of current interest. The progress of science is achieved through debate, the accumulation of evidence and convergence upon explanations and interpretations of the evidence. Questions that may seem to be resolved in this way can be reopened when new data throw an accepted theory into doubt, or when somebody interposes a new explanation or interpretation, as witness the revolution in thinking that came at the start of the twentieth century with relativity theory superseding the previously accepted Newtonian physics. Consider any piece of research that is published in some eminent scientific journal. The authors will present their data and the conclusions that they draw from those data. The data themselves may be considered to be objective, but the conclusions are not. The authors will describe the process by which the data were collected and describe their own interpretation of those data as clearly as they can, to convince the reader to accept their conclusions. The conclusions may indeed be deemed uncontroversial, but often their fellow scientists will apply their own interpretations (and perhaps reach different conclusions) or else reserve judgment until the issues have been debated more or until more data are available. Objectivity in science is really a convergence of subjective opinion, and that agreement may be only temporary.[20]

Subjectivity in frequentist statistics is equally easy to see. In practice, two statisticians faced with the same data will often reach different inferences. This may be because they have chosen to use different inference rules, for instance, two different hypothesis tests. The choice of an estimator, a test, or a confidence interval is one source of subjectivity, and although in some simple problems there are universally agreed "best" inferences this is rarely the case in more complex analyses. A more common reason for reaching different conclusions is that the statisticians model the data differently. The effect of this is that they obtain different likelihoods. From the Bayesian perspective, this is entirely natural because all probabilities are subjective and the likelihood is no exception. But from the perspective of a frequentist who criticizes the Bayesian statistician for being subjective, this is an embarrassment. It is this author's contention that no methods of statistics are objective, just as science is not objective.

This is not to say that we should make a virtue of subjectivity. Like science itself, a Bayesian analysis aspires toward objectivity and attempts to avoid those aspects of subjectivity that have given a derogatory connotation to the word "subjective." Thus, probabilities may be subjective, but they should not be affected by prejudice, superstition, or wishful thinking.

Furthermore, Bayesian analysis reflects the above view of the process of science perfectly. It was explained in the section Prior Distribution how the prior distribution has less influence if the data are strong. Thus, as more data are collected, people who might have begun with very different prior beliefs will find that their posterior distributions converge. Eventually, differences of prior opinion are overwhelmed by the accumulating evidence, which is precisely the way that science progresses. Indeed, the fact that Bayesian methods recognize prior opinion is a positive benefit, because it allows us to see when this convergence has taken place. If the data are not strong enough to yield uncontroversial inferences, then this is an important fact that is not apparent in any frequentist analysis.[21] Howson and Urbach (1993) present a detailed argument in favor of Bayesian statistics from the perspective of the philosophy of science.

Bayesian Statistics Today

Modern Bayesian statistics is a rich and powerful framework in which to make inferences and decisions. We consider here a few of the more striking features of Bayesian statistics today.

The Growth of Bayesian Applications

Since about 1990, there has been a dramatic growth in the use of Bayesian methods. In some application areas today, a Bayesian approach is almost a hallmark of leading-edge research. These are often fields where data are scarce, or have complex structures that are difficult to analyze, whereas frequentist methods are still dominant in the more traditional application areas of statistics. In the social sciences particularly, there is more recognition of the role of judgment in interpreting data, and there is less resistance to the apparent subjectivity of Bayesian methods.

For example, the relatively new field of health economics is concerned with assessing the cost-effectiveness of competing medical technologies (such as alternative drugs, surgical interventions, or vaccinations). Such assessments are typically made by assembling evidence on the effects (both positive and negative) of the treatments and the costs incurred (for the treatments themselves and

[20] I have been told by senior scientists that personal judgment does not play a role in their work, but they are wrong. What makes these people leaders of their own fields is that their opinions and judgments are esteemed by their fellows.

[21] Notice, however, that the convergence of opinion relies on all participants agreeing on the likelihood. This mirrors the need for scientists to agree on the interpretation of data before they can agree on the conclusions that can be drawn from them.

any other medical resources used). The resulting evidence base is complex, and inevitably very weak in some areas. Bayesian methods are acknowledged as essential to produce meaningful statistical analyses in such problems. In contrast, frequentist methods are still the dominant methodology in the more well-established field of analyzing clinical trial data. Clinical trials have traditionally produced high-quality, well-structured data, and have been large enough to ensure that prior information and preexisting opinions would be overwhelmed by the trial evidence. Here too, however, Bayesian methods are beginning to become more attractive, partly driven by the high cost of modern drug development that has led to a desire for smaller trials and more efficient use of all available information.

In the following subsections, we look at some of the factors that have played a part in stimulating this rapid growth in the uptake of Bayesian methodology.

Bayesian Computation

Two distinct steps can be identified in the basic Bayesian method:

1. *Bayesian Modeling.* Identify the unknown parameters and the inference questions about these parameters that are to be answered. Construct the likelihood and the prior distribution to represent the available data and prior information.
2. *Bayesian Analysis.* Obtain the posterior distribution and derive inferences.

We will consider Bayesian modeling in the section One Coherent Framework for Thinking, so concentrate here on the second step, Bayesian analysis.

Until the advent of powerful computational tools, Step 2 represented a major difficulty except in very simple problems. To illustrate these difficulties, first suppose we have a sample of data from a normal distribution with unknown mean μ and known variance σ^2. The unknown parameter that we have generically denoted by θ is, in this example, μ. The likelihood for this sample can be written[22]

$$f(x\,|\,\mu) \propto \exp\left\{-\tfrac{n}{2\sigma^2}(\mu-\bar{x})^2\right\}, \qquad (6.2)$$

where $\bar{x}$ is the sample mean. Now suppose that the prior distribution for μ is normal with mean m and variance v, so that

$$f(\mu) \propto \exp\left\{-\tfrac{1}{2v}(\mu-m)^2\right\}. \qquad (6.3)$$

This is an instance of what is called a conjugate prior distribution, because it combines nicely with the likelihood to produce a posterior distribution that is very easy to analyze. In fact, the combination of likelihood (6.2) and prior (6.3) is easily shown to result in a posterior distribution for μ that is also normal. Derivation of inferences such as the posterior mean or credible intervals is now simple. In this case, the whole Bayesian analysis can be done analytically because the posterior is found to have a well studied, standard distributional form.

However, if the prior distribution is not normal, the posterior will typically no longer be so simple. For instance, if the prior density has the logistic form

$$f(\mu) \propto \exp(p\mu)\left\{1+\exp(\mu)\right\}^{-(p+q)},$$

then the posterior will not have any standard form. To derive any inference such as the posterior mean or a credible interval will now require numerical computation. Because there is only one parameter in this problem, these calculations require only numerical integration in one dimension, which is straightforward. In the period from the birth of modern Bayesian thinking in the 1950s to at least the mid-1980s, Bayesian analysis was restricted to situations in which conjugate prior distributions were available, or where the number of parameters was small enough for computation of posterior inferences by numerical integration to be feasible.

---

[22] We have simplified the likelihood here by writing it as *proportional to* the expression shown. That is, factors that do not depend on the parameter μ have been dropped. We do the same with the prior distribution in the next expression. These are legitimate simplifications because Bayes's theorem says the posterior distribution is proportional to the product of prior and likelihood, and this remains true after removing any such constant factors in either term.

Problems that could be analyzed routinely by frequentist methods, such as generalized linear models with many explanatory variables, were outside the reach of Bayesian methods.

This changed with the development of the computational technique known as Markov chain Monte Carlo, universally abbreviated to MCMC, so that we can now perform those computations even in very complex, multiparameter situations.

MCMC is based on two conceptually very simple ideas. The first is that of sampling-based computation. Suppose that we wish to compute the posterior mean of the parameter θ_1, which is the first element of the vector θ of, say, k parameters. Formally, this is

$$E(\theta_1 \mid x) = \int \theta_1 f(\theta \mid x)\, d\theta$$

and involves integrating over the whole k-dimensional space of the parameter vector θ.[23] If k is more than about 10, this is a very substantial computation using numerical integration. However, imagine that we could take a sample of N values from the posterior distribution $f(\theta \mid x)$. Denote these by $\theta^{(1)}, \theta^{(2)}, \ldots, \theta^{(N)}$. Then we would in particular have a sample of values of the first parameter θ_1, obtained by taking the first element in each of the vectors $\theta^{(i)}, i = 1, 2, \ldots, N$. We could use the sample mean $\bar{\theta}_1$ as an approximation to $E(\theta_1 \mid x)$. If the sample were very large, for instance $N = 10^6$, then we could regard this as effectively an accurate *computation* of $E(\theta_1 \mid x)$.

Direct sampling like this from the posterior is sometimes feasible, even in some quite large and complex problems, and is referred to as Monte Carlo computation. However, in most serious applications of Bayesian analysis the posterior distribution is too complex and high dimensional for this direct approach to be feasible. We then employ the second device, which is based on the theory of Markov chains. We again obtain a series of vectors $\theta^{(1)}, \theta^{(2)}, \ldots, \theta^{(N)}$, but these are not sampled directly from $f(\theta \mid x)$ and they are not independent. Instead, each $\theta^{(i)}$ depends on the previous $\theta^{(i-1)}$ and is sampled from a distribution $g(\theta^{(i)} \mid \theta^{(i-1)})$. This means that the $\theta^{(i)}$s are a Markov chain. The conditional distribution g, which is known as the *transition kernel* of the chain, is chosen so that for sufficiently large i the distribution of $\theta^{(i)}$ converges to the posterior distribution $f(\theta \mid x)$.[24] Markov chain theory provides relatively simple criteria under which this convergence will occur, and in practice there are numerous ways of constructing a suitable transition kernel to sample from any desired posterior distribution.[25]

The combination of the two ideas of sample-based computation and the Markov chain is MCMC. To go more deeply into the technique of MCMC would require more than this chapter, and indeed whole books have been written about it (see, for instance, Gilks, Richardson, & Spiegelhalter, 1995). Instead, we will just note the following important points:

- Although convergence is guaranteed eventually, it is not possible to say how large a sample must be taken before successive values can be considered to be sampled from the posterior distribution. Judging when the sample is large enough is something of an art, although there is a growing body of diagnostics to help with this task.
- Successive points in the Markov chain are correlated, and the strength of this correlation is very important. A highly correlated chain converges slowly and moves around the parameter space slowly, so that a larger

[23]We often think of this integration in two stages. First, we integrate $f(\theta \mid x)$ over all elements of θ except θ_1, a $(k-1)$-dimensional integration, to obtain the marginal density $f(\theta_1 \mid x)$. Then we integrate with respect to θ_1 to obtain its posterior mean as $E(\theta_1 \mid x) = \int \theta_1 f(\theta_1 \mid x)\, d\theta_1$.

[24]This is true no matter what the initial value $\theta^{(1)}$ is. In simple terms, the chain can be said to have converged when it has "forgotten" where it started from.

[25]To understand MCMC, it is helpful to think first of simple Monte Carlo sampling as, for example, shooting randomly into the space of possible values of θ. Each shot is distributed according to the posterior distribution and successive shots are independent. In contrast, MCMC starts at an arbitrary point $\theta^{(1)}$, and then wanders around the space, each successive value being a random move away from the previous one. If the transition kernel is appropriately chosen, this wandering point will make its way into the part of the θ space with appreciable posterior density, and will spend more time in regions with higher density and less in regions with lower density, so that the collection of points behaves like a sample from the posterior distribution.

sample is needed to compute relevant inferences accurately. Devising a chain that has relatively low correlation is another task that is something of an art.

The ability of MCMC to tackle extremely complicated problems with very large number of parameters is a major factor in the growth of applied Bayesian statistics. As remarked above, the practice of MCMC is still under rapid development and is a skilled task. There is a powerful software package available, known as WinBUGS,[26] but this also requires a relatively sound knowledge of MCMC practice. As yet it is not truly easy to use software for Bayesian computation.

One Coherent Framework for Thinking

Another appealing feature of the Bayesian approach is its conceptual simplicity and consistency. In effect, a Bayesian analysis involves only the formulation and manipulation of probabilities. The process of building a Bayesian model is all about formulating beliefs in terms of probabilities, and it does not matter whether these probabilities represent aleatory or epistemic uncertainties. The second step of the Bayesian method, which is the derivation of the posterior distribution and inferences, is in principle simply a matter of manipulating probability distributions. The key requirement for an applied Bayesian statistician is to be able to think in terms of probabilities formulating knowledge and uncertainties.

The frequentist philosophy is different. Probabilistic modeling is used to create the likelihood, but the formulation and choice of inference rules are based on an array of more or less ad hoc criteria for what constitutes a good rule. The frequentist statistician is free to propose new rules, and unless they are demonstrably and uniformly inferior to another rule (which can rarely be shown) it is legitimate to use them.

This aspect of Bayesian inference as a coherent framework for thinking about uncertainty emerges very clearly in the following example, where there are no aleatory uncertainties at all. Mathematical models are widely used in science, engineering, economics, and other fields to describe real-world processes, with a view to understanding and predicting their behavior. Such models are usually implemented in computer programs, which can be very large and take anything from a few seconds to many hours to run. In practice, the user of such a model does not require to run it just once, but wishes to consider what outputs are predicted by the model for a variety of settings of its inputs. In some cases, the number of runs that would, in principle, be required is so large that it is impractical to do so within any realistic time-span. Bayesian methods have been developed to enable such analyses to be done without physically running the model for all the necessary input combinations.[27] The idea is to model uncertainty about what outputs the model would produce at some input settings for which the model has not actually been run. There is no aleatory uncertainty because the model itself is deterministic; running it at any given inputs will always produce the same outputs. However, there is clearly epistemic uncertainty about what the outputs will be before we actually run the model. Bayesian methodology can model this uncertainty as if the relationship between inputs and outputs was a random function.

Design, Decision, and Prediction

We end this chapter by highlighting several kinds of problems where a Bayesian approach is more natural and powerful than frequentist methods. The design of experiments and observational studies is obviously such an area, because before we actually collect the data there is only prior information. Frequentist methods must use prior information, but do so in an informal and oblique way. In a Bayesian approach, the prior information is explicit and is used to identify optimal designs.

Decision theory is a large topic. The most difficult decisions arise when there is uncertainty

[26] See http://www.mrc-bsu.cam.ac.uk/bugs.

[27] See O'Hagan (2006).

about the consequences of our actions. The uncertainty about consequences is invariably (at least partially) epistemic and cannot be addressed by frequentist methods. A Bayesian approach is quite natural in this situation, and decision makers rarely exhibit any resistance to the idea that such uncertainties should, in principle, be expressed as probabilities. Bayesian decision theory chooses the optimal decision by maximizing the expectation of a utility function that represents the value of different consequences for each possible decision. The expectation in question is taken with respect to the uncertainty in the consequences. The Bayesian development of optimal experimental designs is actually an instance of Bayesian decision theory.

Finally, consider the prediction of future data. Suppose that data on the efficacy of some medical treatment in a sample of patients have been obtained in a clinical trial, and a clinician wishes to predict the response of new patients to this treatment. This is another area where frequentist methods have difficulty. The uncertainty in future data is primarily epistemic. Frequentist approaches introduce aleatory uncertainty by regarding the new patient as randomly chosen from the population of all potential patients, but there is still epistemic uncertainty because, despite the clinical trial data, there is still uncertainty about the true mean efficacy of the treatment.

CONCLUSION

This chapter has tried to explain the essence of the Bayesian approach to statistics, how it differs from the frequentist approach and what advantages have caused it to grow dramatically in usage since the late 1980s. The presentation has not been completely impartial because the author has been firmly committed to the Bayesian framework for more than 30 years. It is also important to recognize that within the community of users and advocates of Bayesian methods there is a diversity of opinion on some issues that could not be fully covered within this chapter. The reader is advised to seek other opinions, to which end there are recommendations for further reading at the end of the chapter.

REFERENCES AND FURTHER READING

Berger, J. O. (2006). The case for objective Bayesian analysis. *Bayesian Analysis*, *1*, 385–402. (Also available from http://ba.stat.cmu.edu/vol01is03.php)

Berger, J. O., & Wolpert, R. L. (1988). *The likelihood principle*. Haywood, CA: The Institute of Mathematical Statistics. (An authoritative text on the subject, although now a bit old)

Bernardo, J. M., & Smith, A. F. M. (1994). *Bayesian theory*. New York: Wiley. (A deep and authoritative text with a huge bibliography. Takes a different stance from that presented here on a number of issues)

Berry, D. A. (1996). *Statistics: A Bayesian perspective*. London: Duxbury. (Teaches a substantial amount of Bayesian statistical methods using only elementary mathematics, with an emphasis on medical applications)

Congdon, P. (2001). *Bayesian statistical modelling*. Chichester, UK: Wiley.

Congdon, P. (2003). *Applied Bayesian models*. Chichester, UK: Wiley. (This and the preceding book concentrate on Bayesian modeling and computation in real, sometimes complex situations)

Gilks, W. R., Richardson, S., & Spiegelhalter, D. J. (Eds.). (1995). *Markov chain Monte Carlo in practice*. London: Chapman & Hall. (Although not up-to-date with many modern developments, this is an excellent introduction to the techniques of Markov chain Monte Carlo)

Goldstein, M. (2006). Subjective Bayesian analysis: Principles and practice. *Bayesian Analysis*, *1*, 403–420. (Also available from http://ba.stat.cmu.edu/vol01is03.php)

Howson, C., & Urbach, P. (1993). *Scientific reasoning: The Bayesian approach* (2nd ed.). Chicago: Open Court. (A book that goes deeply into philosophy of science, but generally quite readable)

Lee, P. M. (2004). *Bayesian statistics: An introduction* (3rd ed.). London: Edward Arnold. (A basic text using college level mathematics)

Lindley, D. V. (1980). *Making decisions* (2nd ed.). New York: Wiley. (Deals with subjective probability and decision making in a very clear and non-technical way)

Migon, H. S., & Gamerman, D. (1999). *Statistical inference: An integrated approach*. London: Edward Arnold. (A modern and concise text handling both Bayesian and frequentist theories at an intermediate level)

O'Hagan, A. (1988). *Probability: Methods and measurement*. London: Chapman & Hall. (An elementary but rigorous treatment of subjective probability, leading into exchangeability and basic statistical ideas)

O'Hagan, A. (2006). Bayesian analysis of computer code outputs: A tutorial. *Reliability Engineering and System Safety*, *91*, 1290–1300. (Also available from http://mucm.group.shef.ac.uk)

O'Hagan, A., Buck, C. E., Daneshkhah, A., Eiser, J. R., Garthwaite, P. H., Jenkinson, D. J., et al. (2006). *Uncertain judgements: Eliciting expert probabilities*. Chichester, UK: Wiley. (A survey of the elicitation of subjective probabilities to build prior distributions)

O'Hagan, A., & Forster, J. J. (2004). *Bayesian inference* (2nd ed., Vol. 2B). London: Edward Arnold. (Assumes a strong background in mathematics and statistics but in a readable style)

7

DESIGN OF EXPERIMENTS

MAURO GASPARINI AND MARIA PIERA ROGANTIN

EXPERIMENTS DIFFER FROM OBSERVATIONAL STUDIES

An experiment is a scientific or technological investigation in which the researcher has a good degree of control over all variables and objects involved. For example, to investigate crop yield in an agricultural study, the researcher can choose the plots of lands to use, the different fertilizers to compare, different tools, times of operations, and so on. This is the framework in which the renowned statistician R. A. Fisher worked in the first half of the 20th century and first laid out explicit principles and methods of the *Design of Experiments* (DOE from now on), illustrated in his landmark book (Fisher, 1935).

This control requirement is what distinguishes an *experimental study* from an *observational study*, in which the researcher observes certain aspects of the real world as it is and is unable to manipulate the way in which certain variables affect other variables or experimental units are chosen.

An example of an experimental study is a clinical trial to compare an experimental treatment to a standard treatment. Suppose, for instance, that a new drug has been developed to reduce blood pressure. The manufacturer of the new drug can test it against the best available therapy to reduce blood pressure. To do this, the company selects a group of patients satisfying certain inclusion criteria, then—for reasons to be discussed later—randomly assigns the experimental drug to half of them and the best available therapy to the other half. In a carefully controlled environment, such as a hospital, clinical researchers observe the two groups of patients over time and measure blood pressure and possibly other efficacy and safety variables. At the end of the study, the company applies statistical methods to produce evidence about the new drug, evidence that may be used to apply to the health authorities for a marketing authorization.

An example of an observational study might be the investigation conducted by a researcher about the lifestyles of two different groups of people to identify health hazards that may previously have been unknown. For example, the researcher may compare smokers and nonsmokers, or people living in areas exposed to different doses of a possibly hazardous pollutant. Clearly, the researcher cannot impose smoking on anybody, or force people to live in a certain area for a long time. All that the researcher can do is to measure retrospectively certain variables and apply statistical methods to compare health measurements, such as blood pressure, in an attempt to identify differential risks.

In a modern experiment, the researcher has *some* degree of control, but not *complete* control. The agricultural experiments Fisher designed in the 1930s are closer to the complete control scenario than most modern researchers are able to achieve. Particularly in the social sciences, where experiments usually involve people, the requirements imposed by a modern society clearly limit the scope and the choices available to a scientist. For example, a clinical trial must satisfy a large number of ethical and legislative concerns, symbolized by the declaration of Helsinki (see http://www.fda.gov/oc/health/helsinki89.html). The company testing a new drug designed to reduce blood pressure, as described above, can only test the new drug on patients after a long series of preclinical tests have shown that it is safe to switch to human beings; it can only test the new drug against the best available therapy to avoid subjecting patients to treatments that are known to be suboptimal; it must halt the trial if there is any evidence of a safety hazard associated with the new treatment; it can only examine patients from whom informed consent has been obtained; and so on.

Experiments should possess certain characteristics that facilitate the direct application of statistical concepts and are desirable properties of any study, following what could be called "principles of good statistical practice." It is, therefore, important for any researcher involved in experimentation to understand these characteristics, which are illustrated in the next section.

A Perfect Experiment Is Comparative, Replicated, Not Confounded, Randomized, Blocked, and Optimal

Control

Experiments are usually conducted to prove something, such as the efficacy of a treatment or the correctness of a new concept or conjecture, and to quantify its effects. It is seldom possible to prove something without a term of comparison, which is why experiments are usually *comparative* in nature.

It is perfectly reasonable to claim that after drinking several glasses of water standing on one leg, all patients suffering from a cold will have recovered. It is equally reasonable to observe that the patients would have recovered in any case, given that a cold usually disappears after a few days.

We often hear politicians claim credit for the positive effects of their policies, but we seldom know whether the positive effects would have occurred anyway. It is a fact of life that, like history, most political actions are not comparative. This is why politics and history are so subject to unresolved controversies, which must necessarily rely on ideological arguments (ideological in a neutral sense).

The term of comparison in an experiment is often called a *control*, and a comparative experiment is also called a *controlled* experiment. This may create a certain amount of confusion with the meaning given to the term *control* in the previous section, but the terminology is widely used.

Replication

Experiments should contain *replicates*, that is, distinct applications of the same experimental conditions to different unrelated experimental units.

The very reason for the existence of Probability and Statistics is that most research, especially when complicated units such as human beings are involved, has to take into account natural and artificial variability. The previous chapters have outlined the construction of stochastic models, as opposed to the deterministic models that characterized the first few centuries of modern science. In no other field are stochastic models more evident than in experimental design, as the output responses of different experimental units to the same controlled inputs are usually different. A specific combination of controlled inputs is called a *treatment*. In the search for regularities that characterizes modern research, the experimenter has to observe the responses in a number of cases before being able to test hypotheses about and estimate the effects of the different treatments.

Increased replication will result in accrual of evidence and increasing reliability of the tests and of the estimates the researcher constructs. Consider estimating a quantitative effect, for example estimating the difference $\mu_T - \mu_C$ between a specific new treatment unknown population mean μ_T and the control treatment unknown population mean μ_C. An estimate of $\mu_T - \mu_C$ may be obtained from n observations $t_1, \ldots, t_n$ obtained under the new treatment and, for simplicity, from the same number of observations $c_1, \ldots, c_n$ obtained under the control treatment: Simply compute the sample mean difference

$$\bar{t} - \bar{c} = \frac{\sum_{i=1}^{n} t_i}{n} - \frac{\sum_{i=1}^{n} c_i}{n}.$$

Using the tools indicated in Chapter 5, it can be shown that a measure of variability of this estimate, that is, an *inverse* measure of its reliability, is its standard error given as follows:

$$\text{standard error } (\bar{t} - \bar{c}) = \frac{\sigma_T + \sigma_C}{\sqrt{n}},$$

where σ_T is a measure of variation in the treatment population and σ_C is a measure of variation in the control population. This decrease in the variability of the estimate of an effect with the square root of the number of observations is the single most important rule of statistics. It shows that its inverse, the reliability of the estimate, increases with the number of replicates, although not proportionally to it.

No Confounding of Causes

When planning an experiment, every effort must be made to ensure that differences between groups can be attributed solely to treatments. In other words, it is necessary to avoid *confounding of causes*. Causality is a very sensitive philosophical issue, and the whole of the next chapter is devoted to this subject. Put simply, however, the identification of causes is what one is looking for when planning an experiment and assigning treatments.

For example, suppose a company has to decide whether the presence of a facilitator makes it easier for a group of workers to perform a certain task. To do this, the company plans an experiment in which two groups of workers perform the task, one group with and the other without a facilitator. Suppose also the company has the group without facilitator perform the task under the usual working conditions, whereas the group with facilitator is set to perform the task in a luxurious hotel in an exclusive resort. Regardless of the outcome of the comparative experiment, the company will never know whether an observed difference between the two groups is due to the facilitator or to the different locations in which the experiment has taken place. The facilitator effect is said to be confounded with the site effect.

Another well-known example of confounding of causes arising in an observational setup is the correlation between age and lung cancer: Since smokers tend to be older, such a correlation is probably an effect of smoking.

The possibility of confounding of causes always arises when *historical controls* are used. When planning an experiment, the researcher may be tempted to use past observations on the control treatment as terms of comparison. For example, in a clinical setup the control treatment may be the best available therapy so far, about which many observations from past experiments are available. This should be avoided, in that one can never be sure that the observed differences are due to an actual difference between treatments or to other confounding causes, including the simple passing of time. Historical controls are not correct DOE, in that good experiments should always have *concomitant controls*.

At a more advanced level, the DOE literature on confounding encompasses a deeper discussion on which parameters can be truly estimated based on the data available. Such a discussion is technical and not covered here.

Randomization

Both known and unknown causes may be confounded with the treatments under scrutiny. In the facilitator example above, the presence of an obvious confounding factor was used purely to illustrate the case of a senseless design only for illustrative purposes. However, even in realistic situations, the researcher can never be certain that all potentially confounding variables have been considered. Ideally, experiments should be performed on statistical units that are as homogeneous as possible so that, once treatments have been applied to different units, differential effects can be measured and attributed to treatments. This is the reason why biologists inbreed guinea pigs for generations to obtain litters of totally identical twins, and why industrial experiments should be conducted on material produced in the same batches by the same operators, and so on. However, from a logical standpoint there is no reason why an undiscovered genetic differentiation of guinea pigs or some hitherto unknown characteristic of production runs should not be confounded with two or more given treatments.

To get round this seemingly inescapable logical difficulty, R. A. Fisher, to whom most of the ideas in this section are due, invented a simple and elegant device: *randomization*. Statistical units, rendered as homogeneous as possible by preliminary human intervention, should nonetheless be randomized to different treatment groups by an independent randomization device such as a table of random numbers or, nowadays, a computer program. Before randomization, every statistical unit should have the same probability, for example 1/2, of being assigned to a specific treatment as any other statistical unit. This way, the researcher can reasonably expect the distribution of unknown differences among statistical units to be similar among different treatments and therefore not confounded with them.

It should be pointed out that randomization is a typical *frequentist* device and is used in experimental design to provide reference distributions for typical frequentist procedures such as hypothesis testing and confidence intervals (see Chapters 2 and 5). In fact, R. A. Fisher was himself one of the founders of the frequentist approach to statistics. Bayesian scientists do not have a uniform opinion of randomization: any moderate Bayesian would probably not oppose to it as a precaution against the harmful effects of a poor choice of prior inputs, whereas an extremely subjective Bayesian would not recognize any merit to randomization.

One further remark: Homogeneity is important, as mentioned above, but one should keep in mind that the results of an experiment are often used to make decisions and take actions regarding the members of a population larger than the small sample strictly involved in the experimentation. Often the more general population will be more variable than the smaller experimented sample and, due to a sheer size effect, exhibit rare events that may not have been observed in the experiment. This is sometimes undesirable and some caution should be used. For example, negative side effects of a drug are often not all observed during the course of the clinical trials that precede the marketing authorization. For this reason, a new marketed drug is usually kept under so-called postmarketing surveillance, that is, a system of reporting side effects as they are observed in the general population of everyday users of the drug.

Blocking

Sometimes the experimental units are naturally not homogeneous in a known fashion. Rather than relying purely on randomization in the hope that the distribution of inhomogeneities will be the same in all treatment groups, the researcher may explicitly incorporate inhomogeneity into the design by creating *blocks*. Blocks are groups of units such that units within a block are more homogeneous than units across blocks.

By introducing block membership as an extra variable affecting our responses, the researcher may improve the efficiency of the design by lowering the variability of the estimates of the effects of treatments of interest. For example, if the blocks are of the same size, the researcher may randomize one half of each block to one treatment and the other half to the control within each block, giving rise to what is called a *completely randomized block design*. This way, block membership will be explicitly recognized in the analysis and the treatment effect will then be purged of any possible block effect.

As an example, consider an agricultural experiment in which plots of land are to be treated with two different fertilizers A and B. The design

A A A B B B
A A A B B B

is certainly not efficient, because the fertilizer effect is confounded with a possible left/right fertility difference the researcher may or may not know. The researcher could then choose a randomized design and assign six plots to A and six plots to B in a random fashion, obtaining, for example, the design

A A B B B A
B A A B B A

But suppose the researcher knows for certain that there is a left to right fertility gradient. A more balanced design choice would be to divide the land into three blocks, left to right, of four plots each, then randomize within each plot. A possible result of this operation might be, for example,

A B B A B A
B A A B A B

Example of natural blocks are the two eyes of a patient, which could be randomized to two different treatments by an ophthalmologist, or the four tires of a car, which could be randomized to four different brands to compare them in a comparative quality experiment run by a consumer association.

Blocking is used in experimentation as a device to take into account inhomogeneous units much as stratification and clustering are used in sampling (see Chapters 11 and 12) for very similar reasons.

Optimality

Optimality is the most technical requirement. Experiments should be planned in such a way that the most can be achieved with the limited amount of resources available. For example, an optimality requirement is that treatments be balanced, in the sense that observations should be taken following certain symmetries, for example that the number of observations per treatment be the same, or that certain treatments be symmetric with respect to their composition. At other times, due to limited resources, only a fraction of all possible treatments can be experimented with, giving rise to fractional designs, which should be carefully chosen to optimize efficiency.

A Response Is Explained in Terms of Predictors

Once an experiment has been designed in the best possible way, it should be run and the results collected and analyzed. The results of an experiment are usually stochastic observations and, as discussed in Chapters 5 and 6, should be analyzed using statistical methods, either classical (frequentist) or Bayesian. For simplicity and for reasons of tradition, most of this chapter is written using the terminology of classical statistics, but the discussion could also be approached from a Bayesian perspective.

The purpose of an experiment is usually to learn about a *response variable*. Response variables may be

- categorical, when they merely denote membership to a class, such as political preference, infection type, or the taste of a new beverage;
- ordinal, when there exists an ordering between their values, but the values are not numbers, such as the condition of a patient (worse, stationary, improved, or much improved) or the ability to perform a certain task (low, normal, or high);
- quantitative, that is, numerical values indicating a real measured intensity, quantity, time, space, and so on.

Quantitative responses are more common, but specialized methods exist also for categorical and ordinal responses.

Responses need to be "explained" in terms of other variables (often more than one) called *predictors*, which can be either pure DOE covariates, that is the variables manipulated, controlled, or assigned by the experimenter, or observational covariates that happen to be of some importance, for example, when using blocks.

Predictors may be categorical or ordinal (in one word, qualitative) variables, in which case the predictor is called *factor* and its possible values are called *levels*. For example, an agricultural response might be yield, measured in tons, while the predictors might be fertilizer and type of soil. The fertilizers under comparison may be a few, say three, and the type of soil may be classified simply into two types, such as acidic and nonacidic. As yet another example, the time it takes for an employee to perform a certain task might depend on the employee's literacy level, degree of stress, and, possibly, gender.

Predictors may also be quantitative but, since the researcher cannot experiment with a large number of values of predictors, often a few representative values of the quantitative predictors will be chosen, making them closer to being a factor. Genuine quantitative predictors will also exist if some concomitant variables, thought to be of some value, are recorded for improving the explanatory value of the statistical model. For example, a certain yield may depend on fertilizer, soil type, and, more specifically, the percentage of sand present in the plot used. In this case, the quantitative predictor is often called *explanatory covariate*. The time it takes for an employee to perform a certain task may depend on literacy and stress, but also on personal pay, an explanatory quantitative covariate. The tasting score of a new beverage may depend on the color and the shape of the bottle but also, obviously, on its sugar content and other ingredients, measured quantitatively.

As mentioned before, predictors sometimes combine to establish the notion of *cause* in the eyes of the experimenter. Even if causes cannot be identified directly, manipulated variables are used in an experiment to predict the value of the response, without necessarily being identified as causes of the values assumed by the response. This is why statisticians like to refer to them using the more neutral term *predictors*.

The mathematical details of the statistical models used in the design and analysis of experiments will not be illustrated here as many good textbooks exist at various levels of abstraction. See, for example, Box, Hunter, and Hunter (2005).

A simple pseudocode description may instead be useful, especially in programming the analysis of an experiment using a statistical package. A basic dependence of a response variable on two factors may, for example, be written as

```
response ~ factorA + factorB    (7.1)
```

This formula clarifies that `response` on the left-hand side is to be explained by the combined *additive* effect, symbolized by the + sign, of `factorA` and `factorB`, plus an implicit error term with mean 0, representing natural variability, which does not appear in the formula but is usually understood. Note that sometimes it is better to transform the response variable by taking logarithms, in which case an additive model for logarithms will actually be a multiplicative one in the original scale.

The reason why this basic model with two predictors is called additive and without interactions, is discussed in the next section.

Understanding Main Effects and Interactions

Consider the combinations of factor A, with three levels coded 1, 2, and 3, and factor B, with two levels H and K. There are six combinations possible, that is six treatments: $1H$, $1K$, $2H$, $2K$, $3H$, and $3K$. Suppose, for the sake of simplicity, that the error is identically zero; in other words, we can observe the mean responses exactly, without variability. This will not usually be the case in real-world situations, where mean responses are instead estimated on the basis of several replicates, but it simplifies the explanation of interactions.

Let μ_{ij} be the mean response of the treatment corresponding to level i of factor A and level j of factor B, with $i = 1,2,3$ and $j = H,K$. A common way of rewriting the μ_{ij}s is as follows:

$$\begin{aligned}
\mu_{1H} &= \mu + \alpha_1 + \beta_H + \gamma_{1H},\\
\mu_{1K} &= \mu + \alpha_1 + \beta_K + \gamma_{1K},\\
\mu_{2H} &= \mu + \alpha_2 + \beta_H + \gamma_{2H},\\
\mu_{2K} &= \mu + \alpha_2 + \beta_K + \gamma_{2K},\\
\mu_{3H} &= \mu + \alpha_3 + \beta_H + \gamma_{3H},\\
\mu_{3K} &= \mu + \alpha_3 + \beta_K + \gamma_{3K}.
\end{aligned} \tag{7.2}$$

The following constraints are imposed:

$$\begin{aligned}
\alpha_3 &= -\alpha_1 - \alpha_2,\\
\beta_K &= -\beta_H,\\
\gamma_{3j} &= -\gamma_{1j} - \gamma_{2j} && \text{for } j = H,K,\\
\gamma_{iH} &= -\gamma_{iK} && \text{for } i = 1,2,3,
\end{aligned}$$

but they are justified on technical grounds and can be ignored at a first reading.

Six different values of μ_{ij}s are rewritten in terms of αs, βs, and γs in an apparently complicated but useful way, since the μ_{ij}s stand alone as response means per se, whereas the latter group of parameters can be given a global meaning as follows.

Suppose first $\gamma_{ij} = 0$. Then μ_{ij}s can be written as

$$\begin{aligned} \mu_{1H} &= \mu + \alpha_1 + \beta_H, \\ \mu_{1K} &= \mu + \alpha_1 + \beta_K, \\ \mu_{2H} &= \mu + \alpha_2 + \beta_H, \\ \mu_{2K} &= \mu + \alpha_2 + \beta_K, \\ \mu_{3H} &= \mu + \alpha_3 + \beta_H, \\ \mu_{3K} &= \mu + \alpha_3 + \beta_K. \end{aligned} \tag{7.3}$$

The parameter $\mu = \sum_{ij} \mu_{ij}/6$ is the *grand mean*, that is, the mean of all mean responses. The parameters α_1, α_2 and α_3 are said to be the *main effects* of the three levels of factor A respectively, since they are the deviations from the grand mean of certain partial means. For example,

$$\alpha_1 = \frac{\mu_{1H} + \mu_{1K}}{2} - \mu.$$

Similarly, β_H is said to be the first main effect (or the main effect of level H) of factor B. Model (7.3) is a mathematically explicit way of representing pseudocode (7.1) and is called a *no-interaction additive model*. It is a parsimonious representation which, if true, allows us to represent each μ_{ij} as an overall average plus the ith main effect of factor A plus the j main effect of factor B. Equivalently, the difference between the μ_{ij} at two specified levels of factor B does not depend on which level of factor A is applied:

$$\begin{aligned} \mu_{iH} - \mu_{iK} &= \mu + \alpha_i + \beta_H - \mu - \alpha_i - \beta_K \\ &= \mu + \alpha_i + \beta_H - \mu - \alpha_i + \beta_H = 2\beta_H, \end{aligned}$$

independent of i. An additive model is pictured in Figure 7.1, where the two lines describing the variation in response at varying levels of factor A for the two levels of factor B are parallel, at fixed vertical distance equal to $2\beta_H$.

Consider instead equalities (7.2), with some γ_{ij}s different from 0. The μs do not have the parsimonious interpretation above and, as we explained, can be rewritten equivalently as formulas (7.2). We can still call the αs and the βs main effects of the two factors, but to obtain the μs we also need various quantities γ_{ij}, called *interaction effects*, or simply *interactions*. For example, the interaction effect of level 1 of factor A with level H of factor B is

$$\gamma_{1H} = \mu_{1H} - \alpha_1 - \beta_H - \mu.$$

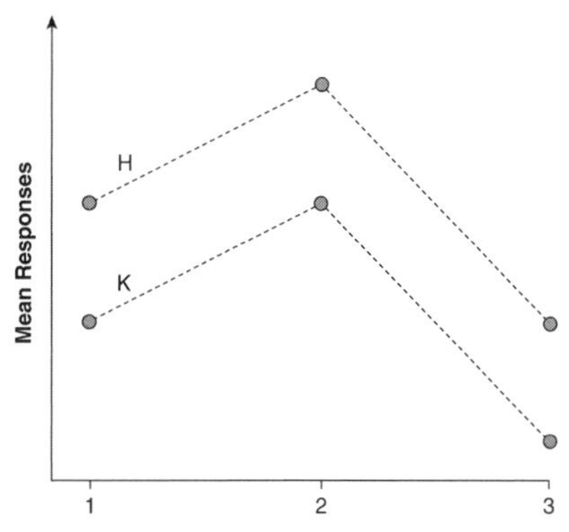

Figure 7.1 No-interaction additive model.
NOTE: On the ordinate, the mean values of the response; on the abscissa, three levels of the factor A. Two separate parallel broken lines corresponding to two levels of factor B.

Similarly, γ_{1K} is the interaction of level 1 of factor A with level K of the second factor, γ_{2H} is the interaction of level 2 of factor A with level H of the second factor, and so on. This model is called a model with interaction. Since the interactions between two factors are not all zero in the simple two-factor model (7.2), they are very important in the explanation of μ_{ij}s. The two lines describing the variation in mean response at varying levels of factor A for the two levels of factor B are not parallel, as can be seen in Figure 7.2.

In the particular case of Figure 7.2, it can be seen that level 1 of factor A and level H of factor B act synergistically to make the average response as high as the mean of treatment $2K$.

The concept of interaction can be extended to the case when one predictor is quantitative (e.g., a covariate) and the other is a factor. The dependence of mean response from a quantitative predictor may be represented, in the simplest case, as a straight line. Suppose mean responses depend on the value of a quantitative predictor according to a certain straight line when the factor is fixed at level H and, when switching to level K of the factor, the straight line is translated to a new position in a parallel way, as in Figure 7.3. Then the linear model contemplating the factor and the covariate as predictors is a no-interaction model, since there is a fixed difference in mean response between the two levels of the factor corresponding to any level of the quantitative predictor.

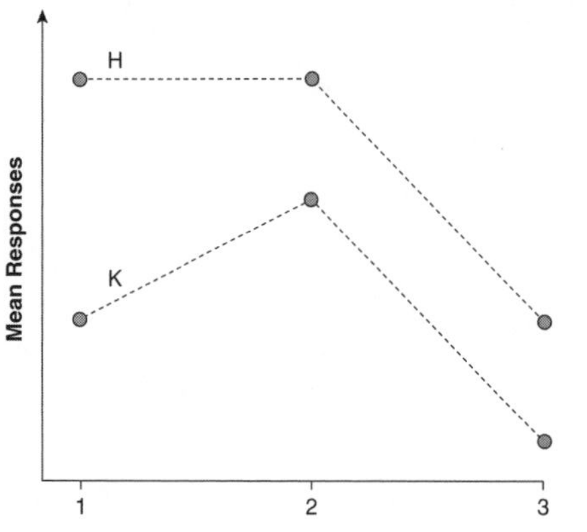

Figure 7.2 Model with some non-null interactions.
NOTE: On the ordinate, the mean values of the response; on the abscissa, three levels of factor A. Two separate broken lines corresponding to two levels of factor B.

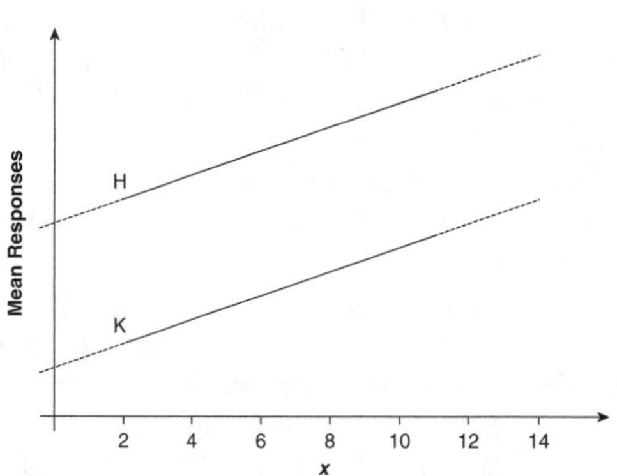

Figure 7.3 No-interaction additive model.
NOTE: On the ordinate, the mean values of the response; on the abscissa, the values of the quantitative predictor x. Two separate parallel lines corresponding to two levels of factor B.

If instead, when switching from one level of the factor to another, the straight line changes not only the intercept, but also the slope, then a non-null interaction is said to be present, as in Figure 7.4.

Interactions and Main Effects Are Tested and Estimated

In real experiments, errors will not be null, as was instead assumed in the previous section to explain

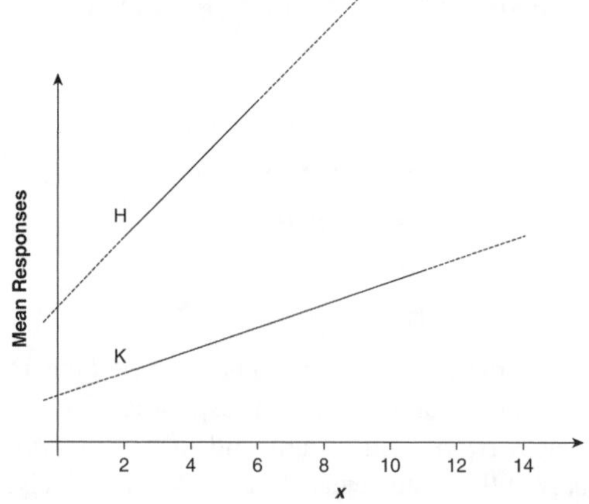

Figure 7.4 Model with non-null interaction.
NOTE: On the ordinate, the mean values of the response; on the abscissa, the values of the quantitative predictor x. Two separate lines corresponding to two levels of factor B.

the concept of interaction in a simplified context. If random errors are thought to add to a systematic component provided by the combination of the predictors to provide a quantitative response, then the result will be a *linear* model. The simplest two-factor additive linear model is pseudocode (7.1)

```
response ~ factorA + factorB,
```

where the error term is understood. Its mathematical description is model (7.3). A more refined model with non-null interations is model (7.2), which can be represented in pseudocode as

```
response ~ factorA + factorB
   + factorA*factorB                    (7.4)
```

where the symbol * represents interaction.

As seen in the previous section, in general predictors may be qualitative (factors) or quantitative and there will be several predictors and their interactions on the right-hand side of pseudocode. Furthermore, the concept of interaction can be generalized to higher-order interactions, for example when three predictors are present, as in pseudocode

```
response ~ pred1 + pred2 + pred3
   + pred1*pred2 + pred1*pred3
   + pred2*pred3 + pred1*pred2*pred3
```

In the presence of observations, the statistical problem arises as to whether the data support the hypotheses of higher-order zero interactions. This can be done, formally, using the technology of hypothesis testing described in Chapter 5. If higher-order interactions do seem null, then we can in turn test whether lower-order interactions are null, still using some tests of hypothesis. If then all interactions appear to be null, we can test whether some of the factors have all zero main effects, depriving them of any explanatory value with respect to the response. If some of the factors are useless, they can be removed from the model, and perhaps other factors introduced, with possibly new data coming from new experiments, and so on. This process of empirical model building has been called the *iterative learning process* and is a fundamental mode of operation for the statistical practitioner.

Once a plausible model has been built, the magnitude of the effects present in the model, whether interactions or main effects, should be estimated together with the uncertainty of the estimates themselves. The theory of estimation has also been described in Chapter 5.

For a researcher in applied social science, the mathematical details of the models used can probably be neglected, whereas the concepts of response, predictor, error, interactions, and so on should be clearly understood. In working practice, a social scientist will use statistical software, possibly in cooperation with a statistician. The software must provide reasonable output based on the state of the art and the specific requirements of the field of application. For example, most current statistical software provides an analysis of variance (ANOVA) table to perform testing in the case of balanced factorial designs, as briefly illustrated in the following section.

AN EXAMPLE: STRESS, ALCOHOL, AND BLOOD PRESSURE

The data in the following example are simulated, but many elements are taken from a real clinical trial. Suppose we want to study the effect on systolic blood pressure (SBP, expressed in mmHg) of a certain factor A with three levels, namely three stress-generating situations, coded 1, 2, and 3. In addition, we want to keep into account the possible effects of a second factor B, standardized alcohol consumption, at nominal levels *H* and *K* (*H* meaning no consumption, and *K* meaning standardized consumption).

SBP *at baseline*, that is, before applying the treatments, is measured first on 12 male healthy volunteers, randomized to the six treatments in a balanced way, two volunteers to each treatment. After randomization, treatments are applied, then SBP is measured again. The trial generates as response variable SBP after treatment (variable `after`), which is to be explained in terms of treatment, that is the combination of the two factors, and possibly the explanatory covariate SBP at baseline (variable `before`). The covariate can be seen as a blocking device, since SBP varies widely across human beings and using SBP at baseline as a covariate is equivalent to using each volunteer as control of himself. Note that we could also use a new difference variable `after-before` as response, but in this case it may be advisable to leave variable `before` as a covariate in order, for example, to be able to test its effects.

The data are collected in a simple rectangular database as follows:

after	before	factA	factB
98.6	99.5	1	H
134.0	133.2	1	H
108.3	108.0	1	K
120.5	118.8	1	K
106.0	108.4	2	H
107.9	106.9	2	H
120.5	120.7	2	K
132.3	133.2	2	K
101.4	97.8	3	H
121.3	115.2	3	H
125.9	119.8	3	K
128.9	125.1	3	K

The first row contains the variable names, then there is one row per volunteer.

Let us neglect at first the baseline values and start the analysis with a simple two-factor interaction model such as model (7.2), in which response `after` is explained in terms of qualitative variables `factA`, `factB`, and their interactions. First, we can produce estimates of the treatment means μ_{ij}, which in this simple, balanced situation will be simple group means:

factA	factB	N	after
1	H	2	116.30
1	K	2	114.40
2	H	2	106.95
2	K	2	126.40
3	H	2	111.35
3	K	2	127.40

It is customary to perform the analysis via statistical software. A package for linear models produces the estimates of main effects and interactions as in the output given in the next page.

For our illustrative purposes, it is sufficient to say that, based on the lines following `Coefficients`, it is possible to reconstruct the estimates of the parameters used in model (7.2), that is, estimates of the αs, the βs, and the γs. The reconstruction is not immediate since a different parametrization is used by the statistical software.

More interestingly, an interaction test can be performed based on the ANOVA table, produced by the statistical package as follows:

```
Analysis of Variance Table

Response: after
            Df  Sum Sq  Mean Sq  F value  Pr(>F)
factA        2   33.66    16.83   0.1036  0.9032
factB        1  376.32   376.32   2.3160  0.1789
factA*factB  2  263.20   131.60   0.8099  0.4882
Residuals    6  974.93   162.49
```

where we can see that, since the so-called *p-value* (column `Pr(>F)`) of the interaction term equals 0.4882, a fairly high value, we cannot reasonably reject the hypothesis of zero interaction, as there would be a chance of about 48% of seeing a value as extreme or more than the one actually observed if the interactions were in fact zero. Note that the main effects are also both nonsignificant, but instead of discussing this let us turn to a more realistic model.

To take covariate `before` into account, we can complicate the model by adding it to the predictors, giving rise to what is sometimes called analysis of covariance (ANCOVA) model. An important step in the analysis is to test whether the two-factor interaction and the baseline are "significant," that is, if there is empirical evidence to support the hypotheses that the interactions are all zeros or that SBP at baseline is useless when predicting SBP after treatment. A more complicated ANOVA (or, better, ANCOVA) table is produced (shown in the next page).

As in the first model above, since the interaction, represented by line `factA*factB` has a high p-value (column `Pr(>F)`), the data do not seem to provide evidence of an interaction between the two factors. As for baseline instead, line `before` has low p-value, which shows that the data support the hypothesis of a linear relationship between SBP at baseline and after treatment, as expected.

At this point, the researcher may choose to remove interactions from the model, retest baseline (just to be on the safe side) and finally test for main effects of the two factors (note that, in the presence of the baseline, the two factors now have a low p-value, making us expect that it will be reasonable to leave them in the model, once interaction is removed). As an alternative, the researcher may decide to leave the interaction term in the model, or return to the laboratory and plan for a new experiment. At some point, the researcher will reach a satisfactory model and will estimate mean responses for different combinations of predictors using tools similar to the ones illustrated with the simpler model.

Social Experimentation Is Difficult

A discussion of the possibility to learn from well-designed experiments in a social context is at hand. We could define a social experiment as one that involves human beings as statistical units.

According to this very general definition, clinical trials (i.e., medical experiments on human beings) are also social experiments. Clinical trials have undergone enormous developments since they were first regulated in the 1960s. The developments include innovative designs, greater scope and applicability, modern ethical regulations, and their application to non–First World countries. The statistical literature has also grown enormously alongside with statistical expertise, and nowadays statisticians are perceived, at least in the major pharmaceutical and biomedical research centers, as equal partners of medical personnel; see, for example, Piantadosi (2005). Clinical trials are a probabilistic success story because in a

```
Call:
lm(formula = after  factA + factB + factA * factB, data = SBP)

Coefficients:
  (Intercept)    factA2  factA3    factBK    factA2*factBK    factA3*factBK
       116.30     -9.35   -4.95     -1.90            21.35            17.95
```

```
Analysis of Variance Table

Response: after
            Df  Sum Sq Mean Sq  F value    Pr(>F)
factA        2   33.66   16.83   7.0710  0.03487 *
factB        1  376.32  376.32 158.0994  0.00005 ***
before       1 1224.24 1224.24 514.3254  0.00000 ***
factA*factB  2    1.99    0.99   0.4176  0.67963
Residuals    5   11.90    2.38
---
Signif. codes:  0 '***' 0.001 '**' 0.01 '*' 0.05 '.' 0.1 '' 1
```

clinical context it is natural and generally agreed to adopt good statistical practice principles such as randomization, controlling, and ethics.

It may be more difficult to replicate this success in other fields of social experimentation such as, for example, intervention studies or training. Proving the success of a training program may be the interest—sometimes vested interest—of some organization. Consider, for example, a situation in which unemployed people are tested on a certain task, perform poorly on the test, are retrained, are finally tested again on a second occasion and perform better. When evaluating whether the good performance on the second occasion is really caused by the retraining program, the researcher should honestly evaluate all possibilities. Would the retested people have improved anyway? Has a control group been used? Has randomization been used, or do units in one group differ systematically from the ones in the other group? May there be confounding causes?

Social experimentation is often difficult, because human beings have fundamental rights and they make for very complex statistical units. Randomization or controlling, for example, may not be possible. Some of these difficulties have already been faced by the discipline of epidemiology, which studies the effects on health of the exposition to environmental risk factors. Epidemiologists would like to identify causes of diseases, much as clinical trialists would like to identify good therapies. (This discussion echoes the examples already mentioned in the section Experiments Differ From Observational Studies.) But epidemiological studies are often—if not always—observational uncontrolled studies: You simply cannot randomize people to risk factors (e.g., smoking) for ethical reasons. Epidemiologists have learned, in the course of time, how to adopt special designs (case-control, to mention one) that allow the use of many statistical tools without surrendering to unrealistic assumptions. Social scientists could learn from epidemiologists and clinical trialists.

Another important kind of social experiments are the psychological ones, where the researcher tries to measure aspects of human personality. A huge difficulty arising here is that the object of measurement itself is difficult to define, let alone test methods and interpretations for it. Part IV of this book covers psychological experimentation in more depth.

Experimentation and Society

Several fields of application of experimental design are of vital importance for society. Modern mechanical and electronic production, for example, rely on experiments to provide products, which are constantly changing to satisfy the requests of fast evolving markets. Modern agriculturists use experimental designs to optimize scarce resources and face an ever increasing world population. But some sectors in which the advantages of experimental designs will be more and more obvious can be identified as follows.

It is often said that the 21st century is the century of biology, in particular molecular biology. After the completion of the decoding of the human genome, genetic experimentation has become an example of the progressive engineerization of biology, which has important and profound implication for our society and our lives. A typical biological postgenomic experiment involves the study of the reactions of some genes or proteins to certain stimuli. The genes and proteins are taken from a sample of biological material, such as a cell culture or a tissue sample, and their activity is measured by sophisticated electronic or nanotech devices.

Modern postgenomic technology is producing an impressive amount of quantitative data that offer hope of solving some of the most critical contemporary medical and environmental problems. The size and complexity of this amount of data requires statistical tools, which are often beyond the traditional education of a biologist. Several new biotechnologies have produced blurred pictures after an initial enthusiasm, due not only to insufficient biological explanation, but also to a predominance of "noise" over "signal." There appears to be extensive scope for applying all the rational tools that modern science has developed in the field of agricultural, medical, and engineering experimentation to the field of biological experimentation.

Strictly related to biological experimentation is clinical experimentation. Many observers of the field speak of *pharmacogenomics* as the new horizon of clinical experimentation. Not only the genetic factors that create predisposition to a disease, but also those that favor the choice of a specific treatment over another are of great interest. The hope is the individualitation of therapy will bring about great benefits. It is expected that genetic driven research will see the greatest development in high-profile fields such as cancer and cardiovascular diseases.

Next, in an engineering context, the expression "design of experiments" is associated to the quality bandwagon. In a global market, continuous improvement of the quality of services and products is a vital necessity for any producer, manufacturer, or service provider. In the last few years of the 20th century, the engineering and business community made great efforts to master the statistical tools necessary for improving quality. Statistical tools are needed to tackle the inevitably large number of sources of variability that affect composite manufacturing and service processes. These tools can be roughly divided into two classes: online tools to monitor quality production and offline tools to experiment with product improvements. Most of the latter technology stems from DOE ideas. In this context, the term *experiment* should be generalized to include virtual experiments that can be run on a computer, also called computer experiments. Interest in these kinds of experiments is prompted by the reduction in costs and times of experimentation that can be brought about by intensive simulation and computational tools.

A related field of experimentation is marketing. DOE techniques are increasingly being adopted to optimize use of the tools available to a business to reach out to customers and to offer better service.

ACKNOWLEDGMENTS

The authors thank John Freeman and Davide Ambrosi for careful reading and suggestions.

REFERENCES

Box, G., Hunter, J. S., & Hunter, W. G. (2005). *Statistics for experimenters* (2nd ed.). New York: Wiley.

Fisher, R. A. (1935). *The design of experiments.* Edinburgh, UK: Oliver & Boyd.

Piantadosi, S. (2005). *Clinical trials: A methodologic perspective* (2nd ed.). New York: Wiley.

8

CAUSATION AND CAUSAL INFERENCE: DEFINING, IDENTIFYING, AND ESTIMATING CAUSAL EFFECTS

MICHAEL SOBEL

INTRODUCTION

This chapter is an introduction to the modern statistical literature on causal inference, which began when Rubin (1974, 1977, 1978, 1980) rediscovered Neyman's (1923/1990) potential outcomes notation and extended the theory of experimental design to observational studies. Workers from other disciplines, for example, economics, have also adopted this framework, sometimes molding it to substantive issues in their disciplines. Although tailored to the concerns of social scientists, this chapter should also be of interest to researchers in public health, psychology, and medicine.

I proceed as follows. Causal inference is the act of making inferences about the causal relation. Thus, it is not possible to compare and evaluate alternative inferential methodologies without discussing causation itself. In the following section, I briefly review several notions of the causal relation, using the discussion to motivate an inferential approach to causation that stems from the requirement that a causal relation sustains a counterfactual conditional statement. The section Unit and Average Casual Effects carries this approach forward, using a notation allowing causal parameters to be defined independently of the methods used to estimate them. Several estimands of interest are defined and discussed. Statistical methods that can be used to estimate causal parameters in observational studies and randomized experiments are considered in the section Identification and Estimation of Average Causal Effect. Methods that can be used when an "ignorability" assumption holds include regression, matching, and matching on the propensity score. Fixed effects regression models and instrumental variables are two methods that can be useful when "ignorability" does not hold. The relationship between instrumental variables and structural equation models is also considered, because the latter are often used to make causal inferences in the social, behavioral, and medical sciences. The final section concludes.

SOME PHILOSOPHICAL CONSIDERATIONS

Hume argued that the causal relation, as it exists in the real world, consists of three components: (1) temporal priority, that is, the cause must precede the effect in time; (2) spatiotemporal contiguity, that is, the cause and effect are "near" in time and space; and (3) constant conjunction, that is, if the same circumstances are repeated, the same outcome will eventuate. Subsequent philosophers have disagreed with all these criteria, arguing that causes and effects occur simultaneously in time, that there can be action at a distance, and that the constant conjunction criterion, which essentially amounts to the idea that the cause is sufficient for the effect, should be replaced by the idea that the cause is necessary (or necessary and sufficient) for the effect, or even by some weaker notion that allows causation to be nondeterministic.

However, the most controversial aspect of Hume's account is the idea that these three components completely characterize the causal relationship. Many philosophers feel that something is missing. For example, Bunge (1979), Harré (1972), and Harré and Madden (1975) have argued that whereas in Hume, the effect is merely that which is preceded by the cause, the causal relation is generative, that is, the cause brings about the effect. This is appealing, especially to modern scientists who speak of mechanisms. But attempts to pin this down by clarifying the notion of a mechanism (or through some other means) have not been entirely successful. (Incidentally, Hume confronted this view directly, arguing that mechanisms, called powers or forces in his time, are mental constructions of observers anxious to "understand" why things happen, not properties of the causal relationship itself.) More generally, while it is easy enough to construct examples of relationships that satisfy Hume's criteria that most persons would not deem causal, it has proven far more difficult to say precisely what is missing from Hume's account.

John Stuart Mill (1843/1973) criticized and refined Hume's analysis in several ways, arguing that causes could be multiple and could consist of conjunctions of events (Hume's analysis does not preclude this). This led him to view a cause (what philosophers call the full cause or philosophical cause) as a disjunction of conjunctions necessary and sufficient for the effect. Mackie (1974) also develops this idea.

Mill also anticipated the modern philosophical literature on causation in several ways that are important for the statistical literature on causal inference discussed herein. Most important (not that his methods reflected this), he argued that the cause must be the invariable antecedent of the effect, by which he meant that a causal statement must satisfy what is now known as a counterfactual conditional statement.

Mill also distinguished between the causes of an effect, the subject of regularity theories of causation (as above), and the effects of causes, the subject of manipulability theories of causation (see Collingwood, 1940/1948, for an early treatment). In the latter type of theory, which is closer to the way an experimentalist thinks of causation, the cause is a state that is manipulated, and the effect is a state following this manipulation, as when one states that turning the ignition on caused the car to start. Such a statement would not satisfy regularity theorists, who would point out that many other conditions must be satisfied for the car to start. To them, these conditions are part of the full cause; to a manipulability theorist, these are part of the causal background (Anderson, 1938). The recent statistical literature on causation is based on the latter type of approach to causation. As I demonstrate below (see also Sobel, 1995), the two approaches are easily reconciled.

There is also a literature on so-called probabilistic causation (e.g., Reichenbach, 1956; Simon, 1954; Suppes, 1970; Yule, 1896). With minor variations, the idea is as follows. First, there is a putative cause Z prior in some sense to an outcome Y. Furthermore, Z and Y are associated (correlated). However, if the $Z - Y$ association vanishes when a (set of) variable(s) X prior to Z is conditioned on (or in some accounts, if such a set exists), this is taken to mean that Z "does not cause" Y. The use of path analysis and structural equation models to make causal inferences is based on this idea. Granger causation (Geweke, 1984; Granger, 1969) extends this approach to time series. The literature on probabilistic causation is problematic because it uses probability to draw causal inferences, but never says what probabilistic causation is (Sobel, 1995). See also Holland (1988) and Sobel (2006c) on the use of structural equation models.

Taking a different tack, some authors have argued explicitly that the causal relationship is probabilistic. However, one need not argue this to use probability to make causal inferences (Sobel, 1995): Probability arises naturally when the statistical approach to causal inference is reconciled with regularity theories of the causal relation. To see this, suppose, as must be the case if the causal relation is deterministic, an outcome y can be described as a function $g(f,b)$, where f (for foreground) and b (for background) are two sets of factors; b may include both known and unknown factors. Suppose the effect of $f(1)$ versus $f(2)$ for a fixed b is defined as $g(f(1),b) - g(f(2),b)$. In virtually any case of interest that is not trivial, the scientist either does not know all the arguments of g (much less g itself) or does not have the ability to measure all the arguments. Thus, the scientist cannot make an inference about this deterministic causal relationship.

Sometimes a much more modest inference can be made. Suppose the scientist takes a random sample from a population $\mathcal{P}$, then uses a fair coin to assign (on average) half the units to receive the value $f(j)$, for $j = 1,2$. He or she does not assign values of the other argument(s), treating these as random variables (whose values may depend on $f(1)$ or $f(2)$). For each unit, he or she then measures the value $Y_i = g(f_i, B_i(f_i))$, where f_i is either $f(1)$ or $f(2)$ and $B_i(f_i)$ is either $B_i(f(1))$ or $B_i(f(2))$, defining the unit effects of $f(1)$ versus $f(2)$ as $g(f(1),B_i(f(1)) - g(f(2),B_i(f(2)))$. By virtue of the random assignment, the set of units receiving $f(1)$ ($f(2)$) constitute a random sample from the set of outcomes $g(f(1),B(f(1))$ ($g(f(2),B(f(2)))$, respectively. The difference between the sample means is thus an unbiased estimator of

$$E(g(f(1),B(f(1)) - g(f(2),B(f(2))). \quad (8.1)$$

I now discuss an approach to causal inference, originating in the statistical literature on experimentation, that relies on averaging (as above) to contend with the problem that only some (not all) causes of the effect are known. Although I shall not discuss the appropriateness or value of this approach generally, several points are in order. First, even if the causal relation is regarded as deterministic, it is not clear that the scientist wishes to know all the causes of a given effect, especially when events that the scientist deems unsystematic and happenstance are determinants. This suggests the scientist wishes to know only the "systematic"factors, and averaging over the unsystematic factors would be a good way to deal with the latter. That said, it is doubtful all "systematic" factors are included in analyses (and were they to be, estimation issues might arise). The approach cannot in general inform us about the interactions among causes in producing the response. Nor can we learn much about the pathways by which a cause produces an effect. That said, approaches purporting to inform us about the way in which causes produces effects (e.g., structural equation models) rest on implicit and often implausible assumptions. A virtue of this account is that it is easily used to reveal such assumptions. Furthermore, this approach, properly implemented, can yield valid inferences about the effects of particular interventions, although it does not indicate in general how or why these work. Whether or not such knowledge is deemed very deep or otherwise, it may nonetheless be of great social value.

Unit and Average Causal Effects

In the modern statistical literature on causal inference, the causal relationship is viewed as singular, in contrast to regularity theories of causation where causal statements about individual events are meaningful only because these belong to a broader class. Various justifications can be given, and the two perspectives can be reconciled, as above. Furthermore, a causal statement must sustain a counterfactual conditional. Thus, stating that going to college caused John to earn more money means that John went to college and subsequently earned y, whereas (the counterfactual conditional) had he not gone to college, he would subsequently have earned $y^* < y$. Note that if we cannot imagine John had not gone to college, it would not make sense to speak of causation in this instance. Note also that only John's education is considered here. Other factors, for example, sex, are treated as part of the causal background.

The key ideas underlying the modern statistical literature on causal inference are that it is meaningful to speak of individual causal effects, which may be heterogeneous, and that a causal statement must sustain a counterfactual conditional. I noted earlier that the first of these ideas can be reconciled with the notion that the causal relation is deterministic. It is also worth noting that not all relationships that sustain a counterfactual conditional are causal (see Mackie, 1974, for an example). Furthermore, in this literature, by virtue of the times at which measurements are taken, causes also temporally precede effects. Some authors (Holland, 1986) have also argued that causes must actually be manipulable. Others have argued that it is enough to imagine a hypothetical manipulation, even if it cannot be implemented.

These ideas may be formalized as follows. Denoting John by the subscript i, let $Y_i(0)$ denote the amount of money John would earn had he not graduated from college and let $Y_i(1)$ denote John's earnings if he graduates from college. To say that acquiring a college degree causes John to earn more money then means $Y_i(1) - Y_i(0) > 0$. However, the scientist does not observe the pair of "potential outcomes" ($Y_i(0)$, $Y_i(1)$), but only one member of the pair; Holland (1986) calls this the fundamental problem of causal inference.

To reconcile this account with regularity theories of causation, suppose the scientist observes the education variable F. Let $Y_i(0) \equiv g(0, B_i(0))$, $Y_i(1) \equiv g(1, B_i(1))$, where $B_i(0)$ is the value of B that occurs if John does not obtain a college degree, and $B_i(1)$ is the value of B that occurs if John obtains a college degree. Some of the arguments may be the same under both treatments, for example, factors prior to or not affected by education, such as income in the family of orientation.

That said, attention herein centers not on knowing g or even taking into consideration jointly education and other factors, but rather the more modest goal of defining and estimating some type of average effect of manipulating or hypothetically manipulating a particular cause or set of causes, in this case education, while the other factors (those in B) run their natural course.

An important aspect of this account is the relativity of causation, discussed by Collingwood (1940/1948) and Anderson (1938). Simply put, the partition into F and B is subjective; the components of F constitute the causal foreground chosen by the investigator and those in B constitute the background. Often investigators invoking one set of causes treat their theory as incompatible with theories that invoke different sets of causes. Clearly, this kind of thinking is misdirected.

The potential outcomes notation was invented by Neyman (1923/1990). It is perhaps the single most important development in the statistical literature on causal inference. As above, this is not the only way one might express the foregoing ideas, but without some way of clearly expressing these mathematically, it is not possible to define causal estimands independently of the methods used to estimate these, making it impossible to formally evaluate alternative methods for causal inference. Furthermore, this notation is simple to use and unlikely to lead a researcher astray.

Using this notation, unit causal effects are defined as a function $h(Y_i(1), Y_i(0))$, for example $Y_i(1) - Y_i(0)$. Averaging these over a population $\mathcal{P}$ gives the average treatment effect (ATE):

$$E(Y(1) - Y(0)) = E(Y(1)) - E(Y(0)). \quad (8.2)$$

The ATE is often a natural parameter of interest. It measures the average effect of universally implementing a new policy, relative to a baseline policy in place; it is also the average effect for a randomly selected element in $\mathcal{P}$. However, because the fundamental problem of causal inference precludes drawing a random sample of the unit effects, estimating (8.2) is not straightforward.

To illustrate these ideas and the problem of making inferences about (8.2) from an empirical study in the simplest possible setting, Table 8.1 records the values of the potential outcomes $Y_i(0), Y_i(1)$ for a population $\mathcal{P}$ of size 12 (remember it is not really possible to observe both values). Also recorded are two different assignment variables: $D_i = 1$ if subject i obtained a college degree, 0 otherwise, and D_i^*, coded in the same way. Finally, the covariate sex (X_i), coded 0 for women and 1 for men, is also recorded.

A sample of size 8 is taken from $\mathcal{P}$. The notation u in the columns headed D and D^* denotes that such units are not in the sample. The unit treatment effects $Y_i(1) - Y_i(0)$ indicate that obtaining a college degree does not always increase earnings; for example, the effect is 0 for

Table 8.1 Hypothetical Data for the Example in the Section "Unit and Average Causal Effects"

Unit	Y_0	Y_1	D	X	D^*
01	0	6	1	0	1
02	2	2	0	0	0
03	3	2	1	0	1
04	2	8	1	0	0
05	2	4	0	1	0
06	4	4	0	1	1
07	5	4	1	1	0
08	2	3	0	1	1
09	4	4	u	0	u
10	6	9	u	0	u
11	10	7	u	1	u
12	6	8	u	1	u

unit 2 and -1 for unit 3. Because the expected value is a linear operator, the ATE can be obtained by averaging the $Y(1)$ column and subtracting the average of the $Y(0)$ column, giving $61/12-46/12=1.25$. To make inferences about the ATE, data from the eight sample units are used. Suppose D is the assignment variable; thus, for unit 1, $D_1 = 1$, indicating that unit 1 receives a college degree. Thus $Y_1(1)$ is observed and the response $Y_1(0)$ is not observed. The observed responses can be used to estimate (8.2):

$$\bar{Y}_1 - \bar{Y}_0 = \frac{\sum_{i=1}^{8} Y_i(1)D_i}{\sum_{i=1}^{8} D_i} - \frac{\sum_{i=1}^{8} Y_i(0)(1-D_i)}{\sum_{i=1}^{8}(1-D_i)}, \tag{8.3}$$

which gives the estimate $20/4-10/4=2.5$. Suppose instead that treatment assignment was governed by the assignment variable D^*. In that case, an estimate of $15/4-11/4=1$ is obtained.

An investigator might wish to know if the college effect differs by sex. This leads to consideration of the average treatment effect within sex X (hereafter ATE(X)):

$$E(Y(1)-Y(0) \mid X) = E(Y(1) \mid X) - E(Y(0) \mid X). \tag{8.4}$$

In $\mathcal{P}$, the six units numbered 1 to 4, 9, and 10 are female; thus, ATE($X = 0$) for the women is $E(Y(1)-Y(0) \mid X=0) = (6+0+-1+6+0+3)/6 = 2.333$; for the men, $E(Y(1)-Y(0) \mid X=1) = 0.1667$. Women benefit more from obtaining a college education than men. Using the treatment variable D, the estimated ATE for the women is $\bar{Y}_{1f} - \bar{Y}_{0f} = (6+3+8)/3-2 = 3.667$, where $\bar{Y}_{1f}$ and $\bar{Y}_{0f}$ are the sample means for women in the treatment and control groups, respectively. A similar calculation gives an estimate of 2 for the men.

But how should these estimates be evaluated? The goal is to estimate (8.2) accurately. From the linearity of expectations, it is clear that one way to do so is to estimate $E(Y(1))$ and $E(Y(0))$ accurately. Thus, if subjects receiving a college degree (not receiving) constitute a random sample from the column $Y(1)$ ($Y(0)$) in Table 8.1, the difference in sample averages (as above) will be an unbiased estimator of (8.2) (and consistent in large samples). Similarly, if female subjects receiving (not receiving) a degree are a random sample from the women's values of $Y(1)$ ($Y(0)$), the difference in the sample averages (for women) will be unbiased for the ATE for women. In the next section, conditions under which the estimators above (and others) are unbiased and consistent for various causal effects are given.

The foregoing example illustrates the basic ideas behind the modern literature on causal inference in a very simple setting; the emphasis on estimating some type of average effect is typical. Because of the fundamental problem of causal inference, it is necessary to compare outcomes between persons in different groups. The resulting estimate is unbiased and consistent for the causal parameter of interest if the data obtained from the treatment and control groups, respectively, can be regarded as a random sample of the population outcomes under these conditions. This highlights the importance of the "assignment mechanism" that sorts subjects into treatment and control groups. Extension to the case with more than two levels of the cause or more than one causal variable is trivial.

An important aspect of Neyman's notation is the assumption that unit i's potential outcomes do not depend on the treatment received by other units. This is the assumption (Cox, 1958) that units do not interfere with one another, and it is part of the stable unit treatment value assumption (SUTVA) (Rubin, 1980). Although standard, there are many instances (especially in the social sciences) where this assumption is not reasonable; this is considered briefly in the discussion.

The ATE is one of many causal parameters that might be of interest. For example, a decision maker (e.g., the subject or a policymaker) might transform the potential outcomes into potential utilities and ask whether average utility (or some other measure of social welfare) is increased. Nor need attention center exclusively on averages or subpopulation averages. For example, Björklund and Moffit (1987) define the marginal treatment effect for those who are indifferent between participating or not in a program (taking or not taking up the treatment) of interest.

If it is possible to draw a random sample from $Y(1)$ and $Y(0)$, as above, it is also possible to estimate their marginal distribution and ask questions that depend on these, for example, whether $Y(1)$ is stochastically larger than $Y(0)$. Doksum (1974) and Lehman (1974) considered quantile treatment effects, the difference between the marginal quantiles of $Y(1)$ and $Y(0)$; these effects have received some attention recently (e.g., Abadie, Angrist, & Imbens, 2002).

Nevertheless, here I focus on various types of average treatment effects, as this should be most useful for applied researchers or persons wishing to obtain familiarity with the subject. I now consider and motivate several parameters that are often of substantive interest. To discuss these, it is useful to make the notation a bit more complicated than before.

First is the intent to treat estimand (ITT). This arises naturally in randomized experiments where subjects do not necessarily take up their assigned treatment, for example, a job training study, where some subjects assigned to receive training do not attend training sessions. In such studies, it is useful to distinguish between the assigned treatment and the treatment received. Let $Z_i = 1$ if subject i is assigned to the treatment group; $Z_i = 0$ otherwise. Consider the two potential outcomes $D_i(0) = 1$ if subject i takes up treatment even though he is assigned to the control group, 0 otherwise; and $D_i(1) = 1$ if subject i takes up treatment when assigned to the treatment group, 0 otherwise. The observed treatment received is $D_i(Z_i)$.

For the response, four potential outcomes may be considered: (1) $Y_i(0,0)$, i's response when he or she is assigned to the control group and does not take up treatment; (2) $Y_i(0,1)$, i's response when he or she is assigned to the control group and takes up treatment; (3) $Y_i(1,0)$, i's response when he or she is assigned to the treatment group and does not take up treatment; and (4) $Y_i(1,1)$, i's response when he or she is assigned to the treatment group and takes up treatment. In studies where subjects assigned to the control group cannot receive the treatment, there is no response of the second type.

The potential outcomes for the response under the two possible treatment assignments may be written as $Y_i(0,D_i(0))$ and $Y_i(1,D_i(1))$, respectively; the former is i's response when he or she is assigned to the control group (and takes up treatment $D_i(0)$), the latter i's response when he or she is assigned to the treatment group. The ITT is defined as the average (over $\mathcal{P}$)

$$E(Y(1,D(1)) - Y(0,D(0))). \tag{8.5}$$

It measures the average effect of treatment assignment (offering the program vs. not offering the program). For example, in a study of the efficacy of birth control methods, the ITT measures the effectiveness (relative to a status quo treatment) of making a particular contraceptive method available, not the effect of actually using the contraceptive. One might object that the ITT is not an interesting parameter because from a scientific standpoint, the effect of the treatment itself is of primary interest. But such an argument ignores the perspective of the policy maker who wants to optimize social welfare. Faced with the choice between two programs (alternative treatments), A, which is very effective but which subjects don't take up, and B, which is less effective, but which subjects are very likely to take up, it is reasonable for the policy maker to choose the program with the larger ITT.

The ITT is likely to be of greatest interest to a policy maker when the policy being evaluated will not require mandatory participation. Here, one might also be interested in the effect of offering the program for those who actually take it up. The following parameter (which is not usually considered in the literature) may be called the "effect of treatment assignment on the treated":

$$E(Y(1,D(1)) - Y(0,D(0)) \mid D(Z) = 1). \tag{8.6}$$

(8.6) is the ITT for those who will actually take up treatment. It combines the effects of treatment with the effects (if any) of assignment; if the latter are 0, (8.6) reduces to the more familiar effect of treatment on the treated considered below.

However, in programs that would require mandatory participation, for example, increasing a sales tax, the average effect of implementing the tax is a natural parameter of interest for both the policy maker and the scientist.

In randomized studies where it is believed that the effect of treatment assignment operates only through the treatment received, the "exclusion restriction" $Y(1,d) = Y(0,d)$ for $d = 0,1$ holds. In this case, the notation can be simplified to $Y(z,d) \equiv Y(d)$. Similarly, in observational studies, subjects are not assigned to treatments. In this case, there is no variable Z and the notation $Y_i(d)$ is used to denote that subject i took up treatment d, as above. In both types of studies, the ATE (8.2) is often of interest, even if subjects take up treatments other than those to which they have been assigned. Here, another parameter of long-standing interest is the "effect of treatment on the treated" (TOT):

$$E(Y(1) - Y(0) \mid D = 1). \tag{8.7}$$

The TOT is the average program effect for those receiving treatment. Some authors claim this parameter is of greater interest than the ATE because the benefits of treatment to those who don't take it up are irrelevant. But were it known that a treatment under consideration were highly effective persons who did not take up this treatment previously may now wish to do so. A policy maker might also want to know the effect of treatment for the untreated, for if this is substantial, he or she might want to pay more attention to delivering the program to such persons. Both considerations suggest the ATE is still of considerable relevance, even in programs with voluntary participation.

Identification and Estimation of Average Causal Effects

Several causal estimands of interest were defined above. All are averages of unit causal effects over $\mathcal{P}$ or a subpopulation of $\mathcal{P}$. If the unit effects could be observed, random samples of these could be drawn from $\mathcal{P}$ and it would be easy to unbiasedly and consistently estimate these parameters. However, as this is not the case, the identifiability of these parameters must be considered.

It is useful to classify approaches to identification and estimation by whether or not the assumption that the potential outcomes are independent of the treatment assignment variable Z (or treatment received D), either conditionally on covariates X, or unconditionally, is made. This is the assumption that treatment assignment is ignorable, and it is key to understanding the literature on causal inference and serves as the basis for much applied work. I first consider this case.

Ignorable Treatment Assignment

To motivate this assumption, consider a large randomized experiment. Here, treatments are assigned without regard to (i.e., independently of) the characteristics of subjects,

$$D(0), D(1), Y(0, D(0)), Y(1, D(1)), X \perp\!\!\!\perp Z, \tag{8.8}$$

$$0 < \Pr(Z = 1) < 1, \tag{8.9}$$

where the symbol "$\perp\!\!\!\perp$" is used to denote statistical independence. Following Rosenbaum and Rubin (1983), when (8.8) and (8.9) hold, treatment assignment is said to be strongly ignorable.

Consider now the ITT (8.5). The observable expectations are $\mathrm{E}(Y(1,D(1)) \mid Z = 1)$ and $\mathrm{E}(Y(0,D(0)) \mid Z = 0)$; in general, $\mathrm{E}(Y(1,D(1)) \mid Z = 1) \neq E(Y(1,D(1))$ and $\mathrm{E}(Y(0,D(0)) \mid Z = 0) \neq E(Y(0,D(0)))$. But if (8.8) holds, the observable expectations reduce, respectively, to $\mathrm{E}(Y(1,D(1)))$ and $\mathrm{E}(Y(0,D(0)))$, and thus the ITT is identified. However, the parameter (8.6) is not identified on the basis of (8.8); intuitively, this is because D is "endogenous."

Often, it is important to know if the value of the ITT depends on the covariates X. If (8.8) holds, the parameter

$$E(Y(1,D(1)) - Y(0,D(0)) \mid X), \tag{8.10}$$

(hereafter ITT(X)) is also identified, because (8.8) implies the potential outcomes are independent of treatment assignment, given the covariates X:

$$D(0), D(1), Y(0, D(0)), Y(1, D(1)) \perp\!\!\!\perp Z \mid X. \tag{8.11}$$

Note also that

$$0 < \Pr(Z = 1 \mid X) < 1. \quad (8.12)$$

Using (8.11), the observable expectations $E(Y \mid X, Z = z) = E(Y(z, D(z)) \mid X = x, Z = z)$ then reduce to $E(Y(z, D(z)) \mid X)$ for $z = 0, 1$.

In a conditionally randomized experiment, randomization is used within subgroups. For example, consider an experiment where subjects are first split by sex, and then 80% of the males and 50% of the females are randomized to the treatment group. Here, if the potential outcomes depend on sex, assumption (8.8) is false. However, treatment assignment is ignorable within levels of X; that is, (8.11) holds. ITT(X) is then identified, and the ITT is obtained by averaging ITT(X) over the marginal distribution of X.

For an observational study with potential outcomes $Y(d)$ for $d = 0, 1$, the assumption $Y(0), Y(1) \perp\!\!\!\perp D$ is often too strong. Rubin (1977, 1978) saw that one way to make valid causal inferences was to view such studies as conditionally randomized experiments:

$$Y(0), Y(1) \perp\!\!\!\perp D \mid X, \quad (8.13)$$

for some set of covariates X. The conditional expectations $E(Y \mid D = d, X = x) = E(Y(d) \mid D = d, X = x)$ are identifiable, and under the additional ignorability assumption (8.13), these reduce to $E(Y(d) \mid X = x)$. Thus, unbiased and/or consistent estimates of $E(Y \mid D = d, X = x)$ are unbiased and/or consistent for $E(Y(d) \mid X = x)$, leading to unbiased and/or consistent estimation of ATE(X). Under (8.13), the parameter TOT(X) $\equiv E(Y(1) - Y(0) \mid X, D = 1)$ is also identified and equals ATE(X). In fact, since $E(Y(1) \mid X = x, D = 1) = E(Y \mid X = x, D = 1)$, TOT($X$) is identified under the weaker assumption $Y(0) \perp\!\!\!\perp D \mid X$; under this weaker assumption, ATE(X) is not identified. Note also that ATE(X) = TOT(X) does not imply ATE = TOT, because the distribution of X may differ for the treated and untreated.

I now consider estimation of causal effects. The simplest case is a large, completely randomized experiment. Here, under random sampling from $\mathcal{P}$,

$$\bar{Y}_1 - \bar{Y}_0, \quad (8.14)$$

where $\bar{Y}_1$ ($\bar{Y}_0$) is the sample average in the treatment (control) group, is unbiased and consistent for the ITT (8.5).

When the conditional ignorability assumption (8.11) holds, but the ignorability assumption (8.8) does not, as would generally be the case in a conditionally randomized experiment, (8.14) is not unbiased and consistent for the ITT. Here, it is necessary to estimate ITT(X) and average the estimate over the distribution of X. For example, suppose X is discrete and there are treatment and control group observations at each level $x \in X$. Then

$$\sum_{\{x \in X\}} \frac{(\bar{Y}_{1x} - \bar{Y}_{0x}) n_x}{n}, \quad (8.15)$$

where $\bar{Y}_{1x}$ ($\bar{Y}_{0x}$) is the mean in the treatment (control) group at level x, n_x is the number of observations at level x, and $n = \sum_{\{x \in X\}} n_x$ is unbiased and consistent for the ITT (8.15).

Unlike the conditionally randomized experiment, in observational studies where (8.11) is presumed to hold for a given set of covariates X, there may be many distinct levels of the covariates and there may not be treatment and control group observations at each level. Thus, the estimator (8.15) cannot be used. This problem and the widespread use of observational studies for causal inference have spurred the development of a large literature on the estimation of causal effects under assumption (8.11). Imbens (2004) gives an excellent overview, from which I draw. He discusses in some detail four types of estimators: (1) regression estimators, (2) matching estimators, (3) approaches based on the propensity score, and (4) methods combining one or more of the other three approaches. Here I focus on the intuition and basic mechanics for these methods (for details on estimation of variances and for results on efficiency, see Imbens, 2004, and references therein).

First consider regression estimators. The basic idea rests on imputing the potential outcomes that are not observed using the regression function from the treatment or control group.

Using (8.13), ATE(X) is the difference between the regression functions $E(Y \mid X = x, D = 1)$ and $E(Y \mid X = x, D = 0)$, and ATE is ATEX(X) averaged over the marginal distribution of X. Under simple random sampling from $\mathcal{P}$, the ATE can be estimated as

$$\frac{\sum_{i=1}^{n} (\hat{Y}_i(1) - \hat{Y}_i(0))}{n}, \quad (8.16)$$

where $\hat{Y}_i(0)$ and $\hat{Y}_i(1)$ are predicted potential outcomes for unit i, based on the estimated regression functions for the untreated ($D = 0$) and the treated ($D = 1$), respectively. Typically, $\sum_{i=1}^{n} D_i\hat{Y}_i = \sum_{i=1}^{n} D_iY_i = n_1\bar{Y}_1$, where Y_i is the observed outcome, so it is not necessary to impute values of $Y(1)$ ($Y(0)$) in the treatment (control) group.

To estimate the TOT, which uses only observations with $D = 1$, note that $\bar{Y}_1$ is unbiased and consistent for $E(Y \mid D = 1)$, so it is not necessary to estimate the regression function $E(Y \mid X = x, D = 1)$. The regression function $E(Y \mid X = x, D = 0)$ is estimated using the controls and, as before, used to impute the values $\hat{Y}_i(0)$ for treated units. Thus, the TOT can be estimated as

$$\frac{\sum_{i=1}^{n} D_i(Y_i - \hat{Y}_i(0))}{\sum_{i=1}^{n} D_i}. \qquad (8.17)$$

Estimates (8.16) and (8.17) are only as good as the imputations, which depend on estimation of the regression function. In many applications, the regression function is specified as linear:

$$Y_i = \alpha + \beta' X_i + \tau D_i + \varepsilon_i, \qquad (8.18)$$

where β is a column vector of parameters, and $E(\varepsilon \mid X, D) = 0$. Under (8.13), τ is the ATE and the least-squares estimate $\hat{\tau}$ is equal to both (8.16) and (8.17). More generally, one might use nonlinear regression for imputing values, or, if the form of the regression is unknown, nonparametric regression. However, if there are many covariates to control for, as is typical in observational studies, the precision of nonparametric regression may be quite low. This problem then spills over to the imputations.

Another problem with regression occurs when there are "regions" with little overlap between covariate values in the treatment and control groups. Imputed values are then based on extrapolations outside the range of the data. For example, suppose the TOT is of interest and a substantial proportion of the treatment group members have "large" values on a covariate X_1, whereas members of the control group are concentrated at the lower end on this covariate. The $Y(0)$ values that are imputed for treatment group members with large values of X_1 then come from extrapolating the control group regression outside the range of the control group data.

In the regression approach, $Y(0)$ ($Y(1)$) is imputed for members of the treatment (control) group using the regression from the control (treatment) group. To estimate the TOT, another method, similar in spirit to nonparametric regression, imputes $Y(0)$ values for treatment group members using the values of one or more "nearby" members of the control group. When the ATE is of interest, $Y(1)$ values for members of the control group are imputed using "matches" from the treatment group. The ATE and TOT can then be estimated as in (8.16) and (8.17).

Many possible matching schemes can be used. A unit can be matched with one or more units using various metrics to measure the distance between covariates X, and various criteria for when two units have covariate values close enough to constitute a "match" can be used. In some schemes, matches are not reused, but in others are used again. In some schemes, not all units are necessarily matched. In practice, matching is most often used to estimate the TOT and works best when the control group is substantially larger than the treatment group, in which case it is often easier to find better matches for the treated units.

While matching is intuitively appealing, insufficient overlap of covariates in the treatment and control groups is also problematic here. Some matches will then be of poor quality. One alternative is not to match in this case, but then the quantity estimated is no longer the TOT or ATE. Abadie and Imbens (2002) have also shown that estimators based on matching on covariates often have poor large sample properties.

In an important paper, Rosenbaum and Rubin (1983) proved that when (8.13) holds,

$$Y(0), Y(1) \perp\!\!\!\perp D \mid e(X), \qquad (8.19)$$

where $e(X)$ is the "propensity score" $\Pr(D = 1 \mid X)$. If also $0 < e(X) < 1, 0 < \Pr(D = 1 \mid e(X)) < 1$. Then, it suffices to match on the scalar propensity score, which is a many to one function of the covariates X. This is useful because the $e(X)$ values may overlap "sufficiently" even if the X values do not.

The propensity score can also be used in the regression-based approach. Using $e(X)$ (as against X) has two potential advantages. First, regression functions can be estimated nonparametrically more precisely using $e(X)$ than X.

Second, the extrapolation problem may be lessened (though lack of overlap in the propensity scores is still a frequent problem in empirical work). However, the gain from using $e(X)$, as against X, is somewhat illusory, because in observational studies satisfying (8.13), the propensity score is unknown and must be estimated. Thus, the dimensionality issue is simply transferred from estimation of the regression function to estimation of the propensity score.

Matching on propensity scores has been widely used in empirical work. Corollary 4.1 in Rosenbaum and Rubin (1983) shows that the ATE can be estimated by drawing a random sample $e(X_1),\ldots,e(X_n)$ from the distribution of $e(X)$, then randomly choosing a unit from the treatment group and the control group with this value $e(x)$, taking the difference $Y(1)-Y(0)$, and then averaging the n differences. To estimate the TOT, one could proceed as above, sampling from the distribution of $e(X)$ among the n_1 treated members of the sample. More commonly, each treated unit is matched to one or more control group units and the TOT is estimated using (8.17). This works best when there are many more controls than treated. In practice, lack of overlap between the propensity scores in the control and treatment groups can be problematic. If poor matches are used, bias is increased, but if no matches are made when the overlap is deemed insufficient, the parameter estimated is an average treatment effect on the intersection of the support of the propensity score in the two groups. This parameter may not be of general interest.

Another approach is to adjust the standard estimator (8.14) to account for the imbalance in the covariates across the two groups; by (8.19), it suffices to adjust for the imbalance in the propensity scores. This may be done by weighting the observations. Using this approach, the ATE may be estimated as

$$\frac{\sum_{i:D_i=1} Y_i/\hat{e}(X_i)}{\sum_{i:D_i=1}(\hat{e}(X_i))^{-1}} - \frac{\sum_{i:D_i=0} Y_i/(1-\hat{e}(X_i))}{\sum_{i:D_i=0}(1-\hat{e}(X_i))^{-1}}. \tag{8.20}$$

The TOT may be estimated using

$$\bar{Y}_1 - \frac{\sum_{i:D_i=0} Y_i\hat{e}(X)_i/(1-\hat{e}(X_i))}{\sum_{i:D_i=0}(\hat{e}(X_i)/1-\hat{e}(X_i))}. \tag{8.21}$$

Rosenbaum and Rubin (1983) also discuss the use of subclassification on the estimated propensity score. Subclassification may be thought of as a very crude form of nonparametric regression. Here the unit interval is divided into L equal length intervals. The ATE (within interval I_ℓ), $\ell = 1,\ldots,L$, can be estimated as

$$\frac{\sum_{i\in I_\ell} D_iY_i}{\sum_{i\in I_\ell} D_i} - \frac{\sum_{i\in I_\ell}(1-D_i)Y_i}{\sum_{i\in I_\ell}(1-D_i)}. \tag{8.22}$$

The ATE is then estimated by averaging the estimates (8.22), with weights

$$\frac{\sum_{i=1}^{n} 1_{A(\ell(i))}}{n},$$

where $1_{A(\ell(i))} = 1$ if $i \in I_\ell$, 0 otherwise. The TOT can be estimated using weights

$$\frac{\sum_{i=1}^{n} 1_{B(\ell)}(i)}{\sum_{i=1}^{n} D_i},$$

where $1_{B(\ell)}(i)) = 1$ if $i \in I_\ell$ and $D_i = 1$, 0 otherwise.

For generalizations of the propensity score to multiple groups, see Imbens (2000). For the case of a continuous treatment, see Imai and van Dyk (2004).

When Ignorability Fails

If the ignorability (or ignorability given covariates) assumption is not reasonable, other procedures must be used to identify or bound causal effects. In a short review, it is not possible to do justice to this subject. Therefore, attention is focused on two important approaches: (1) fixed effects regression models and (2) instrumental variables.

I do not consider bounding causal effects (Manski, 1990; Robins, 1989). Bounds are intellectually appealing because the overly strong assumptions that are often used to point identify causal effects are replaced by weaker assumptions, yielding more principled inferences. However, in practice, the bounds are often too wide to be useful. At the other extreme, the treatment assignment process can be modeled and adjustments for the lack of ignorability made. As such methods can be very sensitive to modeling assumptions that are often difficult to defend (Vella, 1998), I do not consider these further.

Recently, there has been renewed interest in causal inference for the case where subjects are assigned to treatment and control groups using "risk-based" allocation schemes (Finkelstein, Levin, & Robbins, 1996a, 1996b); social and behavioral scientists call this a "regression discontinuity design" (Hahn, Todd, & van der Klaauw, 2001; Thistlethwaite & Campbell, 1960). Here, subjects are assigned to treatment and control groups using a known deterministic rule, for example, $Z = 1$ if $X > 0$, 0 otherwise. In this case, $\Pr(Z = z \mid X = x, Y(0) = y(0), Y(1) = y(1)) = \Pr(Z = z \mid X = x)$, that is, treatment assignment is ignorable, given X. However, $\Pr(Z = z \mid X = x) = 0$ or 1. That is, all subjects with a given value of X are allocated to the treatment (control) group. This is the extreme form of the case where the covariates take nonoverlapping values in the treatment and control groups. Recently, some authors have focused on estimating the causal effect in a "small" neighborhood in which some subjects are allocated to the treatment group, others to the control group. (For example, above one might consider estimating the causal effect on the interval $(-0.1, 0.1)$.) Although this does not actually solve the problem, if it is reasonable to believe the regression functions are sufficiently smooth it may also be reasonable to believe the causal effect can be estimated more or less precisely on a small neighborhood. But this "local" estimate may not be of much interest. However, if the level of scientific knowledge supporting an application is high, the objections above are not insurmountable (Finkelstein et al., 1996b). I now consider fixed effects models.

The use of fixed effects models (including the special case of differences in differences) in conjunction with longitudinal data has a long history. Applications using different types of data structures, for example, siblings in a family, have also been considered. For illustrative purposes, suppose the data are from a panel study. The idea behind fixed effects is that bias due to (constant) omitted variables can be "controlled" for using observations on the same individual over time, and on the same time over individuals. Suppose the outcome is metrical. The researcher considers the linear regression

$$Y_{it} = \alpha + \beta' X_{it} + \tau D_{it} + \gamma_1 \eta_i + \gamma_2 \zeta_t + \varepsilon_{it}, \quad (8.23)$$

where X_{it} is the covariate vector for subject i at time t, $t = 1, \ldots, T$, $D_{it} = 1$ if i receives treatment at time t, 0 otherwise, η_i is a subject specific unobserved variable constant over time and ζ_t is a time-specific unobserved variable constant over subjects. The parameters are identified using the definition $\mathrm{E}(\varepsilon_{it} \mid X_{it}, D_{it}, \eta_i, \zeta_t) = 0$. Thus,

$$\begin{aligned} E(Y_{it} \mid X_{it}, D_{it}, \eta_i, \zeta_t) &\\ = E(Y_{it} \mid X_{it}, D_{it}, \eta_i, \zeta_t) &\\ = \alpha + \beta' X_{it} + \tau D_{it} + \gamma_1 \eta_i + \gamma_2 \zeta_t. & \quad (8.24) \end{aligned}$$

Because there are repeated measures on the same individual and many individuals at each time, the fixed effects $\gamma_1 \eta_i$ and $\gamma_2 \zeta_t$ can be identified; consequently, the "treatment effect" τ is identified.

The description above is conventional. To clarify the assumptions made, I now recast it in terms of potential outcomes. Assuming the potential outcomes can be written as below (a big assumption) consider the causal model:

$$\begin{aligned} Y_{it}(d) = \alpha^{(c)} + \beta'^{(c)} X_{it} + \tau^{(c)} d &\\ + \gamma_1^{(c)} \eta_i + \gamma_2^{(c)} \zeta_t + \varepsilon_{it}(d), & \quad (8.25) \end{aligned}$$

for $d = 0, 1$. The model is identified using the definition $E(\varepsilon_{it}(d) \mid X_{it}, \eta_i, \zeta_t) = 0$. Consequently,

$$\begin{aligned} E(Y_{it}(d) \mid X_{it}, \eta_i, \zeta_t) &\\ = \alpha^{(c)} + \beta'^{(c)} X_{it} + \tau^{(c)} d &\\ + \gamma_1^{(c)} \eta_i + \gamma_2^{(c)} \zeta_t. & \quad (8.26) \end{aligned}$$

As the model is linear, $\tau^{(c)}$ is both the conditional and unconditional ATE. In general, the parameters of (8.24) and (8.26) are not identical. They are identical if

$$Y_{it}(d) \perp\!\!\!\perp D_{it} \mid X_{it}, \eta_i, \zeta_t. \quad (8.27)$$

That is, although treatment is not ignorable given the observed covariates X_{it}, given these, the latent temporal component ζ_t and the latent person-specific variable η_i, treatment is ignorable. Note that under (8.27), $\tau^{(c)}$ is also the TOT.

Fixed effects models only take into account unobserved heterogeneity that does not vary. Using this approach can necessitate using a sample unrepresentative of the population to which inference is desired. For example, researchers have studied the effect of different environments on adult outcomes using monozygotic twins; the results may not generalize well to a broader population. Fixed effects models can also be difficult to estimate when the response is not metrical or the model is nonlinear. Finally, the implicit assumption in (8.27) that covariates whose values change over time are not affected by outcomes at previous times is also problematic in many applications.

In a randomized experiment, assumption (8.8) is reasonable. Under (8.8), the average effect of Z on D, $E(D(1)-D(0))$, and the average effect of Z on Y, the ITT (8.5), are identified. However, treatment received (D) is not ignorable, creating problems when the effect of D on Y is of interest. To estimate this effect, some authors have used per-protocol analyses, discarding data from control (treatment) group subjects who take up (do not take up) treatment. If many cases are discarded and these are "not like" those retained, this analysis may be very misleading. Others have analyzed the data by treatment received. Here, subjects in the control (treatment) group who take up (do not take up) treatment are lumped together with subjects in the treatment (control) group who take up (do not take up) treatment. Nor does this analysis account for the fact that D is self-selected.

Instrumental variable (IV) procedures date back to the 1920s and the work of the geneticist Sewall Wright (or his father, Philip). The rationale offered in many econometrics texts (for the case of linear regression) is that D and ε are correlated in the equation

$$Y_i = \alpha + \beta' X_i + \tau D_i + \varepsilon_i. \tag{8.28}$$

Thus, $E(\varepsilon \mid X=x, D=d) \neq 0$. However, if a variable Z "affects" Y only by affecting D, which is taken to imply Z and ε are uncorrelated, $E(\varepsilon \mid X, Z) = 0$, implying $E(Y \mid X, Z) = \alpha + \beta' X + \tau E(D \mid Z)$. Thus, if $E(D \mid Z=1) - E(D \mid Z=0) \neq 0$,

$$\tau = \frac{E(Y \mid X, Z=1) - E(Y \mid X, Z=0)}{E(D \mid Z=1) - E(D \mid Z=0)}. \tag{8.29}$$

The IV estimand has been used for various purposes, including making inferences about the effect of an "endogenous" treatment D. But the rationale above is unclear. To understand the meaning of the IV estimand, it is useful to use potential outcomes, as in Imbens and Angrist (1994), Angrist, Imbens, and Rubin (1996), and Holland (1988).

I assume the instrument Z is binary and randomly assigned. Two cases are considered: (1) D is binary and (2) D is continuous. For "early" treatments of these cases, see Bloom (1984) and Holland (1988).

Following Angrist et al. (1996), let Z_i denote the treatment to which unit i is assigned, with $Z_i = 1$ if unit i is assigned to the control group, 0 otherwise. For $z = 0, 1$, consider the potential outcomes $D_i(0)$ and $D_i(1)$, respectively, the treatment i takes up when assigned to the control group and the treatment i takes up when assigned to the treatment group; $D_i(Z_i)$ is i's observed treatment. Similarly, for $z = 0, 1$ and $d = 0, 1$, let $Y_i(z, d)$ denote the response when i is assigned to treatment z and receives treatment d; let $Y_i(Z_i, D_i(Z_i))$ denote i's observed response.

The ITT is a weighted average over four compliance types: (1) compliers, with $D_i(0) = 0$, $D_i(1) = 1$; (2) never takers, with $D_i(0) = 0$, $D_i(1) = 0$; (3) always takers, with $D_i(0) = 1$, $D_i(1) = 1$; and (4) defiers, with $D_i(0) = 1$, $D_i(1) = 0$. Often it is reasonable to assume there are no defiers. Never takers and always takers receive the same treatment regardless of treatment assignment, so if there is an effect of treatment assignment Z on Y among these types, it cannot be due to treatment. In some applications, it will also be reasonable to assume that the effect of treatment assignment operates only through treatment, that is, there is no "direct effect" of treatment assignment on Y. Assuming there are no defiers and that the effect of Z on Y is 0 for the never takers and the always takers, the ITT (8.5) reduces to

$$\begin{aligned} &E(Y(1, D(1)) - Y(0, D(0))) \\ &\quad = E(Y(1,1) - Y(0,0)) \\ &\quad\quad \times \Pr(D_i(0) = 0, D_i(1) = 1). \end{aligned} \tag{8.30}$$

Since $\Pr(D_i(0) = 0, D_i(1) = 1) = E(D(1) - D(0))$, provided this is not 0, the IV estimand is the average causal effect of Z on Y for the compliers. If the direct effect of treatment assignment on

Y for the compliers is 0, the IV estimand (8.29) is also the effect of D on Y in this subpopulation; this is sometimes called the local average treatment effect (LATE).

Substantively, the result above may be discouraging. Since compliance is only partially observed, the compliers are a latent subpopulation. It is impossible to identify and treat only these persons. Furthermore, the substantive questions researchers typically ask are "global." Thus, Angrist et al. (1996) asked about the effect of the Vietnam War on excess civilian mortality (not the effect among compliers). They used the draft lottery as an instrument. For every date in a particular birth cohort, a number from 1 to 365 was randomly assigned, then applied to subjects with that birthdate. For each cohort, subjects with a "high enough" number were not called up. Subjects in college due to be called up were allowed a postponement to continue college, and many students avoided serving by remaining in college. If the compliers constitute the overwhelming majority of the population and/or the other types have similar effects, LATE may be a parameter of interest. When the compliers are a small fraction of the population, as in this example (about 16%), LATE may not address an interesting question or be useful for evaluating a social policy under consideration.

It is also important to remember that the exclusion restriction is a very strong assumption, even in randomized experiments (where subjects are not blinded to their assignment). For example, during the Vietnam War, some of the never takers with low draft numbers may have remained in college to avoid the draft, creating an effect on mortality due to education.

The foregoing work makes an important methodological contribution by clarifying the meaning of the IV estimand for the widely encountered case of a binary endogenous treatment. (For an extension to a discrete metrical variable, see Angrist & Imbens, 1995.) Researchers can then ask whether or not LATE generalizes to other parameters of interest, such as the TOT and ATE. For example, TOT is a weighted average of LATE and the average effect of treatment among always takers (TOA); therefore, if the values of TOA and LATE are the same, the values of LATE and TOT are identical. There is another important case where LATE = TOT. In programs where subjects in the control group cannot take up treatment, for example, various job training programs, there are no always takers.

I now consider the case where D is continuous. Substantively, this arises when the researcher believes the effect of Z on the outcome Y stems from the effect Z has on an intervening variable(s) (mediator(s)) D that in turn affect Y. In psychology and medicine, structural equation models (SEMs) are often used to estimate the effect of D on Y (see, e.g., MacKinnon & Dwyer, 1993); this is problematic (Holland, 1988; Sobel, 1998, 2006c).

SEMs were first examined using potential outcomes by Holland (1988), who considered a hypothetical encouragement study with subjects randomly assigned to receive encouragement ($Z = 1$) or not ($Z = 0$) to study for a test. He assumed the effect of encouragement on the test score Y was mediated by the amount of time studied (D). He defined the unit level "total" effects of Z on D and Y, respectively, as $D_i(1) - D_i(0)$ and $Y_i(1, D_i(1)) - Y_i(0, D_i(0))$. He also defined hypothetical outcomes $Y(z, d)$ for all z and d, using these to define "pure" effects of Z on Y as $Y_i(1, d) - Y_i(0, d)$ (assuming this has the same value for all d) and the effect of D (for values d vs. d^*, say) on Y as $Y_i(z, d) - Y_i(z, d^*)$ (assuming this has the same value for $z = 0, 1$).

Holland argued that the "direct effect" of D on Y in the SEM for Z, D, and Y should not be endowed with a causal interpretation. He showed that when the effect of D on Y is linear, all effects have the same value for all individuals (the assumption of constant effects), encouragement has a nonzero effect on D, and the pure effect of encouragement Z on test score Y is 0, the IV estimand (8.29) can be interpreted as the causal effect on Y of a one unit increase in D.

Because the constant effects assumption is almost always implausible in the social and behavioral sciences, Holland's results are of limited utility for empirical researchers. And as this assumption is neither weaker nor stronger than those required to justify using SEMs (Sobel, 2006c), SEMs may sometimes be useful when the constant effects assumption is unreasonable. Nevertheless, the assumptions needed to justify using SEMs are also typically too strong.

Sobel (2006c) replaces the constant effect assumption with a weaker condition, showing that IV estimand (8.29) can still be interpreted as the average effect of a one unit increase in D (assuming the other assumptions hold). Importantly, this condition is also weaker than that needed to justify structural equation modeling (when the other assumptions justifying the use of the IV estimand hold). Nevertheless, this weaker condition is not innocuous. Researchers need to evaluate its plausibility on a case-by-case basis.

In the hypothetical example above, compliance is not an issue: subjects are exposed to encouragement or not and they choose to study a certain number of hours. But in many randomized studies where mediation is of interest and compliance is less than perfect, it is no longer clear how to interpret the IV estimand.

Sobel (2006c) combines the case of a continuous mediator with the case of compliance discussed above, thereby incorporating the previous results on IV into one general framework. Assuming Z affects treatment received D, the effect of the continuous mediator D on Y among compliers can also be equated with the IV estimand (8.29) under a few additional conditions. As above, the complier effect may or may not be of general interest. As before, when there are no always takers, as in programs where subjects cannot receive the treatment except through the program, the IV estimand can be interpreted as the average effect (among the treated) on the outcome of a one unit increase in the mediator.

The results above are for the case of a single mediator, but in most applications, there are several pathways, hence more than one causal parameter of interest. To identify these parameters, the number of treatment groups must be increased and/or covariate information incorporated into the picture. This topic could benefit from further work; for some suggestions, see Genetian, Morris, Bos, and Bloom (2005).

Finally, the case of a continuous mediator could also be approached using the idea of principal stratification (Frangakis & Rubin, 2002). In the case of compliance, the analysis is conditioned on the four values of the potential "endogenous" treatment variables $(D(0), D(1))$. These outcomes are unaffected by the treatment assignment and constitute the four principal strata. Jo (2006) considers the use of principal stratification for the case of a binary mediator; although the problem is formally identical to that of compliance, distinct substantive issues arise. More generally, following this approach, the idea would be to condition on all the potential values $(D(0), D(1))$. One could also extend this to the case where there is a mediator and compliance is also at issue.

In nonrandomized studies or studies with no "natural experiment" yielding a randomized instrument, assumption (8.8) is usually implausible, but (8.11) may be credible. When D is binary, this leads to estimating the parameter LATE(X); LATE is then estimated by averaging over the distribution of X. Similar remarks apply when D is continuous. In both cases, a researcher considering using IV should consider both the issues previously raised and the reasonableness of the ignorability assumption (8.11).

Discussion

During the past three decades, statisticians and others have developed a literature on causal inference where the idea that the causal relation sustains a counterfactual conditional statement is given formal expression using an appropriate notation that allows causal parameters to be defined independently of their estimators. The use of this notation also facilitated understanding the conditions under which various estimators are unbiased (and/or consistent) for these parameters, with the idea of ignorability playing a key role. Certainly, this idea was understood informally in some quarters beforehand, as evidenced by the belief that randomized experiments had greater internal validity than observational studies (Campbell & Stanley, 1963). However, expressing these ideas formally has been very important, especially for social scientists working with observational studies, who have been slow to understand the limited value such studies often have for making causal inference.

As understanding has increased and many social scientists have come to regard structural modeling (as in econometrics) as a failure, enthusiasm for randomized experiments, as well as natural experiments, for example, the Vietnam draft lottery, has grown. Another example occurs when one administrative district institutes a law and another (judged comparable) does not; a before-after comparison of the two jurisdictions then estimates the effect of the law, for example, the effect of a change in the minimum wage on employment. This approach, which has a long history and is a special case of fixed effects, is now called "differences in differences." Yet another example (the case of risk-based allocation) occurs when students are assigned to a remedial reading course based on their test score. In all these cases, the literature on causal inference has clarified the assumptions that are made when data from such studies are used to infer causation. Ironically (given the desire to use such studies in lieu of structural modeling), these assumptions are often too strong. In addition, there is the matter of external validity. Investigators using natural experiments have no control over the treatment, either its form or levels, or over the population to which it is applied. Unless these fortuitously coincide with the treatment(s) and population of interest, the analysis may not answer an interesting or useful question.

Many challenges remain. For social scientists, one of the these is to develop suitable approaches when SUTVA does not hold. This is an important and large topic and little work has been done. Halloran and Struchiner (1995) studied this problem in the context of infectious diseases. Letting vaccination status denote the treatment, whether or not a person becomes infected can depend not only on the person's own vaccination status, but also on that of others. For example, consider the case of a person who is not vaccinated when everyone else in the population is vaccinated and the case where neither that person nor anyone else in the population is vaccinated. Sobel (2006a, 2006b) has studied this problem in the context of neighborhood effects, both in observational and randomized studies. He examines the recent "Moving to Opportunity Demonstration." In five American cities, residents of housing projects in poor neighborhoods who attended a group session and enrolled in the demonstration were randomly assigned to either a control group, a standard group, or an experimental group that received a housing voucher plus other assistance to move to a neighborhood with a poverty rate less than 10%. Because subjects were recruited from a few projects in group sessions, some subjects knew one another and SUTVA is almost certainly violated. Sobel (2006b) showed that when SUTVA fails, mean differences between groups no longer estimate average causal effects. Similar remarks apply to regression adjusted estimates. Nor does the IV estimand (or the IV estimand adjusted for covariates) estimate LATE.

REFERENCES

Abadie, A., Angrist, J., & Imbens, G. (2002). Instrumental variables estimation of quantile treatment effects. *Econometrica, 70*, 91–117.

Abadie, A., & Imbens, G. (2002). *Simple and bias-corrected matching estimators for average treatment effects* (NBER Technical Working Paper No. 283). Cambridge, MA: National Bureau of Economic Research.

Anderson, J. (1938). The problem of causality. *Australasian Journal of Psychology and Philosophy, 16*, 127–142.

Angrist, J. D., & Imbens, G. W. (1995). Two stage least squares estimation of average causal effects in models with variable treatment intensity. *Journal of the American Statistical Association, 90*, 431–442.

Angrist, J. D., Imbens, G. W., & Rubin, D. B. (1996). Identification of causal effects using instrumental variables. *Journal of the American Statistical Association, 91*, 444–472.

Björklund, A., & Moffit, R. (1987). The estimation of wage gains and welfare gains in self-selection models. *The Review of Economics and Statistics, 69*, 42–49.

Bloom, H. S. (1984). Accounting for no-shows in experimental evaluation designs. *Evaluation Review, 8*, 225–246.

Bunge, M. A. (1979). *Causality and modern science* (3rd ed.). New York: Dover.

Campbell, D. T., & Stanley, J. C. (1963). *Experimental and quasi-experimental designs for research*. Chicago: Rand McNally.

Collingwood, R. G. (1948). *An essay on metaphysics*. Oxford, UK: Oxford University Press. (Original work published 1940)

Cox, D. R. (1958). *The planning of experiments*. New York: Wiley.

Doksum, K. (1974). Empirical probability plots and statistical inference for nonlinear models in the two-sample case. *Annals of Statistics, 2*, 267–277.

Finkelstein, M. O., Levin, B., & Robbins, H. (1996a). Clinical and prophylactic trials with assured new treatment for those at greater risk: I. A design proposal. *American Journal of Public Health, 86*, 691–695.

Finkelstein, M. O., Levin, B., & Robbins, H. (1996b). Clinical and prophylactic trials with assured new treatment for those at greater risk: II. Examples. *American Journal of Public Health, 86*, 696–702.

Frangakis, C. E., & Rubin, D. B. (2002). Principal stratification in causal inference. *Biometrics, 58*, 21–29.

Genetian, L. A., Morris, P. A., Bos, J. M., & Bloom, H. S. (2005). Constructing instrumental variables from experimental data to explore how treatments produce effects. In H. S. Bloom (Ed.), *Learning more from social experiments: Evolving analytic approaches* (pp. 75–114). New York: Russell Sage Foundation.

Geweke, J. (1984). Inference and causality in economic time series models. In Z. Griliches & M. E. Intriligator (Eds.), *Handbook of econometrics* (Vol. 2, pp. 1101–1144). Amsterdam: North-Holland.

Granger, C. W. (1969). Investigating causal relationships by econometric models and cross-spectral methods. *Econometrica, 37*, 424–438.

Hahn, J., Todd, P., & van der Klaauw, W. (2001). Identification and estimation of treatment effects with a regression-discontinuity design. *Econometrica, 69*, 201–209.

Halloran, M. E., & Struchiner, C. J. (1995). Causal inference in infectious diseases. *Epidemiology, 6*, 142–151.

Harré, R. (1972). *The philosophies of science*. Oxford, UK: Oxford University Press.

Harré, R., & Madden, E. H. (1975). *Causal powers: A theory of natural necessity*. Oxford, UK: Basil Blackwell.

Holland, P. W. (1986). Statistics and causal inference. *Journal of the American Statistical Association, 81*, 945–970.

Holland, P. W. (1988). Causal inference, path analysis, and recursive structural equation models. In C. C. Clogg (Ed.), *Sociological methodology* (pp. 449–493). Washington, DC: American Sociological Association.

Imai, K., & van Dyk, D. A. (2004). Causal inference with general treatment regimes: Generalizing the propensity score. *Journal of the American Statistical Association, 99*, 854–866.

Imbens, G. W. (2000). The role of the propensity score in estimating dose-response functions. *Biometrika, 87*, 706–710.

Imbens, G. W. (2004). Nonparametric estimation of average treatment effects under exogeneity: A review. *Review of Economics and Statistics, 86*, 4–29.

Imbens, G. W., & Angrist, J. D. (1994). Identification and estimation of local average treatment effects. *Econometrica, 62*, 467–475.

Jo, B. (2006). *Causal inference in randomized trials with mediational processes*. Unpublished manuscript, Stanford University.

Lehman, E. (1974). *Nonparametrics: Statistical methods based on ranks*. San Francisco: Holden-Day.

Mackie, J. L. (1974). *The cement of the universe*. Oxford, UK: Oxford University Press.

MacKinnon, D. P., & Dwyer, J. H. (1993). Estimating mediating effects in prevention studies. *Evaluation Review, 17*, 144–158.

Manski, C. F. (1990). Nonparametric bounds on treatment effects. *American Economic Review Papers and Proceedings, 80*, 319–323.

Mill, J. S. (1973). A system of logic: Ratiocinative and inductive. In J. M. Robson (Ed.), *The collected works of John Stuart Mill* (Vol. 7). Toronto, Ontario, Canada: University of Toronto Press. (Original work published 1843)

Neyman, J. (1990). On the application of probability theory to agricultural experiments. Essays on principles. Section 9 (with discussion). *Statistical Science, 5*, 465–480. (Original work published 1923)

Reichenbach, H. (1956). *The direction of time*. Berkeley: University of California Press.

Robins, J. M. (1989). The analysis of randomized and nonrandomized aids treatment trials using a new approach to causal inference in longitudinal studies. In L. Sechrest, H. Freedman, & A. Mulley (Eds.), *Health services research methodology: A focus on AIDS* (pp. 113–159). Rockville, MD: U.S. Department of Health and Human Services.

Rosenbaum, P. R., & Rubin, D. B. (1983). The central role of the propensity score in observational studies for causal effects. *Biometrika, 70*, 41–55.

Rubin, D. B. (1974). Estimating causal effects of treatments in randomized and nonrandomized studies. *Journal of Educational Psychology, 66*, 688–701.

Rubin, D. B. (1977). Assignment to treatment groups on the basis of a covariate. *Journal of Educational Statistics, 2*, 1–26.

Rubin, D. B. (1978). Bayesian inference for causal effects: The role of randomization. *Annals of Statistics, 6*, 34–58.

Rubin, D. B. (1980). Comment on "randomization analysis of experimental data: The Fisher randomization test" by d. basu. *Journal of the American Statistical Association, 75*, 591–593.

Simon, H. A. (1954). Spurious correlation: A causal interpretation. *Journal of the American Statistical Association*, *49*, 467–492.

Sobel, M. E. (1995). Causal inference in the social and behavioral sciences. In G. Arminger, C. C. Clogg, & M. E. Sobel (Eds.), *Handbook of statistical modeling for the social and behavioral sciences* (pp. 1–38). New York: Plenum.

Sobel, M. E. (1998). Causal inference in statistical models of the process of socioeconomic achievement: A case study. *Sociological Methods and Research*, *27*, 318–348.

Sobel, M. E. (2006a). Spatial concentration and social stratification: Does the clustering of disadvantage "beget" bad outcomes?. In S. Bowles, S. N. Durlauf, & K. Hoff (Eds.), *Poverty traps* (pp. 204–229). New York: Russell Sage Foundation.

Sobel, M. E. (2006b). What do randomized studies of housing mobility demonstrate? Causal inference in the face of interference. *Journal of the American Statistical Association*, *101*, 1398–1407.

Sobel, M. E. (2006c). Identification of causal parameters in randomized studies with mediating variables. *Journal of Educational and Behavioral Statistics*.

Suppes, P. (1970). *A probabilistic theory of causality*. Amsterdam: North-Holland.

Thistlethwaite, D. L., & Campbell, D. T. (1960). Regression-discontinuity analysis: An alternative to the ex post facto experiment. *Journal of Educational Psychology*, *51*, 309–317.

Vella, F. (1998). Estimating models with sample selection bias: A survey. *Journal of Human Resources*, *34*, 208–224.

Yule, G. U. (1896). On the correlation of total pauperism with proportion of out-relief. II: Males over 65. *Economic Journal*, *6*, 613–623.

9

RANDOMNESS AND COMPUTATION

ODED GOLDREICH

INTRODUCTION

While it is safe to assume that any living adult is aware of the revolutionary impact of the computing technology on our society, we fear that few readers have a sense of the theory of computation. This contrast is not so surprising because people seem so overwhelmed by the wonders of this technology that they do not get to wonder about the theory underlying it. Consequently, the fascinating intellectual contents of the theory of computation is rarely understood by nonspecialists.

One goal of this essay is making a tiny contribution toward a possible change in this sour state of affairs, by discussing one aspect of the theory of computation: its connection to randomness. Our guess is that the suggestion that there is a connection between computation and randomness may meet the skepticism of some readers, because computation seems the ultimate manifestation of determinism.

To address this skepticism, we suggest considering what happens when a deterministic machine (or any deterministic process) is fed with a random input or just with an input that looks random. Indeed, one contribution of the theory of computation (further discussed in the section Pseudorandomness) is a definition of "objects that look random" (a notion that makes sense even if the real world is actually deterministic).

Still one may wonder whether we can obtain or generate objects that look random. For example, can we toss a coin (in the sense that one cannot feasibly predict the answer before seeing it)? Assuming a positive answer, we may also assume that unpredictable values can be obtained by other mechanical or electrical processes, which suggests that computers can also obtain such values. The question then is what benefit can be achieved by using such random (or unpredictable) values.

A major application of random (or unpredictable) values is to the area of cryptography (see the section Cryptography). In fact, the very notion of a *secret* refers to such a random (or unpredictable) value. Furthermore, various natural security concerns (e.g., private communication) can be met by employing procedures that make essential use of such secrets or random values.

Another major application of random (or unpredictable) values is to various sampling procedures. In the section Sublinear Time Algorithms, we consider a wider perspective on such procedures, viewing them as a special type of super-fast procedures called *sublinear time algorithms*. Such a procedure cannot afford to scan the entire input, but rather probes few (randomly) selected locations in it and, based on these few values, attempts to make a meaningful assertion regarding the entire input. Indeed, we assume that the reader is aware of the fact that random sampling allows approximation of the fraction of the population that votes for a particular candidate. Our point is that other global properties of the input, which are not merely averages of various types, can also be approximated by sampling.

Last, we mention that randomized verification procedures yield fascinating types of *probabilistic proof systems*, which are discussed in the section Probabilistic Proof Systems. In particular, such proof systems demonstrate the advantage of interaction (over one-directional communication) and the possibility of decoupling proving from learning (i.e., the possibility of proving an assertion without yielding anything beyond its validity). Other forms of probabilistic proof systems allow for superfast verification (based on probing few locations in a redundant proof, indeed as in the aforementioned sublinear-time algorithms).

Before discussing the foregoing applications of randomness in greater length, we provide a somewhat wider perspective on the theory of computation as well as present some of its central conventions. We will also clarify what randomness means in that theory (and in this chapter).

A Wider Perspective on the Theory of Computation

The **theory of computation** aims at understanding general properties of computation be they natural, artificial, or imaginary. Most important, it aims to understand the nature of **efficient computation**. We demonstrate these issues by briefly considering a few typical questions.

A key question is *which functions can be efficiently computed?* For example, it is (relatively) easy to multiply integers, but it seems hard to take the product and factor it into its prime components. In general, it seems that there are one-way computations, or put differently *one-way functions*: Such functions are easy to evaluate but hard to invert (even in an average-case sense). As hinted, it is widely believed that one-way functions exist and this conjecture is related to other fundamental questions.

A related question is that of the comparable difficulty of *solving problems versus verifying the correctness of solutions*. Indeed, our daily experience is that it is harder to solve a problem than it is to check the correctness of a solution (e.g., think of either a puzzle or a research problem). Is this experience merely a coincidence or does it represent a fundamental fact of life (or a property of the world)? Could you imagine a world in which solving any problem is not significantly harder than checking a solution to it? Would the term *solving a problem* not lose its meaning in such a hypothetical (and impossible in our opinion) world? The denial of the plausibility of such a hypothetical world (in which "solving" is not harder than "checking") is what the celebrated "P different from NP" conjecture means, where P represents tasks that are efficiently solvable and NP represents tasks for which solutions can be efficiently checked for correctness.

The theory of computation is also concerned with finding the most efficient methods for solving specific problems. To demonstrate this line of research, we mention that the simple (and standard) method for multiplying numbers that is taught in elementary school is not the most efficient one possible. Multiplying two n-digit long numbers by this method requires n^2 single-digit multiplications (and a similar number of single-digit additions). In contrast, the best-known algorithm for this problem runs in time $(\log n)^2 \cdot n$.

The theory of computation provides a new viewpoint on old phenomena. We have already mentioned the computational approaches to randomness (see the section Pseudorandomness) and to proofs, interaction, knowledge, and learning (see the section Probabilistic Proof Systems). Additional natural concepts given an appealing computational interpretations include the *importance of representation*, the notion of *explicitness*, and the possibility that approximation is easier than optimization (see the section Sublinear Time Algorithms). Let us say a few words about representation and explicitness.

The foregoing examples hint to *the importance of representation*, because in all these computational problems the solution is implicit in the problem's statement. That is, the problem contains all necessary information, and one merely needs to process this information to supply the answer.[1] Thus, the theory of computation is concerned with the manipulation of information and its transformation from one representation (in which the information is given) to another representation (which is the one desired). Indeed, a solution to a computational problem is merely a different representation of the information given; that is, a representation in which the answer is explicit rather than implicit. For example, the answer to the question of whether or not a given system of quadratic equations has an integer solution is implicit in the system itself (but the task is to make the answer explicit). Thus, the theory of computation clarifies a central issue regarding representation; that is, the distinction between what is explicit and what is implicit in a representation. Furthermore, it also suggests a quantification of the level of nonexplicitness.

Important Conventions for the Theory of Computation

In light of the foregoing discussion, it is important to specify the representation used in computational problems. Actually, a computational problem refers to an infinite set of *finite objects*, called the **problem's instances**, and specifies the desired solution for each instance. For example, the instances of the `multiplication problem` are pairs of natural numbers, and the desired solution is the corresponding product. Objects are represented by finite binary sequences, called **strings**.[2] For a natural number n, we denote by $\{0,1\}^n$ the set of all strings of length n, hereafter referred to as **n-bit strings**. The set of all strings is denoted $\{0,1\}^*$; that is, $\{0,1\}^* = \bigcup_{n\in\mathbb{N}}\{0,1\}^n$.

We have already mentioned the notion of an **algorithm**, which is central to the theory of computation and means an automated procedure designed to solve some computational task. A rigorous definition requires specifying a reasonable model of computation, but the specifics of this model are not important for the current essay. We focus on **efficient algorithms**, which are commonly defined as making a number of steps that is polynomial in the length of their input.[3] Indeed, asymptotic analysis (or rather a functional treatment of the running time of algorithms in terms of the length of their input) is a central convention in the theory of computation.

Typically, our notion of efficient algorithms will include also *probabilistic* (polynomial-time) algorithms, that is algorithms that can "toss coins" (i.e., make random choices). For each reasonable model of computation, probabilistic (or randomized) algorithms are defined as standard algorithms augmented with the ability to choose uniformly among a finite number (say two) of predetermined possibilities. That is, at each computation step, such an algorithm makes a move that is chosen uniformly among two predetermined possibilities.

Randomness in the Context of Computation

Throughout the entire essay we will refer only to *discrete* probability distributions. The support of such distributions will be associated with a set of strings, typically of the same length.

For the purpose of asymptotic analysis, we will often consider **probability ensembles**, which are sequences of distributions that are indexed either by integers or by strings. For example, throughout the essay, we let $\{U_n\}_{n\in\mathbb{N}}$ denote the **uniform ensemble**, where U_n is uniform over the set of strings of length n; that is, $\Pr_{z\sim U_n}[z=\alpha]$ equals 2^{-n} if $\alpha \in \{0,1\}^n$ and equals 0 otherwise. More generally, we will typically consider probability ensembles, denoted $\{D_n\}_{n\in\mathbb{N}}$, where there exists some function $\ell : \mathbb{N} \to \mathbb{N}$ such that $\Pr_{z\sim D_n}[z\in\{0,1\}^{\ell(n)}] = 1$. Furthermore, typically, ℓ will be a polynomial.

One important case of probability ensembles is that of ensembles that represent the output of randomized processes (e.g., randomized algorithms). Letting $A(x)$ denote the output of the

[1] In contrast, in other disciplines, solving a problem may also require gathering information that is not available in the problem's statement. This information may either be available from auxiliary (past) records or be obtained by conducting new experiments.

[2] Indeed, in the foregoing example, we used the daily representation of numbers as sequences of decimal digits, but in the theory of computation natural numbers are typically represented by their binary expansion.

[3] In the section Sublinear Time Algorithms, we consider even faster algorithms, which make (significantly) fewer steps than the length of their input, but such algorithms can only provide approximate solutions.

probabilistic (or randomized) algorithm A on input x, we may consider the probability ensemble $\{A(x)\}_{x\in\{0,1\}^*}$. Indeed, if A is a probabilistic polynomial-time algorithm then $A(x)$ is distributed over strings of length that is bounded by a polynomial in the length of x. On the other hand, we say that a probability ensemble $\{D_n\}_{n\in\mathbb{N}}$ is **efficiently sampleable** if there exists a probabilistic polynomial-time algorithm A such that for every $n \in \mathbb{N}$ it holds that $A(1^n) \equiv D_n$. That is, algorithm A makes a number of steps that is polynomial in n, and produces a sample distributed according to D_n.

We will often talk of "random bits" and mean values selected uniformly and independently in $\{0,1\}$. In particular, randomized algorithms may be viewed as deterministic algorithms that are given an adequate number of random bits as an auxiliary input. This means that rather than viewing these algorithms as making random choices, we view them as determining these choices according to a sequence of random bits that is generated by some outside process.

PSEUDORANDOMNESS

Indistinguishable things are identical.[4]

—G. W. Leibniz, 1646–1714

A fresh view at the *question of randomness* has been taken in the theory of computation: It has been postulated that a distribution is pseudorandom if it cannot be told apart from the uniform distribution by any efficient procedure.

At the extreme, this approach says that the question of whether the world is deterministic or allows for some free choice (which may be viewed as sources of randomness) is irrelevant. *What matters is how the world looks to us and to various computationally bounded devices.* That is, if some phenomenon looks random then we may just treat it as if it were random. Likewise, if we can generate sequences that cannot be told apart from the uniform distribution by any efficient procedure, then we can use these sequences in any efficient randomized application instead of the ideal random bits that are postulated in the design of this application.

A Wider Context and an Illustration

The second half of the twentieth century witnessed the development of three theories of randomness, a notion that has been puzzling thinkers for ages. The first theory (cf. Cover & Thomas, 1991), initiated by C. E. Shannon, is rooted in probability theory and is focused at distributions that are not perfectly random (i.e., are not uniform over a set of strings of adequate length). Shannon's information theory characterizes perfect randomness as the extreme case in which the *information contents* is maximized (i.e., the strings contain no redundancy at all). Thus, perfect randomness is associated with a unique distribution: the uniform one. In particular, by definition, one cannot (deterministically) generate such perfect random strings from shorter random seeds.

The second theory (cf. Li & Vitanyi, 1993), initiated by R. J. Solomonov, A. Kolmogorov, and G. J. Chaitin, is rooted in computability theory and specifically in the notion of a universal language (equivalently, universal machine or computing device). It measures the complexity of objects in terms of the shortest program (for a fixed universal machine) that generates the object. Like Shannon's theory, Kolmogorov complexity is quantitative and perfect random objects appear as an extreme case. However, in this approach, one may say that a single object, rather than a distribution over objects, is perfectly random. Yet, Kolmogorov's approach is inherently intractable (i.e., Kolmogorov complexity is uncomputable), and—by definition—one cannot (deterministically) generate strings of high Kolmogorov complexity from short random seeds.

The third theory, initiated by Blum, Goldwasser, Micali, and Yao, is rooted in the notion of *efficient computations* and is the focus of this section. This approach is explicitly aimed at providing a notion of randomness that nevertheless allows for an efficient generation of random strings from shorter random seeds. The heart of

[4]This is the *principle of identity of indiscernibles.* Leibniz admits that counterexamples to this principle are conceivable but will not occur in real life because God is much too benevolent. We thus believe that he would have agreed to the theme of this section, which asserts that *indistinguishable things should be considered as identical.*

this approach is the suggestion to view objects as equal if they cannot be told apart by any efficient procedure. Consequently, a distribution that cannot be efficiently distinguished from the uniform distribution will be considered as being random (or rather called pseudorandom). Thus, randomness is not an "inherent" property of objects (or distributions) but is rather relative to an observer (and its computational abilities). To demonstrate this approach, let us consider the following mental experiment.

> Alice and Bob play "head or tail" in one of the following four ways. In each of them, Alice flips an unbiased coin and Bob is asked to guess its outcome *before* the coin hits the floor. The alternative ways differ by the knowledge Bob has before making his guess.
>
> In the first alternative, Bob has to announce his guess before Alice flips the coin. Clearly, in this case Bob wins with probability $1/2$.
>
> In the second alternative, Bob has to announce his guess while the coin is spinning in the air. Although the outcome is *determined in principle* by the motion of the coin, Bob does not have accurate information on the motion and thus we believe that also in this case Bob wins with probability $1/2$.
>
> The third alternative is similar to the second, except that Bob has at his disposal sophisticated equipment capable of providing accurate *information* on the coin's motion as well as on the environment effecting the outcome. However, Bob cannot process this information in time to improve his guess.
>
> In the fourth alternative, Bob's recording equipment is directly connected to a *powerful computer* programmed to solve the motion equations and output a prediction. It is conceivable that in such a case Bob can substantially improve his guess of the outcome of the coin.

We conclude that the randomness of an event is relative to the information and computing resources at our disposal. Thus, a natural concept of pseudorandomness arises: a distribution is *pseudorandom* if no efficient procedure can distinguish it from the uniform distribution.

The Notion of Pseudorandom Generators

Loosely speaking, a pseudorandom generator is an *efficient* program (or algorithm) that *stretches* short random strings into long *pseudorandom* sequences. We stress that the generator itself is deterministic and that the randomness involved in the generation process is captured by its input (called the **seed**). We emphasize three fundamental aspects in the notion of a pseudorandom generator: efficiency of generation, stretching of the seed, and pseudorandomness of the output. The formulation of the last notion refers to the general concept of **computational indistinguishability** that is the heart of the entire approach. Intuitively, two objects are called computationally indistinguishable if no efficient procedure can tell them apart. Here the objects are (fixed) probability distributions (or rather ensembles), and the observer is given a sample drawn from one of the two distributions and is asked to tell from which distribution it was taken (e.g., it is asked to say "1" if the sample is taken from the first distribution). Following the asymptotic framework (see the sections Important Conventions for the Theory of Complication and Randomness in the Context of Computation), the foregoing discussion is formalized as follows.

Definition 9.1 (Computational Indistinguishability). *Two probability ensembles, $\{X_n\}_{n\in\mathbb{N}}$ and $\{Y_n\}_{n\in\mathbb{N}}$, are called **computationally indistinguishable** if for any probabilistic polynomial-time algorithm A, any positive polynomial p, and all sufficiently large n*

$$\left| Pr_{x\sim X_n}[A(x)=1] - Pr_{y\sim Y_n}[A(y)=1] \right| < \frac{1}{p(n)}. \tag{9.1}$$

The probability is taken over X_n (or Y_n) as well as over the internal coin tosses of algorithm A.

Algorithm A, which is called a potential **distinguisher**, is given a sample (which is drawn either from X_n or from Y_n), and its output is viewed as an attempt to tell whether this sample was drawn from X_n or from Y_n. Equation (9.1) requires that such an attempt is bound to fail; that is, the outcome 1 (possibly representing a verdict that the sample was drawn from X_n) is essentially as likely to occur when the sample is drawn from X_n as when it is drawn from Y_n.

A few comments are in order. First, the distinguisher (i.e., A) is allowed to be probabilistic.

This makes the requirement only stronger, and seems essential to the technical development of our approach. Second, we view events occurring with probability that is upper bounded by the reciprocal of polynomials as **negligible** (e.g., $2^{-\sqrt{n}}$ is negligible as a function of n). This is well coupled with our notion of efficiency (i.e., polynomial-time computations): An event that occurs with negligible probability (as a function of a parameter n) will also occur with negligible probability if the experiment is repeated for poly(n)-many times. Third, for efficiently sampleable ensembles, computational indistinguishability is preserved also when providing the distinguisher with polynomially many samples (of the tested distribution). Last, we note that computational indistinguishability is a coarsening of statistical indistinguishability; that is, waiving the computational restriction on the distinguisher is equivalent to requiring that the variation distance between X_n and Y_n (i.e., $\sum_z |X_n(z) - Y_n(z)|$) is negligible (in n).

An important case in which computational indistinguishability is strictly more liberal than statistical indistinguishability arises from the notion of a pseudorandom generator.

Definition 9.2 (Pseudorandom Generators). *A deterministic polynomial-time algorithm G is called a* ***pseudorandom generator*** *if there exists a* stretching function, $\ell : \mathbb{N} \to \mathbb{N}$ (i.e., $\ell(n) > n$), *such that the following two probability ensembles, denoted* $\{G_n\}_{n\in\mathbb{N}}$ *and* $\{R_n\}_{n\in\mathbb{N}}$, *are computationally indistinguishable.*

1. *Distribution G_n is defined as the output of G on a uniformly selected seed in* $\{0,1\}^n$.

2. *Distribution R_n is defined as the uniform distribution on* $\{0,1\}^{\ell(n)}$.

Note that $G_n \equiv G(U_n)$, whereas $R_n = U_{\ell(n)}$. Thus, pseudorandom generators are efficient (i.e., polynomial-time) deterministic programs that expand short randomly selected seeds into longer pseudorandom bit sequences, where the latter are defined as computationally indistinguishable from truly random bit-sequences. It follows that any efficient randomized algorithm maintains its performance when its internal coin tosses are substituted by a sequence generated by a pseudorandom generator (using a shorter random seed). The point is that the pseudorandom sequence may be generated using much fewer truly random coins, which leads to a saving in randomness while maintaining performance (see further discussion in the section The Applicability of Pseudorandom Generators). In a sense, pseudorandom generators offer a way to recycle randomness, that is generating long random-looking sequences by using only a small amount of randomness.

Amplifying the Stretch Function

Pseudorandom generators as in Definition 9.2 are only required to stretch their input a bit; for example, stretching n-bit-long inputs to $(n+1)$-bit-long outputs will do. Clearly, generators with such moderate stretch functions are of little use in practice. In contrast, we want to have pseudorandom generators with an arbitrary long stretch function. By the efficiency requirement, the stretch function can be at most polynomial. It turns out that pseudorandom generators with the smallest possible stretch function can be used to construct pseudorandom generators with any desirable polynomial stretch function. Thus, when talking about the existence of pseudorandom generators, we may ignore the specific stretch function.

How to Construct Pseudorandom Generators

The known constructions of pseudorandomness generators are based on one-way functions. Loosely speaking, a *polynomial-time computable* function is called one way if any efficient algorithm can invert it only with negligible success probability. For simplicity, we consider only length-preserving one-way functions.

Definition 9.3 (One-Way Function). *A* ***one-way function****, f, is a polynomial-time-computable function such that for every probabilistic polynomial-time algorithm A', every positive polynomial $p(\cdot)$, and all sufficiently large n*

$$Pr_{x\sim U_n}\left[A'(f(x))\in f^{-1}(f(x))\right] < \frac{1}{p(n)},$$

where $f^{-1}(y) = \{z : f(z)=y\}$.

It is widely believed that one-way functions exist. Popular candidates for one-way functions are based on the conjectured intractability of integer factorization, the discrete logarithm problem, and decoding of random linear code. It turns out that pseudorandom generators can be constructed based on any one-way function. Furthermore, this sufficient condition is also necessary.

Theorem 9.4 (Existence of Pseudorandom Generators). *Pseudorandom generators exist if and only if one-way functions exist.*

Pseudorandom Functions

Pseudorandom generators allow one to efficiently generate long pseudorandom sequences from short random seeds (e.g., using n random bits, we can efficiently generate a pseudorandom bit-sequence of length n^2). Pseudorandom functions (defined below) are even more powerful: They allow efficient direct access to a huge pseudorandom sequence (which is infeasible to scan bit by bit). For example, based on n random bits, we define a sequence of length 2^n such that we can efficiently retrieve any desired bit in this sequence while the retrieved bits look random. In other words, pseudorandom functions are indistinguishable from random functions by any efficient procedure that may obtain the function values at arguments of its choice. Such procedures are called **oracle machines**, and if M is such machine and f is a function, then $M^f(x)$ denotes the computation of M on input x when M's queries are answered by the function f (i.e., during its computation, M generates special strings called **queries** such that in response to the query q machine M is given the value $f(q)$).

Definition 9.5 (Pseudorandom Functions). *A* ***pseudorandom function*** (ensemble), *with length parameters* $\ell_D, \ell_R : \mathbb{N} \to \mathbb{N}$, *is a collection of functions* $\{F_n\}_{n\in\mathbb{N}}$, *where*

$$F_n \stackrel{def}{=} \{f_s : \{0,1\}^{\ell_D(n)} \to \{0,1\}^{\ell_R(n)}\}_{s\in\{0,1\}^n},$$

satisfying

- ***(Efficient Evaluation).*** *There exists an efficient* (deterministic) *algorithm that when given a* seed, *s, and an* $\ell_D(n)$*-bit* argument, *x, returns the* $\ell_R(n)$*-bit long value* $f_s(x)$, *where n denotes the length of s.*

  (Thus, the seed s is an "effective description" of the function f_s.)

- ***(Pseudorandomness).*** *For every probabilistic polynomial-time oracle machine M, every positive polynomial p, and all sufficiently large n*

$$\left| Pr_{s\sim U_n}[M^{f_s}(1^n) = 1] - Pr_{\rho\sim R_n}[M^{\rho}(1^n) = 1] \right| < \frac{1}{p(n)},$$

where R_n *denotes the uniform distribution over all functions mapping* $\{0,1\}^{\ell_D(n)}$ *to* $\{0,1\}^{\ell_R(n)}$.

Although pseudorandom functions seem stronger than pseudorandom generators, the former can be constructed using the latter.

Theorem 9.6. *The existence of pseudorandom generators implies the existence of pseudorandom functions* (with any polynomially bounded length parameters $\ell_D, \ell_R : \mathbb{N} \to \mathbb{N}$).

The Applicability of Pseudorandom Generators

Randomness is playing an increasingly important role in computation: It is frequently used in the design of sequential, parallel, and distributed algorithms (see Motwani & Raghavan, 1995) and is of course central to cryptography. Whereas it is convenient to design such algorithms making free use of randomness, it is also desirable to minimize the use of randomness in real implementations since generating perfectly random bits via special hardware is quite expensive. Thus, pseudorandom generators (as in Definition 9.2) are a key ingredient in an "algorithmic tool-box": they provide an automatic compiler of programs written with free use of randomness into programs that make an economical use of randomness.

Indeed, "pseudorandom number generators" have appeared with the first computers. However, typical implementations use generators that are not pseudorandom according to Definition 9.2. Instead, at best, these generators are shown to pass *some* ad hoc statistical test. We warn that the fact that a "pseudorandom number generator" passes some statistical tests does not mean that it will pass a new test and that it is good for a future (untested) application. In contrast, the approach encompassed in Definition 9.2 guarantees that pseudorandom generators can be used for *all* practical purposes (i.e., that the sequences that they produce are as good as truly random ones).

Pseudorandom generators and functions are of key importance in Cryptography. In particular, they are typically used to establish private-key encryption and authentication schemes. For further discussion, see the section Cryptography.

The Intellectual Contents of Pseudorandom Generators

We shortly discuss some intellectual aspects of pseudorandom generators as defined above.

Behavioristic Versus Ontological

Our definition of pseudorandom generators is based on the notion of computational indistinguishability. The behavioristic nature of the latter notion is best demonstrated by confronting it with the Kolmogorov-Chaitin approach to randomness. Loosely speaking, a string is *Kolmogorov-random* if its length equals the length of the shortest program producing it. This shortest program may be considered the "true explanation" to the phenomenon described by the string. Considering the simplest explanation of a phenomenon may be viewed as an ontological approach. In contrast, considering the effect of phenomena (on an observer), as underlying the definition of pseudorandomness, is a behavioristic approach. Furthermore, there exist probability distributions that are not uniform (and are not even statistically close to a uniform distribution) but nevertheless are indistinguishable from a uniform distribution by any efficient procedure. Thus, distributions that are ontologically very different are considered equivalent by the behavioristic point of view taken in Definition 9.1.

A Relativistic View of Randomness

Pseudorandomness is defined in terms of its observer: It is a distribution that cannot be told apart from a uniform distribution by any efficient (i.e., polynomial-time) observer. However, pseudorandom sequences may be distinguished from random ones by infinitely powerful computers (not at our disposal!). Furthermore, a machine that runs in exponential-time can distinguish the output of a pseudorandom generator from a uniformly selected string of the same length (e.g., just by trying all possible seeds). Thus, pseudorandomness is subjective, dependent on the abilities of the observer.

Randomness and Computational Difficulty

Pseudorandomness and computational difficulty play dual roles: The definition of pseudorandomness relies on the fact that placing computational restrictions on the observer gives rise to distributions that are not uniform and still cannot be distinguished from uniform. Furthermore, the known constructions of pseudorandom generators rely on conjectures regarding computational difficulty (e.g., the existence of one-way functions), and this is inevitable: The existence of pseudorandom generators implies the existence of one-way functions.

Randomness and Predictability

The connection between pseudorandomness and unpredictability (by efficient procedures) plays an important role in the analysis of several constructions of pseudorandom generators. We wish to highlight the intuitive appeal of this connection.

Suggestions for Further Reading

A detailed textbook presentation of the material that is reviewed in this section is provided in Goldreich (2001, chap. 3). For a wider perspective, which treats this material as a special case of a general paradigm, the interested reader is referred to (Goldreich, 1999, chap. 3).

PROBABILISTIC PROOF SYSTEMS

The glory attributed to the creativity involved in finding proofs makes us forget that it is the less glorified procedure of verification that gives proofs their value. Philosophically speaking, proofs are secondary to the verification procedure, whereas technically speaking, proof systems are defined in terms of their verification procedures.

The notion of a verification procedure assumes the notion of computation and furthermore the notion of efficient computation. This implicit assumption is made explicit in the following definition in which efficient computation is associated with deterministic polynomial-time algorithms.

Definition 9.7 (NP-Proof Systems). *Let $S \subseteq \{0,1\}^*$ and $v : \{0,1\}^* \times \{0,1\}^* \rightarrow \{0,1\}$ be a function such that $x \in S$ if and only if there exists a $w \in \{0,1\}^*$ that satisfies $v(x,w) = 1$. If v is computable in time bounded by a polynomial in the length of its first argument, then we say v defines an* ***NP-proof system for*** *S and that S is an* ***NP-set***. *The class of NP-sets is denoted $\mathcal{NP}$.*

Indeed, v represents a verification procedure for claims of membership in a set S, and a string w satisfying $v(x,w) = 1$ is a proof that x belongs to S, whereas $x \notin S$ has no such proofs. For example, consider the set of systems of quadratic equations that have integer solutions. Clearly, any integer solution $\overline{v}$ to such a system Q constitutes an "NP-proof" for the assertion `the system` Q `has an solution` (the verification procedure consists of substituting the variables of Q by the values provided in $\overline{v}$ and computing the value of the resulting arithmetic expressions).

We seize the opportunity to note that the celebrated "P different from NP" conjecture asserts that NP-proof systems are useful in the sense that *there are assertions for which obtaining a proof helps to verify the correctness of the assertion.*[5] This conforms with our daily experience by which reading a proof eases the verification of an assertion.

The formulation of NP-proofs restricts the "effective" length of proofs to be polynomial in length of the corresponding assertions (since the running time of the verification procedure is restricted to be polynomial in the length of the assertion). However, longer proofs may be allowed by padding the assertion with sufficiently many blank symbols. So it seems that NP gives a satisfactory formulation of proof systems (with efficient verification procedures). This is indeed the case if one associates efficient procedures with *deterministic* polynomial-time algorithms. However, we can gain a lot if we are willing to take a somewhat nontraditional step and allow *probabilistic* verification procedures. In particular,

- Randomized and interactive verification procedures, giving rise to *interactive proof systems*, seem much more powerful than their deterministic counterparts (see the section Interactive Proof Systems).
- Such randomized procedures allow the introduction of *zero-knowledge proofs*, which are of great conceptual and practical interest (see the section Zero-Knowledge Proof Systems).
- NP proofs can be efficiently transformed into a (redundant) form (called a *probabilistically checkable proof*) that offers a trade-off between the number of bit locations examined in the NP proof and the confidence in its validity (see the section Probabilistically Checkable Proof Systems).

In all these types of probabilistic proof systems, explicit bounds are imposed on the computational resources of the verification procedure,

[5] NP represents sets of assertions that can be efficiently verified with the help of adequate proofs, whereas P represents sets of assertions that can be efficiently verified from scratch (i.e., without proofs). Thus, "P different from NP" asserts the existence of assertions that are harder to prove than to be convinced of their correctness when presented with a proof. This means that the notion of a proof is meaningful (i.e., that proofs do help when trying to be convinced of the correctness of assertions).

which in turn is personified by the notion of a verifier. Furthermore, in all these proof systems, the verifier is allowed to toss coins and rule by statistical evidence. Thus, *all these proof systems carry a probability of error; yet, this probability is explicitly bounded and, furthermore, can be reduced by successive application of the proof system.*

Clarifications

Like the definition of NP-proof systems, the abovementioned types of probabilistic proof systems refer to proving membership in predetermined sets of strings. That is, the assertions are all of the form "the string x is in a set S," where S is a fixed infinite set and x is a variable input. The definition of an interactive proof system makes explicit reference to a prover, which is only implicit in the definition of an NP-proof system (where the prover is the unmentioned entity providing the proof). We note that, as a first approximation, we are not concerned with the complexity of the prover or the proving task. Our main focus is on the complexity of verification. This is consistent with the intuitive notion of a proof, which refers to the validity of the proof and not to how it was obtained.

Interactive Proof Systems

In light of the growing acceptability of randomized and distributed computations, it is only natural to associate the notion of efficient computation with probabilistic and interactive polynomial-time computations. This leads naturally to the notion of an interactive proof system in which the verification procedure is interactive and randomized, rather than being noninteractive and deterministic. Thus, a "proof" in this context is not a fixed and static object but rather a randomized (dynamic) process in which the verifier interacts with the prover. Intuitively, one may think of this interaction as consisting of "tricky" questions asked by the verifier, to which the prover has to reply "convincingly." The above discussion, as well as the following definition, makes explicit reference to a prover, whereas a prover is only implicit in the traditional definitions of proof systems (e.g., NP proofs).

Loosely speaking, an interactive proof is a game between a computationally bounded verifier and a computationally unbounded prover whose goal is to convince the verifier of the validity of some assertion. Specifically, the verifier is probabilistic polynomial-time. It is required that if the assertion holds then the verifier always accepts (i.e., when interacting with an appropriate prover strategy). On the other hand, if the assertion is false then the verifier must reject with probability at least $1/2$, no matter what strategy is being employed by the prover.

Definition 9.8 (Interactive Proofs, IP). *An **interactive proof system for a set** S is a two-party game, between a **verifier** executing a probabilistic polynomial-time strategy* (denoted V) *and a **prover** that executes a computationally unbounded strategy* (denoted P), *satisfying*

- Completeness*: For every $x \in S$ the verifier V always accepts after interacting with the prover P on common input x.*
- Soundness*: For every $x \notin S$ and every possible strategy P^*, the verifier V rejects with probability at least $1/2$, after interacting with P^* on common input x.*

The class of sets having interactive proof systems is denoted by $\mathcal{IP}$.

Recall that the error probability in the soundness condition can be reduced by successive application of the proof system. To clarify the definition and illustrate the power of the underlying concept, we consider the following story.

> One day on Olympus, bright-eyed Athena claimed that Nectar poured out of the new silver-coated jars tastes less good than Nectar poured out of the older gold-decorated jars. Mighty Zeus was annoyed at the claim. He ordered that Athena be served one hundred glasses of Nectar, each poured at random either from an old jar or from a new one, and that she tell the source of the drink in each glass. To everybody's surprise, wise Athena correctly identified the source of each serving, to which the Father of the Gods responded "my child, you are either right or extremely lucky." Since all gods knew that being lucky was not one of the attributes of Pallas-Athena, they all concluded that the impeccable goddess was right in her claim.

Note that the proof system underlying this story establishes the dissimilarity of two objects. Indeed, typically, proving similarity between objects is easy, because one can present a mapping (of one object to the other) that demonstrates this similarity. In contrast, proving dissimilarity seems harder, because in general there seems to be no succinct proof of dissimilarity. More generally, it is typically easy to prove the existence of an easily verifiable structure in the given object by merely presenting this structure, but proving the nonexistence of such a structure seems hard.

Formally speaking, proving the existence of an easily verifiable structure corresponds to NP-proof systems. The foregoing discussion suggests that interactive proof systems can be used to demonstrate the nonexistence of such structures, which is something that NP-proof systems seem unable to do. For example, the set of systems of quadratic equations that have no integer solutions has an interactive proof system, but is believed not to have an NP-proof system. In general, $\mathcal{IP}$ contains co$\mathcal{NP} \stackrel{\text{def}}{=} \{\{0,1\}^* \setminus S : S \in \mathcal{NP}\}$, which is widely believed *not* to be contained in $\mathcal{NP}$. Furthermore, $\mathcal{IP}$ coincides with the class of sets that can be decided using a polynomial amount of work-space, denoted $\mathcal{PSPACE}$.

Theorem 9.9. $\mathcal{IP} = \mathcal{PSPACE}$.

Thus, interactive proofs seem to be more powerful than NP proofs. This conforms with our daily experience by which interaction facilitates the verification of assertions. As we shall argue next, randomness (and the error probability in the soundness condition) play a key role in this phenomenon.

Interactive proof systems extend NP-proof systems in allowing extensive interaction as well as randomization (and ruling based on statistical evidence). As hinted, extensive interaction by itself does not provide any gain (over NP-proof systems). The reason being that the prover can predict the verifier's part of the interaction and thus it suffices to let the prover send the full transcript of the interaction and let the verifier check that the interaction is indeed valid. The moral is that *there is no point to interact with predictable parties that are also computationally weaker*. This moral represents the prover's point of view (with respect to deterministic verifiers). Certainly, from the verifier's point of view it is beneficial to interact with the prover, since the latter is computationally stronger.

We mention that the power of interactive proof systems remains unchanged under several natural variants. In particular, it turns out that, in this context, *asking clever questions is not more powerful than asking totally random questions*. The reason being that a powerful prover may assist the verifier, which may thus refrain from trying to be clever and focus on checking (by using only random questions) that the help extended to it is indeed valid. Also, the power of interactive proof systems remains unchanged when allowing two-sided error probability (i.e., allowing bounded error probability also in the completeness condition). Recall that, in contrast, one-sided error probability (i.e., error probability in the soundness condition) is essential to the power of interactive proofs.

Zero-Knowledge Proof Systems

Standard proofs are believed to yield knowledge and not merely establish the validity of the assertion being proven. Indeed, it is commonly believed that (good) proofs provide a deeper understanding of the theorem being proved. At the technical level, assuming that NP proof is useful at all (i.e., assuming that $\mathcal{P} \neq \mathcal{NP}$, see the section A Wider Perspective on the Theory of Computation), an NP proof of membership in some sets $S \in \mathcal{NP} \setminus \mathcal{P}$ yields something (i.e., the NP proof itself) that is typically hard to find (even when assuming that the input is in S). For example, an integer solution to a system of quadratic equations constitutes an NP proof that this system has an integer solution, but it yields information (i.e., the solution) that is infeasible to find (when given an arbitrary system of quadratic equations that has an integer solution). In contrast to such NP proofs, which seem to yield a lot of knowledge, zero-knowledge proofs yield no knowledge at all; that is, the latter exhibit an extreme contrast between being convincing (of the validity of a statement) and teaching something on top of the validity of the statement.

Loosely speaking, zero-knowledge proofs are interactive proofs that yield nothing beyond the validity of the assertion. These proofs are fascinating and extremely useful constructs. Their fascinating nature is due to their seemingly contradictory definition: Zero-knowledge proofs are both convincing and yet yield nothing beyond the validity of the assertion being proven. Their applicability in the domain of cryptography is vast; they are typically used to force malicious parties to behave according to a predetermined protocol.

Zero knowledge is a property of some interactive proof systems, or more accurately of some prover strategies. Specifically, it is the property of yielding nothing beyond the validity of the assertion; that is, a verifier obtaining a zero-knowledge proof only gains conviction in the validity of the assertion. This is formulated by saying that anything that can be feasibly obtained from a zero-knowledge proof is also feasibly computable from the (valid) assertion itself. Details follow.

The formulation of the zero-knowledge condition refers to two types of probability ensembles, where each ensemble associates a distribution to each valid assertion. The first ensemble represents the output distribution of the verifier after interacting with the specified prover strategy P, where the verifier is not necessarily employing the specified strategy (i.e., V) but rather any efficient strategy. The second ensemble represents the output distribution of some probabilistic polynomial-time algorithm (which does not interact with anyone). The basic definition of zero knowledge asserts that for every ensemble of the first type there exist an ensemble of the second type such that the two ensembles are computationally indistinguishable.

The Power of Zero Knowledge

Zero-knowledge interactive proof systems for every set in $\mathcal{NP}$ can be constructed provided that one-way functions exist, which in turn is a widely believed conjecture (underlying almost all of modern cryptography). Furthermore, these proof systems are efficient in the sense that the prover strategy for them can be implemented in probabilistic polynomial-time provided that it is given an adequate NP proof as auxiliary input. That is:

Theorem 9.10. *Assuming the existence of one-way functions, any NP proof can be efficiently transformed into a zero-knowledge interactive proof.*

Theorem 9.10 has a dramatic effect on the design of cryptographic protocols (cf. Goldreich, 2001, 2004). In a different vein, we mention that, under the same assumption, any set having an interactive proof system also has a zero-knowledge interactive proof system.

The Role of Randomness

Again, randomness is essential to all the aforementioned results. Namely, zero-knowledge proof systems in which either the verifier or the prover is deterministic exist only for sets in $\mathcal{BPP}$, where $\mathcal{BPP}$ is the class of sets for which membership is decidable by some probabilistic polynomial-time algorithm. Note that such sets have trivial zero-knowledge proofs in which the prover sends nothing and the verifier just tests the validity of the assertion by itself. Thus, randomness is essential to the usefulness of zero-knowledge proofs.

Probabilistically Checkable Proof Systems

We now return to the noninteractive mode in which the verifier receives a (or an alleged) written proof. But our focus is on probabilistic verifiers that are capable of evaluating the validity of the assertion by examining few (randomly selected) locations in the alleged proof. Thus, the alleged proof is a string, as in the case of a traditional proof system, but we are interested in probabilistic verification procedures that access only few locations in the proof, and yet are able to make a meaningful probabilistic verdict regarding the validity of the alleged proof. Specifically, the verification procedure should accept any valid proof (with probability 1) but rejects with probability at least $1/2$ any alleged proof for a false assertion.

The main complexity measure associated with probabilistically checkable proof (PCP) systems is indeed their query complexity (i.e., the number of bits accessed in the alleged proof). Another complexity measure of natural concern is the length of the proofs being employed, which in turn is related to the randomness complexity of the system. The randomness complexity of PCPs plays a key role in numerous applications (e.g., in composing PCP systems as well as when applying PCP systems to derive nonapproximability results), and thus we specify this parameter rather than the proof length.

Loosely speaking, a probabilistically checkable proof system consists of a probabilistic polynomial-time verifier having access to an oracle that represents an alleged proof (in redundant form). Typically, the verifier accesses only few of the oracle bits, and these bit positions are determined by the outcome of the verifier's coin tosses. As in the case of interactive proof systems, it is required that if the assertion holds then the verifier always accepts (i.e., when given access to an adequate oracle); whereas, if the assertion is false then the verifier must reject with probability at least $1/2$, no matter which oracle is used. The basic definition of the PCP setting is given in Item 1 of Definition 9.11. Yet, the complexity measures introduced in Item 2 are of key importance for the subsequent discussions.

Definition 9.11 (Probabilistically Checkable Proofs)**.**

1. *A **probabilistically checkable proof (PCP) system for a set** S is a probabilistic polynomial-time oracle machine* (called **verifier**)*, denoted V, satisfying*
   - Completeness: *For every $x \in S$ there exists an oracle π_x so that V, on input x and access to π_x, always accepts x.*
   - Soundness: *For every $x \notin S$ and every oracle π, machine V, on input x and access to π, rejects x with probability at least* $1/2$.
2. *Let r and q be integer functions. The complexity class $\mathcal{PCP}(r(\cdot),q(\cdot))$ consists of sets having a probabilistically checkable proof system in which the verifier, on any input of length n, makes at most $r(n)$ coin tosses and at most $q(n)$ oracle queries, where each query is answered by a single bit.*

We stress that the oracle π_x in a PCP system constitutes a proof in the standard mathematical sense. Yet, this oracle has the extra property of enabling a lazy verifier to toss coins, take its chances, and "assess" the validity of the proof without reading all of it (but rather by reading a tiny portion of it).

We focus on the classes $\mathcal{PCP}(\texttt{log},\cdot)$, where `log` denotes a generic logarithmic function, because in this case the relevant oracles are of polynomial length. In particular, for every constant c, it holds that $\mathcal{PCP}(\texttt{log},c) \subseteq \mathcal{NP}$. The opposite inclusion is a highly nontrivial result.

Theorem 9.12. *There exists a constant c such that $\mathcal{NP} \subseteq \mathcal{PCP}(\texttt{log},c)$.*

Thus, probabilistically checkable proofs in which the verifier tosses only logarithmically many coins and makes only a constant number of queries exist for every set in the complexity class $\mathcal{NP}$. (Essentially, this constant is 3.) Furthermore, NP proofs can be efficiently transformed into NP proofs that offer a trade-off between the portion of the proof being read and the confidence it offers. Specifically, if the verifier is willing to tolerate an error probability of ε then it suffices to let it examine $c\log_2(1/\varepsilon)$ bits of the (transformed) NP proof.[6] These bit locations need to be selected at random. We mention that the length of the redundant NP proofs that provide the aforementioned trade-off can be made almost linear in the length of the standard NP proofs.

PCP and the Study of Approximation

The characterization of $\mathcal{NP}$ in terms of probabilistically checkable proofs has played a central role in developments concerning the study of approximation problems. For details, see Hochbaum (1996, chap. 10). We merely mention

[6] In fact, c can be made arbitrarily close to 1, when ε is small enough.

that Theorem 9.12 implies that, assuming $\mathcal{P} \neq \mathcal{NP}$, there exists a constant $\delta < 1$ such that *given a system of quadratic equations it is infeasible to distinguish the case in which the system has an integer solution from the case that any assignment of integers satisfies at most a δ fraction of the equations.*

The Role of Randomness

The foregoing results rely on the randomness of the verifier and are not possible for deterministic verifiers. Furthermore, $\mathcal{PCP}(0, \texttt{log}) = \mathcal{P}$.

Suggestions for Further Reading

More detailed overviews of the three aforementioned types of probabilistically checkable proof systems can be found in Goldreich (1999, chap. 2). A detailed textbook treatment of zero knowledge is provided in Goldreich (2001, chap. 4).

CRYPTOGRAPHY

In this section, we focus on the role of randomness in cryptography. As stated in the introduction, the very notion of a secret, which is central to cryptography, refers to randomness in the sense of unpredictability (i.e., unpredictability of the secret by other parties). Furthermore, the use of randomized algorithms and/or strategies is essential for achieving almost any security goal. We start with the concrete example of providing secret communication and end with a wider perspective.

Secret Communication

The problem of providing *secret communication over insecure media* is the traditional and most basic problem of cryptography. The setting of this problem consists of two parties communicating through a channel that is possibly tapped by an adversary. The parties wish to exchange information with each other, but keep the "wire-tapper" as ignorant as possible regarding the contents of this information. The canonical solution to the above problem is obtained by the use of encryption schemes.

Loosely speaking, an encryption scheme is a protocol allowing these parties to communicate *secretly* with each other. Typically, the encryption scheme consists of a pair of algorithms. One algorithm, called **encryption**, is applied by the sender (i.e., the party sending a message), while the other algorithm, called **decryption**, is applied by the receiver. Hence, to send a message, the sender first applies the encryption algorithm to the message, and sends the result, called the **ciphertext**, over the channel. Upon receiving a ciphertext, the other party (i.e., the receiver) applies the decryption algorithm to it, and retrieves the original message (called the **plaintext**).

For the foregoing scheme to provide secret communication, the communicating parties (at least the receiver) must know something that is not known to the wire-tapper. (Otherwise, the wire-tapper can decrypt the ciphertext exactly as done by the receiver.) This extra knowledge may take the form of the decryption algorithm itself, or some parameters and auxiliary inputs used by the decryption algorithm. We call this extra knowledge the **decryption-key**. Note that, without loss of generality, we may assume that the decryption algorithm is known to the wire-tapper, and that the decryption algorithm operates on two inputs: a ciphertext and a decryption-key. (The encryption algorithm also takes two inputs: a corresponding encryption-key and a plaintext.) We stress that the existence of a decryption-key, not known to the wire-tapper, is merely a necessary condition for secret communication.

The point we wish to make is that the decryption-key must be generated by a randomized algorithm. Suppose, in contrast, that the decryption-key is a predetermined function of publicly available data (i.e., the key is generated by employing an efficient deterministic algorithm to these data). Then, the wire-tapper can just obtain the key in exactly the same manner (i.e., invoking the same algorithm on the said data). We stress that saying that the wire-tapper does not know which algorithm to employ or does not have the data on which the algorithm is employed just shifts the problem elsewhere; that is, the question remains as to *how do the legitimate parties select this algorithm and the data to which it is applied.* Again, deterministically selecting these objects based on publicly available data will not do. At some point, *the legitimate parties must obtain some object that is unpredictable by the wire-tapper*, and such unpredictability refers to randomness (or pseudorandomness).

However, the role of randomness in allowing for secret communication is not confined to the generation of secret keys. To see why this is the case, we need to understand what is "secrecy" (i.e., to properly define what is meant by this intuitive term). Loosely speaking, we say that an encryption scheme is secure if it is *infeasible for the wire-tapper to obtain from the ciphertexts any additional information about the corresponding plaintexts*. In other words, whatever can be efficiently computed based on the ciphertexts can be efficiently computed from scratch (or rather from the a priori known data). Now, assuming that the encryption algorithm is deterministic, encrypting the same plaintext twice (using the same encryption-key) results in two identical ciphertexts, which are easily distinguishable from any pair of different ciphertexts resulting from the encryption of two different plaintexts. This problem does not arise when employing a randomized encryption algorithm (as presented next).

As hinted, an encryption scheme must specify also a method for selecting keys. In the following encryption scheme, the key is a uniformly selected n-bit string, denoted s. The parties use this key to determine a pseudorandom function f_s (as in Definition 9.5). A plaintext $x \in \{0,1\}^n$ is encrypted (using the key s) by uniformly selecting $r \in \{0,1\}^n$ and producing the ciphertext $(r, f_s(r) \oplus x)$, where $\alpha \oplus \beta$ denotes the bit-by-bit exclusive-or of the strings α and β. A ciphertext (r, y) is decrypted (using the key s) by computing $f_s(r) \oplus y$. The security of this scheme follows from the security of an imaginary (ideal) scheme in which f_s is replaced by a totally random function $F : \{0,1\}^n \rightarrow \{0,1\}^n$.

Public-Key Encryption Schemes

The foregoing description corresponds to the so called model of a *private-key encryption scheme*, and requires the communicating parties to agree beforehand on a corresponding pair of encryption/decryption keys. This need is removed in *public-key encryption schemes*, envisioned by Diffie and Hellman (and materialized by the RSA scheme of Rivest, Shamir, and Adleman). In a public-key encryption scheme, the encryption-key can be publicized without harming the security of the plaintexts encrypted using it, allowing anybody to send encrypted messages to Party X by using the encryption-key publicized by Party X. But in such a case, the need for randomized encryption is even more clear. Indeed, if a deterministic encryption algorithm is employed and the wire-tapper knows the encryption-key, then it can identify the plaintext in the case that the number of possibilities is small. In contrast, using a randomized encryption algorithm, the encryption of plaintext `yes` under a known encryption-key may be computationally indistinguishable from the encryption of the plaintext `no` under the encryption-key. For further discussion of the security and construction of encryption schemes, the interested reader is referred to Goldreich (2004, chap. 5).

A Wider Perspective

Modern cryptography is concerned with the construction of information systems that are robust against malicious attempts to make these systems deviate from their prescribed functionality. The prescribed functionality may be the private and authenticated communication of information through the Internet, the holding of incoercible and secret electronic voting, or conducting any "fault-resilient" multiparty computation. Indeed, the scope of modern cryptography is very broad, and it stands in contrast to "classical" cryptography (which has focused on the single problem of enabling secret communication over insecure communication media).

For a presentation of the foundations of modern cryptography, the interested reader is referred to Goldreich (2001, 2004). Here, we merely note that randomness plays a central role in the treatment of each problem in that vast area. In almost every case, the inputs of the legitimate parties are assumed to be unpredictable by the adversary, and the task is performing some manipulation (of the inputs) while preserving or creating some unpredictability. In all cases, this is obtained by using randomized algorithms.

Sublinear Time Algorithms

For starters, let us consider a well-known example in which fast approximations are possible and useful. Suppose that some cost function is defined over a huge data set, and that one wants to approximate the average cost of an element in the set. To be more specific, let $\mu : S \to [0,1]$ be a cost function, and suppose we want to estimate $\overline{\mu} \stackrel{def}{=} \frac{1}{|S|}\sum_{e \in S}\mu(e)$. Then, for some constant c, uniformly (and independently) selecting $m \stackrel{def}{=} c \cdot \varepsilon^{-2}\log_2(1/\delta)$ sample points, $s_1, \ldots, s_m$, in S we obtain with probability at least $1 - \delta$ an estimate of $\overline{\mu}$ within $\pm\varepsilon$:

$$\mathrm{Pr}_{s_1,\ldots,s_m \in S}\left[\left|\frac{1}{m}\sum_{i=1}^{m}\mu(s_i) - \overline{\mu}\right| > \varepsilon\right] < \delta.$$

We stress the fact that the number of samples *only depends on the desired level of approximation* (and is independent of the size of S). In this section, we discuss analogous phenomena that occur with respect to objectives that are beyond gathering statistics of individual values. We focus on more complex features of a data set; specifically, relations among pairs of elements rather than values of single elements. Such binary relations are captured by graphs (as implicitly defined next): a symmetric binary relation $R \subseteq S \times S$ is represented by a **graph** $G = (S,R)$, where the elements of S are called **vertices** and the elements of R are called **edges**. Each edge consists of a pair of vertices, called its endpoints.

One natural computational question regarding graphs is whether or not they are **bipartite**; that is, whether there exists a partition of S into two subsets S_1 and S_2 such that each edge has one endpoint in S_1 and the other endpoint in S_2. For example, the graph consisting of a cycle of four vertices is bipartite, whereas a triangle is not bipartite. We mention that there exists an efficient algorithm that, given a graph G, determines whether or not G is bipartite. Needless to say, this algorithm must inspect all edges of G, whereas we seek sublinear time algorithms (i.e., algorithms operating in time smaller than the size of the input). In particular, sublinear time algorithms cannot afford reading the entire input graph. Instead, these algorithm can inspect portions of the input graph by querying for the existence of specific edges (i.e., query whether there is an edge between a specific pair of vertices). It turns out that, by making a number of queries that are independent of the size of the graph, one may obtain meaningful information regarding its "distance" to being bipartite. Specifically,

Theorem 9.13. *There exists a randomized algorithm that, on input a parameter ε and access to a graph $G = (S,R)$, makes poly$(1/\varepsilon)$ queries to G and satisfies the following two conditions:*

1. *If G is bipartite, then the algorithm accepts with probability 1.*
2. *If any partition of S into two subsets S_1 and S_2 has at least $\varepsilon|S|^2$ edges with both endpoints in the same S_i, then the algorithm rejects with probability at least 99%.*

The algorithm underlying Theorem 9.13 uniformly selects $m = \mathrm{poly}(1/\varepsilon)$ vertices, and checks whether the induced graph is bipartite; that is, for a sample of vertices $v_1, \ldots, v_m$, it checks whether there exists a partition of $\{v_1, \ldots, v_m\}$ into two subsets V_1 and V_2 such that for every $i \in \{1,2\}$ and every $u, v \in V_i$ it holds that $(u,v) \notin R$.

We stress that the said algorithm does not solve the question of whether or not the graph is bipartite, but rather a relaxed (or approximated) version of this question in which one needs to *distinguish graphs that are bipartite from graphs that are very far from being bipartite*. This phenomenon is analogous to the case of approximating the average value of $\mu : S \to [0,1]$. Also, as in the case of approximating the average value of $\mu : S \to [0,1]$, it is essential that the approximation algorithm be randomized. A similar phenomenon occurs with respect to several other natural properties of graphs, but is not generic. That is, there exist graph properties for which even inspecting a constant fraction of the graph does not allow for an approximate decision regarding satisfiability of the property. For details, the interested reader is directed to Fischer (2001) and Ron (2001).

We note that the notion of approximation underlying Theorem 9.13 refers to disregarding $\varepsilon|S|^2$ edges, where $|S|^2$ is the maximum possible number of edges over S. This notion of approximation is appealing in the case that R is dense (i.e., contains a constant fraction of all possible edges). Going to the other extreme, we may consider the case that R contains only a linear (in $|S|$) number of edges, or even the case that each vertex participates only in a constant number of edges. In this case, we may want to distinguish the case that the graph is bipartite from the case that any partition of S into two subsets S_1 and S_2 has at least $\varepsilon|S|$ edges with both endpoints in the same S_i. It turns out that this problem can be solved by an algorithm that makes $\text{poly}((\log|S|)/\varepsilon)\sqrt{|S|}$ queries (to an adequate data structure), and that these many queries are essentially necessary. We note that this sublinear time algorithm operates by inspecting a graph induced by $\text{poly}((\log|S|)/\varepsilon)\sqrt{|S|}$ vertices that are selected by taking many (relatively short) random walks from few randomly selected starting vertices. For details, the interested reader is directed to Ron (2001, sec. 3).

The aforementioned type of approximation is known by the name *property testing*. One archetypical problem, which played a central role in the construction of PCP systems (see the section Probabilistically Checkable Proof Systems), is distinguishing low-degree polynomials from functions that are far from any such polynomial. Specifically, let F be a finite field (i.e., a set with addition and multiplication) and m, d be integers. Given access to a function $f : F^m \to F$, we wish to make few queries and distinguish the case that f is an m-variate polynomial of total degree d from the case it disagrees with any such polynomial on at least 1% of the domain. It turns out that making $\text{poly}(d)$ random (but dependent) queries to f suffices for making a decision that is correct with high probability.

FURTHER READING

We recommend textbooks such as Sipser (1997) for background on the aspects of the theory of computation that are most relevant for the current essay. We note that randomized algorithms and procedures are valuable also in settings not discussed in the current essay (e.g., for polynomial-time computations as well as in the context of distributed and parallel computation). The interested reader is referred to Motwani and Raghavan (1995).

REFERENCES

Cover, T. M., & Thomas, G. A. (1991). *Elements of information theory*. New York: Wiley.

Fischer, E. (2001). The art of uninformed decisions: A primer to property testing. *Bulletin of the European Association for Theoretical Computer Science, 75*, 97–126.

Goldreich, O. (1999). *Modern cryptography, probabilistic proofs and pseudorandomness*. Berlin, Germany: Springer.

Goldreich, O. (2001). *Foundation of cryptography: Basic tools*. Cambridge, UK: Cambridge University Press.

Goldreich, O. (2004). *Foundation of cryptography: Basic applications*. New York: Cambridge University Press.

Hochbaum, D. (Ed.). (1996). *Approximation algorithms for NP-hard problems*. Boston: PWS.

Li, M., & Vitanyi, P. (1993). *An introduction to Kolmogorov complexity and its applications*. New York: Springer-Verlag.

Motwani, R., & Raghavan, P. (1995). *Randomized algorithms*. Cambridge, UK: Cambridge University Press.

Ron, D. (2001). Property testing. In S. Rajasekaran, P. M. Pardalos, J. H. Reif, & J. D. P. Rolim (Eds.), *Handbook on randomization* (Vol. 2, pp. 597–649). Dordrecht, the Netherlands: Kluwer Academic.

Sipser, M. (1997). *Introduction to the theory of computation*. Boston: PWS.

PART III

APPLICATIONS

10

TIME-SERIES ANALYSIS

MICHAEL ANTHONY LEWIS

INTRODUCTION

As anyone reading this book is likely to be aware, social scientists analyze a great deal of data. Political scientists analyze voting outcomes; psychologists examine response times; sociologists analyze the effects of wealth on numerous outcomes of interest; and economists examine, among other things, the relationship between the unit price of a good and the quantity of that good demanded. Most of the data analyzed by social scientists are cross-sectional, meaning that the variables measured are for a given point in time. But some of the time, social scientists are also interested in dynamic analyses.

The term *dynamic* in the physical/natural sciences (Kaplan & Glass, 1995) refers to change over time. Thus, an ecologist analyzing the change in the population of the members of a particular species over time would be engaging in dynamic analysis. So would a chemist examining the change in the concentration of a substance over time, as would a climate scientist analyzing the change in the global average surface temperature of the earth over time. The term *dynamic* is used in this chapter the way it is in the physical/natural sciences. Thus, an economist analyzing the change in the gross national product (GNP) over time, a sociologist studying change in the divorce rate over time, and a political scientist analyzing change in the proportion of the electorate that voted Republican in the presidential elections over time would all be engaging in dynamic analysis.

It just so happens, however, that in the social sciences, there are different types of dynamic analyses that one can engage in. For instance, an economist might be interested in following a sample of college graduates over time to see how long it takes for members of the sample to obtain their first full-time job. This type of dynamic analysis is referred to as event history or duration modeling (Blossfeld & Rohwer, 1995). As another example, a sociologist might be interested in how social attitudes regarding African Americans have changed over time. To study this, he or she might obtain access to a number of cross-sectional (at a given point in time) samples that were collected at different points in time. These samples could be pooled to form one large sample, and there are certain techniques (Wooldridge, 2000) that would allow the sociologist to analyze the change in social attitudes that interest him or her. This chapter will focus on a third type of dynamic analysis, called time-series analysis. Particular attention will be paid to probability theory and time-series analysis.

The best way to define a time series is through the concept of a *discrete stochastic process*, and defining this concept relies on the notion of a *random variable*. Recall that a random variable is a particular type of function. The range of this function is a subset of real numbers, while the domain is some relevant sample space. A more intuitive definition of random variable, and one that will sometimes be used in this chapter, is a numerical quantity whose value depends on chance (Hassett & Stewart, 1999). This dependence on chance means that the value such a variable will assume cannot be predicted with certainty. Recall also that we can assign probabilities to the values (for discrete random variables) or intervals of values (for continuous ones) that a given random variable can assume. Thus, the concept of a random variable is intimately connected to probability theory.

Having made these points about the notion of a random variable, I can now define discrete stochastic process. A discrete stochastic process is a sequence of random variables. Associated with each number in this sequence is a random variable; together, the members of the sequence and their associated random variables constitute a discrete stochastic process (Wooldridge, 2000).

A somewhat different way of stating this requires a bit of mathematical notation. Let T be the set of natural numbers, and let $\{X_t : t \in T\}$ be a set of random variables indexed by the set T. Then, this set of random variables is a discrete stochastic process. The values available to a social/natural scientist over a given time period—that is, an observed time series—constitute a *realization* of such a stochastic process. By *realization*, I mean a specific set of the possible values, for a given time period, that the random variables making up the stochastic process over that same time period could assume (Wooldridge, 2000). An example should make this clearer.

Again, consider an economist interested in GNP. He or she might have data on GNP for a 25-year period. This would be the time series. Each set of 25 values making up a given series is just one of the possible sets of 25 values that the random variables of interest could have assumed. From a theoretical point of view, if we could somehow run the "experiment" over again—that is, observe this same 25-year period again, we should not be surprised to obtain a different sequence of 25 GNP values. Each of the 25 GNP values that would be obtained from running this experiment over and over again would constitute a realization of the stochastic process that generated these realizations. In other words, we can regard the stochastic process, $\{X_t : t \in T\}$, as a population of all realizations and the actually available values over time as a "sample" from this population.

In the social sciences, the time series of interest are typically measures taken on a single unit of analysis. For example, an economist might be interested in the United States's (unit of analysis) GNP (measure). The sequence of natural numbers represents some unit of time (minute, hour, day, month, year, etc.). Thus, the economist might be interested in observations of yearly GNP levels.

Having gone over these preliminary matters, let me now provide a "map" of the territory that will be covered. The next section discusses the two fundamental applications of time-series analysis in the sciences. Afterward, deterministic time-series models are discussed. The section after that discusses random-walk models. Next, the distinction between stationary and nonstationary time series is discussed. I next focus on autoregressive models. Then, what economists/econometricians call regression analysis with time-series data and intervention models are the focus. I end with a short conclusion. I should add that the purpose of this chapter is not to go into the details of model estimation. I have the more modest goals of showing how some of the concepts from probability theory discussed in earlier chapters are related to time-series analysis and of providing an overview of some of the models frequently used in the social sciences.

The Two Applications of Time-Series Analysis

I said above that scientists (natural and social) use time-series analysis to represent change over time. It's time to get a bit more specific. Scientists use time-series analysis in two main applications: (1) explanation and (2) prediction (forecasting).

Explanation is based on a realization (see above) and involves using the past values of a variable to explain (some would say describe) the level of a later value. Or an analyst might use a realization for one variable to explain the realization for another. For example, an economist may have available a set of inflation levels over time and may use earlier inflation levels to explain later levels. Or he or she might have a realization of money supply values and one of inflation levels and regress inflation values on money supply values to determine if variation in money supply explains variation in inflation. Here, one needs to keep in mind that all the values used in time-series analysis for explanation have been actually observed or are actually available to the analyst. This is in contrast to the use of time-series analysis for prediction or forecasting.

Studenmund (1997) defines forecasting as "the estimation of the expected value of a dependent variable for observations that are not part of the sample data set" (p. 568).[1] An example should make this definition clearer. Let's consider the economist again. He or she has a realization of yearly inflation values from 1950 to 2005. Using (10.11) (see below[2]), the economist models later inflation values (e.g., 2005) as a function of the previous year's value. This is using time series for explanation. Now, here comes the forecasting part. Once our economist obtains an estimate for ρ, he or she can insert his or her 2005 inflation value into his or her equation and obtain the expected value of the 2006 inflation. Note that the economist hasn't observed the 2006 inflation value because he or she only has data up to 2005. This is why the expected value for 2006 is a predicted value or forecast.

Now, let's consider the situation where the economist has a realization of money supply values and one of inflation values. If the economist regresses inflation on money supply, he or she will get an estimate of the effect of money supply on inflation. Using his or her estimated equation, he or she could insert a money supply value that falls at a point beyond the times he or she has observed to obtain a forecast for the inflation level at the time, which is also beyond the times of the observed inflation levels. Since this is a book on probability theory, it's appropriate to go into a brief discussion of how probability is related to all this.

In short, the relevance of probability has to do with the concept of expected value. Recall that an observed time series is a realization or sample from a population of realizations. When time-series analysis is used for explanation, often what is happening is that the analyst is using a realization to create a representation of how earlier values (time $t - 1$) explain later values (time t), where the time t value obtained by the model is the expected value of the time t random variable. To consider inflation again, if (10.11) is used as our model, inflation values in 2004 would be used to obtain inflation in 2005, where inflation in 2005 is the expected value of the distribution of possible inflation values for the year 2005.

As stated above, sometimes when time-series analysis is used for explanation, the analyst is using one realization to explain another (money supply at time t to explain inflation at time t). Here, the value of the explained variable at time t is the expected value of the distribution of the possible values of that variable given a value of the explanatory variable at time t. For example, using an estimated equation, one might find that inflation in 2004 is explained by money supply in 2004, where the 2004 inflation rate is the expected value of the distribution of possible 2004 inflation values for a given 2004 money supply value.

Turning to prediction, recall that Studenmund (1997) defines forecasting in terms of expected

[1]See Chapter 2 in this volume for the definition of expected value. Also, the term sample data set in Studenmund's definition is what I've called a realization.

[2]However, in this context, the $\rho = 1$ condition is not required, unless the economist is assuming a random-walk model.

value. That is, when one forecasts a value of a variable for a time point outside the observed time points, the forecast is the expected value of the distribution of possible values of that variable for the time point of interest. The relevance of the concept of expected value to the different applications of time-series analysis is the crucial probability theoretical link between these types of applications.

Deterministic Time-Series Models

Simple Extrapolation Models

When economists and sociologists use statistical techniques to analyze data, they tend to be concerned with modeling how change in a set of independent variables affects change in a given dependent variable.[3] A time series can be treated in an analogous way, with the values of the time series playing the role of dependent variable and time the role of an independent variable. However, unlike in regression analysis, there is no error or residual term included in the models to be covered in this section. The exclusion of an error term amounts to ignoring the stochastic nature of the data and treating the values of the series as if they were generated by a deterministic process. Time-series models that ignore the stochastic nature of the data generation process are called deterministic models. The simplest types of such models are known as *simple extrapolation models*. These are most appropriate when one believes that trends that seem to be evident in the series will continue (Pindyck & Rubinfeld, 1998) beyond the observed time periods.

The most basic extrapolation model is the *linear trend model*. Letting Y_t denote a given variable at time t and t some unit of time, if one believes that Y_t will increase by a constant absolute amount in each time period, then Y_t can be predicted with the following model:

$$Y_t = a + bt. \qquad (10.1)$$

Here, b is the change in Y_t per unit time and can be thought of as the "effect" of time on Y_t. A positive b would indicate a linear upward trend over time and a negative b a linear downward one.

If one believes that Y_t grows with a constant percentage increase over time, the following extrapolation model, called the exponential growth model, would be appropriate:[4]

$$Y_t = Ae^{rt}. \qquad (10.2)$$

To see that this model is a constant percentage increase model, consider the following. First, take the natural logarithm (ln) of both sides of (10.2) to obtain

$$\ln Y_t = \ln A + rt. \qquad (10.3)$$

One sees that $\ln Y_t$ is a linear function of t, and therefore, r is the change in Y_t for each one-unit change in t. Yet using the rule for calculating derivatives of logarithmic functions as well as the chain rule from calculus (Ash & Ash, 1986), one finds that $d\ln Y_t/dt = (1/Y_t)(dY_t/dt) = (dY_t/Y_t)(1/dt)$, which is the percentage of change in Y_t with respect to time.

A third type of extrapolation model is the *quadratic trend model*:

$$Y_t = a + b_1 t + b_2 t^2. \qquad (10.4)$$

For example, assuming that b_1 is positive and b_2 is negative, this model is useful if one believes that Y_t increases over time, but at a decreasing rate.[5]

More could be said about simple extrapolation methods, but due to space constraints, I won't go into these matters. Instead, I'll move on to another type of deterministic model, the so-called moving average model.

[3] The set of independent variables may be a set with one member; that is, concern may be just with one independent variable.

[4] A constant percentage decrease would be the case if rt were negated.

[5] If b_1 were negative and b_2 positive, this model would be useful for representing Y_t as a decreasing function of time, where Y_t decreases at a decreasing rate.

Moving Average Models and Smoothing

Another category of deterministic time-series models are called moving average models. These are most appropriate when one believes that the value of a time series at a given point in time is a simple average of its values over the past n time periods, where n (the number of time periods) is set by the analyst. For example, suppose an analyst is examining a yearly time series and believes that Y_t is a simple average of Y over the six previous years. Then, the following model would be appropriate:

$$Y_t = \tfrac{1}{6}(Y_{t-1} + Y_{t-2} + \cdots + Y_{t-6}). \qquad (10.5)$$

Sometimes, it may be reasonable to assume that earlier values contribute less to the value of a time series at a given point than more recent values. For example, it may make sense to assume that the population of the United States in 2004 was influenced more by its population in 2003 than by its population in 1920. This assumption can be incorporated into a moving average model by weighting more recent values higher than earlier values, and one way to do this is through the use of an *exponentially weighted moving average model*. This model takes the following form:

$$\begin{aligned} Y_t &= \alpha Y_{t-1} + \alpha(1-\alpha)Y_{t-2} + (1-\alpha)^2 Y_{t-3} + \cdots \\ &= \alpha \sum (1-\alpha)^{\tau} Y_{t-\tau}. \end{aligned} \qquad (10.6)$$

Here, the summation is from $\tau = 1$ to $\tau =$ some finite (possibly very large) number, and $0 < \alpha < 1$. The values of α falling within (0, 1) is what accounts for the fact that earlier values have less of an effect on Y_t than later ones. One can see that (10.6) is a true average by considering the fact that $\alpha \sum (1-\alpha)^{\tau}$ is a geometric series—that is, $(1-\alpha)$ is within $(-1, 1)$, and therefore the series converges to $\alpha/[1-(1-\alpha)] = 1$ (Ash & Ash, 1986). That is, the weights in the exponential moving average model sum to 1.

Some time series are characterized by very volatile short-term fluctuations, and smoothing techniques are useful for removing these fluctuations. Such removal might be desirable because it is often easier to visually analyze a series for trends and periodicity when it has been smoothed (Pindyck & Rubinfeld, 1998). The moving average models discussed above are also useful for this purpose. For example, consider the generalized version of (10.5):

$$\text{sm}Y_t = \tfrac{1}{n}(Y_t + Y_{t-1} + \cdots + Y_{t-n+1}). \qquad (10.7)$$

Here, sm denotes the smoothed series. Thus, (10.7) indicates that each value of the smoothed series is the sum of the nonsmoothed series values from $t-n+1$ to t divided by n. The larger the n, the smoother the series will be (Pindyck & Rubinfeld, 1998).

The exponentially weighted moving average model can also be used to smooth a time series if one wants to weight later values more to create the smoothed series. Slightly modifying (10.7), we find that

$$\text{sm}Y_t = \alpha Y_t + \alpha(1-\alpha)Y_{t-1} + \alpha(1-\alpha)^2 Y_{t-2} + \cdots. \qquad (10.8)$$

Modeling Seasonal Variation

Some time series are characterized by repetitive or periodic patterns, and for obvious reasons, when these patterns have frequencies of less than a year, they are often called seasons (Williams, 1997). Seasonal adjustment methods can be used to separate seasonal patterns from long-term trends in a time series to make it easier to assess such trends. One may assume that (Bowerman, O'Connell, & Koehler, 2005) a time series can be represented as a combination of two parts:

$$Y_t = \text{TR}_t + \text{SN}_t, \qquad (10.9)$$

where TR_t = the long-term trend at time t and SN_t = the seasonal component at time t.[6] There are many ways to separate out SN_t, but due to space constraints, I'll only consider one of the simpler methods—namely, the use of dummy variables.[7]

[6]Bowerman et al. (2005) include an error term in their version of (10.9). This is because they are concerned with the stochastic nature of a time series, while, for the time being, this chapter is focused on models that ignore the stochastic nature of time series. Also, a time series may be represented as having an additional periodic component longer than 1 year, usually called a cycle (see Williams, 1997).

[7]The methods include the ratio-to-moving-average method, the percentage-of-annual-average method, and the use of trigonometric functions. See Gujarati (1995) and Bowerman et al. (2005).

To use the dummy variable method, the analyst must first conceptualize the series in terms of n seasons. For example, suppose one had a relatively long series of monthly GNP figures. We usually think of a year as being made up of four seasons, so we might use $n = 4$ to seasonally adjust such a series. Let $D_2 = 1$ if the value comes from Season 2, 0 if from another season. Let $D_3 = 1$ if the value comes from Season 3, 0 if from another season. Let $D_4 = 1$ if the value comes from Season 4, 0 if from another season.[8]

And finally, let $\text{SN}_t = \beta_2 D_2 + \beta_3 D_3 + \beta_3 D_3$. Then, one might consider the following model:

$$Y_t = \text{TR}_t + \beta_2 D_2 + \beta_3 D_3 + \beta_3 D_4. \tag{10.10}$$

Equation (10.10) can be generalized for n seasons by letting the number of dummy variables (i.e., the D variables) range from 2 to $n - 1$.

More could be said about deterministic time-series models, but I'll neglect the urge to do so. This is because the current chapter appears in a book on probability theory, and it only stands to reason that it should concern itself more with topics related to this area of inquiry. When it comes to time-series models, as these are used in the social sciences, probability theory is most relevant for models that consider the stochastic nature of time series. It is to such models that I will next turn.

Random-Walk Model

The first time-series model that I'll discuss focuses on the stochastic nature of a time series and is called the *random-walk model*. It takes the following form:

$$Y_t = \rho Y_{t-1} + u_t, \tag{10.11}$$

where $\rho = 1$. Here, u_t is the error term, and it is assumed to have the same characteristics as the error term in an ordinary least squares (OLS) regression model—namely, a random variable with a mean of 0 and a constant variance. Error is understood here in the sense of part of the information being unaccounted for, not in the sense that something is wrong. Also, as with regression, error terms at different time points are uncorrelated. Inclusion of the error term in (10.11) is why the random-walk model is one that includes the stochastic nature of a time series. Those familiar with mathematical statistics will recall that a function of a random variable is itself a random variable. Thus, since (10.11) indicates that Y_t is a function of u_t, it follows that Y_t is a random variable. That is, at each time t, Y is a variable that assumes one of a number of possible values, and none of these can be predicted with certainty in advance. This means that Y_t represents a sequence of random variables, and this, of course, is just how I defined a stochastic process earlier.

The random-walk model is of interest to economists and financial engineers because GNP values, stock prices, and other time series of interest to such analysts may be best modeled as random walks (Focardi & Fabozzi, 2004). The random-walk model is probably most associated with financial economics. Assuming that participants in stock and other asset markets are rational, and making other assumptions that together constitute the so-called efficient market hypothesis,[9] many financial economists derive the prediction that stock prices are constant over time, excluding random error. That is, the assumptions of a version of the efficient market hypothesis imply that stock prices must unfold over time, as represented by (10.11). I should add that in spite of the popularity of this model in financial economics, many econophysicists do not believe that the random-walk model is supported by the available evidence. That is, they question the efficient market hypothesis.[10] Due to the popularity of the random-walk model in financial economics, economists have even come up with a way to test whether a time series is appropriately modeled as a random walk. The test in question is called the *unit root test*. Since this chapter and the book aren't about statistics or econometrics but

[8] Season 1 is the reference season.

[9] See Peters (1996) for a discussion of the efficient market hypothesis.

[10] See Peters (1996) for a discussion of this debate. For those unfamiliar with the term, econophysicists are a group of physicists who apply methods of physics, mainly statistical physics, to economic and financial issues. Peters's book is essentially an overview of some of these econophysical methods.

about how probability theory is related to these and other fields, I won't go into the details of the unit root test. Instead, I'll just focus on how probability theory is related to the test.

Essentially, the unit root test is based on an estimate of a regression model like (10.11). The estimate of ρ—let's call it ρ_E—is divided by its estimated standard error to obtain the tau statistic. Here is where probability comes into play. After conducting the unit root test, a statistical test based on Frequentist as opposed to Bayesian statistical theory, one determines whether the particular ρ_E value obtained is likely given that the null is true (Gujarati, 1995). The use of "likely" is an obvious indication of the relevance of probability theory.

STATIONARY AND NONSTATIONARY TIME SERIES

Refer back to (10.11). If $\rho = 1$, Y_t "takes" a random walk, as discussed above. But if $\rho > 1$, this would mean that Y_t trends upward over time, and if $\rho < 1$, this would mean a downward trend in Y_t. Time series with upward (or downward) trends are called nonstationary time series. Since time series are sequences of random variables, one can consider the means and variances of these variables as well as the correlations between them. Nonstationarity of a time series has to do with the means of, variances of, and correlations between the random variables that constitute a time series. Let Y_t be the value of a given variable at time t, and Y_{t-k} the value of this variable k periods earlier. Then, a time series is nonstationary if (1) the mean Y_t is not constant over time, (2) the variance Y_t is not constant over time, and (3) the simple correlation coefficient between Y_t and Y_{t-k} does not depend only on the value of k (Bowerman et al., 2005). The last condition may need some elaboration.

The correlation referred to in Condition 3 is called the autocorrelation of lag k (ACF(k)) and, for the infinite sequence of time-series values, is expressed mathematically as

$$\text{ACF}(k) = \frac{E[(Y_t - \mu_Y)(Y_{t-k} - \mu_Y)]}{\sigma_{Y_t}\sigma_{Y_{t-k}}}, \quad (10.12)$$

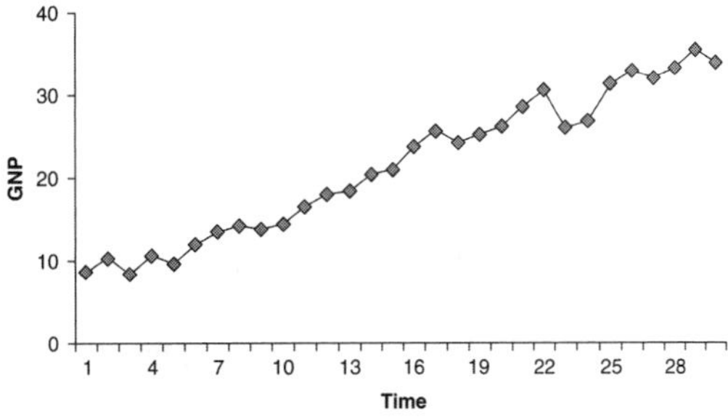

Figure 10.1 Time series of GNP.

SOURCE: Data taken from Griffiths, Hill, and Judge (1993).

where E denotes the expected value, μ_Y denotes the mean of the sequence of time-series values, σ_{Y_t} is the standard deviation of Y_t, and $\sigma_{Y_{t-k}}$ is the standard deviation of Y_{t-k}.

A careful look at (10.12) indicates that when it comes to actually calculating ACF(k), one runs into a problem. To calculate ACF(k), one would need μ_Y, which means that all the values making up the time series would be required. But there are an infinite number of such values, so all of them cannot be obtained. Since all these values cannot be obtained, μ_Y cannot be calculated; and since μ_Y cannot be calculated, the expected value in (10.12) cannot be observed. Thus, ACF(k) cannot be calculated.[11] To address this problem, statisticians have developed the sample autocorrelation of lag k, based on the available time-series values:

$$\text{ACF}(k)_s = \frac{\Sigma[(Y_t - \mu_{Y_s})(Y_{t-k} - \mu_Y)]}{\Sigma(Y_t - \mu Y_s)^2}, \quad (10.13)$$

where s denotes the sample value.

Figure 10.1 is a graph of the United States's GNP values over a 30-year period.

Assuming that the means of the sequence of random variables constituting the time series are linearly and positively related, the realization in the figure clearly indicates the characteristic upward trend of a nonstationary time series. One might wonder how the upward trend is related to the three conditions for the nonstationary series discussed above. From an intuitive point of view,

[11] The standard deviations of Y_t and Y_{t-k}, which appear in the denominator of (10.12), also cannot be observed. This adds to the problem of trying to calculate ACF(k).

this connection is easy to explain. If the line of best fit were fitted to the series in Figure 10.1, it should be clear that this line would trend upward just as the actual date points do. Recall from regression analysis that the points on the line of best fit represent the means of the y-axis random variables with respect to given values of the x-axis variables. Thus, an upward trending line of best fit indicates upward trending means of these random variables, which, clearly, meets Condition 1 for a nonstationary series.

A formal test for stationarity relies on (10.13). Suppose we (really the computer) calculate (10.13) for lags 1,2,3,.... We could then graph the left-hand side of (10.13), for given lags, as a function of the different lags. Such a graph is called the *sample autocorrelation function* (Bowerman et al., 2005). It is an estimate of the relationship between the lags and the true autocorrelations given by (10.12). That is, it estimates how the relationship between all possible time-series values separated by a given lag (provided by (10.12)) is related to that lag. One can transform a given $\text{ACF}(k)_s$ to a t statistic by application of the appropriate formula, the details of which I need not go into here.[12] Delving into the meaning of such a t statistic allows us to further explore the relationship between probability and time-series analysis.

I said above that a time series is a realization from a set of possible realizations. Thus, theoretically speaking, the value of $\text{ACF}(k)_s$ based on a given realization for a given time period is just one possible value this statistic could take. Other realizations over this same time period would often result in other values. That is, for a given lag, we can imagine there being a sampling distribution of $\text{ACF}(k)_s$ values, with the $\text{ACF}(k)_s$ obtained based on the realization with which one is working serving as one of the members of this distribution. This distribution has the shape of a t distribution, and the t value alluded to in the previous paragraph simply locates the $\text{ACF}(k)_s$, for a given realization, on this distribution. Using t tests based on the t statistics associated with given $\text{ACF}(k)_s$ values, for given lags, one can determine if these $\text{ACF}(k)_s$ values tend to 0 as the

[12]See Studenmund (1997, chap. 5) for the formula.

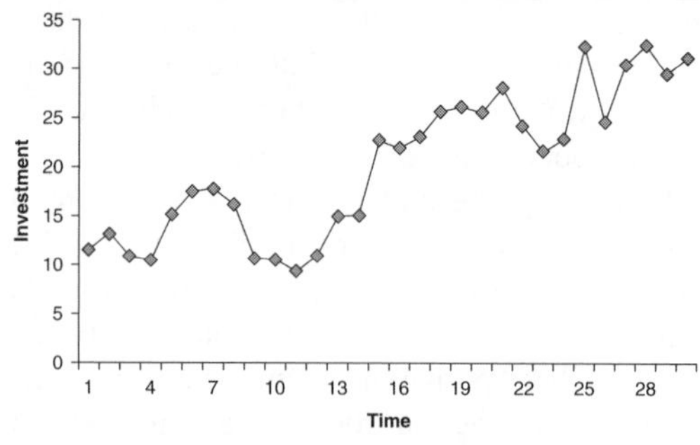

Figure 10.2 Time series of investment.

SOURCE: Data taken from Griffiths et al. (1993).

length of the lag increases. That is, one can determine if the sample autocorrelation function decreases toward 0 as the lag increases. If this were the case, the time series in question would be considered stationary (Gujarati, 1995). What's most relevant for readers of this book is to note the use of the t probability density function in arriving at this decision.

One of the main reasons nonstationarity should be of interest to social scientists is that if one were to model one time series as a function of another series,[13] ignoring nonstationarity could lead to spurious relationships. For example, consider the graph of U.S. investment over time (the same 30-year period as depicted in Figure 10.1) shown in Figure 10.2.

Clearly, investment shows the same upward trend as does GNP, or at least it does from about Year 11 onward. If one were to regress GNP on investment, say to test an economic theory of GNP determination, one would, no doubt, find a very strong relationship between these two variables, as indicated by a very high r^2 value. Yet this strong relationship might not be because investment really affects GNP but simply because both variables are trending upward. In other words, a third variable may be affecting both GNP and investment in such a way that both trend upward; that is, the investment-GNP relationship may be spurious. For example, relying on

[13]This notion of modeling one series as a function of another is the hallmark of so-called regression analysis with time-series analysis data (Wooldridge, 2000). More will be said about this approach later.

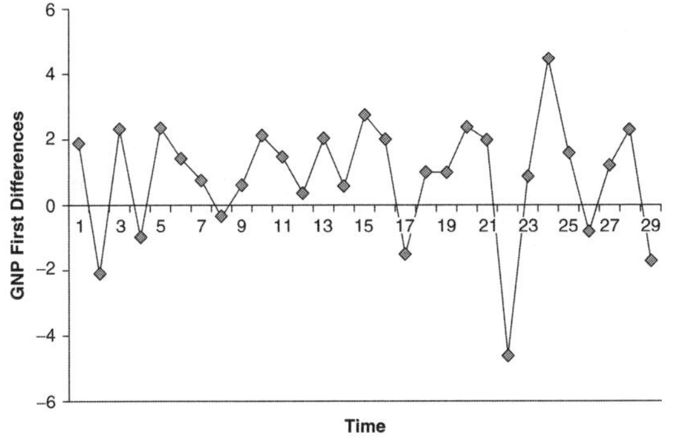

Figure 10.3 First differences of GNP series.

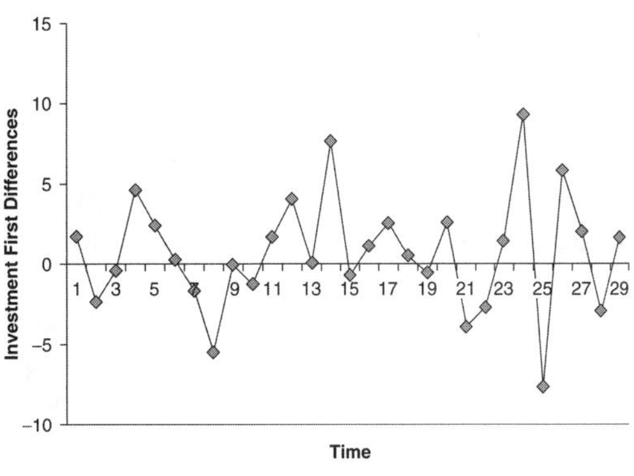

Figure 10.4 First differences of investment series.

Keynesian economic assumptions,[14] an increase in government spending may increase GNP through stimulating more aggregate demand while at the same time increasing investment because private sector investors expect the increase in government spending to result in more people buying their goods and services.

A standard way of addressing this problem is to take what are called first differences (Bowerman et al., 2005). The first differences of Y (ΔY) are obtained as follows:

$$(\Delta Y) = Y_t - Y_{t-1}. \qquad (10.14)$$

That is, a new variable is created by subtracting from each Y value the Y value that preceded it by one unit.

A plot of the first differences of GNP is shown in Figure 10.3 and one of the first differences of investment in Figure 10.4. Note the lack of upward trend in these two graphs, suggesting that the plotted variables may now be stationary over time.[15] According to econometricians, if one were now to regress GNP on investment, the spurious relationship problem may be less likely to occur (Studenmund, 1997).

[14]See Colander and Gamber (2002).

[15]Below, I'll discuss a more formal test for stationarity, since the "eyeballing" method can easily lead one astray.

Autoregressive Models

One of the most influential approaches to analyzing time series, fully taking into account their stochastic natures, is often called the Box-Jenkins (BJ) approach since Box and Jenkins (1976)[16] developed it in their widely acclaimed text on series data. The BJ approach "makes a very big deal" out of the distinction between stationary and nonstationary time series. To see the relevance of this distinction to the BJ approach, one must first get some sense of what this approach involves.

When social scientists, particularly sociologists and economists, use statistical methods in their work, they tend to use some version of regression analysis. As those familiar with such work are most likely aware, social scientists often start with a theory positing the relationship between some dependent variable and a set of independent variables and view the regression techniques as ways of "testing" the theory. Since social scientists, especially economists and sociologists, often deal with observational as opposed to experimental data, they usually are not in a position to conduct experiments. Thus, the testing of theoretical models in social science using regression analysis serves as a kind of second best to experiments in the natural sciences. The BJ approach is different. Instead of the more

[16]See Bowerman et al. (2005) for a more accessible discussion of the BJ approach.

theory-driven approach of social scientists, the BJ approach is more empirically driven, in the sense that it calls for starting with the sequence of data points and simply trying to find out what time-series model adequately represents the process that generated these data. Testing the relationship between/among the variables of interest to sociologists, economists, or any other natural/social scientists is not a major concern in this approach. In fact, in an effort to represent the data-generation processes that produced given time series, the BJ approach often uses models that in a sense don't contain dependent and independent variables in the sense that social scientists are used to. To the average quantitative social scientist, a standard type of BJ approach time-series model might look like a regression model where the dependent variable is regressed on itself. This is because the BJ approach time-series models often take the following form:

$$Y_t = \delta + \rho Y_{t-1} + u_t. \tag{10.15}$$

In (10.15), u_t meets standard OLS assumptions. It is clear that (10.15) does represent Y at a later time as a function of "itself" one period earlier, and for this reason the equation is called an *autoregressive model*. More specifically, (10.15) is called an autoregressive model of order 1 because Y only "goes back" one period or unit of time. Astute readers may have noticed that the random-walk model of (10.11) is a special case of an autoregressive where $\delta = 0$ and $\rho = 1$. From a more general perspective, the autoregressive model of order p takes the following form:

$$Y_t = \delta + \rho Y_{t-1} + \rho Y_{t-2} + \cdots + \rho Y_{t-p} + u_t. \tag{10.16}$$

For an autoregressive model to be used appropriately to represent a time series, the series must be nonstationary (Bowerman et al., 2005). Given that, as stated above, the BJ approach makes frequent use of autoregressive models, it should be clear why the nonstationary/stationary distinction is so important to this approach.

Even though autoregressive models, as used in the BJ approach, tend not to be concerned with testing social scientific theories, such models might be useful to social scientists. A number of variables of interest to social scientists may be autoregressive. For example, there may be good reasons for believing that GNP at one time point may be affected by GNP at earlier time points plus some random or stochastic component, and the same may be true about the effect of the previous year's population on this year's.

The Regression Approach to Times-Series Analysis and Intervention Models

As stated above, social scientists engaged in quantitative research are typically interested in testing for the effects of a set of independent variables on a dependent variable, and OLS regression is used to do this. It's also the case that this use of regression is often on cross-sectional data. Yet this chapter hasn't had much to say about the relationship between time-series analysis and this more traditional OLS approach. It is now time to discuss this relationship.[17]

Social scientists, especially economists, often take a deductive approach to theorizing. That is, they start with a set of assumptions, state these assumptions mathematically in the form of models, and derive predictions from these models. These predictions are then tested using regression analysis. Often, social scientists' mathematical models lead to predictions about how time series are related to one another. For example, an economist might predict that the quantity demanded of some good at a given time is a function of the price of the good at that time. Observations of quantity demanded and price at given time points could be used in a regression analysis to test to see if this relationship takes a certain form. This use of time-series data to test predictions that have been deductively generated by mathematical models (sometimes called structural equation models) is referred to as *regression analysis with time-series data*. In contrast with the more inductive BJ approach, at least this is the way many social scientists see it (Ostrom, 1990; Wooldridge, 2000).

[17]This section will focus on OLS-based intervention and multivariate models since these are likely to be the ones of most interest to social scientists. Box and Jenkins (1976) introduced a more complicated approach to these models.

Suppose there are three time series of interest to a social scientist and the scientist believes that two of these series, represented as X_{1t} and X_{2t}, can be used to predict the conditional means of the variables making up the third, represented by Y_t. By "conditional mean," I'm referring to the mean of Y at a certain point in time, given specific values of X_1 and X_2 at that point in time—that is, (mean $Y_t|X_{1t},X_{2t}$). This belief could be tested by estimating the following model (Wooldridge, 2000):

$$Y_t = \alpha + \beta_1 X_{1t} + \beta_2 X_{2t} + u_t. \qquad (10.17)$$

If the estimates of β_1 and β_2 are statistically significant, this would support the social scientist's hypothesis. Of course, (10.17) could be generalized to include more than two independent variables.

Researchers who use models such as (10.17) need to attend to two crucial issues. First, as stated above, if a set of time-series values (the values being from different series) are all nonstationary, it may appear that the conditional means of the values making up one depend on the values making up the others, when this is not the case. In terms of (10.17), we may get significant β_1 or β_2 estimates, even though the independent variables in the equation have no effect on the dependent one. If it's discovered that nonstationarity is a problem, taking the first differences (see above) of all the variables in (10.17) and rerunning the model with these differences will usually solve the problem.[18]

Second, regression analysis models with time-series data tend to have nonzero correlations between adjacent (separated by one time unit)[19] errors to a greater extent than do cross-sectional regression models (Gujarati, 1995; Studenmund, 1997). This makes a statistical test called the *Durban-Watson d* (DWd) test particularly relevant to regression analysis with time-series data. This test is used to see if there is what is called *first-order serial correlation* between adjacent errors. Of course, since the true errors are typically unobservable, the DWd test is applied to the residuals of the equation used to estimate (10.18). The test is only appropriately used if the following assumptions hold:

1. The regression model includes an intercept term.
2. The serial correlation is first order; that is, $u_t = \rho u_{t-1} + \varepsilon_t$, where ε_t is an error term that meets standard OLS assumptions.
3. The regression model does not include an earlier period dependent variable (called a lagged variable) as an independent variable.[20]

Condition 2 indicates that for the DWd test to be valid, the true error must unfold according to an autoregressive process, and if $\rho = 1$, this would be a random-walk process (see above). If $\rho < 0$, this would indicate no positive serial correlation, and if $\rho = 0$, this would indicate no serial correlation of any kind. If $\rho > 0$, there would be positive serial correlation, and if $\rho \neq 0$, we would have serial correlation. The DWd statistic is used to determine if $\rho > 0$ or if $\rho \neq 0$. If first-order serial correlation is found, alternative estimation (alternative to (10.17)) methods are required.

Like cross-sectional regression models, regression analysis with time-series data can also include dummy variables. Such variables are often used to represent how interventions of various kinds affect the values of a time series (Wooldridge, 2000).[21] For example, slightly modifying (10.17), suppose a researcher believes that in, addition to X_{1t} and X_{2t}, Y_t is also affected by a new law. Some of the values of Y_t preceded and occurred in the same t (e.g., year, month, etc.) as the t when the law was implemented. The rest of the Y_t came after the t of implementation. This scenario could be modeled in the

[18] See Studenmund (1997), Griffiths et al. (1993) and Enders (2004) for details.

[19] These models can have correlations between errors farther apart as well. See Studenmund (1997) for details.

[20] Condition 3 is needed because in the presence of a lagged dependent variable modeled as a dependent variable, the DWd statistic is biased toward 2 (Studenmund, 1997).

[21] Once again, Box and Jenkins (1976) and Bowerman et al. (2005) discuss a more complete method for doing the same thing.

following way:

$$Y_t + \alpha + \beta_1 X_{1t} + \beta_2 X_{2t} + \beta_3 D_t + u_t, \quad (10.18)$$

where $D_t = 1$ if Y_t is before or at the t of implementation of the law and $D_t = 0$ if Y_t is after implementation.

A significant β_3 estimate would indicate support for the hypothesized effect of the law.

Time-series regression models can also include interaction effects. Considering (10.18), suppose the researcher believes that X_{2t} and D_t interact to influence Y_t; that is, the effect of X_{2t} on Y_t depends on the value of D_t. The following model can be estimated using OLS regression:

$$Y_t + \alpha + \beta_1 X_{1t} + \beta_2 X_{2t} + \beta_3 D_t + \beta_4 X_{2t} D_t + u_t, \quad (10.19)$$

A significant estimate of β_4 would indicate an interaction between the two variables in that term. Using the rule, from calculus, for calculating the derivatives of power functions (Ash & Ash, 1986), the effect of X_{2t} on Y_t would be $\beta_2 + \beta_4 D_t$.

Conclusion

This chapter has focused on dynamic modeling in the social sciences—more specifically, time-series modeling. A great deal has been covered in a relatively short amount of space. Unlike in statistics books, the details of estimation have not been the focus. Instead, following the "mission" of the book, I have focused on how probability is related to time-series analysis as well as some of the standard models used in the social sciences. It is hoped that this has been enough to spark the interest of uninitiated readers in the subject. Those interested in finding out more about the details of estimation can start with appropriate books in the list of references.

References

Ash, C., & Ash, R. B. (1986). *The calculus tutoring book*. New York: Wiley-IEEE.

Blossfeld, H.-P., & Rohwer, G. (1995). *Techniques of event history modeling: New approaches to causal analysis*. Mahwah, NJ: Lawrence Erlbaum.

Bowerman, B. L., O'Connell, R. T., & Koehler, A. B. (2005). *Forecasting, time series, and regression*. Belmont, CA: Thomson Brooks/Cole.

Box, G., & Jenkins, G. (1976). *Time series analysis: Forecasting and control*. San Francisco: Holden Day.

Colander, D. C., & Gamber, E. N. (2002). *Macroeconomics*. Upper Saddle River, NJ: Prentice Hall.

Enders, W. (2004). *Applied econometric time series*. New York: Wiley.

Focardi, S. M., & Fabozzi, F. J. (2004). *The mathematics of financial modeling and investment management*. Hoboken, NJ: Wiley.

Griffiths, W. E., Hill, R. C., & Judge, G. G. (1993). *Learning and practicing econometrics*. New York: Wiley.

Gujarati, D. N. (1995). *Basic econometrics*. New York: McGraw-Hill.

Hassett, M. J., & Stewart, D. G. (1999). *Probability for risk management*. Winsted, CT: Actex.

Kaplan, D., & Glass, L. (1995). *Probability for risk management*. New York: Springer-Verlag.

Ostrom, C. W., Jr. (1990). *Time series analysis: Regression techniques*. Newbury Park: CA: Sage.

Peters, E. E. (1996). *Chaos and order in the capital markets: A new view of cycles, prices, and market volatility*. Hoboken, NJ: Wiley.

Pindyck, R. S., & Rubinfeld, D. L. (1998). *Econometric models and economic forecasts*. New York: Irwin McGraw-Hill.

Studenmund, A. H. (1997). *Using econometrics: A practical guide*. New York: Addison-Wesley Educational.

Williams, G. P. (1997). *Chaos theory tamed*. Washington, DC: Joseph Henry Press.

Wooldridge, J. M. (2000). *Introductory econometrics*. Cincinnati, OH: South-Western College.

11

SURVIVAL ANALYSIS

NANCY BRANDON TUMA

INTRODUCTION

In recent decades, social scientists have increasingly collected longitudinal (i.e., overtime) data on widely varying phenomena. They hope that the richness of longitudinal data will help them to better understand the social world and how it changes over time. The challenge for analysts is to find and apply the statistical tools and methods that make the best use of the information in longitudinal data.

One important type of longitudinal data consists of observations on the occurrence of a specific type of nonrepeatable event for members of a sample during a certain interval of time. A "nonrepeatable" event is one that cannot occur more than once for any given individual. Historically, the nonrepeatable event of interest was death, which is why analysis of data on the time of death became known as *survival analysis*.

Researchers in other disciplines have adopted other terms for statistical models and methods that resemble survival analysis. Engineers ordinarily refer to similar analytic techniques as *failure analysis* and study phenomena such as the time of failure of various kinds of equipment or physical structures. Economists typically use the term *duration analysis* and examine phenomena such as the duration of employment or unemployment. Sociologists, and more recently political scientists, usually employ the term *event history analysis* (originally proposed by Tuma, Hannan, & Groeneveld, 1979) for similar models and methods used to analyze data on the timing of repeatable events (i.e., events that can recur for a given individual), such as people's changes of jobs in different occupations or changes in the network ties of organizations.

KEY CONCEPTS AND TERMS

Before considering the *statistical* concepts that are central to survival analysis, certain other concepts and terms need to be introduced.

Units of Analysis

Survival analysis requires data on clearly identifiable units or cases that are similar in essence and can plausibly be considered as members of some population of general scientific interest. For instance, the units or cases might be people, married couples, households, clans, formal organizations (e.g., schools, firms, nonprofit organizations), informal organizations (e.g., friendship cliques, clubs, gangs), or political/administrative units (e.g., census tracts, cities, regions, countries). The units of analysis may even be cultural products (e.g., poems, novels, plays, songs, films, advertisements, blogs).

Event

Another fundamental concept is that of an event, which refers to something that happens to a case almost instantaneously, allowing it to be said that the case is in one condition or status *before* the event and in another condition or status *after* the event. A classic example is the event of "death." Before death, the case (e.g., a person) is "alive," as indicated by vital signs such as breathing, beating of the heart, and electrical activity in the brain. Death is indicated by the absence of these vital signs. As medicine advances, it is sometimes harder to decide the *exact* time when death occurs. Because the ambiguities about when someone is alive or dead are limited in number and (with rare exceptions) to a narrow time interval, scientists can continue to collect data on the time of death and conduct survival analysis.

More generally, to apply survival analysis empirically, one must be able to categorize the cases in a sample as being in various conditions or statuses (such as alive or dead) and to identify a brief interval in which the event or transition from one condition to another occurs. The mathematical formulas for the statistical concepts in survival analysis are clear-cut; however, real-world phenomena are not always neat. Empirical analysts must match fuzzy, real-world phenomena to the clear-cut mathematical formulas in survival analysis. Survival analysis is possible in principle if this matching can be done without too much uncertainty.

Onset of Risk

Empirical analysts must also be able to determine when each unit becomes at risk of the event. For example, if the length of life is being studied and the event is death, an analyst must be able to define and determine when life begins because this moment is when the risk of dying starts. It is just as necessary to recognize the onset of risk as to recognize when the event itself occurs.

Empirical analysis of human survival usually defines the start of "life" as the moment when a newborn infant takes its first breath. In this instance, solving the scientific problem of when the onset of risk begins is fairly easy. In other applications, such as the analysis of organizational survival, it may be as unclear when an organization "begins to exist" as when it "ceases to exist" (see Freeman, Carroll, & Hannan, 1983). Similarly, the start of "marriage" can be ambiguous if one treats cohabitation and legal marriage as equivalent. When ambiguities surround the onset of risk, survival analysis can yield very different conclusions, depending on how the "onset of risk" is defined.

Observation Period

The observation period refers to the time interval (or the points in time) when there are *data* on the process under study. Often the observation period differs from the period when cases in the population or in a sample are at risk of the event. The observation period may start before or after the onset of risk, and it may end before or after all events have occurred. When the observation period begins after the onset of risk or when it ends before all events have occurred, analysts need to take appropriate steps to adjust for the fact that relevant information has not been observed and is therefore missing.

Censoring

If the observation period ends without the occurrence of the event having been observed for some sample members, the data on the timing of their events are said to be censored on the *right*.[1] Censoring is a characteristic of the data collection scheme because the incidence and extent of censoring can, in general, be altered by modifying the research design—in particular, by changing the start and/or end of the observation period.

There may also be censoring on the *left* which happens when some events are known to occur before the start of the observation period but the exact times of these events have not been observed. Censoring on the left is more problematic than censoring on the right because the past

[1]Censoring is said to be "on the right" because the time scale increases from left to right in the standard Cartesian graphical display of axes.

history of a case often affects which events occur in the future and when these events occur.

Risk Set

The set of cases at risk of the event at a given point in time is termed the "risk set." The composition of the risk set tends to vary over time. With the passage of time, some cases leave the risk set, because the event under study occurs, a competing event occurs that removes the case from the risk set, or (in the case of data for a sample) the observation period ends. The *size of the risk set* at a given time is the number of cases in the risk set at that point in time.

Competing Risks

A competing risk is any type of event (other than the one being studied) that may occur and remove cases from the risk set. For example, in a study of "survival in the labor force" in which "retirement" is the event under study, "death during employment" is one possible competing event: Someone who dies while still working is no longer at risk of retiring.

In prospective longitudinal studies (i.e., studies that select a sample and then follow the sample forward in time), attrition from the sample is also a competing risk. In general, survival analysis is not compromised by the existence of competing risks if the occurrence of the event under study and the occurrence of the various competing risks are statistically independent. However, if the event being studied affects the likelihood of attrition, the occurrence of the event and attrition from the sample are *not* statistically independent competing risks. In such situations, survival analysis that assumes competing risks *are* statistically independent leads to biased conclusions.

Truncation

The data may also be truncated, which occurs when cases are excluded from the sample because the timing of their onset of risk and/or the timing of their events fall outside the observation period. Various methods for dealing with sample truncation have been proposed, but they are inherently less satisfactory than methods for dealing with censored observations. Faced with a truncated sample, an analyst must make assumptions about the process that led some unknown fraction of the population to be omitted from the sample. Considerable uncertainty is almost always associated with these kinds of assumptions.

Statistical Concepts

To analyze survival data well, researchers must use appropriate statistical models and methods of estimation. These models and methods are founded on certain statistical concepts. In the following definitions of those concepts, a capital letter refers to a random variable and a lowercase letter to a realization or specific value of a random variable. For example, W may represent a certain random variable; correspondingly, w denotes a specific realization or value of the random variable W.

Survival Probability (Survivor Function)

Since survival analysis is the subject of this chapter, it is appropriate to start with the concept of the *survival probability* also known as the *survivor function.* The time of the occurrence of a *nonrepeatable event*, such as dying or getting married for the first time, is represented by the random variable T. The survival probability, $S(t)$, is the probability that the event has not occurred by some specified time t:

$$S(t) \equiv \Pr(T \geqslant t). \tag{11.1}$$

At t_0, which denotes the starting time (the time when the onset of risk starts for a case), $S(t_0) = 1$.

For many phenomena, the event eventually occurs as t in (11.1) approaches ∞. For instance, death is inevitable for people and all other living creatures. It may also be inevitable for organizations and states, even though the Catholic Church and England have lasted a very long time. If the occurrence of an event is inevitable, then $S(\infty) = 0$.

For some kinds of phenomena, the event may never occur for some cases. For example, certain individuals are biologically unable to give birth, and others have no chance of becoming President of the United States. (According to the U.S. Constitution, only people born in the United States are eligible to become President.) In these instances, $S(\infty) > 0$.

Cumulative Distribution Function

The *cumulative distribution function* (CDF) of T, which is central to the standard literature on statistical analysis, is the complement of $S(t)$:

$$F(t) \equiv \Pr(T < t) = 1 - S(t). \qquad (11.2)$$

That is, $F(t)$ is the probability that the event occurs by time t. In the literature on survival analysis, the survivor function is mentioned more frequently than the cumulative distribution function. In actuality, the cumulative distribution function and the survivor function convey exactly the same information.

Clearly, $F(t_0) = 0$, which means that the event has not occurred by the starting time, which is the start of the onset of risk. This is true by definition. If the event must eventually occur, $F(\infty) = 1$, and the probability distribution of T is said to be *nondefective.* On the other hand, if $F(\infty) < 1$, or, equivalently, if $S(\infty) > 0$, the probability distribution of T is *defective*. Then there is a nonzero probability that the event will not have occurred after an infinite amount of time has elapsed.

The statistical literature mainly focuses on probability distributions that are nondefective; namely, the probability of the event eventually occurring is 1. In empirical applications of survival analysis in the social sciences, however, defective probability distributions of T are fairly common. Some individuals have no chance of having a child, of marrying, of becoming a billionaire, or of getting a job (at least of getting a prestigious job).

Probability Density Function

A *probability density function* (commonly abbreviated "pdf"[2]) is associated with $F(t)$ and equivalently with $S(t)$:

$$f(t) \equiv dF(t)/dt \equiv -dS(t)/dt. \qquad (11.3)$$

[2]This abbreviation needs to be distinguished from the portable data format (PDF) file format developed by Adobe Systems Inc.

The *unconditional* probability that the event occurs between time t and $t + \Delta t$ is determined by integrating $f(t)$ over the interval from t to $t + \Delta t$.

Hazard Rate

The *hazard rate*, which is also called the *failure rate* (especially in the engineering literature) is a key concept in the literature on survival analysis. It is defined as

$$h(t) \equiv \lim_{\Delta t \downarrow 0} \frac{\Pr[t \leqslant T < t + \Delta t | T \geqslant t]}{\Delta t} = f(t)/S(t) = -d \ln S(t)/dt. \qquad (11.4)$$

The hazard rate is a measure of the probability that an event occurs between time t and $t + \Delta t$, as Δt shrinks to 0, *conditional* on the event not having occurred before t. The hazard rate conditions on being at risk at time t (i.e., the event has not occurred by time t). In contrast, the pdf, $f(t)$, is defined unconditionally.

A hazard rate cannot be negative because it is defined as the limit of the ratio of two nonnegative quantities, a probability and Δt. Like a pdf, a hazard rate may exceed 1. Unlike a pdf, a hazard rate is measured "per unit of time" (e.g., per day, per week). Changing the time scale (e.g., from weeks to years) produces a proportional change in the units of the hazard rate. To illustrate, a hazard rate of 0.1 per week is equivalent to a hazard rate of 5.2 per year (0.1 per week is multiplied by 52 weeks in a year).

Equation (11.4) implies that

$$f(t) = h(t)S(t). \qquad (11.5)$$

This equation is sometimes used to estimate $f(t)$ (see the subsection on the probability density function in the section Exploratory Analyses below).

Integrated (Cumulative) Hazard Rate

The integral of the hazard rate is known as the integrated or cumulative hazard rate, $H(t)$. It equals minus the natural logarithm of $S(t)$:

$$H(t) \equiv \int_{t_0}^{t} h(u)du = -\ln S(t). \qquad (11.6)$$

As discussed in the subsection on the integrated (cumulative) hazard rate in the section Exploratory Analyses below, it is useful to examine estimates of the integrated hazard rate in exploratory survival analyses in order to assess whether the hazard rate varies with time and, if so, how it varies with time.

Conditional Transition Probability

Various other types of events, called *competing risks* (see the subsection on competing risks in the section Key Concepts and Terms above), are possible in some applications. For example, when a marriage ends, it may be because the couple divorced or because the husband or the wife died. Divorce and death are two competing risks because the occurrence of either terminates a marriage. Or, viewed slightly differently, divorce, the husband's death, and the wife's death are three competing risks as any of these three events terminates a couple's marriage. When there are K competing risks, the conditional transition probability, $m_k(t)$, is defined as the probability of an event of type k between time t and $t+\Delta t$, as Δt shrinks to 0, conditional on one of the K types of events occurring within this interval.

Transition Rate

When K competing risks exist, the transition rate to $k, k = 1, \ldots, K$ can also be defined. Synonyms are the transition intensity and the instantaneous rate of a transition. All of these equivalent terms are defined as

$$r_k(t) \equiv h(t)m_k(t). \qquad (11.7)$$

Some authors refer to the "hazard rate of a transition rate to k" and do not distinguish it from the hazard rate of *any* type of event. For conceptual clarity, the terms *hazard rate* and *transition rate* are distinguished below.

Since $m_k(t)$ is a probability and varies between 0 and 1, a transition rate $r_k(t)$ has the same basic characteristics as a hazard rate: It is always nonnegative, it may exceed 1, and it is measured per unit of time.

Survival Data

Data suitable for survival analysis have several key features. First, there must be a sample of cases with certain types of information about each case. In most instances, researchers prefer that the cases being studied have been selected according to a well-defined random sampling design. However, in experiments, it suffices for the experimental treatments to be randomly assigned to members of the sample. Second, one must know when the observation period for each case begins and when it ends. Often the observation period is the same for all cases in the sample. In principle, however, both the starting and the ending times of the observation period may vary from one case to another. Third, one should know the time when each case becomes at risk of the event whose occurrence is being studied. The time when a case becomes at risk of the event may coincide with the start of the observation period, it may be *after* the start of the observation period, or it may be *before* the start of the observation period. The last of these possibilities creates problems that are not reviewed in this chapter. Fourth, one needs to know whether each case experiences the event during the observation period and, if so, the time when the event occurred.

Finally, researchers almost always want information on other variables that may influence whether and when the event occurs. The most common type of question in applications of survival analysis is whether some variable x is associated with the event occurring sooner rather than later or perhaps never. Sometimes x refers to environmental conditions that apply to several cases in the sample. For example, in a study of labor force entry, x might describe the demand for workers in the local area. More often x refers to an attribute of an individual case. For example, it might be a person's gender, ethnicity, or educational level.

Exploratory Analyses

The recommended first step is exploratory analysis of the available survival data. This type of analysis largely consists of estimating some of the statistical concepts defined in the previous section. Since most of these statistical concepts are functions of time, the analyst typically estimates the values of a particular statistical concept at a series of time points and then examines how these estimates vary over time.

The analyst may also estimate the statistical concept for subgroups of the sample defined by values of predictor variables (i.e., covariates) and then study how the estimates vary across the subgroups as well as over time. Such exploratory analysis serves a purpose similar to that of estimating means or medians of outcomes in cross-sectional data and then examining how the estimates vary across values of certain covariates. Exploratory analysis of survival data is especially informative because no single statistical concept conveys the myriad ways in which the occurrence of an event varies over time, among subgroups, and across values of various covariates.

Exploratory analysis of survival data (and confirmatory analysis in the last section) is illustrated below using data on age at first marriage of independent random samples of noninstitutionalized U.S. residents aged 18 and older. These data were gathered in the General Social Surveys (GSS), which were conducted almost annually from 1972 through 1996 (Davis, Smith, & Marsden, 1996). Data for the various years are distributed in a single data set as many questions were asked in almost every year of the survey. To illustrate comparisons of subgroups in exploratory analysis of survival data, estimates for the first marriage of males and females are compared.

Number at Risk (Size of the Risk Set)

In analyses of cross-sectional data, the size of a sample is usually clear and fixed, except that missing information on the outcome of interest or on the covariates often reduces the size of the sample that is actually analyzed. In the present example, missing information on individuals' ages when interviewed, whether they had ever been married, and their age at marriage (if they had ever been married) causes the combined GSS sample size to decrease from the 31,863 people who were interviewed in the various years to 31,642 (99.3% of the full sample). These 31,642 cases comprise 17,739 females (56% of the sample) and 13,903 males (44%).

When analyzing longitudinal data, whether survival data or any other type, the size of the analyzable sample often varies over time, sometimes greatly. If the analyzable sample size is much smaller at some times than at others, the *total size* of the sample with no missing information can be misleading when a researcher wishes to draw conclusions based on statistics estimated for a specific time point.

In survival analysis, the relevant sample size at time t is the number at risk at that time. The sample members at risk of the event at a given time t are termed the *risk set* at time t (see the subsection on the risk set in the section Key Concepts and Terms above), denoted here by $\mathcal{R}(t)$. Usually, the analyzable number at risk is depleted with the passage of time both by the occurrence of events in the sample and by censoring on the right. The lack of information on some members of the sample after a certain time point (viz., the time point at which their data are censored on the right) means that these cases are not in the risk set at times after their censoring times.

In the GSS data on first marriage, for example, respondents reported their age at the interview and their age when they first married. If they had never been married before the interview, their age at first marriage is right censored at their age when they were interviewed.

Figure 11.1 shows a plot of the total number of people in the GSS data at risk of marrying for the first time (i.e., who had never been married) by age, along with the breakdown by gender. Although the total number at risk is initially large, it falls below 700 by age 40 and below 250 around age 60. There are sufficient data to study first marriage through early adulthood; however, analyzing these data to study first marriage of older adults is inadvisable because the size of the risk set at older ages is rather small for even this very basic breakdown by gender.

Number of Events

It is equally useful to examine variation in the number of events over time. Estimation of virtually all statistics and statistical concepts defined in the section Key Concepts and Terms above depends on this number as well as on the number at risk.

Figure 11.2 displays a plot of the number of first marriages at each single year of age for the entire analyzable sample and separately for males

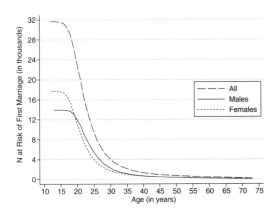

Figure 11.1 Number at risk of first marriage versus age.

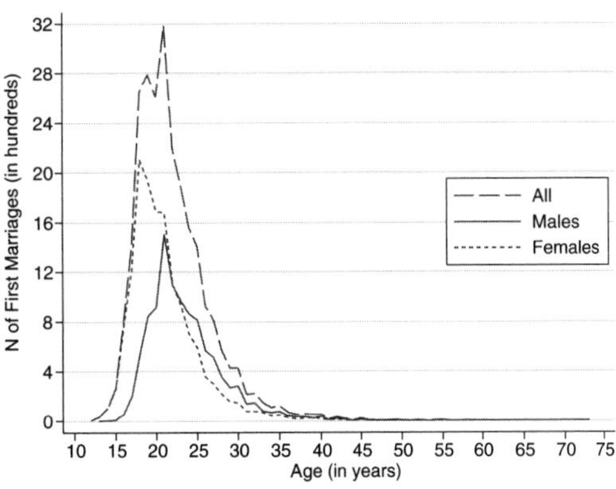

Figure 11.2 Number of first marriages versus age.

and females. Ages below 10 years are omitted because the youngest age at marriage was 12 years for females and 13 years for males. The oldest reported age at first marriage was 61 years for females and 73 years for males. In the late teens and early 20s, first marriages are very numerous. At these ages, the large numbers of first marriages, combined with the large numbers at risk of a first marriage, imply that statistical concepts can be estimated rather accurately during early adulthood.

In contrast, after 45 years of age, the number of first marriages at any given year of age in these data is seven (or fewer) and is typically one or two; for some years of age, it is zero. The rarity of events at older ages is a further sign that even the sample of 31,642 individuals in the GSS data is not large enough for a reliable study of first-marriage patterns among middle-aged and elderly adults.

The reason for examining plots such as Figures 11.1 and 11.2 is as follows. Before embarking on sophisticated forms of survival analysis, a researcher should be well informed about time variation in the size of the analyzable risk set and in the observed number of events for the analyzable risk set. In the present illustration, it appears unwise to attempt to draw conclusions about entry into a first marriage for people older than about age 45. The remaining plots display estimates for ages up to 60 years of age for thoroughness; however, estimates for ages much above 45 should be treated with considerable caution.

Survival Probability (Survivor Function)

The survival probability, $S(t)$, is almost always estimated using the product-limit estimator advanced in 1958 by Kaplan and Meier (KM). The reason for the near-universal use of the KM estimator is that it is unbiased and consistent even if the observations are right censored, as long as the censoring is statistically independent of the occurrence of the event itself. The formula for the KM estimator is

$$\widehat{S}_{\mathrm{KM}}(t) = \prod_{t_{(i)}<t} \left[1 - \frac{d_{(i)}}{n_{(i)}}\right], \qquad (11.8)$$

where (i) signifies the ith event when events are arranged in nondescending time order, $t_{(i)}$ is the time of the (i)th ordered event, $d_{(i)}$ denotes the number of events occurring at $t_{(i)}$, and $n_{(i)}$ refers to the number in the risk set immediately before $t_{(i)}$. By convention, the risk set at time t includes the sample members whose observations are right censored at time t.

A good way to comprehend the empirical findings is to prepare a *survivor plot*, which consists of plotting the estimates of $S(t_{(i)})$ versus time $t_{(i)}$. Although a survivor plot is a *step function* according to the formula in (11.8), the point estimates are sometimes connected by *line segments* if the event could, in principle, have occurred between the event times recorded for the sample. Connecting point estimates with line segments helps to smooth the survivor plot visually, which is useful when an analyst is trying to interpret a survivor plot.

The asymptotic variance of the KM estimator of the survivor probability is usually calculated using Greenwood's formula (Cox & Oakes, 1984, p. 51):

$$\mathrm{Var}[\widehat{S}_{\mathrm{KM}}(t)] = [\widehat{S}_{\mathrm{KM}}(t)]^2 \sum_{t_{(i)}<t} \frac{d_{(i)}}{n_{(i)}[n_{(i)} - d_{(i)}]}. \tag{11.9}$$

This formula is routinely used to estimate a two-sided $(1-\alpha)\cdot 100\%$ *pointwise confidence interval* of the survival probability at time t:

$$\widehat{S}_{\mathrm{KM}}(t) \pm z_{\alpha/2}\sqrt{\mathrm{Var}(\widehat{S}_{\mathrm{KM}}(t))}. \tag{11.10}$$

It is called a "pointwise" confidence interval to emphasize that it is a confidence interval at a particular point in time t.

If the KM estimator of $S(t)$ in (11.8) has a Gaussian distribution, which holds asymptotically, then z in (11.9) has a standard normal distribution. However, (11.10) underestimates the width of the confidence interval when the number at risk at time t is small.

It is tempting to estimate the *set of pointwise confidence intervals* for all event times observed in a sample and then to treat line segments connecting the outer boundaries of the set of pointwise confidence intervals as a *confidence band* for the survivor probability as a function of time. Clearly, pointwise confidence intervals for the distinct event times in a single sample are not statistically independent. Consequently, a band constructed in this manner overestimates the confidence level. That is, a band fabricated by connecting 95% pointwise confidence intervals for a series of event times appears narrower than the true 95% confidence band that results when one considers that the estimates for the set of event times in the sample are not statistically independent. Various ways of calculating simultaneous confidence bands for the survivor probability have been proposed, but reviewing them is beyond the scope of this chapter.

All survivor plots (i.e., graphs of $S(t)$ vs. time t) tend to look similar: $S(t)$ equals 1 at the starting time and tends to decline toward $S(\infty)$ as t increases. All survivor plots have a shape that resembles the letter S written backward, a so-called backward-S shape. Because survivor plots have broadly similar shapes, they rarely give much

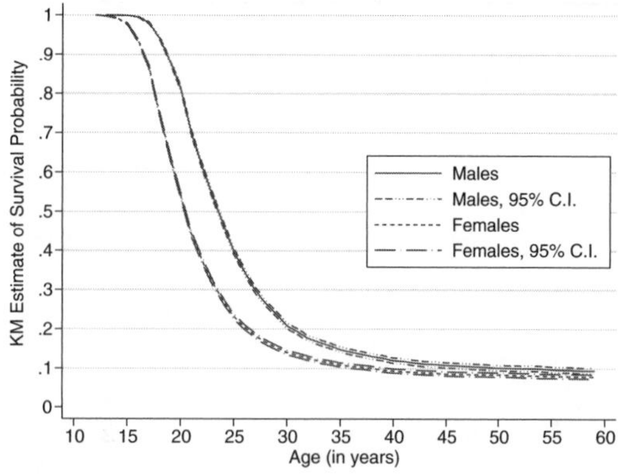

Figure 11.3 KM estimate of survival probability versus age.

insight into the process that generates the event being studied.

Analysts sometimes identify selected percentile values for survival, such as the time at which $S(t) = 0.5$ (the half-life). If the observation period is long enough, a survivor plot may also give a good indication of whether the cumulative distribution function of T is defective. As the observed time t becomes very large, $S(t)$ approaches 0 if the cumulative distribution function is nondefective, whereas $S(t)$ approaches a nonzero asymptote if the cumulative distribution function is defective.

Figure 11.3 shows the KM estimates of the probabilities that males and females in the United States have never married (i.e., $\widehat{S}_{\mathrm{KM}}(t)$) vs. age t), along with the 95% pointwise confidence intervals estimated using Greenwood's formula in (11.9). Even considering that pointwise confidence intervals underestimate the true simultaneous confidence band, it appears clear that the probabilities of males and females still being single differ greatly between 15 and 45 years of age.

Various tests for the equality of survivor functions of different groups have been proposed. Two of the most popular are the log-rank test (Peto & Peto, 1972) and Breslow's (1970) generalization of Gehan's (1965) extension of a Wilcoxon test. In this example, the χ^2 statistic is 1,387.8 for the log-rank test and 2,624.9 for the Wilcoxon-Gehan-Breslow test, both with 1 degree of freedom. Both χ^2 values are statistically significant at a very small probability level, indicating that American males and females indeed have different probabilities of survival in the "never married" state at various ages.

The estimate of $S(t)$ is 1 until the first event in the GSS sample (age 12 for females and age 13 for males). As age increases, the survival probability declines rather rapidly. The estimated quartiles of the survival times are 18, 21, and 25 years of age for females and 21, 24, and 29 years of age for males. Above age 40, the curves for males and females appear to converge, approaching a value of approximately 0.08 for females and 0.09 for males at the last observed age of first marriage. That is, the plots in Figure 11.3 suggest that singleness lasts for life for roughly 8% of females and 9% of males in the United States.

Cumulative Distribution Function

Because the survival probability is the complement of the cumulative distribution function, an unbiased and consistent estimator of $F(t)$ is $1-\widehat{S}_{\mathrm{KM}}(t)$. No further discussion of it is needed here.

Probability Density Function

A relative frequency distribution or histogram of event times (based on Figure 11.2, for example) gives an empirical approximation to the pdf of the time of events. A relative frequency distribution is a biased estimator of the pdf whenever there is extensive censoring of event times in the available survival data. In this situation, an analyst should estimate the pdf another way. For example, it might be estimated by multiplying estimates of the hazard rate at time t and the survival probability at time t after estimating each of these two statistical concepts while taking censoring into account (see (11.5)).

Integrated (Cumulative) Hazard Rate

Nelson (1972) proposed an estimator of the integrated hazard rate, $H(t)$, which turns out to be asymptotically unbiased, as proved by Aalen (1978). This estimator, typically called the Nelson-Aalen (NA) estimator, is

$$\widehat{H}_{\mathrm{NA}}(t)=\sum_{t_{(i)}<t}\frac{d_{(i)}}{n_{(i)}}^{2}. \tag{11.11}$$

Since $H(t)=-\ln S(t)$, $\widehat{H}_{\mathrm{NA}}(t)$ and $-\ln\widehat{S}_{\mathrm{KM}}(t)$ differ very little when the risk set at time t is large enough for asymptotic properties to hold approximately.

The pointwise confidence interval of $H(t)$ is computed by first estimating its asymptotic variance (Cox & Oakes, 1984, p. 56):

$$\mathrm{Var}[\widehat{H}_{\mathrm{NA}}(t)]=\sum_{t_{(i)}<t}\left[\frac{d_{(i)}}{n_{(i)}[n_{(i)}-d_{(i)}]}\right]^{2}. \tag{11.12}$$

Then the two-sided $(1-\alpha)\cdot100\%$ pointwise confidence interval of the integrated hazard rate at time t is

$$\widehat{H}_{\mathrm{NA}}(t)\pm z_{\alpha/2}\sqrt{\mathrm{Var}(\widehat{H}_{\mathrm{NA}}(t))}. \tag{11.13}$$

Again, analysts would ordinarily like to estimate a confidence *band* for $\widehat{H}_{\mathrm{NA}}(t)$. The pointwise confidence intervals for $\widehat{H}_{\mathrm{NA}}(t)$, like those for the survival probability, are not statistically independent within a particular sample. Consequently, the true confidence band is wider than the band obtained by connecting the outer boundaries of the set of pointwise confidence intervals.

A graph of estimates of the integrated hazard rate against time t (an "integrated hazard plot") gives information on how the likelihood of an event varies over time. A plot of the integrated hazard rate against time is approximately a straight line if the likelihood of the event does not vary with time. As time increases, it bends upward if the likelihood of the event increases with time, and it bends downward if the likelihood of the event decreases with time. For example, the integrated hazard rate of retirement from the labor force is upward bending, but the integrated hazard rate of voluntarily quitting from a job and moving to another job is downward bending.

In some instances, the integrated hazard rate is upward bending and then changes direction and becomes downward bending. This pattern suggests that the hazard rate is a nonmonotonic function of time. The plot of the integrated hazard rate

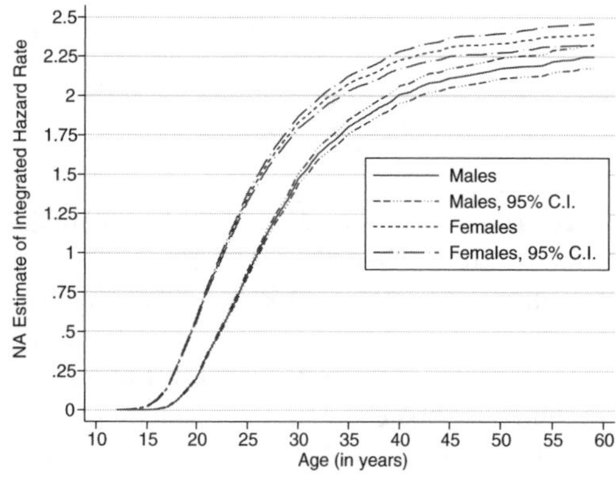

Figure 11.4 NA estimate of integrated hazard rate versus age.

of first marriage for males and females by age in Figure 11.4 has this pattern.

If the integrated hazard rate increases at a decreasing rate and then changes direction and begins to increase at an increasing rate, it suggests that the hazard rate is a nonmonotonic function of time with a so-called bathtub shape. The mortality rates of most living creatures have this pattern.

Often one can detect general tendencies in how a hazard rate varies over time by examining it directly (see below). However, plots of empirical estimates of hazard rates versus time often appear very erratic, especially when the size of the risk set and the number of events are small. In contrast, plots of the integrated hazard rate versus time usually appear relatively smooth. In this situation, general tendencies in the time variation in the hazard rate can often be identified more readily by examining a plot of the integrated hazard rate versus time (like the one in Figure 11.4) than by examining a plot of the hazard rate itself versus time.

Hazard Rate

There are various estimators of hazard rates. It is useful to distinguish between estimators for time intervals and estimators for time points. Estimators for time intervals arose when it was common to have data on the size of the risk set and on the number of events for a few fairly broad *time periods* or *time intervals*. In recent years, there is often little time aggregation in the data, and the timing of events is measured fairly accurately. Estimators for the time points at which events occur have been developed in conjunction with these improvements in data.

Estimator for Time Intervals

One of the oldest estimators of a hazard rate, traditional in demography, is the life-table (LT) estimator. Assume that the entire time interval when cases are at risk of the event is subdivided into P nonoverlapping time intervals. Each time period (or time interval) runs from τ_{p-1} to τ_p, $p = 1,\ldots,P$. For simplicity, assume $\tau_0 = t_0$ and $\tau_P = \infty$.

To give a specific example, demographers studying mortality traditionally had data on the number alive at the start of an age interval (e.g., at age $a = \tau_{p-1}$) and on the number who had died by the end of that age interval (e.g., by age $a+\Delta a = \tau_p$). In a study of human mortality, there might be 20 time intervals starting at age 0 and spanning from age a to age $a+5$. If desired, some time intervals could be narrower or wider than others. In a study of human mortality, Δa might be 5 years for adults but only 1 year for children and even less than 1 year for infants. There might also be an extra open-ended time interval from age 100 to infinity. The final, open-ended time interval in this example is infinitely long, but it may be ignored in the analysis because very few events are likely to be observed after age 100 because so few people survive until that age.

Let n_p denote the number at risk (e.g., "alive") at τ_p, and let d_p represent the number who experience the event (e.g., "die") in the interval τ_{p-1} to τ_p. If cases leave the risk set between τ_{p-1} and τ_p only because they experience the event in the pth interval, then $n_{p-1} = n_p + d_p$. In some data sets, cases may also leave the risk set because a competing risk occurs or because observations are right censored. Let c_p equal the number of cases who leave the risk set between τ_{p-1} and τ_p for any reason *other than* the occurrence of the event itself. Then $n_{p-1} = n_p + d_p + c_p$. Given these definitions, the LT estimator of the hazard rate in the interval between τ_{p-1} and τ_p is

$$\widehat{h}_{\mathrm{LT}}(t) = \frac{d_p}{(\tau_p - \tau_{p-1})(n_{p-1} - 0.5d_p - 0.5c_p)}, \tag{11.14}$$

where $\tau_{p-1} < t \leq \tau_p$.

In (11.14), d_p and c_p are multiplied by 0.5 because it is assumed that both events and departures from the risk set for various other reasons (including censoring) are not concentrated at a single point in time but are spread evenly over the pth time interval.

Estimators for Time Points

There are two main estimators of the hazard rate at a specific point in time. One is based on the KM estimator of the survival probability:

$$\widehat{h}_{\text{KM}}(t_{(i)}) = \frac{1}{\Delta t_{(i)}} \ln\left(1 - \frac{d_{(i)}}{n_{(i)}}\right), \qquad (11.15)$$

where (i) signifies the ith event when events are arranged in nondescending time order, $t_{(i)}$ is the time of the (i)th ordered event, $\Delta t_{(i)}$ equals $t_{(i)} - t_{(i-1)}$, $d_{(i)}$ denotes the number of events occurring at $t_{(i)}$, and $n_{(i)}$ refers to the number in the risk set immediately before $t_{(i)}$. By convention, the risk set at time t includes sample members whose observations are right censored at time t. The second estimator is an extension the NA estimator of $H(t)$:

$$\widehat{h}_{\text{NA}}(t_{(i)}) = \frac{1}{\Delta t_{(i)}} \frac{d_{(i)}}{n_{(i)}}. \qquad (11.16)$$

A Taylor expansion of (11.15) yields (11.16) as a first approximation.

Plots of estimated hazard rates versus time tend to vary greatly and to appear erratic, especially when the number at risk at a given time and the number of events at that time are small (see the subsection on the integrated [cumulative] hazard rate in this section). If the hazard rate is a continuous function of time, as researchers often assume in empirical applications, the underlying hazard rate is discerned more readily by smoothing the point estimates of the hazard rate over time. The LT estimator of the hazard rate smooths by estimating the hazard rate for a time interval rather than at a time point. Another approach is to apply a smoothing algorithm to estimates of the hazard rate at a series of time points. To give a very simple example, an analyst might compute a running mean or median of the hazard rate at several adjacent time points. Better methods of smoothing exist, but they lie outside the scope of the present discussion.

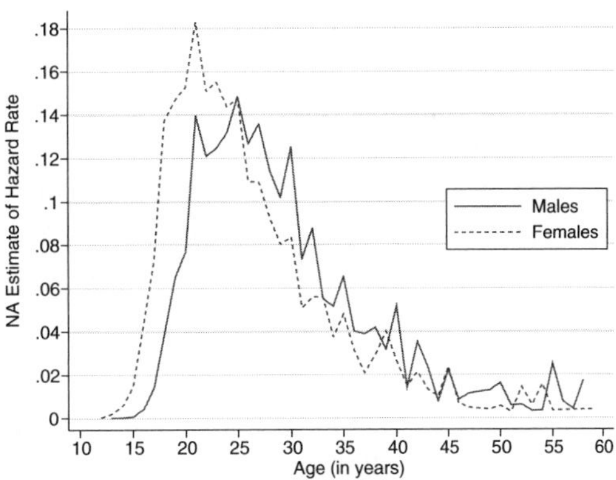

Figure 11.5 Hazard rate of first marriage versus age.

Figure 11.5 displays a plot of the NA estimates of the hazard rate of first marriage by age for males and females based on the GSS data. The estimates exceed 0 only after the first event in the sample, which is around 12–13 years of age in these data. In the teen years, the hazard rate climbs sharply for both males and females, but it climbs more rapidly for females than for males. The peak hazard rate is higher and occurs at a younger age for females than for males. After the peak, the hazard rate declines rather rapidly, but the decline is less steep than the increase in the teen years.

Even though the number at risk and the number of events are sizable between ages 15 and 30, the estimates of the hazard rate fluctuate considerably during this period, more than one would expect in the population. Closer inspection suggests that the upward bump at age 21 may be genuine, reflecting marriage around the usual age of college graduation in the United States. Other upward bumps may result from sample members rounding their age at first marriage to be a multiple of 5. If jaggedness in the hazard plot results from people favoring certain numbers (e.g., multiples of 5), it would be useful to apply some form of smoothing algorithm to the series of point estimates of the hazard rate over time.

Logarithm of the Hazard Rate

A common assumption in many confirmatory survival models is that the effects of various covariates on the hazard rate are multiplicative. This assumption, termed the "proportional hazards" assumption (discussed more fully in the subsection on proportional models of hazard and transition rates in the section Confirmatory Analyses), can simplify survival analysis to a considerable extent. But analysts must consider whether this assumption is valid, or even approximately true.

One way to evaluate this assumption is to estimate the hazard rate for various subgroups and to graph how the estimates vary with time. If the plots for different groups *cross* (i.e., a group with a higher hazard rate than another group in one time period has a lower hazard rate in another time period), it means that the predictor variable defining group membership does *not* have a multiplicative effect on the hazard rate. In fact, if the predictor variable identifying group membership *does* have a multiplicative effect on the hazard rate, the distance between plots of the natural logarithm of the hazard rate for different groups versus time (a so-called plot of the log hazard rate vs. time) should be a time-invariant constant.

Figure 11.6 displays such a plot. It shows the natural logarithm of the estimated hazard rate of first marriage for males and females versus age based on the point estimates plotted in Figure 11.5. Around 25 years of age, the plots for males and females cross. At ages younger than 25, the logarithm of the estimated hazard rate is clearly much higher for females than for males, although the gap between the two decreases in the early 20s. In contrast, above age 25, the logarithm of the estimated hazard rate tends to be slightly higher for males than for females. Figure 11.6 indicates that the effect of gender on the hazard rate of first marriage for Americans is *not* multiplicative. It suggests that a proportional hazard rate model of first marriage that includes gender as a covariate would *not* be appropriate. A similar conclusion is reached in the last section, An Example of Confirmatory Survival Analysis, based on another technique.

Conditional Transition Probability

If there are competing risks (i.e., multiple kinds of events), the conditional transition probability to state k, $m_k(t)$, can be estimated like other probabilities. For instance, it might be estimated as the number of events of type k occurring in some comparatively small interval of time near t divided by the total number of events in the same interval.

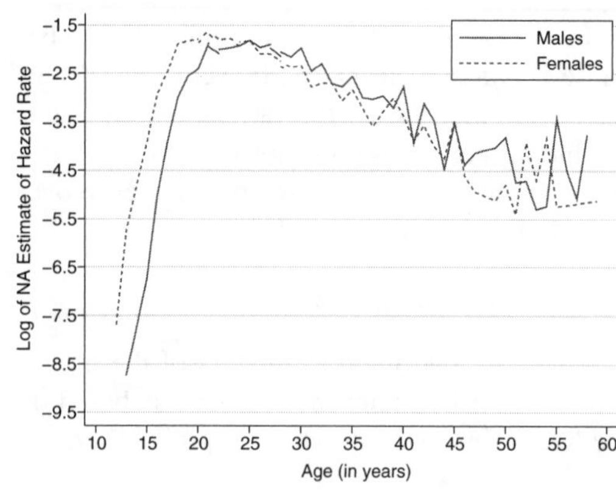

Figure 11.6 Log hazard rate of first marriage versus age.

Transition Rate

The transition rate to state k, $r_k(t)$, can be estimated by analogues to (11.14) through (11.16). The only change is that $d_{k_{(i)}}$, the number of events of type k at time $t_{(i)}$, replaces $d_{(i)}$ in those formulas. For example, the NA estimator is

$$\widehat{r}_k(t_{(i)}) = \frac{1}{\Delta t_{(i)}} \frac{d_{k_{(i)}}}{n_{(i)}}. \tag{11.17}$$

As mentioned in the subsection on the logarithm of the hazard rate in this section and as discussed more fully in the subsection on proportional models of hazard and transition rates in the next section, a common assumption is that a predictor variable has a multiplicative effect on the transition rate to some state k. One way of evaluating this assumption is to examine a plot of the logarithm of the transition rate to some state k versus time. The resulting plot would be comparable with the one in Figure 11.6.

CONFIRMATORY ANALYSES

Exploratory analysis is usually followed by confirmatory analysis, which is typically regarded as the centerpiece of the analysis of survival data.

In this phase of an investigation, researchers typically formulate a model of the process generating the event of interest. The next tasks are to estimate the model's parameters, to assess the overall fit of the model, and to test hypotheses about the effects of covariates included in the model and in some cases also to test hypotheses about patterns of time dependence in the process generating events.

General Issues

A model of the process that generates the event could be based on any statistical concept defined in the section Statistical Concepts. Frequently, however, the most suitable is the *hazard rate* of the event or, if there are competing risks, the *transition rate*. Another common choice is the average time to an event or the average of the natural logarithm of the time to the event. Models of this type are called *accelerated failure time* (AFT) models. Both types of models are reviewed below.

In principle, any model used to analyze longitudinal data, including survival data, must handle two basic issues:

1. *Time dependence:* Does the process that leads to an event vary over time, and if so, how does it vary with time? In some situations, analysts are not interested in how the event-generating process varies over time, net of the effects of covariates that are changing over time. Nevertheless, they must still address this question to a certain extent so that they can control for the consequences of any time variation that does exist.

2. *Population heterogeneity:* How does the process vary with characteristics of the environment and with attributes of the cases at risk of the event? This question is the more familiar issue because it is also central to the analysis of cross-sectional data.

There are two types of approaches to each of these two basic issues: (1) a nonparametric approach and (2) a parametric approach.

1. *Nonparametric approach:* In this approach to these two issues, the analyst categorizes time and/or key predictor variables (i.e., covariates), cross-tabulates the categories, and then estimates the statistic of interest within cells of the cross-tabulation. To illustrate, in analyzing age at first marriage, a researcher might regard age, gender, and ethnicity as key predictors of the hazard rate of first marriage. The researcher might create 5-year categories of age to have enough cases in any given age group and then cross-tabulate the sample by age group, gender, and ethnicity. Finally, the researcher might estimate the hazard rate of the event within each 5-year age category separately for males and females in each ethnic category using the LT estimator in (11.14). The resulting estimates would be an alternative to the type of analysis displayed in Figure 11.5.

Traditionally, demographers adopted a nonparametric approach in empirical studies of rates of mortality, marriage, fertility, migration, and so on. Still other covariates (e.g., year of birth, rural-urban residence) might be added and a higher-dimensional cross-tabulation created. Within each cell of the cross-tabulation of time and the covariates, the researcher then estimates the statistic of interest—for example, the probability of surviving without an event.

A nonparametric approach continues to be favored by some researchers, especially those who routinely use log-linear and log-multiplicative models of cross-tabulations and who prefer to begin with cross-tabulations when they analyze survival data (e.g., Yamaguchi, 1991). In applying log-linear or log-multiplicative models to such cross-tabulations, these analysts are employing a type of parametric model because these models also specify a particular functional relationship in accounting for the number of events in particular cells of the cross-tabulation.

A nonparametric approach suffers from the typical problems found when examining cross-tabulations. For instance, there may be many empty (or nearly empty) cells if more than a few covariates are cross-classified or if time is finely divided. Moreover, trends and patterns over time or with covariates may be obscure with these kinds of models because of a profusion of higher-order interactions of time and the covariates, as well as their main effects. Broad confidence intervals for parameter estimates, which result when cells in the cross-tabulation are sparsely populated and exhibit few events, accentuate the problem of detecting patterns of effects over time and with the covariates.

2. *Parametric approach:* In this approach, the researcher starts by postulating the functional form of various relationships—namely, how some statistic or statistical concept varies with time and the covariates—and then uses survival data to estimate the parameters that specify the function precisely. This approach tends to be more parsimonious than the approach described above, but it suffers noticeably from the possibility that the analyst may unwittingly choose an inappropriate functional form. The customary next step is to test the fit of the function to the data and then to test hypotheses about the values of the parameters in the function. Since choosing an inappropriate functional form often leads to mistaken conclusions, the *functional form* of the postulated relationships should be empirically evaluated whenever feasible. This last type of evaluation is, however, less common than testing hypotheses about the values of the parameters for the chosen functional form.

Patterns of Time Dependence

Whether analysts adopt a parametric or a nonparametric approach to confirmatory analysis of survival data, and whether they use hazard rate models, AFT models, or even models for cross-tabulations, they must deal with the possibility of time dependence in the process generating events and in the hazard or transition rate of the event.

There are three main patterns of time dependence in hazard and transition rates, net of the effects of covariates. These rates may be constant in time, vary monotonically with time, or vary nonmonotonically with time. If a hazard or transition rate does vary monotonically with time, it may be an increasing or decreasing function of time. If a hazard or transition rate varies nonmonotonically with time, by definition it is an increasing function of time in some periods and a decreasing function of time in other periods. In addition, the cumulative distribution function for the event time may be nondefective or defective.

In view of this wide range of possibilities, it is not surprising that there are many named functional forms for models of event times, far more than can be reviewed in this chapter. Examples of each *main type* of time dependence are given below. (For a more extensive set of examples, see Tuma & Hannan, 1984.) To simplify the formulas, the starting time t_0 is assumed to be 0.

1. *Constant hazard rate:* If the hazard rate does not vary with time—that is, $h(t) = \beta$ for all t, then the integrated hazard rate $H(t) = \beta t$. A model with a hazard rate that does not vary with time is also known as the *exponential model.*

2. *Monotonic hazard rate:* The most common survival models in which the hazard rate changes monotonically with time are the Weibull model and the Gompertz/Makeham (G/M) model(s). The hazard rates for these models are as follows:

$$h(t) = \beta t^{\gamma} \quad \text{(Weibull)}, \qquad (11.18a)$$

$$h(t) = \alpha + \beta \exp[\gamma t] \quad \text{(G/M)}. \qquad (11.18b)$$

The Gompertz model is the special case of (11.18b) when $\alpha \equiv 0$. Both the Weibull model and the Gompertz/Makeham model reduce to the exponential model (the constant or time-invariant hazard model) when $\gamma = 0$.

If the hazard rate in (11.18) is an increasing function of time (i.e., $\gamma > 0$), the cumulative distribution function of T is nondefective. Indeed, if the hazard rate exceeds 0 for $t = \infty$, $F(\infty) = 1$, and correspondingly $S(\infty) = 0$.

If the hazard rate in (11.18) is a decreasing function of time (i.e., $\gamma < 0$), the models given by (11.18a) and (11.18b) differ from one another more than when $\gamma \geq 0$. The cumulative distribution function of T associated with a Weibull model is still nondefective: $F(\infty) = 1$, and $S(\infty) = 0$. The Gompertz-Makeham model also yields a nondefective cumulative distribution function if $\alpha > 0$, even if $\gamma < 0$. This is because the hazard rate declines with time but has a plateau at $\alpha > 0$. However, the Gompertz model yields a defective distribution when $\alpha = 0$ and $\gamma < 0$. Consequently, a Gompertz model is ordinarily more appropriate than a Weibull model when the event of interest has a declining hazard rate and a positive probability of never occurring.

3. *Nonmonotonic hazard rate:* There exist even more named models in which the hazard rate is nonmonotonic. In the most common nonmonotonic models, the slope of the hazard rate with respect to time changes sign at most once; that is, it has a single inflection point. The slope of the hazard rate may initially be positive and

then become negative; this is the pattern for the hazard rate of first marriage (see Figure 11.5). Or, the slope of the hazard rate may initially be negative and then turn positive; this is called a bathtub shape. The hazard rate of leaving a job often has this shape as the rate of leaving a job tends to be high initially, declines with time, but then ascends again as jobholders approach typical retirement ages. As noted earlier, mortality rates of living creatures also usually exhibit a bathtub shape.

Three models with the first pattern (i.e., increasing and then decreasing) are the Sickle model, the log-logistic model, and the log-normal model; the equations for their respective hazard rates are

$$h(t) = \beta t \exp[\gamma t] \tag{11.19a}$$

$$= \frac{\alpha\beta t^{\beta-1}}{1+\alpha t^{\beta}} \tag{11.19b}$$

$$= \frac{1}{\sqrt{2\pi}\,\sigma t}\exp\left[\frac{-(\ln t-\mu)^2}{2\sigma^2}\right]\cdot \left[1-\Phi\left(\frac{\ln t-\mu}{\sigma}\right)\right]^{-1}. \tag{11.19c}$$

Mathematically simple models of hazard rates with a bathtub shape (i.e., declining and then increasing) are rarer. Here are three examples:

$$h(t) = \gamma\beta t^{\beta-1}\exp[\gamma t^{\beta}] \quad 0<\beta<1;\ \gamma>0 \tag{11.20a}$$

$$= \beta_1 \exp[\gamma_1 t] + \beta_2 \exp[\gamma_2 t] \quad \beta_1,\beta_2,\gamma_1>0;\ \gamma_2<0 \tag{11.20b}$$

$$= \beta_1 t^{\gamma_1} + \beta_2 t^{\gamma_2} \quad \beta_1,\beta_2,\gamma_1>0;\ \gamma_2<0. \tag{11.20c}$$

The first equation, (11.20a), is called the *exponential power model*. Equations (11.20b) and (11.20c) are the sums of two Gompertz and two Weibull hazard rates, respectively. In each of these two expressions, one component of the hazard rate is strictly decreasing over time and the other component is strictly increasing over time. Initially, the decreasing component of the hazard rate is larger and dominates the sum of the two components. As time increases, the increasing component becomes large enough to dominate the sum. How long it takes for the increasing component to dominate depends on the magnitudes of the parameters in the model.

Population Heterogeneity

Population heterogeneity is a common feature of survival models. Models incorporating observed population heterogeneity fall into four main categories: (1) proportional hazard models, (2) nonproportional hazard models, (3) hazard models that also include unobserved heterogeneity, and (4) AFT models. In the social sciences, empirical applications are usually based on models in the first or fourth category or occasionally on models in the second category. Empirical applications based on models in the third category are rare.

Proportional Models of Hazard and Transition Rates

In general, proportional hazard and transition rate models assume that

$$h(t,\mathbf{x}(t)) = q(\cdot)\theta(\mathbf{x}(t)), \tag{11.21}$$

where $\mathbf{x}(t)$ is a vector of observed covariates that may vary over time. The function $q(\cdot)$ may be specified as an explicit function of time t, or in a Cox model, it may be treated as an unspecified nuisance function of time t that has the same value for all members of a specified (sub)population at every possible time t. Consequently, the ratio of the hazard rates for any two cases i and i' with identical values of $q(\cdot)$ at every possible time t depends only on the observed values of the covariates for i and i', $\mathbf{x}_i(t)$ and $\mathbf{x}_{i'}(t)$, and not on $q(\cdot)$:

$$\frac{h(t,\mathbf{x}_i(t))}{h(t,\mathbf{x}_{i'}(t))} = \frac{q(\cdot)\theta(\mathbf{x}_i(t))}{q(\cdot)\theta(\mathbf{x}_{i'}(t))} = \frac{\theta(\mathbf{x}_i(t))}{\theta(\mathbf{x}_{i'}(t))}. \tag{11.22}$$

Whether $q(\cdot)$ is an explicit function of time or an unspecified nuisance function, an analyst needs to specify the functional form of $\theta(\mathbf{x}(t))$. Because hazard and transition rates must be nonnegative, $\theta(\mathbf{x}(t))$ must be nonnegative at all possible values of time and for all possible values of $\mathbf{x}(t)$. A linear specification in which $\theta(\mathbf{x}(t)) = \beta'\mathbf{x}(t)$ is unsatisfactory, because values of $\theta(\mathbf{x}(t))$ could be negative unless suitable constraints on the parameters β are imposed. Instead, analysts usually specify a functional form such that $\theta(\mathbf{x}(t))$ cannot be negative. It is customary to assume that

$$\ln\theta(\mathbf{x}(t)) = \beta'\mathbf{x}(t) \qquad (11.23a)$$

or, equivalently,

$$\theta(\mathbf{x}(t)) = \exp(\beta'\mathbf{x}(t)) = \prod_{j=1}^{J} \xi_j^{x_j(t)}, \qquad (11.23b)$$

where $\xi_j \equiv \exp(\beta_j)$ and J is the number of covariates. The parameters $\boldsymbol{\xi}$ are called the "relative risks." According to (11.23), the effect of a covariate on the hazard rate or transition rate is *multiplicative*, and its effect on the logarithm of the hazard rate (or the logarithm of the transition rate) is *additive*.

If $\beta_j = 0$, or, equivalently, if $\xi_j = 1$, the covariate $x_j(t)$ does not affect the hazard (or transition) rate. If $\beta_j = 0.5$, so that $\xi_j = \exp(0.5) = 1.65$, then a unit increase in x_j increases the hazard (or transition) rate by 65%. If $\beta_j = -0.5$, so that $\xi_j = \exp(-0.5) = 0.61$, then a one-unit increase in x_j decreases the hazard (or transition) rate by 39%. To calculate the percentage change in the hazard (or transition) rate for a unit change in x_j in a proportional hazards model, one uses the formula $(\xi_j - 1)\cdot 100\%$.

Cox Model. In 1972, the famous British statistician David R. Cox proposed a variation of the proportional model of hazard and transition rates in (11.21), which has become extremely popular. It is typically called the "Cox model" in his honor. In this model, $q(\cdot)$ is treated as a *nuisance function* that is assumed to have the same value at all possible times t for all members of a certain specified (sub)population.

As (11.22) shows, when (11.21) holds, the ratio of the hazard (or transition) rate for two members of the same (sub)population depends only on the values of $\theta(\mathbf{x}(t))$ for those two sample members. Cox took advantage of the fact that this ratio does not depend on $q(\cdot)$ in proposing a new method for estimating the model in (11.21). In a 1975 article, he named this new method "partial likelihood" (PL) (see the subsection on partial likelihood estimation in the section Model Estimation below). Subsequently, PL estimators were shown to be almost as efficient as maximum likelihood (ML) estimators when the hazard (or transition) rates are indeed proportional.

A further advantage of the Cox model is that certain specified control variables $\mathbf{z}(t)$ can be incorporated into the nuisance function, which then becomes $q(t, \mathbf{z}(t))$. Then the proportionality assumption is that (11.22) holds, subject to this specification of the nuisance function. In this extension of a simple Cox model (in which the nuisance function depends only on time t), the analyst *controls* $\mathbf{z}(t)$ but cannot directly estimate the effects of the variables in $\mathbf{z}(t)$. The coefficients of the other observed covariates, $\mathbf{x}(t)$, which do have proportional effects on the hazard (or transition) rate, can be estimated by partial likelihood.

Various tests of the proportionality assumption have been proposed in connection with the Cox model, in addition to the type of graphical examination illustrated in Figure 11.6 as one step in exploratory analysis. To give one example, Schoenfeld (1982) proposed a test based on a set of partial residuals that result from estimating a Cox model. In this test, a partial residual is estimated for each observed event time and for each covariate included in the model. If the proportionality assumption holds for a particular covariate, the set of partial residuals associated with that covariate should not only average zero but also exhibit no trend over time.

The Cox model is a very useful analytical tool when an analyst seeks only to understand how certain covariates act to increase or decrease the hazard (or transition) rate of an event and believes that the effects of those covariates on that rate are proportional.

Explicit Proportional Hazards Models. Analysts who are interested in the pattern of time dependence, and who have arguments or theories about it, typically specify an explicit functional form for $q(\cdot) = q(t)$. For example, analysts interested in the pattern of time dependence who believe that the hazard (or transition) rate declines with time might postulate a Gompertz model in which $q(t) = \exp[-\gamma t]$. Or they might postulate a Weibull model in which $q(t) = t^{\gamma}$. Then analysts seek to estimate γ as well as the effects of the covariates in $\theta(\mathbf{x}(t))$ from available survival data. Ordinarily, when $q(\cdot)$ is specified as an explicit function of time t, ML estimation is used to obtain estimates of the model's parameters and to evaluate model fit. The subsection on maximum likelihood estimation in the section Model Estimation below summarizes these procedures.

Nonproportional Models of Rates

If a hazard or transition rate is thought to be nonproportional, a researcher can and should formulate, estimate, and test a nonproportional model. These models often start with an explicit proportional model, such as those mentioned above, and then allow observed covariates to influence how the hazard (or transition) rate depends on time.

One nonproportional model that has proven especially useful in empirical applications is a piecewise constant hazard (or transition) rate model. It was originally proposed by Tuma et al. (1979) to examine how covariates of marital dissolution varied over the duration of a large social experiment.

$$h(t) = \exp(\boldsymbol{\lambda}_p'\mathbf{x}_p), \qquad \tau_{p-1} < t \leq \tau_p \quad (11.24a)$$

or, equivalently,

$$\ln h(t) = \boldsymbol{\lambda}_p'\mathbf{x}_p, \qquad \tau_{p-1} < t \leq \tau_p. \quad (11.24b)$$

In (11.24), p represents one of a sequence of P nonoverlapping time periods comprising the possible times when an event may occur. Each time period runs from τ_{p-1} to τ_p, where the final time period P may either be open-ended or end at some specific time chosen by the analyst. This model not only permits a hazard or transition rate to vary from one time period to another but also allows the values of the covariates and their effects to vary from one time period to another.

Another approach to constructing a nonproportional model starts with a simple parametric model of time dependence in the hazard or transition rate. The parameters of the simple model are then specified to be functions of covariates, which may vary over time. For example, in a study of the "liability" of organizational newness, Freeman et al. (1983) began with a Makeham model of organizational mortality rates (see (11.18b)):

$$h(t) = a + b\exp(ct) \quad (11.25a)$$

or, equivalently,

$$\ln h(t) = \ln b + ct, \quad (11.25b)$$

where a, b, and c replace α, β, and γ, respectively, to clarify the equations below. These authors then postulated that the parameters a, b, and c in (11.25) were the following functions of observed covariates:

$$a = \boldsymbol{\alpha}'\mathbf{v}, \quad (11.26a)$$

$$b = \boldsymbol{\beta}'\mathbf{x}, \quad (11.26b)$$

$$c = \boldsymbol{\gamma}'\mathbf{z}. \quad (11.26c)$$

Wu and Martinson (1993) proposed a piecewise Gompertz model that combined the two approaches described above. The resulting model possesses the desirable properties of both approaches. They constrained the parameters in the piecewise Gompertz model so that the hazard (or transition) rate at the end of one time period equaled the corresponding rate at the start of the next time period. Constraining the parameters of the model in this way prevents discontinuities in the hazard (or transition) rate at the boundary shared by two adjacent time periods.

Note that the logarithm of the hazard (or transition) rate in a constrained piecewise Gompertz model is piecewise linear. In this respect, it resembles the use of linear splines. Because this model is piecewise linear, with sufficient time periods, it can yield a good approximation to a hazard (or transition) rate that varies nonmonotonically with time and that has nonproportional effects of covariates.

Finally, it should be noted that the effects of covariates on the hazard rate are nonproportional in most AFT models (see the subsection on these models below).

Models With Unobserved Heterogeneity

It is almost impossible to include every predictor of the outcome under study in a model estimated from empirical data. Consequently, in addition to heterogeneity due to the observed covariates that are included in a model, there is also almost always unobserved heterogeneity due to omitted predictors. When unobserved variables are omitted from a *linear* model, standard estimators remain unbiased if the observed covariates are statistically independent of the omitted predictors.

Unfortunately, unobserved heterogeneity invariably causes spurious time dependence in survival models. This conclusion is readily apparent because the expected time of the event is greater for those sample members with values of the unobserved variables causing them to be unlikely to experience the event. Consequently, as time passes, those with a lower unobserved propensity to have the event tend to become a growing proportion of the risk set. For this reason, the estimate of the *overall* hazard rate in a sample appears to decrease as time increases unless the unobserved predictors are properly included in the model, even if each sample member has a constant hazard rate.

Although unobserved heterogeneity may be the result of many different unobserved variables, they are often lumped together as a single composite (like a random disturbance) and referred to as the individual sample member's "frailty." Early models of unobserved heterogeneity usually started from a parametric model of the hazard or transition rate and then assumed that there was an additional frailty variable with some postulated probability distribution. Sometimes the postulated distribution of frailty was assumed to be discrete. The earliest example was a "mover-stayer" model with two groups, one of "movers" at risk of the event and a second group of "stayers" not at risk of the event. Sometimes frailty was assumed to be continuous. For example, frailty has often been assumed to have a gamma distribution because this particular assumption simplifies deductions of the resulting probability distribution of the overall distribution of the time to the event.

The assumption that frailty has a known probability distribution, such as a gamma distribution, is a strong and restrictive one. Usually, it is not derived from any plausible theory of the process generating the event of interest. If the assumption of the distribution of frailty does not hold (at least approximately), the resulting model that includes unobserved heterogeneity may not be superior to a model that ignores unobserved heterogeneity.

In contrast, nonparametric approaches to unobserved heterogeneity make weaker assumptions and are less restrictive than the parametric approach described above. However, they are also computationally intensive and require large samples to estimate the points of support for the distribution of "frailty." Because of these demanding data requirements, and to a lesser extent because of the accompanying computational requirements (which become less important as computers become more powerful), survival models that incorporate unobserved heterogeneity are still not widely used.

Accelerated Failure Time (AFT) Models

AFT models (also called *accelerated life models*) are based on the mean time to an event. In AFT models, there is an underlying baseline random variable for time, T_0, rather than an underlying baseline hazard rate, $q(t)$, as in a proportional hazards model. Thus, T_0 is defined as the random variable describing the time of the event for the baseline; it has the corresponding baseline hazard rate

$$h_0(t) = \frac{f_0(t)}{S_0(t)}. \qquad (11.27)$$

In this subsection on AFT models, the subscript 0 signifies that a quantity refers to the baseline.

AFT models assume that the distribution function of T_i, the time of the event for case i with covariates $\mathbf{x}_i$, is the same as the distribution function for the baseline T_0 multiplied by a certain function of the covariates, $g[\cdot]$. The typical assumption is that $g[\cdot] = \exp(\boldsymbol{\beta}'\mathbf{x}_i)$. Therefore,

$$T_i = \exp(\boldsymbol{\beta}'\mathbf{x}_i)\,T_0. \qquad (11.28)$$

(11.28) implies that on average, T_i is shorter than T_0 if $\boldsymbol{\beta}'\mathbf{x}_i < 0$ and longer than T_0 if $\boldsymbol{\beta}'\mathbf{x}_i > 0$. Thus, the values of the covariates are conceptualized as hastening or delaying the time of the event for a given case, relative to the baseline, in a multiplicative manner. This is why it is called an *accelerated* failure time model.

A series of mathematical manipulations follow from this view of the underlying process. They yield

$$\begin{aligned} h(t\,|\,\mathbf{x}_i) &= \frac{f(t\,|\,\mathbf{x}_i)}{S(t\,|\,\mathbf{x}_i)} \\ &= \frac{f_0(\exp[-\boldsymbol{\beta}'\mathbf{x}_i]t)\exp[-\boldsymbol{\beta}'\mathbf{x}_i]}{S_0(\exp[-\boldsymbol{\beta}'\mathbf{x}_i]t)} \\ &= h_0(\exp[-\boldsymbol{\beta}'\mathbf{x}_i]t)\exp[-\boldsymbol{\beta}'\mathbf{x}_i]. \qquad (11.29) \end{aligned}$$

Usually, someone deduces the hazard rate implied by a particular AFT model, allowing parameters in the model to be estimated by maximum likelihood (see the subsection on maximum likelihood estimation in the next section). Last, define $U_i \equiv \log T_i$. Then

$$E(U_i) = \beta'\mathbf{x}_i + E(\log T_0) \quad (11.30a)$$
$$= \beta'\mathbf{x}_i + \theta. \quad (11.30b)$$

Consequently, the AFT model is equivalent to

$$U = \beta'\mathbf{x}_i + \theta + \varepsilon, \quad (11.31a)$$
$$\varepsilon = \log T_0 - E(\log T_0). \quad (11.31b)$$

Standard statistical models assume that the random disturbance in a linear model has a normal distribution, and one could make the same assumption about ε in (11.31a) above. If one assumes that ε has a different probability distribution, it leads to a different AFT model. For example, it might be more plausible to assume that ε has a log-normal distribution than a normal distribution.

Only the exponential and Weibull models are both proportional hazards models and AFT models. For example, if the time of the event has a log-normal distribution, the resulting model is not a proportional hazards model.

A log-logistic model can be specified either as a proportional hazards model with covariates or as an AFT model with covariates. The two versions of a log-logistic model have different parameterizations, different underlying conceptualizations, and different interpretations. An analyst needs to decide which conceptualization, parameterization, and interpretation are appropriate for a particular empirical application.

Model Estimation

Maximum Likelihood (ML) Estimation

Parametric models of the timing of an event are typically estimated from survival data by the method of ML. If there is a single nonrepeatable event, the log likelihood for a simple random sample of I cases is

$$\ln \mathcal{L} = \sum_{i=1}^{I} (1 - y_i) \ln f(t_i, \mathbf{x}_i(t)) + y_i \ln S(\tau_{ei}, \mathbf{x}_i(\tau_{ei})), \quad (11.32)$$

where (as defined earlier) y_i is 1 if the time of the event is observed for case i and 0 if no event is observed (i.e., the event time is censored on the right), $\mathbf{x}_i(t)$ denotes i's values for the covariates included in the model, t_i is the time of the event for i if $y_i = 1$, and τ_{ei} is the end of the observation period for i if $y_i = 0$.

ML estimation of a parametric model from survival data possesses the typical advantages of ML. Under rather general conditions, which apply in most empirical applications, ML estimators are asymptotically unbiased, efficient, and normally distributed. In addition, improvement in model fit can be tested using a likelihood ratio test based on a pair of nested models. Let $\mathcal{L}_A$ be defined as the likelihood for an unconstrained alternative model with $k_0 + k_A$ parameters, and let $\mathcal{L}_0$ be defined as the likelihood for the constrained, null model with k_0 parameters. It has been shown that $-2\ln(\mathcal{L}_0/\mathcal{L}_A)$ has a χ^2 distribution with k_A degrees of freedom under the null hypothesis (viz., that model A does not improve on the null model 0). The null model must be nested within model A to perform this test. Nesting requires not only that the null model is a subset of model A from a mathematical viewpoint but also that both models are estimated from exactly the same samples.

The asymptotic variance-covariance matrix of the parameters in a model can be estimated from the inverse of the Hessian matrix of the log likelihood, which is ordinarily estimated as the matrix of second derivatives of the log likelihood with respect to the parameters in a given model. The square root of a diagonal element of the asymptotic variance-covariance matrix furnishes an estimate of the asymptotic standard error of the parameter associated with that particular diagonal element. After obtaining the asymptotic standard errors of the model's parameters, an analyst can perform a Wald test of a hypothesis concerning whether a given parameter has a certain value (e.g., whether a parameter or the effect of a covariate equals 0).

To give an example, if β_0 is the parameter's value under the null hypothesis, $\hat{\beta}$ is its ML estimate, and $\widehat{\text{se}(\hat{\beta})}$ is the estimated standard error of $\hat{\beta}$, then the resulting test statistic is $(\hat{\beta} - \beta_0)/\widehat{\text{se}(\hat{\beta})}$. If the sample is sufficiently large for asymptotic properties to hold approximately, the alternative hypothesis that β differs from β_0 can be rejected if the absolute value of the test statistic is greater than the critical value of $z_{\alpha/2}$, where z has a standard normal distribution and α is the significance level.

Partial Likelihood Estimation (PL)

Cox (1975) proposed a method that he named *partial likelihood* to estimate the proportional hazard rate model in which the hazard rate is a product of a nuisance function $q(\cdot)$ and an explicit function of covariates whose values are observed in the data (see the subsection on proportional models of hazard and transition rates in the section Confirmatory Analyses). The PL is

$$\mathcal{L}_p = \prod_{i=1}^{I^*} \frac{\theta(\mathbf{x}_{(i)}(t_{(i)}))}{\sum_{v \in \mathcal{R}(t_{(i)})} \theta(\mathbf{x}_v(t_{(i)}))}, \qquad (11.33)$$

where I^* represents the observed *number of events* in the sample (not the size of the sample or the risk set), $\mathcal{R}(t)$ is the set of cases at risk of the event at time t, and $\theta(\mathbf{x}(t))$ is a specified, explicit function of the covariates. As stated in the subsection on proportional models of hazard and transition rates in the section Confirmatory Analyses, it is typically assumed that $\theta(\mathbf{x}(t)) = \exp(\beta'\mathbf{x}(t))$; however, PL estimation does not require this particular specification.

As indicated in (11.33), the covariates may vary with time, or they may be time invariant. In practice, the inclusion of time-varying covariates is complicated because (11.33) assumes that $\mathbf{x}(t)$ is observed at *every event time* for *every case in the risk set at that event time*. Since information on the time-varying covariates is rarely this complete, the most recent value of each time-varying covariate is ordinarily substituted for its value at the event time. This substitution is satisfactory if a covariate does not change rapidly or substantially between when it is actually measured and the times of events of other members of the sample.

Equation (11.33) also assumes that there are no tied event times in the data. The exact PL equation is more complex when some event times are tied because of imprecise measurement of the actual event times. Several approximate ways of handling tied events have been proposed in addition to the formally correct ways derived from combinatoric principles. Equation (11.33) is, however, a reasonable approximation if the number of ties at any given event time is relatively small.

Although the nuisance function $q(\cdot)$ is typically assumed to depend only on time, an analyst may choose to include various control variables (see the subsection on proportional models of hazard and transition rates in the section Confirmatory Analyses). For example, since the exploratory analysis of first marriage based on the GSS data reported in the section Exploratory Analyses indicates that the pattern of time dependence in the hazard rate of first marriage differs substantially for men and women, it would make sense to include gender in the nuisance function and to estimate a proportional hazard rate model in which other covariates are assumed to have proportional effects on males' and females' hazard rate of first marriage. The next section illustrates this approach.

An Example of Confirmatory Survival Analysis

To illustrate the estimation and testing of a confirmatory survival model, the hazard rate of entering into a first marriage was examined by estimating a Cox model using the GSS data on first marriages of American men and women (see the section Exploratory Analyses). Seven covariates were included in this analysis. Five of them were (0–1) dummy variables: indicators of whether the person was female, was black (i.e., African American), was reared as a Catholic, lived in the South at age 16, and resided at age 16 with a mother who worked. The other two (essentially continuous) covariates were the person's year of birth (minus 1900 and then multiplied by 10) and the years of formal education completed by the person's father. There was little missing information on any of the seven covariates except the indicator of the mother working. In addition, the sample analyzed in this section included a few hundred individuals who were reported as neither black nor white ("other race"), and these few hundred individuals were also excluded from the confirmatory analysis. Omission of the cases with missing information on the seven covariates and the cases of "other race" reduced the analyzable sample size from 31,642 to 26,645. These respondents reported 21,966 first marriages by age 50. Event times were censored at 50 years of age due to the dearth of first marriages at older ages, as discussed earlier.

A series of Cox models of the hazard rate of entry into first marriage were estimated using these seven covariates. Examination of Figures 11.5 and 11.6 strongly suggests that the effect of gender (i.e., the female dummy variable) on the hazard rate of entry into first marriage is not proportional. Nevertheless, the first Cox model estimated the effects of all seven covariates because one objective was to learn whether Schoenfeld's test of partial residuals would confirm the conclusion suggested by visual inspection of Figures 11.5 and 11.6.

Table 11.1 reports the results for a series of Cox models. For a particular model, Panel A gives the estimated coefficients of the covariates, whereas Panel B states the corresponding χ^2 statistics for the Schoenfeld tests of whether each covariate has a nonproportional effect over the event times and whether they jointly (globally) have a proportional effect.

For the moment, ignore the results of the Schoenfeld tests based on partial residuals in Panel B. In Model 1, the likelihood ratio χ^2 statistic for the model as a whole is statistically significant, and each covariate individually has a statistically significant ($p < .01$) effect on the hazard rate of first marriage. In subsequent models (discussed below), the effects of the covariates remain similar in magnitude and in statistical significance, except for the indicator of having a working mother at age 16, which is not significant at the 0.05 level in Models 4–6.

In Model 1, females have a strikingly higher hazard rate than males, blacks have a markedly lower hazard rate, those living in the South of the United States have a higher rate, and those reared as Catholics have a lower rate. Those with working mothers have a somewhat higher rate of first marriage. Those whose fathers had completed more years of schooling had a significantly lower rate, as did those who were born in more recent cohorts.

Now consider the χ^2 statistics for the Schoenfeld tests of proportionality over event time (see Panel B).[3] A statistically significant χ^2 for a Schoenfeld test implies that the effects of the individual covariates or of the set of covariates are not proportional.

In Model 1, gender contributes most to the magnitude of the χ^2 statistic for the global Schoenfeld test of proportionality. Therefore, gender is included in the nuisance function in Model 2; the effects of the other covariates in this model were estimated as if their effects were proportional. (It is conceivable that the effects of the other covariates appear nonproportional in model 1 because it treated gender as having a proportional effect, contrary to the findings.) Again, the χ^2 statistics for the Schoenfeld test for Model 2 imply that the effects of the covariates are not jointly proportional. In Model 2, father's education contributes most to the global χ^2 value. Consequently, in Model 3, father's education as well as gender was included in the nuisance function of the Cox model; the effects of the other variables were estimated as if their effects were proportional. In Models 4 through 6, one additional covariate was included in the nuisance function of the Cox model if it contributed the most to the global χ^2 for the Schoenfeld test in the preceding model.

In Model 6 (the last one estimated), the joint (i.e., global) test of proportionality is just accepted at the 0.05 level of significance. Interestingly, being black has a strong negative effect on the hazard rate of first marriage, and one cannot reject the null hypothesis that this effect is proportional. In contrast, the effect of having a working mother is small and statistically insignificant, but the effect's proportionality is just barely rejected at the 0.05 level. Faced with the ambiguity and borderline nature of the results for having a working mother, most analysts are likely to avoid drawing a firm conclusion about the effect of this variable. The evidence does suggest that the hazard rate of entry into first marriage is about 25% lower for black Americans than for white Americans under 50 years of age, net of the effects of the other covariates that are controlled.

---

[3]Even greater deviations from proportionality are implied by χ^2 statistics for Schoenfeld tests of proportionality over the *logarithm* of event time (results not shown).

Table 11.1 Results for a Series of Cox Models

	Model					
	1	2	3	4	5	6
Panel A: Partial likelihood estimates						
Black	−0.357	−0.342	−0.348	−0.306	−0.303	−0.294
Mother worked	0.065	0.063	0.056	0.025	0.015	0.008
Reared Catholic	−0.180	−0.175	−0.169	−0.201	−0.218	
South at age 16	0.202	0.203	0.210	0.225		
Birth year	−0.011	−0.010	−0.010			
Father's education	−0.039	−0.038				
Female	0.486					
Likelihood ratio χ^2	2,187.5	1,000.7	522.0	430.8	220.5	100.2
df	7	6	5	4	3	2
Panel B: χ^2 values testing proportionality over event time[a]						
Black	0.2	0.5	0.2	0.7	1.3	2.1
Mother worked	1.4	1.8	2.2	2.3	4.0	4.0
Reared Catholic	35.9	35.1	30.9	18.8	13.4	
South at age 16	92.7	85.5	90.3	65.3		
Birth year	156.1	163.3	134.6			
Father's education	182.9	176.3				
Female	1,136.6					
Global	1,844.4	483.7	336.6	121.0	19.3	6.0
df	7	6	5	4	3	2

SOURCE: General Social Surveys, 1972–1996.
NOTE: Sample size = 26,645; number of events = 21,966.
a. Based on Schoenfeld's (1982) estimates of partial residuals.

REFERENCES

Aalen, O. O. (1978). Nonparametric inferences for a family of counting processes. *Annals of Statistics, 6*, 701–726.

Breslow, N. (1970). A generalized Kruskal-Wallis test for comparing K samples subject to unequal patterns of censorship. *Biometrika, 57*, 579–594.

Cox, D. R. (1972). Regression models and life tables (with discussion). *Journal of the Royal Statistical Society Series B, 34*, 187–220.

Cox, D. R. (1975). Partial likelihood. *Biometrika, 62*, 269–276.

Cox, D. R., & Oakes, D. (1984). *Analysis of survival data.* London: Chapman & Hall.

Davis, J. A., Smith, T. W., & Marsden, P. V. (1996). *General social surveys, 1972–1996: Cumulative codebook.* Chicago: National Opinion Research Center.

Freeman, J., Carroll, G. R., & Hannan, M. T. (1983). The liability of newness: Age dependence in organizational death rates. *American Sociological Review, 48*, 692–710.

Gehan, E. A. (1965). A generalized Wilcoxon test for comparing arbitrarily singly-censored samples. *Biometrika, 52*(1–2), 203–223.

Kaplan, E. L., & Meier, P. (1958). Nonparametric estimation from incomplete observations. *Journal of the American Statistical Association, 53*, 457–481.

Nelson, W. (1972). Theory and applications of hazard plotting for censored failure data. *Technometrics, 14*, 945–966.

Peto, R., & Peto, J. (1972). Asymptotically efficient rank invariant procedures. *Journal of the Royal Statistical Society Series A, 135*, 185–207.

Schoenfeld, D. (1982). Partial residuals for the proportional hazards regression model. *Biometrika, 69*, 239–241.

Tuma, N. B., & Hannan, M. T. (1984). *Social dynamics: Models and methods.* Orlando, FL: Academic Press.

Tuma, N. B., Hannan, M. T., & Groeneveld, L. P. (1979). Dynamic analysis of event histories. *American Journal of Sociology*, *84*, 820–854.

Wu, L. L., & Martinson, B. C. (1993). Family structure and the risk of a premarital birth. *American Sociological Review*, *53*, 210–232.

Yamaguchi, K. (1991). *Event history analysis.* Newbury Park, CA: Sage.

12

PROBABILISTIC SAMPLING

JEFFREY M. WOOLDRIDGE

INTRODUCTION

Sampling theory underlies virtually all applications of mathematical statistics. Before one can intelligently analyze a set of data, one must know how the data were obtained. In other words, what was the *sampling scheme*? Were the data obtained by random sampling from the underlying population, with or without replacement? Were some segments of the population oversampled or undersampled? Were some segments systematically excluded? Are the sampling units naturally grouped into clusters?

The random sampling paradigm ensures that a sample of data is, loosely speaking, "representative" of the underlying population. The power of random sampling is undeniable: It simplifies the search for unbiased, or at least consistent, estimators, and it results in rather straightforward statistical inference. Many common estimation techniques, including least squares, method of moments, and maximum likelihood, have desirable statistical properties under random sampling. In most fields where cross-sectional (and longitudinal or panel) data are used, random sampling continues to play a prominent role in the development and analysis of new estimators.

While random sampling is convenient, it can be, and sometimes intentionally is, violated when cross-sectional data and longitudinal data are collected. Rather than draw observations at random from the population, often some subsets of the population are oversampled, undersampled, or not sampled at all. For example, a survey aimed at determining retirement saving behavior might focus on low-income families, even though some high-income families are included. Subsequently, a researcher may decide to use the data to estimate a model relating pension saving to income and other factors. To decide on the appropriate estimation and inference methods, the researcher needs to know how to account for the particular sampling scheme that generates the data. As is well-known (see, e.g., Cochran, 1977) and as we will discuss in the sections Inverse Probability Weighting and Stratified Sampling, failure to reweight the observations can result in biased and inconsistent estimators of the population parameters.

Cluster sampling is another important deviation from random sampling. With a cluster sample, individual units are properly viewed as belonging to a cluster that contains other "similar" units. For example, if a large number of primary schools are sampled and within each school several students are sampled, then the students at a school constitute a cluster. Typically, because a response variable such as test scores would depend on features of the school—some not observed—we should account for correlation in the test scores of students within a school, even after netting out observed school characteristics.

In this chapter, I provide an introduction to several kinds of sampling methods, focusing on the implications for estimation and inference. I begin with random sampling in the first section, and in the second, I introduce a framework for studying so-called selected samples, where certain units in the population are omitted from the sampling scheme. This includes nonrandom sampling for a variety of reasons, including missing data. In this section, I consider cases where the nonrandom sampling can be ignored. In the third section, I allow for more general selected samples, where ignoring the sampling mechanism generally produces inconsistent estimators. Instead, inverse probability weighting can recover the population parameters. The fourth section, Selection on Unobservables, contains a brief discussion of nonignorable sampling schemes that are common in econometrics and other fields where self-selection induces nonrandom sampling. In the next section, I explicitly consider two different kinds of stratified sampling, variable probability sampling and standard stratified sampling. In the final section, I turn to cluster samples, where we can no longer treat outcomes on individual units as independent within a group or cluster.

Random Sampling

When discussing random sampling, it is important to be very precise about the population that is the target of our analysis. For example, if a labor economist plans to study the effects of a job-training program on labor earnings, he or she must decide on the relevant population. Is the appropriate population the entire working population at a particular point in time? Perhaps, but as a policy matter we may not be interested in obtaining average effects of job training that include the effects on high-income workers. Instead, the target population might be a subset of all workers, defined to include only workers who might at some future point be eligible for job training. For example, the researcher may define this to be all members of the population whose previous earnings fell below a certain threshold.

To define random sampling, we start with a *sample space* $\mathcal{W}$, which is the set of possible outcomes on a set of variables, and a probability density function $f(\cdot)$ defined over $\mathcal{W}$. A *random sample* of size n is a set of random vectors $\{W_i : i = 1,2,\ldots,n\}$, where the W_i are independent with density $f(\cdot)$. That is, $\{W_i : i = 1,2,\ldots,n\}$ are *independent and identically distributed*, or *iid*, with density $f(\cdot)$.

In this chapter, I use the definition of random sampling just provided. It applies to infinite populations and also to finite populations when sampling is done with replacement. Some authors prefer to call sampling from a finite population, where each unit has the same probability of being selected, *simple random sampling*. Then, the distinction is made between sampling with and without replacement. As is well-known (see, e.g., Cochran, 1977, chap. 2), sampling with replacement from a finite population induces correlation among the observations, which is a nuisance, especially in general estimation frameworks. In this chapter, I consider only iid sampling schemes and deviations from iid sampling—such as unequal probability sampling and stratified sampling—that can result in systematic bias of basic statistical methods. I follow current usage (see, e.g., Casella & Berger, 2002, chap. 5) and use "random sampling" to refer to iid random vectors drawn from a population.

Given our definition of random sampling, we can use a random vector W with density $f(\cdot)$ to describe the underlying population, and it is often convenient to do so in describing features of the distribution, such as moments. Therefore, W has the same distribution as each random draw W_i over the sample space $\mathcal{W}$. As is common practice, we use $w \in \mathcal{W}$ to represent a possible outcome of W. Similarly, the observed data, $\{w_i : i = 1,\ldots,n\}$, is a particular realization of the set of random vectors, $\{W_i : i = 1,2,\ldots,n\}$.

Random sampling has many important implications for statistical analysis. For example, the sample average of a random sample is an unbiased estimator of the population average or mean. In fact, if $g : \mathcal{W} \to \mathbb{R}$ is a real-valued function with $E[\|g(W)\|] < \infty$, then $n^{-1}\sum_i^n g(W_i)$ is an unbiased estimator of $E[g(W)]$. The sample average is also a consistent estimator of the population average; that is, as $n \to \infty$, the sample average converges in probability to the population average:

$$n^{-1}\sum_{i}^{n} g(W_i) \xrightarrow{p} E[g(W)] \equiv \mu_g. \qquad (12.1)$$

For functions with finite second moment, the standardized sample average converges in distribution to a normal random variable:

$$n^{-1/2}\sum_{i}^{n}[g(W_i) - \mu_g] \xrightarrow{d} \text{Normal}(0, \sigma_g^2), \qquad (12.2)$$

where $\sigma_g^2 = \text{Var}[g(W)]$. These limiting distribution results for random samples are fundamental for estimation and approximate inference in large samples.

In most statistical applications, we are interested in estimating a finite set of parameters that index some feature of the distribution of W. Often we are not interested in the full distribution of W. Rather, we might be interested in a conditional distribution, say $D(Y|X)$, where W is partitioned into X and Y. Or we may be interested in low-order moments, such as means and variances (or, especially, conditional means and variances).

To illustrate the power of random sampling and to provide a springboard for nonrandom sampling in subsequent sections, we consider the problem of *M-estimation*, which dates back to Huber (1967). Let θ be a $P \times 1$ vector of parameters indexing some feature of the distribution of W. We assume that $\theta \in \Theta \subset \mathbb{R}^P$. Let $q(w, \theta)$ be a real-valued function of the data and the parameter vector. In other words, for fixed θ, $q(W_i, \theta)$ is a random variable, and for any outcome w_i, $q(w_i, \cdot)$ is a real-valued function on Θ. We hope to estimate $\theta_o \in \Theta$, which is the unique solution to the population minimization problem

$$\min_{\theta \in \Theta} E[q(W_i, \theta)]. \qquad (12.3)$$

To estimate θ_o, which is sometimes called the "true value of theta," it is natural to solve the sample analog

$$\min_{\theta \in \Theta} n^{-1}\sum_{i=1}^{n} q(W_i, \theta). \qquad (12.4)$$

By the law of large numbers (LLN), it makes sense that the solution to (12.4), say $\hat{\theta}$, is consistent for θ_o. In fact, consistency holds quite generally if $q(w, \cdot)$ is continuous on Θ for each $w \in \mathcal{W}$. Other conditions, such as $E[|q(W, \theta)|]$ bounded on the compact (closed and bounded) set Θ, are typically imposed as sufficient conditions. The key is that the LLN can be shown to hold *uniformly* on Θ; that is, the distance between the sample average and the population average can be bounded over the parameter space. Details can be found in Newey and McFadden (1994) and Wooldridge (2002, chap. 12).

Two leading examples of M-estimation are nonlinear least squares (NLS) and (conditional) maximum likelihood estimation (MLE). In the former case, we take $q(W_i, \theta) = [Y_i - m(X_i, \theta)]^2/2$, where $m(x, \theta)$ is a parametric model for $E(Y_i|X_i = x)$ (i.e., $m(x, \theta)$ is a known function of x and the finite-dimensional vector θ). For maximum likelihood, we take $q(W_i, \theta) = -\log[f(Y_i|X_i, \theta)]$, where $f(y|x, \theta)$ is a parametric model of the density of Y_i given $X_i = x$. Importantly, even though in each case we are modeling a feature of $D(Y|X)$, random sampling still makes sense: We draw $W_i = (X_i, Y_i)$ randomly from the underlying population.

Treatments of NLS and MLE with conditioning variables often assume that the conditioning variables are fixed in repeated samples at the observed values $x_i, i = 1, \ldots, n$, in which case the data $\{(x_i, Y_i) : i = 1, \ldots, n\}$ must be treated as nonidentically distributed: The unconditional distribution of Y_i depends on x_i, often through the mean $E(Y_i)$. For most applications, treating the conditioning variables as random draws along with Y_i is more realistic. Also, random sampling actually simplifies the statistical analysis, which, in the end, is the same when the data are *independent, not identically distributed* (inid).

Turning to inference, if we impose some smoothness on the objective function—the simplest is that $q(w, \cdot)$ is twice continuously differentiable on the interior of the parameter space, $\text{int}(\Theta)$, and that $\theta_o \in \text{int}(\Theta)$, then asymptotic normality of the M-estimator follows under random sampling. In particular,

$$\sqrt{n}(\hat{\theta} - \theta_o) \xrightarrow{d} \text{Normal}(0, A_o^{-1}B_oA_o^{-1}), \qquad (12.5)$$

where $B_o = \text{Var}[\nabla_\theta q(W, \theta_o)] = E[\nabla_\theta q(W, \theta_o)' \nabla_\theta q(W, \theta_o)]$ is the variance of the gradient of the objective function and $A_o = E[\nabla_\theta^2 q(W, \theta_o)]$ is the expected value of the Hessian. (We use prime to denote transpose.) Recall that the gradient of a real-valued differentiable function is the row vector of partial derivatives—in this case, a $1 \times P$ vector with elements $\partial q(W, \theta)/\partial \theta_j$, $j = 1, \ldots, P$. The Hessian is the $P \times P$ symmetric matrix of partial second derivatives. The asymptotic normality result in (12.5) is fundamental for analyzing NLS, maximum likelihood, and many other estimation methods under random sampling.

Selected Sampling

Nonrandom sampling comes in many forms, and we will cover several different kinds in the rest of this article, along with general methods for dealing with nonrandom samples in estimation. First, it is helpful to focus on a particular but still fairly general kind of nonrandom sampling called *selected sampling.*

A Framework for Describing Selected Samples

To define a selected sample, it is useful to define a *selection indicator* that allows us to concisely represent missing data. In particular, on the *i*th random draw from the population, along with W_i we obtain a binary random variable S_i. We define $S_i = 1$ if W_i is kept in the sample and $S_i = 0$ otherwise. This simple mechanism, which has a long history in the missing data and nonrandom sampling literature, covers all kinds of sampling and missing data schemes. For example, in a phone survey, which is intended to be a random sample from a specified population, some individuals or families contacted may refuse to respond to the survey or at least refuse to answer some of the questions. Suppose, for example, that W_i is the amount of time spent watching television per week, but some families refuse to answer the question. Then, we can think of our "data" as $\{(W_i, S_i) : i = 1, 2, \ldots, n\}$, where n is the number of telephone calls made. But the actual number of data points we observe on W is $N_o = \sum_{i=1}^{n} S_i$, which is properly viewed as a random variable (because it is unknown prior to completing the survey). Assumptions about how S_i relates to W_i are critical for determining how to estimate features of the distribution of $f(\cdot)$.

To illustrate the issues in a simple case, suppose that we are interested in estimating the mean of W, say $\mu = E(W)$. We draw units at random from the population, but for some units, we do not observe W_i (perhaps because of nonreporting). Therefore, we cannot compute the average of W_i over all sampled units. Instead, we can use the sample average of the data we do observe—that is, the *selected sample*, which can be written as

$$\hat{\mu} = \left(\sum_{i=1}^{n} S_i\right)^{-1} \left(\sum_{i=1}^{n} S_i W_i\right)$$
$$= \left(n^{-1} \sum_{i=1}^{n} S_i\right)^{-1} \left(n^{-1} \sum_{i=1}^{n} S_i W_i\right). \quad (12.6)$$

Note how S_i selects out the observed data points, so that $\hat{\mu}$ is computable from the observed data. When $S_i = 0$, W_i does not enter the average. Some authors prefer to set the outcome on W_i to a specific value, usually 0, when it is not observed. But this can only sow confusion: It is best to think of W_i as simply being unknown, and the selection indicator setup reflects that reality.

The representation in (12.6) is convenient because it shows that $\hat{\mu}$ is a function of sample averages of the iid random vectors $\{(W_i, S_i) : i = 1, \ldots, n\}$. Treating (W_i, S_i) as random draws from a joint distribution is natural when we assume that the unconditional probability of being selected in the sample is constant across units; that is, $P(S_i = 1) = \rho$ for all i.

Given that we view $\{(W_i, S_i) : i = 1, \ldots, n\}$ as a random sample (from an expanded sample space), it is useful to let (W, S) denote a random vector that has the distribution common to (W_i, S_i). For example, in the context of survey sampling, the subpopulation with $S = 1$ consists of units that would respond if asked, while those with $S = 0$ would not respond if asked. In the context of attrition in a two-period survey, $S = 1$ corresponds to those who would still be available in the second interview period, and $S = 0$ stands for those who would not.

We can easily see that, in general, $\hat{\mu}$ will be biased as well as inconsistent for estimating μ. In fact, it is pretty clear that $\hat{\mu}$ generally estimates

$\mu_1 \equiv E(W|S=1)$, the average of W over the selected subset of the population. Formally,

$$\begin{aligned}
E(\hat{\mu}|\mathbf{S}) &\equiv E(\hat{\mu}|S_1,S_2,\ldots,S_n) \\
&= \left(\sum_{i=1}^{n} S_i\right)^{-1}\left(\sum_{i=1}^{n} S_i E(W_i|S_1,S_2,\ldots,S_n)\right) \\
&= \left(\sum_{i=1}^{n} S_i\right)^{-1}\left(\sum_{i=1}^{n} S_i E(W_i|S_i)\right) \\
&= \left(\sum_{i=1}^{n} S_i\right)^{-1}\left(\sum_{i=1}^{n} S_i[(1-S_i)\mu_0 + S_i\mu_1]\right) \\
&= \left(\sum_{i=1}^{n} S_i\right)^{-1}\left(\sum_{i=1}^{n} S_i\mu_1\right) = \mu_1, \quad (12.7)
\end{aligned}$$

where $\mu_0 \equiv E(W|S=0)$ and we use $E(W|S) = (1-S)\mu_0 + S\mu_1$, $S(1-S)=0$ along with $S^2 = S$ because S is a (0–1) variable. It follows by iterated expectations that $E(\hat{\mu}) = \mu_1$.

Deriving the probability limit is instructive for our subsequent analysis. By the (weak) LLN, $n^{-1}\sum_{i=1}^{n} S_i \xrightarrow{p} \rho$ and $n^{-1}\sum_{i=1}^{n} S_i W_i \xrightarrow{p} E(SW)$. But

$$\begin{aligned}
E(SW) &= P(S=0)\cdot E(SW|S=0) \\
&\quad + P(S=1)\cdot E(SW|S=1) \quad (12.8) \\
&= P(S=1)\cdot E(W|S=1) = \rho\mu_1.
\end{aligned}$$

Therefore,

$$\text{plim}(\hat{\mu}) = \rho^{-1}(\rho\mu_1) = \mu_1. \quad (12.9)$$

These results are, of course, very intuitive. In effect, $\hat{\mu}$ is the sample average of a random sample from the subpopulation with $S=1$, and so we expect $\hat{\mu}$ to be unbiased and consistent for the mean of that subpopulation.

Data Missing Completely at Random

We just saw that the sample average using the observed data points is not generally a good estimator of the population average. But there are situations where $\hat{\mu}$ is unbiased and consistent for μ: when $\mu_1 = \mu$. The weakest form of the assumption is

$$E(W|S) = E(W), \quad (12.10)$$

in which case we say that W is *mean independent* of S. If (12.10) holds, then $\mu \equiv E(W) = E(W|S=1) \equiv \mu_1$, and it follows immediately from the arguments in (12.7) and (12.9) that the sample average based on the selected sample, $\hat{\mu}$, is both unbiased and consistent for the population mean of interest, μ.

A sufficient condition for assumption (12.10) is full independence between W and S, which we can write as

$$D(W|S) = D(W), \quad (12.11)$$

where D denotes distribution. Sometimes it is more convenient to use

$$P(S=1|W) = P(S=1) = \rho > 0. \quad (12.12)$$

Independence between S and W is often called *missing completely at random*, or MCAR, in the statistics literature on missing data (see, e.g., Little & Rubin, 2002). While MCAR is stronger than mean independence, it is probably rare that (12.10) holds but MCAR does not. Also, MCAR has the virtue of implying that the sample average on the selected sample of any function of W, say $(\sum_i^n S_i)^{-1}\sum_i^n S_i g(W_i)$, is unbiased and consistent for $E[g(W)]$. MCAR is an *equal probability sampling* scheme because the probability of keeping an observation does not depend on the outcome W_i.

The analysis of M-estimation under MCAR follows along the same lines. As with random sampling, we let $\hat{\theta}$ denote the M-estimator on the selected sample (which should cause no confusion because it is the only estimator we study in this section):

$$\min_{\theta\in\Theta} n^{-1}\sum_{i=1}^{n} S_i q(W_i,\theta), \quad (12.13)$$

where we divide by n (which often is not known) so that we can directly apply the LLN for an average of iid random variables. When does estimation using the selected sample consistently estimate θ_o, the solution to the population problem (12.3)? Because the sample average in (12.13) converges in probability to $E[Sq(W,\theta)]$, consistency follows (under standard regularity conditions) if θ_o uniquely solves

$$\min_{\theta\in\Theta} E[Sq(W,\theta)]. \quad (12.14)$$

Under independence between S and W, it is easy to show that θ_o uniquely solves (12.14) whenever it uniquely solves (12.3): $E[Sq(W,\theta)] =$

$E(S)E[q(W,\theta)] = \rho E[q(W,\theta)]$. Also, similar manipulations show that the usual estimators of A_o and B_o from the selected sample are consistent. This should not be surprising. Under independence between W and S, the distribution of W given $S = 1$ is the same as the distribution of W. In effect, we just have a smaller random sample from the original population.

Exogenous or Ignorable Sampling

The MCAR assumption is very restrictive in practice. Rarely are observations missing or discarded in a manner that is independent of all data outcomes. A less restrictive assumption allows selection to depend on conditioning variables. We now partition W as (X,Y) and assume that we are estimating some correctly specified feature of $D(Y|X)$. That is, we assume that we have specified a parametric model for, say, the density of Y given X or the mean of Y given X and that model contains the true conditional density or conditional expectation, respectively. Of course, we should also choose an objective function that identifies the feature of interest. As we saw for random sampling, two leading cases are NLS and MLE.

To study NLS when selection depends on conditioning variables, we must use the following basic fact from probability: the conditional mean function minimizes the conditional mean squared error. That is, if $E(Y|X) = m(X,\theta_o)$ then θ_o satisfies

$$E\{[Y - m(X,\theta_o)]^2|X = x\} \leqslant E\{[Y - m(X,\theta)]^2|X = x\}, \quad \text{for all } \theta \in \Theta. \tag{12.15}$$

The proof of (12.15) without conditioning can be found in any introductory probability book. The conditional case follows in a similar manner; Wooldridge (2002, chap. 2) contains a detailed proof.

For conditional MLE, a critical result is the *conditional Kullback-Leibler information inequality*. If $f(y|x,\theta_o)$ is the density of Y given $X = x$, then

$$E\{\log[f(Y|X,\theta_o)]|X = x\} \geqslant E\{\log[f(Y|X,\theta)]|X = x\}, \quad \text{for all } \theta \in \Theta \tag{12.16}$$

for all x (see, e.g., Wooldridge, 2002, chap. 13). Results (12.15) and (12.16) show that for NLS and MLE, the true value of the parameter solves the underlying population optimization problem conditional on any outcome of X. In the context of M-estimation, posed as a minimization problem, we state this property generally as

$$E[q(W,\theta_o)|X] \leqslant E[q(W,\theta)|X], \quad \text{for all } \theta \in \Theta. \tag{12.17}$$

Given this background on estimators of models with conditioning variables, we can now define a sampling scheme that can be ignored in the estimation of conditional models:

$$P(S = 1|X,Y) = P(S = 1|X), \tag{12.18}$$

which is the same as $P(S = 1|W) = P(S = 1|X)$. Condition (12.18), which we can call *selection on conditioning variables*, has been given other names in the literature. It has been called *exogenous sampling*, the idea being that selection is allowed to be a function of X (the "exogenous" variables) but not Y (the "endogenous" variable or variables).

In the econometrics literature, condition (12.18) has been called *selection on observables*. As a general label, this name is less than ideal because (12.18) can apply when X_i is observed only along with Y_i. The term *selection on observables* actually comes from regression analysis, where X_i is always observed, and we write

$$Y_i = m(X_i,\theta_o) + U_i, \quad E(U_i|X_i) = 0, \tag{12.19}$$

where U_i is the unobserved *error term*. In the regression context with always observable X_i, condition (12.18) allows selection to depend in an arbitrary way on the "observables," X_i, but not on the "unobservables," U_i. In the section Selection on Unobservables, we consider the case where selection can be correlated with U_i.

Regardless of what we call (12.18), it is important to know that it means that we can ignore the sampling scheme in estimation and inference concerning features of conditional distributions. Under assumptions (12.17) and (12.18), we can show that the M-estimator on the selected sample, $\hat{\theta}$, which solves (12.13), is generally consistent for θ_o. Why? Using the law of iterated expectations, Wooldridge (2007) shows that

$$E[Sq(W,\theta_o)|X] \leqslant E[Sq(W,\theta)|X], \quad \text{for all } \theta \in \Theta. \tag{12.20}$$

Because (12.20) holds for any outcome on X, we can integrate both sides and apply iterated expectations:

$$E[Sq(W,\theta_o)] \leqslant E[Sq(W,\theta)], \quad \text{for all } \theta \in \Theta. \tag{12.21}$$

In other words, θ_o is a solution to (12.14). At this level, we cannot claim that θ_o is the unique solution, and we need uniqueness for θ_o to be identified by the sampling scheme. In fact, if our sample selection method retains too little of the population (an extreme case in a regression context would be that one of the covariates does not vary in the selected population), then θ_o need not be identified. We can allow for parts of the population, defined by outcomes on X, to be excluded; that is, $p(x) = 0$ for some x. But we need enough variation in the selected population to identify θ_o.

Similarly, the gradient of the selected objective function, evaluated at θ_o, has zero mean conditional on X: $E[S_i\nabla_\theta q(W_i,\theta_o)|X_i] = 0$. Under smoothness conditions on the objective function, it follows that the M-estimator on the selected sample is generally $\sqrt{n}$-asymptotically normal. In particular,

$$\sqrt{n}(\hat{\theta} - \theta_o) \xrightarrow{d} \text{Normal}(0, A_o^{-1}B_oA_o^{-1}), \tag{12.22}$$

where now

$$A_o \equiv E[S_i\nabla_\theta^2 q(W_i,\theta_o)] \tag{12.23}$$

and

$$B_o = E[S_i\nabla_\theta q(W_i,\theta_o)'\nabla_\theta q(W_i,\theta_o)]. \tag{12.24}$$

The asymptotic variance of the M-estimator can be estimated as

$$\left(\sum_{i=1}^{n} S_i\nabla_\theta^2 q(W_i,\hat{\theta})\right)^{-1} \left(\sum_{i=1}^{n} S_i\nabla_\theta q(W_i,\hat{\theta})'\nabla_\theta q(W_i,\theta_o)\right)^{-1} \left(\sum_{i=1}^{n} S_i\nabla_\theta^2 q(W_i,\hat{\theta})\right)^{-1}, \tag{12.25}$$

which is simply the usual Huber (1967)/White (1982) "sandwich" estimator on the selected sample. Wooldridge (2007) contains a careful derivation and shows how $\nabla_\theta^2 q(W_i,\hat{\theta})$ can be replaced with the expected value of the Hessian given X_i, which would be common for NLS and some conditional MLE problems. For NLS, we would have

$$\widehat{\text{Avar}(\hat{\theta})} = \left(\sum_{i=1}^{n} S_i\nabla_\theta\hat{m}_i'\nabla_\theta\hat{m}_i\right)^{-1} \left(\sum_{i=1}^{n} S_i\hat{U}_i^2\nabla_\theta\hat{m}_i'\nabla_\theta\hat{m}_i\right)^{-1} \left(\sum_{i=1}^{n} S_i\nabla_\theta\hat{m}_i'\nabla_\theta\hat{m}_i\right)^{-1}, \tag{12.26}$$

where $\nabla_\theta\hat{m}_i \equiv \nabla_\theta m(X_i,\hat{\theta})$ is the gradient of the regression function, evaluated at the estimates, and the $\hat{U}_i$ are the NLS residuals (computed, of course, only for the selected sample). This expression is the White (1980) heteroskedasticity/robust variance matrix estimator for NLS but where we have been explicit about only using the selected sample.

Wooldridge (2007) shows that the usual NLS variance matrix is valid under the standard homoskedasticity assumption:

$$\text{Var}(Y|X) = \sigma_o^2. \tag{12.27}$$

That is,

$$\widehat{\text{Avar}(\hat{\theta})} = \hat{\sigma}^2\left(\sum_{i=1}^{n} S_i\nabla_\theta m(X_i,\hat{\theta})'\nabla_\theta m(X_i,\hat{\theta})\right)^{-1}, \tag{12.28}$$

where $\hat{\sigma}^2$ is the usual variance estimator based on the sum of squared residuals in the selected sample.

In the conditional MLE case, with a correctly specified density, the conditional information matrix equality holds; that is,

$$E[\nabla_\theta l(W_i,\theta_o)'\nabla_\theta l(W_i,\theta_o)|X_i] = -E[\nabla_\theta^2 l(W_i,\theta_o)|X_i], \tag{12.29}$$

where $l(W_i,\theta) = \log[f(Y_i|X_i,\theta)]$ is the log-likelihood for observation i. It is easy to see that any of the usual estimators on the selected sample can be used as $\widehat{\text{Avar}(\hat{\theta})}$:

$$\left(\sum_{i=1}^{n} S_i \nabla_\theta l(W_i, \hat{\theta})' \nabla_\theta l(W_i, \hat{\theta})\right)^{-1},$$

$$-\left(\sum_{i=1}^{n} S_i \nabla_\theta^2 l(W_i, \hat{\theta})\right)^{-1}, \text{ or}$$

$$-\left(\sum_{i=1}^{n} S_i C(X_i, \hat{\theta})\right)^{-1}, \qquad (12.30)$$

where $C(X_i, \theta_o) = E[\nabla_\theta^2 l(W_i, \theta_o)|X_i]$ is the expected value of the Hessian conditional on X_i.

What is our conclusion of this section? If we have a correctly specified model of some feature of $D(Y|X)$, we have suitably chosen an objective function that identifies the parameters of interest in the population, and selection depends on the conditioning variables in the sense of (12.19), then we can ignore the fact that the sample was nonrandomly selected. Perhaps this seems obvious and unexciting, but one can see that some derivations, albeit fairly straightforward, are necessary to draw general conclusions. The power of the selection setup is that consistency is easily established using just a few basic tools from probability, including the law of iterated expectations and the LLN.

Of course, sample selection does not always just depend on conditioning variables. In the next section, we allow the selection to depend on other variables, but then we must know or be able to estimate the selection probability function.

Inverse Probability Weighting

We now turn to sampling schemes with unequal probabilities where the sampling is not necessarily exogenous. Provided we know or can estimate the sampling probabilities, consistent estimation is possible using inverse probability weighting.

A General Framework

We again start with random draws of the data and selection indicators, $\{(W_i, S_i) : i = 1, \ldots, n\}$, but now we make probabilistic assumptions that are weaker than independence between S_i and W_i. Furthermore, we allow for selection to depend on variables other than conditioning variables, as in (12.19).

A key assumption for various methods that use *probability weights* is the following. We have a random vector Z_i, drawn along with (W_i, S_i), such that

$$P(S_i = 1|W_i, Z_i) = P(S_i = 1|Z_i) = p(Z_i). \qquad (12.31)$$

As stated, this assumption is not easily fitted into the existing literature, although it is related to, and is sometimes the same as, some common assumptions. When Z_i is always observed, (12.31) is called the *missing at random* (MAR) assumption (see, e.g., Little & Rubin, 2002). (The MCAR assumption in (12.12) requires (12.31) with Z_i empty.) Unfortunately, the term *missing at random* does not properly highlight the role of Z_i. Condition (12.31) could hold for some choices of Z_i but not others. Adding the qualifier "conditional on Z_i" is more informative. In the subsection Data Missing Completely at Random, we discussed the case where (12.31) holds for a set of conditioning variables X_i in modeling some feature of $D(Y|X)$.

Wooldridge (2007) uses assumption (12.31), where Z_i might not be always observed and need not be a set of conditioning (or "exogenous") variables. This allows us to consider various sampling schemes in a unified framework, including variable probability stratified sampling, which we turn to in the section Stratified Sampling.

A common setup is where Z_i is always observed and Z_i and W_i contain variables in common. For example, in a regression context, suppose we always observe the conditioning variables, X_i, but we do not always observe Y_i. Then, $W_i = (X_i, Y_i)$ is only fully observed when Y_i is. If R_i is an additional set of variables, always observed, that affect the probability of observing Y_i, then $Z_i = (X_i, R_i)$. In some cases, R_i might contain exogenous variables in the sense that $E(Y_i|X_i, R_i) = E(Y_i|X_i)$, as would be the case if R_i consists of indicators for different interviewers that are randomly assigned or assigned based on values of X_i. In other cases, R_i might contain values on X, Y, and other variables observed in a previous time period, in which case it is not necessarily true that $E(Y_i|X_i, R_i) = E(Y_i|X_i)$. In either case, assumption (12.31) means that X_i and R_i are such good predictors of selection that, conditional on (X_i, R_i), S_i is independent of Y_i.

Inverse probability weighting requires that the probabilities are always strictly positive:

$$p(z) > 0, \quad \text{for all } z \in \mathcal{Z}. \tag{12.32}$$

Under (12.31) and (12.32), we can solve the nonrandom sampling problem if we know the probability function. Let $g(\cdot)$ be a function with finite expected value, and suppose we want to estimate $\mu = E[g(W)]$. We can use the selected sample provided we observe $p_i \equiv p(Z_i)$ whenever $S_i = 1$. Then, the *inverse probability weighted* (IPW) estimator of μ, sometimes called the Horvitz-Thompson estimator after Horvitz and Thompson (1952), is

$$\hat{\mu}_{\text{IPW}} = \left(\sum_{i=1}^{n}[S_i/p(Z_i)]\right)^{-1}\left(\sum_{i=1}^{n}[S_i g(W_i)/p(Z_i)]\right). \tag{12.33}$$

Note that $\hat{\mu}_{\text{IPW}}$ is just a weighted average of the sampled data, where the weight for a sampled point is the inverse of the selection probability. While (12.33) appears to depend on n (the number of times the population was sampled), n is not needed to compute $\hat{\mu}_{\text{IPW}}$ (and often n is not known).

Expression (12.33) is especially convenient for establishing the large sample properties of $\hat{\mu}_{\text{IPW}}$. Using an iterated expectations argument, it is easily shown that

$$E[S_i/p(Z_i)] = 1, \tag{12.34}$$

and so, by the LLN, $n^{-1}\sum_{i=1}^{n}[S_i/p(Z_i)] \xrightarrow{p} 1$. Similarly,

$$E[S_i g(W_i)/p(Z_i)] = E[g(W_i)]. \tag{12.35}$$

(Wooldridge, 2007, contains the proof.) Again, the LLN implies that $n^{-1}\sum_{i=1}^{n}[S_i g(W_i)/p(Z_i)] \xrightarrow{p} E[g(W_i)]$, which establishes consistency of the IPW estimator under (12.31) and (12.32) (assuming, for now, that the sampling probabilities $p(Z_i)$ are known).

We can apply IPW estimation to handle nonrandom samples in the context of M-estimation, too. The IPW estimator now solves

$$\min_{\theta \in \Theta} n^{-1}\sum_{i=1}^{n}[S_i/p(Z_i)]q(W_i,\theta), \tag{12.36}$$

where the division by n does not affect the estimation problem. Under assumption (12.31), we can show that $E\{[S_i/p(Z_i)]q(W_i,\theta)\} = E[q(W_i,\theta)]$, for all θ, and so the weighted objective function on the selected sample identifies θ_o if θ_o is identified in the population.

The asymptotic variance of the IPW M-estimator has the usual sandwich form in (12.22), but with different definitions for A_o and B_o. The score and Hessian for the selected sample are weighted by the inverse probabilities, resulting in the following estimator of the asymptotic variance of the IPW M-estimator:

$$\left(\sum_{i=1}^{n}(S_i/p_i)\nabla_\theta^2 q(W_i,\hat{\theta})\right)^{-1} \left(\sum_{i=1}^{n}(S_i/p_i^2)\nabla_\theta q(W_i,\hat{\theta})'\nabla_\theta q(W_i,\hat{\theta})\right) \left(\sum_{i=1}^{n}(S_i/p_i)\nabla_\theta^2 q(W_i,\hat{\theta})\right)^{-1}. \tag{12.37}$$

Standard errors obtained from the square roots of the diagonal elements in (12.37), or slight variations on it, are commonly reported by statistical packages that support inverse probability weighting. These standard errors can be used to construct asymptotic t statistics and confidence intervals.

Estimating the Sampling Probabilities

Except in special cases, we need to estimate the sampling probabilities. Wooldridge (2007) covers a general setup where $p(\cdot)$ is estimated using a parametric conditional maximum likelihood framework. Here, we consider the case where Z_i is always observed, and then a standard binary response model, such as logit or probit, is specified for $P(S_i = 1|Z_i)$. Among other situations, this setup applies to regression or MLE where the conditioning variables are always observed, Y_i is only observed when $S_i = 1$, and $Z_i = (X_i, R_i)$ for extra variables R_i that are always observed. Wooldridge (2007) considers the case where Z_i is only partially observed.

If we let Z_i be a $1 \times r$ row vector, a standard binary response formulation is

$$P(S_i = 1|Z_i) = F(Z_i\delta_o), \tag{12.38}$$

where $0 < F(\cdot) < 1$ is a known, continuously differentiable cumulative distribution function (such as the standard normal or logistic) and δ_o is the $r \times 1$ vector of parameters. The estimator $\hat{\delta}$ is from a standard binary response MLE (such as probit or logit):

$$\max_{\delta \in \Delta} \sum_{i=1}^{n} \{(1 - S_i)\log[1 - F(Z_i, \delta)] + S_i \log[F(Z_i, \delta)]\}. \qquad (12.39)$$

Given $\hat{\delta}$, we obtain the estimated probabilities $\hat{p}_i = F(Z_i, \hat{\delta})$. Now the IPW estimator solves

$$\min_{\theta \in \Theta} \sum_{i=1}^{n} (S_i/\hat{p}_i) q(W_i, \theta), \qquad (12.40)$$

which, again, is just the objective function for the selected sample weighted by the inverse of the estimated probability of being kept in the sample. Replacing p_i with $\hat{p}_i$ has no effect on the consistency of $\hat{\theta}$ under weak conditions because $\hat{\delta}$ is consistent for δ_o. Practically, a more important issue is the effect of having to estimate the sampling probabilities on the asymptotic variance of the IPW M-estimator. The combination of the selection assumption (12.31), along with the fact that $\hat{\delta}$ is an MLE (conditional on Z_i) leads to the following interesting fact: The asymptotic variance of the IPW M-estimator that uses estimated weights is no larger, and often strictly smaller, than the asymptotic variance of the IPW M-estimator that uses known weights (if they happen to be known). In other words, it is *better* to estimate the probabilities even if we know them! The section Stratified Sampling contains a simple illustration of the case of variable probability sampling.

The finding that it can be more efficient to estimate the sampling probabilities than to know them has a long history in a variety of IPW problems under the MAR assumption (12.31). Wooldridge (2007) contains references and a unified framework, and generally explains the source of the efficiency gain. Furthermore, Wooldridge shows how to obtain simple asymptotic variance estimates that reflect the increased efficiency from using $\hat{\delta}$ in place of δ_o.

What If Selection Is on Conditioning Variables?

In the subsection Data Missing Completely at Random, we discussed how if the sample selection is based on conditioning variables X in a correctly specified model for some feature of $D(Y|X)$, the nonrandom sampling can be ignored. But what are the consequences if we use inverse probability weighting anyway because we suspect that selection depends on other factors?

The answer depends on whether X_i is always observed. To see why, let Z_i denote the vector of observed factors thought to affect selection, so that our inverse probability estimation is based on estimation of $P(S_i = 1|Z_i)$. The assumption that selection is based solely on the conditioning variables X_i is

$$P(S_i = 1|X_i, Y_i, Z_i) = P(S_i = 1|X_i). \qquad (12.41)$$

If we always observe X_i, then X_i can, and should, be included in Z_i. Why? Because if we use a flexible approach to modeling $P(S_i = 1|Z_i)$, we will consistently estimate $P(S_i = 1|X_i)$. Specifically, suppose we can choose $Z_i = (X_i, R_i)$. Then, $P(S_i = 1|X_i, R_i) = P(S_i = 1|X_i)$, and asymptotically, the elements of R_i will simply be redundant in the inverse probability weighting. It is easy to show that under (12.41), weighting by any positive function of X_i does not cause inconsistency in the IPW estimator.

Are there costs to weighting if (12.41) holds and we can always observe X_i and therefore include them in Z_i? Yes, although these are not as serious as if we do not always observe X_i. First, our model for $P(S_i = 1|X_i, R_i)$ might not be such that $\hat{F}(x, r) \xrightarrow{p} P(S = 1|X = x)$. We hope that with a large enough sample size, we can use a flexible enough model to minimize this problem. Second, even if we assume that we consistently estimate the selection probabilities, the IPW estimator can be less efficient than the unweighted estimator. A leading case is (conditional) maximum likelihood where the density $f(y|x)$ is correctly specified. Then, weighting the log-likelihood by any function of X_i is asymptotically inefficient; it is best not to weight at all. Other cases where probability weighting using functions of X_i causes inefficiency is regression (linear or nonlinear) under homoskedasticity and estimation of so-called generalized linear models under the canonical variance-mean relationship. See Wooldridge (2007) for more discussion.

Unfortunately, if X_i is not always observed—due to nonresponse in a survey or attrition in longitudinal data—then weighting can be quite harmful. The problem is that X_i can no longer be included in Z_i because we need to always observe Z_i to estimate $F(z)$. For concreteness, suppose that X_{i1} is always observed along with some other variables R_i, but X_{i2} is observed only along with Y_i. Then $Z_i = (X_{i1}, R_i)$, and X_i is not a subset of Z_i. If selection is based on X in the sense that $P(S=1|X,Y) = P(S=1|X)$, it is not usually true that $P(S=1|X,Y,R) = P(S=1|X_1,R)$—unless R contains very good proxy variables for X_2. In other words, the key MAR condition (12.31) that underlies consistency of IPW for estimating θ_o fails. In effect, we are using the wrong probability weights, which depend on (X_1, R), when, in fact, we would get consistency by not using any weights. This situation presents a conundrum for the applied researcher: If the unweighted and weighted estimators produce very different results, is it because the probability of selection is a function of factors other than X or because Z cannot include all of X? Presently, there is no good way to distinguish between these two possibilities.

Selection on Unobservables

In the previous sections, nonrandom sampling could be either ignored (see Selected Sampling) or corrected by using inverse probability weighting, assuming that we observe the factors that determine selection (see Inverse Probability Weighting). Unfortunately, in some cases, the key assumption—that we have some variables Z_i that are good predictors of selection and such that $P(S_i = 1|Z_i)$ is known or can be estimated—is unrealistic. To take a leading case, consider the linear regression model

$$Y_i = X_i\beta_o + U_i \tag{12.42}$$

$$E(U_i|X_i) = 0, \tag{12.43}$$

where X_i is always observed but Y_i is not. We are often worried that selection depends on U_i. For example, suppose that Y_i is the percentage of voters supporting the incumbent in an election, where interest is on incumbents who are eligible for re-election. The vector X_i may contain variables reflecting voting on various issues. If some incumbents choose not to run, then Y is unobserved for some part of the population. The decision to run (i.e., whether $S_i = 1$) could be correlated with factors that affect support that we do not have data on, such as personality or general "quality" of the candidate.

In such cases, we often model the selection process as, say,

$$S_i = 1[Z_i\delta_o + V_i \geqslant 0], \tag{12.44}$$

where $1[\cdot]$ is the indicator function, which equals 1 when the statement in brackets is true; X_i is a subset of Z_i; (U_i, V_i) is independent of Z_i; and V_i is usually assumed to have a standard normal distribution:

$$V_i|Z_i \sim \text{Normal}(0,1). \tag{12.45}$$

Then, $P(S_i = 1|Z_i) = \Phi(Z_i\delta_o)$; that is, S_i follows a probit model.

Even though the setup here and in the section on inverse probability weighting both rely on a standard binary response model for the sampling probability, there are important differences here compared with the key MAR assumption (12.31). First, the entire vector Z_i, say $Z_i = (X_i, R_i)$, is assumed to be independent of the error U_i in (12.42) (or we could get by with $E(U_i|Z_i) = 0$). In other words, in econometric parlance, the extra variables R_i must be exogenous in (12.42). This means that we have one or more variables in R_i that affect selection but do not affect Y_i once X_i has been conditioned on. For example, perhaps in obtaining data on wealth, some interviewers, who were randomly assigned, were more effective at eliciting a response. Then, R_i could be a vector of interviewer indicators, with the random assignment ensuring that R_i is independent of U_i. For the approach to be convincing, selection should depend on R_i even after X_i has been accounted for; such an assumption is not needed in the IPW framework in the inverse probability weighting section.

The need for R_i to be exogenous in (12.42) is quite different from what we would assume of R_i to apply the IPW method in the inverse probability weighting section. For IPW estimation, we want R_i to satisfy

$$P(S_i = 1|X_i, R_i, U_i) = P(S_i = 1|X_i, R_i), \tag{12.46}$$

which can be interpreted as stating that R_i contains good proxies for the elements of U_i that are correlated with selection. That is, we might choose R_i to be highly correlated with U_i (such as previous outcomes on Y).

In the selection on unobservables setting, we allow the unobservables U_i and V_i to be correlated, which means that (12.46) cannot hold. In the econometrics literature, the correlation between U_i and V_i has been dubbed *selection on unobservables* because S_i is correlated with U_i even after conditioning on Z_i. The celebrated solution to the sample selection problem in this case was provided by Heckman (1976) (and is much different from inverse probability weighting). If we assume that (U_i, V_i) is independent of Z_i and that $E(U_i|V_i) = \rho_o V_i$, then

$$E(Y_i|Z_i,V_i) = X_i\beta_o + E(U_i|Z_i,V_i) = X_i\beta_o + \rho_o V_i, \tag{12.47}$$

and because S_i is a function of (Z_i, V_i), we can use iterated expectations to obtain

$$E(Y_i|Z_i,S_i) = X_i\beta_o + \rho_o E(V_i|Z_i,S_i). \tag{12.48}$$

(Remember, X_i is contained in Z_i, so in (12.47) and (12.48), we are conditioning on X_i.) Equation (12.48) is important. By construction, selection is a function of the conditioning variables because the expectation is conditional on S_i as well as Z_i. From the subsection What If Selection Is on Conditioning Variables? we know that we can use the $S_i = 1$ subsample to consistently estimate β_o and ρ_o from a regression of Y_i on $X_i, \lambda(Z_i\delta_o)$, where $\lambda(Z_i\delta_o) \equiv E(V_i|Z_i, S_i = 1)$. Conveniently, (12.44) and (12.45) imply that

$$\lambda(Z_i\delta_o) = \frac{\phi(Z_i\delta_o)}{\Phi(Z_i\delta_o)}, \tag{12.49}$$

where $\phi(\cdot)$ is the standard normal probability density function (see, e.g., Maddala, 1983, Section 5.7). The function in (12.49) is known as the *inverse Mills ratio*. We have shown that $E(Y_i|Z_i, S_i = 1) = X_i\beta_o + \rho_o\lambda(Z_i\delta_o)$, and so the nonrandom sampling problem caused by selection on unobservables—at least in the linear regression model—is solved by adding $\lambda(Z_i\delta_o)$ as regressor in the regression on the selected sample. In practice, of course, we replace δ_o with a consistent estimator—in this case, the probit maximum likelihood estimator, $\hat{\delta}$. (Therefore, the first-stage estimation of the selection probabilities can be the same as for IPW estimation.) Let $\hat{\lambda}_i \equiv \lambda(Z_i\hat{\delta})$ be the estimated Mills ratio for observation i. Then, β_o and ρ_o are consistently estimated from the regression

$$Y_i \text{ on } X_i, \hat{\lambda}_i, \quad \text{for } S_i = 1. \tag{12.50}$$

A standard test of $H_0 : \rho_o = 0$ is a test for the absence of sample selection bias. If $\rho_o \neq 0$, the asymptotic variance in the second-stage estimation must be adjusted to account for estimation of δ_o. Unfortunately, we cannot conclude, as in the IPW case, that ignoring the first-stage estimation leads to conservative inference; in fact, it can be shown that the asymptotic variance that adjusts for estimation of δ_o is always larger than the incorrect one that does not (see Wooldridge, 2002, Section 17.2 for further details).

Allowing selection to be correlated with U_i is attractive in many applications, but the approach has limited scope. Nonlinear regression functions can be accommodated if we assume an additive error that is independent of X_i, as we essentially did in (12.42). Unfortunately, often we use a nonlinear regression function because Y_i has special features, such as being nonnegative or being bounded in the unit interval, in which case the formulation $Y_i = m(X_i, \beta_o) + U_i$ with U_i independent of X_i is untenable. Terza (1998) has shown how Heckman's approach can be extended to an exponential regression model without assuming an additive error. The case where Y_i is a binary response that itself follows a probit model—so $Y_i = 1[X_i\beta_o + U_i \geqslant 0]$, where (U_i, V_i) follows a bivariate normal distribution with unit variances—has also been derived (see, e.g., Wooldridge, 2002, Section 17.4.3). Such methods have been programmed in popular statistical packages such as Stata.

Before we conclude this section, it is important to understand a further limitation of Heckman's approach to sample selection problems. In the subsection What If Selection Is on Conditioning Variables?, we warned about the dangers of IPW estimation if the conditioning variables, X_i, cannot all be included in the covariates affecting selection, Z_i. The same warning holds here. Suppose that X_{i2} is only observed if $S_i = 1$, and so we take $Z_i = (X_{i1}, R_i)$. Then, we can no longer assume that V_i in (12.44) is independent of X_i unless we assume that $P(S_i = 1|X_{i1}, X_{i2}, R_i) = P(S_i = 1|X_{i1}, R_i)$, a strong assumption that means that X_{i2} has no partial effect on selection once we control for X_{i1} and R_i. If V_i is not independent of X_{i2}, then in general, $E(U_i|X_i, R_i, V_i) \neq E(U_i|V_i)$—in fact, $E(U_i|X_i, R_i, V_i)$ would generally depend on X_i and R_i in addition to V_i, and then (12.47), with Z_i in the conditioning set replaced with (X_i, R_i), does not hold. But then $E(Y_i|X_i, R_i, S_i = 1) \neq X_i\beta_o + \rho_o\lambda(Z_i\delta_o)$, and the Heckman selection correction fails. Wooldridge (2002, Section 17.4.2) shows how partial observability of variables X_{i2} can be solved by an extension of Heckman's method if sufficient instrumental variables—that is, variables that are exogenous in (12.42), like R_i, but also partially correlated with X_{i2}—are available.

Stratified Sampling

I now explicitly consider two common stratified sampling schemes. Stratified sampling is often used when one wants to target certain portions of a population. For example, a survey of income and demographic characteristics may intentionally oversample families with incomes below the median. Because the relative frequencies in a stratified sample may differ systematically from those in the population, it is intuitively clear that using descriptive statistics from such a sample will not necessarily produce satisfying estimates of population moments. Fortunately, if we have enough information about the stratification scheme, we can often modify standard methods and consistently estimate population parameters.

There are two common types of stratified sampling, *variable probability* (VP) sampling and *standard stratified* (SS) sampling. A third type of sampling, typically called *multinomial sampling*, is practically indistinguishable from SS sampling, but it generates a random sample from a modified population (thereby simplifying certain theoretical analyses). See Cosslett (1993), Imbens and Lancaster (1996), and Wooldridge (1999) for further discussion. We focus on VP and SS sampling here.

With VP and SS sampling, the sample space $\mathcal{W}$ is partitioned into J nonoverlapping, exhaustive strata, say $\mathcal{W}_1, \ldots, \mathcal{W}_J$. But VP and SS sampling differ in their particulars. We start with VP sampling.

VP sampling is convenient for telephone or e-mail surveys. A unit is selected randomly from the population, but it is kept in the sample with probability that depends on its strata. The sampling probabilities, $p_1, \ldots, p_J$, are part of the sample design. If we keep all randomly drawn units from stratum j, then $p_j = 1$.

If we keep a random draw W_i—that is, $S_i = 1$, we also know its sampling probability. If $S_i = 0$, we usually do not know which stratum the discarded observation fell into (though we may know the aggregate figures). The idea is that we may stratify the population based on a small number of characteristics, find out those characteristics, and then essentially flip a biased coin to determine whether to continue the interview.

VP sampling falls into the framework of the inverse probability weighting section. We can define Z_i as the J-vector of strata indicators, $Z_{ij} = 1[W_i \in \mathcal{W}_j]$, where again, $1[\cdot]$ is the indicator function. Because the probability of being kept is constant within each stratum, the MAR assumption (12.31) holds by design. Furthermore, the fact that Z_i is observed only when W_i is observed causes no problems because the response probabilities, p_j, are known. Therefore, we can implement VP sampling with a wide variety of estimation methods, including the general class of M-estimators. If we happen to observe the number of times each stratum was sampled, say n_j, then we can apply the efficiency result mentioned in the subsection What If Selection Is on Conditioning Variables? It is more efficient to use the maximum likelihood estimates of p_j—namely, $\hat{p}_j = m_j/n_j$, where m_j is the number of retained observations in stratum j, a figure we always know—than to use the known p_j.

With standard stratified sampling, we take a random sample from each of the J strata. A random draw from stratum j has the distribution $D(W|W \in \mathcal{W}_j)$, so it is useful to denote the random sample from stratum j as $\{W_{ji} : i = 1, \ldots, n_j\}$. With SS sampling, we always know the sample sizes within each stratum, and so we know the total sample size, $n = n_1 + n_2 + \cdots + n_J$.

How can we use the SS sample to estimate population moments? It turns out that we need to know (or be able to estimate) the *population shares*—that is, $\pi_j \equiv P(W \in \mathcal{W}_j)$, $j = 1,\ldots,J$. Then, the population mean is a weighted average of the stratum means,

$$\mu = E(W) = \pi_1 E(W|W \in \mathcal{W}_1) + \pi_2 E(W|W \in \mathcal{W}_2) + \cdots + \pi_J E(W|W \in \mathcal{W}_J). \tag{12.51}$$

We can use the sample average of the random sample from stratum j, say $\bar{W}_j$, as an unbiased, consistent estimator of $E(W|W \in \mathcal{W}_j)$. Therefore, an unbiased, consistent (as $n_j \to \infty$ for each j) estimator of μ is

$$\hat{\mu} = \pi_1 \bar{W}_1 + \pi_2 \bar{W}_2 + \cdots + \pi_J \bar{W}_J, \tag{12.52}$$

and its variance is

$$\text{Var}(\hat{\mu}) = \pi_1^2 \text{Var}(\bar{W}_1) + \pi_2^2 \text{Var}(\bar{W}_2) + \cdots + \pi_J^2 \text{Var}(\bar{W}_J). \tag{12.53}$$

Each variance on the right-hand side is easily estimated using the standard formula for the variance of the average from a random sample (within each stratum in this case).

Generally, estimators from SS sampled data can be defined by weighted averages. For example, if we drop the strata indicators, we can write (12.52) as

$$\hat{\mu} = \frac{1}{(\sum_{i=1}^n v_i)} \sum_{i=1}^n v_i W_i, \tag{12.54}$$

where now the sampling weights $v_i = \pi_{j_i}/h_{j_i}$, where j_i is the stratum for observation i and $h_j = n_j/n$ is the fraction of observations in stratum j. Observations in stratum j receive a weight larger than unity if they are underrepresented in the sample relative to the population—that is, $h_j < \pi_j$. The other case can occur, too. Equation (12.54) effectively has the same form as in the VP sampling case, except that in the VP the weights are inverse probability weights, $v_i = 1/p_{j_i}$, and the sum would be only over data points that we actually observe (with the selection indicator implicit).

Because of the simplicity of (12.54), it is tempting to estimate the variance of $\hat{\mu}$ as

$$\widehat{\text{Var}(\hat{\mu})} = \frac{1}{(\sum_{i=1}^n v_i)^2} \sum_{i=1}^n v_i^2 (W_i - \hat{\mu})^2. \tag{12.55}$$

In fact, if information on the strata is not explicitly included, (12.55) is the estimate reported by standard statistical packages that allow sampling weights in estimating population means (as well as regression parameters). Equation (12.55) turns out to be an overestimate of the actual variance of $\hat{\mu}$, even in large samples, for the following reason. In estimating (12.53), we should compute a sample variance within each stratum. Importantly, this means that we deviate each observation in stratum j, W_{ji}, from the sample mean within that stratum, $\bar{W}_j$. The estimator in (12.55) deviates all observations from the overall mean, $\hat{\mu}$, which means that the probability limit of this equation is usually too large. Therefore, if we only account for the weights and do not exploit the different stratum means in obtaining the variance, our inference will be conservative.

A similar analysis holds for M-estimation with SS samples. Now, the weighted M-estimator solves

$$\min_{\theta \in \Theta} \sum_{i=1}^n v_i q(W_i, \theta) \tag{12.56}$$

for the sampling weights v_i. Wooldridge (2001) established consistency and asymptotic normality of the M-estimator on SS samples. The usual Huber-White sandwich form of the asymptotic variance is

$$\widehat{\text{Avar}(\hat{\theta})} = \left(\sum_{i=1}^n v_i \nabla_\theta^2 q(W_i, \hat{\theta}) \right)^{-1} \left(\sum_{i=1}^n v_i^2 \nabla_\theta q(W_i, \hat{\theta})' \nabla_\theta q(W_i, \hat{\theta}) \right) \left(\sum_{i=1}^n v_i \nabla_\theta^2 q(W_i, \hat{\theta}) \right)^{-1}, \tag{12.57}$$

which simply requires that we compute the gradient (the row vector of partial derivatives) and the Hessian (the matrix of second derivatives) at the estimate $\hat{\theta}$. The estimated variances from (12.57) are conservative in the sense that in large samples, they are at least as large as the actual sampling variances. Therefore, using standard errors computed from (12.57) leads to 95% confidence intervals that have coverage probability greater than 95% (in large samples). An estimator that explicitly recognizes the

SS sampling scheme is obtained by subtracting strata-specific averages of the gradient before computing the middle of the sandwich; that is, $\sum_{j=1}^{J}\sum_{i=1}^{n_j} v_i^2(\nabla_\theta \hat{q}_{ji} - \overline{\nabla_\theta \hat{q}_j})'(\nabla_\theta \hat{q}_{ji} - \overline{\nabla_\theta \hat{q}_j})$, where $\overline{\nabla_\theta \hat{q}_j} = n_j^{-1}\sum_{i=1}^{n_j}\nabla_\theta \hat{q}_{ji}$ is the average of the estimated gradient within stratum j. As in the case of estimating a mean, subtracting off the stratum-specific averages leads to a smaller asymptotic variance estimate, and in large samples, this estimate more properly reflects the sampling variation in $\hat{\theta}$.

One case where the asymptotic variance is not affected by removing strata-specific means is when sampling is exogenous. That is because $E[\nabla_\theta q(W, \theta_o)|X] = 0$ and the stratification is based on X, and so the gradient evaluated at θ_o has a mean of 0 in each stratum. Wooldridge (2001) provides further discussion.

Generally, it is probably not a bad idea to use the easily computable, conservative variance estimator in (12.57). For one, this is the correct estimator to use under exogenous sampling. But even if sampling is endogenous, we might want to recognize that the asymptotic variance estimators have only asymptotic justification. By using conservative inference, we acknowledge that the asymptotic formulas might be too optimistic in actual (finite) samples.

Cluster Sampling

Data obtained from cluster samples share a structure similar to data obtained from standard stratified sampling, but the method of obtaining cluster samples differs. With SS sampling, the population is partitioned, and then random samples are drawn from within each stratum. The most common setup for cluster sampling is when disaggregated units—often people or families—combine naturally as relatively small clusters in the population and then those clusters are sampled from a large population of clusters. For example, to study the effects of school inputs on a national fourth-grade mathematics test, we might randomly sample public schools and obtain test results for all students in each school or for a random sample of students within each school. There may be tens of thousands of primary schools in the country, but perhaps only a few hundred schools are sampled. Under this sampling scheme, it makes sense to think of each fourth grader as belonging to his or her cluster (school). While there is randomness in outcomes within a school, typically we think that the outcomes for students within a school will be correlated, due to both observed and unobserved school characteristics.

A cluster sample presents itself in much the same way as a stratified sample: A cluster or group identifier is included for each observation. But because clusters are sampled, valid inference requires accounting for within-cluster correlation (except in the rare case where none is present). Typically, this correlation is dealt with through variance estimation that accounts for the within-cluster correlation. We can consider general M-estimation to illustrate the approach. As before, this covers a wide range of estimation methods.

Let $\{W_g : g = 1, 2, \ldots, G\}$ be the cluster sample, where g indexes the cluster. Visually, it helps to think of W_g as a matrix where each row is a data point on an individual, say W_{gm}. In other words, W_{gm} is, say, a $1 \times R$ vector of variables on individual (or unit) m in cluster g. We assume that cluster g contains M_g individuals (or other units); in effect, W_g is an $M_g \times R$ matrix.

A typical assumption is that sampling across clusters is independent, so that $\{W_g : g = 1, 2, \ldots, G\}$ are independent. We cannot assume identical distribution because the dimension of W_g generally changes with g. (For example, we might sample 15 students from one school and 25 from another.) But the technical complications that result from nonidentically distributed data are easily overcome by employing the LLN and the central limit theorem for inid observations.

An M-estimator on a cluster sample solves

$$\min_{\theta \in \Theta} \sum_{g=1}^{G} \sum_{m=1}^{M_g} q(W_{gm}, \theta); \qquad (12.58)$$

that is, we pool the data across individuals and groups. Assuming that we have correctly specified the feature we are interested in and have appropriately chosen the objective function, the M-estimator is again consistent, in general, and asymptotically normal. But we must show some care in how we do the asymptotics here. Typically, so that we can allow very general dependence within clusters, it is desirable to view an observation as being W_g with fixed cluster size M_g. Then, the analysis is with M_g fixed and $G \to \infty$. For this to be realistic, we should, of course, have many groups or clusters. But the method may still work well if G is only moderately large.

Consistency of pooled regression—linear or nonlinear—or pooled MLE is relatively straightforward with cluster samples. The more interesting, and difficult, question is inference. With cluster sampling, the summands in the gradient of the objective function are correlated within each group or cluster. An estimator of Avar$(\hat{\theta})$ that properly accounts for the cluster correlation is

$$\left(\sum_{g=1}^{G}\sum_{m=1}^{M_g}\nabla_{\theta}^{2}\hat{q}_{gm}\right)^{-1}\left(\sum_{g=1}^{G}\sum_{m=1}^{M_g}\sum_{r=1}^{M_g}\nabla_{\theta}\hat{q}_{gm}'\nabla_{\theta}\hat{q}_{gr}\right)\left(\sum_{g=1}^{G}\sum_{m=1}^{M_g}\nabla_{\theta}^{2}\hat{q}_{gm}\right)^{-1}, \quad (12.59)$$

where the gradient and Hessian are evaluated at W_{gm} and $\hat{\theta}$. In some cases, including NLS and common maximum likelihood problems—such as probit and logit—the Hessian is replaced with the expected Hessian conditional on exogenous variables.

The matrix in (12.59) is yet another example of a robust sandwich estimator. For linear regression, (12.59) becomes

$$\left(\sum_{g=1}^{G}\sum_{m=1}^{M_g}X_{gm}'X_{gm}\right)^{-1}\left(\sum_{g=1}^{G}\sum_{m=1}^{M_g}\sum_{r=1}^{M_g}\hat{U}_{gm}\hat{U}_{gr}X_{gm}'X_{gr}\right)\left(\sum_{g=1}^{G}\sum_{m=1}^{M_g}X_{gm}'X_{gm}\right)^{-1}, \quad (12.60)$$

where X_{gm} is a $1 \times K$ vector of regressors and $\hat{U}_{gm} = Y_{gm} - X_{gm}\hat{\theta}$ is the pooled ordinary least squares residual for unit m within group g. When $m = r$, the summand in the middle term in (12.60) is $\hat{U}_{gm}^{2}X_{gm}'X_{gm}$, which shows that the matrix is robust to heteroskedasticity in Var$(Y_{gm}|X_{gm})$. The term $\hat{U}_{gm}\hat{U}_{gr}X_{gm}'X_{gr}$ for $m \neq r$ accounts for possible correlation between the unobservables U_{gm} and U_{gr} for any two units within group g, and this correlation is entirely unrestricted. In the context of cluster sampling, within-group correlation is often called *cluster correlation.* For nonlinear regression, the gradient of the mean function simply replaces X_{gm} everywhere. See Wooldridge (2003) for further discussion.

Conveniently, many statistical packages now report "cluster robust" variance matrices as a simple option with a variety of estimation commands, including regression and preprogrammed likelihood methods such as probit, logit, Tobit, and Poisson regression. Typically, one just uses the same command as for a cross-sectional data set, but then one uses a clustering option (that requires having a variable that identifies clusters). When the cluster option is added, expression (12.60) is computed. This should not be confused with the variance matrix estimate that is robust only to heteroskedasticity, which omits the terms $\hat{U}_{gm}\hat{U}_{gr}X_{gm}'X_{gr}$ for $m \neq r$. The estimator in (12.60) is robust to heteroskedasticity and cluster correlation. One must be cautious in applying the cluster option when the number of groups or clusters, G, is small.

A special case of cluster sampling is panel or longitudinal data. In that case, g indexes an individual, family, firm, and so on, and m indexes time periods. For each cross-sectional unit g, we have, say, M_g time periods. (In the *balanced* case we have the same time periods for each g.) Then, formulas such as (12.59) and (12.60) allow for general dependence over time within each unit. Because the estimators are justified only for a fixed M_g, $G \to \infty$ asymptotic analysis, they apply to the panel data case when we have many cross-sectional units over relatively few time periods, as is common in data sets on individuals, families, firms, and even schools, cities, and counties. See Arellano (1987) and Wooldridge (2002) for more discussion on panel data applications.

Acknowledgment

I would like to thank the editor, Tamás Rudas, for very helpful comments and suggestions on an earlier draft.

REFERENCES

Arellano, M. (1987). Computing robust standard errors for within-groups estimators. *Oxford Bulletin of Economics and Statistics*, *49*, 431–434.

Casella, G., & Berger, R. L. (2002). *Statistical inference* (2nd ed.). Pacific Grove, CA: Duxbury.

Cochran, W. G. (1977). *Sampling techniques* (3rd ed.). New York: Wiley.

Cosslett, S. R. (1993). Estimation from endogenously stratified samples. In G. S. Maddala, C. R. Rao, & H. D. Vinod (Eds.), *Handbook of statistics* (Vol. 11, pp. 1–43). Amsterdam: North-Holland.

Heckman, J. J. (1976). The common structure of statistical models of truncation, sample selection, and limited dependent variables and a simple estimator for such models. *Annals of Economic and Social Measurement*, *5*, 475–492.

Horvitz, D. G., & Thompson, D. J. (1952). A generalization of sampling without replacement from a finite universe. *Journal of the American Statistical Association*, *47*, 663–685.

Huber, P. J. (1967). The behavior of maximum likelihood estimates under nonstandard conditions. In L. M. LeCam & J. Neyman (Eds.), *Proceedings of the fifth Berkeley symposium in mathematical statistics* (Vol. 1, pp. 221–233). Berkeley: University of California Press.

Imbens, G. W., & Lancaster, T. (1996). Efficient estimation and stratified sampling. *Journal of Econometrics*, *74*, 289–318.

Little, R. J. A., & Rubin, D. B. (2002). *Statistical analysis with missing data.* Hoboken, NJ: Wiley.

Maddala, G. S. (1983). *Limited dependent and qualitative variables in econometrics.* Cambridge, UK: Cambridge University Press.

Newey, W. K., & McFadden, D. (1994). Large sample estimation and hypothesis testing. In R. F. Engle & D. McFadden (Eds.), *Handbook of econometrics* (Vol. 4, pp. 2111–2245). Amsterdam: North-Holland.

Terza, J. V. (1998). Estimating count models with endogenous switching: Sample selection and endogenous treatment effects. *Journal of Econometrics*, *84*, 129–154.

White, H. (1980). A heterosekdasticity-consistent covariance matrix estimator and a direct test for heteroskedasticity. *Econometrica*, *48*, 817–838.

White, H. (1982). Maximum likelihood estimation with misspecified models. *Econometrica*, *50*, 1–26.

Wooldridge, J. M. (1999). Distribution-free estimation of some nonlinear panel data models. *Journal of Econometrics*, *90*, 77–97.

Wooldridge, J. M. (2001). Asymptotic properties of weighted M-estimators for standard stratified samples. *Econometric Theory*, *17*, 451–470.

Wooldridge, J. M. (2002). *Econometric analysis of cross section and panel data.* Cambridge: MIT Press.

Wooldridge, J. M. (2003). Cluster-sample methods in applied econometrics. *American Economic Review*, *93*, 133–138.

Wooldridge, J. M. (2007). Inverse probability weighted estimation for general missing data problems. *Journal of Econometrics*, *141*, 1281–1301.

13

PANEL STUDIES

EDWARD W. FREES AND JEE-SEON KIM

INTRODUCTION

What Are Longitudinal and Panel Data?

Longitudinal data represent a marriage of cross-sectional and time-series data. Unlike purely cross-sectional data typically used in regression, with longitudinal data we observe subjects over time. Unlike time-series data, with longitudinal data we observe many subjects. Observing a broad cross-section of subjects over time allows analysts to study dynamic, as well as cross-sectional, aspects of a problem.

The descriptor *panel data* comes from surveys of individuals. In this context, a "panel" is a group of individuals surveyed repeatedly over time. Historically, panel data methodology within economics had been largely developed through labor economics applications. Now, economic applications of panel data methods are not confined to survey or labor economics problems and the interpretation of the descriptor "panel data analysis" is much broader. Hence, we will use the terms *longitudinal data* and *panel data* interchangeably although, for simplicity, we often use only the former term.

Prevalence of Longitudinal and Panel Data Analysis

Longitudinal and panel databases and models have taken an important role in the literature. They are widely used in the social science literature, where panel data are also known as *pooled cross-sectional time series* and in the natural sciences, where panel data are referred to as longitudinal data. To illustrate, an index of business and economic journals, ABI/INFORM, lists 685 articles in 2004 and 2005 that use panel data methods. Another index of scientific journals, the ISI Web of Science, lists 1,137 articles in 2004 and 2005 that use longitudinal data methods. And these are only the applications that were considered innovative enough to be published in scholarly reviews!

Longitudinal data methods have also developed because important databases have become available to empirical researchers. Within economics, two important surveys that track individuals over repeated interviews include the Panel Survey of Income Dynamics (PSID) and the National Longitudinal Survey of Labor Market Experience (NLS). In contrast, the Consumer Price Survey (CPS) is another survey conducted repeatedly over time. However, the CPS is generally not regarded as a panel survey because individuals are not tracked over time. For studying firm-level behavior, databases such as Compustat and CRSP (the University of Chicago's Center for Research on Security Prices) have been available for several decades. More recently, the National Association of Insurance Commissioners (NAIC) has made insurance company financial statements available electronically. With the rapid pace of software development within the database industry, it is easy to anticipate the development of many more databases that would benefit from longitudinal data analysis. To illustrate, within the marketing area, product codes are scanned in when customers check out of a store and are transferred to a central database. These so-called scanner data represent yet another source of data information that may reveal new information to marketing researchers about purchasing decisions of buyers over time or the efficiency of a store's promotional efforts.

Some Notation

Models of longitudinal data are sometimes differentiated from regression and time series through their "double subscripts." With this notation, we may distinguish among responses by subject and time. To this end, define y_{it} to be the response for the ith subject during the tth time period. A longitudinal data set consists of observations of the ith subject over $t = 1,\ldots,T_i$ time periods, for each of $i = 1,\ldots,n$ subjects. Thus, we observe

$$\begin{array}{ll} \text{First subject} & \left\{y_{11}, y_{12}, \ldots, y_{1T_1}\right\} \\ \text{Second subject} & \left\{y_{21}, y_{22}, \ldots, y_{2T_2}\right\} \\ \vdots & \vdots \\ n\text{th subject} & \left\{y_{n1}, y_{n2}, \ldots, y_{nT_n}\right\} \end{array}.$$

For many data sets, it is useful to let the number of observations depend on the subject; T_i denotes the number of observations for the ith subject. This situation is known as the *unbalanced* data case. In other data sets, each subject has the same number of observations, known as the *balanced* data case.

Benefits and Drawbacks of Longitudinal Data

There are several advantages of longitudinal data compared with either purely cross-sectional or purely time-series data. We focus on two important advantages: the ability to study dynamic relationships and to model differences, or heterogeneity, among subjects. Of course, longitudinal data are more complex than purely cross-sectional or time-series data and so there is a price in working with them. The most important drawback is the difficulty in designing the sampling scheme to reduce the problem of subjects leaving the study prior to its completion, known as *attrition*.

Dynamic Relationships

Dynamic relationships can only be studied with repeated observations, and we have to think carefully about how we define our "subject" when considering dynamics. To illustrate, suppose that we are looking at the event of divorce on individuals. By looking at a cross-section of individuals, we can estimate divorce rates. By looking at cross-sections repeated over time (without tracking individuals), we can estimate divorce rates over time and thus study dynamic movement. However, only by tracking repeated observations on a sample of individuals can we study the duration of marriage or time until divorce, another dynamic event of interest.

With longitudinal data, we use several (repeated) observations of subjects, over time. Repeated observations from the same subject tend to be correlated. A model that we use is

$$y_{it} = \mathrm{E}y_{it} + \varepsilon_{it},\ t = 1,\ldots,T_i,\ i = 1,\ldots,n.$$

Here, ε_{it} represents the deviation of the response from its mean; this deviation may include dynamic patterns. Intuitively, if there is a dynamic pattern that is common among subjects, then by observing this pattern over many subjects, we hope to estimate the pattern with fewer time-series observations than required of conventional time-series methods.

For many data sets of interest, subjects do not have identical means. As a first-order approximation, a linear combination of known, explanatory variables, such as $\mathrm{E}y_{it} = \alpha + \mathbf{x}_{it}'\beta$, serves as a useful specification of the mean function. Here, $\mathbf{x}_{it} = \left(x_{it,1}, \ldots, x_{it,K}\right)'$ is a vector of explanatory, or independent, variables. The slope parameters β_1, β_2, ..., β_K are associated with the K explanatory variables. For a more compact expression, we summarize the parameters as a column vector of dimension $K \times 1$, denoted by $\beta = (\beta_1, \ldots, \beta_K)'$.

Heterogeneity

By tracking subjects over time, we may model subject behavior. In many data sets of interest, subjects are unlike one another, that is, they are *heterogeneous*. In (repeated) cross-sectional regression analysis, we use models such as $y_{it} = \alpha + \mathbf{x}'_{it}\beta + \varepsilon_{it}$ and ascribe the uniqueness of subjects to the disturbance term ε_{it}. In contrast, with longitudinal data we have an opportunity to capture this uniqueness. A basic longitudinal data model that incorporates heterogeneity among subjects is based on

$$\mathrm{E}\,y_{it} = \alpha_i + \mathbf{x}'_{it}\beta, \qquad t = 1,\ldots,T_i, \quad i = 1,\ldots,n. \tag{13.1}$$

In cross-sectional studies, where $T_i = 1$, the parameters of this model are unidentifiable. However, in longitudinal data, we have a sufficient number of observations to estimate β and $\alpha_1,\ldots,\alpha_n$. Allowing for subject-specific parameters, such as α_i, provides an important mechanism for controlling heterogeneity of individuals. Models that incorporate heterogeneity terms such as in (13.1) will be called *heterogeneous models*. Models without such terms will be called *homogeneous models*.

We may also interpret heterogeneity to mean that observations from the same subject tend to be similar compared with observations from different subjects. Based on this interpretation, heterogeneity can be modeled by examining the sources of correlation among repeated observations from a subject. That is, for many data sets, we anticipate finding a positive correlation when examining $\mathbf{y} = (y_{i1},\ldots,y_{iT_i})'$. As noted above, one possible explanation is the dynamic pattern among the observations. Another possible explanation is that the response shares a common, yet unobserved, feature that induces a positive correlation.

Failure to include heterogeneity quantities in the model may introduce serious bias into the model estimators. To illustrate, suppose that a data analyst mistakenly uses the function $\mathrm{E}\,y_{it} = \alpha + \mathbf{x}'_{it}\beta$ when (13.1) is the true function. This is an example of *heterogeneity bias*.

Omitted Variables

Incorporating heterogeneity quantities into longitudinal data models are often motivated by the concern that important variables have been omitted from the model. The section Correlated Effects provides additional discussion of this important topic.

Efficiency of Estimators

A longitudinal data design may yield more efficient estimators than estimators based on a comparable amount of data from alternative designs. To illustrate, suppose that the interest is in assessing the average change in a response over time, such as the proportion of a population whose marital status is "divorced." Thus, let $\bar{y}_{\bullet 1} - \bar{y}_{\bullet 2}$ denote the difference between divorce rates between two time periods. In a repeated cross-sectional study, such as the CPS, we would calculate the reliability of this statistic assuming independence among cross-sections to get

$$\mathrm{Var}\,(\bar{y}_{\bullet 1} - \bar{y}_{\bullet 2}) = \mathrm{Var}\,\bar{y}_{\bullet 1} + \mathrm{Var}\,\bar{y}_{\bullet 2}.$$

However, in a panel survey that tracks individuals over time, we have

$$\mathrm{Var}\,(\bar{y}_{\bullet 1} - \bar{y}_{\bullet 2}) = \mathrm{Var}\,\bar{y}_{\bullet 1} + \mathrm{Var}\,\bar{y}_{\bullet 2} - 2\mathrm{Cov}\,(\bar{y}_{\bullet 1}, \bar{y}_{\bullet 2}).$$

The covariance term is generally positive because observations from the same subject tend to be positively correlated. Thus, other things being equal, a panel survey design yields more efficient estimators than a repeated cross-section design.

For some situations, a researcher may obtain more information by sampling each subject repeatedly. Thus, some advocate that an advantage of longitudinal data is that we generally have more observations, due to the repeated sampling, and greater efficiency of estimators compared with a purely cross-sectional regression design. The danger of this position is that generally observations from the same subject are related. Thus, although more information is obtained by repeated sampling, researchers need to be cautious in assessing the amount of additional information gained.

Correlation and Causation

For many statistical studies, analysts are pleased to be able to describe associations among variables. This is particularly true of forecasting studies, where the goal is to predict the future. However, for other analyses, researchers are interested in assessing causal relationships among variables.

Longitudinal and panel data are sometimes touted as providing "evidence" of causal effects. Just as with any statistical methodology, longitudinal data models in and of themselves are not enough to establish causal relationships among variables. However, longitudinal data can be more useful than purely cross-sectional data in establishing causality. To illustrate, consider the three ingredients necessary for establishing causality, taken from the sociology literature (see, e.g., Taris, 2000):

- A statistically significant relationship is required.
- The association between two variables must not be due to another, omitted, variable.
- The "causal" variable must precede the other variable in time.

Longitudinal data are based on measurements taken over time and thus address the third requirement of a temporal ordering of events. Moreover, as described above, longitudinal data models provide additional strategies for accommodating omitted variables that are not available in purely cross-sectional data.

Observational data are not from carefully controlled experiments, where random allocations are made among groups. Causal inference is not directly accomplished when using observational data and only statistical models. Rather, one thinks about the data and statistical models as providing relevant empirical evidence in a chain of reasoning about causal mechanisms. Although longitudinal data provide stronger evidence than purely cross-sectional data, most of the work in establishing causal statements should be based on the theory of the substantive field from which the data are derived.

Drawback: Attrition

Longitudinal data sampling design offers many benefits compared with purely cross-sectional or purely time-series designs. However, because the sampling structure is more complex, it can also fail in subtle ways. The most common failure to meet standard sampling design assumptions is through difficulties that result from *attrition*. In this context, attrition refers to a gradual erosion of responses by subjects. Because we follow the same subjects over time, nonresponse typically increases through time. To illustrate, consider the U.S. Panel Study of Income Dynamics (PSID). In the first year (1968), the nonresponse rate was 24%. However, by 1985, the nonresponse rate grew to about 50%.

Attrition can be a problem because it may result in a selection bias. Selection bias potentially occurs when a rule other than simple random (or stratified) sampling is used to select observational units. Examples of selection bias often concern endogenous decisions by agents to join a labor pool or participate in a social program. To illustrate, suppose that we are studying a solvency measure of a sample of insurance firms. If the firm becomes bankrupt or evolves into another type of financial distress, then we may not be able to examine financial statistics associated with the firm. Nonetheless, this is exactly the situation in which we would anticipate observing low values of the solvency measure. The response of interest is related to our opportunity to observe the subject, a type of selection bias.

Student Achievement Data

To develop intuition, we consider a data set regarding student academic achievement during elementary schools. These data were gathered to assess the relationship between student achievement and education initiatives. Moreover, they can also be used to address related interesting questions, such as how one can rank the performance of schools, or how one can forecast a child's future performance on achievement tests based on their early test scores.

Webb et al. (2002) investigated relationships between student achievement and Texas school district participation in the National Science Foundation Statewide Systemic Initiatives program between 1994 and 2000. They focused on the effects of systemic reform on performance on a state mathematics test. We consider here a subset of these data to model trajectories of students' mathematics achievement over time. This subset consists of a random sample of 20 elementary schools in Dallas, with 20 students randomly selected from each school. All available records for these 400 students during elementary school are included. In Dallas, Grades 3 through 6 correspond to elementary school.

Table 13.1 Variable Descriptions of Student Achievement Data

Variable	*Description*
Level-1 variables (replications over time)	
GRADE	Grade when assessment was made (3–6)
YEAR	Year of assessment (1994–2000)
TIME	Observed repeated occasions for each student
RETAINED	Retained in grade for a particular year (1 = yes, 0 = no)
SWITCH_SCHOOLS	Switched schools in a particular year (1 = yes, 0 = no)
DISADVANTAGED	Economically disadvantaged (1 = free/reduced lunch, 0 = no)
TLI_MATH	Texas Learning Index on mathematics—assessment measure
Level-2 variables (replications over child)	
CHILDID	Student identification number
MALE	Gender of students (1 = male, 0 = female)
ETHNICITY	Caucasian, African American, Hispanic, Other
COHORT	Elementary school graduating class of 1994 to 2004 (1 to 10)
Level-3 variables (replications over school)	
SCHOOLID	School identification number
USI	Urban System Initiative cohort (1993, 1994, 1995)
N_TEACHERS	Total number of teachers in the school

SOURCE: Adapted from Webb et al. (2002).

Table 13.1 describes variables in the data set. Although there exists a natural hierarchy at each time point (students are nested within schools), this hierarchy was not maintained completely over time. Several students switched schools (see variable SWITCH_SCHOOLS) and many students were not promoted (see variable RETAINED). To maintain the hierarchy of students within schools, a student was associated with a school at the time of selection. To maintain a hierarchy over time, a cohort variable was defined as 1, 2, 3, and 4 for those in Grades 6, 5, 4, and 3, respectively, in 1994, and a 5 for those in Grade 3 in 1995, and so on up to a 10 for those in Grade 3 in 2000. The response variable (y) is TLI_MATH. Level 2 and 3 variables contain child and school information, respectively, both of which are constant over time. Level 1 variables do vary over time.

Accounting for Heterogeneity

Basic Setup

We focus attention on assumptions that concern the observable variables, $\{x_{it,1},\ldots,x_{it,K},\, y_{it}\}$.

Assumptions of the Observables Representation of the Linear Regression Model

F1. $\mathrm{E}\, y_{it} = \alpha + \mathbf{x}_{it}'\boldsymbol{\beta}$.

F2. $\{x_{it,1},\ldots,x_{it,K}\}$ are nonstochastic variables.

F3. $\mathrm{Var}\, y_{it} = \sigma^2$.

F4. $\{y_{it}\}$ are independent random variables.

The "observables representation" is based on the idea of conditional linear expectations (see Goldberger, 1991, for additional background). One can motivate assumption F1 by thinking of $(x_{it,1},\ldots,x_{it,K}, y_{it})$ as a draw from a population, where the mean of the conditional distribution of y_{it} given $\mathbf{x}_{it} = (x_{it,1},\ldots,x_{it,K})'$ is linear in the explanatory variables. Inference about the distribution of y is conditional on the observed explanatory variables, so that we may treat $\{\mathbf{x}_{it}\}$ as nonstochastic variables. When considering types of sampling mechanisms for thinking of $(\mathbf{x}_{it},\, y_{it})$ as a draw from a population, it is convenient to think of a stratified random sampling scheme, where values of $\{\mathbf{x}_{it}\}$ are treated as the strata. That is, for each value of $\{\mathbf{x}_{it}\}$, we draw a random sample of responses from a population. This sampling scheme also provides motivation for assumption F4, the independence among responses. To illustrate, when drawing from a database of firms to understand stock return performance (y), one can choose large firms, measured by asset size, and focus on an industry, measured by standard industrial classification, and so forth. You may not select firms with the largest stock return performance because this is stratifying based on the response, not the explanatory variables.

A fifth assumption that is often implicitly required in the linear regression model is

F5. $\{y_{it}\}$ is normally distributed.

This assumption is not required for all statistical inference procedures because central limit theorems provide approximate normality for many statistics of interest. However, formal justification for some, such as t statistics, do require this additional assumption.

We call the representation in assumption F1 cross-sectional because, although it relates the explanatory variables to the response, it does not use the information in the repeated measurements on a subject. Because it also does not include (subject specific) heterogeneous terms, we also refer to the assumption F1 representation as part of a *homogeneous* model.

Fixed Effects Models

Our first representation that uses the information in the repeated measurements on a subject is

$$\mathrm{E}y_{it} = \alpha_i + \mathbf{x}'_{it}\beta. \qquad (13.2)$$

Equation (13.2) and assumptions F2 to F4 comprise the *basic fixed effects model.* Unlike assumption F1, in (13.2) the intercept terms, α_i, are allowed to vary by subject.

Parameters of Interest

The parameters $\{\beta_j\}$ common to each subject are called *population* parameters. The parameters $\{\alpha_i\}$ vary by subject and are known as *subject-specific* parameters. In many applications, population parameters capture broad relationships of interest and hence are the parameters of interest. The subject-specific parameters account for the different features of subjects, not broad population patterns. Hence, they are often of secondary interest and are called *nuisance* parameters.

The subject-specific parameters represent our first device that helps control for the heterogeneity among subjects. Estimators of these parameters use information in the repeated measurements on a subject. Conversely, recall that the parameters $\{\alpha_i\}$ are nonestimable in cross-sectional regression models without repeated observations (with $T_i = 1$). An important advantage of longitudinal data models when compared with cross-sectional regression models is the ability to separate the effects of $\{\alpha_i\}$ from the disturbance terms $\{\varepsilon_{it}\}$. By separating out subject-specific effects, our estimates of the variability become more precise and we achieve more accurate inferences.

Subject and Time Heterogeneity

We will argue that the subject-specific parameter, α_i, captures much of the time-constant information in the responses. However, the basic fixed effects model assumes that $\{y_{it}\}$ are independent terms and, in particular, that there is

- no serial correlation (correlation over time) and
- no contemporaneous correlation (correlation across subjects).

Thus, no special relationships between subjects and time periods are assumed. By interchanging the roles of "i" and "t," we may consider the regression function

$$\mathrm{E}y_{it} = \lambda_t + \mathbf{x}'_{it}\beta. \qquad (13.3)$$

Here, the parameter λ_t is a time-specific variable that does not depend on subjects.

For typical longitudinal data applications, the number of subjects, n, substantially exceeds the maximal number of time periods, T. Furthermore, generally the heterogeneity among subjects explains a greater proportion of variability than the heterogeneity among time periods. Thus, we begin with the "basic" function $\mathrm{E}y_{it} = \alpha_i + \mathbf{x}'_{it}\beta$. This model allows explicit parameterization of the subject-specific heterogeneity.

Both functions in (13.2) and (13.3) are based on traditional one-way analysis of covariance models. For this reason, the basic fixed effects model is also called the *one-way fixed effects model.* By using binary (dummy) variables for the time dimension, we can incorporate time-specific parameters into the population parameters. In this way, it is straightforward to consider the function

$$\mathrm{E}\, y_{it} = \alpha_i + \lambda_t + \mathbf{x}_{it}'\beta. \qquad (13.4)$$

Equation (13.4) with assumptions F2 to F4 is known as the *two-way fixed effects model.*

Random Effects Models

Basic Model and Assumptions

The *error components model* equation is

$$y_{it} = \alpha_i + \mathbf{x}_{it}'\beta + \varepsilon_{it}. \qquad (13.5)$$

The notation in (13.5) is the same as an error representation of the basic fixed effects model in (13.1). However, now the term α_i is assumed to be a random variable not a fixed, unknown parameter. The term α_i is known as a *random effect. Mixed effects models* are ones that include random as well as fixed effects. Because (13.5) includes random effects (α_i) and fixed effects (β), the error components model is a special type of mixed effects model.

To complete the specification of the error components model, we assume that $\{\alpha_i\}$ are identically and independently distributed with mean zero and variance σ_α^2. Furthermore, we assume that $\{\alpha_i\}$ are independent of the error random variables, $\{\varepsilon_{it}\}$. For completeness, we still assume that $\mathbf{x}_{it}$ is a vector of covariates or explanatory variables and that β is a vector of fixed, yet unknown, population parameters. Note that because E $\alpha_i = 0$, it is customary to include a constant within the vector $\mathbf{x}_{it}$. This was not true of the fixed effects models, where we did not center the subject-specific terms about 0.

Linear combinations of the form $\mathbf{x}_{it}'\beta$ quantify the effect of known variables that may affect the response. Additional variables that are either unimportant or unobservable comprise the "error term." In the error components model, we may think of a regression model $y_{it} = \mathbf{x}_{it}'\beta + \eta_{it}$, where the error term η_{it} is decomposed into two components so that $\eta_{it} = \alpha_i + \varepsilon_{it}$. The term α_i represents the time-constant portion, whereas ε_{it} represents the remaining portion. To identify the model parameters, we assume that the two terms are independent. In the biological sciences, the error components model is known as the *random intercepts* model; this descriptor is used because the intercept α_i is a random variable. We will use the descriptors "error components" and "random intercepts" interchangeably although, for simplicity, we often use only the former term.

Sampling and Model Assumptions

The basic fixed effects and error components models are similar in appearance yet can lead to different substantive conclusions in the context of a specific application. The choice between these two models is dictated primarily by the method in which the sample is drawn. On the one hand, selecting subjects based on a two-stage sample implies use of the random effects model. On the other hand, selecting subjects based on exogenous characteristics suggests a stratified sample and thus using a fixed effects model.

The sampling basis allows us to restate the error components model as follows.

Error Components Model Assumptions

R1. $\mathrm{E}\,(y_{it}|\alpha_i) = \alpha_i + \mathbf{x}_{it}'\beta$.

R2. $\{x_{it,1}, \ldots, x_{it,K}\}$ are nonstochastic variables.

R3. Var $(y_{it}|\alpha_i) = \sigma^2$.

R4. $\{y_{it}\}$ are independent random variables, conditional on $\{\alpha_1, \ldots, \alpha_n\}$.

R5. y_{it} is normally distributed, conditional on $\{\alpha_1, \ldots, \alpha_n\}$.

R6. E $\alpha_i = 0$, Var $\alpha_i = \sigma_\alpha^2$, and $\{\alpha_1, \ldots, \alpha_n\}$ are mutually independent.

R7. $\{\alpha_i\}$ is normally distributed.

Assumptions R1 to R5 are similar to the fixed effects models assumptions F1 to F5; the main difference is that we now condition on random subject-specific terms, $\{\alpha_1, \ldots, \alpha_n\}$. Assumptions R6 and R7 summarize the sampling basis of the subject-specific terms. Taken together, these assumptions comprise our error components model.

However, assumptions R1 to R7 do not provide an "observables" representation of the model because they are based on unobservable quantities, $\{\alpha_1, \ldots, \alpha_n\}$. We summarize the effects of assumptions R1 to R7 on the observable variables, $\{\mathbf{x}_{it}, y_{it}\}$.

Observables Representation of the Error Components Model

RO1. $\mathrm{E}\, y_{it} = \mathbf{x}'_{it}\boldsymbol{\beta}$.

RO2. $\{x_{it,1}, \ldots, x_{it,K}\}$ are nonstochastic variables.

RO3. $\mathrm{Var}\, y_{it} = \sigma^2 + \sigma^2_\alpha$ and $\mathrm{Cov}(y_{ir}, y_{is}) = \sigma^2_\alpha$, for $r \neq s$.

RO4. $\{\mathbf{y}_i\}$ are independent random vectors.

RO5. $\{\mathbf{y}_i\}$ is normally distributed.

To reiterate, the properties RO1 to RO5 are a consequence of R1 to R7. As we progress through more complex situations, the strategy will consist of using sampling bases to suggest basic assumptions, such as R1 to R7, and then convert them into testable properties such as RO1 to RO5. Inference about the testable properties then provides information about the more basic assumptions. When considering nonlinear models, this conversion is not as direct. In some instances, we will focus on the observable representation directly and refer to it as a *marginal* model. The marginal version emphasizes the assumption that observations are correlated within subjects (assumption RO3), not the random effects mechanism for inducing the correlation.

For more complex situations, it is useful to describe these assumptions in matrix notation. Assumption R1 can be expressed more compactly as $\mathrm{E}(\mathbf{y}_i|\alpha_i) = \alpha_i\mathbf{1}_i + \mathbf{X}_i\beta$ and thus,

$$\mathrm{E}\,\mathbf{y}_i = \mathbf{X}_i\beta. \tag{13.6}$$

Here, $\mathbf{1}_i$ is a $T_i \times 1$ vector of ones, and $\mathbf{X}_i$ is a $T_i \times K$ matrix of explanatory variables, $\mathbf{X}_i = \left(\mathbf{x}_{i1} \;\cdots\; \mathbf{x}_{iT_i}\right)'$. Equation (13.6) is a restatement of assumption RO1. Alternatively, (13.6) is due to the law of iterated expectations and assumptions R1 and R6, because $\mathrm{E}\,\mathbf{y}_i = \mathrm{E}(\mathrm{E}(\mathbf{y}_i|\alpha_i)) = \mathrm{E}(\alpha_i\mathbf{1}_i + \mathbf{X}_i\beta) = \mathbf{X}_i\beta$. For Assumption RO3, we have

$$\mathrm{Var}\,\mathbf{y}_i = \mathbf{V}_i = \sigma^2_\alpha\mathbf{J}_i + \sigma^2\mathbf{I}_i.$$

Here, $\mathbf{J}_i$ is a matrix of ones and $\mathbf{I}_i$ is an identity matrix, both of dimension $T_i \times T_i$.

Subject-Specific Slopes

In addition to letting intercepts vary by subject, it can be also useful to let one or more slopes vary by subject. Returning to the fixed effects model, we define the subject-specific slope parameters to be $\alpha_i = (\alpha_{i1}, \ldots, \alpha_{iq})'$ and the q explanatory variables are $\mathbf{z}_{it} = (z_{it1}, \ldots, z_{itq})'$; both column vectors are of dimension $q \times 1$. We will consider regression functions of the form

$$\mathrm{E}\, y_{it} = \mathbf{z}'_{it}\alpha_i + \mathbf{x}'_{it}\beta. \tag{13.7}$$

To provide a more compact representation using matrix notation, we define $\mathbf{Z}_i = (\mathbf{z}_{i1}, \ldots, \mathbf{z}_{iT_i})'$, a $T_i \times q$ matrix of explanatory variables. With this notation, a matrix form of (13.7) is

$$\mathrm{E}\,\mathbf{y}_i = \mathbf{Z}_i\alpha_i + \mathbf{X}_i\beta.$$

The responses between subjects are independent, yet we allow for temporal correlation and heteroskedasticity through the assumption that $\mathrm{Var}\,\mathbf{y}_i = \mathbf{R}_i$. Taken together, these assumptions comprise the fixed effects linear longitudinal data model.

Assumptions of the Fixed Effects Linear Longitudinal Data Model

F1. $\mathrm{E}\mathbf{y}_i = \mathbf{Z}_i\alpha_i + \mathbf{X}_i\beta$.

F2. $\{x_{it,1}, \ldots, x_{it,K}\}$ and $\{z_{it,1}, \ldots, z_{it,q}\}$ are nonstochastic variables.

F3. $\mathrm{Var}\,\mathbf{y}_i = \mathbf{R}_i$.

F4. $\{\mathbf{y}_i\}$ are independent random variables.

F5. $\{y_{it}\}$ are normally distributed.

Note that we use the same letters, F1 to F5, to denote the assumptions of the fixed linear longitudinal data model and the linear regression model. This is because the models differ only through their mean and variance functions.

In a similar fashion, one can easily extend the error components model by rewriting the conditional regression function as

$$\mathrm{E}(\mathbf{y}_i|\alpha_i) = \mathbf{Z}_i\alpha_i + \mathbf{X}_i\beta$$

and conditional variance as

$$\mathrm{Var}(\mathbf{y}_i|\alpha_i) = \mathbf{R}_i,$$

where (α_i) are iid, mean zero with $\mathrm{Var}\,\alpha_i = \mathbf{D}$.

Robust Standard Errors

We now consider the fixed effects model. It is common practice to ignore serial correlation and heteroskedasticity initially when estimating β so that one can assume $\mathbf{R}_i = \sigma^2 \mathbf{I}_i$. With this assumption, the least squares estimator of β is

$$\mathbf{b} = \left(\sum_{i=1}^{n} \mathbf{X}_i' \mathbf{Q}_i \mathbf{X}_i \right)^{-1} \sum_{i=1}^{n} \mathbf{X}_i' \mathbf{Q}_i \mathbf{y}_i,$$

where $\mathbf{Q}_i = \mathbf{I}_i - \mathbf{Z}_i \left(\mathbf{Z}_i' \mathbf{Z}_i \right)^{-1} \mathbf{Z}_i'$. This is an unbiased and asymptotically normal estimator of β. Basic calculations show that it has variance

$$\operatorname{Var} \mathbf{b} = \left(\sum_{i=1}^{n} \mathbf{X}_i' \mathbf{Q}_i \mathbf{X}_i \right)^{-1} \left[\sum_{i=1}^{n} \mathbf{X}_i' \mathbf{Q}_i \mathbf{R}_i \mathbf{Q}_i \mathbf{X}_i \right] \left(\sum_{i=1}^{n} \mathbf{X}_i' \mathbf{Q}_i \mathbf{X}_i \right)^{-1}.$$

To get an estimate of $\operatorname{Var} \mathbf{b}$ that is robust to unsuspected serial correlation and heteroskedasticity, Huber (1967), White (1980), and Liang and Zeger (1986) suggested replacing $\mathbf{R}_i$ by $\mathbf{e}_i \mathbf{e}_i'$, where $\mathbf{e}_i$ is the vector of residuals. Thus, a robust standard error of b_j is

$$se(b_j) = \sqrt{j\text{th diagonal element of} \left(\Sigma_{i=1}^{n} \mathbf{X}_i' \mathbf{Q}_i \mathbf{X}_i \right)^{-1}} \times \sqrt{\left[\Sigma_{i=1}^{n} \mathbf{X}_i' \mathbf{Q}_i \mathbf{e}_i \mathbf{e}_i' \mathbf{Q}_i \mathbf{X}_i \right] \left(\Sigma_{i=1}^{n} \mathbf{X}_i' \mathbf{Q}_i \mathbf{X}_i \right)^{-1}}. \quad (13.8)$$

This is also known as a *cluster-based* standard error.

In contrast, consider a pooled cross-sectional regression model so that $\mathbf{Q}_i = \mathbf{I}_i$ and assume no serial correlation. Then, the ordinary least squares estimator of β has variance

$$\operatorname{Var} \mathbf{b} = \left(\sum_{i=1}^{n} \mathbf{X}_i' \mathbf{X}_i \right)^{-1} \left[\sum_{i=1}^{n} \mathbf{X}_i' \mathbf{R}_i \mathbf{X}_i \right] \left(\sum_{i=1}^{n} \mathbf{X}_i' \mathbf{X}_i \right)^{-1},$$

where $\mathbf{R}_i = \sigma_i^2 \mathbf{I}_i$ for heteroskedasticity. Further, using the estimator $s_i^2 = \mathbf{e}_i' \mathbf{e}_i / T_i$ for σ_i^2 yields White's robust standard errors. By way of comparison, the robust standard error in (13.8) accommodates heterogeneity (through the $\mathbf{Q}_i$ matrix) and also accounts for unsuspected serial correlation by using the $T_i \times T_i$ matrix $\mathbf{e}_i \mathbf{e}_i'$ in lieu of the scalar estimate $s_i^2 = \mathbf{e}_i' \mathbf{e}_i / T_i$.

Example

Table 13.2 displays the mean Texas Learning Index on mathematics (TLI_MATH) score for different levels of explanatory variables. This table suggests that student scores increase over time (with GRADE) and that lower scores are obtained for those RETAINED.

Table 13.3 summarizes the corresponding random effects and fixed effects solutions for the error components models in (13.5). Here, for both fixed and random effect estimators, we see statistically significant effects for both GRADE and RETAINED. Both estimators also show that the variable DISADVANTAGED is not statistically significant. Moreover, both fits show a strong serial correlation effect (even after including the linear effect of GRADE); the autoregressive of order one (AR1) correlation parameter ρ is about 0.30 and is statistically significant. Table 13.3 also reminds us that variables such as ETHNICITY and gender (MALE) do not vary over time and hence are inestimable with the fixed effects estimators. This can be a critical point; for example, it may be that the purpose of the data modeling is to investigate the effects of gender or ethnicity on mathematics achievement. A model that is silent on this issue would be of little interest to analysts wishing to investigate these effects.

Because the subjects (children) were selected via a probability sampling scheme, one would typically use random effects estimators for these data. For these data, there is little difference in estimates of the time-varying variable coefficients. The following section describes tactics and potential explanations when there are strong differences in these two types of estimators.

Correlated Effects

In regression modeling, it is customary to assume that explanatory variables in a model are uncorrelated with the error term. As in single-level regression, in panel data models the consistency of standard estimation methods depends on the assumption that the predictors are uncorrelated with any random component. The implicit assumption is that all predictors are uncorrelated with all random components.

Table 13.2 Summary Statistics of TLI_MATH by Level of Explanatory Variables

Variable	*Time-Varying Variables*			*Variable*	*Time-Constant Variables*		
	Level	*Number*	*Mean*		*Level*	*Number*	*Mean*
GRADE	3	218	66.38	ETHNICITY	African American	565	69.52
	4	271	72.33		Hispanic	32	74.29
	5	260	72.80		Other	19	75.68
	6	263	75.81		Caucasian	105	78.35
YEAR	1994	122	66.49	GENDER	Male	483	71.34
	1995	145	66.04		Female	529	72.74
	1996	126	70.75	USI	1993	110	70.74
	1997	147	73.52		1994	388	73.72
	1998	167	73.05		1995	514	71.11
	1999	163	76.01				
	2000	142	77.03				
RETAINED	Yes	14	64.71				
	No	998	72.18				
SWITCH	Yes	101	70.25				
SCHOOLS	No	911	72.27				
DISADVANTAGED	Yes	696	71.40				
	No	181	72.27				
	Missing	135	75.27				

To illustrate the consequences of the correlated effects, consider

$$\mathbf{y}_i = \mathbf{1}_i\alpha_i + \mathbf{X}_i\beta + \varepsilon_i,$$

where $\mathbf{1}_i$ is a vector of ones. Suppose that the joint distribution of α_i and $\mathbf{X}_i$ can be defined by a multivariate normal distribution

$$\begin{pmatrix} \alpha_i \\ \mathbf{x}_i \end{pmatrix} \sim N\left(\begin{bmatrix} 0 \\ \mu_{\mathbf{X}} \end{bmatrix}, \begin{bmatrix} \sigma_\alpha^2 & \Sigma_{\alpha\mathbf{X}} \\ \Sigma_{\mathbf{X}\alpha} & \Sigma_{\mathbf{XX}} \end{bmatrix}\right),$$

where $\mathbf{x}_i$ is the column vector associated with $\mathbf{X}_i$. Then, standard calculations show that expected value of the outcome variable $\mathbf{y}_i$ given the set of predictors is

$$\mathrm{E}(\mathbf{y}_i|\mathbf{x}_i) = \mathbf{X}_i\beta + \mathbf{1}_i\mathrm{E}(\alpha_i|\mathbf{x}_i),$$

where $\mathrm{E}(\alpha_i|\mathbf{x}_i) = \Sigma_{\alpha\mathbf{X}}\Sigma_{\mathbf{XX}}^{-1}(\mathbf{x}_i - \mu_{\mathbf{X}})$. Thus, $\mathrm{E}(\alpha_i|\mathbf{x}_i)$ is nonzero unless $\mathrm{Cov}(\alpha_i, \mathbf{x}_i) = \Sigma_{\alpha\mathbf{X}} = \mathbf{0}$. Therefore, $\mathrm{E}(\mathbf{y}_i|\mathbf{x}_i) \neq \mathbf{X}_i\beta$ so that the usual estimators provide biased estimates of β if α_i and $\mathbf{X}_i$ are correlated.

There are three common sources of correlated effects: First, some unobserved effects can induce *omitted variable bias*. Second, predictors might be measured imprecisely and result in *measurement error* or *error-in-variables bias*. Third, some predictors may not only cause but also be influenced by the outcome variable, yielding *simultaneity bias*. If any variable in a model suffers from one of these problems, all regression coefficients and variance component estimates in the model may be biased (Frees, 2004; Hayashi, 2000; Wooldridge, 2002).

Omitted Variables

To illustrate the problem of omitted variables mathematically, consider a generic "true" model

$$\mathbf{y} = X\beta + \mathbf{U}\gamma + \varepsilon, \tag{13.9}$$

where $\mathbf{y}$ is the outcome variable, $\mathbf{X}$ are observed and $\mathbf{U}$ are unobserved predictors that affect the outcome, and ε is an error term. Since the $\mathbf{U}$ are unobserved—hence omitted in the analysis—the "fitted" model is $\mathbf{y} = \mathbf{X}\beta + \eta$, where $\eta = \mathbf{U}\gamma + \varepsilon$. The expected value of the least squares estimates for the regression coefficients associated with $\mathbf{X}$ can be shown to be $\beta + (\mathbf{X}'\mathbf{X})^{-1}\mathbf{X}'\mathbf{U}\gamma$. Unless either $\mathbf{X}'\mathbf{U} = \mathbf{0}$ or $\gamma = \mathbf{0}$, the least squares estimator of β is biased and inconsistent.

Table 13.3 Random Effects Model and Fixed Effects Model Solutions

	Random Effects Model		*Fixed Effects Model*	
	Estimate	*t-Statistic*	*Estimate*	*t-Statistic*
Time-Varying Variables				
GRADE	3.82	13.40	3.64	12.71
SWITCH_SCHOOLS	−0.11	−0.12	0.52	0.49
RETAINED	9.30	2.81	11.04	3.32
DISADVANTAGED				
Yes	−0.40	−0.34	−0.07	−0.06
Missing	0.20	0.17	−0.17	−0.13
No				
Time-Constant Variables				
MALE	−2.23	−1.60		
ETHNICITY				
African American	−10.13	−4.71		
Hispanic	−7.23	−3.12		
Other	−6.69	−1.27		
Caucasian				
COHORT	1.85	5.76		
USI				
1993	0.86	0.35		
1994	2.53	1.66		
1995				
N_TEACHERS	−0.03	−0.39		

	Estimate	*Standard Error*	*Estimate*	*Standard Error*
Variance Components				
AR(1) parameter (ρ)	0.30	0.09	0.29	0.09
Var ε_{it}	75.48	8.67	75.09	8.61
Var α_i	150.93	9.51		
Model Fit Indices				
−2 log(likelihood)	7759.0		4537.0	
AIC	7793.0		5353.0	
BIC	7810.1		5763.1	

Thus, the omission of relevant predictor variables causes bias because it induces a correlation between the disturbance term and the explanatory variables. There are many ways in which omitted variables may enter a problem that are far more complex than the simple linear mechanism described in (13.9). To employ procedures that provide some protection against omitted variable bias, analysts must have a sense of the source of potentially important omitted variables.

A panel data model that includes omitted variables can be written as

$$y_{it} = \alpha_i + \mathbf{x}_{it}'\beta + u_i + \varepsilon_{it}. \qquad (13.10)$$

Equation (13.10) includes the latent intercept variable α_i that is constant over time. This latent variable induces a correlation among individual responses over time and serves as a proxy for unobserved time-constant characteristics, such as "ability," that are uncorrelated with the explanatory variables. Without the omitted variable u_i, the model in (13.10) is a random intercepts model.

Unlike α_i, u_i may be correlated with one or more of the explanatory variables in $\mathbf{x}_{it}$. Thus, this variable may create a bias in the usual least squares estimates of β. To mitigate the effects of u_i, one can apply a fixed effects transformation such as $\mathbf{Q}_i$ introduced in the section Robust Standard Errors, "sweeping out" the time-constant omitted effects. Here, the phrase *sweeping out* refers to the fact that $\mathbf{Q}_i$ is orthogonal to time-constant variables. Recall that **b** is our symbol for the fixed effects estimator; this estimator has desirable properties even in the presence of time-constant omitted variables.

To determine the importance of omitted variables, we again consider the model in (13.10) but now assume that there are no omitted variables so that $u_i = 0$. We retain, however, the random effects α_i. Then, estimating β via the usual generalized least squares (GLS) routines, we denote the resulting estimator as $\mathbf{b}_{REE}$. The test statistic

$$\chi_H^2 = (\mathbf{b} - \mathbf{b}_{REE})' \left(\mathrm{Var}\left(\mathbf{b} - \mathbf{b}_{REE}\right)\right)^{-1} (\mathbf{b} - \mathbf{b}_{REE})$$

measures the distance between vectors **b** and $\mathbf{b}_{REE}$. Hausman (1978) showed that χ_H^2 has a chi-square distribution under the null hypothesis of no omitted variables with degrees of freedom equal to the number of parameters in β.

This simple setting underscores the major strengths and limitations of this approach to testing for omitted variables. One important strength is that there are relatively few assumptions needed; these procedures are robust to different types of omitted variables and are easy to understand and interpret by analysts. The robust procedures are essentially determined by "sweeping out" unobserved variables and then using standard inference procedures. In contrast, an alternative procedure, instrumental variable estimation (the section Exogeneity, Endogeneity, and Instruments), requires the analyst to identify a proxy for the omitted variable. Similarly, simultaneous equations modeling requires specifying a model for the latent, unobserved, omitted variables. Although these alternatives are certainly appropriate in many circumstances, they do require additional (and sometimes unavailable) knowledge by the analyst.

Exogeneity, Endogeneity, and Instruments

Collecting the random effects terms on the right-hand side, we may write the linear model

$$\mathbf{y} = \mathbf{X}\beta + \boldsymbol{\delta},$$

where $\boldsymbol{\delta}$ is a mean zero random variable. Following standard econometrics literature, a set of variables that comprise the columns of the matrix **H** is said to be predetermined if $\mathrm{E}\,(\mathbf{H}\boldsymbol{\delta}) = \mathbf{0}$, that is, they are uncorrelated with $\boldsymbol{\delta}$. Because of our focus on linear models, we primarily use $\mathrm{E}\,(\mathbf{H}\boldsymbol{\delta}) = \mathbf{0}$ as our condition for *exogeneity*; a variable that does not satisfy this condition is said to be *endogenous*. We also find it useful to examine the more restrictive assumption $\mathrm{E}\,(\delta|H) = \mathbf{0}$. Exogenous variables in **H** that are useful for estimating β are said to be *instruments*. In most applications, there is a large overlap between model-based variables **X** and instrumental variables **H**.

In a linear model context, an instrumental variable (IV) estimator is

$$\mathbf{b}_{IV} = \left(\mathbf{XW'PWX}\right)^{-1}\mathbf{XW'PWy},$$

where $\mathbf{P} = P(\mathbf{H}) = \mathbf{H}(\mathbf{H'H})^{-1}\mathbf{H'}$ is the projection onto the linear space spanned by the columns of

H. The matrix **W** is assumed to be known and is for weighted regression. Recall that in a classic regression problem (where $\mathbf{W} = \mathbf{I}$) one decomposes model variables **X** as $(\mathbf{X}_1, \mathbf{X}_2)$, where $\mathbf{X}_1$ represents exogenous variables and $\mathbf{X}_2$ represents endogenous variables. The instruments **H** are decomposed as $(\mathbf{H}_1, \mathbf{H}_2)$, where $\mathbf{H}_1 = \mathbf{X}_1$ represents exogenous model variables included as instruments and $\mathbf{H}_2$ represents nonmodel variables. For consistent estimation, one requires that the number of instruments not from the model ($rank(\mathbf{H}_2)$) be at least as large as the number of endogenous model variables ($rank(\mathbf{X}_2)$). Thus, IV estimators readily accommodate the presence of endogenous model-based variables. Moreover, because both the responses and model-based variables are projected onto the space of instruments (**Py** and **PX**, respectively), they could be computed in "two stages," which is helpful in interpreting results.

Correlated Effects Models

The drawback of classical IV estimation is the need for the analyst to develop the appropriate instruments. The Hausman and Taylor (1981) method mitigates this drawback for special types of endogeneities. Hausman and Taylor showed how one could use the hierarchical structure of a panel data set to create additional instruments that one could use in the estimation. Another widely cited model is due to Arellano and Bond (1991). Endogeneity and correlated effects have been extensively studied in the context of two-level panel data models (e.g., Arellano, 1993, 2003; Arellano & Bover, 1995; Breusch, Mizon, & Schmidt, 1989). We refer to Baltagi (2001, chap. 8) for further discussion.

A Large Number of Replicates

The difference between fixed effects estimator (**b**) in the section Fixed Effects Models and random effects estimator ($\mathbf{b}_{REE}$) in the section Random Effects Models may be due to omitted variables that can be detected using the Hausman test. Under what types of designs are we likely to observe important differences? In the panel data context, Maddala (1971) observed that one could express

$$\mathbf{b}_{REE} = (I - \Delta)\mathbf{b} + \Delta\mathbf{b}_B,$$

where $\mathbf{b}_B$ is the between-groups estimator and Δ is a measure of the relative precision of the estimators. In a balanced design ($T_i = T$), one computes the between-groups estimator as

$$\mathbf{b}_B = \left(\sum_{i=1}^{n}(\bar{\mathbf{x}}_i - \bar{\mathbf{x}})(\bar{\mathbf{x}}_i - \bar{\mathbf{x}})'\right)^{-1} \left(\sum_{i=1}^{n}(\bar{\mathbf{x}}_i - \bar{\mathbf{x}})(\bar{\mathbf{y}}_i - \bar{\mathbf{y}})'\right).$$

Note that an omitted variable u_i does not induce a bias in **b** but will affect $\mathbf{b}_B$. Furthermore, as the number of replicates (T) or the variability at the time level increases, the difference between $\mathbf{b}_{REE}$ and **b** becomes less prominent. Conversely, for a given impact of an omitted variable at the individual level, one can anticipate more prominent differences between $\mathbf{b}_{REE}$ and **b**, when the number of replicates per individual is small or the variability at the individual level is small (see, e.g., Blundell & Windmeijer, 1997). This pattern also holds in a higher-order multilevel/hierarchical designs, the subject of the next section.

With many observations per subject, analysts have several options for introducing more complex dynamic model features that address questions of interest or that represent important tendencies of the data (or both). One option is based on the serial correlation structure; another dynamic option is to allow parameters to vary over time. Moreover, for a data set with a long time dimension relative to the number of subjects, we have an opportunity to model the cross-sectional correlation, an important issue in many studies. Alternatively, the Kalman filter approach allows the analyst to incorporate many of these features simultaneously (see Frees, 2004, chap. 8). Finally, one can consider lagged dependent variables as explanatory variables, another way of introducing dynamic features into the model.

Multilevel Models

This section describes a modeling framework that takes into account clustered data structures. Such structures, known as *m*ultilevel or *h*ierarchical structures, are common in the educational, social, and behavioral sciences. Multilevel models are specified through conditional relationships, where the relationships described at one level are expressed conditional on the (generally unobserved) random coefficients of higher levels. Longitudinal data can also be viewed as possessing a multilevel structure, where measurement occasions are "Level-1" units of observation and individuals are "Level-2" units. In such settings, we can also imagine additional higher-level data being collected through a cluster sampling scheme involving, say, classes, schools, or districts.

Multilevel models may be written as linear mixed effects models with the advantage that properties of the parameter estimates are known from a broad statistics literature in this area (see, e.g., McCulloch & Searle, 2001; Pinheiro & Bates, 2000, among others). On the other hand, the hierarchical framework of multilevel models allows analysts to develop and test hypotheses regarding relationships at each level of the nesting as well as across levels. As important examples of involving consideration of different hierarchical units, we present multilevel model prediction in the section Multilevel Model Prediction, omitted variable tests and generalized method of moments techniques in the section Omitted Variables Tests and Model Estimators.

Although multilevel models can be used for any clustered structure, this chapter considers multilevel models for time-ordered data. An important feature of the longitudinal multilevel model that distinguishes it from its cross-sectional counterpart is that some measure of time generally enters the Level-1 model. There are a number of ways that this can be specified. One way is to let one or more of the explanatory variables be defined as a function of time. This is the approach historically taken in growth curve modeling. Another approach is to let one of the explanatory variables serve as a lagged response variable. This approach is particularly prevalent in economics. Yet another approach is to model the serial correlation of the response variables through the variance-covariance matrix of the vector of disturbance terms, a widely adopted approach in biostatistics and educational research.

The natural development or aging of an individual or a process is often represented as a growth curve model. In growth curve modeling, one often uses a polynomial function of age or time to represent growth. Because growth curve data often reflect observations from a developmental process, it is intuitively appealing to think of the expected response as a function of time. In *l*atent growth curve models for multilevel data, individual variability in growth is accounted for through varying the coefficients that represent the growth process. For example, the variability of random coefficients associated with the intercepts and slopes of the time-related explanatory variables (e.g., time or time^2), referred to as *r*andom intercepts and *r*andom slopes, can be quantified and/or explained in understanding individual differences.

There are many introductions to multilevel modeling available in the literature. Widely cited references include Raudenbush and Bryk (2002), Goldstein (2003), and Snijders and Bosker (1999). For an introduction that employs a minimal amount of mathematics, see Kreft and de Leeuw (1998).

Given the increasingly important role that multilevel models play in analyzing hierarchical data structures, issues related to their estimation and interpretation have received much recent attention. Such issues are naturally involved owing to the complexity of the models. In this section, we provide an overview of several recent advances related to (a) the concept of multilevel predictors and development of best linear unbiased predictors (BLUPs) and (b) the development of omitted variable tests and robust estimators. Prior to discussing these issues, we provide a short illustration of a common multilevel model.

Three-Level Model Example

Although multilevel models may theoretically consist of many levels, two- and three-level models are the most commonly applied designs in the social sciences. We focus on a three-level "time-child-school" model in the context of the section Student Achievement Data example. For models with additional levels, Frees and Kim (2006) provide a recursive notation system that allows for multilevel modeling with an arbitrary number of levels. Consider three levels of nesting, where the subscript s identifies a school, the subscript

c identifies a child within school s, and the subscript t denotes the time that a child has taken an achievement test. The Level-1 model is

$$y_{s,c,t} = \mathbf{Z}^{(1)}_{s,c,t}\beta^{(1)}_{s,c} + \mathbf{X}^{(1)}_{s,c,t}\beta_1 + \varepsilon^{(1)}_{s,c,t}. \quad (13.11)$$

In this expression, the variable $y_{s,c,t}$ denotes the response variable (achievement test score) and there are $s = 1,\ldots,S$ schools, $j = 1,\ldots,S_c$ children within schools, and $t = 1,\ldots,T_{s,c}$ test scores for child c in school s. The explanatory variables $\mathbf{Z}^{(1)}_{s,c,t}$ and $\mathbf{X}^{(1)}_{s,c,t}$ represent characteristics that depend on time, child, or school. The parameters that may depend on either school s or child c appear as part of the $\beta^{(1)}_{s,c}$ vector, whereas parameters that are constant appear in the β_1 vector. Conditional on child and school, the disturbance term $\varepsilon^{(1)}_{s,c,t}$ has a mean of zero.

The Level-2 model describes variability at the child level. It is of the form

$$\beta^{(1)}_{s,c} = \mathbf{Z}^{(2)}_{s,c}\beta^{(2)}_{s} + \mathbf{X}^{(2)}_{s,c}\beta_2 + \varepsilon^{(2)}_{s,c}.$$

Analogous to (13.11), the explanatory variables $\mathbf{Z}^{(2)}_{s,c}$ and $\mathbf{X}^{(2)}_{s,c}$ may depend on the child or school but not on time. The parameters associated with $\mathbf{Z}^{(2)}_{s,c}$, $\beta^{(2)}_{s}$, may depend on school s, whereas the parameters associated with $\mathbf{X}^{(2)}_{s,c}$, β_2, are constant. The random component $\varepsilon^{(2)}_{s,c}$ has a mean of zero. The Level-1 parameter $\beta^{(1)}_{s,c}$ may vary nonstochastically or stochastically. Within this notation, we use a zero variance to model parameters that are varying but nonstochastic.

The Level-3 model describes variability at the school level. Analogous to the Level-2 model, the Level-2 parameter $\beta^{(2)}_{s}$ may vary nonstochastically or stochastically. The Level-3 model is of the form

$$\beta^{(2)}_{s} = \mathbf{X}^{(3)}_{s}\beta_3 + \varepsilon^{(3)}_{s}.$$

The variables $\mathbf{X}^{(3)}_{s}$ may depend on the school, while the random component $\varepsilon^{(3)}_{s}$ has a mean of zero.

For example, it is natural to consider the child-specific intercept and school-specific intercept as random quantities. The parameters associated with the other variables are treated as fixed in this example, making the model a three-level random intercept model. For illustration purposes, suppose the variables in our model are

$y_{s,c,t}$ = Texas Learning Index on Mathematics (TLI_MATH),

$\mathbf{X}^{(1)}_{s,c,t}$ = GRADE, RETAINED, SWITCHING_SCHOOLS,

$\mathbf{X}^{(2)}_{s,c}$ = GENDER, ETHNICITY, COHORT, and

$\mathbf{X}^{(3)}_{s}$ = USI, N_TEACHERS.

See the section Student Achievement Data and Table 13.1 for further descriptions of these variables. For further discussion of this example, see Kim and Frees (2005).

Multilevel Model Prediction

The complex structures of multilevel models often rely explicitly on many unobserved random variables, so inference from multilevel models depends heavily on how one "summarizes" the random variables from available sample information. In model prediction, we wish to estimate an unobserved quantity that we model stochastically.

Best Linear Unbiased Predictors

We can consider predictors that are optimal in the sense that they are derived as minimum mean square (best) linear unbiased predictors. We refer to these predictors as *BLUPs*. Goldberger (1962) introduced these predictors in a mixed linear model setting. A general extension of the Gauss-Markov theorem was provided by Harville (1976); this extension covers the random effects of interest here. Harville also showed that Bayesian posterior mean predictors with a diffuse prior are equivalent to BLUPs, thus providing additional motivation for these predictors. Robinson (1991) provides an overview of the broad variety of fields in which BLUPs have been used. Afshartous and de Leeuw (2005) conducted a Monte Carlo study examining the problem of predicting a future observable in multilevel models.

Frees and Kim (2006) expanded this literature by distinguishing different types of random variables in multilevel models. They showed that the structure of multilevel models allows the development of special forms of predictors that can be of interest to applied researchers. Specifically, Frees and Kim distinguished three types of random variables in multilevel modeling—model disturbances, random coefficients, and forecasts of future responses—and provided explicit representations for predicting realizations of each of these random variables. They also derived the variances of predictors and forecasts. It is shown that BLUPs and their prediction intervals can be computed in closed forms and have desirable interpretations.

Multilevel Model Predictors

It is also possible to develop readily interpretable expressions for predictors of random variables in multilevel models. Formulas for computation of the variances of multilevel predictors of disturbance terms, random coefficients, and future outcomes are provided by Frees and Kim (2006). The predictors can be computed recursively, thus enhancing interpretability, as follows:

- Predictors of higher-level disturbance terms are based on Level-1 predictors of disturbance terms that, in turn, are based on GLS estimators of the disturbance terms.
- Predictors of random coefficients are based on predictors of disturbance terms and lower-level random coefficients, recursively.
- Forecasts of future outcomes are based on predictors of random coefficients and disturbance terms.

For the formulas in the three types of BLUPs as well as extensions to an arbitrary number of levels, see Frees and Kim (2006) and Kim and Frees (in press).

Omitted Variables Tests and Robust Estimators

Multilevel models can be viewed as a special type of panel data model (and vice versa). Thus, the potential difficulties of correlated effects described in the section Correlated Effects for panel data models may also be present in multilevel models. To assist researchers with these problems, Kim and Frees (2006, in press) developed statistical methods that can test the severity of bias and further provide consistent regression coefficient estimators even in the presence of omitted and/or correlated effects in multilevel models. Specifically, Kim and Frees (2006) presented three types of omitted variable tests: single-, multiple-, and intermediate-level tests. The first and second tests compare a robust estimator with an estimator that is efficient assuming no omitted variables. The third test compares results from robust estimators at different levels. For more general cases and further details, readers should consult their original article.

Kim and Frees (2006, in press) provided another statistical technique that overcomes the limitations of fixed effects estimators and provides estimated effects of variables at all levels in the presence of omitted effects, or more generally, correlated effects. Their method can be viewed as a *generalized method of moments* (GMM) extension of instrumental variable (IV) estimators in multilevel modeling. Using a GMM framework, Kim and Frees extended IV estimators by (a) incorporating weights to accommodate the variance structure of a multilevel model and (b) specifying more general projections to take advantage of the hierarchical structure of multilevel models.

The GMM approach provides an overarching framework that unifies well-known estimators such as fixed effects estimators and random effects estimators and also provides more options. Kim and Frees (2006, in press) also showed that GMM estimators can be expressed as IV estimators, which further enhances the interpretability of the estimates. Moreover, unlike traditional IV methods, the GMM technique can obtain robust IV estimators without requiring additional variables by exploiting the hierarchical structure of the data.

NONLINEAR MODELS

Nonlinear models represent an area of recent development, where examples of their importance to statistical practice appear with greater frequency. The phrase "nonlinear models" in this context refers to instances where the distribution of the response cannot be reasonably approximated using a normal curve. Some examples of this occur when the response is binary or other types of count data, such as the number of accidents in a state, and when the response is from a very heavy-tailed distribution, such as with insurance claims.

Modeling Approaches

As described by Diggle, Heagarty, Liang, and Zeger (2002), there are three basic approaches to handling nonlinear modeling. The first is the conditioning approach, where one traces the development of a dependent variable over time and represents the distribution of its current value as a function of its history. To this end, define H_{it} to be the history of the ith subject up to time t. For example, if the explanatory variables are assumed to be nonstochastic, then we might use $H_{it} = \{y_{i1}, ..., y_{i,t-1}\}$. With this information set, we may partition the likelihood for the ith subject as

$$L(\mathbf{y}_i) = \mathrm{f}(y_{i1}) \prod_{t=2}^{T_i} \mathrm{f}(y_{it}|H_{it}),$$

where $\mathrm{f}(y_{it}|H_{it})$ is the conditional distribution of y_{it} given its history and $\mathrm{f}(y_{i1})$ is the marginal distribution of y_{i1}. This is the topic of the following section.

A second approach is the so-called marginal model. Here, one focuses on the parameters of the marginal distributions, typically related to the first and second moment. Rather than accounting for dependencies via a full probabilistic model, patterns over time are accounted for with approximate relationships, known as "working correlations." Marginal models are useful when the primary scientific interest is to analyze the influence of the covariates.

The third approach is a full probabilistic model of the multivariate distribution of $\mathbf{y}_i = (y_{i1}, \ldots, y_{iT_i})'$. Typically, dependencies over time are accounted for by a latent random effect that is common to all observations, hence the name "random effects" model. For an alternative approach that is useful for long-tailed data, see Frees and Wang (2005) who use a copula specification to account for heterogeneity.

Conditional Model With Categorical Responses

We now consider a response that is an unordered categorical variable that may take on values $1, \ldots, c$, corresponding to c categories. In many social science applications, the response categories correspond to an attribute possessed or choices made by individuals, households, or firms. Some applications of categorical dependent variable models include (a) employment choice, such as Valletta (1999); (b) mode of transportation choice, such as the classic work by McFadden (1978); (c) choice of political party affiliation, such as Brader and Tucker (2001); and (d) marketing brand choice, such as Jain, Vilcassim, and Chintagunta (1994).

To simplify our discussion, we also assume discrete unit time intervals and consider Markov models of order 1. Thus, the history H_{it} need only contain $y_{i,t-1}$. More formally, we assume that

$$\begin{aligned}\pi_{it,jk} &= \Pr(y_{it} = k|y_{i,t-1} = j) \\ &= \Pr(y_{it} = k|y_{i,t-1} = j, y_{i,t-2}, ..., y_{i,1}).\end{aligned}$$

That is, given the information in $y_{i,t-1}$, there is no additional information content in $y_{i,t-2}, \ldots, y_{i1}$ about the distribution of y_{it}.

Without covariate information, it is customary to organize the set of transition probabilities $\pi_{it,jk}$ as a matrix of the form

$$\mathbf{\Pi}_{it} = \begin{pmatrix} \pi_{it,11} & \pi_{it,12} & \cdots & \pi_{it,1c} \\ \pi_{it,21} & \pi_{it,22} & \cdots & \pi_{it,2c} \\ \vdots & \vdots & \ddots & \vdots \\ \pi_{it,c1} & \pi_{it,c2} & \cdots & \pi_{it,cc} \end{pmatrix}.$$

Here, each row sums to one. With covariate information and an initial state distribution $\Pr(y_{i1})$, one can trace the history of the process knowing only the transition matrix $\mathbf{\Pi}_{it}$. We call the row identifier, j, the state of origin and the column identifier, k, the destination state.

We can parameterize the problem by choosing a multinomial logit, one for each state of origin. Thus, we use

$$\pi_{it,jk} = \frac{\exp(\eta_{it,jk})}{\sum_{h=1}^{c} \exp(\eta_{it,jh})},$$

where the systematic component $\eta_{it,jk}$ is given by $\eta_{it,jk} = \mathbf{x}'_{it,jk}\beta_j$. With this parameterization, estimation may proceed using maximum likelihood. See Frees (2004) for further details.

Historical Notes

The term *panel study* was coined in a marketing context when Lazarsfeld and Fiske (1938) considered the effect of radio advertising on product sales. Traditionally, hearing radio advertisements was thought to increase the likelihood of purchasing a product. Lazarsfeld and Fiske considered whether those that bought the product would be more likely to have heard the advertisement, thus positing a reverse in the direction of causality. They proposed repeatedly interviewing a set of people (the "panel") to clarify the issue.

Taris (2000) cites Engels's 1857 budget survey, examining how the amount of money spent on food changes as a function of income, as perhaps the earliest example of a study involving repeated measurements from the same set of subjects. Baltes and Nesselroade (1979) trace the history of longitudinal data and methods with an emphasis on childhood development and psychology. They describe longitudinal research as consisting of "a variety of methods connected by the idea that the entity under investigation is observed repeatedly as it exists and evolves over time." Moreover, they trace the need for longitudinal research to at least as early as the 19th century.

In early panel data studies, pooled cross-sectional data were analyzed by estimating cross-sectional parameters using regression and using time-series methods to model the regression parameter estimates, treating the estimates as known with certainty. Dielman (1989) discusses this approach in more detail and provides examples. Early applications in economics of the basic fixed effects model include Kuh (1959), Johnson (1960), Mundlak (1961), and Hoch (1962). Balestra and Nerlove (1966) and Wallace and Hussain (1969) introduced the (random effects) error components model, the model with $\{\alpha_i\}$ as random variables.

Wishart (1938), Rao (1965), and Potthoff and Roy (1964) were among the first contributions in the biometrics literature to use multivariate analysis for analyzing growth curves. Specifically, they considered the problem of fitting polynomial growth curves of serial measurements from a group of subjects. This approach to analyzing longitudinal data was extended by Grizzle and Allen (1969), who introduced covariates, or explanatory variables, into the analysis. Laird and Ware (1982) made the other important transition from multivariate analysis to regression modeling as discussed in this chapter. They introduce the two-stage model that allows for both fixed and random effects.

References

Afshartous, D., & de Leeuw, J. (2005). Prediction in multilevel models. *Journal of Educational and Behavioral Statistics, 30*, 109–139.

Arellano, M. (1993). On the testing of correlated effects with panel data. *Journal of Econometrics, 59*, 87–97.

Arellano, M. (2003). *Panel data econometrics*. Oxford, UK: Oxford University Press.

Arellano, M., & Bond, S. (1991). Some tests of specification for panel data: Monte Carlo evidence and an application to employment equations. *Review of Economic Studies, 58*, 277–297.

Arellano, M., & Bover, O. (1995). Another look at the instrumental-variable estimation of error components models. *Journal of Econometrics, 68*, 29–51.

Balestra, P., & Nerlove, M. (1966). Pooling cross-section and time-series data in the estimation of a dynamic model: The demand for natural gas. *Econometrica, 34*, 585–612.

Baltagi, B. H. (2001). *Econometric analysis of panel data* (2nd ed.). New York: Wiley.

Baltes, P. B., & Nesselroade, J. R. (1979). History and rational of longitudinal research. In P. B. Baltes & J. R. Nesselroade (Eds.), *Longitudinal research in the study of behavior and development.* New York: Academic Press.

Blundell, R., & Windmeijer, F. (1997). Cluster effects and simultaneity in multilevel models. *Health Economics, 6*, 439–443.

Brader, T., & Tucker, J. A. (2001). The emergence of mass partisanship in Russia, 1993–1996. *American Journal of Political Science, 45*, 69-83.

Breusch, T. S., Mizon, G. E., & Schmidt, P. (1989). Efficient estimation using panel data. *Econometrica, 57*, 695–700.

Dielman, T. E. (1989). *Pooled cross-sectional and time series data analysis.* New York: Marcel Dekker.

Diggle, P. J., Heagarty, P., Liang, K.-Y., & Zeger, S. L. (2002). *Analysis of longitudinal data* (2nd ed.). London: Oxford University Press.

Frees, E. W. (2004). *Longitudinal and panel data: Analysis and applications in the social sciences.* Cambridge, UK: Cambridge University Press.

Frees, E. W., & Kim, J.-S. (2006). Multilevel model prediction. *Psychometrika, 71*, 79–104.

Frees, E. W., & Wang, P. (2005). Credibility using copulas. *North American Actuarial Journal, 9*, 31–48.

Goldberger, A. S. (1962). Best linear unbiased prediction in the generalized linear regression model. *Journal of the American Statistical Association, 57*, 369–375.

Goldberger, A. S. (1991). *A course in econometrics.* Cambridge, MA: Harvard University Press.

Goldstein, H. (2003). *Multilevel statistical models* (3rd ed.). London: Oxford University Press.

Grizzle, J. E., & Allen, M. D. (1969). Analysis of growth and dose response curves. *Biometrics, 25,* 357–381.

Harville, D. (1976). Extension of the Gauss-Markov theorem to include the estimation of random effects. *Annals of Statistics, 2,* 384–395.

Hausman, J. A. (1978). Specification tests in econometrics. *Econometrica, 46,* 1251–1271.

Hausman, J. A., & Taylor, W. E. (1981). Panel data and unobservable individual effects. *Econometrica, 49,* 1377–1398.

Hayashi, F. (2000). *Econometrics.* Princeton, NJ: Princeton University Press.

Hoch, I. (1962). Estimation of production function parameters combining time-series and cross-section data. *Econometrica, 30,* 34–53.

Huber, P. J. (1967). The behaviour of maximum likelihood estimators under non-standard conditions. In L. M. LeCam & J. Neyman (Eds.), *Proceedings of the fifth Berkeley symposium on mathematical statistics and probability* (Vol. 1, pp. 221–233). Berkeley: University of California Press.

Jain, D. C., Vilcassim, N. J., & Chintagunta, P. K. (1994). A random-coefficients logit brand choice model applied to panel data. *Journal of Business and Economic Statistics, 12,* 317–328.

Johnson, P. R. (1960). Land substitutes and changes in corn yields. *Journal of Farm Economics, 42,* 294–306.

Kim, J.-S., & Frees, E. W. (2005). *Fixed effects estimation in multilevel models.* Madison: University of Wisconsin. (Retrieved from http://www.research.bus.wisc.edu/jfrees/)

Kim, J.-S., & Frees, E. W. (2006). Omitted variables in multilevel models. *Psychometrika, 71,* 659–690.

Kim, J.-S., & Frees, E. W. (in press). Multilevel modeling with correlated effects. *Psychometrika.*

Kreft, I., & de Leeuw, J. (1998). *Introducing multilevel modeling.* Thousand Oaks, CA: Sage.

Kuh, E. (1959). The validity of cross-sectionally estimated behavior equation in time series application. *Econometrica, 27,* 197–214.

Laird, N. M., & Ware, J. H. (1982). Random-effects models for longitudinal data. *Biometrics, 38,* 963–974.

Lazarsfeld, P. F., & Fiske, M. (1938). The panel as a new tool for measuring opinion. *Public Opinion Quarterly, 2,* 596–612.

Liang, K. Y., & Zeger, S. L. (1986). Longitudinal data analysis using generalized linear models. *Biometrika, 73,* 12–22.

Maddala, G. S. (1971). The use of variance components models in pooling cross section and time series data. *Econometrica, 39,* 341–358.

McCulloch, C. E., & Searle, S. R. (2001). *Generalized, linear, and mixed models.* New York: Wiley.

McFadden, D. (1978). Modeling the choice of residential location. In A. Karlqvist, L. Lundqvist, F. Snickers, & J. Weibull (Eds.), *Spatial interaction theory and planning models* (pp. 75–96). Amsterdam: North-Holland.

Mundlak, Y. (1961). Empirical production function free of management bias. *Journal of Farm Economics, 43,* 44–56.

Pinheiro, J. C., & Bates, D. M. (2000). *Mixed-effects models in S and S-plus.* New York: Springer.

Potthoff, R. F., & Roy, S. N. (1964). A generalized multivariate analysis of variance model useful especially for growth curve problems. *Biometrika, 51,* 313–326.

Rao, C. R. (1965). The theory of least squares when the parameters are stochastic and its application to the analysis of growth curves. *Biometrika, 52,* 447–458.

Raudenbush, S. W., & Bryk, A. S. (2002). *Hierarchical linear models: Applications and data analysis methods* (2nd ed.). London: Sage.

Robinson, G. K. (1991). The estimation of random effects. *Statistical Science, 6,* 15–51.

Snijders, T. A. B., & Bosker, R. J. (1999). *Multilevel analysis: An introduction to basic and advanced multilevel modeling.* London: Sage.

Taris, T. J. (2000). *A primer in longitudinal data analysis.* London: Sage.

Valletta, R. G. (1999). Declining job security. *Journal of Labor Economics, 17,* S170–S197.

Wallace, T., & Hussain, A. (1969). The use of error components in combining cross section with time series data. *Econometrica, 37,* 55–72.

Webb, N. L., Clune, W. H., Bolt, D. M., Gamoran, A., Meyer, R. H., Osthoff, E., et al. (2002). *Models for analysis of NSF's systemic initiative programs: The impact of the urban system initiatives on student achievement in Texas, 1994–2000* (Technical Report). Madison, WI: Wisconsin Center for Education Research.

White, H. (1980). A heteroskedasticity-consistent covariance matrix estimator and a direct test for heteroskedasticity. *Econometrica, 48,* 817–838.

Wishart, J. (1938). Growth-rate determinations in nutrition studies with the bacon pig, and their analysis. *Biometrika, 30,* 16–28.

Wooldridge, J. M. (2002). *Econometric analysis of cross section and panel data.* Cambridge: MIT Press.

14

Probabilistic Methods in Surveys and Official Statistics

Vasja Vehovar, Matka Zaletel, and Rudi Seljak

Introduction

Historically, the development of probabilistic methods in survey sampling has been closely linked to official statistics. One of the first large-scale attempts to infer about a target population from partial observations came in the 1890s when Anders Kiaer, the director of Statistics Norway, challenged the discussion of "representative" samples—not yet based on probabilistic theory—with partial observations of the Norwegian population (Schweder, 1999). The well-known session of the International Statistical Institute in 1895 condemned such a practice—that is, inferring from partial observations to the total population. Kiaer argued in vain for his "representative" method at the next three consecutive sessions of the International Statistical Institute. Finally, he also had to admit defeat at home as some important estimates from such surveys were proved to be wrong in 1906 (Lie, 2002). On the other hand, the theoretical development of the probabilistic approach was slowly expanding to its first peaks in the 17th (Pascal, Fermat), 18th (Bernoulli, Bayes, de Moivre), and 19th (Laplace, Thiele, Gauss) centuries, followed by rapid developments in the early decades of the 20th century (Pearson, Fischer) (Hald, 2003; Kotz, 2005). However, it was only in 1934 that Jerzy Neyman summarized, upgraded, and built the foundations for modern probabilistic sampling using a randomization approach, sometimes also labeled scientific sampling (Neyman, 1934). After the *Literary Digest* debacle in 1936, when a survey of 10 million respondents failed to predict the winner of the U.S. presidential elections—while modern pollsters (Gallup, Roper, Crossley) using some elements of probabilistic methods got it right—survey sampling finally became a discipline based on probabilistic theory. Since then, it has rapidly expanded in several directions. Early developments in official statistics—particularly in the United States (Frankel & Frankel, 1987), where Morris Hansen joined the Census Bureau in 1935; in India (i.e., Mahalanobis); and also in Poland, Russia, and other countries—contributed crucially to modern sampling theory and practice. This close relationship also continued after World War II, and the first textbooks and major monographs on survey sampling were closely related to the official statistics (i.e., Hansen, Hurvitz, & Madow, 1953; Kish, 1965).

Of course, official statistics encompasses other areas such as national accounts, index theory, and so on, but the application of probabilistic methods is still one of its essential components. Probabilistic methods are closely related to official statistics in various areas, such as small-area estimation, sample selection, variance calculations, and statistical disclosure. Other than that, official statistics is predominantly an area where numerous general statistical methods are applied. Official statistics has only partially established itself as an articulated discipline with its journals (e.g., *Survey Methodology*, *Journal of Official Statistics*), associations (e.g., International Association of Official Statistics), various conferences, and so on, but specialized educational programs are still relatively rare (e.g., MA in Official Statistics, University of Southampton), and we can hardly find a textbook focusing specifically on official statistics.

Nevertheless, in this chapter, we focus on and systematically overview the existing applications of probabilistic methods in official statistics or, more precisely, in the practice of public statistical offices. We first discuss (in the next section) the most typical official surveys that are present in almost all statistical offices. There, we expose the corresponding specifics of the probabilistic approach and discuss the major challenges. In the third section, we focus on those probabilistic methods that are most closely related to official statistics. In the fourth section, we overview some related methodological issues. Finally, in the last section, we summarize and outline trends and point out certain challenges. Throughout the chapter, we use some illustrations from the Statistical Office of the Republic of Slovenia, whose activities are harmonized with the Eurostat regulations so that it also corresponds to global trends in other statistical offices (e.g., the United States, Canada, and Australia).

Major Official Sample Surveys

Official surveys use a probabilistic sample selection, which is based on randomization. This usually requires that all units in the population have a positive probability of being included in the sample. In addition, all these probabilities have to be known before the sample selection. Here, we present a few of the better-known official surveys.

Household Surveys

Household surveys are often the central surveys of any statistical office. Correspondingly, these surveys have a long history of methodological developments. Here are the main specific elements of these surveys:

- Probabilistic methods are essential here to properly estimate the size and structure of the population. Complex samples and complicated estimators of the target variables are usually used in these surveys.

- Household surveys often use so-called area sampling, which enables a probabilistic sample selection even if we have no lists of dwellings or persons. The area sample was a major innovation in probabilistic sampling as it assigns a known and positive selection probability to all households in a target population. In the first step, we select (with some randomization and often in several stages) the spatial/area units (e.g., towns, settlement, districts, and census enumeration areas). We usually use here the estimated size from the most recent census (e.g., number of households). When the final area units are selected, all dwellings are identified. In the second step, they are enumerated (listed) by specially trained enumerators. In the third step, some of those dwellings are randomly selected into the sample, and interviewers approach their inhabitants with questionnaires.

- The target population in household surveys is quite homogeneous. As a consequence, the stratification—that is, splitting of the target population into homogeneous parts (i.e., strata) with independent sample selection in each stratum—brings little improvement to the sampling variance. However, the stratification helps when we need to provide estimates of the target variables for predefined domains of the study (e.g., regions).

- Most of the national statistical institutes have developed their specific sampling frames of the population to optimize the stratification and perform effective multistage sampling. The practices vary considerably since some countries apply area samples, while others use lists of the population (e.g., a register of the population) to select the sample.

- Administrative sources were not very important for household surveys until recent years, with the notable exception of Scandinavian countries. However, this situation is now changing very rapidly. Statistical offices are increasingly combining data from administrative sources and existing surveys with various forms of matching.

- Only a small proportion of all household surveys in a certain country is carried out by the national statistical institute. There are many other institutions dealing with them, from universities and nonprofit research institutes, on one hand, to market research companies on the other. The methodology for household surveys had thus often been developed outside national statistical offices, which have later applied it with some modification.

- Longitudinal surveys, which focus on changes to observed phenomena over time, are ever more important in household surveys. These surveys are designed as panel surveys, surveying the same unit for several consecutive time periods. Cross-sectional surveys focus on a detailed description of the observed phenomena at a certain point in time. In other words, these surveys seek to take a snapshot of the observed population. Since longitudinal surveys are quite costly, statistical offices increasingly use one survey implementation for various purposes (cross-sectional and longitudinal). For example, one wave of the Labor Force Survey (LFS), which is initially a longitudinal survey measuring changes in employment, can be expanded by a separate block of questions related to lifelong learning (i.e., a cross-sectional survey). This approach is usually not applied to business surveys.

- Household surveys and censuses of the population often spend a majority of the budget of national statistical institutes, so the methodology is exposed to many revisions in an attempt to lower the related expenditure. This creates a very specific environment for the development of the methodology. In particular, the new survey modes—for example, computers, mobile phones, Web surveys, and so on—have dramatic consequences for household surveys because these surveys are largely performed with expensive personal interviewing, which can be significantly reduced with the introduction of new technologies.

The three main and most typical household surveys carried out by almost all national statistical offices are briefly described below.

Labor Force Survey

The LFS is a household survey using international (i.e., International Labor Organization, ILO) methodology to measure employment statuses. Statistical offices usually provide annual and quarterly estimates of the ILO unemployment rate, activity rates, and so on, while some (e.g., the United States) also provide monthly estimates. Many of these data are important short-term indicators and of particular interest to the media, politicians, and researchers. In addition to estimating the quarterly and yearly change of the unemployment rate, estimates of the transitions—that is, entries and exits to and from a specific employment status—are needed, and a rotational sample pattern is used to ensure the balance between the quality of quarterly and yearly estimates. Often the "3-1-2" pattern is used: One household is interviewed for three consecutive quarters, then it is excluded for one quarter, and then it is interviewed again for two quarters. Accordingly, we always have a considerable share of the sample where all units are interviewed in a 4-month interval, along with a share interviewed in a 1-year interval.

Samples of LFS are usually stratified as two stage (or multistage), but again, the decision on the sample design varies from country to country and depends mostly on the population frame and mode of data collection. Increasingly, however, the samples are simple random samples (in each stratum) whereby stratification is usually performed by the size and type of settlement and by region. Since the majority of interviews in second and later waves are carried out by telephone, travel costs are no longer an issue. On the other hand, the design effects (i.e., a specific increase in sampling variance caused by multistage sampling) would imply larger samples—and consequently higher costs, so within given data quality requirements, a simple random sample is often more cost-effective.

Household Budget Survey

The Household Budget Survey (HBS) is another typical survey carried out by national statistical institutes. The results of the survey (the consumption of households) are used by price statisticians, national accounts along with the media, politicians, researchers, and the general public. This is a very special survey: The respondents' burden is one of the highest, the costs are also very high, and the methodology is extremely complicated. Generally, data are collected through two instruments:

1. *Diary:* The respondents write down their daily consumption for a period of 2 weeks.
2. *Questionnaire:* The interviewer fills in all the other data, including products not purchased on a daily basis.

The practice is very different across countries; some carry out the HBS every 5 years, some carry out the survey every 3 years, some have a "large" 5-yearly survey and "small" yearly surveys. Many countries in Europe nowadays use the Danish or Norwegian model of the HBS, which minimizes the costs and ensures the required data quality. The essence of this model is within estimation, whereby data from three consecutive survey years are analyzed together. Typically, a yearly survey would include around 1,200 households per year and thus provide a 3-yearly estimate involving 3,600 households. This kind of estimate is produced every year.

Since intensive personal interviewing is involved here, the sample design for this type of surveys is often a stratified multistage sample. In the first stages, the enumeration areas are selected with a probability proportional to the size, where the size is the estimated number of households in the area. In the final stage, a fixed number of households are selected. This is performed either with area sample procedures (i.e., an enumeration of the dwellings) or directly from the central register of the population (in countries where such a register exists).

Post-Enumeration Surveys

One of the largest household surveys is the so-called post-enumeration survey, which follows the decennial censuses to evaluate their quality. Due to various problems with fieldwork, censuses typically suffer from certain undercounts; sometimes they underestimate the population by 1% or more. Post-enumeration surveys usually have very large sample sizes; they typically involve tens or even hundreds of thousands of households. Because of a sufficiently large sample size, the sampling error is almost negligible. At the same time, we have much more control over field operations and other types of errors than in censuses, where it is difficult to provide control over the huge number of staff involved. The probabilistic methods used in post-enumeration surveys can thus provide much better counts of the population than a census, which sometimes seems surprising to laymen and might also be in conflict with the legal role of the census. This discussion in the United States has even been the subject of court processes, as some states complained about the undercount from the 1990 Census, where a post-enumeration survey showed that the census undercount was 1.6% (i.e., 4 million people). The problem was that different groups had different relative undercounts. However, the Supreme Court rejected the corrections based on the post-enumeration survey for the U.S. 1990 Census (U.S. Census Bureau, 2007).

Business Surveys

The methodology of business surveys differs in many respects from that of other surveys. Here are the main specifics (Cox, Binder, Chinnappa, & Christianson, 1995; Silver, 1997):

- The target population of the business surveys is very heterogeneous, meaning that we have few large and many small units. As a consequence, the key variables (e.g., number of employees, turnover) tend to have a very skewed distribution.

- There are many different observational units that vary not only in their conceptual definitions but also in the context of their usage across surveys in countries. Businesses, establishments, enterprises, and specific local types of activity units are just some examples. In addition, the dynamics of demographic changes (e.g., births, cessations, mergers, takeovers) among business entities introduces substantial complications.
- A large number of secondary data sources, most of them coming from administrative bases, are available for use in business surveys. These data are used in various stages of the survey process, from sample design, data collection, data editing, and imputation to estimation procedures and tabulations.
- Business surveys are largely carried out by the statistical offices or other agencies funded directly by governments. Consequently, most of the methodology is developed inside these institutions. Very often, the companies are legally obliged to fill in the questionnaires, so the response rates are usually high. Commercial surveys, on the other hand, either fail to achieve an acceptable response rate or do not have a probabilistic approach at all.

There are many different classifications of business surveys, but probably the most commonly used of them groups business surveys into longitudinal and cross-sectional ones. In the remainder of the section, we briefly describe the three typical business surveys, with two of them being longitudinal and one cross-sectional.

Retail Trade Survey

The Retail Trade Survey (RTS) is a monthly survey whose purpose is to measure the monthly movement of turnover in retail trade. This is typically a random sample (with some stratification) of at least 1,000 enterprises, where the units stay in the panel for 12 consecutive months. Most often, the data are collected by a mail questionnaire, but they can also be collected through the Internet. We can find this type of survey in European Union (EU) countries ("Methodology of Short-Term Business Statistics", 2002) and—with some specifics—in the United States (Monthly Retail Trade Survey, 2007). Results are published as indices that are seasonally adjusted with the autoregressive moving average (ARIMA) models initially developed by Box and Jenkins (1976).

Industrial Production Index

The Industrial Production Index is a monthly indicator with the purpose of estimating monthly changes of the industrial production value; it conceptually originates in the national accounts. It is one of the key measures of economic activity. Typically, this is a mail survey of at least a few thousand companies selected by so-called cutoff sampling (described in the subsection Deviations From Probability Samples). The results are usually published as indices within 1–2 months of the end of the reference month.

PRODCOM Survey

The PRODCOM survey denotes the group of annual structural surveys carried out to provide detailed data on industrial production outputs. For members of the EU, the basis of the survey is the PRODCOM regulation (1991), which stipulates that annual production is to be reported according to the PRODCOM list of products, consisting of about 4,500 products based on a statistical classification of products by activity. Here, once again, cutoff sampling is frequently used, usually on at least a few thousand companies. The selected units report data on the quantity of production and the quantity and value of the sales of goods and services. These data are also used in the construction of the weights needed for the Industrial Production Index.

Selected Probabilistic Topics

Here, we discuss some specific probabilistic topics where the corresponding methodological developments are closely related to official statistics.

Small-Area Estimation

The users of official surveys are increasingly often interested in small areas such as towns or municipalities. There are various reasons for this interest, from public administrative needs (e.g., the distribution of governmental funds), insight into the expansion of a certain phenomenon (e.g., a disease), and market intelligence information for business decisions (e.g., measuring the economic potential of a certain area) to local estimates of standard official surveys (e.g., unemployment statistics). The key problem we usually face is the fact that data from a sample survey do not provide acceptable direct estimates. Very often there are fewer than 10 elements from a specific area in the sample, so either the corresponding estimates are impossible to calculate or the estimates have unacceptably wide confidence intervals. SAE procedures use data from neighboring areas, auxiliary information, and modeling assumptions to produce estimates for small areas, which are also called small domains of interest.

The beginnings of SAE go back to the 17th century in Canada and England; however, modern statistical methods started in the 1970s in the United States and Canada. With regard to the EU, we note the EURAREA Project 2001–2004, which integrated the leading European statisticians in this field. The project's aim was the empirical evaluation of various SAE methods and to make these methods more user-friendly. Yet it is true that European statistical offices have still not fully accepted this approach as one of their routine practices. Among the reasons for this are the complexities of the procedures and the complicated computer implementation, along with a certain lack of pressure from the users.

In SAE, we can use the so-called design-based approach where the distribution of the estimator depends on the sampling design, and so standard estimation approaches can be used (e.g., Horvitz-Thompson). Of course, we also use auxiliary information correlated with our target variable. A well-known example of this approach is the Generalized Estimation System from Statistics Canada. We can additionally assume a model for this relationship as in so-called model-assisted estimators. However, as is usual in post-survey adjustments, an improvement in precision (reduction of sampling variance) is paid for with increased bias.

On the other hand, model-based approaches are increasingly being used. In this approach, we first construct model-dependent estimators. If the assumed model is valid for our data, this approach is often better than the design-based one. Of course, the model needs to be tested carefully before being applied. With the model-based approach, we may also obtain estimates for areas where we otherwise have no elements in our sample survey. The Fay-Herriot model is frequently used when we have auxiliary data for the area but not for the observed units in our sample. Another frequently used model is the Battese-Harter-Fuller model, which assumes that we have the auxiliary information for the units. Again, bias and variance should be considered together when evaluating SAE approaches. The mean squared error (MSE) as a measure of accuracy is very important here since it integrates precision (sampling variance) and bias.

A more detailed overview of the methods can be found in Rao (2003) and Longford (2005).

Data Linkage and Data Fusion

Modern information communication technologies increasingly enable several options for comparing, merging, and linking data from various sources. The procedures of merging records for the same units are even more common in contemporary e-government services, specifically in the so-called G2G component, where government institutions merge data from various sources and thus save time for the citizens. For example, when applying for some welfare benefits, the applicants do not need to enclose their income tax report because the employment office obtains this directly from the tax office.

In statistical offices, this type of linkage is also being increasingly used for analytical studies. For example, nonrespondents of LFSs can be linked to the census and tax information so that we can obtain insight into their characteristics.

Data are also linked into surveys to shorten the questionnaire. For example, in the European survey of households, the data related to social benefits are obtained from the corresponding government office, and respondents do not need to be asked these questions. Particularly in Scandinavian countries, register-oriented statistics provide rich options for data linkage, so censuses are no longer needed. Of course, such linkages face severe problems with respect to data protection; however, the majority of countries allow this for statistical purposes. Various codes regulate the privacy aspects of these practices, such as the Protocol on Data Matching (e.g., Office of National Statistics, 2004).

Much more problematic—but also of much greater potential—is so-called statistical matching, sometimes also referred to as data fusion. Here, we do not have the same identifiers or the same units, but we combine data from different units. For example, we may have separate data from the LFS and separate data from the Family Budget survey, whereby no unit responded to both surveys. If we are interested in consumer expenditure variables across employment characteristics, we may use the variables common to both files (i.e., sociodemographic variables) and match similar records with some probabilistic methods. The recipient record from the LFS sample would thus receive the (consumption) data from the most appropriate donor record from the Family Budget survey. Obviously, this is a dangerous practice and is subject to various legal restrictions in some countries. On the other hand, it may be very fruitful, particularly in official statistics (D'Orazio, Di Zio, & Scanu, 2001). It has been shown that such statistical matching works well if the basic assumption holds: The target variables from two sources should be conditionally independent given the common sociodemographic block of questions. A good overview of this practice is provided in D'Orazio, Di Zio, and Scanu (2006) and Raessler (2002), who elaborated the Bayesian approach and multiple imputations (Rubin, 1987). Another very promising result of this approach is the split of questionnaires, where we allocate blocks of questions to different subgroups of the same sample and then use data-matching techniques to create the full data set.

Statistical Disclosure

The problem of statistical disclosure relates to the danger that an individual unit will be recognized from the corresponding public statistical publications. This recognition can occur spontaneously or through the use of some additional data. In any case, this may have harmful consequences for the responding unit. Particularly when we have a very small number of respondents in a certain segment, it is increasingly possible to infer about an individual from aggregate results. For example, if there is only one large company in a certain sector, its characteristics (e.g., annual value of investments) could be identified from the aggregate presented in the table. A problem also exists if one or two units have a dominant role in a certain segment or when we have three or fewer units in the cell (the so-called sensitivity problem). Similarly, when an anonymous sample—with direct identifiers removed—from the census is publicly provided, someone could still be identified if too many matching identifiers are revealed (e.g., age group, gender, type of settlement). Consequently, some sensitive information of the disclosed unit could be identified—for example, an individual's answer to a question on religion.

Of course, statistical offices—as well as other survey organizations—promise respondents that their individual responses will never be revealed but will only appear in an aggregate form. Statistical offices also assure respondents of their privacy, which means that each individual has the right to decide which information about him or her will be publicly revealed. Related to this is the concept of confidentiality, which in our context refers to the relationship between the respondent and the survey organization. The latter usually ensures that the respondent's individual data will not be revealed to third parties. However, a certain probability—although negligible and close to 0—that the unit will be identified often exists. Consequently, statistical offices have to deal with this very carefully because a clear contradiction exists: On one hand, statistical data must be presented in a form that is useful to users, while on the other, they have to provide sufficient protection of the individuals or businesses to which the data refer.

Various strategies have been developed to reduce the probability of identifying the responding unit (statistical disclosure control). When dealing with micro data, one popular approach is to add various forms of random noise (errors). The data can also be changed between units (i.e., data swapping). If performed properly, this will change the individual data without harming the quality of the estimates for the aggregates. Another solution is the direct collapsing of small segments; for example, instead of two age categories, one for 30–40 years and another for 40–50 years, we aggregate them to only one category of 30–50 years. With these methods, the probability of disclosure decreases significantly.

With respect to aggregate tables, cell suppression is the most frequent among the existing approaches. However, in multidimensional tables, this poses a very complex optimization problem.

More about disclosure issues can be found in Willenborg and de Waal (2001).

Panels, Attrition, and Seam Effects

Panel surveys—sometimes also referred to as longitudinal surveys—are used in official statistics to analyze changes to the units in a target population. The most well-known examples of panels in official statistics are the LFSs described above, where members enter a panel and are interviewed over several waves about their employment status. If we want to detect not only the net change (e.g., unemployment change from 6% to 7%) but also the gross change (e.g., 20% of unemployed persons obtained work), this is impossible with cross-sectional surveys.

All panels suffer from the same methodological problems as cross-sectional surveys and, in addition, from their own specific problems, particularly those related to attrition. In each wave, additional members of the panel are lost because of refusals, noncontacts, or movers or because panel members die. This all adds up and can reduce the sample size dramatically in later waves. Survey organizations try to reduce attrition by improving refusal-conversion practices, providing incentives, updating contact information, and switching the mode of contact (Schneider et al., 2005). Surveys have different strategies here: Some panels follow all members of the original family (e.g., the new family of the children becomes eligible), while other surveys simplify the tracking. To fight nonresponse and save resources, some panels allow proxy interviews whenever the target member cannot be interviewed. On the other hand, as we saw with the LFS example, complex rotating schemes are also used whereby the sample is refreshed with new members, which preserves the sample size but still provides overlaps for periodical estimates.

A very special methodological problem related to panel surveys is the so-called seam effect. This effect occurs when respondents are surveyed, say, every 4 months, and at each interview, they provide data (e.g., the social benefits they received) for each of the past 4 months. It has been observed that changes between reported monthly figures are much smaller for adjacent months within a wave (e.g., among the 4 months reported at the first interview) than for the adjacent months reported between two waves (i.e., when comparing the most recent month from the first interview with the earliest month reported in the second interview).

The term *seam* was introduced by Burkhead and Coder (1985) in their analysis of the 1983–1984 Survey of Income and Program Participation (SIPP) data. Seam effects have been observed in different panels, with various reference periods and with data collected using different modes. Among the strategies to reduce seam effects, the so-called dependent interviewing (Lynn, Jackle, Jenkins, & Sala, 2004) seems to be the most effective even if it does not completely reduce the seam effect problem. With dependent interviewing, the interviewer—when asking questions—uses the responses from previous interviews along with auxiliary information.

More about panel surveys can be found in Frees (2004) and Duncan, Kalton, Kasprzyk, and Singh (1989).

Related Methodological Issues

The issues of probabilistic sample surveys are closely related to more general survey methodology problems. They are, in fact, so interwoven that sometimes they cannot be separated, so we briefly overview the most important ones.

Survey Modes

Historically, mail surveys and face-to-face data collection have prevailed in official statistics' survey data collection. Telephone surveys started a few decades ago and have now become one of the main data collection modes. With telephone surveys, the principles of probabilistic sampling do not change, but due to sampling frame problems, the key important surveys often perform the initial contact in a face-to-face interview (e.g., the LFS). On the other hand, some attitude surveys—for example, opinions of consumers—are often based on telephone surveys.

A more radical transformation began with the introduction of computers to data collection, where *computer-assisted data collection* (CADAC) changed many aspects of administrative procedures. The corresponding applications in survey data collection are labeled *computer-assisted survey information collection* (CASIC). Starting with *computer-assisted telephone interviewing* (CATI) in the 1970s, computers further penetrated the survey process through *computer-assisted personal interviewing* (CAPI) and *computer-assisted self-interviewing* (CASI), *computerized self-administered questionnaires* (CSAQ), *touch-tone data entry* (TDE), and *interactive voice response* (IVR). Despite bringing a considerable simplification of data collection and cost savings, official statistics is relatively conservative when it comes to the introduction of new modes. The introduction of Internet data collection for LFSs is thus still in its early development, and in census data collection, it is used to a limited extent, while even business surveys, which are the most convenient for this type of data collection, are moving to the Web only relatively slowly.

In any case, new technology did not bring many changes to the principles of probability sample design, except that dual sampling frames—where we combine two sampling frames (e.g., telephone list and personal addresses)—are considered much more often. In addition, the new technologically supported modes often lack corresponding sampling frames (e.g., there is no list of e-mails for the general population), so statistical offices have to rely on their traditional sampling frames. On the other hand, many potential problems arise due to potential mode effects. This is particularly important when we combine different modes in the so-called mixed-mode surveys. Modes may be combined in different ways:

- We can combine various modes on the same persons, as in the case of nonresponse (e.g., first mail, then telephone, the third attempt in person) (Voogt & Saris, 2005).
- We can apply different modes for parts of the surveys (e.g., a personal interview for those who do not own a telephone).
- We can apply different modes for different waves of surveys (e.g., first contact in person, then by telephone, as in LFSs).
- We can also allow respondents to select the mode by themselves (e.g., Web or mail).

In all these cases, the particular mode effects need to be carefully studied. Sometimes, the questions need rewording to fit into another mode. An excellent overview of mixed methods issues is provided by De Leeuw (2005).

We should add that costs have usually been the key factor driving the introduction of new modes. Telephone surveys are several times cheaper than face-to-face surveys, and Web surveys have even more advantages. However, on the other hand, mobile phone surveys are starting to become—even though they are a more expensive mode compared with a fixed-line telephone—a necessary option as individuals tend not to have a fixed-line telephone.

Deviations From Probability Samples

Despite the theoretical advantages of probabilistic sampling, we often face situations where cost savings and other practical benefits outweigh the merits of the probabilistic approach. We now present four typical examples of this.

Representative Sampling Approach: Consumer Price Index

Due to their importance for macroeconomic policy, price indices have always been considered one of the most important statistical indicators. The consumer price index (CPI) is an indicator measuring changes in the level of retail prices of goods and services (products) and should reflect the change of prices of all products produced and provided in a particular economy. However, due to the large number of these commodities, it would be very complicated to use a proper probabilistic sample. As a consequence, many statistical offices do not sample them with a random mechanism; instead, they do it purposively. The universe of products is first clustered into groups, and then the "representative" products with the most important share in total consumption, and whose price changes best reflect changes in prices of related products, are selected. Retail stores, on the other hand, are often selected with probabilistic approaches, yet many statistical offices also select them purposively: First, they select the most typical or most important cities, and in the next step, they also purposively select retail points (shops, marketplaces, craftsmen, and other retail locations).

The rationale for not using probabilistic sampling is very practical, while the theoretical justification relies on the assumption that the price increase is, in general, very robust. In any case, the collected prices are compiled into the CPI by using the Laspeyres-index approach (Allen, 1975). An important role in the calculation procedures is played by weights, which in the definition of the Laspeyres index, refer to the base period and should reflect the consumption pattern of households in the base period. These weights are determined on the basis of data obtained from the HBS.

Cutoff Sampling: Monthly Report on Turnover

In business surveys, a small number of units usually represent a significant share of the total aggregate of some key variable—for example, number of employees or turnover. This characteristic of the population is especially distinctive for the area of industry. Therefore, the use of cutoff instead of random sampling is quite a common approach when surveying this population. Cutoff sampling is a procedure where only the units with values of a certain key variable greater than the threshold value are selected. In the surveys of monthly turnovers—which are used to estimate the industrial production index—the key variable in the selection procedure is often the number of employees. The selection procedure is typically carried out in two steps. In the first step, units with at least 20 employees are selected. In the second step, the population of enterprises can be further divided by the two-digit activity classes, and inside each of the groups, the units are sorted by a descending number of employees until we achieve, say, 75% coverage of the total number of employees.

Cutoff sampling causes a certain degree of bias in the estimate, along with a bias in the estimated sampling variance, which follows directly from the design. It is almost impossible to estimate such bias for each survey, but it is advisable to perform an evaluation at least once a year by using some kind of exhaustive administrative data.

Quota Selection: Sampling of Travelers

When studying travels across borders, the sampling unit is usually the vehicle (car, truck, bus, etc.). For this type of sampling, the days within the year and the border crossing points are selected with probabilistic sampling (i.e., stratified probability proportional to site). When an interviewer surveys specific cross-border traffic on a selected day, the vehicles and then the travelers within the vehicles have to be selected. However, to perform the correct random procedure, a second interviewer would be needed to count and select the vehicles. Instead, quotas are often used instructing the interviewers to get, say, 40 filled-in questionnaires for each of the 8-hour shifts. Further instructions are provided to ensure the approximately right ratio of trucks, buses, and cars. Later in the stage of weighting, however, quota sampling is treated as simple random sampling where all vehicles have equal chances of being selected.

Field Substitutions: Household Surveys

Relatively often in official statistics (even in some LFSs), in the last stage of the probabilistic sample design, we have a very small number of units, particularly in cluster sample designs with high intracluster correlation, where we select only three to five units. A similar situation occurs with stratified cluster samples, with a two-per-strata selection strategy. In such situations, we may end up (due to nonresponse) with no observations in a certain cluster or strata, so it is very natural to apply a substitution procedure. During the field stage of the survey, we replace nonresponding units with a substitute (reserve) one from the same cluster/strata. The substitute unit can be selected randomly, but sometimes simply the neighboring unit (e.g., household) is selected or some quotas are used. Despite the procedure being seemingly beneficial, Vehovar (1999) showed that it could not be justified even if it is performed with randomization. It is disadvantageous from both bias and variance points of view when compared with the simple alternative of an increased sample size and corresponding weighting adjustment. In addition, it suffers from very serious complications in field procedures, including considerable delays in timing. Instead, supplement samples should be used, or the increased size of the cluster size should be implemented (based on estimates of anticipated nonresponse). Nevertheless, there are still some very specific circumstances where this may be a useful approach, such as matched substitutes (Rubin & Zanutto, 2001) or modified Waksberg-Mitofski telephone sampling (Brick & Waksberg, 1991).

Editing, Imputation, Estimation, and Adjustments

Editing

Survey data are inevitably contaminated by different types of errors. Typically, these include

- an inconsistent answer of the respondent (e.g., a company first says that there are 100 employees in total, while later it reports 120 employees working in administration),
- a wrong recording of the answer by the interviewer, and
- error in data input (i.e., a "typo").

The goal of data editing processes is to find and correct as many of these errors as possible and to improve the data quality.

Many empirical studies have pointed out that, in addition to data collection, data editing is often the most costly part of the statistical process. It is estimated that, particularly in mail surveys of enterprises, data editing costs can represent up to 40%–60% of the whole survey budget. Typically, editing involves the specific cleaning of computerized data where special software is used to detect and remove inconsistencies.

Crucial progress in this area occurred in the second half of the 20th century, when the development of computer technology enabled the introduction of new procedures. The first cornerstone of a new paradigm was the automated data-editing approach (Fellegi & Holt, 1976). The main principle of this approach is that the procedure should always keep as much of the reported data as possible unchanged. If there is an alternative to correct two variables by 10% each or one variable by 30%, the system would choose the latter option.

Another important aspect of modern data editing is the role of data editing in the statistical process. While the "classical" approach isolates the editing procedures, we now understand data editing in a much broader sense as an integral part of the statistical process.

Imputation

Closely related to the data-editing activities are data imputation procedures, which are often understood merely as procedures for replacing missing values. However, in a broader sense, they should also be considered as the replacement of incorrect values. Various imputation methods have been developed in statistical theory (Cox et al., 1995), but only a few of them are broadly used in the practice of official statistics. We can group these methods into stochastic and deterministic procedures. The former use some kind of probabilistic mechanism and can thus give different results in different executions for the same data. The latter group, on the contrary, yields the same result in each execution for the same data.

Two of the most popular imputation methods (Pannekoek & Waal, 2005) are hot-deck (we use responses from other units in the same sample) and historical (we use responses from previous surveys of this unit) data imputation, which can have a deterministic or stochastic realization. In both cases, the imputed values are "borrowed" from the set of existing data. Considerable theoretical research has been devoted lately to the development of more advanced methods such as multiple imputation methods or neural network imputations, but so far, these methods have not yet been broadly used in official statistics.

Estimation

The estimation of the statistical parameters (e.g., totals, means, and proportions) and corresponding variances (including confidence intervals) is the final stage of the statistical production process. Only for all estimates that are based on probabilistic samples can the sampling variance, standard errors, and confidence intervals be calculated. The calculation usually applies specialized software packages; increasingly, this is often also integrated with weight calculations.

Adjustments

In practice, the estimation procedures require the proper construction of the weights, which are then attached to each of the records. Weight construction usually consists of three consecutive steps. The first step is the calculation of the sampling weight, which is just the inverse value of the selection probability and is already determined at the time of the sampling (i.e., design weight). In the second step, the weights are adjusted for the nonresponse and coverage errors. The *missing at random* (MAR) response mechanism is usually assumed for this adjustment. It means that the probability of a missing value depends only on the observed data (and not on the missing data). In the final stage, the weights are usually adjusted according to some external source, such as auxiliary variables. These auxiliary variables are obtained from administrative sources or from some larger surveys or censuses. The basic condition for the effective use of the auxiliary variables is that these variables are closely correlated to the target variables. The use of auxiliary variables is in practice realized through several different approaches. The regression approach, poststratification, and calibration are just some of these (Sarndal, Swenson, & Wretman, 1992). The final weight used in the estimation procedure can be decomposed into three factors, with each of them coming from the aforementioned steps.

Data Quality and Reporting

The final outputs of the official statistics production process are various types of statistical results describing certain social, economic, or other phenomena. Of course, the results should reach the users in a quick, clear, and user-friendly way. The standard paper publications disseminated at a fixed and previously announced time are supplemented with ad hoc tables as required by some demanding users. In fact, the preparation of the standard data releases used to be one of the most important tasks of the dissemination units. The Internet's rapid development introduced an entire new universe for the dissemination of statistical data. The majority of statistical agencies are now turning their dissemination policy from a paper-based to an Internet-based dissemination, where the users increasingly create their own output. However, this also changes several issues from disclosure risks to the reporting of sampling errors.

When national statistical offices plan the release of their materials, they devote more and more attention to various aspects of quality reporting. Quality information is usually provided in two different ways. The first provides basic quality information along with the results themselves, which is usually limited to some core quality indicators (e.g., standard errors, response, and eligibility rates) and to key survey design and processing characteristics. However, even here, in the case of sampling error, which is still considered one of the most important quality indicators, we can find diverse practices in different countries. Nevertheless, there are three basic approaches to providing the evaluation of sampling error:

- The first approach is to denote the quality of the results with a special label. Typically, estimates with a coefficient of variation larger than 0.15 (15%) are put in brackets; sometimes even two brackets are used for estimates with a coefficient of variation within the interval 0.2–0.3. The estimates with a coefficient of variation above 0.3 are usually not published at all. Instead, a dot (.) is used to indicate that an estimate does exist and it has a "nonzero" value, but it is unreliable. If published, the corresponding 95% confidence interval would extend more than 60% of the mean in each direction, which is unacceptable because users cannot be prevented from using the estimates uncritically.

- Sometimes, additional restrictions are imposed in terms of the number of units for which the estimate is provided. Typical benchmarks are 10, 20, or 30 and sometimes even 100 units as the cell minimum.
- A more demanding approach to documenting the precision of estimates is to explicitly disseminate the estimated errors either in the form of coefficients of variation and standard errors or by providing a model specification that allows the user to estimate the sampling error.

Of course, the precision and the corresponding sampling error are only one component of data quality. Other errors (e.g., measurement error) and biases (e.g., nonresponse bias) also exist, particularly nonresponse bias.

When observing errors and biases simultaneously, a smaller sampling error, which requires a larger sample size, may be traded for a smaller nonresponse bias, which requires increased fieldwork efforts. Within the same budget, we may thus prefer a smaller sample with a smaller nonresponse bias to a larger sample with a sizeable nonresponse bias. We also examined this bias-variance balance in the discussion of SAE, where bias and sampling error were jointly controlled within the context of accuracy (i.e., MSE).

In recent years, however, the MSE approach has been substantially broadened. Various statistical offices (e.g., Canada, Sweden, the United Kingdom, etc.) have developed frameworks that include other aspects of data quality, from dissemination aspects to the user-friendliness of the data. The main guidelines for preparing a quality report inside the European statistical system is provided by the Standard Quality Report (2003), which defines six quality dimensions: relevance, accuracy, timeliness and punctuality, accessibility and clarity, comparability, and coherence.

At the same time, most national statistical offices have found that they cannot ensure the quality of products without maintaining the quality of the whole organization. Some statistical offices have obtained the ISO 9001 qualification, while others have been using total quality management models (European Foundation for Quality Management [EFQM] Excellence Model or Common Assessment Framework [CAF]). A very important development in Europe came with the European Statistics Code of Practice (2005), which was addressed to governments, national statistical institutes, users, and other data providers. This Code of Practice describes quality standards from three different aspects: (1) institutional environment, (2) statistical processes, and (3) statistical output. It addresses most of the contemporary problems in official statistics: human resources management, relations with users, the burden on respondents, technological issues, data reporting, and so on.

Conclusion

Official statistics is one of the leading fields where probabilistic approaches to sample surveys have developed. It is also an area where they are increasingly being applied and upgraded. Of course, probabilistic methods can be used differently in the design, estimation, and postsurvey adjustment stages. They are also used in some other specific applications (e.g., statistical matching, disclosure issues, SAE). In the past few years, alongside the rapid development of probabilistic methods, corresponding applications in official statistics have also been evolving. It is, however, sometimes true that statistical offices are quite slow and conservative when it comes to applying new methods.

When discussing the application of probabilistic methods in official statistics, we should mention the trend of the global harmonization of these surveys. Key official surveys are increasingly using common methodological approaches because international comparisons are becoming ever more important. On the other hand, we can also observe a trend of the integration of the probabilistic aspects of sample survey data collection into broader processes of data collection where issues of management, technology, costs, and data quality are receiving greater attention. From this broader prospective, we sometimes even abandon the principles of the probabilistic approach. Yet it is still true that compared with other areas (i.e., the commercial sector), official statistics remains one of the cornerstones of the application of probabilistic methods in sample survey data collection.

ACKNOWLEDGMENTS

We wish to thank Mario Callgaro from the University of Lincoln, Nebraska, for his valuable comments on the draft section related to the seam effect and Boro Nikić from the Statistical Office of the Republic of Slovenia for his comments on the section on small-area estimation (SAE).

REFERENCES

Allen, R. G. D. (1975). *Index numbers in theory and practice.* Chicago: Aldine.

Box, G., & Jenkins, F. M. (1976). *Time series analysis: Forecasting and control.* Oakland, CA: Holden-Day.

Brick, J. M., & Waksberg, J. (1991). Avoiding sequential sampling with RDD. *Survey Methodology, 17*(1), 27–41.

Burkhead, D., & Coder, J. (1985). Gross changes in income recipiency from the Survey of Income and Program Participation. In *Proceedings of the Social Statistics Section* (pp. 351–356). Washington, DC: American Statistical Association.

Cox, B. G., Binder, D. A., Chinnappa, B. N., & Christianson, A. (1995). *Business survey methods.* New York: Wiley.

De Leeuw, E. D. (2005). To mix or not to mix data collection modes in surveys. *Journal of Official Statistics, 21*(2), 233–255.

D'Orazio, M., Di Zio, M., & Scanu, M. (2001). *Statistical matching: A tool for integrating data in national statistical institutes.* Retrieved September 28, 2007, from http://www.webfarm.jrc.cec.eu.int/etk-ntts/Papers/final_papers/43.pdf

D'Orazio, M., Di Zio, M., & Scanu, M. (2006). *Statistical matching: Theory and practice.* New York: Wiley.

Duncan, G., Kalton, G., Kasprzyk, D., & Singh, M. P. (1989). *Panel surveys.* New York: Wiley.

EURAREA Project. (2001–2004). Retrieved September 28, 2007, from http://www.statistics.gov.uk/eurarea

European Statistics Code of Practice. (2005). Retrieved September 28, 2007, from http://www.epp.eurostat.cec.eu.int/pls/portal/docs/PAGE/PGP_DS_QUALITY/TAB47141301/CODE_OF_PRACTICE-EN.PDF.

Fellegi, I. P., & Holt, D. (1976). A systematic approach to automatic editing and imputation. *Journal of the American Statistical Association, 71*, 17–35.

Frankel, M. R., & Frankel, L. R. (1987). Fifty years of survey sampling in the United States. *Public Opinion Quarterly, 51*(4), S127–S138.

Frees, E. W. (2004). *Longitudinal and panel data: Analysis and applications in the social sciences.* Cambridge, UK: Cambridge University Press.

Hald, A. (2003). *A history of probability and statistics and their applications before 1750.* New York: Wiley.

Hansen, M., Hurvitz, W., & Madow, W. (1953). *Sample survey methods and theory.* New York: Wiley.

Kish, L. (1965). *Survey sampling.* New York: Wiley.

Kotz, S. (2005). Reflections on early history of official statistics and a modest proposal for global coordination. *Journal of Official Statistics, 21*(2), 139–144.

Lie, E. (2002). The rise and fall of sampling surveys in Norway, 1985–1906. *Science in Context, 15*(3), 385–409.

Longford, N. T. (2005). *Missing data and small area estimation.* New York: Springer-Verlag.

Lynn, P., Jackle, A., Jenkins, S. P., & Sala, E. (2004). *The effects of dependant interviewing on respondents to questions on income sources.* Retrieved September 28, 2007, from http://www.iser.essex.ac.uk/pubs/workpaps/pdf/2004-16.pdf.

Methodology of short-term business statistics: Interpretation and guidelines. (2002). In *Eurostat Manual of Business Statistics* (sect. 3), Luxembourg.

Monthly Retail Trade Survey. (2007). U.S. Census Bureau. Retrieved September 28, 2007, from http://www.census.gov/mrts/www/ndesign.html.

Neyman, J. (1934). On the two different aspects of the representative method: The method of stratified sampling and the method of purposive selection. *Journal of the Royal Statistical Society, 97*, 558–606.

Office of National Statistics. (2004). *Protocol on data matching.* Retrieved September 28, 2007, from http://www.statistics.gov.uk/about/national_statistics/dcop/downloads/NSCoPDatamatching.pdf.

Pannekoek, J., & Waal, T. de. (2005). Automatic edit and imputation for business surveys: The Dutch contribution to the EUREDIT project. *Journal of Official Statistics, 21*(2), 257–286.

PRODCOM regulation (EEC) No 3924/91. (1991, December 31). *Official Journal of the European Communities*, L 374/1.

Raessler, S. (2002). *Statistical matching*. New York: Springer.

Rao, J. N. K. (2003). *Small area estimation*. New York: Wiley.

Rubin, D. B. (1987). *Multiple imputation for nonresponse in surveys*. New York: Wiley.

Rubin, D. B., & Zanutto, E. (2001). Using matched substitutes to adjust for nonignorable nonresponse through multiple imputations. In R. Groves, R. Little, & J. Eltinge (Eds.), *Survey nonresponse* (pp. 389–402). New York: Wiley.

Sarndal, C. E., Swenson, B., & Wretman, J. (1992). *Model assisted survey sampling*. New York: Springer-Verlag.

Schneider, S. J., Cantor, D., Malakhoff, L., Arieira, C., Segel, P., Nguyen, K. L., et al. (2005). Telephone, Internet, and paper data collection modes for the Census 2000 short form. *Journal of Official Statistics, 21*(1), 89–101.

Schweder, T. (1999). *Early statistics in the Nordic countries: When did the Scandinavians slip behind the British?* Retrieved September 28, 2007, from http://www.stat.fi/isi99/proceedings/arkisto/varasto/schw0844.pdf.

Silver, M. (1997). *Business statistics*. Berkshire, UK: McGraw-Hill.

Standard Quality Report. (2003). Retrieved September 28, 2007, from http://www.epp.eurostat.ec.europa.eu/pls/portal/docs/PAGE/PGP_DS_QUALITY/TAB47143233/STANDARD_QUALITY_REPORT_0.PDF. Eurostat.

U.S. Census Bureau. (2007). *What is 1990 Census undercount?* Retrieved September 28, 2007, from http://www.census.gov/dmd/www/techdoc1.html.

Vehovar, V. (1999). Field substitution and unit nonresponse. *Journal of Official Statistics, 15*(2), 335–350.

Voogt, R. J. J., & Saris, W. E. (2005). Mixed mode designs: Finding the balance between nonresponse bias and mode effects. *Journal of Official Statistics, 21*(3), 367–387.

Willenborg, L., & de Waal, T. (2001). *Elements of statistical disclosure control*. New York: Springer.

15

PROBABILISTIC MODELS OF MEASUREMENT ERRORS

NICHOLAS T. LONGFORD

INTRODUCTION

Measurement error or, more generally, recording the values of a related (*manifest*) variable instead of the *ideal* or *latent* variable is a common feature of many studies. Often, the definition of the latent variable precludes establishing its values with precision. For example, physical, mental, and intellectual abilities have no clinical definitions, and their levels can merely be estimated for human subjects by their performances on tasks and tests constructed for the specific purpose. Such instruments are bound to be imperfect because they cannot capture the entire domain, are contaminated by context not relevant to the domain (such as the need to understand instructions in a particular language), and rely on the motivation of the subject, which can be maintained for an extended period of time only in some unusual circumstances or by providing incentives. In some settings, the values of the latent variable could be established with precision, but it would be practical only if extensive resources (funding, time, expertise, equipment, subjects' goodwill, etc.) were available. For example, the outcome of an invasive surgery might be defined by the extent of the patient's recovery and ability to return to his or her presurgery lifestyle, allowing some time for recuperation. Instead of waiting for several months, a consultant may assess the patient a few days after the surgery. Although such an assessment is fallible, it may be preferred to a more exact but greatly delayed assessment.

By measurement error, we understand the deviation of a manifest variable X from its underlying latent variable U. The deviation need not be "linear," $X - U$; it can be any function $e(X,U)$ such that $e(X,U) = 0$ if and only if $X = U$ and for each fixed value of U, $e(X,U)$ is an increasing function of X. The value of a manifest variable can be regarded as an estimate of the corresponding value of the latent variable. In our liberal definition of a manifest variable, any variable qualifies as an (imperfect) substitute for a given latent variable. We define criteria by which alternative manifest variables can be compared; such comparisons are meaningful only by reference to the same latent variable. One such criterion is the mean squared error of measurement (MSEm), defined as $\mathrm{E}\left\{(X-U)^2\right\}$ or, more generally, as $\mathrm{E}\left[f\{e(X,U)\}\right]$, where f is an even function, satisfying the condition $f(y) = f(-y)$ for all y, increasing for $y > 0$ and such that $f(0) = 0$. Small MSEm is preferred.

Another criterion states that the manifest variable is not contaminated by any of a given set of auxiliary (background) variables $\mathbf{Z}$. That is, the conditional distribution of X given U and $\mathbf{Z}$, denoted by $(X \mid U, \mathbf{Z})$, coincides with the conditional distribution $(X \mid U)$. We refer to this property as *impartiality* (of X for U with respect to $\mathbf{Z}$). We motivate it by an example from educational testing related to *differential item functioning* (DIF). A highly desirable property of an educational test is that it imparts no advantage—is *fair*—to any of the subpopulations defined by one or several categorical variables $\mathbf{Z}$ (sex, race, socioeconomic category, etc.); that is, it has no DIF. Thus, for the examinees with the same ability $U = u$, the conditional distributions of the test scores X should be the same for the strata defined by the categories of a background variable in $\mathbf{Z}$. Although this motivation has an obvious appeal, its drawback is that it is absolute—the definition is not accompanied by a measure of departure from impartiality. The two criteria, MSEm and impartiality, represent distinct characteristics; it is easy to construct manifest variables that have small MSEms but that are partial (i.e., not impartial), as well as variables that have large MSEms but are impartial.

In some settings, we need not pursue the recovery of the value of U and would be satisfied with a manifest variable X highly correlated with U. This is particularly practical when U is defined only as a class of equivalence of variables that are related by increasing linear transformations. Further generality is gained by defining such a class of equivalence by a family of smooth increasing functions. For example, scholastic aptitude does not have an unambiguous definition, but we are in general agreement about what we regard as higher aptitude. A test score as a manifest version of the aptitude remains equally valid (or invalid) when linearly transformed, so long as the transformation used is increasing.

Throughout, we are concerned with making inferences using manifest variables. That is, if the values of the latent variables $\mathbf{U}$ were available, we would have evaluated the statistic $g(\mathbf{U})$; this could be an estimate, a confidence limit, the outcome of a hypothesis test, or the like. We say that we can ignore the measurement error if the distributions of $g(\mathbf{U})$ and $g(\mathbf{X})$, the manifest version of $g(\mathbf{U})$, coincide. A weaker version of this condition (weak ignorability) is that $g(\mathbf{X})$ and $g(\mathbf{U})$ have identical expectations. This can be further weakened by allowing some adjustments of $g(\mathbf{X})$—that is, if there is a statistic $g^*(\mathbf{X})$ that is a good replacement (e.g., weakly ignorable) for $g(\mathbf{U})$.

Estimators are usually accompanied by their (estimated) standard errors or other (estimated) measures of their quality. We can reasonably expect that $\mathrm{MSE}\{g(\mathbf{X}); \theta\} > \mathrm{MSE}\{g(\mathbf{U}); \theta\}$ for the two estimators of a parameter θ; here, $\mathrm{MSE}(\hat{\theta}; \theta)$ stands for the mean squared error of an estimator $\hat{\theta}$ in estimating the parameter θ. Thus, a secondary task is to estimate $\mathrm{MSE}\{g(\mathbf{X}); \theta\}$, preferably by an adjustment of the estimator of $\mathrm{MSE}\{g(\mathbf{U}); \theta\}$. Formally, let $h(\mathbf{U})$ be an unbiased estimator of $\mathrm{MSE}\{g(\mathbf{U}); \theta\}$. Then, $h(\mathbf{X})$ is likely to underestimate $\mathrm{MSE}\{g(\mathbf{X}); \theta\}$, because it would have been unbiased had $\mathbf{X}$ been the values of the latent variables.

In a seminal paper, Prentice (1989) proved that impartiality is the necessary and sufficient condition (with an unimportant qualification) for ignorability of a null-hypothesis test in the setting of a clinical trial for comparing two randomized treatments. This result has been inappropriately extrapolated to estimators; Begg and Leung (2000) and Baker, Izmirlian, and Kipsnis (2005) highlight this misunderstanding and discuss it in detail.

The study of measurement processes has a long history in most areas of statistical applications. Much of the terminology in current use can be traced to applications in the physical sciences, where the exact value of a quantity is a realistic goal, so that any deviation from it is rightly regarded as an *error* (see Airy, 1861, for an early example). In the behavioral sciences, concerned with measurement of human attributes, such as abilities; skills; attitudes; and states of economic, mental, and other aspects of well-being or deficiency, it is more appropriate to refer to *inconsistency*, uncertainty, or *deviation* (from a long-term trend), to reflect the human idiosyncracies and short-term inconsequential changes that result from everyday influences and distractions. In the setting of an experimental measurement, such changes cannot be undone or separated from the stable underlying quantities, even when the instruments applied are perfect. Early references to measurement issues in the behavioral sciences include Gulliksen (1950) and Cronbach, Gleser,

Nanda, and Rajaratnam (1972). The latter text introduced several quantitative characteristics of the measurement process, such as the Cronbach α coefficient, outlined their uses, and derived their estimators. It highlighted, in various forms, the role of replication in quantifying the inconsistency and its potential to reduce it. The strength in this aspect is not matched by prescriptions for how to make inferences when some or all the variables involved in the analysis are measured inconsistently. The only prescription, not always practicable, is to have measurement instruments sufficiently long, involving replication when feasible, so that the inconsistency could be ignored.

A particularly strong motivating force for developments has been the measurement of abilities related to education and its outcomes (Lord & Novick, 1968). Here, several sources of uncertainty are compounded, making the measurement (assessment) particularly challenging. First, a subject can be assessed (by an educational test) for a particular purpose only once; replication is not feasible. Second, the domain of the test has to be well represented by the items (questions) in the test. Third, the issue of deviation of the performance on the day from the (longer term and stable) ability has to be addressed; the former is observed, whereas the latter is desired, especially when assessing the potential of a subject for an engagement in the future (as an employee, student, member of a professional organization, etc.). And finally, the artificial setting of the test, with its rules of no conferring, no aids, time limits, and format that facilitates easy and unambiguous scoring, introduces further distortions. In contrast to Cronbach et al. (1972), the focus of *item response theory* (Lord, 1968) has been on assessment—making inferences about subjects' abilities and properties of the test items.

Fuller (1987) contains a comprehensive account of methods for analysis with normally distributed (continuous) variables subject to measurement error up to its publication. Carroll, Ruppert, and Stefanski (1995) focus on computationally intensive methods for nonlinear models and, in particular, on the method called SIMEX, outlined in the section Simulation-Extrapolation. Measurement error is closely related to structural equation modeling (Marcoulides & Schumacher, 2001).

The next section defines the measurement process and analyzes a well-known example, which leads to the section Connection to Missing Data Methods, in which measurement error is described as a problem involving missing data. The section Impartiality and Regression discusses impartiality, a key property of manifest variables, and shows that it is not sufficient for straightforward use of manifest variables in place of their latent counterparts. In the section Other Methods and Processes, we review an alternative approach to dealing with measurement error based on simulations. The section Design Issues outlines some design issues, focusing on the split of the resources available for the study into replication of the measurement process and observation (indirectly) of the studied data-generating process. Two applications (case studies) are discussed in the applications section. The chapter is concluded by a discussion.

Measurement Process

The measurement process is defined as the distortion (alteration) of U resulting in X. We regard this distortion as a *nuisance*, in that if it were absent, the inferential goals related to the latent variable U would be easier to accomplish. All the information about the measurement process is contained in the joint distribution (U,X). It may be more convenient to consider the class of conditional distributions $(X\,|\,U = u)$ for all possible values u of U (i.e., for the *support* of U), because they describe the distortion directly. In contrast, the conditional distribution $(U\,|\,X = x)$ is related to inference about individual values of U. The two conditional distributions are connected by the Bayes theorem, establishing that properties of the measurement process have an effect on the information about the latent variable and, through it, on inferences in general.

The simplest nontrivial setting involves bivariate normally distributed (X, U), such that

$$X = U + \varepsilon, \qquad (15.1)$$

with ε centered and independent of U. For this model,

$$\begin{pmatrix} U \\ X \end{pmatrix} \sim \mathcal{N}\left\{ \begin{pmatrix} \mu \\ \mu \end{pmatrix}, \begin{pmatrix} \sigma_{\mathrm{u}}^2 & \sigma_{\mathrm{u}}^2 \\ \sigma_{\mathrm{u}}^2 & \sigma_{\mathrm{u}}^2 + \sigma_{\mathrm{e}}^2 \end{pmatrix} \right\},$$

where $\sigma_e^2 = \text{var}(\varepsilon)$ and $\sigma_u^2 = \text{var}(U)$. The conditional distribution $(X \mid U = u)$ is also normal, $\mathcal{N}(u, \sigma_e^2)$. Furthermore,

$$(U|X=x) \sim \mathcal{N}\left\{\mu + \frac{\sigma_u^2}{\sigma_e^2+\sigma_u^2}(x-\mu), \frac{\sigma_e^2\sigma_u^2}{\sigma_e^2+\sigma_u^2}\right\}.$$

As $\text{E}(U) = \text{E}(X)$, the sample mean of X, $\bar{x}$, is weakly ignorable for (has the same expectation as) its latent counterpart $\bar{u}$ in estimating μ. However, direct substitution of X for U is not appropriate for most other common estimators. The most widely studied example is the simple regression of an outcome variable on a latent variable U. If the values of U were observed, as $\mathbf{u}$, the slope of a variable Y on U would be estimated by

$$\hat{\beta}_u = \frac{\mathbf{y}^\top(\mathbf{u}-\bar{u}\mathbf{1})}{(\mathbf{u}-\bar{u}\mathbf{1})^\top(\mathbf{u}-\bar{u}\mathbf{1})}, \qquad (15.2)$$

where $\bar{u}$ is the sample mean of $\mathbf{u}$, $\bar{y}$ is the mean of the observed values $\mathbf{y}$ of Y, and $\mathbf{1}$ is the (column) vector of ones of length implied by the context. Regarding $\mathbf{u}$ and $\mathbf{y}$ as fixed, but the observed values $\mathbf{x}$ of X as random, the manifest version of $\hat{\beta}$,

$$\hat{\beta}_x = \frac{\mathbf{y}^\top(\mathbf{x}-\bar{x}\mathbf{1})}{(\mathbf{x}-\bar{x}\mathbf{1})^\top(\mathbf{x}-\bar{x}\mathbf{1})},$$

has the numerator with the same expectation as in (15.2),

$$\text{E}\left\{\mathbf{y}^\top(\mathbf{x}-\bar{x}\mathbf{1}) \mid \mathbf{u},\mathbf{y})\right\} = \mathbf{y}^\top(\mathbf{u}-\bar{u}\mathbf{1}),$$

but the expectations of the two denominators differ:

$$\text{E}\left\{(\mathbf{x}-\bar{x}\mathbf{1})^\top(\mathbf{x}-\bar{x}\mathbf{1}) \mid \mathbf{u},\mathbf{y}\right\}$$
$$= (\mathbf{u}-\bar{u}\mathbf{1})^\top(\mathbf{u}-\bar{u}\mathbf{1}) + (n-1)\sigma_e^2,$$

where n is the sample size. The (positive) denominator is overestimated, and therefore the regression slope is estimated with a bias toward 0. This phenomenon is referred to as *attenuation*. Figure 15.1 gives an illustration based on artificially generated data. Here, $\sigma_u^2 = 2.1$, $\sigma_e^2 = 2.25$, and the residual variance in the regression of Y on U is 1.0. The regression slope β_u is equal to 0.6; its ordinary least squares (OLS) estimator with the latent values $\mathbf{u}$ is unbiased and has sampling variance $\text{var}\{\hat{\beta}_u(\mathbf{u})\} = 0.069^2$, whereas the expectation of the OLS estimator with $\mathbf{x}$ in place of $\mathbf{u}$ is only $\hat{\beta}_x = 0.28$, with conditional sampling variance (given $\mathbf{x}$) equal to $\text{var}\{\hat{\beta}_x(\mathbf{x})\} = 0.048^2$. The variance reduction (compared with 0.069^2) is more than offset by the substantial bias.

The obvious remedy for attenuation is to adjust the centered sum of squares of the xs by $(n-1)\hat{\sigma}_e^2$, using an unbiased estimator of σ_e^2; it is referred to as correcting for attenuation. This highlights the need for collecting information about the measurement process. In particular, the variance σ_e^2 cannot be estimated from $\mathbf{x}$. A practical proposition is to observe the values of X for some units two or more times so that the realizations of ε in (15.1) are independent even within a unit.

We note in passing that correction for attenuation does not yield an unbiased estimator of the slope β_u because even though the numerator and denominator are estimated without bias, the ratio of the estimators is not unbiased for the ratio of their respective targets (underlying quantities). However, this is a nontrivial issue only in small samples. In very small samples, the estimate of the denominator in (15.2) could even be negative, even though its expectation is positive.

Connection to Missing Data Methods

Correction for attenuation can be interpreted as an application of the EM algorithm (Dempster, Laird, & Rubin, 1977). In the standard terminology for incomplete data, the values of the latent, manifest, and outcome variables—$(\mathbf{u},\mathbf{x},\mathbf{y})$—are regarded as the complete data, $(\mathbf{x},\mathbf{y})$ as the incomplete (recorded) data, and $\mathbf{u}$ as the missing data. The complete-data analysis is defined as the analysis we would apply with the complete data if it were available. (We may refer to it here as the latent-values analysis.) The corresponding likelihood is given by the conditional distribution of $\mathbf{y}$ given $\mathbf{u}$. In the simple regression discussed in the previous section, it involves the missing data only through a set of sufficient statistics, comprising its sum of squares, $\mathbf{u}^\top\mathbf{u}$, and the sums of its cross products with the other variables, $\mathbf{u}^\top\mathbf{y}$ and $\mathbf{u}^\top\mathbf{1}$. These statistics are selected so that the log-likelihood depends on them linearly.

In the EM algorithm, the values of these sufficient statistics are estimated by their conditional expectations given model parameters (including

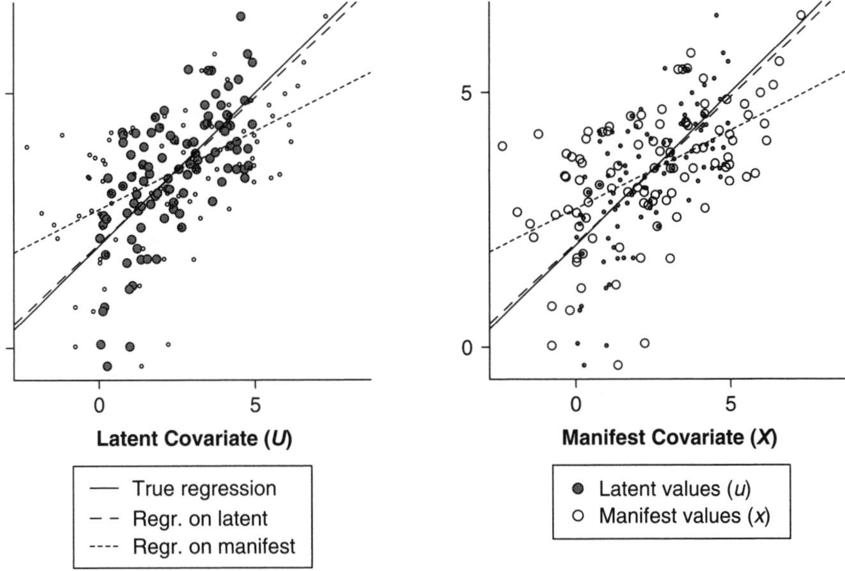

Figure 15.1 Example of attenuation in ordinary regression.

NOTE: In the left-hand panel the latent values (and the regression based on them) and in the right-hand panel the manifest values are highlighted.

σ_e^2) and the recorded (incomplete) data **y** and **x**. Then, the complete-data analysis is applied, with the sufficient statistics replaced by their estimates. These two steps, estimation (E) and likelihood maximization (M), form an iteration, and the iterations have to be executed in general several times until convergence is achieved. This particular EM algorithm, however, requires only one iteration.

The EM algorithm yields the maximum likelihood (ML) estimators under some mild regularity conditions. Inasmuch as ML is appropriate, the EM algorithm indicates that separate optimal estimation of each missing item is not a good strategy, except in the very unusual setting when the log-likelihood is a linear function of the missing values. For example, in our setting of normally distributed outcomes, it is a quadratic function.

The EM algorithm can be applied whenever the log-likelihood depends on the missing data **u** only through a short list of sufficient statistics. When the EM algorithm is too difficult to implement, multiple imputation (MI) (Rubin, 1996, 2002) is a practical alternative. In MI, a complete-data estimator $\hat{\theta}(\mathbf{u})$ is considered, together with a model for how **u** is related to the incomplete data. A small number of independent completions $\mathbf{u}^{(m)}$, $m = 1, \ldots, M$, are generated according to this model; the complete-data estimator $\hat{\theta}$ is applied to each completion, yielding so-called completed-data estimates $\hat{\theta}^{(m)} = \hat{\theta}\left(\mathbf{u}^{(m)}, \mathbf{y}\right)$; and the MI estimator is defined as the average of these M estimates:

$$\hat{\theta}_{\mathrm{MI}} = \frac{1}{M} \sum_{m=1}^{M} \hat{\theta}^{(m)}.$$

If the complete-data estimator is accompanied by an unbiased estimator $\hat{s}^2(\mathbf{u})$ of its sampling variance—that is, $\mathrm{E}\left\{\hat{s}^2(\mathbf{u})\right\} = \mathrm{var}\{\hat{\theta}(\mathbf{u})\}$, then the variance of the MI estimator $\hat{\theta}_{\mathrm{MI}}$ is estimated as

$$\begin{aligned} \hat{s}^2_{\mathrm{MI}} &= \frac{1}{M} \sum_{m=1}^{M} \hat{s}^2\left(\mathbf{u}^{(m)}\right) \\ &\quad + \frac{M+1}{M(M-1)} \sum_{m=1}^{M} \left(\hat{\theta}^{(m)} - \hat{\theta}_{\mathrm{MI}}\right)^2 \\ &= \widehat{W} + \left(1 + \frac{1}{M}\right) \widehat{B}, \end{aligned}$$

with implicitly defined $\widehat{W}$ and $\widehat{B}$. They are unbiased estimators of the complete-data variance

$s^2(\mathbf{u})$ and of the inflation of the variance due to missing data, respectively; B/M can be interpreted as the inflation due to using only M sets of completions. See Rubin (2002) for theoretical background and Longford (2005) for applications.

The values generated for a single completion are called a set of *plausible values*. They have to be generated in such a way as to reflect our uncertainty about the values that they are replacing. This usually involves two contributions to uncertainty. The first is about the model parameters that link the missing data to the incomplete data; in our case, it is about σ_e^2. For each completion, a plausible value has to be drawn from the (estimated) sampling distribution of $\hat{\sigma}_e^2$, and these values have to be independent across the completions. Next, for a given set of plausible values $\tilde{\sigma}_u^2$, $\tilde{\sigma}_e^2$, and $\tilde{\mu}$, a vector $\mathbf{u}^{(m)}$ is drawn from the corresponding conditional distribution given $\mathbf{x}$:

$$(\mathbf{u}|\mathbf{x}) \sim \mathcal{N}\left\{\mu\mathbf{1} + \frac{\sigma_u^2}{\sigma_u^2+\sigma_e^2}(\mathbf{x}-\mu\mathbf{1}), \frac{\sigma_e^2\sigma_x^2}{\sigma_x^2+\sigma_e^2}\mathbf{I}\right\}, \tag{15.3}$$

with each parameter replaced by its plausible value ($\mathbf{I}$ denotes the identity matrix). The plausible values are themselves drawn from their approximate (joint) sampling distribution. In our setting, the sampling distributions of $\hat{\sigma}_u^2$, $\hat{\sigma}_e^2$, and $\hat{\mu}$ are mutually independent, so this task reduces to independent draws from three univariate distributions. For example, if $r\hat{\sigma}_e^2/\sigma_e^2 \sim \chi_r^2$ for some $r > 0$, then a plausible value $\tilde{\sigma}_e^2$ is set to $r\hat{\sigma}_e^2/\xi^2$, where ξ^2 is a random draw from χ_r^2. The sampling distribution of $\hat{\mu}$ depends on σ_u^2 and σ_e^2, $\hat{\mu} \sim \mathcal{N}\{\mu, (\sigma_u^2+\sigma_e^2)/n\}$, and so the plausible values for these variances are used in drawing a plausible value of $\tilde{\mu}$:

$$(\tilde{\mu}\,|\,\hat{\mu}, \tilde{\sigma}_u^2, \tilde{\sigma}_e^2) \sim \mathcal{N}\left\{\hat{\mu}, \frac{\tilde{\sigma}_u^2+\tilde{\sigma}_e^2}{n}\right\}.$$

Finally, a plausible vector $\mathbf{u}^{(m)}$ is drawn at random from its plausible joint distribution derived from (15.3).

In more complicated settings, the sampling distributions are more involved, but the implementation of MI is not any more difficult, except for drawing samples from less common distributions. An undisputed advantage of MI is that the analysis uses the estimators that would have been appropriate for the complete data and often were constructed with the intention to apply them to the complete data or to a completed data set. These estimators have to be applied several times, but that is hardly a drawback, since this is straightforward to program.

The assumptions underlying MI are that the complete-data estimator $\hat{\theta}(\mathbf{u})$ is unbiased and efficient, its sampling variance s^2 is estimated without bias and with sampling variance that is of lower order of magnitude than s^4, and the model for missing values is correctly specified. Furthermore, the sets of plausible values have to be generated *properly*— that is, with variation and a correlation structure that reflects our uncertainty about the missing values. The latter condition may appear to be a tall order in many settings, although not in many problems involving measurement error where the measurement process can be observed (in replications). However, single-imputation procedures can be related to MI procedures with $M = 1$ and very poor representation of the uncertainty about the missing values. Therefore, MI is definitely an improvement over them.

Note that the M sets of plausible values have to be generated only once, and then they can be used in several analyses, irrespective of their type or complexity. The number of sets, M, does not have to be very large; it depends on the relative sizes of complete-data sampling variance W and the between-imputation variance B. These quantities can only be estimated and depend on the target of estimation. Greater M improves the precision of estimating W and B, but an appropriate setting of M can be justified only post hoc, when estimates of W and B become available. Erring on the side of greater M does no harm, except for having to deal with a greater number of completions (data sets). The returns in terms of greater precision diminish with increasing M.

An analyst provided with the M completions requires no expertise in methods for missing data, except for the formulae for combining the completed-data estimators $\hat{\theta}^{(m)}$ and $\hat{s}^2(\mathbf{u}^{(m)})$. The M completions can be supplied as separate data sets. When only a few variables are subject to completion, a more practical option may be a single file with the completions as its separate columns. The program to generate a completion can be provided to the analyst directly, in the form of a black box, with the instruction to execute it before every completed-data analysis.

Misclassification and MI

We use the term *misclassification* for measurement error with categorical variables when both X and U are categorical. In this section, we discuss measurement processes and imputation for such variables.

The measurement process that results in a particular manifest variable is characterized by a *transition matrix* $\mathbf{T}$ of the conditional probabilities $\mathrm{P}(X = k \,|\, U = h)$. An example of a transition matrix is given in Table 15.1. When X and U have the same categories, $\mathbf{T}$ is a square matrix. It need not be symmetric, and its diagonal need not be constant. A "good" measurement process has high probabilities on the diagonal of $\mathbf{T}$, and when the categories are ordinal, the probabilities decline (rapidly) with the distance $|k - h|$, as in Table 15.1. We assume that the number of categories of U is known. Of course, the properties of the measurement process are highly contingent on the definition of U.

Table 15.1 Example of a Transition Matrix

Latent (U)	*Manifest (X)*			
	1	2	3	4
1	0.82	0.11	0.05	0.02
2	0.09	0.77	0.09	0.05
3	0.04	0.08	0.81	0.07
4	0.01	0.04	0.11	0.84

The manifest and latent variables need not have the same categories. For example, the manifest variable may attain the value 3.5, even when the latent variable attains only integer values. It would indicate uncertainty as to whether $U = 3$ or $U = 4$, although even $\mathrm{P}(U = 2 \,|\, X = 3.5)$ may be positive.

We describe the MI procedure for imputing values of the latent variable in the simplified setting of impartiality, in which auxiliary variables have no influence on the conditional probabilities in $\mathbf{T}$; that is,

$$\mathrm{P}(X = k \,|\, U = h, \mathbf{Z} = \mathbf{z}) = \mathrm{P}(X = k \,|\, U = h)\,.$$

According to the Bayes theorem,

$$\mathrm{P}(U = h \,|\, X = k) = \frac{\mathrm{P}(X = k \,|\, U = h)\,\mathrm{P}(U = h)}{\mathrm{P}(X = k)}\,,$$

and so, apart from $\mathbf{T}$, we require the marginal distributions of U and X. These distributions are connected by the identity $\mathbf{p}_{\mathrm{x}} = \mathbf{p}_{\mathrm{u}}\mathbf{T}$, where $\mathbf{p}_{\mathrm{u}}$ and $\mathbf{p}_{\mathrm{x}}$ are the respective (row) vectors of marginal probabilities for U and X. We observe $\mathbf{p}_{\mathrm{x}}$, so $\mathbf{p}_{\mathrm{u}}$ can be recovered by solving the system of linear equations $\mathbf{p}_{\mathrm{u}} = \mathbf{p}_{\mathrm{x}}\mathbf{T}^{-1}$, assuming that $\mathbf{T}$ is nonsingular.

As in the continuous case, information about the measurement process can be gathered by replications—applying the process independently several times to each of a sample of subjects. Of course, a better alternative is to observe both U and X on a subsample of subjects, but this is often infeasible or unaffordable.

For each subject, a plausible value of U is drawn from a plausible (multinomial) conditional distribution of U given $X = k$, and the plausible distribution is drawn using the estimated joint distribution of the parameters it involves. For an example, see the section Applications. We generate M alternative completions of the data set, apply the complete-data method to each of them, and average the results as described in the section Connection to Missing Data Methods.

Suppose a conditional distribution $\mathrm{P}(U = h \,|\, X = k)$, with k fixed, is estimated by the vector $\hat{\mathbf{p}}_{\cdot k}$, with sampling variance matrix $\mathbf{S}_k = \mathrm{var}(\hat{\mathbf{p}}_{\cdot k})$. Then, a plausible conditional distribution (vector of probabilities $\mathbf{p}_{\cdot k}^{(m)}$) is generated by a draw from the estimated (approximate) sampling distribution $\mathcal{N}(\hat{\mathbf{p}}_{\cdot k}, \hat{\mathbf{S}}_k)$. For each subject with $X = k$, a plausible latent value is drawn independently from this plausible distribution. An example is discussed in the section Applications.

The method described here is based on a complete-data analysis, which has to be well identified and efficient. That is, deficiencies of the complete-data analysis cannot be undone by imprecise measurement or MI. Furthermore, (nearly) unbiased estimators of the parameters involved in the description of the measurement process have to be available, together with estimators of their sampling variances. These are usually derived from replications of the process.

Impartiality and Regression

Although MI offers a near-universal recipe for dealing with measurement error, it is instructive to explore the consequences of replacing a latent variable by its manifest version. Here, we study this issue in the context of ordinary regression and comparisons of within-group probabilities, when the manifest variable is impartial; that is, $(X\,|\,U,\mathbf{Z}) \sim (X\,|\,U)$, where $\mathbf{Z}$ is a column vector. We show that this condition is far from sufficient for the replacement of U by X to be weakly ignorable.

We assume first that the variables involved have a joint multivariate normal distribution. Thus, for a given set of auxiliary variables $\mathbf{Z}$, we explore how close $\mathrm{E}(Y\,|\,X)$ is to $\mathrm{E}(Y\,|\,U)$. Let the respective expectations of U, X, and $\mathbf{Z}$ be μ_u, μ_x, and $\boldsymbol{\mu}_z$ and their variance matrix be

$$\mathrm{var}\begin{pmatrix} U \\ X \\ \mathbf{Z} \end{pmatrix} = \begin{pmatrix} \sigma_u^2 & \sigma_{ux} & \boldsymbol{\sigma}_{uz} \\ \sigma_{xu} & \sigma_x^2 & \boldsymbol{\sigma}_{xz} \\ \boldsymbol{\sigma}_{uz}^\top & \boldsymbol{\sigma}_{xz}^\top & \boldsymbol{\Sigma}_z \end{pmatrix}.$$

The conditional expectations of U given X and $(X,\mathbf{Z})$ are

$$\mathrm{E}(U\,|\,X=x) = \mu_u + \frac{\sigma_{ux}}{\sigma_x^2}(x-\mu_x)$$

$$\mathrm{E}(U\,|\,X=x,\mathbf{Z}=\mathbf{z})$$

$$= \mu_u + (\sigma_{ux}\;\boldsymbol{\sigma}_{uz})\begin{pmatrix} \sigma_x^2 & \boldsymbol{\sigma}_{xz} \\ \boldsymbol{\sigma}_{zx} & \boldsymbol{\Sigma}_z \end{pmatrix}^{-1}\begin{pmatrix} x-\mu_x \\ \mathbf{z}-\boldsymbol{\mu}_z \end{pmatrix}. \qquad (15.4)$$

It can be shown that impartiality is equivalent to the absence of the partial (or conditional) correlation of X and $\mathbf{Z}$ given the value of U; that is, $\boldsymbol{\sigma}_{xz} = \boldsymbol{\sigma}_{uz}\sigma_{xu}/\sigma_u^2$ or $\boldsymbol{\rho}_{xz} = \rho_{xu}\boldsymbol{\rho}_{uz}$ for the corresponding correlations. Under normality, this partial correlation does not depend on the value of U in the condition.

We compare the regression slopes in $\mathrm{E}(U\,|\,\mathbf{Z})$ and $\mathrm{E}(X\,|\,\mathbf{Z})$. We assume that $\boldsymbol{\Sigma}_z$ is nonsingular. These regression slopes are equal to $\mathrm{cov}(U,\mathbf{Z})\{\mathrm{var}(\mathrm{Z})\}^{-1} = \boldsymbol{\sigma}_{uz}\boldsymbol{\Sigma}_z^{-1}$ and $\boldsymbol{\sigma}_{xz}\boldsymbol{\Sigma}_z^{-1}$, respectively, and so they coincide when $\boldsymbol{\sigma}_{xz} = \boldsymbol{\sigma}_{uz}$. Owing to impartiality, this condition is equivalent to $\sigma_{xu} = \sigma_u^2$, or $\mathrm{cov}(U, X-U) = 0$. Thus, replacement of U by a manifest variable impartial with respect to the regressors is weakly ignorable only when X differs from U by white noise: $X = U + \varepsilon$, where ε is independent of both U and Z. Of course, even in this setting, the measurement error brings about an inflation of the residual variance and, consequently, inflation of the sampling variance of the OLS estimator of the regression slope.

Next, we compare the regression slopes in $\mathrm{E}(Y\,|\,U)$ and $\mathrm{E}(Y\,|\,X)$, assuming that X is impartial for Z with respect to Y. The regression slopes coincide when $\sigma_{uz}/\sigma_u^2 = \sigma_{xz}/\sigma_x^2$, and this condition, together with impartiality, $\sigma_{xz} = \sigma_{xu}\sigma_{uz}/\sigma_u^2$, yields the condition $\sigma_x^2 = \sigma_{xu}$. This is the same condition as for replacing U with X as the outcome variable but with the roles of X and U interchanged. Therefore, the replacement of the covariate U with an impartial X is appropiate only when U is a noisy version of X; $U = X + \varepsilon$ with ε independent of both X and the outcome Y. This is a rather unusual condition, implying that $\mathrm{var}(X) < \mathrm{var}(U)$, given that X is meant to be a version of U contaminated with error.

These two examples demonstrate that the appropriateness of the replacement of a latent variable by a manifest one depends, among other conditions, on the role of the latent variable in the complete-data analysis. We reinforce this message by the corresponding examples with categorical variables, in which we compare the conditional probabilities $\mathrm{P}(U\,|\,\mathbf{Z})$ and $\mathrm{P}(X\,|\,\mathbf{Z})$.

It suffices to explore the setting in which the manifest and latent variables are binary and there is a single auxiliary variable Z that is also binary. We compare the differences $\mathrm{P}(U=1\,|\,Z=1) - \mathrm{P}(U=1\,|\,Z=0)$ and $\mathrm{P}(X=1\,|\,Z=1) - \mathrm{P}(X=1\,|\,Z=0)$, to assess the impact of replacing U with X when making inferences about the influence of the variable Z. We assume impartiality; that is,

$$\mathrm{P}(X=x\,|\,U=u, Z=z) = \mathrm{P}(X=x\,|\,U=u)$$

for all combinations of values of U, X, and Z. Using this identity we obtain

$$\begin{aligned} &\mathrm{P}(X=1\,|\,Z=1) \\ &\quad= \mathrm{P}(X=1\,|\,U=1)\,\mathrm{P}(U=1\,|\,Z=1) \\ &\qquad+ \mathrm{P}(X=1\,|\,U=0)\,\mathrm{P}(U=0\,|\,Z=1) \\ &\quad= \mathrm{P}(X=1\,|\,U=0) \\ &\qquad+ \mathrm{P}(U=1\,|\,Z=1) \\ &\qquad\times\{\mathrm{P}(X=1\,|\,U=1) - \mathrm{P}(X=1\,|\,U=0)\}. \end{aligned}$$

Hence,

$$\begin{aligned} &\mathrm{P}(X=1\,|\,Z=1)-\mathrm{P}(X=1\,|\,Z=0)\\ &\quad=\{\mathrm{P}(X=1\,|\,U=1)-\mathrm{P}(X=1\,|\,U=0)\}\\ &\qquad\times\{\mathrm{P}(U=1\,|\,Z=1)-\mathrm{P}(U=1\,|\,Z=0)\}\\ &\quad\leqslant \mathrm{P}(U=1\,|\,Z=1)-\mathrm{P}(U=1\,|\,Z=0), \end{aligned}$$

with equality only when either U and Z are independent or $\mathrm{P}(U=X)=1$. Therefore, the substitution of U by an impartial X is appropriate (weakly ignorable) only in trivial cases—when the auxiliary information is irrelevant (independence) or when the measurement process is perfect ($X=U$).

The implications of using a manifest conditioning variable are explored similarly, by comparing the manifest and latent contrasts $\Delta_{\mathrm{x}} = \mathrm{P}(Z=1\,|\,X=1)-\mathrm{P}(Z=1\,|\,X=0)$ and $\Delta_{\mathrm{u}} = \mathrm{P}(Z=1\,|\,U=1)-\mathrm{P}(Z=1\,|\,U=0)$. First, for $k=0,1$,

$$\begin{aligned} &\mathrm{P}(Z=1\,|\,X=k)\\ &\quad=\mathrm{P}(X=k\,|\,Z=1)\,\frac{\mathrm{P}(Z=1)}{\mathrm{P}(X=k)}\\ &\quad=\mathrm{P}(Z=1)\sum_{h=0}^{1}\frac{\mathrm{P}(X=k\,|\,U=h)}{\mathrm{P}(X=k)}\,\mathrm{P}(U=h\,|\,Z=1)\\ &\quad=\mathrm{P}(Z=1)\sum_{h=0}^{1}\mathrm{P}(U=h\,|\,X=k)\,\frac{\mathrm{P}(U=h\,|\,Z=1)}{\mathrm{P}(U=h)}\\ &\quad=\sum_{h=0}^{1}\mathrm{P}(U=h\,|\,X=k)\,\mathrm{P}(Z=1\,|\,U=h). \end{aligned}$$

Hence,

$$\begin{aligned} \Delta_{\mathrm{x}}-\Delta_{\mathrm{u}} &= \mathrm{P}(Z=1\,|\,U=1)\\ &\quad\times\{\mathrm{P}(U=1\,|\,X=1)-P(U=1\,|\,X=0)-1\}\\ &\quad+\mathrm{P}(Z=1\,|\,U=0)\\ &\quad\times\{\mathrm{P}(U=0\,|\,X=1)-P(U=0\,|\,X=0)+1\}\\ &= -\Delta_{\mathrm{u}}\{\mathrm{P}(U=0\,|\,X=1)+\mathrm{P}(U=1\,|\,X=0)\}. \end{aligned}$$

Therefore, replacing U with X is appropriate only when either U and Z are independent ($\Delta_{\mathrm{u}}=0$) or the classification is perfect—$\mathrm{P}(U=0\,|\,X=1)=\mathrm{P}(U=1\,|\,X=0)=0$. Both conditions correspond to trivial cases. The two examples with categorical variables confirm that impartiality does not imply weak ignorability even for some simple inferences.

OTHER METHODS AND PROCESSES

This section reviews other methods for dealing with manifest variables and discusses a common class of measurement processes that include rounding and coding into ordinal categories.

Simulation-Extrapolation

An alternative to MI is based on the following scheme, due to Cook and Stefanski (1994) and Carroll et al. (1995). Suppose a manifest variable can be altered to increase its measurement error with respect to the original latent variable. For example, if $X=U+\varepsilon$ and $\varepsilon\sim\mathcal{N}(0,\sigma_{\mathrm{e}}^2)$, the measurement-error variance can be increased by Δ^2 by adding $\delta\sim\mathcal{N}\left(0,\Delta^2\right)$, independent of ε, to X. Suppose we would evaluate $\hat\theta(\mathbf{u})$ if the values of the latent variable U were available. We can evaluate $\hat\theta(\mathbf{x})$ and also $\hat\theta(\mathbf{x}_{\Delta^2})$ for $\mathbf{x}_{\Delta^2}=\mathbf{x}+\boldsymbol{\delta}$, where $\boldsymbol{\delta}\sim\mathcal{N}\left(\mathbf{0},\Delta^2\mathbf{I}\right)$ for a range of positive values of Δ^2. In fact, for each $\Delta^2>0$, $\mathbf{x}_{\Delta^2}$ is subject to randomness, and so is $\hat\theta(\mathbf{x}_{\Delta^2})$. We can estimate the conditional expectation of $\hat\theta(\mathbf{x}_{\Delta^2})$ given $\mathbf{x}$ for each conceivable Δ^2. Thus, with sufficient computing power, we can construct $\mathrm{E}_\delta\left\{\hat\theta(\mathbf{x}_{\Delta^2})\right\}$ as a function of Δ^2, with the expectation taken over the additional error $\boldsymbol{\delta}$. The estimate $\hat\theta(\mathbf{u})$ corresponds formally to the setting $\Delta^2=-\sigma_{\mathrm{e}}^2$, and so it can be approximated by extrapolation. The two components of the method, *sim*ulation (of manifest variables with additional measurement error) and *ex*trapolation (to zero measurement-error variance) give rise to its acronym SIMEX.

The extrapolation step is a weakness of the method, because the choice of the functional form for it is crucial. However, it can be informed by simulations from settings similar to that of the analyzed study. The computational intensity of the approach is less of a problem because the computation is repetitive and therefore easy to program. Nevertheless, the choice of the values of Δ^2 at which $\hat\theta_{\Delta^2}$ is evaluated is important.

Figure 15.2 illustrates the method on an example of ordinary regression. This example is instructive because we have an alternative solution, by correcting for attenuation. In the left-hand panel, the estimates of the regression slope

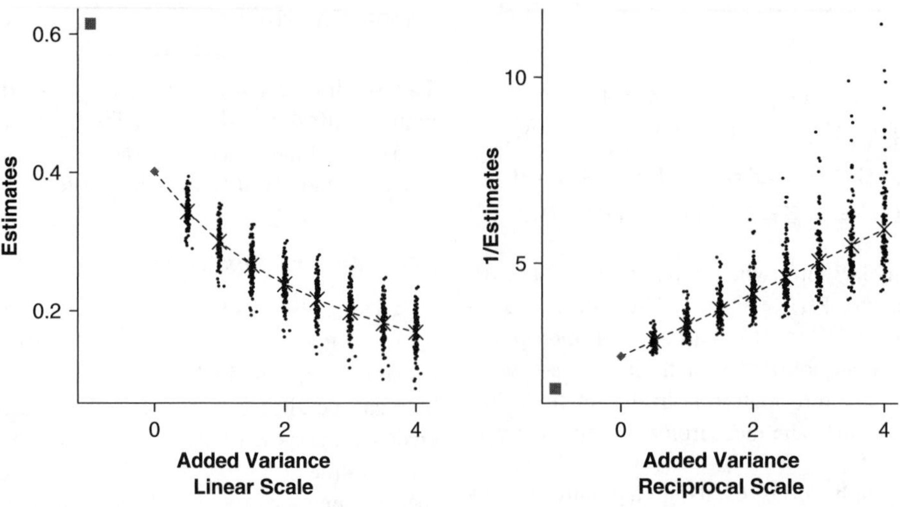

Figure 15.2 Illustration of the simulation-extrapolation method on an ordinary regression.

NOTE: In the left-hand panel the simulated estimates are drawn on the original scale, and in the right-hand panel their reciprocals are drawn.

are plotted, obtained by fitting OLS to the outcomes Y on perturbed values of the (manifest) regressor, $X+\delta$, where $\delta \sim \mathcal{N}(0,\sigma_{\mathrm{a}}^2)$. The added variance σ_{a}^2 is indicated on the horizontal axis. The measurement error variance is $\sigma_{\varepsilon}^2 = 1.0$. For each value of $\sigma_{\mathrm{a}}^2 = 0.5, 1, \ldots, 4$, 100 replicate estimates are generated. A modicum of horizontal random noise (jigging) is added to the points, to distinguish among near-identical values. The OLS fit using X is marked by a dot at $\sigma_{\mathrm{a}}^2 = 0$ (no added variance), and the target, the estimated regression slope on U, is marked by a large square at $\sigma_{\mathrm{a}}^2 = -1$. The means of the estimates within the values of σ_{a}^2 are connected by dashes.

The left-hand panel highlights the nontrivial nature of the task, as the extrapolation is substantial and distinctly nonlinear. However, the task on the reciprocal scale in the right-hand panel is much easier because it involves linear approximation. This can also be confirmed analytically, as the reciprocal of the slope is

$$\frac{1}{\beta} = \frac{\mathrm{var}(U)}{\mathrm{cov}(U,Y)} + \frac{\sigma_{\mathrm{e}}^2 + \sigma_{\mathrm{a}}^2}{\mathrm{cov}(U,Y)},$$

a linear function of σ_{a}^2. Note, however, the difficulties that might arise when β, and with it $\mathrm{cov}(U,Y)$, is close to 0.

Coarsening Processes

Coarsening (Heitjan & Rubin, 1990) is a class of processes that can be regarded as measurement processes. Coarsening is defined by a mapping from a partition of the support of U to the support (set of values) of the (manifest) coarse version X of U. For example, a partitioning of a continuous variable U may be to three intervals, $(-\infty,-2)$, $[-2,3)$, and $[3,+\infty)$, and the corresponding values of X are -5, 0, and 5. Various forms of rounding are other examples of coarsening. Different "rules" (mappings) may apply to distinct subsets of the sample, but the mapping applicable for each subject has to be known with certainty.

Heitjan and Rubin (1990) applied MI in an analysis with a coarse variable and demonstrated by an extensive sensitivity analysis that coarsening is far from ignorable. The principal difficulty is the specification (or estimation) of the conditional distribution $(U \mid X)$. With very crude coarsening (e.g., to X with only a few categories), the distribution of X provides too little information about the distribution of U.

Surveys in which subjects are asked to classify themselves into a category are common examples of coarsening. They define ordinal categories according to income, age, opinion or viewpoint, dietary habit, product preference, and the like. For example, in the Women's Cohort Study (Nur, 2005), the Food Frequency Questionnaire (FFQ) comprises questions with the common introduction

> In the last 12 months, how frequently did you eat the following foods:

and offers 10 ordered response options, ranging from "Never" to "Several times a day." In the planned analyses, inferences are sought about the association of cancer contracted in the years after enrollment in the study with the subject's diet. Information about new cases of cancer is obtained from a national register. The responses to the FFQ items are converted to "typical" quantities that represent the marked category and then converted to nutrients and other components of food, such as vitamins, protein, fat, and carbohydrates. A profound problem with this process is that the conversion is deterministic and the resultant error is ignored in the subsequent analyses. In fact, several sources of measurement error are compounded in this example; first, the responses marked by the subjects (categories) may be error prone or affected by everyday influences, such as perceived desirability of a particular consumption pattern, and also by fatigue in completing a lengthy, mundane questionnaire. The impact of these processes, when ignored in the analysis, is bound to be inflation of the sampling variances of the estimators applied, although bias is likely to be present also.

Design Issues

A key issue in the design of a study in which one or several manifest variables are recorded is how to split the available resources to the tasks of observing X and other relevant variables (outcomes and covariates) and gathering information about the measurement process by replicating it on (some) subjects. In some settings, the latent variable U can be observed directly, enabling us to estimate the measurement-error variance, σ_e^2, directly from the within-subject differences $X - U$. Otherwise, σ_e^2 can be estimated from a pair of replicate measurements $(X^{(1)}, X^{(2)})$ on the same subject, using the identity $\operatorname{var}\left(X^{(1)} - X^{(2)}\right) = 2\sigma_e^2$. Note that independence of these two observations on a subject (conditionally on U) is essential for this identity to hold. Also, unbiasedness of the measurement, $\mathrm{E}(X \mid j) = U_j$ for every subject j is an implied assumption that is frequently very easy to challenge.

Independence of repeated measurements is difficult to ensure when the measurement entails a substantial involvement of the human subject so that he or she might recall details of the measurement process for a considerable time. When the measurements are separated by a lot of time, changes of the values of the latent variable are plausible, and so estimation of σ_e^2 is contaminated by the trend over time. The trend itself can be inferred about, albeit subject to uncertainty, and the variation of U around the trend is confounded with measurement error.

Characteristics of the measurement process are a property of the population, and so care has to be exercised in basing inferences about it on samples in which the population is well represented, preferably by a probability sampling design. The same applies to the substantive inference. A study is on safe ground when the measurement process is replicated on a random subsample of subjects who participate in the study, because then the inferences about the measurement process and the substance of the study refer to the same population. Of course, this is not always feasible, and ignoring other studies in which measurements were replicated might be wasteful. An appropriate perspective weighs the bias of such a data source against the variance reduction that would result by its inclusion in the analysis.

A particularly challenging setting involves a past study in which X and U are observed (the latter at a considerable expense) and a recent study (either conducted or being planned) records the values X and $\mathbf{Z}$. The latent variable and the auxiliary variables are never observed together, yet we wish to make inferences about their association. This example highlights the central role played by the assumption of impartiality.

Applications

As part of designing a study of an imperfect manufacturing process, a simulation exercise was conducted in which the values of the key latent covariate U were generated by a random process that results in U being approximately uniformly distributed on $(0.25, 1.25)$, with about 1% of the values outside this range, by 0.025 at most. The values of U were then distorted by the measurement process $X = U + \varepsilon$ with $\varepsilon \sim \mathcal{N}(0, 0.012)$, independent of one another and of U. The binary outcomes (success or failure in the manufacture) were generated by the cubic logistic regression

$$\text{logit}\{\mathrm{P}(Y = 1 \mid U = u)\} = -2.5 + 1.25u + 0.25u^2 - 0.2u^3.$$

The sample size was set to $n = 18{,}400$.

The regression fit with the latent variable U is

$$\widehat{\text{logit}}\{\mathrm{P}(Y = 1 \mid U = u)\} = \underset{(0.18)}{-2.30} + \underset{(0.80)}{0.67u} + \underset{(1.09)}{0.61u^2} - \underset{(0.46)}{0.21u^3}$$

(the estimated standard errors are given in parentheses). In a realistic setting, this fit would not be available. With the manifest variable X, we obtained a substantially different regression fit:

$$\widehat{\text{logit}}\{\mathrm{P}(Y = 1 \mid X = x)\} = \underset{(0.30)}{-3.26} + \underset{(1.34)}{4.54x} - \underset{(1.83)}{4.27x^2} + \underset{(0.77)}{1.75x^3}.$$

The difference of the two fitted regressions cannot be judged merely by comparing the corresponding pairs of coefficients, because the estimators of the coefficients are highly correlated in both model fits. However, some difference can be expected since it arises even in some simple models, as the examples in the section Impartiality and Regression show.

In MI, we generate $M = 10$ plausible sets of latent regressors U and fit the posited logistic regression model for each set. The averaging of these results yields the MI estimator

$$\widehat{\text{logit}}\{\mathrm{P}(Y = 1 \mid U = u)\} = \underset{(0.23)}{-2.21} + \underset{(1.01)}{0.23u} + \underset{(1.37)}{1.25u^2} - \underset{(0.57)}{0.49u^3}.$$

This fit is somewhat closer to the regression on U, but a much more reliable judgment can be formed by plotting the fitted cubic regressions (see the left-hand panel of Figure 15.3). The MI fit recovers the latent regression almost exactly, whereas the "manifest" regression differs from the "latent" regression at both extremes, 0.25 and 1.25.

Comparing the estimated standard errors of the regression parameters is not very illuminating because the components of each estimator are highly correlated and the expectations and variances are related, owing to the binary nature of the outcomes. Better insight can be gained by comparing the estimated (pointwise) sampling variances for a range of realistic values of the covariate. The estimated pointwise standard errors (the square roots of the estimated variances) based on the three regression fits are plotted in the right-hand panel. The standard errors for the manifest regression display an erratic pattern; at around $x = 1.1$, they are very close to their counterparts for the latent regression, whereas at both extremes, $x = 0.25$ and $x = 1.25$, they are much greater. The estimated standard errors based on MI regression exceed its latent counterparts by an even margin, except for the extremes, where they are somewhat greater.

The MI sampling variance of the prediction of the logit at any point u, $s^2_{\mathrm{MI}}(u)$, comprises two components, the complete-data variance $W(u)$ and the between-imputation variance $(1 + 1/M)\,B(u)$. The former approximates the sampling variance that would be obtained with the complete data $(\mathbf{y}, \mathbf{u})$. With our realization, the estimate $\widehat{W}$ differs from its complete-data target by between -0.004 and $+0.001$ throughout the range $(0.25, 1.25)$; the average difference is -0.0004.

Finally, we comment on the information lost due to the measurement error, equal to B. This is estimated to be less than 10% for all values $u \in (0.25, 1.25)$, except in the narrow neighborhood of 0.25, where it reaches 25%. It is probably no coincidence that the manifest regression performs so poorly in this neighborhood. In MI, we incur an additional component of the sampling variance $B(u)/M$, due to using only $M = 10$ sets of plausible values; it is easy to see that this component is very small.

The following is an example of dealing with misclassification. The Scottish House Condition Survey engages qualified surveyors who visit selected residential properties and assess the quality of the elements, such as roof (when applicable), doors, floor, plumbing, outer walls, decoration, structural soundness, and the like. For each of a large number of elements, the surveyor marks, according to his or her best

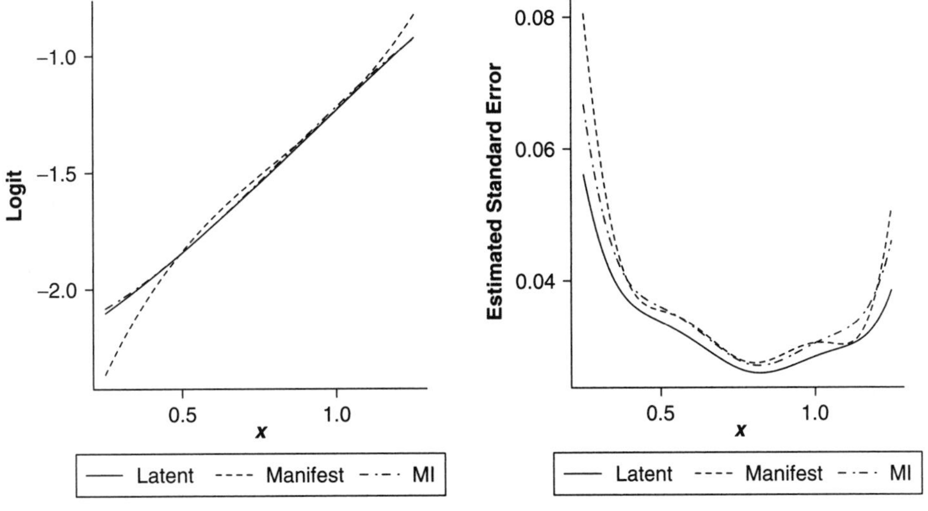

Figure 15.3 Logistic polynomial regression with the latent and manifest covariate and with multiple imputation.

judgment, an integer score in the range 0–10, indicating the estimated value of the repairs required as a percentage (0, 10%, ..., 100%) of the replacement value of the element. Although the surveyors are trained and instructed about the specific tasks, their assessment is not perfect. A subsample of the properties is visited by a second surveyor, who assesses all the elements independently of the previous visiting surveyor. Any discrepancies between the pairs of surveyors are evidence of imperfect assessment.

The misclassification process considered in Longford (2005, chap. 5) posits that there are minor discrepancies, resulting in deviations from the ideal by a single category (above or below the ideal), and gross errors that result in a category unrelated to (independent of) the ideal. The corresponding probabilities p_d and p_g, specific to each element, are estimated from the twice-surveyed properties. Let L_k be the number of neighbors of category k. Categories 0 and 10 have one neighbor each, 1 and 9, respectively. The other categories, 1, ..., 9, have two neighbors each. The probability of assessing a property by the ideal category (for a given element) is given by

$$\begin{aligned}\mathrm{P}(X = k \mid U = k) \\ = 1 - L_k p_d - (K-1)p_g + (K-1)L_k p_d p_g,\end{aligned}$$

where $K = 11$ is the number of categories. If there were no minor discrepancies—that is, $p_d = 0$, the probability p_g would be estimated from the twice-surveyed properties. The probability of a disagreement between two surveyors of a dwelling would be

$$\begin{aligned}d &= 2(K-1)p_g\{1-(K-1)p_g\} \\ &\quad + (K-1)(K-2)p_g^2 \\ &= 2(K-1)p_g - K(K-1)p_g^2.\end{aligned}$$

From this identity, p_g would be estimated by moment matching, leading to a quadratic equation, with $\mathrm{var}(\hat{p}_g)$ approximated by the Taylor expansion.

If gross errors were absent—that is, $p_g = 0$, the probability of minor discrepancy would be estimated similarly, with an adjustment for the numbers of neighbors of each category. When $p_d > 0$ and $p_g > 0$, a disagreement by a single category may arise due to a discrepancy in one of the two assessments or due to a gross error. Therefore, the sum $p_d + p_g$ can be estimated from the disagreements by a single category, disregarding all the disagreements by two or more points. Then, p_g is estimated from the latter (substantial) disagreements, and p_d is estimated as its complement in the estimate of $p_d + p_g$.

After estimating p_d and p_g, plausible pairs of probabilities p_d and p_g are drawn from the estimated sampling distributions of $\hat{p}_d$ and $\hat{p}_g$, and plausible assessment categories are drawn according to the probabilities $P(U = h | X = k)$ derived by the Bayes theorem, with the probabilities p_d and p_g replaced by their plausible versions.

The plausible scores are substituted in a formula that yields the total cost of repairs for a property, which is the principal outcome variable in the survey. The formula is not linear, since it involves discounts when a lot of work is required on a property, details of various maintenance agreements, and the like. Note that the rounding (coarsening) implied by the integer scores can also be addressed by MI, although this is of secondary importance.

Discussion

The method described in the section Connection to Missing Data Methods can be adapted for settings with several latent variables replaced by their manifest versions, even when the manifest variables are partially correlated after conditioning on the latent values. A difficulty associated with MI is in the untestable nature of the assumptions, such as impartiality. We emphasize that applications of simpler and less principled methods have to face the same difficulty because their validity is also contingent on impartiality *and* on other assumptions that relate to ignorability of some sources of variation. The principled nature of MI rests in not ignoring them and in reflecting them in the generation of plausible (latent) values.

Impartiality is difficult to establish, and its presence can at best be argued by discussing the process of measurement qualitatively. Sensitivity analysis provides a general tool for assessing how much the results of the analysis depend on departures from the assumptions, such as impartiality. To implement sensitivity analysis, we require mechanisms that alter the values of the manifest variables in such a way as to make them partial. One such simple mechanism adds a constant to the manifest value of each unit in one category and subtracts the constant for each unit in another category (of a binary variable) in the sample. The result of sensitivity analysis is the function that relates the result of the original analysis to the value of the constant for a range of the constants judged to be plausible in the particular context. The desirable outcome is that the result is not affected by the choice of the constant, in which case the caveat that refers to the explored assumption (impartiality) can be dropped.

The applications described in the section Applications show that the method is relatively easy to implement and can be made modular—separate modules generate plausible values of the latent variable and fit the complete-data model. There are alternatives to MI for dealing with measurement error or misclassification, but none of them are applicable as universally as MI. They require analytical work to develop approximations, cannot handle the entire range of measurement processes, or can be applied with only a narrow range of complete-data methods.

Acknowledgments

This chapter was written while the author was an academic visitor at the Department of Economics and Business, University of Pompeu Fabra, Barcelona, Spain. Funding by grants SEC2003-04476 and SAB2004-0190 from the Spanish Ministry of Science and Technology is acknowledged.

References

Airy, G. B. (1861). *On the algebraical and numerical theory of errors of observations and the combination of observations.* London: Macmillan.

Baker, S. G., Izmirlian, G., & Kipsnis, V. (2005). Resolving paradoxes involving surrogate end points. *Journal of the Royal Statistical Society Series A, 168*, 753–762.

Begg, C. B., & Leung, D. H. Y. (2000). On the use of surrogate end points in randomized trials. *Journal of the Royal Statistical Society Series A, 163*, 15–28.

Carroll, R. J., Ruppert, D., & Stefanski, L. A. (1995). *Measurement error in nonlinear models.* London: Chapman & Hall.

Cook, J. R., & Stefanski, L. A. (1994). Simulation-extrapolation estimation in parametric measurement error models. *Journal of the American Statistical Association, 89*, 1314–1328.

Cronbach, L. J., Gleser, G. C., Nanda, H., & Rajaratnam, N. (1972). *The dependability of behavioral measurements: Theory of scores and profiles.* New York: Wiley.

Dempster, A. P., Laird, N. M., & Rubin, D. B. (1977). Maximum likelihood from incomplete data via the EM algorithm. *Journal of the Royal Statistical Society Series B, 39*, 1–38.

Fuller, W. A. (1987). *Measurement error models.* New York: Wiley.

Gulliksen, H. (1950). *Theory of mental tests.* New York: Wiley.

Heitjan, D. F., & Rubin, D. B. (1990). Inference from coarse data via multiple imputation with application. *Journal of the American Statistical Association, 85*, 304–314.

Longford, N. T. (2005). *Missing data and small-area estimation. Modern analytical equipment for the survey statistician.* New York: Springer-Verlag.

Lord, F. M. (1968). *Application of item response theory to practical testing problems.* Hillsdale, NJ: Lawrence Erlbaum.

Lord, F. M., & Novick, M. (1968). *Statistical theories of mental test scores.* Reading, MA: Addison-Wesley.

Marcoulides, G. A., & Schumacher, R. E. (2001). *New developments and techniques in structural equation modeling.* Mahwah, NJ: Lawrence Erlbaum.

Nur, U. A. M. (2005). *Handling missing data in analyses of the Women's Cohort Study.* Unpublished doctoral dissertation, Leeds University, Leeds, UK.

Prentice, R. L. (1989). Surrogate end points in clinical trials: Definitions and operational criteria. *Statistics in Medicine, 8*, 473–489.

Rubin, D. B. (1996). Multiple imputation after 18+ years. *Journal of the American Statistical Association, 91*, 431–440.

Rubin, D. B. (2002). *Multiple imputation for nonresponse in surveys* (2nd ed.). New York: Wiley.

16

STATISTICAL MODELS FOR THE DEVELOPMENT OF PSYCHOLOGICAL AND EDUCATIONAL TESTS

KLAAS SIJTSMA AND WILCO H. M. EMONS

INTRODUCTION

The general idea behind modern measurement in the social and behavioral sciences is that human behavior is driven by a limited number of traits, attitudes, opinions, skills, and abilities. Each of these attributes serves as an explanation of the cohesion in certain sets of observable behaviors and constitutes what the researcher is really interested in. Examples are as follows. Clinical and personality psychologists may be interested in traits such as introversion and anxiety, sociologists in attitudes toward euthanasia or religiosity, and developmental psychologists in the Piagetian developmental abilities of conservation and transitive reasoning. Many interesting applications can be found in other disciplines such as education (e.g., knowledge of disciplines taught at school), marketing research (e.g., service quality of medical facilities), political science (e.g., opinions about government policy), and social medicine (e.g., quality of life after surgery). The philosophical status of these attributes has been debated in several sources (e.g., Borsboom, 2005; Michell, 1990). Here, we will simply take them for granted as organizing principles behind cohesive sets of observable behaviors.

This takes us to the way these attributes are measured. Because these attributes are latent, conclusions about them have to be inferred from sets of cohesive behaviors that are assumed to be driven by these attributes. Thus, in practice, evidence on the unifying cause comes from what is believed to be its effect—that is, the data collected on the set of observable behaviors that are assumed to be typical of this cause. This is done as follows. A set of J stimuli—questions, statements, tasks: *items*, for short—is presented to a representative sample of N respondents from the population of interest, and each respondent provides responses to each item. Responses can be choices from a set of answers, as in selected-response items (e.g., multiple-choice items) for measuring knowledge of national history, or sentences reflecting the answer to a question, as in constructed-response items, ratings on an ordered scale for each attitude statement in a set, or verbal accounts of the process that lead to the solution of transitive reasoning problems.

Tests can have different appearances. For example, the respondent may react to a paper-and-pencil test and encircle response options, write down answers, rate statements, or manipulate real objects, such as a pen through a maze as in intelligence testing. In computerized testing, similar actions may be performed by pressing keys on a keyboard, moving a mouse, or touching a screen. Likewise, surveys including sets of items for measuring attitudes and opinions need not only be verbal (i.e., as in a street or a telephone interview) or in writing (e.g., as in mail surveys) but may also be administered through the Internet, which in principle enhances their possibilities comparable with computerized testing.

The qualitative responses to items—choices from a number of precoded options or written sentences, ratings on discrete ordinal scales, verbal explanations—are coded next as integers, following the principle that the more evidence a response gives of a higher level of, in these examples, knowledge, attitude, and ability, the higher the item score. Obviously, whether this coding is meaningful depends on the degree to which the items adequately reflect relevant aspects of the attribute of interest. If the theory or the operationalization of this attribute is primitive, or even wrong, responses may have a muddled relationship to the attribute and responses to different items may exhibit little cohesion. Thus, the use of a sound theory and a meaningful operationalization into a set of items are prerequisites for the production of a set of cohesive quantitative item scores that form the basis for the construction of a measurement instrument—a *test*, for short.

Numerous statistical models have been proposed for analyzing the item scores produced by N respondents who reacted to J items (Boomsma, Van Duijn, & Snijders, 2001; Van der Linden & Hambleton, 1997). The application of such models produces information on the following:

- *Dimensionality of the data*—that is, the number of mathematical dimensions needed to explain the data structure. The relations among these dimensions are described in a probabilistic model and are often taken as evidence of one or more explanatory attributes. This may enlighten the meaning of measurement and may or may not confirm the researcher's expectations. From a practical angle, one dimension supports the use of one "measurement rod" or scale for the attribute of interest, and multiple dimensions may call for several scales.
- *Quality of individual items*, such as an item-difficulty parameter, which indicates the ability level required for solving the problem with average probability, and an item-discrimination parameter, which indicates how well the item separates lower ability levels from higher levels. Items that are too easy or too difficult and items that discriminate weakly may be rejected from the final test because they are not properly tuned to the group to be measured.
- *Quality of the whole test*, such as the accuracy of measurement that is possible with a set of items of good quality that together constitute a scale. This accuracy may be expressed in one summary statistic, known as reliability, or as a function of the scale indicating how accurately the test measures at different scale levels. Quality is also expressed as scale validity, indicating the degree to which test performance is driven by the attribute(s) of interest and the degree to which performance on individual items is driven by these attributes. Validity takes the form of a series of results from research rather than a single index or function.

After a scale has been constructed on the basis of information on dimensionality and item and test quality, measurement values for individuals locating them on the scale are determined. These measurement values express the individual's attribute level and can be used to classify the individual for entry or nonentry in a course, for receiving or not receiving therapeutic treatment—either psychological or medical—and for admittance to or rejection from a job. Each of these uses of measurements emphasizes the need for reliable and valid instruments.

The statistical models referred to are united in the family of *item response theory* (IRT) models. The purpose of this chapter is to discuss a few well-known and regularly used models that are representative of the IRT family. Four of these IRT models are used to analyze data from an arithmetic test. It is explained how these models can be used to construct tests and also how they are complementary to one another. Finally, we discuss other possibilities offered by IRT for data analysis and the construction of scales for the measurement of attributes.

Assumptions of Item Response Theory

We assume that a test or a questionnaire consists of J items, which are meant to measure the latent attribute(s) of interest. The scores on items are modeled by random variables, X_j, indexed $j = 1, \ldots, J$, and are usually integer valued: $X_j = x_j$, with $x_j = 0, 1$, for example, expressing incorrect or correct responding, and $x_j = 0, \ldots, m$, for example, expressing the degree to which someone agrees with an attitude statement. These are the most frequently used possibilities, referred to as dichotomous and polytomous scoring, respectively. The latent attribute is often called the latent trait, where the word *trait* is assumed to also capture personality traits, attitudes, opinions, skills, and abilities, but a neutral term such as *latent variable* would probably fit in better with mainstream statistics. Latent variables are denoted θ_q, with $q = 1, \ldots, Q$, and collected in vector $\boldsymbol{\theta}$.

Three classes of assumptions are relevant for IRT models. The first class of assumptions describes the relationship between the probability of a particular score on item j and the latent variables, denoted $P(X_j = x_j|\boldsymbol{\theta})$. This is the response function. For dichotomously scored items, it is known as the item response function (IRF), $P(X_j = 1|\boldsymbol{\theta}) \equiv P_j(\boldsymbol{\theta})$. Most IRT models assume that the IRF is monotone nondecreasing in $\boldsymbol{\theta}$, coordinate-wise in each element θ_q, $q = 1, \ldots, Q$. This is the monotonicity (M) assumption that says that the probability of, for example, a correct response does not decrease—that is, remains constant or increases—when either one of the θs increases while the others are kept constant. If one latent variable, say alienation, drives item responses (and thus $\boldsymbol{\theta} = \theta$), then Assumption M says that the probability of saying "Yes" to the question whether one avoids neighborhood festivities does not decrease—often increases—with higher values of θ.

For polytomously scored items, several possibilities for defining response probabilities exist (e.g., Mellenbergh, 1995). One such possibility is $P(X_j \geqslant x_j|\theta)$, with $x_j = 1, \ldots, m$, which is the item step response function (ISRF). Assumption M says that $P(X_j \geqslant x_j|\theta)$ is nondecreasing in θ. For example, a respondent rates on a 5-point scale *to what degree* he or she avoids neighborhood festivities; and Assumption M says that the probability of rating at least the $(x_j + 1)$st category—that is, obtaining at least score x_j—does not decrease when level of alienation increases.

The second class of assumptions describes the relationships between the items. Specifically, conditioning on $\boldsymbol{\theta}$ simplifies the joint conditional distribution of the J item scores, collected in vector $\mathbf{X} = (X_1, \ldots, X_J)$ with realization $\mathbf{x}$, into the product of marginal conditional distributions, such that

$$P(\mathbf{X} = \mathbf{x}|\boldsymbol{\theta}) = \prod_{j=1}^{J} P(X_j = x_j|\boldsymbol{\theta}). \qquad (16.1)$$

This is the assumption of local independence (LI), in statistics better known as conditional independence. Equation (16.1) implies that for two items j and k,

$$\mathrm{Cov}(X_j, X_k|\boldsymbol{\theta}) = 0, \qquad j,k = 1, \ldots, J; \quad j < k, \qquad (16.2)$$

but reversely, LI is not implied by this set of zero covariances. Thus, LI represents a stronger independence property than that represented by the set of $\frac{1}{2}J(J-1)$ conditional covariances in (16.2). Consequently, (16.2) is known as weak local independence (WLI) (Stout, 2002) or, using a more general terminology, conditional uncorrelatedness. Obviously, LI and WLI only hold when $\boldsymbol{\theta}$ contains all Q latent variables relevant for measurement, and failure of these properties in real data is an indication that the dimensionality of the data is different from what the researcher expected. Several procedures have been proposed that explore the data for dimensionality in an effort to approach (16.2) (Stout et al., 1996).

The third set of assumptions refers to the number of latent variables. Typical of psychological measurement is the requirement that the test measure one latent variable. This renders measurements to unambiguously reflect one "thing" at a time and not a mixture, just as one wants the scale of a thermometer to reflect only temperature and not a mixture of temperature, air pressure, humidity, and wind velocity. Thus, the majority of IRT models assume that $\boldsymbol{\theta} = \theta$ and thus $Q = 1$ (for an overview, see Van der Linden & Hambleton, 1997). This is Assumption $D = 1$. This simplifying assumption is somewhat at odds with psychological reality, whereby responses to items are usually driven by multiple psychological properties (an arithmetic item requires not only arithmetic ability but also reading skills, verbal comprehension, and sometimes also spatial orientation), so that unidimensionality is an ideal and multidimensional models are more realistic (thus assuming $D \geqslant 2$). Nevertheless, unidimensional IRT models are often seen as reasonable approximations to the real dimensionality, which may be defendable when one dominant property drives item responses and the influence of others is minor or may be ignored.

Special Cases of (M, LI, $D = 1$) Models

In this section, several well-known and much used IRT models are discussed. The most important distinctions are between nonparametric and parametric models and between models for dichotomous and polytomous item scores.

Monotone Homogeneity Model for Dichotomous Items

Model Formulation

Mokken (1971) introduced the monotone homogeneity model (MHM) for dichotomously scored items. The MHM is defined by the assumptions of M, LI, and $D = 1$. This model is important in practice because it implies that individuals are measured on an ordinal scale. To see this, define the observable total score

$$X_+ = \sum_{j=1}^{J} X_j, \qquad (16.3)$$

and note that for two individuals, v and w, with total scores $x_{+v} < x_{+w}$, the MHM implies for each value t of θ that

$$P(\theta > t | X_+ = x_{+v}) \leqslant P(\theta > t | X_+ = x_{+w}) \qquad (16.4)$$

(Grayson, 1988; Hemker, Sijtsma, Molenaar, & Junker, 1997). Equation (16.4) is known as stochastic ordering of the latent variable by the total score (SOL). SOL implies that for expected values (E)

$$E(\theta | X_+ = x_{+v}) \leqslant E(\theta | X_+ = x_{+w}). \qquad (16.5)$$

SOL means that the observable total score X_+ orders individuals on the scale of latent variable θ; thus, a fitting MHM implies an ordinal scale for person measurement.

The fit of the MHM can be investigated in two steps. First, the dimensionality of an item set is investigated, and second, the monotonicity of the IRFs is investigated.

Mokken Scaling and Dimensionality Investigation

Mokken (1971, chap. 5) and Sijtsma and Molenaar (2002, chap. 5) proposed an *exploratory* item selection procedure that combines the investigation of the dimensionality of the data with an evaluation of the quality of the items found to assess the same dimension. This method selects items into clusters on the basis of the strength of their relationships with the latent variables such that each cluster measures a different θ. Items that predominantly measure a θ that is not shared by any of the other items are declared unscalable.

Strength of relationship is indexed by means of the item scalability coefficient H_j, which is defined as follows. Let $\mathrm{Cov}(X_j, X_k)$ denote the covariance between item scores X_j and X_k and $\mathrm{Cov}(X_j, X_k)_{\max}$ the maximum possible covariance given fixed marginals of the 2×2 frequency table of bivariate counts; then, H_j is defined as

$$H_j = \frac{\sum\limits_{k \neq j} \mathrm{Cov}(X_j, X_k)}{\sum\limits_{k \neq j} \mathrm{Cov}(X_j, X_k)_{\max}}, \qquad j = 1, \ldots, J. \qquad (16.6)$$

For a set of J items evaluated as one test, coefficient H is defined as

$$H = \frac{\sum_{j=1}^{J-1} \sum_{k=j+1}^{J} \text{Cov}(X_j, X_k)}{\sum_{j=1}^{J-1} \sum_{k=j+1}^{J} \text{Cov}(X_j, X_k)_{\max}} \quad (16.7)$$

and is seen to be a positively weighted average of the J item coefficients, H_j $(j = 1, \ldots, J)$ (Mokken, 1971, pp. 148–153),

$$H = \frac{\sum_{j=1}^{J} \sum_{k \neq j} \text{Cov}(X_j, X_k)_{\max} H_j}{\sum_{j=1}^{J} \sum_{k \neq j} \text{Cov}(X_j, X_k)_{\max}}, \quad (16.8)$$

such that H is bounded by

$$\min(H_j) \leqslant H \leqslant \max(H_j), \qquad j = 1, \ldots, J. \quad (16.9)$$

Given the interpretation of H_j, coefficient H indexes the average strength of relationship of the J items with the latent variable θ. The stronger this relationship, the better—more accurately—the test separates relatively low θs from relatively high θs (Mokken, Lewis, & Sijtsma, 1986). Thus, if the MHM holds, a high H indicates accurate person ordering by means of X_+.

For the class of (M, LI, $D = 1$) models—MHM and special cases that we shall encounter shortly—it can be shown that

$$\text{Cov}(X_j, X_k) \geqslant 0, \qquad \text{for all } (j,k), \quad j \neq k. \quad (16.10)$$

Because IRFs are nonlinear, other association measures may be in order; see Holland and Rosenbaum (1986) for suggestions and also a more general positive covariance condition known as conditional association of which (16.10) is a special case. Using the positive-sign property of (16.10), it follows that

$$0 \leqslant H \leqslant 1 \quad (16.11)$$

and, similarly, for the item coefficients, that

$$0 \leqslant H_j \leqslant 1, \qquad j = 1, \ldots, J. \quad (16.12)$$

Thus, positive values of H and H_j are necessary conditions for the MHM model to hold; hence, negative values are in conflict with the model.

Mokken (1971, p. 184) defined a scale as a set of items for which, denoting correlation by ρ and given a suitably chosen constant c,

1. $\rho_{jk} > 0$ for all item pairs (j,k), $j \neq k$ and
2. $H_j \geqslant c > 0$ for all items j.

Positive correlations and positive H_js both are implied by (16.10), and requiring a positive lower bound c means that only those items are admitted in the scale that have a positive relationship with θ, the strength of which is controlled by the magnitude of c.

Exploratory item analysis focuses on selecting items in the same subset that have high H_js relative to one another and low H_js relative to items that are in another subset. High H_js are due to the same common θ assessed by the items in the same subset, and low H_js express a weak relationship with the θ assessed by the items in the other subset.

The algorithm that does the item selection is a bottom-up procedure that selects items one by one, starting with the pair out of $\frac{1}{2}J(J-1)$ candidate pairs that has the highest, significantly positive H_{jk} value (this is H for two items). In each of the next selection steps, from the unselected items an item is selected such that (1) it has a positive correlation with the items already selected and (2) its H_j relative to the items already selected is significantly greater than 0 and also $H_j > c$, and if more items satisfy Conditions (1) and (2), from this set the item is selected that (3) together with the items already selected in previous steps of the algorithm produces the greatest common H. This results in a subset of items that predominantly measure the same θ, while a high value of H in (16.8) guarantees accuracy of ordinal person measurement in the sense of SOL (16.4) that is controlled by the choice of lower bound c.

If the data are unidimensional, in principle all items fit in the same cluster. However, if the items have different H_js, which is the common situation in practice, higher c values may cause more items to remain unselected. This is not because they do not assess θ but because they do so more weakly than c allows. The researcher should decide what he or she considers a desirable outcome and may take considerations into account such as the degree to which only few items can adequately cover the attribute well.

For multidimensional data—say each subset of items assesses a particular θ, and different subsets assess different θs, to keep things simple—the typical sequence of outcomes is that, first, low c values (near 0) lead to the selection of (nearly) all items in one cluster and, second, higher c values result in the clustering that reflects true dimensionality. Hemker, Sijtsma, and Molenaar (1995) recommended running the cluster algorithm for different c values, starting at 0, using increments of 0.05, and stopping at 0.6. The data section in this chapter will offer an example.

Confirmatory item analysis evaluates a set of J items as a given scale. This situation is relevant when the researcher is interested in testing the hypothesis that a newly constructed test represents a scale. Also, he or she may consider one or more items in an existing test to have become archaic—for example, due to the use of old-fashioned words—and have them replaced by others or the instrument may be investigated for use in another population. In each of these cases, the researcher takes the J-item test as given and estimates its H and H_j coefficients to assess test score and item quality, respectively.

Stout et al. (1996) have proposed a method for dimensionality investigation that searches for the partitioning of the item set that approximates WLI (16.2) as well as possible but without taking item quality into consideration (Van Abswoude, Van der Ark, & Sijtsma, 2004) as Mokken's method typically does. These and other methods have been compared by Van Abswoude et al. (2004).

Monotonicity Investigation

In real data, the relationship between item and latent variable may be monotone, as the MHM assumes, but it is regularly found that for some items in the test the relationship is either monotone by approximation—the empirical curve tends to increase but shows several small local decreases—or sometimes even distinctly nonmonotone. Mokken's method selects items having H_js of at least c in subsets, which ascertains IRFs that show at least a tendency to increase in θ, just as a regression curve with a positive regression coefficient does. The higher the value of c, the stronger this tendency and, roughly, the smaller the chances that local decreases are such that the curve can no longer be evaluated to be approximately monotone. Thus, for most c values, within selected item subsets the additional investigation of Assumption M is useful, and this is true a fortiori the smaller c is. Assumption M is investigated as follows.

Define a total score without Item j, called a restscore and denoted $R_{(-j)}$, as

$$R_{(-j)} = \sum_{k \neq j} X_k. \tag{16.13}$$

Like X_+, restscore $R_{(-j)}$ estimates person ordering on θ, which is justified by the same stochastic ordering results (16.4). The MHM implies manifest monotonicity (MM) (Junker, 1993),

$$P[X_j = 1 | R_{(-j)} = r] \text{ nondecreasing in } r = 0, \ldots, J-1. \tag{16.14}$$

Junker and Sijtsma (2000) showed that an MM result as in (16.14) is not obtained when $R_{(-j)}$ is replaced by X_+. MM can be used to estimate the IRF by means of nonparametric regression. One straightforward possibility is to estimate for each value of r the proportion of the population that have Item j correct, plotting these proportions as a function of r and then checking visually for MM and testing local decreases for significance by means of a normal approximation to the binomial test (Molenaar & Sijtsma, 2000). This approach yields a limited number of at most J discrete points of the IRF. Ramsay (1991) proposed a kernel smoothing approach to obtain a continuous estimate of the IRF. Karabatsos and Sheu (2004) discuss a Bayesian approach to evaluating Assumption M.

Computer Software

In our data example, we used the program MSP (Molenaar & Sijtsma, 2000) to estimate the H and H_j coefficients and select items into clusters for different c values, and also to estimate discrete versions of the IRFs. The program TestGraf98 (Ramsay, 2000) was used to estimate continuous versions of the IRFs.

Monotone Homogeneity Model for Polytomous Items

Molenaar (1997) generalized the MHM to polytomous item scores by redefining Assumption M for conditional probability $P(X_j \geqslant x_j|\theta)$, for $x_j = 1,\ldots,m$. Obvious as this choice may seem, it has been found to have many far-reaching consequences at the theoretical level, which show that the generalization of dichotomous-item models to polytomous-item models may be problematic. Here are two consequences.

First, Hemker et al. (1997) found that the SOL property does not hold for the polytomous-item MHM or for most other IRT models for ordered polytomous items. Van der Ark (2005) established SOL in many data sets by producing a wealth of robustness results for several, much used polytomous-item models, thus demonstrating convincingly that ordinal measurement properties could be maintained at the practical level.

Second, $P[X_j \geqslant x_j|R_{(-j)}]$ has been shown not to be monotone in general, thus losing MM (Junker & Sijtsma, 2000). Specifically, a nondecreasing observable curve, $P[X_j \geqslant x_j|R_{(-j)}]$, is neither a necessary nor a sufficient condition for Assumption M, but much practical experience with simulated data suggests that such monotone curves tend to be supportive of Assumption M. Software for estimating these curves is available (Molenaar & Sijtsma, 2000; Ramsay, 2000).

Fortunately, as concerns dimensionality analysis, Mokken's item selection method has been generalized successfully by defining coefficients H_j and H for polytomous items, maintaining the properties in (16.8), (16.9), (16.11), and (16.12). The program MSP can be used here as well.

The Three- and Two-Parameter Logistic Models

Model Formulation

The three-parameter logistic model (3PLM) (Birnbaum, 1968) is an (M, LI, $D = 1$) model that specializes Assumption M to a logistic IRF with three item parameters,

$$P_j(\theta) = \gamma_j + \frac{(1-\gamma_j)\exp[\alpha_j(\theta-\delta_j)]}{1+\exp[\alpha_j(\theta-\delta_j)]}, \quad 0 < \gamma_j < 1, \quad \alpha_j > 0. \quad (16.15)$$

In (16.15), parameter γ_j is the lower asymptote for $\theta \to -\infty$, parameter δ_j is the location or difficulty parameter, and parameter α_j is the steepest slope or discrimination parameter of the IRF, evaluated at the point with coordinates $(\delta_j, \frac{1+\gamma_j}{2})$. After it has been established whether the data are unidimensional and the smooth S-shaped IRFs in (16.15) fit the data, these item parameters are estimated and then summarize three important aspects of the item: Positive (i.e., nonzero) γ_j indicates that people with low θs have a nontrivial probability of giving the correct answer, as in multiple-choice items; δ_j indicates the degree to which the item is difficult for the population of interest; and α_j indicates the degree to which the item separates θs that are low compared with δ from θs that are high compared with δ.

The two-parameter logistic model (2PLM) (Birnbaum, 1968) specializes Assumption M of the 3PLM by assuming that $\gamma_j = 0$, $j = 1,\ldots,J$, resulting in

$$P_j(\theta) = \frac{\exp[\alpha_j(\theta-\delta_j)]}{1+\exp[\alpha_j(\theta-\delta_j)]}, \qquad \alpha_j > 0. \quad (16.16)$$

The interpretation of the remaining two item parameters is the same as in the 3PLM.

Estimating the 3PLM and the 2PLM

The estimation of the item parameters and the latent variable is straightforward. Let $\mathbf{X}_{N\times J}$ be the data matrix produced by a sample of N individuals, indexed by v, who responded to J items. Also, let $\boldsymbol{\theta}_N = (\theta_1,\ldots,\theta_N)$ and $\boldsymbol{\omega} = (\boldsymbol{\gamma},\boldsymbol{\delta},\boldsymbol{\alpha}) = (\gamma_1,\ldots,\gamma_J,\delta_1,\ldots,\delta_J,\alpha_1,\ldots,\alpha_J)$; then, assuming independent and identically distributed (iid)-sampled individuals and LI (16.1), the likelihood of the data can be written as

$$L(\mathbf{X}_{N\times J} = \mathbf{x}_{N\times J}|\boldsymbol{\theta}_N,\boldsymbol{\omega}) = \prod_{v=1}^{N}\prod_{j=1}^{J} P_j(\theta_v)^{x_{vj}}[1-P_j(\theta_v)]^{1-x_{vj}}, \quad (16.17)$$

with (16.15) inserted for $P_j(\theta_v)$ or (16.16) inserted for $P_j(\theta_v)$ and $\omega^* = (\delta, \alpha)$ replacing ω. Several methods have been proposed for estimating the parameters taking this likelihood as a starting point. The oldest method is joint maximum likelihood (JML) estimation, which maximizes the likelihood in (16.17) simultaneously for all parameters in $\boldsymbol{\theta}$ and ω. However, JML has been shown to fail because in the presence of N incidental parameters in $\boldsymbol{\theta}$, the structural parameters in ω are estimated inconsistently (Neyman & Scott, 1948). Marginal maximum likelihood (MML) estimation of the item parameters does not suffer from this problem and yields consistent estimates for the item parameters in ω as the number N of respondents grows. We will briefly review the much used MML method.

Define the problem as follows. Let $f(\theta)$ denote the probability density of θ with parameters collected in $\boldsymbol{\tau}$; then, the marginal likelihood is

$$P[\mathbf{X}_{N\times J} = \mathbf{x}_{N\times J}|\omega, \boldsymbol{\tau}] = \prod_{v=1}^{N} \int_\theta \prod_{j=1}^{J} P_j(\theta)^{x_{vj}} [1 - P_j(\theta)]^{1-x_{vj}} f(\theta) d\theta. \quad (16.18)$$

The integral gives the marginal probability of the item-score vector of person v, $\mathbf{x}_v$, which can be denoted by $P(\mathbf{x}_v|\omega, \boldsymbol{\tau})$, so that we may define

$$P(\mathbf{x}_v|\omega, \boldsymbol{\tau}) = \int_\theta \prod_{j=1}^{J} P_j(\theta)^{x_{vj}} [1 - P_j(\theta)]^{1-x_{vj}} f(\theta) d\theta \quad (16.19)$$

and write the marginal likelihood as

$$P[\mathbf{X}_{N\times J} = \mathbf{x}_{N\times J}|\omega, \boldsymbol{\tau}] = \prod_{v=1}^{N} P(\mathbf{x}_v|\omega, \boldsymbol{\tau}). \quad (16.20)$$

Often, the normal density is chosen for $f(\theta)$, with parameters $\boldsymbol{\tau} = (\mu, \sigma^2)$.

The probability on the left in (16.20) is a function of $3J$ parameters in ω, and these, as well as those in $\boldsymbol{\tau}$, can be estimated by MML (see Bock & Lieberman, 1970, for details;, also see Baker & Kim, 2004, chap. 6). Estimation of $\boldsymbol{\theta}_N$ then follows from evaluating the posterior distribution of each θ_v, denoted $P(\theta_v|\mathbf{x}_v; \omega, \boldsymbol{\tau})$ and computed by means of Bayes's theorem,

$$P(\theta_v|\mathbf{x}_v; \omega, \boldsymbol{\tau}) = \frac{P(\mathbf{x}_v|\theta_v; \omega) f(\theta_v|\boldsymbol{\tau})}{P(\mathbf{x}_v|\omega, \boldsymbol{\tau})}. \quad (16.21)$$

In (16.21), $f(\theta_v|\boldsymbol{\tau})$ serves as the prior density of θ_v and is assumed to be the same for each θ value. The probability of person v's data in $\mathbf{x}_v$ is weighted by the density of each θ from the prior, and given the marginal likelihood in the denominator, which is independent of θ, this results in the posterior of θ_v. The mean of this posterior often is taken as the estimate of θ_v (e.g., Bock & Mislevy, 1982).

Measurement Accuracy

Fisher's information function expresses the measurement quality of one or more items relative to the latent variable. Let $P_j'(\theta)$ be the first derivative of the IRF with respect to θ. Then, for $Q_j(\theta) \equiv 1 - P_j(\theta)$, Fisher's information function for item j, denoted $I_j(\theta)$, is

$$I_j(\theta) = \frac{[P_j'(\theta)]^2}{P_j(\theta) Q_j(\theta)}, \quad (16.22)$$

and given LI, Fisher's information function for the J-item test equals

$$I(\theta) = \sum_{j=1}^{J} I_j(\theta). \quad (16.23)$$

Insertion of (16.15) and (16.16) in (16.23) gives the test information functions for the 3PLM and the 2PLM, respectively.

The test information function provides the statistical information in the J items together for estimating θ, and $I(\theta)^{-1/2}$ gives a lower bound on the standard error for estimated θ, which is achieved asymptotically for maximum likelihood (ML) estimation as $J \to \infty$. Suppose one wants a test to measure accurately at a cutoff score denoted θ_0, then test information, $I(\theta_0)$, should have a value high enough to result in a standard error that is sufficiently small for the test application envisaged. This can be accomplished by selecting items that contribute relatively large $I_j(\theta_0)$ values to $I(\theta_0)$. Equation (16.22) shows that the IRFs of these items have relatively steep slopes at θ_0. Van der Linden (2005) discusses many examples of test construction based on this item selection principle.

Fitting the 3PLM and the 2PLM

For short tests ($J < 20$), the standardized posterior residuals, also known as root-mean square deviates (RMSDs), are evaluated (Zimowski, Muraki, Mislevy, & Bock, 1996). The RMSD is based on the standardized differences between the posterior probability of a correct response at selected values of θ and the expected probability at those θ values. RMSD > 2.0 indicates item misfit.

Computer Software

The program BILOG-MG (Zimowski et al., 1996) was used to estimate both the 3PLM and the 2PLM and evaluate their fit. Parameters were estimated using MML, and the RMSD was used to assess item fit.

The Graded Response Model

To our knowledge, a feasible generalization of the 3PLM to polytomous items does not exist to date. The most direct generalization of the 2PLM to polytomous items is the graded response model (GRM) (Samejima, 1997). The GRM is an (M, LI, $D = 1$) model that specializes the ISRF, $P(X_j \geqslant x_j|\theta)$, as

$$P(X_j \geqslant x_j|\theta) = \frac{\exp[\alpha_j(\theta - \delta_{jx_j})]}{1+\exp[\alpha_j(\theta - \delta_{jx_j})]}, \quad x_j > 0, \quad \alpha_j > 0. \tag{16.24}$$

Note that this response function is equivalent to that of the 2PLM but that the difference lies in the item score that is modeled: Polytomous $X_j \geqslant x_j$ in the GRM and binary $X_j = 1$ in the 2PLM, and that they coincide when $m = 1$. The GRM has been characterized as a cumulative probability model (Hemker et al., 1997; Mellenbergh, 1995). Such models are sometimes associated with data stemming from a respondent's global assessment of the rating scale and the consecutive choice of a response option from all available options. Baker and Kim (2004, chap. 8) discuss ML estimation of the item and person parameters of the GRM, and Samejima (1997) discusses goodness-of-fit methods. The program MULTILOG (Thissen, Chen, & Bock, 2003) can be used to estimate parameters and evaluate the fit of the GRM to the data.

The Rasch Model

Model Formulation

The Rasch (1960) model, also known as the one-parameter logistic model (1PLM), is obtained from the 2PLM by setting $\alpha_j = 1$, for $j = 1, \ldots, J$, which results in

$$P_j(\theta) = \frac{\exp(\theta - \delta_j)}{1+\exp(\theta - \delta_j)}. \tag{16.25}$$

Thus, within the same test, items are assumed to separate θs equally well at different item difficulty levels. Item parameters can be estimated by means of MML (Thissen, 1982), and assuming these estimates to be the true values, person parameters can be estimated by means of ML. Because the Rasch model is a member of the exponential family (Fischer, 1974), conditional maximum likelihood (CML) estimation is another possibility. In this sense, the Rasch model is unique in IRT, and therefore we will discuss CML in some detail.

Estimating the Rasch Model

Let $\xi = \exp(\theta)$ and $\varepsilon_j = \exp(-\delta_j)$; then (16.25) becomes

$$P_j(\xi) = \frac{\xi\varepsilon_j}{1+\xi\varepsilon_j}. \tag{16.26}$$

Let $\boldsymbol{\xi} = (\xi_1, \ldots, \xi_N)$ and $\boldsymbol{\epsilon} = (\varepsilon_1, \ldots, \varepsilon_J)$. Also, let $x_{v+} = \sum_{j=1}^{J} x_{vj}$ and $x_{+j} = \sum_{v=1}^{N} x_{vj}$. Using this notation, the likelihood in (16.17) can be written as

$$\begin{aligned} L(\mathbf{X}_{N\times J} = \mathbf{x}_{N\times J}|\boldsymbol{\xi}, \boldsymbol{\epsilon}) &= \prod_{v=1}^{N}\prod_{j=1}^{J} P_j(\xi)^{x_{vj}}[1 - P_j(\xi)]^{1-x_{vj}} \\ &= \frac{\prod_{v=1}^{N} \xi_v^{x_{v+}} \prod_{j=1}^{J} \varepsilon_j^{x_{+j}}}{\prod_{v=1}^{N}\prod_{j=1}^{J}(1+\xi_v\varepsilon_j)}. \end{aligned} \tag{16.27}$$

Note that in (16.27) the marginals of the data matrix $\mathbf{X}_{N\times J}$ are sufficient statistics for estimation of the latent parameters of the model. CML proceeds as follows.

Let the person marginals of $\mathbf{X}_{N\times J} = \mathbf{x}_{N\times J}$ be collected in $\mathbf{x}_{N+} = (x_{1+}, \ldots, x_{N+})$. Consider the probability of the data conditional on these person marginals $\mathbf{x}_{N+}$,

$$P(\mathbf{X}_{N\times J}=\mathbf{x}_{N\times J}|\mathbf{x}_{N+};\boldsymbol{\xi},\boldsymbol{\epsilon})=\frac{P(\mathbf{X}_{N\times J}=\mathbf{x}_{N\times J}|\boldsymbol{\xi},\boldsymbol{\epsilon})}{P(\mathbf{x}_{N+}|\boldsymbol{\xi},\boldsymbol{\epsilon})}. \tag{16.28}$$

Standard texts on the Rasch model (e.g., Fischer, 1974) explain in much detail that this equation can be shown to depend only on the item parameters $\boldsymbol{\epsilon}$ and the sufficient statistics for $\boldsymbol{\xi}$ and $\boldsymbol{\epsilon}$ but not on $\boldsymbol{\xi}$. The resulting equation is then taken as a so-called conditional likelihood and solved for $\boldsymbol{\epsilon}$; this yields CML estimates for $\boldsymbol{\epsilon}$. These CML estimates are consistent and close to being maximally efficient (Eggen, 2000). In practice, the CML estimates of $\boldsymbol{\epsilon}$ are used to estimate ξ by means of ML (for details, see Fischer, 1974; Hoijtink & Boomsma, 1995). Fisher's information functions for items and tests are found by deriving the typical expressions for the Rasch model for $I_j(\theta)$ (16.22) and $I(\theta)$ (16.23).

CML thus enables us to estimate one set of parameters independently of the other set. Statistically, this is known as parameter separability. At the theoretical level, the possibility of making statements about items irrespective of the person distribution and, reversely, about persons irrespective of the difficulty level of the test is known as specific objectivity. Fischer (1974) considers specific objectivity crucial for measurement, but this point of view also has met with criticism (e.g., Borsboom, 2005). At the practical level, parameter separation is considered convenient for equation of scales, constructing item banks, and adaptive testing; these topics are discussed later.

Fitting the Rasch Model

Goodness-of-fit tests for the Rasch model have been summarized by Glas and Verhelst (1995). Here, we mention the asymptotic χ^2 tests, R_1 and R_2. The R_1 statistic tests the null hypothesis that the J IRFs are parallel logistic curves as in (16.25), and R_2 tests whether WLI (16.2) holds under the Rasch model for all $\frac{1}{2}J(J-1)$ item pairs simultaneously. Rejection of parallel logistic curves for all items simultaneously could be indicative of different slopes between IRFs, and the approximate standard normal statistic called U_j (Molenaar, 1983) may be used to test whether observed IRFs are steeper (say, $U_j < -1.645$) or flatter (say, $U_j > 1.645$) than expected under the Rasch model. Rejection of WLI (indicated by a significant R_2) may be taken as evidence of multidimensionality.

Computer Software

The program RSP (Glas & Ellis, 1993) was used in our data example. Item parameters were estimated using CML, and person parameters using ML assuming item parameter estimates to be the true values. Fit of the Rasch model to J items was assessed using statistics R_1 and R_2 and fit to individual items using statistic U_j.

The Partial Credit Model

Masters's (1982) partial credit model (PCM) is an extension of the Rasch model to polytomous item scores and is often used for practical data analysis. For ordered, polytomous item scores, $0,\ldots,m$, the PCM models m adjacent score pairs, $(0,1),\ldots,(m-1,m)$, as separate Rasch models:

$$P(X_j=x_j|\theta;X_j=x_j-1\vee X_j=x_j) = \frac{\exp(\theta-\delta_{jx_j})}{1+\exp(\theta-\delta_{jx_j})}, \qquad x_j=1,\ldots,m. \tag{16.29}$$

As in the Rasch model, parameter δ_{jx_j} locates this response function on the θ scale, and for $\theta=\delta_{jx_j}$, the probabilities of having an item score of either x_j-1 or x_j both equal 0.5. Combining the $m-1$ conditional probabilities in (16.29) yields the PCM

$$P(X_j=x_j|\theta)=\frac{\exp\left[\sum_{s=1}^{x_j}(\theta-\delta_{js})\right]}{\sum_{q=0}^{m}\exp\left[\sum_{s=1}^{q}(\theta-\delta_{js})\right]}. \tag{16.30}$$

Note that $x_j=0$ creates a problem in the numerator; hence, one chooses $\sum_{s=1}^{0}(\theta-\delta_{js})\equiv 0$, which results in $\sum_{x_j=0}^{m}P(X_j=x_j|\theta)\equiv 1$. This choice also defines $P(X_j=0|\theta)$ to be decreasing, which is seen as a desirable property.

Masters (1982) used data matrix $\mathbf{X}_{N\times J}$ with elements $x_{vj} = 0,\ldots,m$, and decomposed item scores x_{vj} into m binary scores x_{vjs} ($s = 1,\ldots,m$), with $x_{vjs} = 1$ if $x_{vj} = s$, and $x_{vjs} = 0$ otherwise. The marginal person total scores $x_{v+} = \sum_{j=1}^{J} x_{vj}$, with $v = 1,\ldots,N$, are sufficient statistics for estimating $\boldsymbol{\theta}_N$. The counts for each separate score on item j, $x_{+js} = \sum_{v=1}^{N} x_{vjs}$, with $s = 1,\ldots,m$, are the m sufficient statistics for each of the parameters δ_{js}, with $s = 1,\ldots,m$. Following a two-stage approach, CML is used for estimating the item parameters and ML for estimating the person parameters assuming that the item parameter estimates are the true values. Goodness-of-fit assessment is directed primarily at evaluating response functions, but the investigation of Assumption LI has met with considerable numerical problems. The program OPLM (Verhelst, Glas, & Verstralen, 1994) can be used for estimating and fitting the PCM.

COMPARING IRT MODELS

The 3PLM, the 2PLM and its generalization, the GRM, and the Rasch model and its generalization, the PCM, define response curves by means of parametric functions—here, logistic functions. Hence, these are parametric IRT models. Within the classes of models for dichotomous item scores, different models take different sets of item parameters into account. Hence, they provide descriptions of the data at different levels of complexity, each allowing for interesting explanations of the responses provided by the respondents. The GRM and the PCM provide models for different response probabilities but define similar item parameters.

Unlike parametric IRT models, the MHM imposes order restrictions on response functions, thus leaving them free to vary as long as Assumption M is satisfied. This is a nonparametric IRT model (e.g., Junker, 2001; Sijtsma & Meijer, 2007; Stout, 2002). In general, nonparametric models are based on weaker assumptions than parametric models. This is true within the set of models discussed here but not between any pair of nonparametric and parametric IRT models conceivable (e.g., Hemker et al., 1997).

The MHM is more general than the parametric models discussed here. For dichotomous-item models, in the nested sequence MHM-3PLM-2PLM-1PLM, each next model is a special case of the previous model. For polytomous-item models, Hemker et al. (1997) have shown not only that the GRM and the PCM are both special cases of the MHM but also that they do not imply one another and, even stronger, that they cannot be true simultaneously: There is no set of response functions in one model that can be transformed into another set that also satisfies the other model. However, differences between these models are often so small that in real-data analysis it may be difficult to distinguish the fit of one model from that of the other.

Because of their generality, nonparametric models have proven to be excellent starting points for deriving properties of IRT models in general (e.g., Ellis & Van den Wollenberg, 1993; Hemker et al., 1997; Holland & Rosenbaum, 1986; Junker, 1991, 1993; Stout, 2002). For example, Ellis and Van den Wollenberg (1993) showed that IRT models in general are true for subpopulations that have the same θ but not for individual respondents. This implies that for a particular θ value, say θ_d, a response probability like $P(X_j = 1|\theta_d) = 0.7$ (dichotomous scoring) means that 70% of the respondents having the same θ_d provide a 1 score and 30% a 0 score, whereas the same individual is assumed to provide the same item score across independent replications. This is the random sampling interpretation of response probabilities (Holland, 1990). This interpretation contradicts general notions about human behavior, which assume that individuals show variation in response to the same item. This would imply the stochastic subject interpretation of response probability (Holland, 1990): $P(X_j = 1|\theta_d) = 0.7$ now means that respondent v produces a 1 score in 70% and a 0 score in 30% of the random draws from his or her personal distribution of scores on item j. This has led Borsboom (2005) to argue that models for individual performance should be based on locally independent, repeated measurements, but he also noted that such repetitions usually are not available. This is a challenging conclusion that will need more attention in future developments.

Also interesting is the stochastic ordering result in (16.4). SOL holds for all dichotomous-item (M, LI, $D = 1$) models, including logistic models and also the MHM, which allows for irregular IRFs that are flat in some regions of θ and jagged elsewhere. SOL also holds for the PCM but not for the GRM and the polytomous-item MHM (Hemker et al., 1997).

Finally, for sets of either dichotomous or polytomous items that subsume under relaxed versions of each of the assumptions in (M, LI, $D = 1$), if $J \to \infty$, then the total score X_+ is a consistent ordinal estimator of θ (Junker, 1991). Thus, in nearly each IRT model, there is an intimate relationship between ordering according to the observable X_+ and the latent θ, even in models that do not imply the SOL property. This suggests that, in general, little harm is done if the intuitively sensible total score X_+ is used for ordering persons (Van der Ark, 2005) under nearly any model that either assumes (M, LI, $D = 1$) or even violates these assumptions in controlled ways.

Due to the complexity of many test data sets, IRT models, either nonparametric or parametric, will not readily fit at the first attempt unless the data set is supported by sound empirical research that is based on well-articulated substantive theory. However, in most research, this is more the exception than the rule. Thus, IRT models are often rejected, which marks the beginning of multiple, complicated rounds of data analysis, in which several likely possibilities—leaving out items, trying subdivisions of the item set, fitting other models—are tried and overfitting is a realistic danger. Nevertheless, such data exploration may yield an acceptable result that, although it is different from what one had in mind at the outset, may provide a better understanding of what caused the model misfit. On the other hand, it rarely happens that a researcher starts an item analysis without at least a hunch or, better, an idea about the structure of his or her test. So rather than adopting a purely exploratory attitude, in practice, researchers often will look for a confirmation of their expectations and not just take any outcome for granted.

Even though nonparametric models are often considered exploratory and parametric models confirmatory data tools, in our opinion both approaches basically are used in the same way when analyzing complex test data. Nonparametric models may be a little more "open minded" because they use item selection procedures such as Mokken's (1971) and because they estimate the full response function, thus allowing many peculiarities of the data to become visible (Ramsay, 1991). Thus, in this sense, they are exploratory methods that let the data "speak for themselves." However, in those cases in which the researcher expects his or her item set to be (M, LI, $D = 1$), Assumptions LI and $D = 1$ can be evaluated using methods proposed by Stout et al. (1996) (not discussed here), Assumption M can be tested using the regression of an item score on the rest score (16.13), and measurement quality can be assessed using the H and H_j coefficients. Thus, the same methods that were considered exploratory tools when the researcher did not have a strong belief about his or her data have become confirmatory tools for testing his or her hypothesis about the test.

More than nonparametric models, probably due to their orientation toward statistical model testing, parametric models are often considered null hypotheses that are evaluated by means of formal statistical tests for the fit of the model to the data. First, statistical tests are used to find out whether a particular assumption of the model fits the data for all J items simultaneously. For example, the 1PLM may be evaluated by means of the R_1 statistic, which assesses whether J IRFs are parallel logistic curves, and the R_2 statistic, which assesses WLI for all $\frac{1}{2}J(J-1)$ item pairs. Second, because models often are found not to fit the data for the whole J-item test, one starts searching for items that could be deleted such that the model fits the data of the remaining item subset, one tries to find a subdivision of the item set in dimensionally distinct item clusters, or one uses other models to explain the data structure. This may involve several rounds of statistical testing of particular aspects of the model on (parts of) the data.

Thus, both parametric and nonparametric IRT data analyses often proceed in an exploratory rather than confirmatory manner, and as with most analyses of complex, highly multivariate data, the nature of the process depends much on whether one has strong hypotheses about one's measurement instruments or not.

Table 16.1 MHM Analysis Results—"Scale Analysis": P_j Values and H_j Values for Total Test (15 Items); "Dimensionality Assessment": H_j Values for Several Lower-Bound c Values; and Total H Values (Last Row)

	Scale Analysis		*Dimensionality Assessment*						
j	P_j	H_j	$c = 0.30$	$c = 0.35$	$c = 0.40$		$c = 0.45$		
1	0.34	0.17	us	us	us	us	us	us	us
2	0.48	0.31	0.33	us	us	us	us	us	us
3	0.31	0.35	0.37	0.39	0.42	—	0.47	—	—
4	0.48	0.36	0.39	0.41	—	0.45	us	us	us
5	0.24	0.40	0.43	0.42	—	0.47	—	0.52	—
6	0.42	0.36	0.40	0.43	0.45	—	us	us	us
7	0.64	0.26	us	us	us	us	us	us	us
8	0.22	0.43	0.46	0.46	0.48	—	0.46	—	—
9	0.90	0.31	0.33	0.36	0.41	—	—	—	0.60
10	0.68	0.35	0.36	0.39	0.43	—	0.55	—	—
11	0.12	0.48	0.49	0.48	0.51	—	0.52	—	—
12	0.32	0.37	0.40	0.41	—	0.42	—	—	0.60
13	0.08	0.46	0.48	0.46	0.48	—	—	0.52	—
14	0.64	0.31	0.36	0.40	us	us	us	us	us
15	0.75	0.28	0.31	us	—	0.42	—	0.65	—
Total H		0.34	0.39	0.42	0.45	0.44	0.49	0.56	0.60

NOTE: "us" means the item was unscalable due to negative H_{jk} with one of the selected items or because the H_j value was smaller than lower-bound c.

A Practical Data Example: Arithmetic of Proportions and Ratios

The nested sequence of dichotomous-item MHM, 3PLM, 2PLM, and 1PLM was used to analyze correct (score 1)/incorrect (score 0) scores from a 15-item arithmetic test. Dutch primary school students ($N = 612$) were asked to solve problems involving proportions and ratios. A typical constructed-response item is "If 10 oranges cost $7.50, what do 3 oranges cost?" The MHM, the 3PLM, the 2PLM, and the 1PLM were fitted, in that order. This order of analysis shows neatly that as models impose more structure on the data, from the point of view of the model this may lead to simpler results and a test that is "pure" in terms of formal, psychometric properties, but from the point of view of the data this may lead to a loss of items and thus a loss of information on classifying individuals on the basis of their test scores.

MHM Analysis

The proportions of correct answers (P-values, second column of Table 16.1) varied greatly. Item 13 was the most difficult item (smallest P) and Item 9 the easiest item (largest P). The third column shows the 15 item-scalability values (all H_js significantly larger than 0; test results not tabulated). In an MHM analysis, $c = 0.3$ is considered the minimum for inclusion of items in a scale (Sijtsma & Molenaar, 2002, chap. 5). Because $H_j < 0.3$ for three items and because H_j was small for several other items, the possibility of nonmonotonicities in the IRFs was evaluated next.

As an example, we discuss the IRF of Item 15 ($H_{15} = 0.28$). Its low H_j value does not contradict the MHM but suggests that this item contributes little to an accurate person ordering. This suggestion would be supported by a violation of Assumption M. The discrete IRF estimate (Figure 16.1: left-hand panel, adapted from MSP) shows a significant decrease between two groups

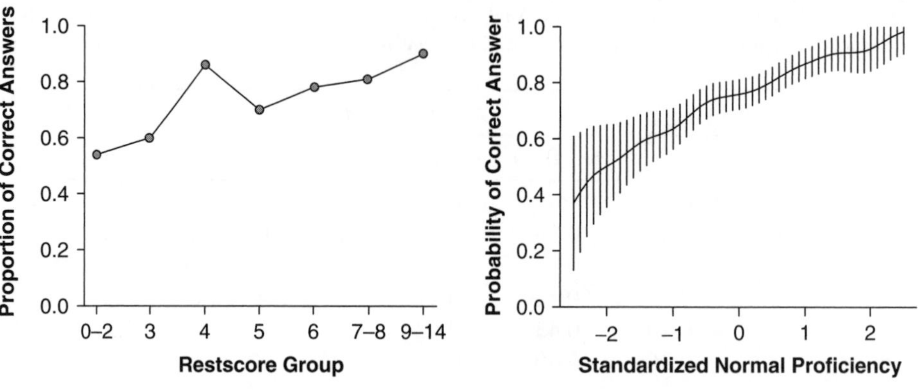

Figure 16.1 IRF estimates of Item 15.

NOTE: (Left-hand side panel) Discrete estimate. (Right-hand side panel) Quasi-continuous estimate. Vertical bars indicate 95% confidence intervals.

based on rest scores (16.13) without Item 15, for that reason called restscore groups (two-tailed normal 5% test of $P[X_{15} = 1|R_{(-15)} = 4] = P[X_{15} = 1|R_{(-15)} = 5]$; $Z = 2.11$, $p = 0.035$). The continuous IRF estimate (right-hand panel, adapted from TestGraf98) is based on weighted averages of $P[X_{15} = 1|R_{(-15)}]$ across neighboring rest-score groups, but it does not pick up this violation. Based on this result and the large p-value of the normal test, we do not take this violation very seriously. Because none of the other 14 estimated IRFs showed significant violations, we conclude that the data support Assumption M for all items.

To assess dimensionality, items were clustered using $c = 0.30, 0.35, 0.40,$ and 0.45. For $c = 0.30$, a 13-item cluster without Items 1 and 7 was found (note that now $H_{15} = 0.31$). Compared with the 15-item test, H increased from 0.34 to 0.39. The IRFs estimated from the data without Items 1 and 7 did not show violations of Assumption M. Thus, the 13-item cluster satisfies the MHM and allows for sufficiently accurate measurement. A higher c of 0.35 led to the additional rejection of Items 2 and 15. For $c = 0.40$, two clusters were found, and for $c = 0.45$, three clusters were found, while several other items proved unscalable. This sequence of outcomes—first, (nearly) all items are in the same cluster, and later, the cluster is split into smaller clusters while other items are unscalable—is taken as evidence of unidimensionality ($D = 1$) (Hemker et al., 1995). This conclusion was corroborated by inspection of the item content, which was highly similar both for items that were in the same cluster and for items that were in different clusters.

3PLM and 2PLM Analysis

Based on the MHM analysis, Items 1 and 7 were removed from the test, and then BILOG-MG (Zimowski et al., 1996; default settings were used) was used to first fit the 3PLM to the data and then the 2PLM. The γ estimates ranged from 0.011 (SE = 0.008) to 0.102 (SE = 0.068); none was significantly larger than 0. A likelihood ratio test that compared the fit of the 2PLM and the 3PLM resulted in $\chi^2_{(df=13)} = 17.98$ ($p = 0.16$); hence, the fit of the models could not be distinguished, which confirmed that the γ parameters could be dropped. In addition, for the 2PLM, the RMSD item fit statistics did not suggest misfit for any of the 13 items. Table 16.2 shows the α and δ estimates. Figure 16.2 (solid curve) shows the standard error for $\hat{\theta}$ (i.e., $I(\theta)^{-1/2}$; see (16.23)) based on all 13 items. The highest measurement precision was obtained for $0.75 < \theta < 1.00$. Thus, the test seems to measure the most accurate at the higher region of the scale.

Table 16.2 Estimated Item Parameters and Item Fit Statistics for the 2PLM and the Rasch Model

	2PLM / MML Estimation					*Rasch /CML Estimation*		
j	$\hat{\alpha}_j$	(*SE*)	$\hat{\delta}_j$	(*SE*)	*RMSD*	$\hat{\delta}_j$	(*SE*)	U_j
2	0.73	(0.09)	0.11	(0.09)	1.20	—	—	—
3	0.90	(0.10)	0.73	(0.09)	0.60	−0.38	(0.10)	0.36
4	0.92	(0.10)	0.07	(0.08)	1.45	−1.43	(0.10)	0.49
5	1.08	(0.14)	0.97	(0.10)	0.76	0.17	(0.11)	−0.41
6	1.00	(0.14)	0.30	(0.08)	0.66	−1.04	(0.10)	0.04
8	1.24	(0.16)	0.99	(0.09)	0.42	0.27	(0.11)	−0.31
9	0.52	(0.09)	−2.80	(0.44)	0.94	—	—	—
10	0.69	(0.08)	−0.83	(0.11)	0.64	—	—	—
11	1.11	(0.17)	1.56	(0.15)	1.37	1.11	(0.13)	−0.53
12	1.01	(0.12)	0.67	(0.09)	0.81	−0.44	(0.10)	−0.15
13	1.01	(0.15)	1.95	(0.19)	0.62	1.74	(0.15)	0.39
14	0.72	(0.09)	−0.60	(0.10)	0.94	—	—	—
15	0.52	(0.08)	−1.46	(0.21)	0.75	—	—	—

NOTE: Item difficulties under MML and CML have been estimated using different norming of latent variable scale.

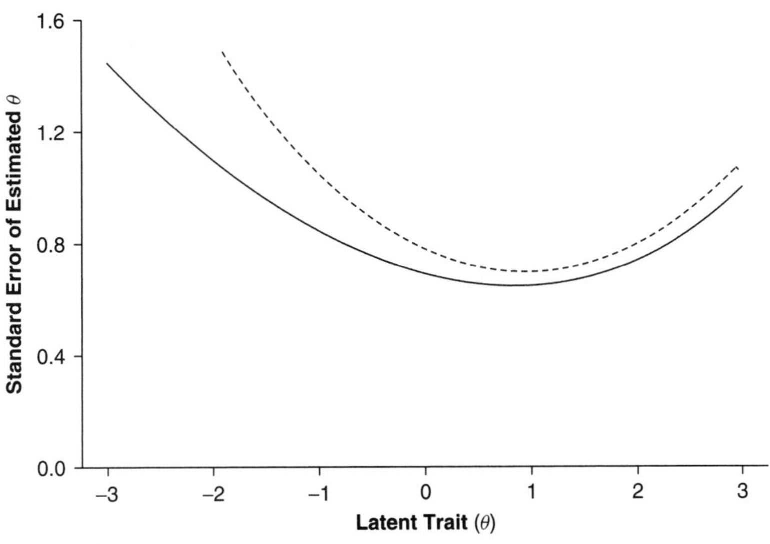

Figure 16.2 Standard error of $\hat{\theta}$ based on 13 2PLM items (solid curve) and 8 Rasch items (dashed curve).

Rasch Analysis

The different slope parameters found in the 2PLM analysis suggest that the Rasch model will not fit the data for all 13 items. Indeed, using RSP (Glas & Ellis, 1993) resulted in significant misfit ($R_1 = 64.20$, $df = 36$, $p = 0.003$; $R_2 = 128.07$, $df = 72$, $p = 0.000$). Next, a subset of 8 items with nearly the same IRF slopes was selected (based on the $\hat{\alpha}$s; the resulting item subset can be found in Table 16.2). For this subset, RSP analysis supported the hypothesis of equal slopes ($R_1 = 29.44$, $df = 21$, $p = 0.10$). This was further corroborated by the standard normal U_j values ($|U_j| < 1.645$ for all j). In addition, support was obtained for Assumption LI ($R_2 = 36.62$, $df = 24$, $p = 0.05$). Figure 16.2 (dashed curve) shows the standard error (i.e., $I(\theta)^{-1/2}$) for $\hat{\theta}$ based on the 8 items. Eight Rasch items selected from 13 2PLM items necessarily provide less statistical information for the ML estimation of θ, but the loss of precision was small because the 5 excluded items had relatively flat IRFs.

Summary of Data Analysis

The MHM analysis of the 15 items showed that the H_js were relatively small and the IRFs were monotone. A dimensionality analysis using varying lower-bound c values suggested that 13 items with $H_j \geqslant 0.3$ together measured one latent trait. Together these results suggest that the IRFs had relatively weak, positive slopes and that the 13 selected items contributed modestly to accurate person ordering using X_+. The 3PLM analysis supported the conclusion that each of the IRF lower asymptotes was 0. The 2PLM fitted the data for the 13 items. A further selection of 8 items with approximately equal slopes led to a fitting Rasch model, but given that the items contributed modestly to person ordering, one may seriously wonder whether one is prepared to sacrifice 5 items to have a fitting Rasch model. Also, note that item selection was data driven and that this provides less compelling evidence for rejecting so many items than substantive reasons would.

Discussion

In this chapter, we have introduced IRT as a family of related models for measurement. We have concentrated on the analysis of data from a single test or questionnaire, because they represent the majority of IRT applications in most areas of science that use tests and questionnaires for measurement. This chapter has emphasized the estimation and fit evaluation of IRT models for single-test data, but several other analyses such as the following are possible:

- Differential item functioning (DIF) is aimed at checking whether an IRF or ISRF of an item is the same in different groups from the population of interest, such as boys and girls and different ethnic groups. If the response function of item j is different, the item is said to exhibit DIF. DIF is often taken as a sign that in one group the item measures abilities or skills that are irrelevant for item performance in the other group. An example is an arithmetic test that also requires elementary language skills and a low-level group that varies considerably with respect to these language skills so that language skills level affects item performance differentially, whereas the individuals in the other group all have a skills level high enough not to affect item performance differentially.

- Person-fit analysis is aimed at identifying respondents who produce patterns of item scores, $\mathbf{x}$, that are atypical for the group to which they belong or relative to the IRT model that was fitted to the test data for this group. An example is students who have guessed excessively for correct answers in educational tests and thus produced patterns of 1s and 0s that are unrelated to item difficulty.

- Cognitive skills diagnosis is aimed at modeling the skills necessary to complete a task successfully or the cognitive process that underlies the response to a cognitive task. Models may formulate linear restrictions on item parameters to formalize skill contributions, assume multidimensional latent variables to formalize a more complex ability structure, or assume a multiplicative structure for noncompensatory response processes. A fitting model provides information on skill deficiencies that require additional training or on the strategies used by children to solve complex cognitive problems. This may provide information on the developmental phase in which they are. This kind of information contributes to a better understanding of what a test measures—that is, to its validity.

Large-scale educational testing done by large testing agencies, such as Educational Testing Service (Princeton, NJ) and CITO National Institute for Educational Measurement (Arnhem, The Netherlands), uses possibilities offered by IRT such as the following:

- *Equating:* Items from different tests measuring the same ability or skill are displayed on a common scale, and students who have taken these different tests are comparable with one another on this scale and also with cutoff scores used for decision making.
- *Item banking:* This refers to the composition of a large set—hundreds—of items that measure the same ability or skill or sets of abilities and skills in a particular domain that is of interest for the evaluation of educational goals. An item bank contains the psychometric properties of all the items and also their position on a common, calibrated scale that is obtained by equating a large number of tests. In addition, an item bank contains information on item content, frequency of item use in tests, dates when they have been used, and so on, and together with the psychometric information on item difficulty and other item properties, this information can be used to assemble tests from the bank that simultaneously agree with a list of specifications deemed necessary for a particular application.
- *Adaptive testing:* This is aimed at presenting by computer to the examinee the smallest number of items that provides the most accurate estimate of his or her θ value in terms of $I(\theta)^{-1/2}$. The items are presented consecutively, and after each response, the estimation of θ is updated; the next item from the item bank to be presented is the one suited best to the examinee's $\hat{\theta}$ as we know it at that point in the testing process. This adaptive testing procedure stops if a formal criterion is satisfied—for example, if the standard error of $\hat{\theta}$ drops below a preset maximum value.

Equating, item banking, and adaptive testing require large-scale research and funding and are only feasible when the scale of the test application is such that the investments pay off. They are of more general interest because they make full use of the possibilities that parametric IRT models, in particular the 1PLM, the 2PLM, and the 3PLM, have to offer. Central is the possibility of equating scales, and the θ scale is a convenient tool for this.

ACKNOWLEDGMENTS

The authors wish to express their gratitude to CITO National Institute for Educational Measurement for generously making the data available that we used for illustrating IRT model analysis.

REFERENCES

Baker, F. B., & Kim, S.-H. (2004). *Item response theory: Parameter estimation techniques.* New York: Marcel Dekker.

Birnbaum, A. (1968). Some latent trait models and their use in inferring an examinee's ability. In F. M. Lord & M. R. Novick (Eds.), *Statistical theories of mental test scores* (pp. 395–479). Reading, MA: Addison-Wesley.

Bock, R. D., & Lieberman, M. (1970). Fitting a response model for *n* dichotomously scored items. *Psychometrika, 35*, 179–197.

Bock, R. D., & Mislevy, R. J. (1982). Adaptive EAP estimation of ability in a microcomputer environment. *Applied Psychological Measurement, 6*, 431–444.

Boomsma, A., Van Duijn, M. A. J., & Snijders, T. A. B. (2001). *Essays on item response theory.* New York: Springer-Verlag.

Borsboom, D. (2005). *Measuring the mind: Conceptual issues in contemporary psychometrics*. Cambridge, UK: Cambridge University Press.

Eggen, T. J. H. M. (2000). On the loss of information in conditional maximum likelihood estimation of item parameters. *Psychometrika, 65*, 337–362.

Ellis, J. L., & Van den Wollenberg, A. L. (1993). Local homogeneity in latent trait models: A characterization of the homogeneous monotone IRT model. *Psychometrika, 58*, 417–429.

Fischer, G. H. (1974). *Einführung in die Theorie psychologischer Tests*. Bern, Switzerland: Huber.

Glas, C. A. W., & Ellis, J. L. (1993). *User's manual RSP: Rasch scaling program*. Groningen, The Netherlands: iecProGAMMA.

Glas, C. A. W., & Verhelst, N. D. (1995). Testing the Rasch model. In G. H. Fischer & I. W. Molenaar (Eds.), *Rasch models: Foundations, recent developments, and applications* (pp. 69–95). New York: Springer-Verlag.

Grayson, D. A. (1988). Two-group classification in latent trait theory: Scores with monotone likelihood ratio. *Psychometrika, 53*, 383–392.

Hemker, B. T., Sijtsma, K., & Molenaar, I. W. (1995). Selection of unidimensional scales from a multidimensional item bank in the polytomous Mokken IRT model. *Applied Psychological Measurement, 19*, 337–352.

Hemker, B. T., Sijtsma, K., Molenaar, I. W., & Junker, B. W. (1997). Stochastic ordering using the latent trait and the sum score in polytomous IRT models. *Psychometrika, 62*, 331–347.

Hoijtink, H., & Boomsma, A. (1995). On person parameter estimation in the dichotomous Rasch model. In G. H. Fischer & I. W. Molenaar (Eds.), *Rasch models: Foundations, recent developments, and applications* (pp. 53–68). New York: Springer-Verlag.

Holland, P. W. (1990). On the sampling theory foundations of item response theory models. *Psychometrika, 55*, 577–601.

Holland, P. W., & Rosenbaum, P. R. (1986). Conditional association and unidimensionality in monotone latent variable models. *Annals of Statistics, 14*, 1523–1543.

Junker, B. W. (1991). Essential independence and likelihood-based ability estimation for polytomous items. *Psychometrika, 56*, 255–278.

Junker, B. W. (1993). Conditional association, essential independence and monotone unidimensional item response models. *Annals of Statistics, 21*, 1359–1378.

Junker, B. W. (2001). On the interplay between nonparametric and parametric IRT, with some thoughts about the future. In A. B. and M. A. J. Van Duijn & T. A. B. Snijders (Eds.), *Essays on item response theory* (pp. 247–276). New York: Springer-Verlag.

Junker, B. W., & Sijtsma, K. (2000). Latent and manifest monotonicity in item response models. *Applied Psychological Measurement, 24*, 65–81.

Karabatsos, G., & Sheu, C.-F. (2004). Order-constrained Bayes inference for dichotomous models of unidimensional nonparametric IRT. *Applied Psychological Measurement, 28*, 110–125.

Masters, G. N. (1982). A Rasch model for partial credit scoring. *Psychometrika, 47*, 149–174.

Mellenbergh, G. J. (1995). Conceptual notes on models for discrete polytomous item responses. *Applied Psychological Measurement, 19*, 91–100.

Michell, J. (1990). *An introduction to the logic of psychological measurement*. Hillsdale, NJ: Lawrence Erlbaum.

Mokken, R. J. (1971). *A theory and procedure of scale analysis*. Berlin, Germany: De Gruyter.

Mokken, R. J., Lewis, C., & Sijtsma, K. (1986). Rejoinder to "The Mokken Scale: A Critical Discussion." *Applied Psychological Measurement, 10*, 279–285.

Molenaar, I. W. (1983). Some improved diagnostics for failure of the Rasch model. *Psychometrika, 48*, 49–72.

Molenaar, I. W. (1997). Nonparametric models for polytomous items. In W. J. van der Linden & R. K. Hambleton (Eds.), *Handbook of modern item response theory* (pp. 369–380). New York: Springer-Verlag.

Molenaar, I. W., & Sijtsma, K. (2000). *MSP5 for Windows: User's manual*. Groningen, The Netherlands: iecProGAMMA.

Neyman, J., & Scott, E. L. (1948). Consistent estimation from partially consistent observations. *Econometrica, 16*, 1–32.

Ramsay, J. O. (1991). Kernel smoothing approaches to nonparametric item characteristic curve estimation. *Psychometrika, 56*, 611–630.

Ramsay, J. O. (2000). *A program for the graphical analysis of multiple choice test and questionnaire data*. Montreal, Quebec, Canada: McGill University, Department of Psychology.

Rasch, G. (1960). *Probabilistic models for some intelligence and attainment tests*. Copenhagen, Denmark: Nielsen & Lydiche.

Samejima, F. (1997). Graded response model. In W. J. van der Linden & R. K. Hambleton (Eds.), *Handbook of modern item response theory* (pp. 85–100). New York: Springer-Verlag.

Sijtsma, K., & Meijer, R. R. (2007). Nonparametric item response theory and related topics. In C. R. Rao & S. Sinharay (Eds.), *Handbook of statistics, Vol. 26: Psychometrics* (pp. 719–746). Amsterdam: Elsevier.

Sijtsma, K., & Molenaar, I. W. (2002). *Introduction to nonparametric item response theory.* Thousand Oaks, CA: Sage.

Stout, W. F. (2002). Psychometrics: From practice to theory and back. *Psychometrika, 67*, 485–518.

Stout, W. F., Habing, B., Douglas, J., Kim, H., Roussos, L., & Zhang, J. (1996). Conditional covariance based nonparametric multidimensionality assessment. *Applied Psychological Measurement, 20*, 331–354.

Thissen, D. (1982). Marginal maximum likelihood estimation for the one-parameter logistic model. *Psychometrika, 47*, 175–186.

Thissen, D., Chen, W.-H., & Bock, R. D. (2003). *MULTILOG (Version 7.0).* Lincolnwood, IL: Scientific Software International. Computer software.

Van Abswoude, A. A. H., Van der Ark, L. A., & Sijtsma, K. (2004). A comparative study of test data dimensionality assessment procedures under nonparametric IRT models. *Applied Psychological Measurement, 28*, 3–24.

Van der Ark, L. A. (2005). Practical consequences of stochastic ordering of the latent trait under various polytomous IRT models. *Psychometrika, 70*, 283–304.

Van der Linden, W. J. (2005). *Linear models for optimal test design.* New York: Springer-Verlag.

Van der Linden, W. J., & Hambleton, R. K. (Eds.). (1997). *Handbook of modern item response theory.* New York: Springer-Verlag.

Verhelst, N. D., Glas, C. A. W., & Verstralen, H. H. F. M. (1994). *OPLM: Computer program and manual.* Arnhem, The Netherlands: CITO.

Zimowski, M. F., Muraki, E., Mislevy, R. J., & Bock, R. D. (1996). *BILOG-MG: Multiple-group IRT analysis and test maintainance for binary items.* Chicago: Scientific Software.

17

PROBABILISTIC SIMULATION MODELS OF SOCIETY

KLAUS G. TROITZSCH

INTRODUCTION

From the very beginning, it should be clear that throughout this chapter, stochastic processes are used as models of dynamic processes in a society. This does not in any way mean that real processes in societies are stochastic or in any way random; we do not even discuss the question of randomness or determination in the real world. But in many cases, we can only estimate probabilities of state changes as we do not know enough about the underlying process in the target system.

When we restrict ourselves, as we do, on stochastic models that deal with individual agents who interact with each other and/or with the population they are members of, then we have to think both of individual transition probabilities (there might be probabilistic laws according to which individuals behave) and of probabilities of transition between different states of the macroentity, and perhaps we will have to define more than two levels besides the level of the individual and the level of the population.

Probabilistic laws can be defined as axioms that do not directly connect the current state of an individual, a group of individuals, or a population as a whole to the future state of the same or other entities but that connect the current state to a probability with which a certain entity can be found at a point of time in the future. In some simple cases, even a time-dependent distribution over the possible states of an entity can de derived from the assumptions, as some of the examples below will illustrate.

This chapter is organized as follows. It starts with a short taxonomy of stochastic processes (although part of this is also covered in Chapters 9 and 10 on time-series and survival analysis). Three more detailed sections then cover the classical stochastic approach in social simulation: microanalytical simulation models (leaving out another, even more classic approach—namely, queuing models, which are covered in Chapter 19); multilevel models, where the interactions between individuals and the population(s) to which they belong are analyzed; and multi-agent models, where interactions between individuals are the focus of research.

A SHORT TAXONOMY OF STOCHASTIC PROCESSES

Generally speaking, a stochastic process is a series $\{X_t\}, t \in T$ of random variables X_t. Here, t—the time parameter—is an element of the index set T, which is often identified with the set of (positive) integers (stochastic process in discrete time) or with the set of (positive) real numbers (stochastic process in continuous time).

In the case of continuous-state space models, a random variable X is a mapping $X : \Omega \to \Re$, which attributes real numbers $X(\omega)$ to the outcomes ω of a random process; in the case of discrete-state space models, the range of the mapping is some finite or countable set. Thus, a result ω of a random process corresponds to the time series $\{X_t\}, t \in T$.

A white-noise process $\{\varepsilon_t\}, t \in T$ is a series of identically and independently distributed random variables ε_t.

If $\{\varepsilon_t\}, t \in T$ is a white-noise process, then $\{X_t\}$ with

$$X_t = \begin{cases} \varepsilon_t & \text{for } t = 1 \\ X_{t-1} + \varepsilon_t & \text{for } t > 1 \end{cases}$$

is a random-walk process.

A Gauss process (or normal process) is a process whose random variables have a joint normal distribution for any finite selection of time points.

The Classical Approach: Microanalytical Simulation Models

Microanalytical simulation models (MSM) were first developed to predict demographic processes and their consequences for tax and transfer systems (Orcutt, Merz, & Quinke, 1986). They consist of at least two levels:

- The level of individuals or households (or in the rare case of simulating enterprises, the level of enterprises)
- The aggregate level (e.g., national economy level)

More sophisticated MSMs distinguish between the individual and the household levels, thus facilitating models in which persons move between households and can form and dissolve new households (e.g., by marriage and divorce).

The classical microsimulation comes in three different types, the first of which is the most common, but does not actually describe a stochastic process:

- *Static microsimulation:* Change of the demographic structure of the model population is performed by reweighting the age class according to external information; that is, the model population remains the same over time, but the individual members of the model population are differently weighted from period to period to make it representative, particularly for the changing age structure (which, in turn, would have to be estimated separately, e.g., in a difference equation model that takes into account the birth, death, and aging process on the level of cohorts instead of individuals!).
- *Dynamic microsimulation:* Change of the demographic structure of the model population is performed by aging the model persons individually (and by having them give birth to new persons and by having them die) according to life tables.
- *Longitudinal microsimulation:* Simulation is done on an age cohort and over the whole life of this cohort, thus omitting a population's age structure (but children of the cohort members may still be simulated).

This chapter will concentrate on the so-called dynamic microsimulation. All types of microsimulation, in contrast to many other simulation approaches, are data driven instead of concept driven: Starting from data of a population or rather a sample from some population, normally on the nation-state level, this approach models individual behavior in terms of reproduction, education, and employment; simulates this individual behavior; and aggregates it to the population level to generate predictions about the future age or employment structure (see Figure 17.1).

To realize the simulation, several subprocesses have to be modeled:

- Demographic processes such as aging, birth, death, marriage, divorce, regional mobility, household formation, and dissolution
- Participation in education and employment, employment income
- Social transfers

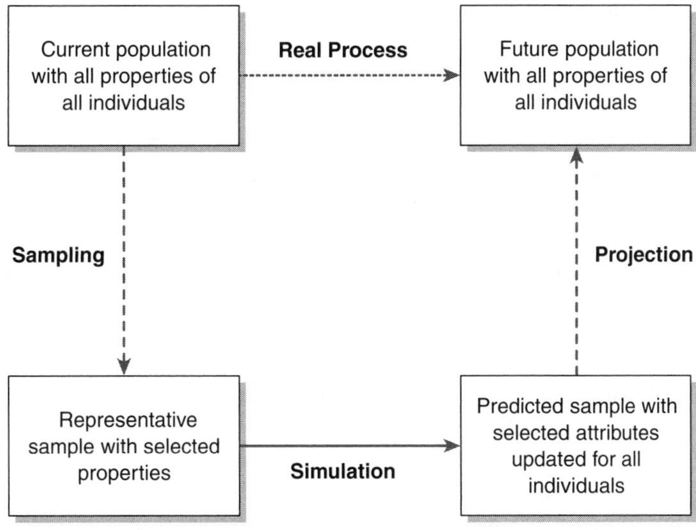

Figure 17.1 The process of microanalytical simulation.

- Taxes and social security
- Consumption
- Wealth

The initial states of MSMs are read from databases in which individual and/or household and/or enterprise characteristics are stored from an empirical sample. It is difficult to construct a sample of households or individuals that is representative both in terms of the structure of the individuals and households and in terms of the enterprises that employ the individuals: Every closed sample of individuals and households will contain persons employed by any number of firms, but to arrive at a contiguous sample, one would have to include at least a sample of the other individuals in these firms, which would then have new employees who are not in the individual sample and so forth; moreover, this sample of firms will not necessarily be representative even if the household and/or individual sample is. Over the years, it has become much easier to get contiguous data for individuals and households as in most developed countries there are long-term panels available (e.g., the German Socio-Economic Panel since 1984). In the case of panels, it is possible, at least in principle, to calibrate model parameters and algorithms to panel data by estimating parameters of birth, death, and other processes from the panel data.

Birth and Death Processes

In the simplest case, the demographic part of a microsimulation model is just a birth-and-death process, which is usually characterized by population-wide birth and death rates. If the probabilities of a birth or a death are called β and δ, respectively, and thought to depend on the current population size n, then these probabilities are often written as $\beta(n) = a_1 n$ and $\delta(n) = a_2 n + b_2 n^2$, where often the carrying capacity K is introduced, such that $b_2 = (a_1 - a_2)/K$. In this—rather simple—case, the overall probability $p(n)$ of finding a population with time-constant coefficients a_1, a_2, and K or b_2 with n members can be calculated with the help of the master equation of this probability (Weidlich & Haag, 1983, p. 113ff.), which reads (with the additional assumption $\beta(-1) = \delta(-1) = 0$),

$$\begin{aligned} dp(n;t)/dt = {} & \beta(n-1)p(n-1;t) \\ & - [\beta(n) - \delta(n)]p(n;t) \\ & + \delta(n+1)p(n+1;t). \end{aligned} \tag{17.1}$$

This master equation is in fact a large (potentially infinite) system of linear differential equations in the functions $p(n)$, where $dp(n;t)/dt$ is the change of the values of these functions in infinitesimal time. The idea behind this system of differential equations is that the probability of finding a population with exactly n members changes over time and this change is due to the fact that within very short time intervals, events such as births and deaths occur with certain (very small) probabilities. In each of these very short time intervals, at most one of these events occurs, and it occurs with a certain probability depending on the current size of the population. And when a birth has a certain probability, then with a certain probability every conceivable population of size n leaves this state and acquires the state $n+1$ instead, thus increasing the probability of finding any conceivable population in state $n+1$ (and the same idea holds for deaths that move a population from state n into state $n-1$).

The only stationary solution—that is, a solution that does not change any longer—of this system of differential equations is $p_{st}(0) = 1$ and $p_{st}(n) = 0$ for $n > 0$; that is, a population with no members cannot change any longer, whereas any other population can increase or decrease, which means that in the long run, all members of the population are dead, as $n = 0$ is an absorbing state that cannot be left once it is reached. Nevertheless, for a long time in this stochastic process, we will find a population size near the carrying capacity with a relatively high probability (i.e., a local maximum of the function $p(n)$).

More Complex Processes

For the case of human populations (and many animal populations), this model of the birth-and-death process is much too simple, as the probability that a child is born of a woman (within a certain period of time) does not only (and in the case of a modern society, not at all) depend on the current size of the population but also on (biological and socially attributed) individual and other social properties, such as age and health (as examples of biological and individual properties), education and employment (as examples of socially attributed individual properties) or marital status, kinship, and friendship network (as examples of social attributes). The same is true for the probability that a person dies within a certain period of time; this probability depends on age, sex, health, as well as education and employment (at least insofar as health partly depends on these) and the state of the society he or she lives in (war and peace, wealth and poverty, etc.).

This is why microsimulation models will always simulate births and deaths with transition probabilities that depend on the named attributes of the model individuals. This makes it necessary to collect data about property-dependent birth and death rates and to make assumptions about their future development. As even the short history of the developed nations in the past half-century shows, death and (even more so) birth rates are by no means constant on the population level, life tables change from decade to decade (due to the progress in medical treatment), and even age-dependent probabilities of giving birth to first and subsequent children have changed in the past five decades. It might still be an open question if this change is only due to a hidden and changing heterogeneity (e.g., in the structure of education and employment of women in their second to fifth decades) or due to a long-term process that extends to all subgroups of women (e.g., as a consequence of the availability and acceptance of contraceptives, at least in Western societies).

Other demographically relevant properties and transitions must also be taken into account. Besides marriage and divorce, we have, for instance, to think of the transition from primary to different types of secondary and tertiary education, the transition from education to employment, the transition between different types and places of employment, migration, and so forth.

For designing simulation models that take all these effects into account, these different types of individual-state transitions are not the central problem; instead, the problem lies in the availability of empirical transition frequencies that can be taken as estimates of transition probabilities (if we consider the real-world demographic as inherently stochastic, perhaps probability is only a surrogate of propensities). Given that we have complex life tables, separately for men and women, migrants and indigenous people, speakers of different languages, adherents of different religions, and so forth, we can easily program a function or method that yields the (empirically estimated or otherwise assumed) probability that a simulated individual with certain values in all these attributes will die during the current simulation period and then execute this death with the given probability. The same applies to a simulated individual representing a real-world woman: The probability of initializing a new simulated individual can also be read from a table of estimated or assumed probabilities (even yielding the probability that twins or triplets, boys or girls are born).

For marriage and divorce, a marriage market has to be set up bringing together (the simulated representatives of real-world) single men and women and having them select among potential partners, according to assumptions that, too, have to be derived from empirical analysis. Designing such a simulated marriage market (and, on the other hand, algorithms for divorce, household dissolution, etc.) is a little more complicated than in the case of birth and death, but still designing the algorithm is the easier task as compared with getting hold of empirically sound assumptions of coefficients and parameters. The same applies to processes in education, employment, unemployment, and retiring.

A typical microsimulation model will have the following structure:

- Initialize the individuals from an empirical database.
- Link them together according to their current household structure and to other information on networks (kinship or friendship networks, where the latter information will usually not be available).
- Then, for every simulated period,
    - ∘ organize the marriage market,
    - ∘ and for every simulated individual,
        - ▷ increase its age,
        - ▷ decide whether it dies,
        - ▷ decide whether, if it represents a woman, it gives birth to one or more children,
        - ▷ decide whether, if it represents a person currently married, it is divorced,
        - ▷ decide whether and whom it will marry,
        - ▷ decide whether it will move from one household to another or form a new household,
        - ▷ decide on transitions in education and employment, and execute all these transitions and changes.
    - ∘ Store all the data needed for the analysis and interpretation of the simulated history and perhaps output some intermediate results.
- Analyze and interpret the collected data, aggregate them, calculate distributions, and so on.

What such a microanalytical simulation model yields is in a way prediction, but not in the strict sense. It is the outcome of one realization of a stochastic process whose parameters are not exactly known but are estimated on the base of more or less reliable empirical data. The distribution of the outcome of this stochastic process can only be estimated (as it were, on a higher level of estimation) if a large number of parallel runs of the same model were run; then, confidence intervals can be estimated on a Monte Carlo base. This means that a large number of identical simulations are run, which differ only in the seed of the random number generator; the limits of a 95% confidence interval can then be estimated as the first and last 2.5 percentiles of the estimates calculated from the simulation runs. After this time-consuming procedure, we arrive at an estimate of, for example, the age distribution among women 10 years from now or the distribution of the proportion of people over 65 years of age with living daughters (to nurse them in case of sickness)—but only for the one set of parameters with which we initialized our simulation model earlier on, and not much is then known about the sensitivity—namely, the dependence—of the distribution of the outcomes of the stochastic process to slight changes on one or several of the large number of input parameters.

Although the preceding paragraph might sound overly pessimistic, results of microanalytical simulation models have their value as they show possible paths into the future, and Monte Carlo simulations of this type even show the reliability of the predictions, while multiple runs of similarly parameterized models give a first glance at the validity of the model: If there is no sensitive dependence on initial conditions, then the problem of estimating parameters is not a difficult one. And if we happen to have a long panel or a series of cross sections, then we can validate our model in comparing the results of simulations of past periods with the empirical data of the same period.

MULTILEVEL MODELS

Discrete-State Space Models

One of the simplest stochastic process models of a dynamic process in a society was first described by (Weidlich & Haag, 1983). It is about a population whose members have to make a decision between two mutually exclusive options at any time and base their decision only on the current majority within their population. If we call the two options "Yes" and "No" for the sake of simplicity, then the individual transition probabilities from Yes to No and vice versa depend on the current number or proportion of individuals who have decided on one of the two options. This means that on the individual level, the state space has exactly two members (Yes and No), while on the macrolevel of the population, the state space has $2N + 1$ elements if there are $2N$ members in the society (from 0 members who say Yes to the case where all $2N$ members say Yes; note that for some technical reasons, Weidlich and Haag called the size of the population $2N$). Then, the individual transition probabilities depend, in some way, on the state of the population: The more the members who have already decided on the Yes option, the more likely it will be that one of the members who still says No will change his or her opinion and the less likely it will be that one of the Yes members switches to No.

Thus, on the individual level, the process is not a white-noise process as the transition probabilities are different from time point to time point and, even more, X_{t-1} and X_t are not independent. On the population level, as is easily seen from Figures 17.2 and 17.3, the population state is not identically distributed over time, although for $t \to \infty$, the distribution of X_t converges to a stationary distribution—that is, a distribution that does not change any longer.

The process can be formulated mathematically or programmed into a computer to see what the long-term behavior of the population is. "Long-term behavior" can here be interpreted as a time-dependent distribution function over the state space of the population. (Figures 17.2 and 17.3 both show that the distribution is different for different early points of time; only for t $\to\infty$ does the distribution converge into a stationary distribution.) The way of solving this problem mathematically is over the so-called master equation (for a full treatment, see, e.g., Haken, 1978; Weidlich & Haag, 1983). The master equation is a system of differential equations for the probabilities of the population being in one of its possible states. Its right-hand sides contain the contributions of the individual-state changes that occur with a certain probability, and its solution—if a closed solution can be derived with the help of some simplifications and approximations—is the time-dependent distribution over the state space of the population $p(n;t)$, telling how probable it is to find a population in state n at time t.

To construct this process, we just have to define the individual transition probabilities (other ways of modeling these individual transition probabilities are, of course, possible; see Lumsden & Wilson, 1981, p. 135—this is the simplest and the only one that allows for an approximate analytical solution):

$$\mu_{\text{yes}\leftarrow\text{no}} = \nu \exp(\pi + \kappa x)$$
$$\mu_{\text{no}\leftarrow\text{yes}} = \nu \exp[-(\pi + \kappa x)],$$

where ν is a volatility parameter (the higher the value of ν, the higher the probability that anything happens), π is a preference parameter, κ is a coupling parameter, and x is the state of the population ($-1 \leqslant x \leqslant +1$: -1 means "all no," $+1$ means "all yes"). The parameter ν is used to ensure that $\mu_{\text{yes}\leftarrow\text{no}}$ and $\mu_{\text{no}\leftarrow\text{yes}}$ never exceed 1, and at the same time it controls the speed of the process or the frequency of any switching (regardless of the direction). With π different from 0, the individuals have a generic bias for Yes ($\pi > 0$) and for No ($\pi < 0$). The higher the value of κ, the stronger is the dependence of μ on x (with $\kappa = 0$, the individual transition probability does not depend on x at all).

With the individual transition probabilities, it is already possible to program an algorithm that calculates and visualizes the stochastic process of one population or of a small number of populations. Figure 17.2 shows 20 realizations of our process on the population level (with $\kappa = 1.5$); all these populations start with more or less the same number of members saying Yes and No, and some of them end up with a high majority of Yes, while most others end up with a high majority of No, and only one population still has approximately as many Yes as it has No.

The state of the population is described in terms of the state variable n ($-N \leqslant n \leqslant +N$, from which it becomes clear that the size of the population is more easily handled as $2N$). The state change of the population can now be derived from the individual-state changes. Again, following Weidlich and Haag (1983, pp. 41–42), we define the population transition probability rates (the probability of a transition within a short time interval is of course proportional to the length of the time interval—which was not essential up to here as we assumed time intervals of length 1!) as follows:

$$\begin{aligned} w[(n+1) \leftarrow n]\Delta t &= w_{\uparrow}(n)\Delta t = n_{\text{no}}\mu_{\text{yes}\leftarrow\text{no}} \\ &= (N-n)\mu_{\text{yes}\leftarrow\text{no}} \\ w[(n-1) \leftarrow n]\Delta t &= w_{\downarrow}(n)\Delta t = n_{\text{yes}}\mu_{\text{no}\leftarrow\text{yes}} \\ &= (N+n)\mu_{\text{no}\leftarrow\text{yes}} \\ w[n \leftarrow n]\Delta t &= w_0(n)\Delta t \\ &= 1 - [w_{\uparrow}(n)\Delta t + w_{\downarrow}(n)\Delta t] \\ w[j \leftarrow i]\Delta t &= 0 \text{ for } \mid i-j \mid > 1. \qquad (17.2) \end{aligned}$$

Then, the probability that the population is still in state n at time $t + \Delta t$ is given by the sum of the probabilities to be in one of the neighboring states $n+1$ and $n-1$ at time t, multiplied by the respective transition probability rates $w_{\uparrow}(n-1)\Delta t$ and $w_{\downarrow}(n+1)\Delta t$, and of the probability of the actual state n multiplied with the probability rate $w_0(n)\Delta t$ to remain there:

$$\begin{aligned} p(n;t+\Delta t) = p(n+1;t)w_{\downarrow}(n+1)\Delta t \\ + p(n;t)w_0(n)\Delta t \\ + p(n-1;t)w_{\uparrow}(n-1)\Delta t. \quad (17.3) \end{aligned}$$

Further simplifications lead to

$$\begin{aligned} &[p(n;t+\Delta t) - p(n;t)]/\Delta t \\ &\quad = p(n+1;t)w_{\downarrow}(n+1) - p(n;t)[w_{\downarrow}(n) \\ &\qquad + w_{\uparrow}(n)] + p(n-1;t)w_{\uparrow}(n-1). \quad (17.4) \end{aligned}$$

Again, as in the discussion of birth and death processes, we assume that in each of the short time intervals of length Δt, at most one individual change occurs; thus, the population transition probabilities are probabilities that something happens within a short time interval (probability rates).

Taking the limit $\Delta t \rightarrow 0$, one gets the derivative of $p(n)$ with respect to t:

$$\begin{aligned} p^{\bullet}(n;t) = p(n+1;t)w_{\downarrow}(n+1) \\ - p(n;t)[w_{\downarrow}(n) + w_{\uparrow}(n)] \\ + p(n-1;t)w_{\uparrow}(n-1), \quad (17.5) \end{aligned}$$

which—as in the case of the simple birth and death process—is a linear differential equation in $p(n;t)$, coupled with the neighboring population states $p(n+1;t)$ and $p(n-1;t)$.

Furthermore, simplification yields the system of linear differential equations consisting of $2N+1$ functions $p(n;t), n \in -N, \ldots, N$:

$$\mathbf{p}^{\bullet}(t) = \mathbf{L}\mathbf{p}(t),$$

where $\mathbf{L}$ is a tridiagonal matrix with constant elements:

$$\begin{aligned} l_{ii} &= -w_{\downarrow}(i) - w_{\uparrow}(i), \\ l_{ij} &= w_{\downarrow}(j) \quad j = i+1, \\ l_{ij} &= w_{\uparrow}(j) \quad j = i-1, \\ l_{ij} &= 0 \quad \mid i-j \mid > 1. \end{aligned}$$

This, by the way, leads to $\sum_i p^{\bullet}(i;t) = 0$ for all t, which also fulfills the condition $\sum_i p(i;t) = 1$. The algorithm allows for a straightforward calculation of the graphs in Figure 17.3—which, at the

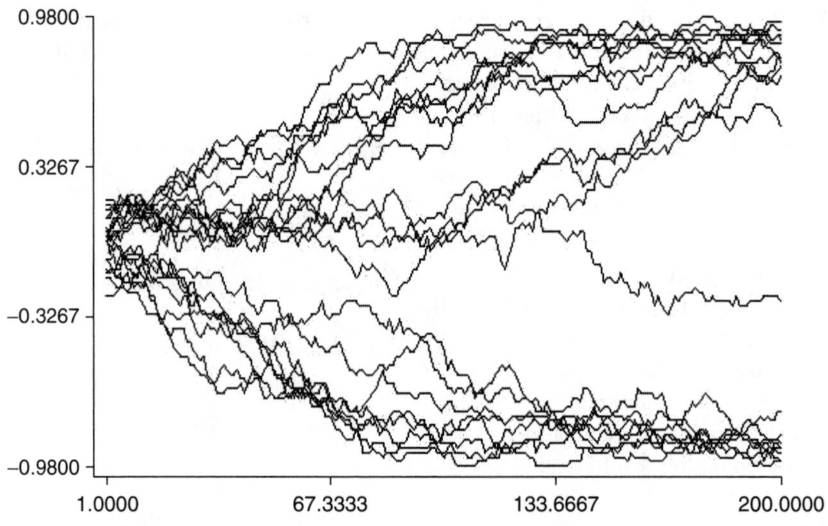

Figure 17.2 Twenty realizations of the opinion formation process.

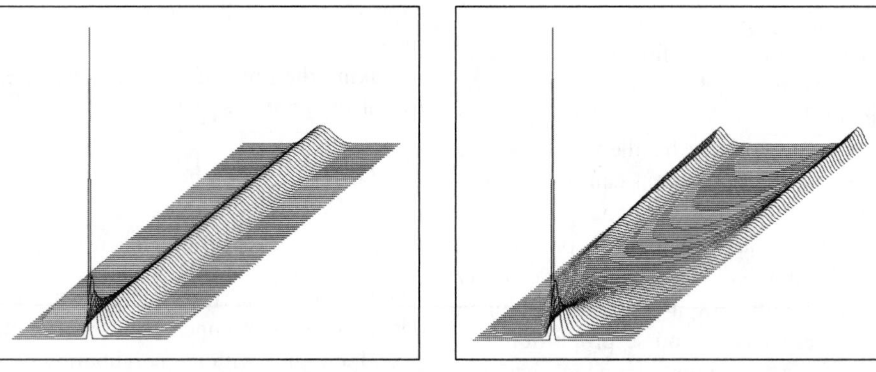

Figure 17.3 Long-term behavior of a two-level opinion formation process.

NOTE: Solutions of the master equation for $\kappa = 0.5$ (left) and $\kappa = 1.5$ (right); horizontal axis: state space of the population; vertical axis: probability of finding a population at a certain point in state space; third axis: time; populations start at a point in state space where the numbers of members saying Yes and No, respectively, are equal.

same time, explains why κ is a coupling parameter. For $\kappa < 1$, the distribution over the ensemble of populations remains unimodal with a mode at $x = 0$ (or $n_{\text{no}} = n_{\text{yes}}$), while for $\kappa > 1$, the distribution becomes bimodal after some time—which means that every single population is likely to have either a high Yes majority or a high No majority but that populations with as many members voting for Yes and No, respectively, are extremely unlikely.

The model can be applied not only to voting processes in referendum campaigns (where voters have only two choices, Yes and No) but also to model consumer behavior, when consumers have a choice between two (more or less compatible) types of devices (e.g., types of video cassettes or DVDs or computer operating systems, to name some devices where compatibility is desirable—as opposed to, e.g., cigarette brands, which are easily substituted). There is some empirical evidence (in the sense of "stylized facts") that real-world processes are similar to the opinion formation process of Weidlich and Haag.

This type of processes can also be extended to several interacting populations and to populations whose members have more than two choices, such that, for instance, processes of migration among several regions can be modeled (Weidlich & Haag, 1988). Another model of this type is a model of a population in which birth and death occur (the opinion formation model has a constant population and is thus not very realistic) and where people either speak one of two languages or are bilingual (Troitzsch, 2004). The bilingual state is of course an absorbing state on the individual level, thus here we have the choice of becoming bilingual as a once-and-forever choice (in the real world, of course, one would learn a third language, but in the model and in the real world one cannot unlearn any second language). Another complication, as compared both with simple birth-and-death models and the opinion formation model, is the fact that the language of a newborn child depends in a way on the language or languages of his or her parents and that later on in his or her life, the propensity to learn the second language depends on the prevailing proportions of language skills in the population. In the most sophisticated version of this model, we have the following situation:

- The state of the population has to be described with three numbers (whose sum is not a constant): the number of speakers of Language 1, the number of speakers of Language 2, and the number of bilinguals.
- The possible events that are interesting in this model are
    - a child is born (and here it is interesting which language[s] he or she will learn, depending on the languages of his or her parents),
    - a person dies, and
    - a unilingual person decides to learn the second language.
- These three events occur with particular probabilities, some of which are independent of the proportions of the subpopulations (the death probability, e.g., can be expected to be the same for all linguistic groups, whereas the probability of learning the majority language will be higher, the smaller the minority group is, etc.).

Without giving the mathematical derivation of the master equation (which here, too, is the way to the solution), one can say that the main parameters of the model can be identified as the propensities or probabilities of learning the mother's and the father's native languages if these are different (in the case of unilingual families, it is obvious that second-language acquisition is a decision that must be modeled differently). One has to consider the following cases:

- Mother and father are unilingual and speak different native languages (a case that is not very likely): These children should have a high probability of becoming "native bilinguals."
- One parent is bilingual, and the other is unilingual: These children's native language will either be the language of the unilingual parent, or they will be bilingual.
- Both parents are bilingual: Here the probability of the children becoming bilingual would also be high, but there should also be a nonvanishing probability that the children learn only one language as their native language.

If we restrict the model to learning languages only during early childhood, then, roughly speaking, bilingualism has a chance only if the probability of children from the second type of families becoming bilingual is at least 0.5 (or some other positive threshold, depending on the exact formulation of the model), whereas the population falls apart linguistically if the probability of learning only the unilingual partner's language is higher than 0.5 (or the same threshold).

If languages are also learnt later on in persons' lives, the situation becomes different. Similar to the opinion formation model, one would find that the higher the probability of learning the other language, the greater its majority. Then, in the long run, the proportion of bilinguals will always rise up to at least half the population even if all children grow up only with one of the languages (the obvious reason is that learning a language takes a short time as compared with the average lifetime of humans; again, "one half" is the outcome of a particular modeling of the transition probabilities, and other models might result in different but positive thresholds).

Continuous-State Space Models

While in the previous section, the individuals on the individual level had a binary attribute (Yes-No), one could also be interested in stochastic processes on two levels, where individuals have an attribute that is continuous. The classical case is Downs's (1957) model of attitude changes in voters. Downs talks about voters whose left-right orientation can be measured on a one-dimensional, more or less continuous scale, either with maximum density in the center or with density maxima toward the extremes. Under certain circumstances of party-voter interaction, these voters "can somehow be *moved* to the center of the *scale* to eliminate their *polar split*" [italics added] (p. 122).

He also postulates that "the political cycle typical for revolutions can be viewed as a *series of movements of men along the political scale.* Preliminary to the upheaval, the once *centralised distribution* begins to *polarise* into two extremes as the incumbents increasingly *antagonize* those who feel themselves oppressed" [italics added] (Downs, 1957, p. 120). Although Downs never took the trouble of explaining in any formal detail how this process should work, it is not too difficult to reconstruct his idea.

We model voters as objects that have one real-valued attribute ("opinion," "attitude"), which at the start of the process is normally distributed (say, with mean 0 and variance 1). Moreover, they can "perceive" the overall distribution in every time step and tend to change their opinion in a way that the new state of the opinion is a more probable state; that is, they move along the gradient (the direction of the steepest ascent) of the frequency density function toward one of its peaks and thus change the shape of the distribution in the successive time step. To simulate this process (analytical treatment of this process is not known), the simulated frequency density function has to be estimated in every time step. The algorithm of this simulation is as follows:

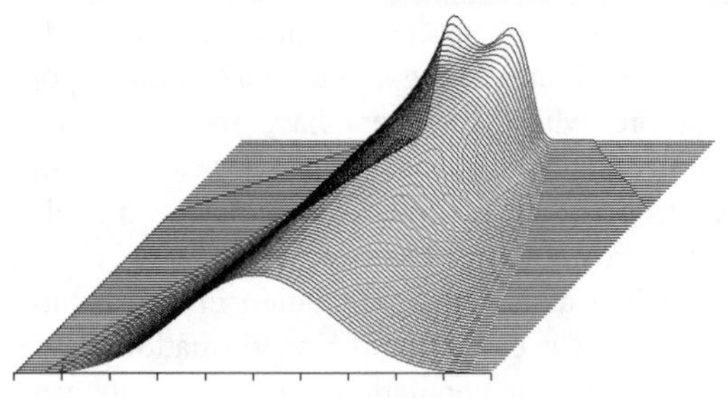

Figure 17.4 Long-term behavior of one population whose members move in continuous-state space.

NOTES: The horizontal axis is the voters' one-dimensional attitude space, the vertical axis is the probability of finding the voters of a certain attitude in the population, and the third axis is time. Curves are frequency density (vertical axis) functions over the individual-state space (horizontal axis). After some time (third axis), the unimodal distribution changes into a bimodal one. The frequency density distribution is modeled as $f(x) = \exp(a_4x^4 + a_3x^3 + a_2x^2 + a_1x + a_0)$.

- Initialize all simulated voters.
- In every time step,
  - estimate the current frequency density function and its gradient, and
  - for all voters,
    - ▷ calculate the new attitude value according to the gradient,
    - ▷ add some random effect to this attitude, and
    - ▷ move to the new attribute value.

While most of the steps of this algorithm are easy to program, the estimation of the frequency density function is intricate when this function should be multimodal. For this example, an algorithm developed by Cobb (1978) is used, where the frequency density function is modeled as an exponential of a polynomial up to some even-numbered order $2n$ (other, even more resource-consuming algorithms for the same type of function are known—see Troitzsch (1987)); the Cobb algorithm approximates the first moments up to order $4n$, while Troitzsch's algorithm yields a distribution function whose first $2n$ moments are exactly equal to the simulated or empirical moments). Figure 17.4 shows an example of the history of the frequency density function of this process for one population. In the beginning, the distribution is nearly exactly normal—as the number of simulated individuals is finite, the distribution cannot be exactly normal—and after some time, the slopes of the graph become steeper until in the end two peaks, separated by a minimum, develop. Here, the polarization postulated by Downs is an emergent phenomenon of this stochastic process. The same phenomenon can also be observed in two dimensions (Troitzsch, 1998, pp. 29–31).

MULTI-AGENT MODELS

In a way, multi-agent models are not—or should not be—stochastic models at all, although in practice they often are. To discuss this properly, we will have to start with a definition of the terms *agent* and *multi-agent simulation models*. According to the standard definition provided by Wooldridge and Jennings (1995), agents are software objects that have the following properties:

- *Autonomy:* They operate without others having direct control of their internal states and actions.
- *Reactivity:* They can perceive their environment and can react on it.
- *Proactivity:* They can take the initiative and display goal-directed behavior.
- *Social ability:* They can interact with other agents by some kind of language, and they can develop and have models of other agents and of their environment.

This, of course, does not mean that agents must be deterministic in any sense, although, generally speaking, one would say that agents obeying certain rules to determine their behavior should be deterministic. But, of course, an agent still fulfills the above definition if, for instance, its reaction to a certain state of its environment is a choice between two or more alternatives that have different probabilities, as in the case of the objects of micro- or multilevel simulation. For the same reason, the perception of an agent can be superimposed by a random variable, thus, for instance, taking into account that rationality of human actors is bounded (see, e.g., the "trembling hand" in game theory, Selten, 1975).

So from the point of view of this chapter, the main difference between the microanalytical and multilevel models dealt with so far and multi-agent models is the fact that the latter always deal with relations and dependencies among objects of the same level. In the case of microanalytical simulation, relations between objects were restricted to certain kinship relations (is married to, is child of, etc.) with some very special relevance to these objects, and in the case of multilevel simulation, there is usually no interaction between objects of the same kind; instead in this case the state of a collection of these objects depends on what happens on the level of these objects, and then the state of the collection determines the behavior of the lower-level objects.

A multi-agent simulation model will follow a much more complicated algorithm (compare the following with the respective descriptions of the algorithms of microanalytical and multilevel models):

- Initialize the individual agents according to theoretical assumptions, and place them in an environment that, too, has to be initialized (perhaps as an instance of a very special sort of agent).
- In every time step,
    - have all agents perceive their environment,
    - have all agents become aware of their goals,
    - have them plan and evaluate possible actions,
    - have them make a decision on which of their alternative actions to take, and
    - have each of them execute its preferred action (given that it is possible).

This algorithm describes a synchronous model world, where in every time step every agent has a chance to act. There is, of course, another alternative that introduces features of discrete-event simulation in multi-agent models:

- Initialize the individual agents according to theoretical assumptions, and place them in an environment that, too, has to be initialized (perhaps as an instance of a very special sort of agent).

- Have all individual agents schedule their first awakening for a certain time in the future, and insert these future events into an event list.
- For every event in this event list,
    - awake this agent and have it perform an action defined at an earlier event, if there is one and if it is possible at this time (e.g., an agent to which a message was to be sent at this time could be out of reach now);
    - have it perceive its environment or at least some part of its environment;
    - have it become aware of (some of) its goals;
    - have it plan and evaluate possible actions;
    - have it make a decision which of its alternative actions to take at what time (immediately or at a later time), and insert a future action or event for this agent into the event list; and
    - have it execute this action (given that it is possible and that is to be executed immediately).

This simulation mode is still replicable as it would be executed according to a deterministic schedule (even when it has random features, in this case the random number generator will have to be started with the same seed to produce the same behavior as in the earlier run).

Synchronous and asynchronous models will have different results even if the rules according to which individual agents behave are the same. In the synchronous case, every agent "sees" the effects of all the others' behavior at the same time, and all agents change their world at the same time—and then it is the order in which the individual agents' calculations are done by the simulation software that decides what exactly happens, whereas in the asynchronous case every agents looks at a world that in a way is frozen until this agent makes its decision and acts correspondingly—and then the world continues to change. In the synchronous case, inconsistent behavior may occur if there are local interactions: The operation that Agent 1 tries to perform with respect to Agent 2 might be incompatible with the action the latter takes on the former. Thus, in the discrete-event (asynchronous) simulation type, one would be on the safe side.

The third version (and complication) of multiagent modeling would then necessitate a grid of computers, with possibly one processor per agent such that there is no central scheduling but only a protocol that tells the individual software agents under which conditions it is their turn to participate in the game. Generally speaking, there is no replicability on multiprocessor systems as there will be external demands (say, from other users of the same processor) on some of the processors in the network that have nothing to do with the simulation running.

So if a stochastic simulation model is executed on a one-processor computer and its pseudorandom number generator is started with the same seed, then actually the behavior of the simulation is replicable. If the pseudorandom number generator is started with, say, the current time of the computer's clock or if the model is run on a grid, then the model is not replicable. Stochasticity in the strict sense would be reached only if one used a physical stochastic process as random number generator, such as a nuclear fission process.

In some of the models discussed in this chapter, structures on the population level *emerged*—for example, substructures such as local density maxima in an originally unstructured and homogeneous population of voters. The clustering of voters, or their polarization, can be seen as an emergent property of the electorate; it is not a property that the individual voters can possess, and it cannot (at least not easily) be calculated from the properties of the voters or, more generally speaking, of the lower-level entities.

While this emergence can occur in systems of nonliving things and living things that do not posses a mind and can be simulated already in multilevel models, another type of feedback between levels can only be observed in societies of humans (and perhaps some other kinds of animals) and can only be simulated in multi-agent models as this feedback necessitates that the lower-level entities can become aware of what happens at some higher level. This phenomenon is called immergence and is defined as the "feedback effect of the emergent phenomenon on its ground elements (the agents): The emergent phenomenon changes their representations in a special way: it is (partially) represented in their minds" (Castelfranchi, 1998, p. 38). Thus, the agents in multi-agent systems that are built to represent human societies and to reflect this special feature of human societies must be capable of representing other agents and their environment and, moreover, of detecting emergent properties of their environment. To put it in terms of one of the earlier examples of this chapter, they must be capable of detecting that the distribution of attitudes became bimodal, not only of "feeling" the local gradient of this density function and of moving accordingly. Instead, they should be able to change the rules of their behavior and to choose to move against the gradient to occupy a location in attitude space that could be attractive enough for other agents in order to fill the valley between the two peaks of the emerging bimodal distribution. For this reason, the software objects representing individual voters in that model would have to be endowed with the capability of not only feeling the local gradient but also evaluating the numbers of minima, maxima, and saddles of the density function and of behaving differently according to these numbers. But why should they react on their notion of the overall gradient field? Obviously, this representation of emergent phenomena would not be sufficient for simulating a human society; instead, goals and foresight seem to be necessary to model the agents' reaction on the emergent phenomenon. The agents should be in a position to predict what could come out of the emergent phenomenon, evaluate this outcome, and decide whether they should behave in the traditional way or in some other way (in the example, move in the direction or against the direction of the gradient). This decision could again be a probabilistic one, for instance: The deeper or wider the valley between the peaks of the density function, the higher the probability of behaving differently.

But still, this extension of the multilevel stochastic model would contain no local interaction between agents. Individuals in a political system do not usually change their attitudes as a reaction to some globally felt opinion climate (Noelle-Neumann, 1993), and at least to some extent also as a reaction of communication with their friends and neighbors, so local interaction has to be taken into account, as has been done from the earliest time of social science computer simulation (Abelson & Bernstein, 1963). This local interaction makes the mathematical analysis of the stochastic process much more intricate than in the relatively simple case of the master equation of two of the earlier examples (Helbing, 1995, pp. 71ff., 164ff.).

Local interaction would also be an alternative to the model of emerging bilingualism or unilingualism in the other model referred to earlier. Proportions of speakers of this or that or both languages are not homogeneous over a country, so local majorities would influence people much more than nationwide proportions, and even this might be an approach that is too simple: A person could find a potential mate or an open job position that gives him or her the idea that it might be useful to learn a second language and use it in everyday life. To model effects such as this appropriately, it would be necessary to describe the entities of a model in much more detail than in the cases reported above.

Thus, it does not seem very promising to mathematically analyze agent-based models as more realistic models of human societies in terms of stochastic processes. Much like other mathematical models of human societies, stochastic processes have their virtues whenever it seems appropriate to simplify the assumptions of a model to a certain degree. In more realistic models, however, a large number of simulation runs with identical parameterization and different seeds of the random number generator (Monte Carlo simulations) could be used as a surrogate of a more serious mathematical analysis, yielding estimates of confidence intervals for outcomes. Changes in the parameters would additionally allow for sensitivity analysis.

REFERENCES

Abelson, R. P., & Bernstein, A. (1963). A computer simulation of community referendum controversies. *Public Opinion Quarterly, 27*, 93–122.

Castelfranchi, C. (1998). Simulating with cognitive agents: The importance of cognitive emergence. In J. S. Sichman, R. Conte, & N. Gilbert (Eds.), *Multi-agent systems and agent-based simulation* (pp. 26–44). Berlin, Germany: Springer.

Cobb, L. (1978). Stochastic catastrophe models and multimodal distributions. *Behavioral Science, 23*, 260–374.

Downs, A. (1957). *An economic theory of democracy*. New York: Harper.

Haken, H. (1978). *Synergetics: An introduction. Nonequilibrium phase transitions and self-organization in physics, chemistry and biology* (2nd enlarged ed.) (Springer Series in Synergetics, Vol. 1). Berlin, Germany: Springer-Verlag.

Helbing, D. (1995). *Quantitative sociodynamics: Stochastic methods and models of social interaction processes*. Dordrecht, the Netherlands: Kluwer.

Lumsden, C. J., & Wilson, E. O. (1981). *Genes, mind and culture, the coevolutionary process*. Cambridge, MA: Harvard University Press.

Noelle-Neumann, E. (1993). *The spiral of silence: Public opinion—our social skin*. Chicago: University of Chicago Press.

Orcutt, G. H., Merz, J., & Quinke, H. (Eds.). (1986). *Microanalytic simulation models to support social and financial policy* (Series in Information Research and Resource Reports, Vol. 7). Amsterdam: North-Holland.

Selten, R. (1975). Reexamination of the perfectness concept for equilibrium points in extensive games. *International Journal of Game Theory, 4*, 25–55.

Troitzsch, K. G. (1987). Interactions between party members and local party activists: A formal model and its empirical application. *Journal of Mathematical Sociology, 12*(4), 415–438.

Troitzsch, K. G. (1998). Multilevel process modeling in the social sciences: Mathematical analysis and computer simulation. In W. B. G. Liebrand, A. Nowak, & R. Hegselmann (Eds.), *Computer modeling of social processes* (pp. 20–36). Thousand Oaks, CA: Sage.

Troitzsch, K. G. (2004). A multi-agent model of bilingualism in a small population. In H. Coelho & B. Espinasse (Eds.), *5th workshop on agent-based simulation* (pp. 38–43). Erlangen, San Diego: SCS.

Weidlich, W., & Haag, G. (1983). Concepts and models of a quantitative sociology. In *Springer series in synergetics* (Vol. 14, chap. The dynamics of interacting populations). Berlin, Germany: Springer-Verlag.

Weidlich, W., & Haag, G. (1988). *Interregional migration: Dynamic theory and comparative analysis*. Berlin, Germany: Springer-Verlag.

Wooldridge, M., & Jennings, N. R. (1995). Intelligent agents: Theory and practice. *Knowledge Engineering Review, 10*, 115–152.

18

PROBABILISTIC NETWORK ANALYSIS

PHILIPPA PATTISON AND GARRY ROBINS

INTRODUCTION

The aim of this chapter is to describe the foundations of probabilistic network theory. We review the development of the field from an early reliance on simple random graph models to the construction of progressively more realistic models for human social networks. Hence, we show how developments in probabilistic network models are increasingly able to inform our understanding of the emergence and structure of social networks in a wide variety of settings.

SOCIAL NETWORKS

Growing numbers of social scientists from an increasingly diverse set of disciplines are turning their attention to the study of social networks. The precise reasons vary, but almost certainly, there are at least two key factors at work. The first is an increasing recognition that networks matter in many realms of social, political, and economic life. Networks both potentiate and constrain the social interactions that, for instance, underpin the dissemination of knowledge, the exercise of power and influence, and the transmission of communicable diseases. Ignoring the structured nature of these interactions often leads to erroneous conclusions about their consequences, as social scientists from a number of disciplines have repeatedly pointed out (e.g., Bearman, Moody, & Stovel, 2004; Kretzschmar & Morris, 1996). The second reason for a heightened focus on social networks is our increasing capacity to measure, monitor, and model social networks and their evolution through time and hence to draw social networks into a more general program for a quantitative social science. Probabilistic models for social networks have played—and will likely increasingly play—a vital role in these developments. In this chapter, we review the progress in attempts to develop probabilistic network models and point to areas of ongoing development.

WHAT IS DISTINCTIVE ABOUT MODELS FOR SOCIAL NETWORKS?

At the outset, it is important to recognize that social networks pose particular challenges as far as probability modeling is concerned. Unlike observations on a set of distinct actors, where an assumption of independent observations may often seem reasonable, social relationships are much less plausibly regarded as independent. Relational observations may share one or more actors and hence be subject to influences such as the goals and constraints of a particular actor.

Alternatively, they may be linked by other relationships (e.g., the relationship between actors i and j may be linked with the relationship between actors k and l by a relationship involving actors j and k) and hence dependent, for example, by virtue of competition or cooperation regarding relational resources involving actors j and k. As we see below, the development of probabilistic network models began with simple models that assumed independent relational ties, but empirical researchers quickly confronted the problem that social networks appeared to deviate from simple random structures in seemingly systematic ways. Hence, the story of the development of probabilistic network models is a story of alternatively probing and parameterizing progressively more complex systematicities in network structure.

Notation and Some Basic Properties of Graphs and Directed Graphs

We begin with some notations and some important definitions, referring the reader to Wasserman and Faust (1994); see also Bollobás (1998) for a fuller exposition of key concepts.

Graphs and Directed Graphs

We let $N = 1,2,\ldots,n$ be a set of network *nodes*, with each node representing a social *actor*. The actors are often persons but may also be groups, organizations, or other social entities. An observed social network may be represented as a *graph* $G = (N,E)$ comprising the *node set* N and the *edge set* E comprising all pairs (i,j) of distinct actors who are linked by a network tie. The tie, or edge, (i,j) is said to be *incident* with nodes i and j. In this case, the network ties are taken to be *nondirected*, with no distinction between the tie from actor i to actor j and the tie from actor j to actor i; in other words, the edges (i,j) and (j,i) are regarded as indistinguishable. If it is desirable to distinguish these ties—as it often is—the network may be represented instead by a *directed graph* (N,E) on N: The node set is then also N, and the *arc set* E is the set of all *ordered* pairs (i,j) such that there is a tie *from* actor i to actor j. The convention of using the term *edge* in the case of a nonordered pair (i.e., a *nondirectional* tie) and *arc* in the case of an ordered pair (i.e., a *directional* tie) is widely adopted by graph theorists, although network researchers are inclined to use the term *tie* interchangeably in both cases. In many cases, by convention, ties of the form (i,i), known as *loops*, are excluded from consideration.

Graphs and directed graphs can be conveniently represented by a *graph drawing*. The elements of the node set N are represented by points in the drawing, and a nondirected line connects node i and node j if (i,j) is an edge in the edge set E. In the case of a directed graph, an arc represented by a directed arrow is drawn from node i to node j if (i,j) is in the arc set E. Figures 18.1 and 18.2 show examples of a graph and a directed graph, respectively.

Order, Size, and Density

The *order* and *size* of a graph are defined to be the number of nodes and edges, respectively; likewise, the order and size of a directed graph are the number of nodes and arcs, respectively. For example, the graph in Figure 18.1 has order 17 and size 34; the directed graph in Figure 18.2 has order 37 and size 169. The size of a graph of order n varies between 0 for an *empty* graph and $n(n-1)/2$ for the *complete* graph of order n (i.e., the graph in which every pair of nodes is linked by an edge). For a directed graph of order n, size varies between 0 and $n(n-1)$. The *density* of a graph or directed graph is a ratio of its actual size to the maximum possible size for n nodes, and it is in the range [0, 1]. The densities of the graph and directed graph of Figures 18.1 and 18.2 are 0.25 and 0.13, respectively.

Adjacency Matrix

Graphs and directed graphs can be represented by a binary *adjacency matrix*. For example, in the case of a graph, we can define $\mathbf{x}$ to be an $n \times n$ matrix with entries $x_{ij} = 1$ if there is an edge between i and j and $x_{ij} = 0$ otherwise. Since $x_{ij} = 1$ if and only if $x_{ji} = 1$, $\mathbf{x}$ is necessarily a *symmetric* matrix. In the case of a directed graph, unit entries in $\mathbf{x}$ correspond to arcs in E (i.e., $x_{ij} = 1$ if and only if

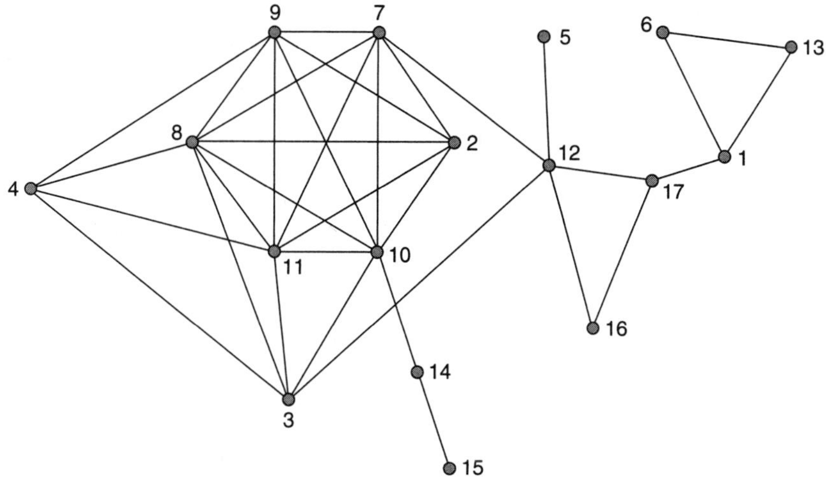

Figure 18.1 A graph on 17 nodes (mutual friendship network).

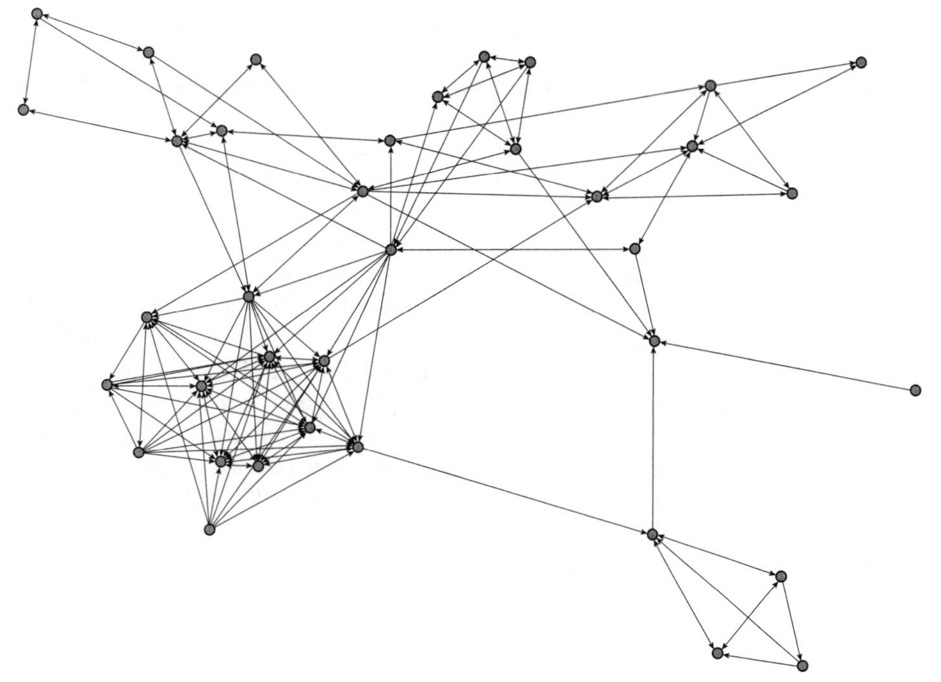

Figure 18.2 A directed graph on 37 nodes (reported collaboration network).

there is an arc from i to j, and $x_{ij} = 0$ otherwise). In this case, symmetry is not necessarily implied. The adjacency matrix corresponding to the graph of Figure 18.1 is shown in Table 18.1. Note that the size of a graph is $x_{++}/2$, whereas the size of a directed graph is x_{++}, where $x_{++} = \sum_{ij} x_{ij}$ is the sum of entries in the adjacency matrix.

Degree, Degree Sequence, and Degree Distribution

The number $k(i)$ of edges incident with a given node i is termed its *degree*: $k(i) = \sum_j x_{ij}$ is the sum of row i in the adjacency matrix $\mathbf{x}$. The *degree sequence* $(k(1), k(2), \ldots, k(n))$ of a

Table 18.1 Adjacency Matrix for Graph of Figure 18.1

	1	2	3	4	5	6	7	8	9	10	11	12	13	14	15	16	17
1	0	0	0	0	0	1	0	0	0	0	0	0	1	0	0	0	1
2	0	0	0	0	0	0	1	1	1	1	1	0	0	0	0	0	0
3	0	0	0	1	0	0	0	1	0	1	1	1	0	0	0	0	0
4	0	0	1	0	0	0	0	1	1	0	1	0	0	0	0	0	0
5	0	0	0	0	0	0	0	0	0	0	0	1	0	0	0	0	0
6	1	0	0	0	0	0	0	0	0	0	0	0	1	0	0	0	0
7	0	1	0	0	0	0	0	1	1	1	1	1	0	0	0	0	0
8	0	1	1	1	0	0	1	0	1	1	1	0	0	0	0	0	0
9	0	1	0	1	0	0	1	1	0	1	1	0	0	0	0	0	0
10	0	1	1	0	0	0	1	1	1	0	1	0	0	1	0	0	0
11	0	1	1	1	0	0	1	1	1	1	0	0	0	0	0	0	0
12	0	0	1	0	1	0	1	0	0	0	0	0	0	0	0	1	1
13	1	0	0	0	0	1	0	0	0	0	0	0	0	0	0	0	0
14	0	0	0	0	0	0	0	0	0	1	0	0	0	0	1	0	0
15	0	0	0	0	0	0	0	0	0	0	0	0	0	1	0	0	0
16	0	0	0	0	0	0	0	0	0	0	0	1	0	0	0	0	1
17	1	0	0	0	0	0	0	0	0	0	0	1	0	0	0	1	0

graph is the sequence of the degrees of its nodes, indexed by the labels $1,2,\ldots,n$ of nodes in N. The *degree distribution* is $(d_0,d_1,\ldots,d_{n-1})$, where d_k is the number of nodes in G of degree k. For example, the degree distribution of the graph in Figure 18.1 is shown in Figure 18.3. In a directed graph, the concept of degree is more complex, since there may be an arc directed from node j toward a given node i or away from node i toward node j, or there may be arcs in both directions between nodes i and j. We therefore characterize each node i in a directed graph by its outdegree $\text{out}_i = x_{i+} = \sum_j x_{ij}$, indegree $\text{in}_i = x_{+i} = \sum_j x_{ji}$, and mutual degree $\text{mut}_i = \sum_j x_{ij}x_{ji}$.

Subgraphs and the Dyad and Triad Census

Each subset S of the node set N of a graph $G = (N,E)$ gives rise to an *induced subgraph* H of G with node set S and edge set E' containing all edges in G that link pairs of nodes in S. More generally, any graph $H = (N',E')$ is a *subgraph* of G if $N' \subseteq N$ and $E' \subseteq E$. For example, the subgraph induced by the node set 1, 6, 13 of the graph of Figure 18.1 has edge set (1, 6),(1, 13),(6, 13); the graph comprising the node set 1, 6, 13 and the edge set (1, 6),(1, 13) is a subgraph of the graph of Figure 18.1 but not an induced subgraph. If every pair of nodes in the subgraph H is connected by an edge, then H is said to be a *clique*; for example, the subgraph induced by 2, 7, 8, 9, 10, 11 in Figure 18.1 is a clique of order 6.

A useful set of descriptive statistics for a graph or directed graph is a summary of the form of all of its small subgraphs. For example, the *dyad census* is a count of the number of each possible type of two-node induced subgraphs, and the *triad census* is the set of counts of three-node induced subgraphs. For example, the graph of Figure 18.1 has 102 null dyads and 34 linked dyads; its triad census comprises 279, 322, 49, and 30 induced three-node subgraphs with zero, one, two, and three edges, respectively. The dyad census and the triad census for directed graphs are defined similarly, but the number of forms of two-node and three-node subgraphs is greater in the directed graph case.

Implicit in the description of the dyad and triad census is the notion that two graphs (or subgraphs) can have the same form. We can make this notion more explicit by defining an isomorphic mapping between graphs. Specifically, two graphs $G = (N,E)$ and $H = (N',E')$ are *isomorphic* if there is a one-to-one mapping φ from N onto N' such that (i, j) is an edge in E if and only if $(\varphi(i), \varphi(j))$ is an edge in E'.

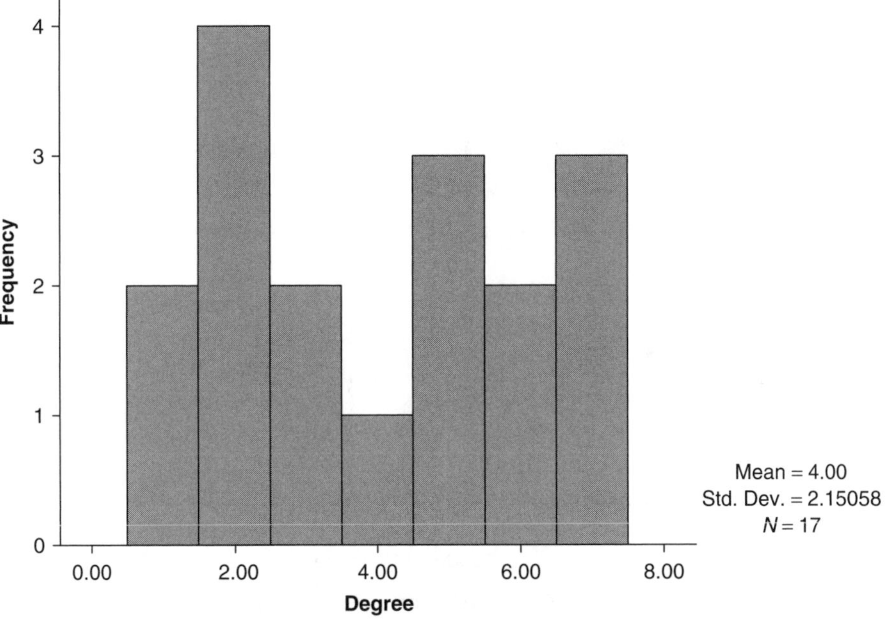

Figure 18.3 The degree distribution for the mutual friendship graph.

Paths, Reachability, and Connectedness

Social networks are often important to understand because social processes—such as the diffusion of information, the exercise of influence, and the spread of disease—are potentiated by network ties. Not surprisingly, therefore, pathlike structures in networks that might be associated with the flow of social processes are important concepts. A *path* from node i to node j is an ordered sequence $i = i_0, i_1, \ldots, i_l = j$ of distinct nodes in which each adjacent pair (i_{j-1}, i_j) is linked by an edge or an arc. The *length* of the path is l. If there is a path from a node i to a node j, then j is said to be *reachable* from i. If node j is the same as node i, then the path is termed a *cycle* of length l.

A *geodesic* from node i to another node j is a path of minimum length, and the *geodesic distance* d_{ij} from node i to node j is the length of the geodesic. If there is no path from i to j, the geodesic distance is *infinite*. The geodesic distance d_{ij} for distinct nodes i and j is either an integer in the range from 1 to $n-1$ or infinite. For a graph, geodesic distances are symmetric, that is $d_{ji} = d_{ij}$; this is not necessarily the case however, for directed graphs. The *geodesic distribution* of a graph or directed graph is the distribution of frequencies of geodesic distances—that is, the distribution of counts of the number of ordered pairs of nodes having each possible geodesic distance. The geodesic distribution of the graph of Figure 18.1 is presented in Figure 18.4 in the form of a histogram. The geodesic distribution can be seen as a useful summary of internode distances. Later, we refer to the quartiles of this distribution as simple summary statistics for internode distances.

If each node in a graph G is reachable from each other node, then G is *connected*. A *component* of G is a maximal connected subgraph—that is, a connected subgraph with vertex set W for which no larger set Z containing W is connected. The graph of Figure 18.1 is clearly connected.

In the case of a directed graph, we may also define a *semipath* from node i to node j as an ordered sequence $i = i_0, i_1, \ldots, i_l = j$ of distinct nodes in which either (i_{j-1}, i_j) or (i_j, i_{j-1}) is an arc. The *length* of the semipath is m. If each node in a directed graph G is reachable from each other node, then G is *strongly connected*. If there is a semipath from each node in G to each other node, then G is said to be *weakly connected*.

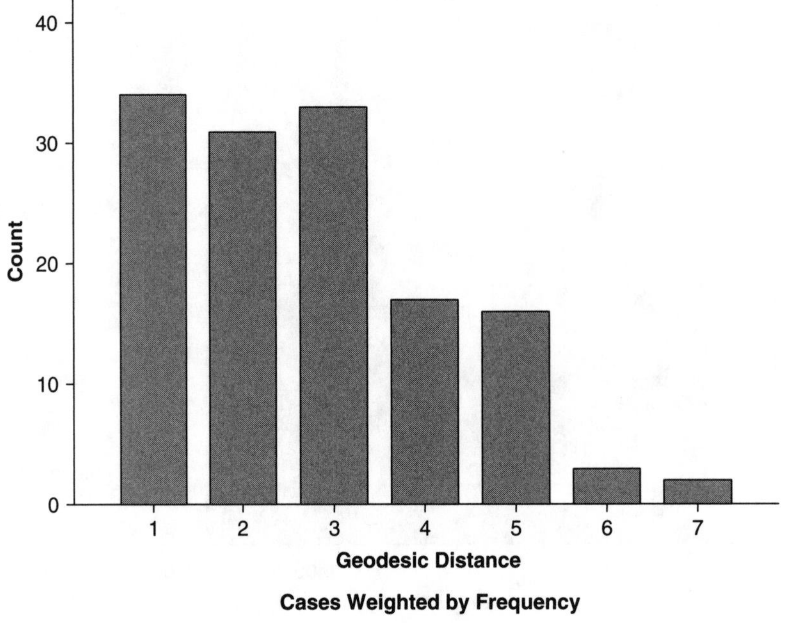

Figure 18.4 Geodesic distribution for the mutual friendship graph.

Simple Random Graphs and Directed Graphs

The Hungarian mathematicians Paul Erdős and Alfréd Rényi initiated an important approach to the study of random graph structures with a foundational series of papers beginning in 1959 (Erdős & Rényi, 1959). They introduced two primary random graph distributions on a fixed node set $N = 1,2,\ldots,n$. The probability distributions are defined on the set of all graphs on n distinct nodes; this set contains $2^{n(n-1)/2}$ graphs, since each of the $n(n-1)/2$ pairs of nodes may or may not be linked by an edge. Each of the two random graph distributions that we introduce below associates a probability with every graph in this set.

$\mathcal{G}(n,p)$

In the first case, the edges of a graph are regarded as a set of independent Bernoulli variables. If we let X_{ij} denote the edge variable for the pair of nodes i and j and p be the (uniform) probability that the edge between i and j is present, then we can write $\Pr(X_{ij} = 1) = p$ and, hence, $\Pr(X_{ij} = 0) = 1 - p$. Since the edge variables are independent, it is then easy to write down the probability of any particular graph H of order n and size m:

$$\Pr(G = H) = p^m(1-p)^{m^*-m},$$

where $m^* = n(n-1)/2$ is the maximum number of edges in a graph of order n. The set of all possible graphs of order n and their corresponding probabilities is the *random graph distribution* $\mathcal{G}(n,p)$.

In the special case where $p = 0.5$, the probability of each graph H on n nodes is

$$\Pr(G = H) = (0.5)^m(0.5)^{m^*-m} = (0.5)^{m^*},$$

and hence, every graph on n nodes is equiprobable. This distribution is often termed the *uniform* random graph distribution and is denoted by U.

$\mathcal{G}(n,m)$

The second random graph distribution associates nonzero probabilities only with graphs of order n and size m; furthermore, every such graph is assumed to be equiprobable. Since there are

$n!/(m!(n-m)!)$ distinct graphs in the class, the probability of any particular graph of order n and size m is

$$\Pr(G = H) = m!(n-m)!/n!.$$

The distribution $\mathcal{G}(n,m)$ may be regarded as the uniform random graph distribution on n nodes, conditional on the property of having m edges. It may also be designated $U \mid x_{++} = m$. More generally, we can define a conditional uniform random graph distribution in terms of any graph property $\mathcal{Q}$ (Bollobás, 1985). If $\mathcal{Q}$ is a subset of all possible graphs on n nodes, then the distribution $U \mid \mathcal{Q}$ assigns equal probabilities (viz., $1/\mid \mathcal{Q} \mid$) to all graphs in the subset $\mathcal{Q}$ and zero probability to all graphs not in $\mathcal{Q}$. We term $U \mid \mathcal{Q}$ the uniform random graph distribution *conditional on* $\mathcal{Q}$.

Some Results for Simple Random Graphs

The field of random graphs in $\mathcal{G}(n,p)$ and $\mathcal{G}(n,m)$ has grown rapidly since its inception. Much work has explored the features of various random graph classes, particularly as n becomes large, and the way in which these features change, often very rapidly, as a function of p. Bollobás (1998) contains an excellent introduction to the field, as does the review by Albert and Barabási (2002); here, we illustrate just two aspects of this literature by considering the expected values of some statistics in $\mathcal{G}(n,p)$ and by reviewing properties of a graph as a function of p in $\mathcal{G}(n,p)$.

We begin by determining the expected number of cliques in a graph. Let $Y_s = Y_s(G)$ be the number of cliques of order s in the graph G. Then, the expected value of Y_s can readily be computed as

$$E(Y_s) = (n!/[s!(n-s)!])p^u,$$

where $u = s(s-1)/2$ is the number of edges in a clique of order s (e.g., see Bollobás, 1998). In $\mathcal{G}(17, 0.25)$, for example, the expected number of cliques of order 3 is 10.6, and the expected number of cliques of order 4 is 0.58. The graph of Figure 18.1 has 17 nodes and a density of 0.25, and it is therefore interesting to compare the expected values for $\mathcal{G}(17, 0.25)$ with those observed for the graph of Figure 18.1—namely, 34 cliques of order 3 and 18 cliques of order 4.

Indeed, if F is any subgraph with s nodes and t edges and Y_F is the number of subgraphs of G that are isomorphic to F, then the expected value of Y_F can readily be shown to be

$$E(Y_F) = (n!/[(n-s)!a])p^t,$$

where a is the number of distinct ways in which the nodes of the graph F can be labeled with the integers $1, 2, \ldots, s$ to yield the same graph. For example, in the case of a cycle of order s, F has s edges and s nodes, and there are $2s$ distinct ways in which nodes can be labeled to yield the same graph; hence,

$$E(Y_F) = (n!/[(n-s)!2s])p^s.$$

The expected number of *induced* subgraphs isomorphic to F may be similarly derived:

$$E(Y_F) = (n!/[(n-s)!a])p^t(1-p)^{s(s-1)/2-t}.$$

The latter formula may be used, for example, to compute the expected triad census for a graph of a given order and density.

The expression for the expected number of subgraphs isomorphic to F in $\mathcal{G}(n,p)$ allows us to explore features of random graphs as n tends to infinity. Since

$$E(Y_F) = (n!/[(n-s)!a])p^t \approx n^s p^t/a,$$

it is clear that if $p = cn^{-s/t}$, then $E(Y_F) \approx c^t/a$ and the expected number of subgraphs isomorphic to F, denoted by $\lambda = c^t/a$, is a finite number. If, however, $pn^{s/t}$ tends to 0 or ∞ as n tends to ∞, then the probability that a random graph in $\mathcal{G}(n,p)$ contains at least one subgraph F converges to 0 or 1, respectively (e.g., Albert & Barabási, 2002). Thus, $p = cn^{-s/t}$ is a critical probability below which graphs with large n rarely contain F and above which they almost certainly do. An important set of results in random graph theory documents the many graph properties that show this form of rapid transition from being very unlikely to very likely as a function of the edge probability p.

Application of this approach allows us to infer for large n some expected features of random graphs in $\mathcal{G}(n,p)$ as a function of p, relative to n. Thus, for example, if $p < 1/n$, then almost every graph in $\mathcal{G}(n,p)$ comprises a number of components, each without any cycles; if p lies between $1/n$ and $(\ln n)/n$, then almost every graph has a so-called giant component (i.e., a component including a large proportion of the nodes in N); and if $p > (\ln n)/n$, then almost every graph is connected (e.g., see Albert & Barabási, 2002).

Random directed graph distributions may be similarly defined, though interest in them has largely come from social scientists with applications to network data in mind. It is to this literature that we now turn.

Applications of Random Graph and Directed Graph Distributions to Social Network Data

Before describing the application of random graphs to social networks, it is important to say something about typical sources of social network data (e.g., Wasserman & Faust, 1994). A common method of measuring social networks is to survey all members of a circumscribed population about their ties. In this case, ties are typically directional, and there may or may not be a limit imposed on the maximum number of ties reported by each respondent. Occasionally in this case, it is fruitful to consider the graph constructed from mutual ties only. For example, the graph of Figure 18.1 is the set of mutual ties observed among the girls in a Grade 8/9 high school class, obtained in response to the question "Who are your best friends in the class?" Networks are also commonly inferred from archival data, such as communication logs or membership or attendance lists. Less common strategies include direct observation and more elaborate survey techniques.

Application of Directed Random Graph Distributions

In the 1930s, the psychiatrist Jacob Moreno and colleagues reported using random directed graph distributions to compute quantities such as the expected number of mutual ties (i.e., $\sum_{i,j} X_{ij}X_{ji}/2$), where X_{ij} denotes the random variable for the tie from node i to node j. Moreno and colleagues also calculated properties of the indegree distribution in a random directed graph distribution (see, e.g., the very interesting historical account in Freeman, 2004).

Consider, for example, the random graph distribution $\mathcal{DG}(n,p)$ with a fixed set of n nodes and uniform but unknown arc probability p; this is the directed graph analog of $\mathcal{G}(n,p)$. The expected number of mutual ties for directed graphs in this distribution is $n(n-1)p^2/2$, and the expected number of nodes with indegree k is $np^k(1-p)^{n-1-k}$. If a social network with n nodes and $x_{++} = \sum_{ij} x_{ij}$ arcs has been observed, then the arc probability p can be estimated from the network data as $p^* = x_{++}/(n[n-1])$. This estimate of the arc probability can be used to compute the expected number of mutual ties and the expected number of nodes with each possible indegree k, on the assumption that the observed network was generated from $\mathcal{DG}(n,p^*)$. These expected values can be compared with the observed number of mutual ties and the observed indegree distribution in the network $\mathbf{x}$. If the observed values are markedly different from the expected ones, then it can be argued that there is reason to question the suitability of the assumption of independent random arcs with uniform probability that underpinned the computation of expected values.

The computations by Moreno and colleagues revealed what would later become a very common finding: that the observed number of mutual ties in an observed human social network is much greater than the number expected on the basis of arc probability alone and the indegree distribution is more heterogeneous than expected—that is, there are more nodes with very low and very high indegree than expected. These and similar findings suggest that tendencies toward mutuality and heterogeneity in partner "attractiveness" are systematic features of observed social networks comprising ties of affiliation.

Most important for our purposes here, Moreno introduced the idea of using random directed graph distributions as *null distributions*. The features of this null distribution could be compared with features of an observed network, a comparison enabling researchers to identify the ways in which the observed network appeared to be systematically different. In this early example, and in many to follow, it was important that the expected features of the null distribution could be derived mathematically. Much later, when fast computers and more versatile simulation algorithms were introduced, this restriction could be relaxed, but it was an important reason for the focus of early applications on this "null distribution" approach. Moreover, although this early application assumed very simple null distributions (such as independent arcs with uniform tie probability), more complex distributions were soon developed. Indeed, the strategy continues to be used in new ways (e.g., Bearman et al., 2004; Pattison, Wasserman, Robins, & Kanfer, 2000) and to be rediscovered in new fields (e.g., Milo et al., 2002). It remains an important means by which some of the systematic structural properties of human social networks can be and have been uncovered.

Holland, Leinhardt, and colleagues were responsible for developing a number of important elaborations of this basic strategy. For example, Holland and Leinhardt (1975) computed the expected mean vector and variance-covariance matrix for the triad census in the uniform random directed graph distribution $U \mid$ mut, asym, null[1] conditional on fixed numbers mut, asym, and null of mutual, asymmetric, and null ties, respectively (mut $= \sum_{ij} x_{ij}x_{ji}/2$, asym $= \sum_{ij}[x_{ij}(1-x_{ji}) + x_{ji}(1-x_{ij})]$, null $= \sum_{ij}(1-x_{ij})(1-x_{ji})$). In other words, they computed the expected distribution of the triad census while conditioning on the dyad census. This allowed them to construct a test statistic for any linear combination of triad counts and, hence, assess whether the observed combination of triad counts is in the upper or lower tail of the expected distribution. For example, they could test for the presence of *transitivity* (i.e., the property that arcs from nodes i to j and from j to k are accompanied by an arc from i to k).

Similar calculations can be made for other distributions of possible interest, including the uniform distribution $U \mid \{x_{i+}\}$,mut conditional on the outdegrees of each node in the directed graph as well as the number of mutual ties. Of course, for some desirable combinations, such as $U \mid \{x_{i+}\}, \{x_{+i}\}$,mut, the calculations are very difficult and have prompted alternative parametric approaches. In some of these difficult cases, clever simulation strategies have been devised to circumvent the difficult mathematics. For example, Snijders (1991) used an importance-sampling approach to simulate $U \mid \{x_{i+}\}, \{x_{+i}\}$, and McDonald, Smith, and Forster (2007) have described a Markov chain Monte Carlo algorithm to simulate the distribution $U \mid \{x_{i+}\}, \{x_{+i}\}$, mut.

[1] In fact, Holland and Leinhardt (1975) termed this the $U \mid$ MAN distribution, but we have attempted to keep notation consistent in the chapter.

BIASED NETS

One other early probabilistic approach deserves mention. In a series of papers, Rapoport and colleagues developed the theory of *biased nets*—that is, random networks with biases toward symmetry, transitivity, and other features characteristic of observed social networks (Rapoport, 1957). Although a full and satisfactory mathematical treatment proved elusive, Rapoport and colleagues employed their conceptualization of biased nets to conduct some illuminating studies of the connectivity structure of a large friendship network (e.g., Rapoport & Horvath, 1961). In part, their work can be seen as the intellectual precursor to the more general probabilistic developments described below, but a different framing of the "biases" has proved more useful.

THE p_1 MODEL

Comparison of observed social networks with random directed graph distributions consistently revealed a greater than expected number of mutual ties and greater than expected degree heterogeneity. As a consequence, it was felt desirable to compare observed networks with graph distributions that resembled observed networks in these fundamental respects. The problem of satisfactorily simulating the random graph distribution conditional on the number of mutual ties and the in-degree and out-degree sequences is arguably still not resolved. In the meantime, Holland and Leinhardt (1981) developed an alternative approach: a probability model that parameterized these tendencies. This model was an important step toward the development of a more general framework.

The p_1 model developed by Holland and Leinhardt (1981) assumes *independent dyads* $D_{ij} = (X_{ij}, X_{ji})$. The distribution of the entire network $\mathbf{X} = [X_{ij}]$ can then be determined by specifying the probability of each possible dyadic form for D_{ij} since the probability of the entire network $\mathbf{X}$ is the product of the dyad probabilities. The individual dyad probabilities can be expressed in terms of the probability of occurrence of a mutual dyad, an asymmetric dyad, and a null dyad. Thus, we define

$$\begin{aligned}\Pr(D_{ij} = (1,1)) &= m_{ij} = m_{ji},\\ \Pr(D_{ij} = (1,0)) &= a_{ij}, \text{ and}\\ \Pr(D_{ij} = (0,0)) &= n_{ij} = n_{ji},\end{aligned}$$

where $m_{ij} + a_{ij} + a_{ji} + n_{ij} = 1$ for all $i \neq j$.

The resulting probability distribution

$$\Pr(\mathbf{X} = \mathbf{x}) = \prod_{i<j} m_{ij}^{X_{ij}X_{ji}} \prod_{i \neq j} a_{ij}^{X_{ij}(1-X_{ji})} \prod_{i<j} n_{ij}^{(1-X_{ij})(1-X_{ji})}$$

may then be reexpressed in the exponential form

$$\Pr(\mathbf{X} = \mathbf{x}) = K \exp[\sum_{i<j} \rho_{ij} X_{ij} X_{ji} + \sum_{ij} \theta_{ij} X_{ij}],$$

where, for all $i \neq j$,

- $\rho_{ij} = \log\{m_{ij} n_{ij}/(a_{ij} a_{ji})\}$ is an index of reciprocity,
- $\theta_{ij} = \log\{a_{ij}/n_{ij}\}$ is a log-odds measure of the probability of an asymmetric dyad between i and j, and
- $K = \prod_{i<j}[1/(1 + \exp(\theta_{ij}) + \exp(\theta_{ji}) + \exp(\rho_{ij} + \theta_{ij} + \theta_{ji}))]$ is a normalizing quantity.

Holland and Leinhardt added two useful restrictions to this general dyad-independent model. The first was that the reciprocity parameter ρ_{ij} is a constant for all dyads; that is, $\rho_{ij} = \rho$ for all $i \neq j$. The second was that the parameter θ_{ij} depended additively on the propensity of arcs to emanate from node i and the propensity of arcs to have node j as a target; in other words,

$$\theta_{ij} = \theta + \alpha_i + \beta_j, \quad \text{for } i \neq j.$$

The resulting model is termed the p_1 model:

$$\begin{aligned}p_1(\mathbf{x}) &= \Pr(\mathbf{X} = \mathbf{x})\\ &= K \exp\left[\rho \sum_{i,j} X_{ij} X_{ji} + \theta X_{++} + \sum_i \alpha_i X_{i+} + \sum_i \beta_i X_{+i}\right].\end{aligned}$$

The parameters ρ and θ can be interpreted as uniform *reciprocity* and *density* parameters, and the node-dependent parameters α_i and β_i reflect the *expansiveness* and *attractiveness*, respectively, of each node i.

The development of the p_1 model was an important step in probabilistic network theory, not the least because much of the machinery of statistical modeling could be brought to bear on the problem of assessing model adequacy. The model could be estimated from data, and its goodness of fit could be subjected to careful scrutiny, as Brieger (1981) demonstrated. Such scrutiny led to the recognition that observed networks often exhibited structural properties not captured by the parameters of the p_1 model and spawned the development of two important lines of further model development.

Latent Variable Models

The first line of development is a series of latent variable models in which the assumption of independent dyads is replaced by an assumption of independent dyads conditional on unobserved variables representing some potential underlying structure.

One such model was inspired by the concept of structural equivalence in a graph (Lorrain & White, 1971). Two nodes are structurally equivalent if they have identical patterns of relationships to other nodes. The concept of structural equivalence has been very influential in the social networks literature because it can be used to represent the idea that two actors have the same social position in a network; that is, that they are indistinguishable from a relational point of view.

Formally, two nodes i and j are *structurally equivalent* in a directed graph G with adjacency matrix $\mathbf{x}$ if $x_{ik} = x_{jk}$ and $x_{ki} = x_{kj}$ for all nodes $k \neq i, j$ in N. Structurally equivalent nodes can be partitioned into *blocks*. Nowicki and Snijders (2001) assumed that the blocks to which nodes belong are unobserved. They defined a set of independent and identically distributed latent random variables $\mathbf{Z} = [Z_i]$, where Z_i denotes the *block* of node i and $\Pr(Z_i = k) = \theta_k$. They assumed the dyads $D_{ij} = (X_{ij}, X_{ji})$ to be conditionally independent given the blocks and the probability that a dyad has a particular relational form to depend only on the (unobserved) blocks of the nodes. In other words,

$$\Pr(D_{ij} = \boldsymbol{a} \mid \mathbf{Z} = \mathbf{z}) = \eta_{\boldsymbol{a}}(z_i, z_j),$$

where $\boldsymbol{a}$ is a vector of possible values for the dyad, with $\boldsymbol{a} \in \{(1,1),(1,0),(0,1),(0,0)\}$ for a directed graph and $\boldsymbol{a} \in \{(1,1),(0,0)\}$ for a graph, and $\eta_{\boldsymbol{a}}(z_i, z_j)$ is the block-dependent probability of observing the vector $\boldsymbol{a}$.

In this model, two nodes i and j are *stochastically equivalent* if they belong to the same block and hence the same dyad probabilities ($\Pr(D_{ik} = \boldsymbol{a} \mid \mathbf{Z} = \mathbf{z}) = \Pr(D_{jk} = \boldsymbol{a} \mid \mathbf{Z} = \mathbf{z})$) for all nodes k. Since the dyads are assumed to be conditionally independent given the blocks $\mathbf{Z}$, the joint distribution of the D_{ij} given $\mathbf{Z}$ is the product of the conditional dyad probabilities. Nowicki and Snijders (2001) developed a Bayesian approach to the estimation of θ and η and, hence, the computation of the posterior probabilities that any pair of nodes are in the same block and that a dyad has any particular relational form.

Several other important latent variable models have been developed for particular types of social networks that are likely to reflect some form of proximity among actors, such as friendship or collaboration. In cases such as these, it may be reasonable to assume that tie probabilities are monotonically related to proximity in a latent space. For example, Hoff, Raftery, and Handcock (2002) proposed a model that assumes that nodes have latent locations in some low-dimensional Euclidean space and that given these latent locations, tie variables are conditionally independent. Schweinberger and Snijders (2003) developed a similar model based on an ultrametric rather than Euclidean space; in their model, every pair of nodes is associated with an unobserved distance in an ultrametric space corresponding to a discrete hierarchy of "settings," and tie probabilities are conditionally independent given these latent ultrametric distances. (Distances in an ultrametric space satisfy the *ultrametric inequality*; i.e., $d(i,j) \leqslant \max\{d(i,k), d(j,k)\}$ for any triple of nodes i, j, k.) They developed approaches for estimating the unobserved ultrametric distances. Handcock, Raftery, and Tantrum (2005) have recently extended Hoff et al.'s (2002) model by assuming that the latent locations are drawn from a finite mixture of multivariate normal distributions, each of which represents a different group of nodes.

MARKOV RANDOM GRAPHS

The second recent line of development has been to build probabilistic network models in which conditional dependencies among tie variables are permitted. This work began with the recognition by Frank and Strauss (1986) that a general approach for modeling interactive systems of variables (Besag, 1974) could be usefully applied to the problem of modeling systems of interdependent network tie variables on a fixed set of nodes. This was an important step because it permitted models to go beyond the limiting assumption of dyad independence in quite a general way. Frank and Strauss (1986) introduced a *Markov dependence* assumption for network tie variables: Two network tie variables were assumed to be conditionally independent given the values of all other network tie variables, unless they had a node in common. Thus, whereas a tie between nodes i and j was assumed to be conditionally independent of ties involving all other distinct pairs of nodes k and l, it could be conditionally dependent on *any* other ties involving i and/or j.

Assumptions about which pairs of tie variables are conditionally dependent, given the values of all other tie variables, can be represented as a dependence graph. The node set of the *dependence graph D* is the set of tie variables $\{X_{ij}\}$, and two tie variables are joined by an edge in D if they are assumed to be conditionally dependent given the values of all other tie variables. In the case of $\mathcal{G}(n,p)$, D is an empty graph since all pairs of variables are assumed to be mutually independent. In the Markov case, the variable X_{ij} is connected to X_{ik} and X_{jk} for all $k \neq i$ or j, and the dependence graph is connected. Figure 18.5

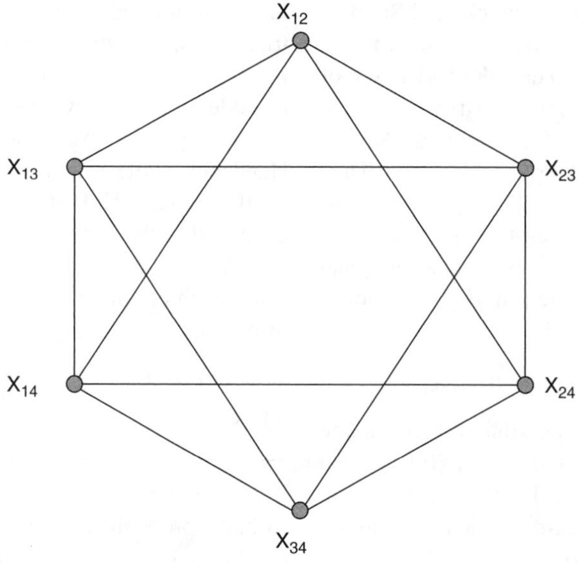

Figure 18.5 Dependence graph for a Markov random graph on four nodes.

shows the Markov dependence graph for a random graph of order 4.

As Frank and Strauss originally outlined, the consequences of any proposed assumptions about potential conditional dependencies among network tie variables can be inferred from the Hammersley-Clifford theorem (Besag, 1974). The theorem establishes a model for the interacting system of tie variables in terms of parameters that pertain to the presence or absence of certain configural forms in the network. The model, known as an *exponential random graph model*, takes the general form

$$\Pr(\mathbf{X}=\mathbf{x}) = \exp\left(\sum_A \gamma_A z_A(\mathbf{x})\right) / \kappa,$$

where A is a subset of tie variables (defining a potential network *configuration*), γ_A is a model parameter associated with the configuration A (to be estimated) and is nonzero only if the subset A is a clique in the dependence graph D, $z_A(\mathbf{x}) = \prod_{X_{ij}\in A} x_{ij}$ is the sufficient statistic corresponding to the parameter γ_A and indicates whether or not all tie variables in the configuration A have values of 1 in the network $\mathbf{x}$, and κ is a normalizing quantity.

To reduce the number of model parameters, Frank and Strauss (1986) introduced a *homogeneity* constraint that parameters for isomorphic configurations are equal. With this constraint, there is a single parameter $\gamma_{[A]}$ for each class $[A]$ of isomorphic configurations that correspond to cliques in the dependence graph. The sufficient statistic in the model corresponding to the class $[A]$ is then

$$Z_{[A]}(\mathbf{x}) = \sum_{A\in[A]} \prod_{X_{ij}\in A} x_{ij},$$

that is, a count of all observed configurations in the graph $\mathbf{x}$ that are isomorphic to the configuration corresponding to A. For example, in the case of a homogeneous Markov random graph, it is readily seen that cliques A in the dependence graph D correspond to graph configurations that are edges, stars, and triangles (see Figure 18.6), and the model therefore takes the form

$$\Pr(\mathbf{X}=\mathbf{x}) = \exp(\theta L(\mathbf{x}) + \sum_k \sigma_k S_k(x) + \tau T(\mathbf{x}))/\kappa,$$

where $L(\mathbf{x})$, $S_k(\mathbf{x})$, and $T(\mathbf{x})$ are the number of edges, k-stars $(2 \leqslant k \leqslant n-1)$, and triangles in the network $\mathbf{x}$ and θ, $\sigma_k (2 \leqslant k \leqslant n-1)$, and τ are the corresponding parameters.

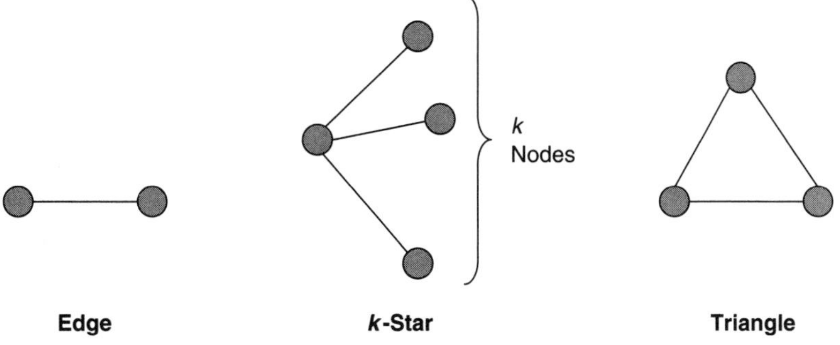

Figure 18.6 Markov model configurations: edges, stars, and triangles.

In many circumstances, the parameters may be interpreted by observing that if a configuration class $[A]$ has a large positive (or negative) parameter in the model, then the presence of many configurations in the class enhances (or reduces) the likelihood of the overall network, net of the effect of all other configurations. It should be noted, though, that the function relating the value of one of the model's parameters, say $\lambda_{[A]}$, to the expected value of the corresponding sufficient statistic $z_{[A]}(\mathbf{x})$ may be markedly nonlinear and exhibit a sharp and rapid transition from lower average counts to higher average counts, with a relatively small change in the parameter (holding constant the values of all other model parameters). For example, the expected number of triangles in a graph as a function of the triangle parameter τ is shown for a graph on 17 nodes in Figure 18.7. The values of the parameters θ, σ_2, and σ_3 are fixed at $-1.2558, -0.0451$, and -0.1084, respectively, and τ takes values in the range $[0.05, 1.70]$. Figure 18.7 shows the distribution of the triangle statistic in the form of a box plot for each value of τ. It can be seen that for low values of τ, small increases in τ are associated with small and steady increases in the triangle statistic. As τ approaches 1.40, though, the impact of small changes in τ increases rapidly in magnitude, and there is a sharp transition to a higher value of the triangle statistic. Near the point of transition, the triangle statistic may take values typical of the graphs on either side of this apparent threshold. This form of nonlinear relationship is common, and the location of this threshold and the sharpness of the rise in the region of greatest sensitivity are likely to depend on other parameter values.

It is important to emphasize that even though this model is well understood in the case where only the parameter θ is nonzero (since this is just the model $\mathcal{G}(n,p)$ with $p = \exp(\theta)/[1+\exp(\theta)]$), more complex instantiations can be seen as models for self-organizing network processes (Robins, Pattison, & Woolcock, 2005). Robins et al. (2005) have demonstrated that specific sets of parameter values for the homogeneous Markov model can characterize very diverse network structures, including small worlds, caveman worlds, long-path worlds, and so on.

For some parameter values, the model may accord very high probability to a small set of graphs and very low probability to the rest, as Handcock (2004) and Snijders (2002) have demonstrated. Handcock termed these models *near-degenerate*. For detailed investigation of the behavior of specific models, see Handcock (2004), as well as Park and Newman (2004) and Burda, Jurkiewicz, and Krzywicki (2004).

Model Simulation

To understand properties such as near-degeneracy of the exponential random graph model $\Pr(\mathbf{X} = \mathbf{x}) = \exp(\sum_A \gamma_A z_A(\mathbf{x}))/\kappa$, it is helpful to be able to simulate it efficiently (i.e., to draw graphs $\mathbf{x}$ with probability $Pr(\mathbf{X} = \mathbf{x})$), and this generally means circumventing the need to compute the normalizing quantity κ, since κ is a function of *all* graphs in the distribution. As Strauss (1986) and others have observed, the *Metropolis algorithm* can be used for this purpose. The algorithm sets up a Markov chain on the space of all possible graphs of order n in such

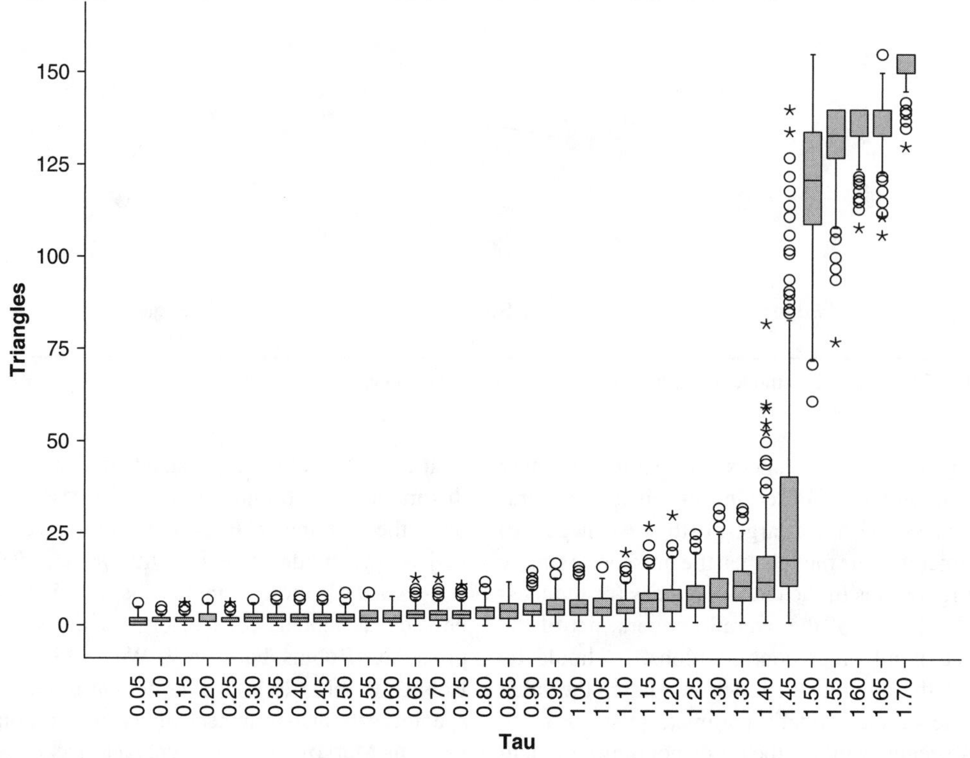

Figure 18.7 Boxplots for the triangle statistic as a function of the triangle parameter for a Markov model on a graph of 17 nodes ($\theta = -1.2558$, $\sigma_2 = -0.0451$, $\sigma_3 = -0.1084$, τ between 0.00 and 1.75).

a way that the Markov chain has the model as its stationary distribution. It may be described as follows:

1. Begin with some graph **x**.
2. At each step, select an edge at random, say the (i, j) edge, and let $\mathbf{x}'$ be the graph that is identical to **x**, except that the edge from i to j is switched to absent if it is present in **x** or to present if it is absent in **x**.
3. Replace **x** by $\mathbf{x}'$ with probability $\min[1, \exp\{\sum_A \gamma_A(z_A(\mathbf{x}') - z_A(\mathbf{x})\}]$.
4. Return to Step 2, unless some specified target number of steps has been taken.

To sample from $\Pr(\mathbf{X} = \mathbf{x})$, it is usual to begin sampling graphs from the chain after some initial number of steps have been completed (the *burn-in* period); graphs are then sampled at a rate that may depend on n. Many variations of this approach may also be used; a valuable discussion may be found in Snijders (2002).

Estimation of Model Parameters

In many settings, primary interest lies in estimating exponential random graph model parameters from observed network data. For example, given the graph of Figure 18.1, there may be interest in estimating the parameters of a Markov model from which it might have been generated. In the early applications of these models to observed data, an approximate form of estimation known as pseudolikelihood estimation was often used (Strauss & Ikeda, 1990; Wasserman & Pattison, 1996), even though the properties of the estimates were not well understood. Initial attempts to apply the very promising approach of Markov chain Monte Carlo maximum likelihood estimation (MCMCMLE) were not always successful because the properties of the models under consideration were not always fully appreciated, as Snijders (2002) and Handcock (2004) demonstrated. However, with a growing understanding of model properties and more careful attention to model adequacy, substantial progress has now been made in implementing MCMCMLE approaches (see Handcock, Hunter, Butts, Goodreau, & Morris, 2004; Snijders, 2002).

As an example of MCMCMLE, we estimate the parameters of the model

$$\Pr(\mathbf{X}=\mathbf{x}) = \frac{\exp(\theta L(\mathbf{x})+\sigma_2 S_2(\mathbf{x})+\sigma_3 S_3(\mathbf{x})+\tau T(\mathbf{x}))}{\kappa}$$

for the mutual friendship network of Figure 18.1 using the approach proposed by Snijders (2002). The resulting estimates and estimated standard errors for the parameters θ, σ_2, σ_3, and τ are shown in Table 18.2.[2] Also displayed in Table 18.2 are convergence t statistics, computed as the difference between the observed value of the sufficient statistic for a parameter and its average simulated value, divided by the standard deviation of simulated values. If the estimated value is indeed the maximum likelihood estimate, the simulated values should be centered on the observed value and the t statistics should all be small, preferably below 0.1 (Snijders, 2002). It can be seen from Table 18.2 that the t statistics satisfy this requirement. Although the edge, 2-star, and 3-star parameters are negative and within about 1 standard error of 0, the triangle parameter is positive and approximately seven times its estimated error. This suggests that, other graph features (edges, 2-stars, and 3-stars) being equal, graphs with more triangles are more likely. That such a model is needed for the graph of Figure 18.1 is consistent with the earlier computations based on $G(17, 0.25)$.

Goodness of Fit

A good statistical model should not be unnecessarily complex, but it should be adequate: that is, the data should resemble realizations from the model in many important respects. We can assess model adequacy by comparing the observed network with graphs generated by the model in features that are not necessarily parameterized within the model. What is important in such comparisons is very much a function of the modeling context, but there are often good reasons to require that the model captures the degree of clustering in a network, the distribution of degrees, and the connectivity structure that is represented by the geodesic distribution (e.g., Goodreau, 2007; Robins, Snijders, Wang, Handcock, & Pattison, 2007). It is important to note that only some of these characteristics need be associated with model parameters; others might be seen as consequences of these parameterized tendencies.

For example, if we simulate the model

$$\Pr(\mathbf{X}=\mathbf{x}) = \frac{\exp(\theta L(\mathbf{x})+\sigma_2 S_2(\mathbf{x})+\sigma_3 S_3(\mathbf{x})+\tau T(\mathbf{x}))}{\kappa}$$

using the parameter estimates in Table 18.2, we can not only compare the observed graph with the simulated graph in terms of its sufficient statistics (viz., the number of edges, 2-stars, 3-stars, and triangles), but we can also make the comparison in relation to any unmodeled network characteristic, such as the number of nodes of degree 4 or more, the number of geodesic distances of length 3, and so on.

Table 18.3 summarizes these comparisons for the graph of Figure 18.1 and the parameter estimates of Table 18.2. It can be seen that the t statistics are all less than 1 for

- the *local clustering coefficient* (the average across all nodes i of the proportion of pairs of nodes j and k incident with $i(x_{ij} = 1 = x_{ik})$ that are themselves connected $(x_{jk} = 1)$,
- the *global clustering coefficient* (the proportion of the triples of nodes $\{i, j, k\}$ with $x_{ij} = 1 = x_{ik}$ for which $x_{jk} = 1$),
- the *standard deviation* of the degree distribution, and
- the *skewness coefficient* of the degree distribution.

[2]The estimation was conducted using PNet (Wang, Robins, & Pattison, 2006), an implementation of the estimation approach in Snijders (2002). Retrieved from http://www.sna.unimelb.edu.au/pnetpnet.html.

Table 18.2 MCMCMLEs for Markov Model of the Graph of Figure 18.1

Parameter	*Estimate*	*s. e.*	*t*
Edge	−1.2558	1.3561	0.047
2-Star	−0.0451	0.3551	0.060
3-Star	−0.1084	0.0974	0.073
Triangle	1.4438	0.2073	0.058

Table 18.3 Goodness of Fit for Markov Model for the Mutual Friendship Network (Figure 18.1)

		Simulated		
	Observed	*Mean*	*Std dev*	*t*
Edges	34	34.07	8.91	−0.0077
2-Stars	139	138.35	77.45	0.0084
3-Stars	181	178.05	156.49	0.0189
Triangles	30	29.34	28.39	0.0231
Std dev degrees	2.09	1.71	0.46	0.8296
Skew degrees	0.08	−0.26	0.62	0.5480
Global clustering	0.65	0.54	0.21	0.5246
Mean local clustering	0.64	0.47	0.19	0.4917
Variance local clustering	0.14	0.10	0.04	0.9899

The observed graph, in other words, exhibits levels of clustering and degree heterogeneity that fall within the envelope of values expected for the model. The 1st, 2nd, and 3rd quartiles of the observed geodesic distribution are 1, 3, and 4, respectively; the median values for the distribution of these quartiles across simulations were 2, 2, and 4, suggesting that the model is associated with somewhat more homogeneous internode distances than the data. In Figure 18.8, the distributions of the number of edges, 2-stars, 3-stars, and triangles for the Markov random graph model with these parameter values are shown. While the mean of each distribution is close to the observed value for the Figure 18.1 graph, as expected, it can be seen that the distributions are positively skewed. Indeed, Figure 18.7 shows the impact on one of these statistics—the number of triangles—of changing its corresponding parameter value τ while holding all other parameters constant. It can be seen from Figure 18.7 that the estimated value of 1.4438 is very close to the point of transition between low and high values of the triangle statistic and the positively skewed distribution of the triangle statistic is consistent with the estimated value of τ being just below this point.

Related Model Parameters

In the Markov model just fitted, parameters for 2-stars and 3-stars were included, but parameters for higher-order stars (4-stars, 5-stars, and so on) were assumed to be 0. Arguably, fitting higher-order star parameters might be desirable, because more star parameters will lead to better characterizations of the degree distribution for the network. Indeed, Snijders, Pattison, Robins, and Handcock (2006) proposed that all star parameters be used, but they also imposed a hypothesis about the relationships among stars parameters. Specifically, they assumed that

$$\sigma_{k+1} = (-1/\lambda)\sigma_k, \quad \text{for } k > 1 \text{ and } \lambda \geqslant 1 \text{ a (fixed) constant,}$$

a hypothesis they termed *the alternating k-star hypothesis*. It follows from this hypothesis that

$$\sum_k \sigma_k S_k(\mathbf{x}) = \left[\sum_k (-1)^k S_k(\mathbf{x})/\lambda^{k-2}\right] \sigma_2$$

and, hence, that the entire set of starlike terms in the model can be captured by a single star parameter (σ_2) with a single *alternating k-star* statistic:

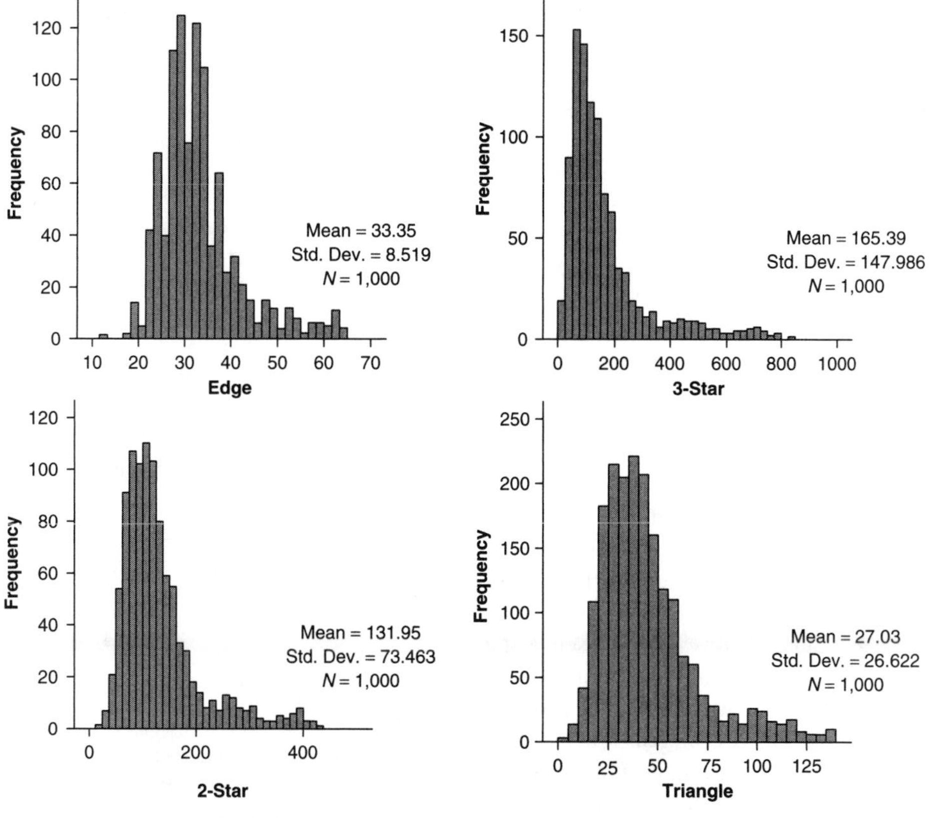

Figure 18.8 Distribution of edge, 2-star, 3-star, and triangle statistics in the Markov random graph distribution with parameters $\theta = -1.2558$, $\sigma_2 = -0.0451$, $\sigma_3 = -0.1084$, $\tau = 1.4438$.

$$S^{[\lambda]}(\mathbf{x}) = \sum_k (-1)^k S_k(\mathbf{x})/\lambda^{k-2}$$

It is of course an empirical matter whether this is an appropriate hypothesis to make. This expression can be simplified to yield a simpler form of the alternating k-star statistic:

$$S^{[\lambda]}(\mathbf{x}) = \lambda^2 \sum_i \{(1 - 1/\lambda)^{k(i)} + k(i)/\lambda - 1\},$$

recalling that $k(i)$ denotes the degree of node i.[3]

Fitting the model

$$\Pr(\mathbf{X} = \mathbf{x}) = \exp(\theta L(\mathbf{x}) + \sigma_2 S^{[\lambda]}(\mathbf{x}))/\kappa$$

to the friendship network in Figure 18.1 yields estimates (standard errors) of −2.7454 (1.3794) and 0.4822 (0.4098) for θ and σ_2, respectively (as before, θ is an edge parameter, and $L(\mathbf{x})$, the number of edges in the network **x**, is its sufficient statistic). Although this model does a reasonable job in reproducing the standard deviation and the skewness coefficient for the degree distribution, not surprisingly, it does a poor job in recovering network clustering. We present a better-fitting model below.

In some applications to date (e.g., Goodreau, 2007; Snijders et al., 2006), a fixed value of λ (such as 2) has been assumed; Hunter and Handcock (2006) have shown that λ can be treated as a variable within a curved exponential family model, and they have developed an associated estimation method.

[3]Hunter and Handcock (2006) proposed an alternative statistic based on geometrically weighted degree statistics; the resulting model is equivalent, provided that the edge parameter is included.

Realization-Dependent Models

A critique of the Markov dependence assumption led Pattison and Robins (2002) to construct a more general class of "realization-dependent" network models. They argued that conditional dependencies among tie variables may emerge from the network processes themselves, with new dependencies created as network ties are generated. For instance, X_{ij} and X_{kl} might become conditionally dependent *if* there is an observed tie between, say, j and k. Baddeley and Möller (1989) termed such models *realization dependent*.

The 4-Cycle Hypothesis

Snijders et al. (2006) argued that in addition to the Markov assumption, two network ties, X_{ij} and X_{kl}, might be conditionally dependent in the case where there is an observed tie between, say, j and k and between l and i; that is, if the presence of a tie from i to j and from k to l would create a 4-cycle in the graph. The rationale for this assumption is that a 4-cycle is a closed structure that can sustain mutual social monitoring and influence, as well as levels of trustworthiness within which obligations and expectations might proliferate (e.g., Coleman, 1988).

Snijders et al. (2006) showed that this assumption led to additional nonzero parameters in an exponential random graph model, including those referring to collections of 2-paths with common starting and ending nodes and collections of triangles with a common base (see Figure 18.9). We define a *k-2-path* to be a subgraph comprising two nodes, i and j, and a set of k paths of length 2 from i to j through distinct intermediate nodes $m_1, m_2, \ldots, m_k$. A *k-triangle* is a subgraph comprising two *connected nodes*, i and j, and a set of k paths of length 2 from i to j through distinct intermediate nodes $m_1, m_2, \ldots, m_k$. If we let ν_k be the model parameter associated with a k-2-path and τ_k the parameter associated with a k-triangle, we can entertain assumptions about the relationships among related parameters (as in the case of k-stars earlier)—namely,

$$\nu_{k+1} = -\nu_k/\lambda$$

and

$$\tau_{k+1} = -\tau_k/\lambda.$$

As for the star parameters, this is just a hypothesis, and its adequacy needs to be assessed. Under this assumption, the statistics

$$U^{[\lambda]}(\mathbf{x}) = \sum_k (-1)^k U_k(\mathbf{x})/\lambda^{k-2}$$

and

$$T^{[\lambda]}(\mathbf{x}) = \sum_k (-1)^k T_k(\mathbf{x})/\lambda^{k-2}$$

become single statistics associated with the parameters ν_1 and τ_1, respectively, where $U_k(\mathbf{x})$ and $T_k(\mathbf{x})$ are the number of k-2-paths and k-triangles in the network $\mathbf{x}$. It should be noted that the value of λ need not be the same for each statistic; as before, Hunter and Handcock have shown how to estimate these parameters.

The parameter estimates presented in Table 18.4 are for a model fitted to the mutual friendship network of Figure 18.1. The positive τ_1 estimate suggests that networks with relatively many triangles are more likely, other statistics being equal, with the cumulative impact of multiple triangles with a common base pair of nodes diminishing as the number of such triangles increases. Likewise, the negative ν_1 estimate suggests that networks with relatively few 2-paths among a pair of nonconnected nodes are more likely, other statistics being equal. Both of these effects are consistent with a pressure toward closure for mutual friendship ties.

The goodness of fit for this model is summarized in Table 18.5. The median values of the quartiles of the geodesic distribution for the random graph distribution simulated from the parameter estimates in Table 18.4 are 2, 3, and 5, suggesting better recovery of short distances than the Markov model, though not of longer ones. Overall, the model of Table 18.4 appears to do a reasonably good job of characterizing the features of the mutual friendship network.

Directed Graph Models

The derivation of similar classes of models for directed graphs is, in principle, very similar to the derivation of models for their nondirected counterparts. Directed graphs give rise, however, to substantially more complicated parameterizations, as a comparison between triadic

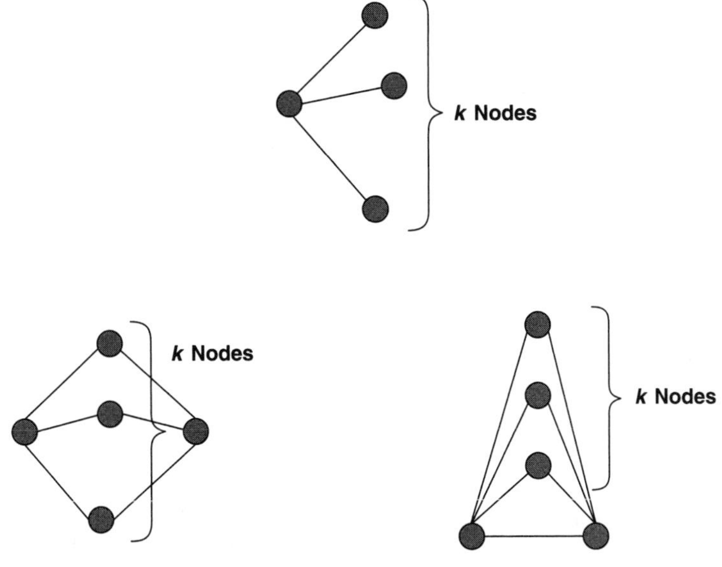

Figure 18.9 The k-star, k-2-path, and k-triangle.

Table 18.4 MCMCMLEs for Realization-Dependent Exponential Random Graph Model for the Mutual Friendship Network (Figure 18.1)

Parameter	*estimate*	*s.e.*	*t*
Edge	−0.0354	1.7851	−0.037
2-Star	−0.0520	0.1094	−0.038
k-Star	0.0674	0.8689	−0.040
k-Triangles	0.7250	0.3159	−0.043
k-2-Paths	−0.5583	0.1727	−0.025

Table 18.5 Goodness of Fit of Realization-Dependent Model for the Mutual Friendship Network

		Simulated		
Statistic	*Observed*	*Mean*	*Std dev*	*t*
Edges	34	34.44	9.33	−0.047
2-Stars	139	145.13	94.54	−0.065
k-Stars	77.8	79.73	34.68	−0.054
k-Triangles	46.0	47.01	28.39	0.023
k-2-Paths	83.3	85.30	30.68	−0.064
Std dev degrees	2.09	1.77	0.60	0.522
Skew degrees	0.08	−0.17	0.46	−0.548
Global clustering	0.65	0.55	0.14	0.696
Mean local clustering	0.64	0.50	0.15	0.439
Variance local clustering	0.14	0.09	0.04	1.207

forms in graphs and directed graphs quickly suggests. There are, as a result, some subtleties to the development of models in the directed graph case (see Robins, Pattison, & Wang, 2006, for further details).

Exogenous Covariates

The general modeling framework can readily accommodate covariates at the node or dyad level, and, of course, if such covariates are regarded as important influences on network tie formation, then they should be included in models for the network. For example, a general and systematic approach to the inclusion of node-level covariates has been outlined by Robins, Elliott, and Pattison (2001), who extended the dependence graph formulation described earlier to include directed dependence relationships from exogenous node-level variables to endogenous tie variables. These developments offer an important means for exploring a wide range of interesting interactions among actor-level and network tie variables, including *homophily* effects (e.g., McPherson, Smith-Lovin, & Cook, 2001) and the effects of spatial locations (e.g., Butts, 2003; Wong, Pattison, & Robins, 2006).

EXTENSIONS

There are a variety of ways in which the models just described may be extended to incorporate richer data forms, including multiple networks, longitudinal data, and changing node and tie sets. In addition, some initial progress has been made on the problem of dealing with missing data. We do not have space for a full account of these interesting and important developments but point to some key developments in each case.

The development of probabilistic models for graphs and directed graphs has been loosely shadowed by the construction of a parallel, albeit generally later, set of models for multiple networks measured on a common node set. Multivariate exponential random graph models are described by Pattison and Wasserman (1999); see also Koehly and Pattison (2005).

Although networks are often measured at a single point in time, they are, in reality, dynamic entities, and there is considerable interest in the processes that underpin their evolution. An important line of work has developed continuous-time Markov process models for network evolution (e.g., see Snijders, 2001). More recently, this framework has been extended to accommodate the possibility of co-evolutionary mechanisms by which network tie change depends on and contributes to change in node attributes (Snijders, Steglich, & Schweinberger, 2007).

CONCLUSION

The field of probabilistic network theory has progressed rapidly in the past 10 years, and as Goodreau (2007) and Robins et al. (2007) have cogently demonstrated, it is now possible to build plausible models for many small and large social networks. Undoubtedly, experience with the current generation of realization-dependent network models will lead to further improvements in model specification and a clearer understanding of how the content of network ties and the contexts in which they are observed might inform model building. Perhaps most important though, the field has now advanced to the point where the promise of a step-change in our understanding of social processes on networks and their consequences might be realized.

ACKNOWLEDGMENTS

We are grateful to Peng Wang and Galina Daraganova for helpful comments on this chapter.

REFERENCES

Albert, R., & Barabási, A. (2002). Statistical mechanics of complex networks. *Reviews of Modern Physics*, *74*, 47–97.

Baddeley, A., & Möller. (1989). Nearest-neighbor Markov point processes and random sets. *International Statistical Review*, *57*, 89–121.

Bearman, P., Moody, J., & Stovel, K. (2004). Chains of affection: The structure of adolescent romantic and sexual networks. *American Journal of Sociology*, *110*, 44–91.

Besag, J. (1974). Spatial interaction and the statistical analysis of lattice systems (with discussion). *Journal of the Royal Statistical Society Series B, 36*, 96–127.

Bollobás, B. (1985). *Random graphs*. London: Academic Press.

Bollobás, B. (1998). *Modern graph theory*. New York: Springer.

Brieger, R. (1981). Comment on "An exponential family of probability distributions for directed graphs". *Journal of the American Statistical Association, 76*, 51–53.

Burda, Z., Jurkiewicz, J., & Krzywicki, A. (2004). Network transitivity and matrix models. *Physical Review E, 69*, 026106.

Butts, C. (2003). Predictability of large-scale spatially embedded networks. In R. L. Breiger, K. M. Carley, & P. E. Pattison (Eds.), *Social network models: Workshop summary and papers* (pp. 313–323). Washington, DC: National Academies Press.

Coleman, J. (1988). Social capital in the creation of human capital. *American Journal of Sociology, 94*(Suppl.), S95–S120.

Erdős, P., & Rényi, A. (1959). On random graphs I. *Publicationes Mathematicae Debrecen, 6*, 290–297.

Frank, O., & Strauss, D. (1986). Markov graphs. *Journal of the American Statistical Association, 81*, 832–842.

Freeman, L. (2004). *The development of social network analysis: A study in the sociology of science*. Vancouver, British Columbia: Booksurge.

Goodreau, S. (2007). Advances in exponential random graph (p*) models applied to a large social network. *Social Networks, 29*, 231–248.

Handcock, M. (2004). *Assessing degeneracy in statistical models for social networks* (Working Paper No. 39). Center for Statistics in the Social Sciences, University of Washington.

Handcock, M., Hunter, D., Butts, C., Goodreau, S., & Morris, M. (2004). *Statnet manual for R* (Tech. Rep.). Center for Statistics in the Social Sciences, University of Washington.

Handcock, M., Raftery, A., & Tantrum, J. (2005). *Model-based clustering for social networks* (Working Paper No. 46). Center for Statistics in the Social Sciences, University of Washington.

Hoff, P., Raftery, A., & Handcock, M. (2002). Latent space approaches to social network analysis. *Journal of the American Statistical Association, 97*, 1090–1098.

Holland, P., & Leinhardt, S. (1975). Local structure in social networks. In D. Heise (Ed.), *Sociological methodology 1976* (pp. 1–45). San Francisco: Jossey-Bass.

Holland, P., & Leinhardt, S. (1981). An exponential family of probability distributions for directed graphs. *Journal of the American Statistical Association, 76*, 33–50.

Hunter, D., & Handcock, M. (2006). Inference in curved exponential families for networks. *Journal of Computational and Graphical Statistics, 15*, 565–583.

Koehly, L., & Pattison, P. (2005). Random graph models for social networks: Multiple relations or multiple raters. In P. Carrington, J. Scott, & S. Wasserman (Eds.), *Models and methods in social network analysis* (pp. 162–191). New York: Cambridge University Press.

Kretzschmar, M., & Morris, M. (1996). Measures of concurrency in networks and the spread of infectious disease: The AIDS example. *Social Science and Medicine, 21*, 1203–1216.

Lorrain, F., & White, H. (1971). Structural equivalence of individuals in social networks. *Journal of Mathematical Sociology, 1*, 49–80.

McDonald, J., Smith, P., & Forster, J. (2007). Markov chain Monte Carlo exact inference for analysing social networks data. *Social Networks, 29*(1), 127–136.

McPherson, M., Smith-Lovin, L., & Cook, J. (2001). Birds of a feather: Homophily in social networks. *Annual Review of Sociology, 27*, 415–444.

Milo, R., Shen-Orr, S., Itzkovitz, S., Kashtan, N., Chkovskii, D., & Alon, U. (2002). Network motifs: Simple building blocks of complex networks. *Science, 298*, 824–827.

Nowicki, K., & Snijders, T. (2001). Estimation and prediction for stochastic blockstructures. *Journal of the American Statistical Association, 96*, 1077–1087.

Park, J., & Newman, M. (2004). Solution of the 2-star model of a network. *Physical Review E, 70*, 066146.

Pattison, P., & Robins, G. (2002). Neighbourhood-based models for social networks. *Sociological Methodology, 32*, 301–337.

Pattison, P., & Wasserman, S. (1999). Logit models and logistic regressions for social networks: II. Multivariate relations. *British Journal of Mathematical and Statistical Psychology, 52*, 169–193.

Pattison, P., Wasserman, S., Robins, G., & Kanfer, A. (2000). Statistical evaluation of algebraic constraints for social networks. *Journal of Mathematical Psychology, 44*, 563–568.

Rapoport, A. (1957). Contributions to the theory of random and biased nets. *Bulletin of Mathematical Biophysics, 19*, 257–277.

Rapoport, A., & Horvath, W. (1961). A study of a large sociogram. *Behavioral Science, 6*, 279–291.

Robins, G., Elliott, P., & Pattison, P. (2001). Network models for social selection processes. *Social Networks, 23*, 1–30.

Robins, G., Pattison, P., & Wang, P. (2006). *Closure, connectivity and degrees: New specifications for exponential random graph models for directed social networks.* University of Melbourne, Melbourne, Australia.

Robins, G., Pattison, P., & Woolcock, J. (2005). Small and other worlds: Global network structures from local processes. *American Journal of Sociology, 110*, 894–936.

Robins, G., Snijders, T., Wang, P., Handcock, M., & Pattison, P. (2007). Recent developments in exponential random graph (p*) models. *Social Networks, 29*, 192–215.

Schweinberger, M., & Snijders, T. (2003). Settings in social networks: A measurement model. *Sociological Methodology, 33*, 307–341.

Snijders, T. (1991). Enumeration and simulation models for 0–1 matrices with given marginals. *Psychometrika, 56*, 397–417.

Snijders, T. (2001). The statistical evaluation of social network dynamics. In M. Sobel & M. Becker (Eds.), *Sociological methodology 2001* (pp. 361–395). Boston: Basil Blackwell.

Snijders, T. (2002). Markov chain Monte Carlo estimation of exponential random graph models [electronic version]. *Journal of Social Structure, 3*(2). Available from http://www.cmu.edu/joss/content/articles/volume3/Snijders.pdf.

Snijders, T., Pattison, P., Robins, G., & Handcock, M. (2006). New specifications for exponential random graph models. *Sociological Methodology, 36*, 99–153.

Snijders, T., Steglich, C., & Schweinberger, M. (2007). Modeling the co-evolution of networks and behavior. In K. van Montfort, H. Oud, & A. Satorra (Eds.), *Longitudinal models in the behavioral and related sciences* (pp. 41–71). Mahwah, NJ: Lawrence Erlbaum.

Strauss, D. (1986). On a general class of models for interaction. *SIAM Review, 28*, 513–527.

Strauss, D., & Ikeda, M. (1990). Pseudolikelihood estimation for social networks. *Journal of the American Statistical Association, 85*, 204–212.

Wang, P., Robins, G., & Pattison, P. (2006). *Pnet: Program for the estimation and simulation of p* exponential random graph models [User manual].* Melbourne, Australia: University of Melbourne, Department of Psychology.

Wasserman, S., & Faust, K. (1994). *Social network analysis: Methods and applications.* New York: Cambridge University Press.

Wasserman, S., & Pattison, P. (1996). Logit models and logistic regressions for social networks, I. An introduction to Markov graphs and p*. *Psychometrika, 61*, 401–425.

Wong, L., Pattison, P., & Robins, G. (2006). A spatial model for social networks. *Physica A: Statistical Mechanics and Its Applications, 360*, 99–120.

19

GAMBLING

CHAS FRIEDMAN

INTRODUCTION

The present chapter is intended to be an elementary introduction to the applications of probability (and some statistics) to gambling. It is certainly not comprehensive; very thorough treatises (e.g., Epstein, 1977) already exist, and this chapter in no way attempts to compete with those. However, the material is intended to be a practical discussion of typical applications of probability to gambling theory and strategy and should be quite useful to those who gamble or wish to improve their results. We note that a large number of excellent treatises with exhaustive analysis and commentary on particular games as well as some general works on gambling (written by folks who make a living doing what they preach) are available from Two Plus Two Publishing, Las Vegas, Nevada. Malmuth (1994) and Sklansky (1994) are examples.

We first make a few remarks concerning the history, origins, and even psychology of gambling, drawing some material from several excellent references on the subject but including some of our own observations as well.

The following sections present a quick review of foundational material; present many examples of games (roulette, craps, poker, sports betting, etc.) and the relevant probabilistic analysis and calculations; and finally discuss in some detail the long-term aspects of gambling—variance and applications of the central limit theorem, the (sometimes maligned) subject of money management, the probability of ruin, "best" strategies, and so on.

Some of the material is taken from existing work of the present author—for example, material for a text part of which appears on the Web (Friedman, 2006), notes handed out in his classes at University of Texas–Austin, and some of his publications (Friedman, 1999).

HISTORY AND ORIGINS

Gambling has been with us for a long time. John Scarne (self-proclaimed as the "world's foremost gambling authority") notes in Scarne (1986) that dice have been found in ancient tombs in Egypt and the Orient and in prehistoric American graves. Many of the earliest writers on probability were concerned with gambling. Scarne recounts that Pascal analyzed the questions posed by a noted gambler, The Chevalier de Méré, concerning the probabilities that a six would come up at least once in 4 rolls of a single die and of a double six coming up at least once in 24 rolls with two dice. Galileo wrote a treatise on dice, and the mathematicians Blaise Pascal and Pierre

Fermat wrote about applications of probability to gambling games, and so did Bernouillis, Laplace, Von Mises, and many others. Many references to such work can be found in Feller's (1968) classic text. However, much of the history of gambling is fairly uncertain. For example, even concerning poker—the classic American game, the origins are open to much speculation; Scarne (1986) has some interesting discussion about this.

Why do we gamble? This is a complicated subject. One possible reason is to "make money." Of course, gambling establishments such as casinos make a profit and in many cases a large one. But what about individuals? A few people have won substantial sums at blackjack but usually only for a short period of time (before being banned from the casinos), and most casinos have changed the game (specifically, the way the cards are dealt) to nullify the advantage that card counting might afford the expert. There are some sports bettors (usually groups) who make a profit but not, to our knowledge, very many. The author knows some poker players who make a relatively small amount playing in home games, but this is somewhat limited. If one makes too much, then one may not get invited again to play the game. There are some professional poker players who make a living playing the game, especially at the present time, when there is sponsorship for many tournaments, some of which are televised on major sports channels. It is a fact, however, that the variance in poker is often rather large, and someone can do well for a period of time approaching a year (or even more) without really having the skill to win over a longer period of time (we discuss this in a later section). Nevertheless, there are some individuals who have done well for a long time playing in tournaments and/or high-stakes casino poker games, but it takes a lot of skill, discipline, and the right personality, and there are many pitfalls. As the saying goes, "it's a tough way to make an easy living."

Another motivation is recreation. Playing cards at home as a regular social activity can be stimulating and highly entertaining, and so can gambling at a casino. Even in games where the casino has an edge, this may be fairly small if one has some skill, and the variance is often large enough that even in games unfavorable to the player, a reasonable amount can be won in the short term; this, of course, is by design, and this is what helps retain the players' interest in the game.

For some, gambling can be a kind of addiction. People become addicted to many things, however—hobbies, games, playing musical instruments, work, and so on. Of course, for some this addiction is carried too far and becomes a liability, but that's true of many things indulged in excess, and so also with gambling. Hence, this is not always a completely negative thing, and it seems unfair to condemn a pastime just because it can be abused.

We conclude with two fairly well-known quotes relevant to the present discussion. A gambler named Canada Bill, who lived during the American riverboat era (1800s), was warned that a certain card game was crooked; he replied, "I know, but it's the only game in town." (Goldblatt & Messick, 1976—the title is just that quote). Nick ("The Greek") Dandalos, who played high-limit poker with Johnny Moss at Binion's in Las Vegas for 5 months (a game that inspired the "World Series of Poker"), says, "The next best thing to gambling and winning is gambling and losing."

We now turn to the applications of probability to gambling, and in the subsequent section we discuss some foundations and practical applications.

Probability and Applications

The notions of random variable and expectation play a central role in probability and in its application to gaming. As an elementary example, consider the experiment $\mathcal{E}$ of tossing a coin, for which the probability of obtaining a head is $P(H) = p$. As we know, it is probably not possible to give this a concrete operational meaning because in the real world things seem to happen on the basis of dynamical causes (but see Friedman, 1999, for a discussion of the frequency interpretation of probability from a more operational point of view than the usual one). We define a *sample space* S whose members are the *elementary outcomes* H and T of $\mathcal{E}$—that is,

$$S = \{H, T\} \qquad (19.1)$$

and a *probability* P on *events* (subsets of S) for which

$$\begin{aligned} P(\emptyset) &= 0, \\ P(S) &= 1, \\ P(\{H\}) &= p, \\ P(\{T\}) &= q = 1-p. \end{aligned} \tag{19.2}$$

(The meaning of *event* is as follows: When we say an "event occurs," we mean that the outcome of the experiment is a member of the event. In this example, the points H, T in S are the things of most interest, and the notion of *event* isn't especially interesting, but in more complicated examples the events are of primary importance.)

We usually identify a singleton set with its single member, in which case $P(\{H\})$ is denoted $P(H)$, and so on, so we just write $P(H) = p$, $P(T) = q$.

The pair $\{S, P\}$, consisting of a sample space and a probability defined on the events of S, is called a *probability space*. We will frequently use this terminology.

The notion of *odds* is important and frequently appears in the analysis of games and gambling situations for reasons that will be clear shortly. For an event A with probability p (such as the event $\{H\}$ in the present example), we say that *the odds against A are q to p* (where $q = 1-p$). This is interpreted in the sense of a ratio, so one could equally well say that the *the odds against A are kq to kp*, where k is any positive real number. One often chooses k, so that kq and kp are whole numbers; for example, if $P(H) = 1/3$, one would say that they are 2 to 1, rather than 2/3 to 1/3, against H.

We remark that sometimes the notion of *odds in favor* of an event is expressed; in the last example, one could say that they are 1 to 2 in favor of H, although one usually sees odds expressed so that the larger number comes first and odds against is more commonly seen in gambling situations. This is likely because gamblers often like to bet on something that has a large payoff if the bet is won, and as we will see, a fair bet on some event for which the odds are 2 to 1 against has a winning payoff of 2 units if 1 unit is bet.

The above discussion shows how to convert a probability to odds. The other way around is equally simple: If the odds against the occurrence of an event A are α to β, then $P(A) = \beta/(\alpha+\beta)$.

To continue with our coin-tossing example with probabilities as in (19.2), suppose that we bet that the outcome will be H and win an amount a when we are correct but lose b when T occurs. Consider the function $X : S \to \mathbf{R}$, where $\mathbf{R}$ is the set of real numbers and

$$X(H) = a, \qquad X(T) = -b. \tag{19.3}$$

X is a *random variable* equal to our winnings on the bet made.

A *random variable* is, by definition, a function from a sample space equipped with a probability (i.e., a probability space) to the real numbers, and we sometimes indicate that by the notation $X : \{S, P\} \to \mathbf{R}$.

The *expectation* (also called the *mean*) of a random variable X defined on a probability space $\{S, P\}$ when S is finite (or countable) is

$$E(X) = \sum_{s \in S} X(s) P(s). \tag{19.4}$$

Another expression for the expectation, which is obtained by rearranging the terms in (19.4), is

$$E(X) = \sum_{x} x P(X = x). \tag{19.5}$$

In (19.5), the sum is over all real values (only the actual values of X of which the number is finite or countable contribute to the sum).

The definition of expectation as a weighted sum over the sample space is perhaps a bit difficult to interpret in a concrete operational sense. A possibly more intuitive meaning follows from the *weak law of large numbers*; if independent repetitions of the associated experiment are performed and the values x_i, $i = 1, 2, 3, \ldots$ of X that occur in each repetition are collected, then the ordinary average

$$\frac{x_1 + \cdots + x_n}{n} \tag{19.6}$$

will be close to $E(X)$, with probability close to 1 for large n. Note that (19.6) is *not* the average of the possible values of X but rather the average of the observed values of X that occur in a sequence of distinct repetitions of the experiment.

For our coin-tossing case with (19.3), we have

$$E(X) = aP(H) - bP(T) = ap - bq. \tag{19.7}$$

Note that $E(X) = 0$ when the ratios $a:b$ and $q:p$ are equal (assuming that b and p are nonzero, this is the same as saying that $a/b = q/p$). When $E(X) = 0$, we say "the bet is fair"; this means that "on average," we neither win nor lose by making the bet. Note that the bet is fair exactly when the ratio $a:b$ is the same as the odds against the event (H) on which we have bet. Furthermore, if the ratio $a:b$ is greater than the odds against H, our expectation is positive (and if it is less, then our expectation is negative). This is one reason why knowing the probabilities in the form of odds is convenient—we can immediately see if win/lose amounts produce a favorable (i.e., positive win expectation) situation. For example, if $P(H) = 1/3$, then if we bet on H and lose one unit when H fails to occur, we should win more than two units when H occurs to have a positive expectation or "edge" (since $P(H) = 1/3$ is 2 to 1 against expressed as odds). In discussions intended for those with no background in probability or technical mathematics, one might analyze the last situation by saying that on average in three tosses, one expects to get 1 H and 2 Ts, so that (assuming we win \$2 or lose \$1) we will win \$2 once and lose \$1 twice for a net gain of zero—hence, the bet is "fair" (to either side).

This kind of calculation comes up all the time in poker play. If the pot contains \$10 and you have to call a bet of \$1 to stay in the hand and draw another card that will likely make you the winner, then you are getting 10 to 1 "pot odds," so you should risk the \$1 if you think the odds against making your hand are less than 10 to 1 against. For example, if there are 47 cards you haven't seen and 9 make your hand (say you have 4 to a flush and need 1 of 9 remaining cards of that suit), then the odds against making your hand are roughly 4 to 1 (actually 38 to 9), so you should call the \$1. (In fact, this kind of reasoning is most accurate when there are no further bets to come; also you have to take into account that you might make your hand and lose to a better hand, so sometimes you might adjust your odds against winning to take these other things into account). We will discuss many more poker situations shortly.

Someone seeing the type of card calculation we have just considered may point out that the probability or odds against getting a needed card really depend on whether someone else already has some of the cards we need. In a sense, this is true, but if we don't know, then we can assume that we are drawing a card from all the *unseen* cards, and the result of our calculation will be correct on average. This follows from a result called "the theorem on total probability," but in fact a little thought should serve to convince one of the truth of what we are saying. The following is a very simple example involving the same kind of reasoning: Suppose we have a box containing a \$1 and a \$10 bill. I reach in and take one out, and then you reach in and take the remaining one. What is the probability that you get the \$10 bill? Well, you could say that it depends on what I got, but if you don't know, then it is clearly correct to say that you get the \$10 bill with probability 1/2 (clearly, I get it with probability 1/2 also). Now, if there were eight \$1 bills and two \$10 bills and we did the same thing, the probability that you get the \$10 is 2/10. (Use of the theorem on total probability would involve computing the conditional probabilities that you get a \$10 bill given what I drew; when I get one, then you are less likely to also get one, and when I don't get one, you are more likely to get one. These situations average to make the probability that you get a \$10 bill the same as if I hadn't drawn one out at all.) This is quite an important principle, which comes up often in computing probabilities in the examples we will consider in this chapter.

Another simple example comes from the game of roulette. American-style roulette wheels have 18 red and 18 black numbers and green 0 and 00 numbers. (European-style wheels have only one green number—a 0). The rules of the game have changed, but at the present time, a bet that the ball will land on red pays off at even odds (i.e., you may win as much as your bet—and similarly for black); if the ball lands on a green number, the bet is lost. (One can also bet on individual numbers that pay off at 35 to 1 odds.) Well, the payoff odds that would make the game fair would be 20 to 18 for a bet on red (or black) and 37 to 1 for a bet on a number for the American-style wheels, so the player has a negative expectation. If you bet one unit on, say, red and X is your winnings, then

$$\begin{aligned} E(X) &= 1(18/38) - 1(20/38) \\ &= -2/38 \approx -0.053. \end{aligned} \tag{19.8}$$

Similarly, if you bet 1 unit on a number and X is your winnings, then

$$\begin{aligned} E(X) &= 35(1/38) - 1(37/38) \\ &= -2/38 \approx -0.053. \end{aligned} \tag{19.9}$$

Thus, the house has an edge over 5%! This is a terrible disadvantage for the player. On the European-style wheels, the house edge is 1/37 instead of 2/38, which is about half as much but still fairly tough on the player. Of the standard table games, roulette is one of the worst for the player with regard to house advantage. We'll see later that for pass line bets in casino craps, the house edge is a little less than 1.5% (and in blackjack it is about that much or less with proper play). One remark about the house advantage (which exists in all casino games except for very rare occasions, such as errors by the casino)—it is not necessarily the case that one should never play such games; as we will see later, the fact that the variance is quite large means that the player has some chance of making a good win in the short run, and so occasionally taking a chance and playing is reasonable; however, games with a negative expectation for the player clearly can't be beaten in the long run, and no allowed schemes of play can change this (we discuss the last fact later).

Sports betting is another situation where much of the analysis involves simple calculations of expectations. Probably, the most popular betting is in football. Suppose two teams, the Bunkos and the Spoilers, are going to play. Football is a sport for which many people can do pretty well in predicting the winner, so unless there were a huge payoff for betting the underdog, the betting would mostly be on the probable winner. The sports books (where legal, e.g., Las Vegas) or your local bookie would like to have moderately equal betting on both sides and then charge the losers more than the winners are paid, thereby ensuring a profit. Equalizing the betting is effected by a marvelous invention—the pointspread. If, say, the Bunkos are the favorite, the bookie might quote a line such as "Bunkos -10." This means that team must win by more than 10 points to make a bet on them a winner. If they win, but by less than 10 points (or actually lose), then a bet on the Spoilers is a winner. If the Bunkos win by exactly 10 points, then no bets win, and all money bet is returned. Typically, to bet either side you have to bet \$110 to win \$100; that is, if you win your bet, you get back your \$110 plus \$100, while if your bet is a loser, you lose your \$110. (With a local bookie, you might just call in a \$100 bet on one side; if you win, you collect the \$100, otherwise you pay \$110 on the settlement day.) If the betting is equal on both sides this is a sure winner for the bookie. For each \$110 risked, he or she wins that with probability 1/2 and loses \$100 with probability 1/2 with an expected win of \$5. Since $5/110 \approx 0.045455$, this is about a 4.55% edge. Of course, if the betting is not equal on both sides, then the bookie might lose money (or make a lot more than 4.55%). From the point of view of the bettor, the analysis is similar, with possibly some small differences. If the pointspread is really such that it is equally likely (whatever that means!) that the Bunkos win by more than 10 or fail to "cover the spread," then the bettor's win expectation is just $-\$5$ on each \$110 risked with a 4.55% disadvantage. On the other hand, it might be that the line was made to equalize betting due to public perception that was inaccurate, and the bettor knows the true situation; then, he or she might be able to make a winning bet with probability greater than 0.5. However, to make anything, he or she must be able to make a winning bet with probability p, where

$$p(100) - (1 - p)(110) > 0, \tag{19.10}$$

requiring $p > 11/21 \approx 0.5238$. This isn't easy to achieve, and most bettors lose in the long run. It isn't always easy being the bookie either. He or she has to worry about (besides the law if he or she isn't legal) losing money due to unequal betting and a resulting big loss. The bookie can adjust the line to try to equalize things, but this can be dangerous. Suppose there is a disproportionately large number of bets on Bunkos -10, and the bookie adjusts the line to Bunkos -12. Suppose that results in most new bets being on the Spoilers, or "Spoilers +12." Now, if the Bunkos win by exactly 11, both these bets win. If an individual made both bets, then the bettor is in a great situation; he or she can win both bets or, at worst, win one and lose the other and have to pay the 4.55%, but he or she can't lose both. Of course, one can only be in this situation if the line moves in an advantageous direction given the initial bet. Finally, we mention the payoffs on *parlays* as a good example of (unfavorable to the bettor) odds. In a parlay, one bets on several games and has to win all the bets for a payoff. Assuming that in each game either side is equally likely to win, then in a two-game parlay, the odds against picking the winner correctly for both games are 3 to 1 (the probability is $(1/2)^2 = 1/4$). Similarly, in three- and four-game parlays, the odds against picking all the winners correctly are 7 to 1 and 15 to 1, respectively. But the payoff odds for two-, three-, and four-game parlays are typically 2.6 to 1, 5 to 1, and 10 to 1, respectively. If you bet \$100 16 times on four-game parlays, you would on average expect to lose \$100 15 times and win \$1,000 once for a net loss of \$500, which is more than a 31% loss.

All things considered, it isn't easy to win at sports betting; besides the fact that one has to be more knowledgeable and cleverer than the bookie (which some people may achieve), there is still enough randomness in the results to considerably dilute the possible advantage.

The calculation of advantage in dice problems is somewhat more rigorous than in the previous problems we have considered. Standard dice are cubes with sides marked with one to six spots. A pair is rolled, and the result is the sum of the numbers of spots on the sides ending on top. The possible sums are thus 2 through 12. If we consider that there are 36 possible ordered pairs that may occur when we roll two dice, then we see that there is exactly one way to make a total of 2 or 12 (with (1,1) and (6,6)), two ways to make a 3 or an 11 ((1,2) or (2,1) for a 3 and (5,6) or (6,5) for 11), three ways to make a 4 or a 10, four ways to make a 5 or a 9, five ways to make a 6 or an 8, and six ways to make a total of 7. So for the totals, we have

$$\begin{aligned} &P(2) = P(12) = 1/36 \\ &P(3) = P(11) = 2/36 \\ &P(4) = P(10) = 3/36 \\ &P(5) = P(9) \ \ = 4/36 \\ &P(6) = P(8) \ \ = 5/36 \\ &P(7) = 6/36. \end{aligned}$$

There are various bets one can make in the standard casino game. One of these is the *pass* (or *pass line*) bet. In this bet, the payoff odds are 1 to 1; the way it works is as follows: The dice are rolled, and if a 7 or an 11 occurs, this is an immediate winner; if 2, 3, or 12 occurs, the bet loses. Otherwise if 4, 5, 6, 8, 9, or 10 occurs, that number becomes the "point," and then the dice are rolled until the point again occurs that makes the bet a winner, or else a 7 occurs and the bet is a loser. The win expectation for the bettor is a little complicated to compute due to the various possibilities that can occur and the fact that if, for example, an 8 occurred on the first roll, the number of rolls till the point or 7 occurs does not have an a priori bound—we have to consider that it might take any number of trials (although in practice not too large a number). For our calculations, it will be useful to have a simple result concerning the following general situation: Suppose A and B are events in a probability space $\{S, P\}$ that are mutually exclusive ($A \cap B = \emptyset$). Suppose $P(A) = a$, $P(B) = b$. If we do independent repetitions of the experiment $\mathcal{E}$ associated with S (S is the set of possible outcomes of $\mathcal{E}$), then what is the probability that A occurs before B? It is fairly elementary to show that

$$P(A \text{ occurs before } B) = \frac{a}{a+b}. \tag{19.11}$$

One way is to sum the probabilities that A occurs on the first trial and that something other than A or B occurs on the first trial (probability $1 - a - b$), and then A occurs on the second trial, and so on. This gives

$$\begin{aligned} &a + (1-a-b)a + (1-a-b)^2 a + \cdots \\ &\quad = a[1 + (1-a-b) + (1-a-b)^2 + \cdots] \\ &\quad = \frac{a}{a+b} \end{aligned} \tag{19.12}$$

(using the formula for the sum of a geometric series).

Another way to get this result is to consider that when we do the trials, we observe whether A or B occurs each time and essentially ignore the times when neither occurs, so we could replace the experiment with an equivalent one in which A and B are the only possibilities and where these events have probabilities in the same ratio as in the original experiment—this would make the probabilities $a/(a+b)$ and $b/(a+b)$. But then, in this new experiment, we just have to see if A occurs at the first trial, and the probability of this is $a/(a+b)$.

Now, to continue with our calculation of the win expectation for the pass line bet of one unit, we need to compute the sum

$$P(7,11)-P(2,3,12) \\ +P(4)[P(4 \text{ before } 7)-P(7 \text{ before } 4)]+\cdots, \quad (19.13)$$

where the dots indicate that we sum additional terms for the cases of 5, 6, 8, 9, and 10 before 7 or 7 before one of these. This gives

$$\begin{aligned}
&\frac{8}{36}-\frac{4}{36}+\frac{3}{36}\cdot\frac{\frac{3}{36}-\frac{6}{36}}{\frac{3}{36}+\frac{6}{36}}+\cdots \\
&=\frac{1}{36}\left(4+3\cdot\frac{3-6}{3+6}+4\cdot\frac{4-6}{4+6}+5\cdot\frac{5-6}{5+6}\right. \\
&\qquad\left.+5\cdot\frac{5-6}{5+6}+4\cdot\frac{4-6}{4+6}+3\cdot\frac{3-6}{3+6}\right) \\
&=-\frac{7}{495}\approx -0.014.
\end{aligned}$$

There is also a *don't pass* bet in which the bettor and the house essentially switch sides, except that since this would give the bettor an advantage, the house takes away the win in case a 2 is rolled initially; in some cases, it is the win on 12 that is taken away, but this has the same probability. The win expectation on the don't pass bet is about the same as for the pass bet. There are many other bets available in the casino game; some are much more unfavorable to the bettor and are considered "sucker bets"; a very complete discussion of all the possible bets can be found in Scarne (1986).

The calculation of probabilities involving card hands in games such as poker involves some additional ideas due to the fact that as cards are dealt from a deck, the set of remaining cards is constantly changing, and therefore the probabilities of drawing various cards change. The appropriate way to calculate usually involves counting *combinations*. We recall that if we have a set of n distinct objects, the number of combinations of size k from n (this is also the same thing as the number of subsets of size k; note that subsets are *unordered* collections) is

$$\begin{aligned}
C(n,k)&=\binom{n}{k}=\frac{n!}{(n-k)!k!} \\
&=\frac{n(n-1)\cdots(n-k+1)}{k(k-1)\cdots 1}. \qquad (19.14)
\end{aligned}$$

We will now calculate various probabilities that arise in the game of poker. The discussion is taken from Friedman (2006).

There are many variants of the game of poker, but in all of them, the object is to make the best five-card poker hand. The following is the ranking of hands (from lowest to highest):

1. High-card hand (no pair, straight, or flush)
2. One pair
3. Two pairs
4. Three of a kind ("trips")
5. Straight (five cards in numerical sequence; ace counts as "1" or "14")
6. Flush (five cards of the same suit)
7. Full house (three of one kind, two of another)
8. Four of a kind
9. Straight flush (five cards in numerical sequence, all of the same suit)

Within each group, ranking is determined by comparing the highest cards or the second highest cards if the highest cards are equal, and so on.

In a five-card draw, usually, each player antes some fixed amount (so there is something to play for) and then is dealt five cards. The players then bet. (Sometimes, there is a minimum requirement to open the betting, e.g., a pair of Jacks). Then, each player may discard up to five cards if desired and draw (receive) replacements for those discarded (usually to try to make a better hand). Then, there is another round of betting, after which the hands are shown down. The highest hand takes the pot, unless there is a tie, in which case the pot is split. (This is just a bare outline of the game, of course.)

We calculate the probability of being dealt various hands in a five-card draw. There are $\binom{52}{5}=2{,}598{,}960$ possible five-card hands (more if a Joker is being used).

One pair: There are $\binom{4}{2}$ ways of picking a pair from some particular rank and 13 ranks. To get a pair, you must be dealt 2 of 1 rank and then 3 other cards of different ranks (with no further pair). The number of ways of getting the latter is $\binom{12}{3} \cdot 4^3$ (the factor 4^3 occurs because there are four suits in which each of the three can be). Thus, the probability of being dealt a pair is

$$\frac{\binom{4}{2} \cdot 13 \cdot \binom{12}{3} \cdot 4^3}{\binom{52}{5}} \approx 0.422569.$$

Two pairs: To get two pairs, you must be dealt pairs from two different ranks and then one other card of a further rank. The probability of this is

$$\frac{\frac{1}{2} \cdot \binom{4}{2} \cdot 13 \cdot \binom{4}{2} \cdot 12 \cdot 11 \cdot 4}{\binom{52}{5}} \approx 0.047539.$$

The initial factor $\frac{1}{2}$ is present so that the ways of picking one pair and then another are not counted twice in different orders.

Trips: The probability of being dealt trips is

$$\frac{\binom{4}{3} \cdot 13 \cdot \binom{12}{2} \cdot 4^2}{\binom{52}{5}} \approx 0.021128.$$

Straight: The probability of being dealt a straight is

$$\frac{10 \cdot 4^5}{\binom{52}{5}} \approx 0.003940$$

Flush: The probability of being dealt a flush is

$$\frac{\binom{13}{5} \cdot 4}{\binom{52}{5}} \approx 0.001981.$$

Full house: The probability of being dealt a full house is

$$\frac{\binom{4}{3} \cdot 13 \cdot \binom{4}{2} \cdot 12}{\binom{52}{5}} \approx 0.001441.$$

Four of a kind: The probability of being dealt four of a kind is

$$\frac{\binom{4}{4} \cdot 13 \cdot 48}{\binom{52}{5}} \approx 0.000240.$$

Straight flush: The probability of being dealt a straight flush is

$$\frac{10 \cdot 4}{\binom{52}{5}} \approx 0.000015.$$

The probabilities computed for straights and flushes include the probability of being dealt a straight flush. To get the probabilities for exactly straights or flushes, one should subtract the probability of a straight flush.

One can also compute the probabilities of improving various hands by discarding and drawing cards. Suppose you have the hand

$$A\heartsuit, \quad A\diamondsuit, \quad K\spadesuit, \quad 7\clubsuit, \quad 8\diamondsuit.$$

You could keep the pair of Aces and discard three, or keep the Aces and King kicker and discard two. (A "kicker" is an "extra" card that is contained in a hand; in this case, the primary value is the pair of Aces, and the extra card is the King, which might have some value later.)

First, we consider what happens if you discard three:

Probability of improving to exactly two pairs: This can occur if you draw a pair of one of the three ranks you discarded (K, 7, 8) and then another card from 42 others (52 – the original 5 – 3 of the rank that produced the new pair – the 2 remaining Aces), or a pair of one of the nine ranks different from the ranks originally held and then another card from 41 others (52 – the original 5 – 4 of the rank that produced the new pair – 2 Aces.) The probability is thus

$$\frac{\binom{3}{2} \cdot 3 \cdot 42 + \binom{4}{2} \cdot 9 \cdot 41}{\binom{47}{3}} \approx 0.159852.$$

Probability of improving to exactly trips: This occurs if you draw one of the Aces and one each from two of the three ranks you discarded, or one Ace and one of the three ranks you discarded and one from one of the remaining nine ranks, or one Ace and two others from different ranks from the nine ranks remaining. The probability of this is

$$\frac{2 \cdot \binom{3}{1}^2 \cdot \binom{3}{2} + 2 \cdot \binom{3}{1} \cdot 3 \cdot \binom{4}{1} \cdot 9 + 2 \cdot \binom{4}{1}^2 \cdot \binom{9}{2}}{\binom{47}{3}} \approx 0.114339.$$

Probability of improving to a full house: This occurs if you draw another Ace and either a pair from one of the three discarded ranks or one of the nine remaining ranks, or three from one of the three discarded ranks or nine remaining ranks. The probability is thus

$$\frac{2 \cdot \left[\binom{3}{2} \cdot 3 + \binom{4}{2} \cdot 9\right] + \binom{3}{3} \cdot 3 + \binom{4}{3} \cdot 9}{\binom{47}{3}} \approx 0.010176.$$

Probability of improving to four of a kind: There are 45 combinations of 3 cards that include the remaining 2 Aces from the 47 cards you draw from, so the probability is

$$\frac{45}{\binom{47}{3}} \approx 0.002775.$$

Now, suppose you discard two, keeping the 2 Aces and the King:

Probability of improving to exactly two pairs: This occurs if you draw 1 of the remaining Kings and 1 from among 42 cards (52 − the original 5 − 2 Aces − 3 Kings), or two 7s or two 8s, or 2 of one of the nine remaining ranks, so the probability is

$$\frac{3 \cdot 42 + \binom{3}{2} \cdot 2 + \binom{4}{2} \cdot 9}{\binom{47}{2}} \approx 0.172063.$$

Probability of improving to exactly trips: For this to occur, you must draw 1 Ace and 1 of 42 cards (52 − the 5 original − 3 Kings − 2 Aces), so the probability is

$$\frac{2 \cdot 42}{\binom{47}{2}} \approx 0.077706.$$

Probability of improving to a full house: You must draw one Ace and one King, or two Kings, so the probability is

$$\frac{\binom{2}{1} \cdot \binom{3}{1} + \binom{3}{2}}{\binom{47}{2}} \approx 0.008326.$$

Probability of improving to four of a kind: You must draw the two remaining Aces. The probability is

$$\frac{1}{\binom{47}{2}} \approx 0.000925.$$

Note that if you keep the King kicker and draw two, you have a better chance of improving to two pairs, but the chances of making the other (stronger) hands are decreased. So what should you do? As usual, "it depends." If you are trying to beat two pairs smaller than Aces up, you should keep the kicker, but if you think an opponent has trips, you should draw three, and so on.

How do you decide what actions to take in playing a hand (i.e., bet, raise, check, call, etc.)? Generally, it is important to determine whether a given action has a positive expectation with regard to the amount that can be won. In a 5-card draw, when deciding whether to bet or call after receiving the initial cards, this is often fairly straightforward and involves calculating whether the odds you will be getting from the pot are greater than the odds against winning. For example, if you start with 5 cards that include 4 of one suit, then the probability of completing the flush by drawing 1 card is $9/47$ (9 cards out of 47 unseen help you), so the odds against making your flush are 38 to 9 or approximately 4 to 1. Suppose you have to call a $20 bet to stay in the hand and draw, but you estimate that if you make the flush, you will be ahead $100. Since you are getting 5 to 1 odds, you may decide to play. Generally, you want the pot odds to be somewhat greater than the odds against making your hand, because you are playing to make money, not to break even; and in addition, you must take into account that there may be raises that decrease your pot odds, and you might make your hand and lose to a better hand if someone makes a miracle draw (or you understimated the strengths of your opponents hands).

When we calculate the probability of completing a 4 flush by drawing one card as equal to $9/47$, we are ignoring the possibility that some of our opponents may hold the cards we need, and in fact, there aren't 47 cards left that we are drawing from. In actuality, sometimes the probability of making the flush is greater than 9/47 and sometimes less; but it is not difficult to see that on average the probability is 9/47, and we get the correct result by ignoring the fact that some cards are unavailable because they are in other players' hands. All that matters is how many *unseen* cards remain. This has been discussed earlier in the present section. In draw poker, which we have been considering, the cards are all concealed; of course, in games where some of the opponents' cards are seen, these should be taken into account, and even when the cards are hidden, one might have some reason to believe that the opponent(s) has certain cards. And then one could take this into account when computing the probabilities of making various hands. We don't consider the latter situation, which would lead us to much greater complications. (Often, a guess about what an opponent holds is difficult to use in our calculation of the probability of making a certain hand; for example, suppose we think that the opponent has two pairs, and we are trying to make a flush to beat that hand; if that opponent holds the flush cards we need, that reduces our chances, but we may have no information about this.)

We make a few comments concerning straights. If you have

$$7\heartsuit,\quad 8\diamondsuit,\quad 9\clubsuit,\quad 10\heartsuit,\quad A\spadesuit,$$

you can discard the Ace and draw to the *open-ended straight*; there are eight cards that help you (four 6s and four Jacks), so the probability of making the straight is $8/47$.

If you have instead

$$7\heartsuit,\quad 8\diamondsuit,\quad 9\clubsuit,\quad J\heartsuit,\quad Q\spadesuit,$$

you can discard the 7 and draw to the *inside straight*. Here, there are only four 10s that help you, so the probability of making your straight is $4/47$. One sometimes hears the advice "never draw to an inside straight," but this can be incorrect if the pot odds are favorable.

Of course, you can also discard the 7 and 8 and draw 2 to the King high straight, but you must draw both a 10 and a King to make this hand. The probability of this is $\binom{4}{1} \cdot \binom{4}{1} / \binom{47}{2} \approx 0.014801$. We hope our opponents routinely make draws like this!

Poker is a very subtle game, and the calculation of probabilities is only part of the strategy. Reading your opponents, bluffing, and causing your opponents to fear you and thus not call bluffs (or the opposite strategy of inducing calls when you are not bluffing) are very important. There are always "mathematically" correct actions in various situations in the game, but if you never deviate from these, then you will be too predictable and lose a fair amount of advantage for that reason. In addition, playing well takes a lot of self-discipline—something that a large number of players lack.

Gambling in the Long Run

In this section, we discuss what happens over a period of time—"the long run"; of course, the notion of *long* is relative and perhaps the title of this section should have been "Gambling in the Short Run and the Long Run". One of the author's favorite quotes is from the economist John Maynard Keynes, who in response to someone's use of the locution *long run* retorted, "In the long run we're all dead!" In fact, it can take a very long time for some of the expected long-range probabilistic behavior to appear, and it is often quite important to discover at least qualitatively the length of time involved. One point worth mentioning in this regard is that often various technical results of the theory of probability and statistics are not correctly understood by non-mathematicians. As an example, the author has read a book on poker in which the author of that text indicated that he had programmed two poker players with equal ability, to play "heads up"; it was reported that after a large number of hands (i.e., approaching 1 million), one of the virtual players was a lot ahead in winnings, and it was stated that this was an example of the fact that it can take a long time for the winnings to become approximately "even." However, this is just incorrect; one expects fluctuations from the mean to occur, and in the situation mentioned, it was actually the case that the fluctuations were about a standard deviation from the mean, which is not at all surprising and is likely to occur often as the number of hands increases.

The fluctuations from the mean are quantified by the *central limit theorem*, which guarantees that the sum of a large number of random variables that are mutually independent and have all the same distribution has a distribution that is approximately *normal*—that is, with a probability density of the form

$$N(\mu,\sigma^2)(x) = \frac{1}{\sqrt{2\pi}\sigma} e^{-(x-\mu)^2/2\sigma^2}. \qquad (19.15)$$

In (19.15), μ and σ are the expectation (mean) and standard deviation of the associated random variable; σ^2 is the variance $V(X)$. For a random variable X, $V(X)$ is defined by

$$V(X) = E(X - E(X))^2 = E(X^2) - (E(X))^2. \qquad (19.16)$$

$V(X)$ is a measure of how much the values of X vary from $E(X)$.

A more precise statement of the result is the following:

Theorem 19.1 (Central Limit Theorem). *Suppose $X_1, \dots, X_n$ is a sequence of independent and identically distributed random variables each with mean μ and standard deviation σ. Then*

$$\lim_{n\to\infty} P\left(a < \frac{\sum_{i=1}^{n} X_i - n\mu}{\sqrt{n}\sigma} < b\right) = \frac{1}{\sqrt{2\pi}} \int_a^b e^{-x^2/2}\, dx.$$

How large does n have to be for the normal approximation to be a good one? The conventional wisdom is that for many common distributions, $n \geqslant 35$ suffices; for $n \geqslant 100$, the approximation is likely very good in almost any case.

Now, for a normal random variable X with mean μ and standard deviation σ, we have

$$P\left(a < \frac{X-\mu}{\sigma} < b\right) = \frac{1}{\sqrt{2\pi}} \int_a^b e^{-x^2/2}\, dx. \tag{19.17}$$

If we put $a = -k$, $b = k$, we can rewrite (19.17) in the form

$$P(\mu - k\sigma < X < \mu + k\sigma) = \frac{1}{\sqrt{2\pi}} \int_{-k}^{k} e^{-x^2/2}\, dx. \tag{19.18}$$

The integral in (19.18) can't be evaluated explicitly in a simple way, but tables of values are available. For our purposes, it will suffice to know that for $k = 1, 2, 3$, the values of $\frac{1}{\sqrt{2\pi}} \int_{-k}^{k} e^{-x^2/2}\, dx$ are approximately 0.6826, 0.9544, and 0.9974, respectively. These are the probabilities that a normal random variable is within k standard deviations of its mean for $k = 1, 2, 3$. Similarly, the probabilities that a normal random variable is no more than k standard deviations above its mean (or no less than k standard deviations below its mean) are 0.8413, 0.9772, and 0.9987, respectively.

These results are quite useful in quantifying long-term results in gambling. If we have an advantage (i.e., the expectation of our winnings is positive), we should eventually win, and if we have a disadvantage, we expect to eventually lose, but the fluctuations from the mean can be significant and usually need to be taken into account. In this context, variance is a measure of risk.

Next, we discuss some applications of the central limit theorem that the present author first read in Malmuth (1994) (although we have added some of our own analysis in the discussion of the probability of ruin). Consider the situation of a gambler playing a repetitive game (hands of poker or blackjack, spins of a roulette wheel, sports bets, etc.) Let X be the random variable equal to his or her hourly win. Suppose X has mean μ and variance σ^2. How could one know μ and σ? One could use some standard statistical estimators: keep track of hourly wins $x_1, x_2, \dots, x_n$ for some time (with n at least 100—1,000 would be extremely good) and then use

$$\bar{x} = \frac{1}{n}\sum_{i=1}^{n} x_i, \qquad s^2 = \frac{1}{n-1}\sum_{i=1}^{n} (x_i - \bar{x})^2 \tag{19.19}$$

as estimates of μ and σ^2, respectively.

First, suppose that $\mu > 0$. This means that our gambler should eventually win, and on average his or her win per hour will be μ. However, if he or she is quite unlucky, his or her total winnings after n hours (which is approximately normal by the central limit theorem since it is a sum of hourly wins) could be less than or equal to a value 3 standard deviations to the left of the mean (the probability that this happens is $1 - 0.9987 = 0.0013$). Now, the mean of a sum of random variables is always the sum of the means; and the variance of a sum is the sum of the variances if the random variables are independent. Hence, after n hours, if our gambler is as unlucky as just described, then his or her winnings $w(n)$ could be less than or equal to

$$f(n) = n\mu - 3\sqrt{n\sigma^2} = n\mu - 3\sqrt{n}\sigma, \tag{19.20}$$

and this occurs with probability 0.0013.

If we want to be 99.87% sure that $w(n) \geqslant 0$, then by (19.20) we need

$$n\mu - 3\sqrt{n}\sigma \geqslant 0$$

or

$$n \geqslant \left(\frac{3\sigma}{\mu}\right)^2. \tag{19.21}$$

We note that the 99.87% figure is likely a bit too large due to the fact that the approximation of normality isn't accurate until n is sufficiently large, and we don't take into account the possibility of going broke at some early time (the latter possibility becomes less likely with a reasonably large bankroll). For similar reasons, the estimates we make below using normality concerning the probability of ruin and the bankroll needed to avoid ruin are likely a bit too small. However, these results seem to be well-known and used by gamblers (at least the more mathematically inclined ones), so familiarity with the arguments seems useful. A more precise discussion of the probability of ruin will be given later.

To put this in perspective, consider that our gambler is playing in a \$5–\$10 poker game and $\mu = \$10, \sigma = \$100$. These are actually reasonable figures for an expert and conservative player. In this case, the result given by (19.21) is $n \geqslant 900$. At about 40 hours per week, this is close to half a year of play to be reasonably sure of winning anything! Of course, if our gambler is really a professional, then he would be playing at higher limits, but in that case the standard deviation might easily be even larger in relation to the mean.

On the other hand, suppose μ is negative, say, equal to $-\$10$, and $\sigma = \$100$ as before. Even though he or she must eventually lose, if our gambler is very lucky and his or her win is at least 3 standard deviations above the mean, then essentially the same calculation shows that it could take 900 hours until he or she is fairly sure of losing. This explains why some good players can be losing for quite a while and some bad players may win for quite a period of time (and think they are experts while it lasts). As another example, consider casino craps (dice); as we discussed earlier, for the better bets (pass or don't pass), the win expectation on a \$1 bet is about -1.4 cents. However, the standard deviation is very close to \$1. So with good luck, one can be winning for a reasonable length of time, although eventually one must lose; this is of course by design—if the game were designed so almost everyone would lose quickly, then very few people would play. This also means that it might be worth taking a chance that one's luck will be good and playing once in a while; the same holds for other games such as slot machines.

In Malmuth (1994), the question of how much money is needed to play and be reasonably sure of not going broke eventually is considered. Of course, in this case, we need $\mu > 0$ (or else going broke eventually is a certainty). To analyze this question, assume that the winnings after n hours are not less than 3 standard deviations to the left of the mean, and consider (19.20) again. How negative can $f(n)$ be? For large n, $f(n)$ will eventually be positive and, in fact, arbitrarily large since n increases much faster than $\sqrt{n}$. But for a while, $f(n)$ can be negative, and we can find the minimum value using a little calculus. From (19.20) (and treating n as a continuous variable), we have

$$f'(n) = \mu - 3\sigma/2\sqrt{n} = 0, \qquad \text{for } n_0 = (3\sigma/2\mu)^2 \tag{19.22}$$

and

$$f(n_0) = -\frac{9}{4}\frac{\sigma^2}{\mu}. \tag{19.23}$$

If we have an initial bankroll z, then ruin (going broke) occurs if

$$-\frac{9}{4}\frac{\sigma^2}{\mu} \leqslant -z, \tag{19.24}$$

and to avoid this, we need

$$z > \frac{9}{4}\frac{\sigma^2}{\mu}. \tag{19.25}$$

For the case of a poker player in a \$5–\$10 game with $\mu = \$10, \sigma = \$100$, as discussed earlier, this gives $z =$ \$2,250. For many players, $\sigma =$ \$200 might be a reasonable figure, and in this case, $z = \$9,000$! (As mentioned earlier, due to the approximations made, these may even be a bit smaller than the true values.)

It is interesting to consider (19.22) and the resulting (19.23) and (19.25) in case we replace 3 with k. We see that to avoid ruin, we then need

$$z > \frac{k^2}{4}\frac{\sigma^2}{\mu}, \tag{19.26}$$

and solving this for k, we see that with an initial bankroll z, ruin occurs if

$$k \geqslant 2\sqrt{z\mu}/\sigma, \tag{19.27}$$

which has probability

$$R(z) = \frac{1}{\sqrt{2\pi}} \int_{2\sqrt{z\mu}/\sigma}^{\infty} e^{-x^2/2}\,dx. \tag{19.28}$$

Again, this is an approximation that is generally a bit too small but not too far off if z is large compared with σ.

A precise analysis of the probability of ruin (in a slightly different but closely related situation) is given in Feller (1968), and we give some of the details here so we can compare with the result just derived.

Consider a gambler making successive bets of one unit that he or she wins or loses with respective probabilities p and q (with $p+q=1$). Suppose also that he or she begins with a bankroll of z units but his or her adversary can't go broke (i.e., has an infinite bankroll). Then, in Feller (1968) it is shown that the gambler's probability of ruin (going broke) is

$$r(z) = \begin{cases} 1 & \text{if } p \leqslant q \\ (q/p)^z & \text{if } p > q \end{cases} . \tag{19.29}$$

It is difficult to compare this directly with (19.28), since (19.28) involves parameters relating to the hourly win, and we don't know the number of bets per hour or the total bet per hour. However, to make a comparison, consider the case of the gambler playing in a \$5–\$10 poker game and with $\mu = \$10$, $\sigma = \$100$. If we think of this as betting approximately \$100 per hour and winning with probability $p = 0.55$, losing with probability $q = 0.45$, so the expected win is $\$100(0.55-0.45) = \$10$, then with a bankroll of z bets (which is \$100z), the probability of ruin given by (19.29) is $(0.45/0.55)^z$. And if we want this to be $1-0.9987 = 0.0013$, then we can solve $(0.45/0.55)^z = 0.0013$, and this has the solution $z \approx 33$. This is \$3,300; recall that the value computed using (19.28) was \$2,250. Note also that if we use $z = 22.5$ in (19.29) with $p = 0.55$, then we get $r(z) \approx 0.01$, whereas the value using (19.28) was 0.0013. Hence, compared with (19.29), (19.28) somewhat underestimates the required bankroll and the probability of ruin. Undoubtedly, (19.29) is the more accurate result for the calculations considered here.

We next turn to the general question of strategy in long-term gambling situations; as mentioned earlier, the notion of *long* is relative—it could be a few hours, a few weeks, or a few months, and so on.

The gambler making successive bets over a period of time generally has various choices to make, the most likely of these being when and how much to bet. Of course, both these can be quite important; for example, in poker a bet might be made for value with a good hand, it might be made with a medium-quality hand to drive others out of the pot, or it might be a bluff, and the amount bet clearly is relevant in all these situations. However, we want to consider right now a much simpler situation—that of a gambler making successive bets on the outcome of independent repetitions of some random experiment, such as tossing a coin, spinning a roulette wheel, rolling dice, or playing hands of blackjack. We can model the outcomes as a sequence $X_1, X_2, \ldots, X_n, \ldots$, which are independent and identically distributed, and let's say that the event to bet on is $\{X_i \in A_i\}$. (The value of A_i can depend on i; e.g., if the experiment is tossing a coin and X_i is the result of the ith toss, then one might bet on H or T at different times; in the case we are modeling blackjack, the X_i would be more complicated and might have values that are the various sets of cards that could occur assuming some a priori strategy of the player, and A_i might then be independent of i and consist of the collection of configurations that are winning for the player.) Let's ignore the question of bet size (this will be considered later) and ask if any advantage can be obtained merely by deciding when to bet based on what has occurred so far (note that in the case of poker, the phrase "when to bet" would for us mean deciding in advance "when to play a hand" and not when to bet in the middle of some hand being played). For example, some roulette players may have systems of the following type: Don't bet until red has occurred five times in succession, and then bet on black the next spin (or some similar scheme). Well, assuming that the spins are independent, it should be clear that this won't change the expected win (although it may prolong the time it takes to go broke and be advantageous in that respect!). However, one might wonder if anything at all can be changed by any kind of scheme of selective betting. That the answer is negative follows from the following theorem, which is proved in Friedman (1999). The present author later found essentially the same result and proof in Doob (1967), although there are a few typos in the discussion in the latter reference. We omit the proof in the following discussion.

Theorem 19.2. *Suppose $X_1, X_2, \dots$ are independent and identically distributed. Let $\mathcal{F}$ be the sigma algebra of measurable sets in the underlying sample space S for the process, and let $\mathcal{F}_k = \mathcal{F}(X_1, X_2, \dots, X_k)$ be the sub-sigma-algebra generated by $X_1, \dots, X_k$ (i.e., $\mathcal{F}_k$ is the smallest sub-sigma-algebra of $\mathcal{F}$ with respect to which $X_1, \dots, X_k$ are measurable). Suppose that $n_1, n_2, \dots$ are natural number-valued random variables satisfying $n_1 < n_2 < \cdots$ pointwise with probability 1, $\{n_i = k+1\} \in \mathcal{F}_k$ for each i and $k \geqslant 1$, and $\{n_1 = 1\}$ is independent of $\mathcal{F}_1$. Then, the $X_{n_i}, i = 1, 2, \dots$ are independent and identically distributed with the same distribution as the X_i.*

In Theorem 19.2, the variable X_i is the result (gain) of the ith repetition of the game. The random variables $n_1, n_2, \dots$ are the occasions when the player decides to bet for the first time, the second time, and so on. These may be defined arbitrarily, but the conditions on $\{n_i = k+1\}$ and $\{n_1 = 1\}$ imply that a decision to bet on the kth repetition only depends on the results of previous repetitions and a decision to bet on the first repetition is independent of the result of that repetition. (Equivalently, one could also just make the hypothesis that for each k, sets of the form $\{n_i = k\}$ are independent of sets of the type $\{X_k \in A\}$.) This implies that a decision to bet on the kth repetition is independent of the results of that repetition. It should be emphasized that the n_i are not "random" in the everyday sense; they are determined by whatever consideration the player uses to decide whether to bet or not—as long as these decisions only depend on the results of previous bets. The result is that the distribution of the gains from the games when the player chooses to bet is the same as that from the original games, so no advantage may be obtained by selection based on the observation of the results of the games.

Considering the independence of the X_i, we should expect that information about previous results would not be useful in deciding future actions, and this is just what the theorem indicates (in a rather strong sense.)

The question of how much to bet is more subtle. Of course, this is mainly of interest in situations where one has an advantage, since with negative expectation one will certainly eventually go broke. However, even in situations where one has negative expectation, the question of bet size has some relevance. For example, suppose you have \$1,000 and intend to use it to play roulette. You could bet it all on red for one spin, and then you would double your bankroll with probability $18/38$ (assuming an American-style wheel) and lose it all with probability $20/38$. On the other hand, you could make 10 successive bets of \$100 on red, in which case your probability of doubling your bankroll and of going broke would both be much smaller than in the former scenario (you win all 10 times with probability $(18/38)^{10}$, lose everything with probability $(20/38)^{10}$), but now there are many other possibilities. Furthermore, in the second situation, you get to gamble for a longer time, which may have some entertainment value. In both cases, the expected win is the same (negative), but expectation is just a single number and there are many other considerations.

Let's now consider the case in which our gambler has an edge—specifically, we suppose that his or her probability of winning each bet is $p > 0.5$; we set $q = 1 - p$ as usual. Suppose also that the gambler may bet any amount up to his or her total bankroll each time. It turns out to be notationally and computationally convenient to consider the *fraction*, r_i, of the gambler's bankroll bet each time; r_i can be any value between 0 and 1 (inclusive), so this includes all possible cases of bet sizes. On the ith bet, a win means that the gambler's total bankroll gets multiplied by $1 + r_i$, and this occurs with probability p; in case of a loss the bankroll is multiplied by $1 - r_i$, this occurring with probability q. If the initial bankroll is a unit amount, then after n bets, the gambler's total bankroll will be of the form

$$\prod_{j=1}^{k}(1 - r_{i_j}) \prod_{j=k+1}^{n}(1 + r_{i_j}) \quad \text{(with probability } q^k p^{n-k}\text{)}, \tag{19.30}$$

where the $r_{i_j}, j = 1 \dots n$ are the fractions bet and k could be 0 or n if all bets are either won or lost. Note that the probability $q^k p^{n-k}$ refers to *one* particular sequence of possible losses and wins during the n bets; there might be more than one such expression with the same value (especially if some of the r_{i_j} are the same).

Expression (19.30) gives the *distribution* of the total bankroll after n bets. To get the bankroll expectation after n bets, we have to sum all the amounts in (19.30) multiplied by their respective probabilities, and this gives

$$\prod_{i=1}^{n}[(1+r_i)p+(1-r_i)q]=\prod_{i=1}^{n}[1+r_i(p-q)]. \tag{19.31}$$

Suppose we want to maximize this expectation; it's clear that this occurs when all $r_i = 1$. This corresponds to the case of betting everything each time. That is, bet the entire bankroll on the first bet; if that wins, let it all ride, and so on. But this is clearly an extremely risky strategy, since the probability that the bankroll is positive after n bets is p^n—which tends to 0 rapidly as n increases (assuming $p < 1$); even one loss means ruin!

The previous example (for which maximizing the expected bankroll leads to a strategy unlikely to be acceptable to most) indicates that the notion of a "best" strategy really doesn't make sense; different strategies produce different results, with advantages and disadvantages, and one can't generally order these with regard to desirability unless it has been decided exactly what characteristics are necessary (and even with such a decision, there may be no best strategy.)

There is an often quoted result due to J. L. Kelly (see Epstein, 1977, for some background) concerning the fraction of total bankroll that should be bet each time, assuming that this fraction is constant. The idea is as follows: Assuming the situation described preceeding (19.30), we know that the number of bets won out of a total of n is binomial based on n and p; that is, the probability that k are won is

$$\binom{n}{k}p^k q^{n-k}, \tag{19.32}$$

and the expectation of a binomially distributed random variable is np; the largest of the values in (19.32) is also approximately np (actually $[(n+1)p]$, where $[x]$ is the greatest integer not exceeding x). We expect the fraction of bets won and lost to be close to p and q, respectively (this follows from the weak law of large numbers). Therefore, in view of (19.30), it makes some sense to find the value of r, which maximizes

$$(1-r)^{nq}(1+r)^{np}$$

or, equivalently,

$$(1-r)^q(1+r)^p. \tag{19.33}$$

This is an elementary calculus problem; the derivative of $\ln((1-r)^q(1+r)^p)$ is $p/(1+r)-q/(1-r)$, and setting this equal to 0 yields the result: (19.33) is maximized when

$$r=p-q. \tag{19.34}$$

This means that one should bet each time a fraction of the entire present bankroll equal to one's edge. This is known as the *Kelly criterion*. Recall, however, that we assumed a constant probability p of winning each bet, so the analysis is not so suited to bets in poker but could reasonably be applied to roulette, blackjack, and many other games in which the fixed parameters of the game and/or one's skill determine a certain constant probability of winning each bet. Note that in blackjack, the probability of winning a hand once the initial cards are dealt isn't constant; but, of course, one has to bet before receiving cards, so one could model the probability of winning a hand as a constant (we ignore "doubling down" here). The Kelly criterion seems to have been extensively used by blackjack players, some of whom are probably among the most technically minded of gamblers due to the complicated nature of the game and the analysis that has been done with regard to winning it. Of course, the Kelly criterion could be applied to other endeavors, such as investing in stocks (which many consider a form of gambling!).

REFERENCES

Doob, J. L. (1967). *Stochastic processes*. Hoboken, NJ: Wiley.

Epstein, R. (1977). *The theory of gambling and statistical logic*. New York: Academic Press.

Feller, W. (1968). An introduction to probability theory and its applications. In *Wiley series in probability and mathematical statistics* (3rd ed., Vol. 1). Hoboken, NJ: Wiley.

Friedman, C. (1999). The frequency interpretation in probability. *Advances in Applied Mathematics, 23*, 234–254.

Friedman, C. (2006). *Probability and statistical theory.* Partially completed text posted on www.ma.utexas.edu/users/friedman/prob.pdf.

Goldblatt, B., & Messick, H. (1976). *The only game in town: An illustrated history of gambling.* New York: Thomas Y. Crowell.

Malmuth, M. (1994). *Gambling theory and other topics* (4th ed.). Las Vegas, NV: Two Plus Two.

Scarne, J. (1986). *New complete guide to gambling.* New York: Simon & Schuster.

Sklansky, D. (1994). *The theory of poker.* Las Vegas, NV: Two Plus Two.

20

INSURANCE

RICHARD A. DERRIG AND KRZYSZTOF OSTASZEWSKI

INTRODUCTION

The business of insurance is inherently tied to all forms of the science of uncertainty. It was the development of modern probability theory with the measure theory of Henri Lebesgue, the axiomatic foundation of Andrey Kolmogorov, and theories that describe the limiting behavior of random phenomena (such as the central limit theorem or the laws of large numbers) that gave the stimulus to the foundation and growth of the modern insurance industry. All insurance contracts, in one form or another, transfer the risk of the financial consequences of a future uncertain event from one party (the *insured*) to another party (the *insurer*), in exchange for some form of financial consideration. Examples of such contracts include

- life insurance, where a fixed payment is made on death of the insured;
- life annuity, where a prescribed series of payments are made until the death of the insured;
- property insurance, for example, automobile insurance or home insurance, where reimbursement for losses is made on the occurrence of accidental events;
- liability insurance, for example, auto bodily-injury liability or medical malpractice insurance, where the insurer covers the financial consequences of at-fault events; and
- reinsurance, where the insured party (the *ceding company*) itself is an insurance firm and the insurer (*reinsurer*) is a firm in the business of providing insurance coverage to other insurers.

The business of insurance is viable only if the risk transfer resulting from the existence of the insurance contract brings about some reduction in the severity of the financial consequences of future events. But as the events themselves are unchanged by the existence of insurance contracts (unless the contract changes the participants' incentives to prevent losses, which in fact is a serious practical issue in the business of insurance), the reduction occurs in the variance of the financial position of the insured. In fact, the reduction is achieved by changing the relationship of the consequences of risk to the participants' capacity to bear it. The insurer removes the unknown consequences, or at least a part of them, from the insured party's future for a known price in the present. The insurer combines the risk exposures of the numerous parties insured and collects their payments (*premiums*), thus making the risk more predictable (because of a combination of many—mostly uncorrelated—risks) and more bearable (because of the combined financial resources from collected premiums). There are also more consequences in the longer run. Because of less exposure to the unexpected financial consequences of risk, the insured parties can now assume a more risky posture in their business and personal activities (this is commonly referred to as *moral hazard* when the altered activity affects the probability of loss, sometimes deliberately in the case of fraud), thus undertaking more projects and projects of larger scale. This, in turn, can benefit the entire society if it expands the set of opportunities in terms of production output, or other desirable activities, but it may also create more risk, because of less restraint on the part of the insured participants.

The science of mathematical models applicable to insurance in particular, and to financial risk modeling in general, is known as *actuarial science* (Bowers, Gerber, Hickman, Jones, & Nesbitt, 1997; Sundt & Teugels, 2004). Actuaries are financial professionals who are typically employed by insurance companies and other entities involved in financial consequences of risk (e.g., consulting companies, governments, etc.). Actuaries perform the following key duties:

Setting the premiums for insurance products:
While the process of pricing insurance is a dynamic one, involving many parties including the market for insurance products, insurance company management and marketing divisions, insurance regulators, and others, actuaries create the core portion of this process by balancing the premium income of insurance firms and the payments made by the insurance firms for benefits, claims, expenses, and distribution of profits to the firm owners.

Setting insurance reserves:
Reserves are defined as expected future payments on policies already underwritten and currently in force. They are the liabilities of insurance companies that represent claim and expense payments, or benefits promised to the insured parties, when the events named in the insurance policies occur.

Assuring solvency of the insurance firm, in both the short-term context and the long run:
This solvency requirement does not just mean the standard ability to make scheduled payments, which applies to all firms, but also an additional requirement of appropriate level of *surplus* (or *capital*)—defined as the excess of the firm's assets over the liabilities—needed to assure the payment of all insured obligations with high probability. Insurance firms' liabilities consist nearly entirely of reserves. When an insurance premium is collected by an insurance company, a portion of it is used to pay expenses, such as marketing, administrative, or salaries of actuaries (this is a sizable expense, as actuaries are consistently among the highest-paid professionals) and other personnel, while the rest is placed in reserve to pay future claims or benefits. In addition to making certain that those reserves are large enough to cover actual promised payments, actuaries have to assure that assets and liabilities of the firm are managed properly, so that the difference between the assets and liabilities (the surplus) remains at a level required by insurance regulators, or higher. This form of management of an insurance firm (or any other entity involved in risk management) is termed *asset-liability management* and is a part of a larger field of *enterprise risk management*, a field of study of proper management of risky activities in which any business entity can and should be engaged.

Insurance Pricing Fundamentals

The key principle of private insurance contracts is a form of a "law of conservation": The totality of funds that are paid out to the insured parties must be originally obtained from the same insured parties in the form of premium payments (Bowers et al., 1997; Klugman, Panjer, & Willmot, 2004; Sundt & Teugels, 2004) While the owners of the insurance firm do provide capital to start the company, and possibly additional capital for its continuing functioning, they expect the opportunity to earn a return on their investment comparable with that available from other sources in the markets for capital of similar risk. Thus, insurance consumers as a whole cannot expect to be subsidized by the insurance firm but rather should expect to pay for their own claims and expenses and, additionally, for the cost of the capital supplied to the insurance firm by its owners. Thus, actuaries begin the process of pricing insurance by forecasting the future costs of claims in property, casualty, and liability insurance, or benefits in the case of life, disability, or health insurance, and life annuities. For example, in the case of life insurance, this begins with the study of the future lifespan of a given insured. If we denote by T the future length of life (a real number) of an insured aged x, then the cost of a life insurance policy in a specified amount is the present value of that amount discounted from the moment of payment (on death or just immediately following it), T years in the future (or a number close to T), to the present moment. This cost is likely to be increased by all policy expenses, such as marketing, administrative, and settlement expenses. Furthermore, starting an insurance enterprise or issuance of new policies requires an outlay of capital by the enterprise owner or owners, and that capital must be paid for. This cost of capital becomes another expense, added to the cost charged to the insured party. If the insurance premium is set as the expected value of the random variable describing future payment of benefits/claims and expenses, this method of pricing is called the *equivalence principle* (Bowers et al., 1997). This most basic principle of pricing insurance calls for the premium to be set at the level equal to the expected value (or mean) of future payouts, modeled as random variables. The process of diversification of many risks combined from various insured parties makes the average payout approximately equal to the theoretical expected value, as a consequence of limit theorems from the probability theory, such as the central limit theorem and the law of large numbers. But this diversification may not always be enough, and some provision for what actuaries call the adverse deviation (deviation of the actual amount of total claims or benefits from the expected amount, in a manner detrimental to the insurance company) must be made by appropriately increasing the insurance premium to cover this risk to the insurer's capital. Thus, the premium is typically set as the expected value of claims or benefits (adjusted for discounted value of money) plus the expected value of all expenses and taxes plus a provision for risk of adverse deviation—commonly called the *risk loading*—covered by the proper estimate of the cost of capital commensurate with the total risk of the insurer.

The key part of the calculation of the insurance premium is the estimate of the future losses or benefits. In the case of life insurance, since the amount to be paid is set in advance, the uncertainty is only twofold—unknown time of death and unknown rate of return that the firm will earn on the premium or premiums collected. While the simplest method of calculation of life insurance would use one amount paid up-front (single premium), real-life policies are nearly always paid for with a series of periodic (annual, quarterly, or monthly) premiums. Those periodic premiums are paid for a set period of time (e.g., 5 or 10 years), but only if the insured is alive, or for the entire remaining life of the insured person. This means that in the calculation of premium, not only is the time of payment of the death benefit uncertain (modeled as a random variable T, remaining time until death), but so is the length of time over which the premium will be paid. Luckily, the underlying random variable, T, is the same for both phenomena, although its practical implications on the present value of the death benefit and the present value of the remaining premium payments are somewhat different (as the death benefit is paid at one time—some time soon after death, while payment of premium is spread over time and stops at the moment of death). Ideally, estimates involving the random variable T would be based on data concerning the exact length of life of all people in the population. But historically, accurate data about the exact length of life have not always been easy to collect, and instead, annual data (expressing the length of life in full years) have been common. A table starting with a given population of newborn persons in a given year and then showing the population alive at any future age is called a *mortality table*. Population alive at age x is denoted by l_x, and number dying between ages x and $x+1$ is denoted by d_x. The ratio $q_x = d_x/l_x$ is a natural estimate of the probability of dying between ages x and $x+1$, and $p_x = 1 - q_x$ is the natural estimate of the probability of surviving that year. The first mortality table is generally attributed to Sir Edmund Halley (Greenwood, 1938; see also

Bowers et al., 1997), who in 1683, created it for the city of Breslau (now Wroclaw, Poland). In the United States, commonly used tables are generally created by the Society of Actuaries, usually using data collected in the national census. Insurance companies commonly undertake their own mortality studies, to better understand the risks of the populations they insure, and subsequently modify the published tables.

The other uncertain element in pricing of life insurance (or other products related to human mortality) is the interest rate that will be earned on the insurance company investments. Modeling of that rate of return is complicated enough if the period over which the return is considered is fixed—for example, 1 year. One-period models of rates of return are usually derived based on an *equilibrium* approach or an *arbitrage-free* approach (Hull, 2006; see also Ostaszewski, 2002). The equilibrium models take into consideration consumption and risk preferences of the participants in the economy and derive expected rates of return corresponding to varying levels of risk. Their crowning achievement is the *capital asset pricing model* (CAPM), widely used but derived under severely restrictive assumptions and thus limited in its applicability. CAPM is basically a one-period model and thus of very limited applicability to the business of life insurance, life annuities, and pensions (which are, by nature, long-term and multiperiod contracts). The second approach to modeling rates of return, the no-arbitrage approach, is rooted in the idea that capital markets would not allow arbitrage to exist, at least not in any persistent fashion. *Arbitrage* is defined as creation of an investment portfolio that does not require any outlay of funds yet allows positive returns with positive probability and never loses any money. In other words, arbitrage is a "free lunch." Given the no-arbitrage condition, two investment portfolios that generate the same cash flows in the future must have identical prices today. The no-arbitrage approach starts with observed prices and rates of return of assets traded in capital markets and attempts to derive appropriate rates of return for other assets of comparable risk that are not directly priced by the market. These two methodologies are of significance to insurance because insurance products are not continuously traded in the markets, but they are priced by insurance firms, and their prices must relate to risk-tolerance and other preferences of market participants, as well as prices of similarly risky capital assets traded in the markets. In other words, an actuary deriving an insurance premium must be aware of the value placed on the insurance product by the firm's customers and prices of capital assets that can be possibly used to replicate some, or even all, of the features of the insurance product under consideration. The actuary must make certain that the estimate of the interest rate used in the calculations of present values of future cash flows of the policy under consideration corresponds realistically to the interest rate that will be earned on the company's investments, after consideration of possible additional investment expenses and taxes (Cummins, 1990).

Methodologies of life insurance and life annuities are quite naturally extended to the area of pricing and planning of retirement. Retirement is usually expected to be funded by a combination of government social insurance pension, employer-sponsored pension or savings plan, and private savings. The problem of providing appropriate amounts of savings for the purpose of obtaining the desirable level of income on retirement is a natural actuarial model problem but compounded not just by the uncertainty of the length of life but also by the length of period of employment, date of retirement, desired level of income replacement (in relation to preretirement income) on retirement, as well as additional complications of possible disability and provision for the spouse and the survivors of the individual under consideration.

Life insurance models do not, however, extend naturally to insurance coverage of property; protection against liability; group insurance, including group health insurance, policies; or workers' compensation insurance. Life insurance policies are typically issued for long time-periods, possibly the entire life of the insured party. In contrast with that approach, automobile insurance or homeowner's insurance is usually issued for a relatively short period of time to individuals (personal) and corporations (commercial), 6 months to 1 year, and requires a different modeling approach. Actuarial models for these forms of insurance covering accidental and at-fault events forecast the random variable, counting the number of claims per insured received in the period of insurance (termed *frequency*) and, separately, the probability distribution of the size of those claims, termed *severity* (Klugman et al., 2004). The two random variables so modeled are then combined in a *collective risk* model of the form

$$S = X_1 + X_2 + \cdots + X_n,$$

where S is the *aggregate claims* random variable, N is the claim frequency random variable, and each X_i represents individual claim severity. Examples of commonly used probability distributions describing N are The Poisson distribution, the binomial distribution, and the negative binomial distribution. If the random variables X_i are assumed to be identically distributed and independent, the resulting distribution of S is termed a *compound distribution*, derived from combining the distribution of N and the distributions of X_i.

Estimation of the frequency and severity distributions is an integral part of the work of an actuary in the areas of property, casualty, liability insurance, and other similar forms of insurance. These estimates are continuously updated based on the claim data, as well as other data collected by insurance enterprises. The challenge is additionally complicated by the fact that not all losses are covered by insurance contracts, and even those that are covered are typically not covered in full (with the use of deductibles, i.e., amounts paid by the insured party before insurance coverage starts, or co-insurance, requiring the insured party to share in the payment for the losses); thus the actuary does not always have full access to the data describing the losses. Furthermore, the cost of items or events insured changes continuously. This is not only due to inflation but also due to changes in relative prices of items or events insured. In the United States, for example, the health insurance industry struggles with increases in costs of health care well in excess of overall inflation, as well as with nearly continuous introduction of new medical technologies and new prescription drugs, which may have not been considered in historical models used for pricing of health insurance. Liability insurance, especially policies covering general (pain and suffering) and punitive damages, are not tied closely to general inflation but, rather, to current and future laws and their interpretations by the court. Thus, the actuary must consider not just the estimates for frequency and severity based on historical data but also adjustments to those estimates for the *trend* (or changes) of the cost of coverage provided. This requires development of *forecasting* methodologies for projecting future costs of claims (Klugman et al., 2004; Sundt & Teugels, 2004). Standard forecasting methodologies are typically based on either *regression* or *time series*, both created within probability theory. Basic linear regression models assume that a predicted random variable Y is related to a predictor variable X via a linear model of the form

$$Y = a + bX + \varepsilon,$$

where a and b are parameters derived in the model estimation, and ε is a *residual* random variable, typically assumed to be normally distributed with mean 0 and a relatively small standard deviation. If empirical values of the predictor variable X are $x_1, x_2, \ldots, x_n$ and the corresponding value of the predicted variable Y are $y_1, y_2, \ldots, y_n$, then the standard methodology for estimation of parameters a and b is to minimize the Euclidean distance or *mean square error*:

$$\sum_{i=1}^{n} (y_i - (ax_i + b))^2 .$$

This approach dates back to Gauss. The relationship between the predictor and the predicted variable can be generalized to allow either X or Y to be replaced by functions of them. For example, if we know that Y is expected to grow exponentially with X, then it would be natural to consider a model of the form

$$\ln Y = a + bX + \varepsilon.$$

One can also have a general multivariate model of the form

$$Y = a + b_1X_1 + b_2X_2 + \cdots + b_mX_m + \varepsilon.$$

Note that in this general model, given the values $X_1 = x_1, X_2 = x_2, \ldots, X_m = x_m$, the predicted value of Y given these values of the predictor variables is

$$y = a + b_1x_1 + b_2x_2 + \cdots + b_mx_m,$$

as the expected value of the residual random variable is 0. Thus, this model gives the predicted value as the mean of the probability distribution of Y given that $X_1 = x_1, X_2 = x_2, \ldots, X_m = x_m$. One can, in fact, generalize this approach to regression analysis to *nonparametric regression models*, under which the distribution of the residuals is allowed to be completely arbitrary, instead of the normal distribution, and if that arbitrary distribution can somehow be estimated or theoretically established, the predicted value of Y is the mean of its conditional distribution.

The second set of methodologies deals with the situation when the variables modeled are time dependent, so that their historical observations do not constitute independent observations of the same random variable. *Time-series analysis* takes into consideration the time structure of data and accounts for phenomena such as *autocorrelation*, *trend*, or *seasonal variation*, all of which are common in real-life insurance data. The following is an example of an autoregressive model, which assumes a regression-type relationship of the value of a variable X_t at time t to the preceding values:

$$X_t = \left(1 - \sum_{i=1}^{p} \phi_i\right)\mu + \phi_1 X_{t-1} + \cdots + \phi_p X_{t-p} + \varepsilon_t.$$

One additional set of prediction methodologies has been created with the arrival of *fuzzy-set theory*. A fuzzy set $\tilde{E}$ is defined by its *membership function* μ_E in the universe of consideration U, so that for every element u of U, there is a value $\mu_E(u)$ where $0 \leqslant \mu_E(u) \leqslant 1$. Prediction methodologies typically use the concept of a *fuzzy number*, for which U is the set of all real numbers, and special generalizations of arithmetic operations developed for fuzzy numbers. The use of fuzzy-set theory is an important supplement to probability theory in that the variability that commonly arises from vague or ambiguous sources, rather than structural randomness, can be accommodated in the modeling process. Applications of fuzzy-set theory and fuzzy logic to insurance have been discussed by Ostaszewski (1993); Cummins and Derrig (1993, 1997); Derrig and Ostaszewski (1999, chap. 16); Shapiro and Jain (2003); and Young (1997). One vitally important area of actuarial science for both life and nonlife insurance is *risk classification* (Sundt & Teugels, 2004; see also Ostaszewski, 1993). If two insured parties have significantly different risk profiles in relation to expected claims yet are charged the same premium for insurance, one of them (the low-risk party) effectively subsidizes the other one (the high-risk party), and if the insurance contracts are voluntary, the low-risk party will avoid obtaining insurance, or minimize its amount, while the high-risk party will seek to maximize the coverage. If the combined or community insurance coverage is desirable for public policy reasons, this *adverse selection* is commonly resolved by making the purchase of the insurance contract compulsory and often administered by a government entity. But in private voluntary markets, when competition among insurance providers is present, the insured parties must be classified in reasonably homogeneous risk classes, within each of which the twisted incentives of inequitable premiums are no longer present. This requires that actuaries collect data concerning potential risk classes and classify insured parties accordingly. Various approaches have been developed to address this problem. *Bayesian* methodologies adjust the premium based on observed experience (Conger, 1988; DuMouchel, 1983). For contracts that bundle insured events (*perils*), such as auto liability, damage to vehicles, and theft, the diversification benefit becomes an important risk class pricing variable. The diversification benefit value is derived from low cross-correlations of random events insured in a bundle that tends to reduce variability. *Credibility theory* treats the premium rate for a given insured party (usually a group) as a weighted average of a premium derived based on that party's historical experience and a premium rate derived for a general population. The credibility weight assigned to the insured party's experience (i.e., history of loss frequency, and severity) is reflective of the accuracy of the empirical sample mean as a predictor of the true mean (Frees, Young, & Luo, 2001; Klugman et al., 2004). Classification methods can also be derived from methodologies used in other areas of mathematics. General and fuzzy clustering, principal component, and kernel-smoothing algorithms have been proposed and used for risk classification in insurance.

RESERVES

Once an insurance contract is in place and premium is collected, some portion of that premium must be placed in reserve for the purpose of payment of future benefits, claims, and expenses. Life insurance, life annuities, and pensions, as well as long-term health insurance contracts (such as disability insurance, and nonstatutory private health insurance in Germany, which is a type of contract not in existence in North America), all have a long-term nature, with risks generally increasing with age but with premium set in advance and rarely changed over time and, even when changed, generally not changed as rapidly as the increase in risk occurs. Such contracts must effectively have a level of premium that is too large in relation to risk in the early part of the policy and too small in the later part. As a result, a reserve must account for this divergence between the premiums and the payments made by the insurance company (Bowers et al., 1997; see also Sundt & Teugels, 2004). In actuarial terminology, the expected value (i.e., the probability mean) of the present value of all future cash flows (i.e., accounting for the time value of money and the risk of adverse development) is termed the *actuarial present value* and represents a *fair value* of the reserve. The most standard formula for the reserve in all forms of long-term insurance contracts is the difference between the actuarial present value of future benefits, claims, and expenses to be paid and the actuarial present value of future premiums to be collected. Of course, if future premiums were sufficient to pay future benefits, claims, and expenses (including the cost of capital) at all times, reserves would not be needed. The only long-term contract that does not use such an approach to reserving is the deferred-annuity contract in the accumulation phase in the United States, which requires the reserve to be the highest possible present value (not adjusted for any probability of occurrence) of guaranteed future account balances under the contract. The *commissioners annuity reserve valuation method*, required for deferred annuities by insurance regulators in the United States, is a unique exception in the actuarial methodology of reserving: It actually never uses any probability concepts.

The process of calculation of reserves for long-term contracts is commonly called *valuation*. The interest rate used in the process of calculation of present values in that process is called the *valuation interest rate*, and the mortality table used is the *valuation mortality table*. In combination, the interest rate and mortality table form the *valuation basis*. It would seem natural that the judgment concerning the mortality table and the valuation rate belongs with the actuarial professional. This is generally the approach adopted in Great Britain, Australia, and Canada. However, in many countries, including the United States (until 1980 and, to lesser degree, still so), this decision is taken away from the actuary, or even from the insurance firm management, and instead, the mortality and interest rate parameters are prescribed by law. The process of valuation based on the methodology prescribed by law is called the *statutory valuation* and is required in the United States of all insurance companies for the purpose of submission of their financial statements to the insurance regulators. Insurance is regulated in the United States separately in each state, and statutory valuation reports must be submitted to each state in which an insurance firm is engaged in the business of insurance. Interestingly enough, a separate valuation methodology required of insurance companies that issue their shares for trading in public stock exchanges in the United States (e.g., the New York Stock Exchange) is prescribed by the generally accepted accounting principles (GAAP). To make things even more complicated, and possibly to create more employment opportunities for actuaries, the accounting rules for the calculation of the income tax due to the federal government in the United States are different from the statutory, or GAAP, rules and are prescribed separately in the tax laws and their interpretations by the tax agency, the Internal Revenue Service. These peculiar regulatory and accounting complexities in the insurance industry in the United States are perceived by some as barriers to the entry of foreign insurers.

Private pensions in the United States are, however, regulated by the federal government (Department of Labor), and a valuation basis chosen by the pension plan actuary, on the basis of that actuary's professional judgment, is generally used. The GAAP rules for pension plans are, however, different from the valuation for regulatory purposes.

The past quarter-century has witnessed increased interest in making the reserving methodologies less *command based* (with formulas and valuation bases prescribed by law) and more *principle based.* This has been especially important in view of dramatic changes in the level of interest rates experienced in the 1970s and 1980s, as well as improvements in longevity of the general population, making the older mortality tables, still used for older policies (as the valuation basis for a long-term policy in the United States is assigned to a policy based on the date of its issue and remains unchanged unless a change would result in an increase in statutory reserves), quite obsolete in many cases. Older mortality tables exhibit mortality levels in excess of those experienced currently, although such policies tend to also have higher premiums, which drive away healthy insured individuals (who switch to newer, cheaper policies), leaving the insurance firm with a high-mortality pool, for which higher premiums may indeed be justified. The principle-based approach to reserving usually requires a complex long-term model of the insurance company. Since 1991 in the United States, such long-term models are effectively required for most long-term contract companies—that is, life insurance, life annuities, and so on—and the process of creating them is called *cash flow testing*. In the long-term model, the set of cash flows generated by an insurance firm is generally treated as a stochastic process (i.e., a series of time-dependent random variables), with financial outcomes such as payments of benefits and claims, payments of expenses, profits generated, and the level of surplus held (assets minus liabilities) modeled in each realization of the stochastic process generated. The stochastic process under consideration is influenced the most by the future scenarios of interest rates, but it is also affected by random outcomes of mortality or any other basis for benefit payments (e.g., payments of any amounts, known as *nonforfeiture amounts*) on policy termination. All these phenomena must be modeled by the valuation actuary. The resulting set of generated scenarios of the future creates an empirical distribution of financial outcomes describing the company's solvency under all the scenarios. Actuaries say that the company *passes a scenario* if it remains solvent during its entire duration. The minimum period modeled is 10 years, although the frequency of cash flows considered during those years need not be very high (quarterly cash flows can be acceptable, and hourly, or even daily or weekly, cash flows are generally not required). Long-term insurance firms are required to pass seven scenarios of the future prescribed by the regulators (those scenarios are termed the *New York 7* because they originate from seven scenarios considered in Regulation 126 in the State of New York) and an overwhelming majority (e.g., 95%) of random scenarios generated by the insurance company internal model. In effect, the regulators want the insurance company to remain solvent with 95% probability, based on the large random sample of the probability distribution describing the future financial situation of the company. This regulatory approach has created a significantly increased demand for applications of stochastic processes to the modeling of insurance firms.

For short-term insurance policies, such as automobile insurance or homeowner's insurance, or even workers' compensation, the emphasis in reserving is not on the long-term discrepancy between payouts to be made and premiums collected but rather on the claim payments that must be made within the remaining term of the policy. Because for short-term policies the premium is typically paid up-front (e.g., for a 6-month automobile policy, the premium payment occurs at the beginning of the 6-month period), payments to be made cannot be offset by any future premiums. The emphasis is therefore on forecasting the claim payments. Those payments come in three major categories:

- Payments for future claims during the unexpired term of the policy
- Payments yet to be made on claims that have already occurred and have been reported to the insurance company
- Payments yet to be made for claims that have already occurred but have not yet been reported (commonly called *Incurred but not reported*, or IBNR)

If a claim has already been reported to the insurance company and is reasonably well-evaluated, it is generally not necessary to use any probability-based methods to estimate its value. Similarly, the value of claims arising in the future during the unexpired term of the policy can be estimated by the expected claims in the premium proportioned to the remaining time to expiration, the *unearned premium reserve*. But for a claim that is entirely unknown to the company, some form of estimation must be made. The traditional approach to this problem has been completely deterministic (i.e., devoid of any probability applications). An actuary establishing IBNR considers the period of time since a theoretical claim has occurred and, based on the company's own data (from historical experience), estimates how long it will take for that claim to be reported and fully paid and what portion of it will be paid at what moment in time. Then, the actuary applies the knowledge so obtained to all data about claims already known and claims not yet known, assuming that the estimates can be applied to the current situation. By applying these estimates, the actuary projects what the ultimate full amount that will be paid is and compares it with the amount that has already been paid. The difference of the two represents the amount that will be paid in the future on the claims already in existence. That difference is the IBNR reserve, the largest liability item in a typical property/casualty insurance company financial statement. The process of paying the claim from the date when the claim is incurred to the date when it is fully settled is called *development* (in property/casualty insurance) or *completion* (in health insurance). The last quarter-century has witnessed a gradual increase in interest in applying probability-based methodologies to estimation of the IBNR reserves and loss development in general. In such probability-based approaches, the final amount to be paid is typically modeled as a random variable dependent on, at the very minimum, time, and then typically, in addition to time, other variables describing the process of development or completion, the entity insured, the nature of the claim, and so on. Regression-based models are the most common. In property-casualty insurance reserving, models may use hundreds of variables, including interactions of those variables, and all such variables must be always very carefully examined for multicollinearity—that is, dependence of the variables on each other, which reduces or even eliminates the model's predictive power.

Asset-Liability Management

The cash-flow-testing models required in life insurance and life annuities in the United States for the purpose of establishing statutory reserves are an example of the expansion of sophisticated asset-liability management models that gradually have entered insurance practice in the past quarter-century. The practice of asset-liability management began in response to the increased volatility of assets held in insurance companies' portfolios in the 1970s and 1980s (Ostaszewski, 2002). Varying interest rates were the greatest concern initially. Insurance companies have traditionally provided long-term guarantees of interest rates paid on policies used for accumulation of wealth for retirement, but those guarantees were at relatively low levels. When interest rates rose, those policies became unattractive and were abandoned by their owners in the process of *disintermediation*—that is, flight from low-interest-rate insurance and bank products to higher-return investment products. Insurance companies responded by offering higher rates of return and pursuing higher returns themselves by investing in riskier bonds and mortgages. High rates of return in the stock markets have been countered by offering new variable annuity products tied to the performance of the stock market. But some of those strategies of insurance firms have resulted in a significant increase of their risk exposure, and this was a new type of exposure: not the familiar diversifiable risk of insuring individuals or firms against death or perils but the nondiversifiable risk of the bond market (in the form of both the risk of changing interest rates and the risk of default of risky bonds) and the stock market. In 1991, the United States life insurance industry experienced two insolvencies of large and established insurance firms: Executive Life and Mutual Benefit. Both these companies had sizable portfolios of risky assets that resulted in a panic of withdrawals from their retirement-type policies when risky investments declined in value and rumors of insolvency spread, so-called systemic risk, similar to the run-on-the-bank risk.

Those developments illustrated the dangers of any divergence between the value of insurance firms' assets and liabilities. The difference between assets and liabilities, the surplus (or capital), is carefully watched by insurance regulators. Since the mid-1990s, the level of surplus required is a function of risks undertaken by the company, in its asset portfolio, in the structure of the insurance products it offers, and in the interaction of its assets and liabilities. While the early models used for asset-liability management called for elimination of risks of divergence of assets and liabilities, by matching assets and liabilities cash flows, in a process called *immunization*, or matching the values of assets and liabilities under changes of interest rates, recent developments in this area are more significantly oriented toward managing the divergence using techniques based on probability models.

One particularly important area of significance for understanding asset-liability management is the study of the *options* embedded in the insurance contracts and the relationship between the insured party and the insurer. Options are defined as contracts between two parties, one of which, for a fee, acquires the right to perform a certain transaction and the other one, receiving the fee (called the *option premium*), assumes the responsibility of accommodating that transaction (Hull, 2006). Options are typically defined in a prescribed period of time and specify, in detail, the nature of the transaction to be performed. For example, an option to buy (termed a *call*) gold at a prescribed price (*strike price*, or *exercise price*) of $500 per ounce within the next 3 months would give the party buying that option (the party with a *long position* in the option) the right to buy gold for $500 per ounce, while the party selling the option (the party with a *short position* in the option) would have to deliver the gold and sell it for $500 when called on to do so (this is termed the *exercise* of the option).

Life insurance policies, as well as life annuities, traditionally contain minimum interest rate guarantees. When interest rates fall, such guarantees are equivalent to the option (granted to the insured) to receive income at the level of the minimum interest rate guarantee, regardless of the current level of interest rates. Life insurance policy or disability insurance policy can be viewed as an option to receive a certain monetary value when the human capital (the ability to generate income through work) of the insured person disappears due to death or disability (Ostaszewski, 1993).

But most important, any insurance company creates an option by the very process of issuance of insurance contracts. The policyholder is promised certain monetary values on the occurrence of insured events, a call option on the company's assets. This promise will be kept only if the insurance company is still in business. If the company is not in business, the insured can only make a claim on the company's remaining assets. In effect, the insurance company holds an insolvency *put*, an option to sell its assets at a predetermined price—that is, the current value of its liabilities. If the value of the assets exceeds the obligation to the policyholder, the insurance company has an incentive to make good on that obligation. But as soon as the value of the assets falls below the value of the obligation, under *limited liability*, the insurance company can just walk away from the obligation and let the policyholders take and divide the assets instead. The risk of such irresponsible behavior by the insurance firm or the unfortunate occurrence of a catastrophe such as an earthquake or a hurricane is the very reason for the existence of insurance regulation. The government regulates insurance firms and prescribes their (minimum) level of surplus, because as soon as that surplus becomes negative, the insurance firm has little financial incentive to serve the best interests of its policyholders.

Pricing options is a complex mathematical problem, requiring a combination of financial mathematics and probability. The most celebrated methodology of pricing options has been developed by Fisher Black and Myron Scholes—who received the Nobel Prize in Economics for this achievement—and is known as the *Black-Scholes formula* (Hull, 2006). Their methodology assumes that the changes in the value of an asset on which the option is issued (*the underlying*) follow a *log-normal process* (stochastic process in which incremental changes are described by the log-normal probability distribution), and it derives the value of the option as the discounted present value of future cash flows generated by the option under an appropriate probability measure (the *risk-neutral measure*). Practical evaluations of various options embedded in insurance contracts generally follow some variation of the Black-Scholes methodology or its simplified version, the *binomial model*, using a stochastic process derived from the binomial probability distribution. This is also the underlying theoretical justification of the cash-flow-testing methodologies used by long-term insurance companies and the *dynamic solvency testing* models used for long-term models of companies issuing short-term insurance contracts.

Insurance Pricing Models

Insurance pricing begins with the fact that both the cost and the expected return (profit) are not known with certainty. Rather, the ultimate cost derives from a stochastic process that commences when the insurance is purchased and is resolved when the final claim, expense, and tax payments are made. The ultimate profit too results from an interrelated stochastic process that depends on the ultimate costs, the premium charged at the time of sale, and the returns on invested premiums (between the time of collection and the payment of costs) and capital. Thus, the determination of an appropriate premium by the actuary or available in the market, prior to sale, is key to the opportunity to earn a profit consistent with the risk of adverse development. Of course, in complete or workably competitive markets, where equilibrium supply and demand prices are equal, those prices may or may not agree with the actuary's calculation of prices and expected profits. We turn next to two comprehensive pricing models developed for insurance in the past 30 years and illustrate their use in the property-casualty context.

Policyholder Demand Side Model

A policyholder purchases insurance to trade risky and uncertain future adverse financial events for the near (because of insolvency potential) certainty of a premium payment. In decision theory, the premium would be the certainty equivalent of the uncertain future liabilities. An insured should be willing to pay a premium equal to the present value of expected future claims, expenses, and taxes, adjusted in the discount rate both for the time value of money and for the risk of adverse deviations from the expectations. The latter is the expected profit to the company for accepting the risk transfer from the insured. The key to the demand model is then the identification of all expected costs: payments to (claims) or on behalf of (expenses and taxes) the policyholder and a market price for the transfer of risk. Proper policyholder demand pricing models should not directly include consideration of the insurer's invested assets and expected investment income above the riskless rate, the time value of money. Policyholders are generally unwilling, except in explicit investment-insurance-linked products such as variable annuities, to trade uncertain adverse accidental events for certain premiums plus uncertain insurer investment returns. Policyholder demand models assume the presence of a supplier at the policyholder demand price in equilibrium.

The paradigm demand model, developed at the Massachusetts Institute of Technology (MIT) by Stewart C. Myers and Richard A. Cohn, posits that the appropriate premium P at the beginning of the policy equals the present value (PV) of losses L, expenses E, and taxes T (because of double taxation in the United States):

$$\mathrm{PV}(L+E+T),$$

where PV incorporates a negative adjustment to the riskless discount rate to provide the necessary profit incentive for the insurer assuming the risk (Derrig, 1993, 1994). In practice, those risk-adjustments have been difficult to model and calculate from empirical data.

Shareholder Supply Side Model

Insurers offer policies precisely to capitalize on the diversification benefits of pooling uncertain adverse future financial event consequences from personal and commercial risks. Insurers count on low levels of adverse event correlations among risks (those risks are often assumed to be independent and identically distributed, to invoke the central limit theorem or the law of large numbers) to provide a substantial risk-spreading benefit across the insured population. A certain premium is traded by the insurer for the uncertain risk of collective adverse events in excess of the premiums and expected riskless investment income from premiums (time value of money) over the life of the policy. If the certain premium, combined with the after-tax investment income from the insurer's asset portfolio, is expected to provide returns to shareholders (investors of capital in the insurer) commensurate with the combined underwriting (insurance) and investment risk, then the insurer offers the insurance contract at the price that produces expected *fair* returns equal to the cost of capital for those risks.

The paradigm supply model is the internal rate of return (IRR) model used for capital budgeting and project decision making in corporate finance (Automobile Insurers Bureau, 2005). The fundamental concept is that the flow of invested capital and the return of that capital with realized profit, if any, should be expected to have an NPV of 0 when discounted at the cost of capital of the insurance firm (the internal rate of return). Nominal policyholder premium, loss, and expense flows and company-invested asset flows with after-tax returns are used to estimate (1) the size and timing of the shareholder investment to back the outstanding liabilities, (2) the size and timing of the return of that invested capital to shareholders as liabilities are resolved and paid, and (3) the size and timing of any assets in excess of (1) to be returned as income to shareholders. Figure 20.1 shows the relative value of the outstanding loss and expense flow for auto bodily injury liability insurance by quarter measured from the issuance of the policy, the commitment of surplus backing those liabilities (proportional to an assumed fixed value of 0.67 surplus/liabilities for all quarters), and the expected profit to be realized by quarter.

In regulatory settings such as personal automobile insurance in Massachusetts, the estimate of the required invested capital used is the book value of surplus measured in units proportional to outstanding costs as in the 0.67 proportion of losses (L) and expenses (E) illustrated in Figure 20.1. This creates a financial mismatch between the proxy for the investors' capital (book value—as reported in the financial statement—of surplus) and the data source for estimating the cost of capital and the actual returns on the market value of the firm. Generally, the market value of insurance companies is higher than the conservative regulatory book value of assets net of liabilities. Insurers may use market or economic values of the firm for internal pricing in less regulated markets, bringing the pricing closer to the supply-demand equilibrium price of traditional economics.

There are two principal methods for estimating the cost of capital for the entire firm, the CAPM and the Gordon growth model (GGM). The simple CAPM models the expected return on a security as the risk-free rate plus a risk premium dependent only on the covariance of the firm's returns, the market returns, and the overall market risk premium (Derrig & Orr, 2004). At this point in time, the use of empirical data and simple regressions of firm returns on market returns (the *market beta*) has provided unsatisfactory results in predicting actual firm returns. The simple CAPM discussed above suffers from an omitted- or confounding-variable problem. The extended three-factor CAPM model of Fama and French developed in the 1990s included two important variables omitted in the simple formulation, the size of the insurer and the ratio of book to market valuations (Fama & French, 1995). The former is well-known in finance as the size effect on stock market returns: Smaller capitalized stocks (need to) earn higher percentage rates of return than large cap stocks. Recent research shows that once the omitted CAPM variables are introduced, the market beta for property-liability companies is about 1; that is, property casualty insurers are about average market risk (Cummins & Phillips, 2005).

The GGM is built on the common assumption that the current price per share P is equal to the present value of all future dividend payments D, discounted at the cost of capital rate. In a simple GGM formulation, the growth rate of dividends and the cost of capital are assumed constant in perpetuity, leading to a simple estimation equation:

$$k = \frac{D}{P} + g,$$

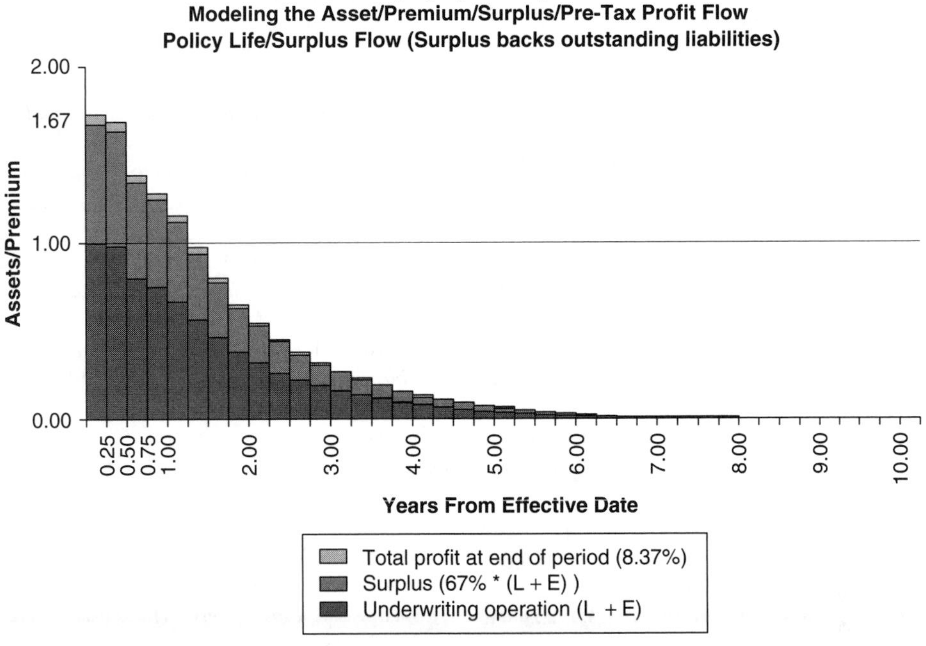

Figure 20.1 Relative value of outstanding loss and expense flow for auto bodily injury liability insurance.

SOURCE: Automobile Insurance Bureau.

where D/P is current dividend rate, k is cost of capital, and g is dividend growth rate.

The dividend growth rate, g, is, of course, key, and many ways of estimation have been used. Most often, the growth rate is estimated as an average of some recent historical rate and some forecasted (by analysts) rate. At the heart of all these cost-of-capital models are probabilistic estimation error models that are rarely calculated in the "real" world.

SUMMARY

This chapter shows that probability methodologies are widely used in, and form the core of, actuarial science—that is, the science of mathematical models used in insurance and risk management. Probability models underlie the pricing of insurance, from mortality tables and interest-rate models in life insurance to frequency, severity, and capital charge predictive models in property/casualty insurance. Stochastic processes are also prevalent in models used for reserve calculations and in asset-liability management. The acknowledgement that insurance represents a bundle of financial assets and options places it squarely in the modern financial asset pricing problem and, therefore, is susceptible to the development of financial engineering techniques, which notably rely on sophisticated empirical parametric and nonparametric probabilistic models and stochastic calculus.

REFERENCES

Automobile Insurers Bureau. (2005). *2005 underwriting profit filing for 2006 rates*. State of Massachusetts, DOI Docket R2005–09: Author.

Bowers, N. L., Gerber, H. U., Hickman, J. C., Jones, D. A., & Nesbitt, C. J. (1997). *Actuarial mathematics* (2nd ed.). Schaumburg, IL: Society of Actuaries.

Conger, R. F. (1988). The construction of automobile rating territories in Massachusetts. *Proceedings of the Casualty Actuarial Society*, *74*, 1–74.

Cummins, J. D. (1990). Multi-period discounted cash flow ratemaking models in property liability insurance. *Journal of Risk and Insurance*, *57*(1), 79–109.

Cummins, J. D., & Derrig, R. A. (1993). Fuzzy trends in property-liability insurance claim costs. *Journal of Risk and Insurance*, *60*(3), 429–465.

Cummins, J. D., & Derrig, R. A. (1997). Fuzzy financial pricing of property-liability insurance. *North American Actuarial Journal*, *1*(4), 21–44.

Cummins, J. D., & Phillips, R. D. (2005). Estimating the cost of equity capital for property-liability insurers. *Journal of Risk and Insurance*, *72*(3), 441–478.

Derrig, R. A. (1993). Price regulation in US automobile insurance: A case study of Massachusetts private passenger automobile insurance 1978–1990. *Geneva Papers on Risk and Insurance*, *67*, 158–173.

Derrig, R. A. (1994). Theoretical considerations of the effect of federal income taxes on investment income in property-liability ratemaking. *Journal of Risk and Insurance*, *61*(4), 691–709.

Derrig, R. A., & Orr, E. (2004). Equity risk premium: Expectations great and small. *North American Actuarial Journal*, *8*, 45–69.

Derrig, R. A., & Ostaszewski, K. M. (1999). Fuzzy sets methodologies in actuarial science. In H. J. Zimmerman (Ed.), *Practical applications of fuzzy technologies* (pp. 531–556). Norwell, MA: Kluwer Academic.

DuMouchel, W. H. (1983). The 1982 Massachusetts automobile insurance classification scheme. *The Statistician*, *32*, 69–81.

Fama, E. F., & French, K. R. (1995). Size and book-to-market factors in earnings and returns. *Journal of Finance*, *50*, 55–84.

Frees, E. W., Young, V., & Luo, Y. (2001). Credibility ratemaking using panel data models. *North American Actuarial Journal*, *5*(4), 24–42.

Greenwood, M. (1938). The first life table. *Notes and Records of the Royal Society of London*, *1*(2), 70–72.

Hull, J. C. (2006). *Options, futures, and other derivatives* (6th ed.). Englewood Cliffs, NJ: Prentice Hall.

Klugman, S. A., Panjer, H. H., & Willmot, G. E. (2004). *Loss models: From data to decisions* (2nd ed.). Somerset, NJ: Wiley.

Ostaszewski, K. M. (1993). *An investigation into possible applications of fuzzy sets methods in actuarial science (Monograph).* Schaumburg, IL: Society of Actuaries.

Ostaszewski, K. M. (2002). *Asset-liability integration (monograph).* Schaumburg, IL: Society of Actuaries.

Shapiro, A., & Jain, L. C. (2003). *Intelligent and other computational techniques in the insurance industry: Theory and applications.* Hackensack, NJ: World Scientific.

Sundt, B., & Teugels, J. L. (Eds.). (2004). *The encyclopedia of actuarial science.* Chichester, UK: Wiley.

Young, V. R. (1997). Adjusting indicated insurance rates: Fuzzy rules that consider both experience and auxiliary data. *Proceedings of the Casualty Actuarial Society*, *84*, 734–765.

21

Credit Scoring

Ad Feelders

Introduction

When you apply for a loan at a bank, the loan officer has to make an assessment of the risk that you will not be able (or willing) to repay the loan and interest. In making this assessment, it is assumed that this risk depends on characteristics of the applicant, such as age, income, occupation, and marital status. Depending on the predicted risk, the applicant is either rejected or accepted. Nowadays, this decision is often made (or supported) by a computer model that makes a risk assessment on the basis of the characteristics of the applicant. Such a computer model is typically based on the analysis of historical data. Repayment behavior of the applicants who have been accepted in the past is observed by the bank, usually leading after some time to a classification as either a defaulted or a nondefaulted loan.

In this chapter, we discuss how such a model can be constructed and what problems we may encounter in trying to do so.

Formal Statement of the Problem

We start by introducing some notation. We assume that some vector of variables $\mathbf{x} = (x_1, \ldots, x_k)$ is completely observed for each applicant. It contains the information that is filled in on the loan application form, typically supplemented with information concerning the credit history of the applicant that is obtained from a central credit bureau.

The outcome of the loan (default or nondefault) is denoted by y. Without loss of generality, we assume that $y \in \{0, 1\}$, with the convention that a default is labeled 1 and a nondefault is labeled 0. So $\Pr(y = 1|\mathbf{x})$ denotes the probability that an applicant with attribute vector $\mathbf{x}$ will default. The basic assumption we make is that

$$\Pr(y = 1|\mathbf{x}) = f(\mathbf{x}); \qquad (21.1)$$

that is, the probability that an applicant will default depends in some (as yet unspecified) way on his or her characteristics. This assumption seems plausible and is supported by empirical evidence.

We assume that historical data on y and $\mathbf{x}$ are available on applicants who have been accepted in the (recent) past. For applicants who have been rejected, we may have data on $\mathbf{x}$, or perhaps only part of $\mathbf{x}$, but obviously not on the outcome y of the loan. For now, we assume that only data on accepted applicants are used to estimate (21.1); in the section Reject Inference, we turn to the problem of the rejected applicants. Equation (21.1), however, is still too general; to get a grip, we need to further specify what f may look like. We briefly discuss two popular techniques to build credit-scoring models from data—namely, linear regression and logistic regression. We start however with a short description of a credit data set we use to illustrate the different techniques.

The Data

We use a publicly available data set known as the *German Credit* data, which can be downloaded from the UCI machine learning repository (Newman, Hettich, Blake, & Merz, 1998). This data set contains 1,000 loans, 300 of which were classified as defaulted ("bad" loans) and 700 as nondefaulted ("good" loans). The definition of defaulted is not given in the documentation but typically is related to the number of arrears that have been recorded for a client. In Feelders, le Loux, and van't Zand (1995), for example, a client is marked as a defaulter if there has been an arrear of 60 days or more, primarily because the bank is legally obliged to report such arrears to the Dutch Credit Registration Bureau. The percentage of defaults (30%) is unusually high in this data set and probably does not reflect the true percentage of defaults among the accepted applicants. For each applicant, 20 variables have been recorded; this set contains numeric variables such as age and credit amount, as well as qualitative variables such as type of occupation and personal status. We analyze the German Credit data using R, a free software environment for statistical computing and graphics (see http://www.r-project.org).

Linear Regression

Linear regression is a popular technique to build credit-scoring models from data, even though it has some shortcomings from a theoretical viewpoint. The linear probability model can be stated as follows:

$$\Pr(y=1|\mathbf{x}) = E(y|\mathbf{x}) = \beta_0 + \beta_1 x_1 + \cdots + \beta_k x_k. \qquad (21.2)$$

The disadvantage of the model is that it may yield "probabilities" smaller than 0 and larger than 1 for some values of **x**; in other words, the function is not bounded between 0 and 1. This can of course be remedied by setting estimated probabilities above 1 to 1 and estimated probabilities below 0 to 0. As an example, we fit a linear regression model with one explanatory variable (the duration of the loan in months) to the German Credit data (see Printout 21.1).

In the first command, we assign the result of the call to `lm` (for linear model) to the variable `german.linreg1`; the symbol `<-` is one of the ways to denote assignment in R. The first argument of the call to `lm` gives a formula that specifies the model to be estimated; here, the formula indicates that `default` is the response variable and `duration` the explanatory variable. The second argument of `lm` gives the name of the data set to be used for fitting the model. From the model summary, we read that the fitted equation is

$$\Pr(\text{Default}=1) = 0.13 + 0.008 \times \text{Duration}$$

The intercept doesn't have a useful interpretation here, since a loan with a duration of 0 months is of course nonsensical. The coefficient of duration (0.008172) can be interpreted as follows: For every extra month duration of the loan, the default probability goes up by approximately 0.008.

Logistic Regression

Another popular technique for building credit-scoring models is called *logistic regression*. This model is more suited for fitting probabilities than the linear regression model. The basic assumption of the logistic regression model is that

$$\ln \frac{\Pr(y=1|x)}{\Pr(y=0|x)} = \beta_0 + \beta_1 x. \qquad (21.3)$$

The expression on the left-hand side is called the *logit transformation* of the probability $\Pr(y=1|x)$. The ratio $\Pr(y=1|x)/\Pr(y=0|x)$ is called the *odds*.

Now, suppose we want to estimate the unknown parameters β_0 and β_1 from a sample of n data points $(y_1,x_1),\ldots,(y_n,x_n)$. We state the simple logistic regression model as follows: The y_i are independent Bernoulli random variables with expected values $E(y_i) = \Pr(y_i=1)$, where

$$E(y_i) = \Pr(y_i=1) = \frac{e^{\beta_0+\beta_1 x_i}}{1+e^{\beta_0+\beta_1 x_i}}. \qquad (21.4)$$

Printout 21.1

```
> german.linreg1 <- lm(default ~ duration,data=german.dat)
> summary(german.linreg1)


Coefficients:
             Estimate Std. Error t value Pr(>|t|)
(Intercept) 0.129187   0.028361   4.555 5.88e-06 ***
duration    0.008172   0.001175   6.952 6.49e-12 ***
---
```

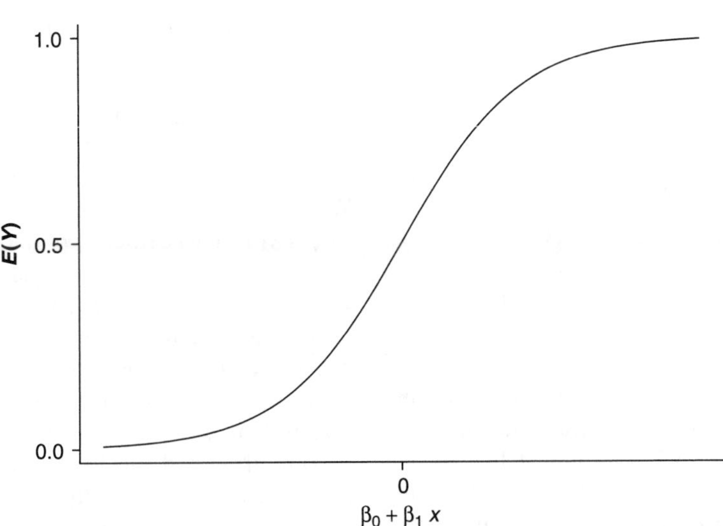

Figure 21.1 Logistic response function.

This response function is plotted in Figure 21.1 and is called the *logistic response function*. Since each y_i observation is a Bernoulli random variable, we can represent its probability distribution as follows:

$$p_i(y_i) = \Pr(y_i = 1)^{y_i}(1 - \Pr(y_i = 1))^{1-y_i}, \quad \text{where } y_i = 0, 1; \; i = 1, \ldots, n. \quad (21.5)$$

Note that $p_i(1) = \Pr(y_i = 1)$, $p_i(0) = \Pr(y_i = 0) = 1 - \Pr(y_i = 1)$ as required.

Since the y_i observations are assumed to be independent (e.g., because they were obtained by random sampling), their joint probability is simply the product of their individual probabilities; that is,

$$p(y_1, \ldots, y_n) = \prod_{i=1}^{n} p_i(y_i) = \prod_{i=1}^{n} \Pr(y_i = 1)^{y_i} (1 - \Pr(y_i = 1))^{1-y_i}. \quad (21.6)$$

When viewed as a function of the unknown parameters of the model, the joint probability of the observed data defines the so-called likelihood function. For convenience, we work with the log-likelihood, since products become sums, and if we take the natural log, we can get rid of some powers of e.

$$
\begin{aligned}
\ln p(y_1,\ldots,y_n) &= \ln\prod_{i=1}^{n}\Pr(y_i=1)^{y_i}(1-\Pr(y_i=1))^{1-y_i} \\
&= \sum_{i=1}^{n} y_i \ln\left(\frac{\Pr(y_i=1)}{1-\Pr(y_i=1)}\right) \\
&\quad + \sum_{i=1}^{n}\ln(1-\Pr(y_i=1)) \\
&= \sum_{i=1}^{n} y_i(\beta_0+\beta_1 x_i) - \sum_{i=1}^{n}\ln(1+e^{\beta_0+\beta_1 x_i}).
\end{aligned}
$$

In the last step, we use the assumption that

$$\ln\left(\frac{\Pr(y_i=1)}{1-\Pr(y_i=1)}\right) = \beta_0+\beta_1 x_i,$$

and as a consequence,

$$1-\Pr(y_i=1) = (1+e^{\beta_0+\beta_1 x_i})^{-1}.$$

Hence, the log-likelihood function is

$$\mathcal{L}(\beta_0,\beta_1) = \sum_{i=1}^{n} y_i(\beta_0+\beta_1 x_i) - \sum_{i=1}^{n}\ln(1+e^{\beta_0+\beta_1 x_i}). \tag{21.7}$$

The maximum likelihood estimates of β_0 and β_1 are those values $\hat{\beta}_0$ and $\hat{\beta}_1$ that maximize the log-likelihood in (21.7). Unfortunately, there are no formulas that give us the values of $\hat{\beta}_0$ and $\hat{\beta}_1$, as there are in least squares estimation of the linear regression model. Computer-intensive numerical search procedures are required to find the maximum likelihood estimates. Once they are found, we substitute these values into the response function in (21.4) to obtain the *fitted response function*

$$\widehat{\Pr}(y_i=1) = \frac{e^{\hat{\beta}_0+\hat{\beta}_1 x_i}}{1+e^{\hat{\beta}_0+\hat{\beta}_1 x_i}}. \tag{21.8}$$

As an example, suppose we use duration of the loan as an explanatory variable, just like in the linear regression example in the section Linear Regression. We fit a logistic regression model with `duration` as the explanatory variable (see Printout 21.2). *Generalized linear model* is abbreviated as GLM; logistic regression models belong to this class of models. By typing `family=binomial`, we indicate that we want to fit a logistic regression model. Next, we view the results (see Printout 21.3).

In the `Estimate` column of the `Coefficients` table, we find $\hat{\beta}_0 = -1.666351$ and $\hat{\beta}_1 = 0.037538$. This means that

$$\widehat{\Pr}(y_i=1) = \frac{e^{-1.666351+0.037538x_i}}{1+e^{-1.666351+0.037538x_i}}.$$

So, for example, if the duration of the loan is 8 months, we would estimate the default probability to be

$$\widehat{\Pr}(y_i=1) = \frac{e^{-1.666351+0.037538(8)}}{1+e^{-1.666351+0.037538(8)}} \approx 0.20.$$

If the duration of the loan is 48 months, we would estimate the default probability to be

$$\widehat{\Pr}(y_i=1) = \frac{e^{-1.666351+0.037538(48)}}{1+e^{-1.666351+0.037538(48)}} \approx 0.53.$$

With a p-value of `4.63e-11` (see the column `Pr(>|z|)`), the coefficient of duration is significant at any conventional significance level. To test whether the model provides an adequate fit of the data, we use the model deviance as a test statistic. The model deviance is defined as $-2\mathcal{L}^*$, that is, minus twice the value of the log-likelihood function evaluated at its maximum. A high value of the (log)likelihood function indicates a high probability of the data given the model and hence a good fit of the data. Therefore, a high model deviance indicates a bad fit of the data, and vice versa. The alternatives of interest are

$$H_0: E(Y) = (1+e^{-\beta_0-\beta_1 x})^{-1}$$

and

$$H_a: E(Y) \neq (1+e^{-\beta_0-\beta_1 x})^{-1}.$$

If the logistic function is the correct response function and the sample size n is large, then the deviance will follow approximately a chi-square distribution with $n-p$ degrees of freedom, where p denotes the number of parameters of the model. Hence, we can use the decision rule (as usual, α denotes the significance level of the test):

$$\text{If } \{-2\mathcal{L}^* \leqslant \chi^2(1-\alpha, n-p)\}, \text{ accept } H_0,$$

otherwise reject H_0. As indicated in the `R` output, the model deviance is 1,199.1 on $n-p = 1000-$

Printout 21.2

```
> german.logreg1 <- glm(default ~ duration,data=german.dat,
                        family=binomial)
```

Printout 21.3

```
> summary(german.logreg1)

Coefficients:
             Estimate Std. Error z value Pr(>|z|)
(Intercept) -1.666351   0.146615 -11.365  < 2e-16 ***
duration     0.037538   0.005703   6.582 4.63e-11 ***
---

Residual deviance: 1199.1  on 998  degrees of freedom
```

2 = 998 degrees of freedom. Using $\alpha = 0.05$, we compare this number with $\chi^2(0.95, 998) = 1072.6$, so we conclude that the model does not provide an adequate fit.

Figure 21.2 plots the fitted default probabilities for different durations of the loan, both for the logistic regression model and for the linear regression model. Despite the theoretical shortcomings of the linear probability model, its fitted probabilities remain well between 0 and 1 for the observed range of values, and furthermore, it approximates the logistic curve quite well within this range.

Now, let's look at the interpretation of the coefficient $\hat{\beta}_1$. Unfortunately, it is not as simple as in the linear regression model. There, $\hat{\beta}_1$ indicated the expected change in y when x increased by one unit. Since $\hat{\beta}_1$ is positive, we can first of all conclude that the longer the duration of the loan, the higher the estimated default probability. To give a quantitative interpretation of $\hat{\beta}_1$, we observe that for any value x_j of x, we have

$$\ln(\text{odds}(x_j+1)) - \ln(\text{odds}(x_j)) = \ln\left(\frac{\text{odds}(x_j+1)}{\text{odds}(x_j)}\right) = \hat{\beta}_1.$$

It follows that the *odds ratio*

$$\frac{\text{odds}(x_j+1)}{\text{odds}(x_j)} = e^{\hat{\beta}_1}.$$

We compute

$$e^{\hat{\beta}_1} = e^{0.037538} \approx 1.04.$$

This means that the odds of defaulting increase with about 4% with every extra month of duration of the loan.

As in linear regression, we usually want to include more than one explanatory variable in a logistic regression model. Basically, we just replace

$$\beta_0 + \beta_1 x$$

by

$$\beta_0 + \beta_1 x_1 + \beta_2 x_2 + \cdots + \beta_k x_k$$

in all formulas. So we get, for example,

$$E(y) = \frac{\exp(\beta_0 + \beta_1 x_1 + \beta_2 x_2 + \cdots + \beta_k x_k)}{1 + \exp(\beta_0 + \beta_1 x_1 + \beta_2 x_2 + \cdots + \beta_k x_k)}.$$

As an example of multiple logistic regression, we consider a model with three explanatory variables: amount of the loan (`amount`), duration of the loan (`duration`), and a qualitative variable containing information about the gender and marital status of the applicant (`stat.sex`). We start by fitting the model (see Printout 21.4). The results, with some output omitted, are given in Prinout 21.5.

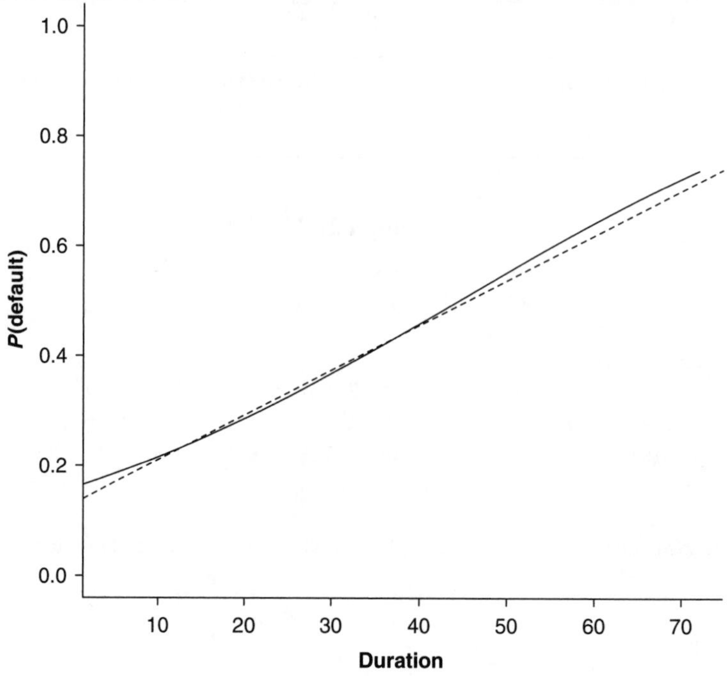

Figure 21.2 Fitted default probabilities of logistic regression (solid) and linear regression (dashed) for different values of duration (in months).

Printout 21.4

```
> german.logreg.mult <- glm(default ~ amount + duration + stat.sex,
                                data=german.dat,family=binomial)
```

The single females are absent in the data, so actually we have four possible values (*levels*) for `stat.sex`. These four values are modeled as three binary attributes (see Printout 21.5). This coding is done automatically in `R` for variables of type *factor*. Indicator variables are created for all levels except the first. From the output, we read that the coefficient of `stat.sex3` is approximately -0.68. We interpret this qualitatively as saying that single males have a lower default probability than divorced/separated males (assuming that `amount` and `duration` are equal). To test whether the model provides an adequate fit, we use the chi-square test on model deviance that we introduced earlier. We read from the `R` output that the model deviance is 1,162.0 on $1000-6=994$ degrees of freedom. Since $\chi^2(0.95, 994) = 1068.5$, we conclude that this model does not provide an adequate fit (at $\alpha = 0.05$) of the data either.

Latent Variable Formulation

We can arrive at the logistic regression model and similar models via another path as well. We discuss this alternative formulation here because it yields additional insights and because it will prove useful in the subsection Nonignorable Selection in Reject Inference.

We view the outcome $(y = 0, 1)$ as a discretization of an underlying regression. We model the

Printout 21.5

```
> summary(german.logreg.mult)

Coefficients:
              Estimate Std. Error z value Pr(>|z|)
(Intercept) -1.296e+00  3.226e-01  -4.016 5.92e-05 ***
amount       2.960e-05  3.121e-05   0.948   0.3430
duration     3.606e-02  7.400e-03   4.872 1.10e-06 ***
stat.sex2   -1.232e-01  3.202e-01  -0.385   0.7003
stat.sex3   -6.830e-01  3.122e-01  -2.188   0.0287 *
stat.sex4   -4.173e-01  3.820e-01  -1.093   0.2746
---
Residual deviance: 1162.0  on 994  degrees of freedom


Personal status and sex                    stat.sex2 stat.sex3 stat.sex4
1 : male, divorced/separated                   0         0         0
2 : female, divorced/separated/married         1         0         0
3 : male, single                               0         1         0
4 : male, married/widowed                      0         0         1
5 : female, single
```

risk score as an unobserved (latent) numeric variable y^*, such that

$$y^* = \beta_0 + \beta_1 x + \varepsilon.$$

We typically assume that ε has a logistic or standard normal distribution. We do not observe the risk score itself but only whether the person defaulted or not. Therefore, our observation is that

$$y = \begin{cases} 1 & \text{if } y^* > 0 \\ 0 & \text{if } y^* \leqslant 0 \end{cases},$$

where a person is assumed to default when his or her risk score is greater than 0.

Now, the probability that $y = 1$ is given by

$$\begin{aligned} \Pr(y=1) &= \Pr(y^* > 0) \\ &= \Pr(\beta_0 + \beta_1 x + \varepsilon > 0) \\ &= \Pr(\varepsilon > -\beta_0 - \beta_1 x). \end{aligned}$$

If the distribution of ε is symmetric with mean 0 (e.g., standard normal or logistic), then

$$\begin{aligned} \Pr(\varepsilon > -\beta_0 - \beta_1 x) &= \Pr(\varepsilon < \beta_0 + \beta_1 x) \\ &= F(\beta_0 + \beta_1 x), \end{aligned}$$

where F is the cumulative distribution function (cdf) of ε.

In the so-called probit model, we assume that $\varepsilon \sim N(0,1)$, where the assumption of unit variance is actually a harmless normalization. To see this, suppose we had assumed instead that $\varepsilon \sim N(0,\sigma^2)$, then

$$\Pr(\varepsilon < \beta_0 + \beta_1 x) = \Pr\left(\frac{\varepsilon}{\sigma} < \frac{\beta_0 + \beta_1 x}{\sigma}\right).$$

Clearly, $\varepsilon/\sigma \sim N(0,1)$, so we can divide β_0 and β_1 by σ and get exactly the same probabilities as the model with unit variance. Since we only observe whether y is 0 or 1 (and not the value of y^* itself), these models cannot be distinguished on the basis of the observed data. In a similar way, we can show that the value of zero for the threshold is also arbitrary if the model contains a constant term β_0.

So for the probit model we have,

$$\Pr(y=1) = \Phi(\beta_0 + \beta_1 x),$$

where $\Phi(\cdot)$ is the standard normal distribution function.

And for the logit model,

$$\Pr(y = 1) = \Lambda(\beta_0 + \beta_1 x) = \frac{e^{\beta_0+\beta_1 x}}{1 + e^{\beta_0+\beta_1 x}},$$

where $\Lambda(\cdot)$ denotes the cumulative logistic distribution function. The probit and logit models are virtually identical; the logistic distribution has somewhat fatter tails than the standard normal distribution. From a computational viewpoint, the logistic distribution has the advantage that its cdf is given by a simple formula, whereas the normal cdf has no closed-form expression.

Model Selection an Model Evaluation

We have shown some examples of how to fit simple linear regression and logistic regression models on the credit data. In the actual practice of building a credit-scoring model from data, we are confronted with the problem that the "correct" model specification is not known to us, and we have to choose from a vast collection of "possible" models. Of course, when a bank has been building such models for a longer period of time, a lot of experience is available, and existing models are updated rather than completely built from scratch. Suppose, however, that we are building a model from scratch. The German data set has 20 attributes, so if we were to try every subset of these 20 attributes as a possible model (assuming that the form of the functional relationship is fixed), we would have to try 2^{20} = a huge number of models. So clearly, exhaustive search (i.e., simply try all models) is out of the question. Typically, heuristic search methods are employed that will usually find good models but not necessarily the best one. We will give an example of such a heuristic search strategy as it is implemented in the `MASS` library of `R`. The algorithm uses a so-called hill-climbing strategy that works as follows:

1. Start with some initial model—for example, the model including all attributes, and compute the score of this model.
2. Look at all neighbors of the current model, and compute the score of each neighbor. Neighbors can, for example, be defined as models having one less or one more attribute than the current model.
3. Move to the neighbor that gives the biggest improvement in score, and make it the current model. If none of the neighbors gives an improvement, stop and select the current model.

We still have to specify how we are going to compute a score for each model. Intuitively, it makes sense to choose some measure of how well the model fits the data. For a regression model, for example, it would make sense to look at the sum of squared errors or, alternatively, the proportion of variance explained by the model as expressed by R^2. For a logistic regression model, which is estimated by maximum likelihood, a comparable measure of fit is given by the value of the likelihood function evaluated at its maximum. Since the likelihood represents the probability of the data given the model, higher values would indicate a better fit. Using only a measure of how well the model fits the data to score models may, however, lead to a phenomenon called *overfitting*. More complex models will always give a better fit of the data that are used to estimate the model, and so the most complex model will always win. However, simpler models may actually give better predictions on data not used to estimate the model: The complex models may have been adapted too much to the peculiarities of the sample, hence the term *overfitting*. There are two basic approaches to try to avoid this problem:

- Compute the model fit on data not used to construct the model and use that to score the models.
- Include some penalty term for model complexity in the scoring function, so more complex models may actually lose if the improvement in fit does not outweigh their extra complexity.

In the first approach, we use part of the data (the training sample) to fit the models and another part (the test sample) to compute the score of the models. Since the test sample was not used to construct the model, a model that has been fitted too much to the peculiarities of the training sample will be "punished" when its score on the test sample is computed. In the second approach, we include some penalty term for model complexity in the scoring function. Several alternative penalized scoring functions have been proposed in the literature, usually having some theoretical justification if we are willing to make certain assumptions. One of these is the Akaike Information Criterion (AIC):

$$\text{AIC}(M) = \mathcal{L}^*(M) - p(M).$$

Here, $\mathcal{L}^*(M)$ is the value of the log-likelihood function for model M evaluated at its maximum, and $p(M)$ is the number of independent parameters of model M. We will perform an example search using the `stepAIC` function from the `MASS` library (Venables & Ripley, 2002). We first load the `MASS` library and then fit a logistic regression model that includes all attributes as explanatory variables (this is the meaning of the dot in the first argument in the call to `glm`). Hence, the model `german.full` is a logistic regression model that includes all attributes. We use this model as the starting point of our search. The function `stepAIC` performs the hill-climbing search described above, where in this case we only consider the removal of single variables in each step. We assign the result of this analysis to the variable `german.step`. The ANOVA component of this object contains a summary of the search process: We see the initial model, the final model, and a table showing which variable was removed in each step. The AIC scores of the models are given in the last column of the table in Printout 21.6, where a slightly different form of AIC is used:

$$\text{AIC}(M) = -2\mathcal{L}^*(M) + 2p(M).$$

This is just the earlier definition multiplied by -2; because of this, lower values are now better. The first term in this sum $(-2\mathcal{L}^*(M))$ is the (residual) deviance, which we used earlier as a test statistic, and is given in the last column but one. In counting the parameters of a model, we should note that a factor with m distinct values counts for $m-1$ parameters, since it is translated to $m-1$ binary variables. Looking at the last row of the table, we conclude that the final model has $(982.4980 - 910.4980)/2 = 36$ parameters.

Table 21.1 Confusion Matrix for the Model Selected With `stepAIC`

	Good	*Bad*	*Total*
Accept	627	143	670
Reject	73	157	230
Total	700	300	1,000

Its residual deviance is 910.5 on $1000 - 36 = 964$ degrees of freedom. The test of model fit we introduced earlier yields $\chi^2(0.95, 964) = 1037.3$, so this time we conclude that the model provides an adequate fit of the data, since the model deviance is smaller than 1,037.3.

The criterion we use to evaluate the selected model may be different from the scoring function we use in model selection. It is, for example, customary to evaluate a classification model on the basis of its error rate—that is, the percentage of cases that are allocated to the wrong class by the model. In a confusion matrix, we tabulate the predicted class against true class. In Table 21.1, we give the confusion matrix for the model selected by our hill climber, where we assign to class good (i.e., accept) if the fitted default probability is smaller than 0.5 and to class bad otherwise. From this table, we calculate that the error rate of the selected model is $(143 + 73)/1000 = 21.6\%$. The error rate achieved by assigning to the majority class is 30%, so the predictive performance of our model does not appear to be spectacular. However, in credit scoring, and in many other applications, error rate is not the most useful evaluation criterion. For one thing, this has to do with the often very skewed distribution of the classes: Typically, the proportion of defaults is very small compared with the proportion of nondefaults. For example, for the case study discussed in Feelders et al. (1995), the proportion of defaults was only about 2.5%. Hence, it is very hard to beat the simple rule "Assign every applicant to the class of nondefaults," in terms of classification accuracy: It would have an accuracy of 97.5% in this case.

A more useful evaluation criterion for credit-scoring models is to determine to what extent the model gets the default probabilities in the correct order. If we order the applicants from low to high (fitted) default probabilities, then ideally, the true

Printout 21.6

```
> library(MASS)
> german.full <- glm(default ~ .,data=german.dat,family=binomial)
> german.step <- stepAIC(german.full)
> german.step$anova
Stepwise Model Path
Analysis of Deviance Table

Initial Model:
default ~ acc.stat + duration + history + purpose + amount +
    savings + empl.since + rate + stat.sex + other + curr.address +
    property + age + plans + housing + num.cred + job + num.prov +
    phone + foreign

Final Model:
default ~ acc.stat + duration + history + purpose + amount +
    savings + rate + stat.sex + other + age + plans + housing +
    phone + foreign


              Step Df   Deviance Resid. Df Resid. Dev      AIC
1                                      951   895.8178 993.8178
2            - job  3 0.73855851       954   896.5563 988.5563
3       - property  3 3.23574958       957   899.7921 985.7921
4   - curr.address  1 0.02024351       958   899.8123 983.8123
5       - num.prov  1 0.99789651       959   900.8102 982.8102
6       - num.cred  1 1.99124290       960   902.8015 982.8015
7     - empl.since  4 7.69651997       964   910.4980 982.4980
```

defaults will all be at the bottom of the list (i.e., they will have the highest fitted default probabilities), and the nondefaults will be ranked above this group. If this were the case, there would be some "cutoff" default probability we could use to completely separate the defaults from the nondefaults. Of course, this ideal situation does not occur in practice, but we can measure to what extent the model gets the applicants in the right order. A popular method to do this goes by the name of ROC (receiver operator characteristic) analysis. We order the applicants from low to high probability of default, according to our model. Then, we compute for different cutoff probabilities the fraction of the defaults that would be accepted at this cutoff (this is called the false-positive rate in the ROC jargon) and the fraction of the nondefaults that would be accepted (called true-positive rate). A plot in which the false-positive rate is plotted on the x-axis against the true-positive rate on the y-axis is called an ROC curve. We can calculate one point on the ROC curve from the confusion matrix given in Table 21.1. This is the point on the curve that corresponds to a cutoff probability of 0.5. The false-positive rate at this point is $143/300 \approx 0.47$, and the true-positive rate is $627/700 \approx 0.90$.

The random model is represented by the line $y = x$: If we randomly accept applicants, then we tend to accept defaults and nondefaults in their population proportions. So, for example, for the German Credit data, 30% of the accepted applicants would be defaults, and 70% would be nondefaults, and the true-positive rate would always be equal to the false-positive rate. So at the point where the random model has a false-positive rate of 0.47, it would also have a true-positive rate of 0.47. A better model would of course accept a

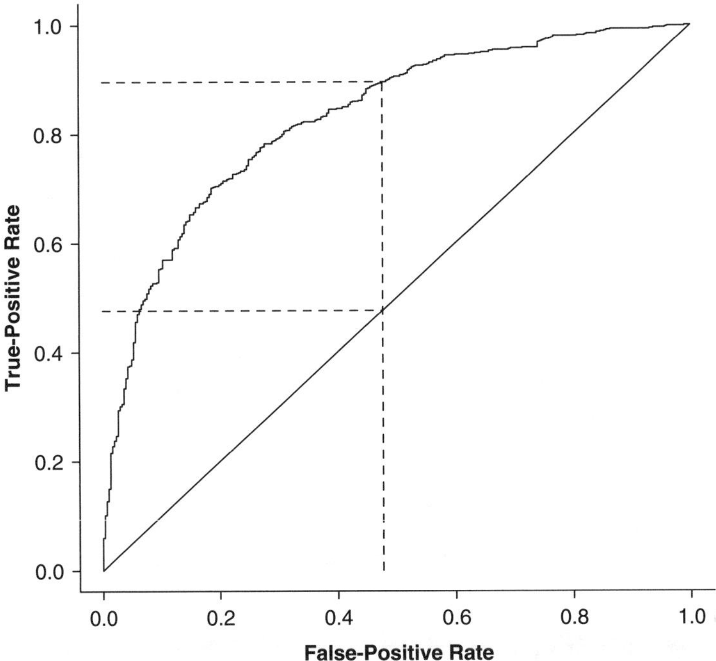

Figure 21.3 ROC curve for model found with stepwise search (area under the curve [AUC] = 82.8%).

bigger percentage of the nondefaults at this point and so should be represented by a point above the line $y = x$. As we already calculated from the confusion matrix in Table 21.1, and as can be read from the graph in Figure 21.3, our selected model has a true-positive rate of 0.9 at this point. The "perfect" model, which has all nondefaults ordered before all defaults, will have true-positive rate of 1 when the false-positive rate is still 0, and so its ROC curve will go straight from the origin to the point (0,1) (e.g., see the left curve in Figure 21.4). As an overall measure of performance of a model, we can look at the true-positive rate at different false-positive rates, where points high above the line $y = x$ are good. This can be summarized by one number: the area under the curve (AUC). The ideal model has area 1, and the random model has area 0.5. The values closer to 1 are better.

In the previous analysis, we used a scoring measure (AIC) during model selection that was different from the measure used to evaluate the final model (AUC). One is tempted to ask the following question: If AUC is really what we are interested in, then why not use it as a scoring function for model selection as well? This is indeed possible, although it requires some more computation, since for each model we consider, we have to sort the data on fitted default probabilities and compute the area under the curve. The parameter values for each model would still be chosen by maximum likelihood, however, even in this scenario. If we were to choose this approach, we should again guard against overfitting—for example, by computing the AUC on an independent test sample. To illustrate why, we consider an extreme example where we fit a model that includes not only all attributes but also all possible interactions between pairs of attributes. The model is fitted on two thirds of the German data; that is, the training sample contains 667 out of the 1,000 observations. The remaining 333 points are used as an independent test sample. The plots in Figure 21.4 give the ROC curve of the fitted model on the training sample (left) and test sample (right). The

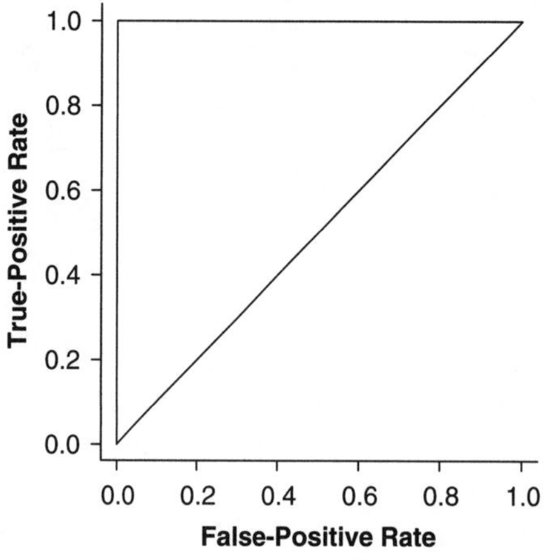

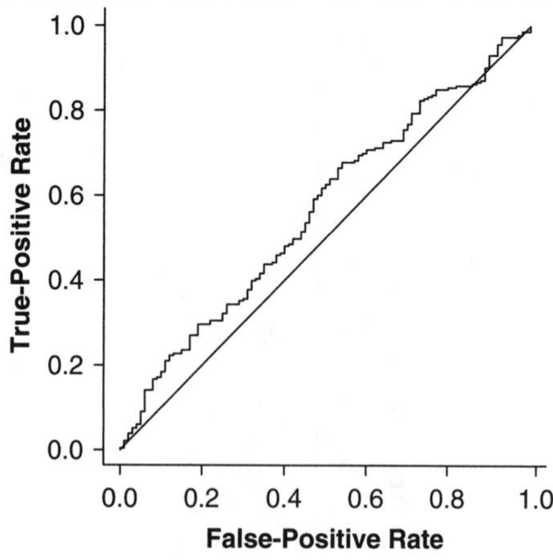

Figure 21.4 In-sample (left; AUC = 100%) and out-of-sample (right; AUC = 56.5%) ROC curves for the model that includes all attributes and all interactions between pairs of attributes as predictors.

in-sample curve suggests that we have the perfect model, with AUC = 1. The out-of-sample curve shows that we have fallen prey to overfitting: The out-of-sample AUC is only 0.56, so in fact this is an inferior model.

Reject Inference

As repayment behavior of rejects is for obvious reasons not observed, complete data are available only for accepted applicants. Since the creditor presumably does not accept applicants at random, this constitutes a nonrandom sample from the population of applicants. Construction of a new decision rule based on accepted applicants only may therefore lead to incorrect results. In particular, one should be careful in using such a rule to assess the default risk of rejected applicants. This is, in a nutshell, what is called the *reject inference* problem in the credit-scoring literature.

To structure the following discussion, we distinguish between the *selection mechanism* that determines whether an applicant is rejected or accepted by the creditor and the *outcome mechanism* that determines the response (good or bad loan) of the applicant. We also refer to selection as the *missing-data mechanism*, since it determines for which applicants the outcome is observed. In credit scoring, the primary objective is to model the outcome mechanism. The creditor is interested in using historical data to learn an updated rule that can be used to make acceptance decisions for new applicants.

The class label y is observed for the accepted applicants but is missing for the rejected applicants. We assume that $y \in \{0, 1\}$, with the convention that a bad loan is labeled 0 and a good loan is labeled 1. (Note that this coding is different from the one we introduced in the section Formal Statement of the Problem; which class is labeled 0 and which is labeled 1 is, of course, completely arbitrary.) Furthermore, we define an auxiliary variable a, with $a = 1$ if the applicant is accepted and $a = 0$ if the applicant is rejected. Note that y is observed if $a = 1$ and missing if $a = 0$. The structure of the observed data is given in Table 21.2.

Following the analysis of Manski (1995), we write the distribution of the outcome as

$$\Pr(y \mid \mathbf{x}) = \Pr(y \mid \mathbf{x}, a = 1)\Pr(a = 1 \mid \mathbf{x}) + \Pr(y \mid \mathbf{x}, a = 0)\Pr(a = 0 \mid \mathbf{x}).$$

Note that the sampling process identifies the acceptance/rejection probability $\Pr(a \mid \mathbf{x})$ and the outcome conditional on acceptance $\Pr(y \mid \mathbf{x}, a = 1)$ but is uninformative on the outcome conditional on rejection $\Pr(y \mid \mathbf{x}, a = 0)$.

Table 21.2 Structure of Loan Application Data

x_1	x_2	$\ldots$	x_k	a	y
				1	
				1	
				1	
				1	
				1	
				0	
				0	
				0	
				0	
				0	

One way to identify $\Pr(y \mid \mathbf{x}, a = 0)$ is to assume that

$$\begin{aligned}\Pr(y = 1 \mid \mathbf{x}, a = 1) &= \Pr(y = 1 \mid \mathbf{x}, a = 0)\\ &= \Pr(y = 1 \mid \mathbf{x}).\end{aligned}$$

Now, $\Pr(y \mid \mathbf{x})$ coincides with the observable distribution $\Pr(y \mid \mathbf{x}, a = 1)$. Hence, we can use $\Pr(y = 1 \mid \mathbf{x}, a = 1)$ to estimate $\Pr(y = 1 \mid \mathbf{x})$. Since $y \perp\!\!\!\perp a \mid \mathbf{x}$, it follows that

$$\Pr(a = 1 \mid \mathbf{x}, y) = \Pr(a = 1 \mid \mathbf{x}). \qquad (21.9)$$

That is, acceptance depends on $\mathbf{x}$, but conditional on $\mathbf{x}$ does not depend on y. This is to say that the class label is missing at random (MAR), in the terminology of Little and Rubin (2002). This situation frequently occurs in practice, since many creditors nowadays use a formal selection model. In that case, y is observed only if some function g of variables occurring in $\mathbf{x}$ exceeds a threshold value, say $g(\mathbf{x}) \geqslant c$, where c is some constant (the cutoff value).

The missing-data mechanism is also called *ignorable*, because there is no need to include it in the model in case we are only interested in the outcome mechanism (there is a technical distinction between MAR and ignorability, but they may be treated as equivalent conditions for all practical purposes).

If MAR does not apply—that is, $y \not\!\perp\!\!\!\perp a \mid \mathbf{x}$, the missing-data mechanism is called *nonignorable*. In that case, the missing-data mechanism must be included in the model to get good estimates of the parameters of the outcome mechanism. In the following sections, we discuss ignorable and nonignorable cases.

Ignorable Selection

In this section, we assume that the acceptance/rejection decision depends only on the observed attributes of the applicant, recorded in the feature vector $\mathbf{x} = (x_1, \ldots, x_k)$. We are interested in modeling the outcome mechanism—that is, the dependence of the probability of a good loan on feature vector $\mathbf{x}$. We write,

$$\Pr(y = 1|\mathbf{x}) = 1 - \Pr(y = 0|\mathbf{x}) = f(\mathbf{x}).$$

The goal of a classification procedure is to produce an estimate $\hat{f}(\mathbf{x})$ of $f(\mathbf{x})$ at every point in the feature space.

If the selection mechanism is deterministic—that is, the probability of acceptance is either 0 or 1 (depending on $\mathbf{x}$)—then we have to *extrapolate* into the reject region. This means that we can't learn anything about $f(\mathbf{x})$ for $\mathbf{x}$ in the reject region unless we are willing to make global parametric assumptions. Only in that case can we infer something about $f(\mathbf{x})$ for $\mathbf{x}$ in the reject region from data in the accept region.

There are two basic approaches to producing such an estimate, sometimes called *function estimation* and *density estimation* (Friedman, 1997). We give a short description of the two approaches because, as noted by Hand and Henley (1994), they have quite different implications for handling reject inference.

Function Estimation

We have discussed the techniques for building credit-scoring models in the sections Linear Regression and Logistic Regression. These are examples of what is sometimes called the function estimation approach to building classification models. In the function estimation setting, one only models the *conditional* distribution of y given $\mathbf{x}$. For binary classification problems, we may write, in general,

$$y \sim B(1, f(\mathbf{x})).$$

That is, y is a Bernoulli random variable with "probability of success" $f(\mathbf{x})$. The goal is to obtain an estimate $\hat{f}(\mathbf{x}|T)$ using training set T.

It is important to note that no assumptions are made concerning the probability distribution of $\mathbf{x}$. Under the MAR assumption, at any particular point $\mathbf{x}$, the distribution of the observed y is the same as the distribution of the missing y. Clearly then, using a function estimation technique on just the accepted loans (complete case analysis) yields unbiased estimates of $\Pr(y = 1|\mathbf{x})$ (provided of course that the functional form of f has been specified correctly).

Furthermore, we observe that the rejects do not provide any information concerning $\Pr(y = 1|\mathbf{x})$, so it is useless to include them in the estimation process. This is quite clear if we consider the contribution of the different observations to the likelihood function. Under the usual assumption that observations are independent, the likelihood L of n observations is simply $L = \prod_{j=1}^{n} L_j$, with

$$L_j = \begin{cases} \Pr(y = i \mid \mathbf{x}_j) & \text{if } y_j = i \ (i = 0, 1) \\ \sum_{i=0}^{1} \Pr(y = i \mid \mathbf{x}_j) & \text{if } y_j \text{ is missing,} \end{cases}$$

where we obtain the marginal probability of an incomplete observation by summing over the possible values of the missing variable y. Clearly, if y_j is missing, it contributes a factor 1 to the likelihood, leaving it unchanged. Thus, including the rejects results in the same likelihood as ignoring them altogether.

Density Estimation

An alternative paradigm for estimating $f(\mathbf{x})$ in the classification setting is based on density estimation. Here, Bayes's theorem,

$$f(\mathbf{x}) = \frac{\pi_1 p_1(\mathbf{x})}{\pi_0 p_0(\mathbf{x}) + \pi_1 p_1(\mathbf{x})}, \tag{21.10}$$

is applied, where $p_i(\mathbf{x}) = p(\mathbf{x}|y = i)$ are the class-conditional probability density functions and $\pi_i = \Pr(y = i)$ are the unconditional ("prior") probabilities of each class. The training data are partitioned into subsets $T = \{T_0, T_1\}$ with the same class label. The data in each subset are separately used to produce estimates $\hat{p}_i(\mathbf{x}|T_i)$ of the class-conditional densities. The prior probabilities π_i are usually estimated by $\hat{\pi}_i = n_i/n$, where n_i is the number of observations from class i. These estimates are plugged into (21.10) to obtain an estimate $\hat{f}(\mathbf{x}|T)$. Examples of this approach are linear and quadratic discriminant analysis (McLachlan, 1992).

Now, let $T^{\mathrm{A}} = \{T_0{}^{\mathrm{A}}, T_1{}^{\mathrm{A}}\}$ denote the training data of the accepted loans. Because the sampling fraction depends on $\mathbf{x}$, $\hat{p}_i(\mathbf{x}|T_i{}^{\mathrm{A}})$ is distorted, and if the probability of a bad loan depends (as we hope) on $\mathbf{x}$, then $\hat{\pi}_i|T^{\mathrm{A}}$ is biased as well (Avery, 1981).

To illustrate these effects, we consider a simple example where selection is based on a single variable x. Suppose that within the class of bad loans, x follows a normal distribution; that is, $p_0(x)$ is $N(\mu, \sigma^2)$. If we accept all applicants with $x > b$, then

$$E[x|x > b] = \mu + \sigma\lambda(\alpha),$$

where $\alpha = (b - \mu)/\sigma$, and

$$\lambda(\alpha) = \frac{\phi(\alpha)}{1 - \Phi(\alpha)}$$

is called the inverse Mills ratio or hazard function for the distribution (Greene, 1993). In this expression, $\phi(\cdot)$ denotes the standard normal density function, and $\Phi(\cdot)$ the standard normal cdf. For the variance of the truncated variable, we get

$$\mathrm{Var}[x|x > b] = \sigma^2(1 - \delta(\alpha)),$$

where $\delta(\alpha) = \lambda(\alpha)(\lambda(\alpha) - \alpha)$.

As an illustrative example, suppose $p_0(x) = N(2, 1)$ and $p_1(x) = N(6, 1)$, $\pi_0 = \pi_1 = 1/2$, and suppose an applicant is accepted if $x > 3$ (i.e., $b = 3$). Then, $E[x_0|x_0 > 3] \approx 3.53$ and $E[x_1|x_1 > 3] \approx 6.00$. Likewise, $\mathrm{Var}[x_0|x_0 > 3] \approx 0.2$ and $\mathrm{Var}[x_1|x_1 > 3] \approx 0.99$. See Figure 21.5 for the truncated densities.

We observe that the distribution of the bads is extremely distorted by the truncation: The mean has increased from 2 to 3.53, whereas the variance has decreased from 1 to 0.2. On the other hand, the distribution of the goods is hardly affected since only a small proportion of the goods is rejected. Furthermore, conditional on $x > 3$, we have $\pi_0 \approx 0.14$ and $\pi_1 \approx 0.86$; that is, the proportion of good loans in the population is of course overestimated if the selection mechanism is any good.

How do all these distortions influence the estimated probability of a good loan? On the basis of the true distributions, we would compute

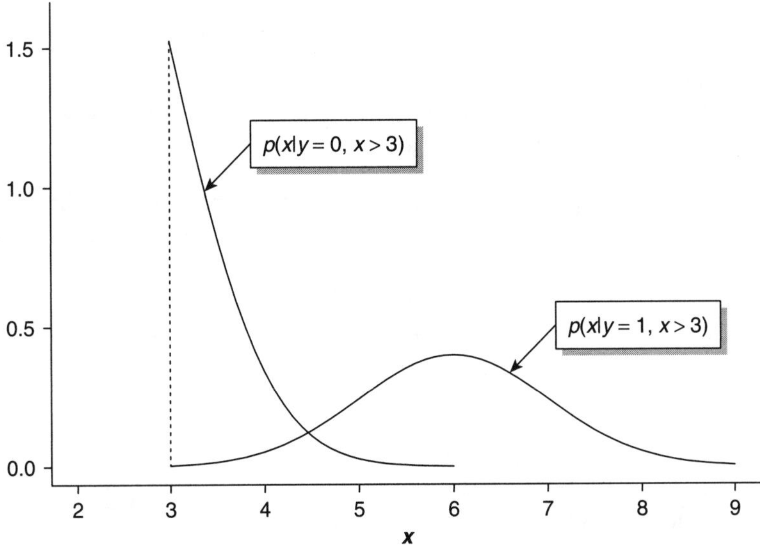

Figure 21.5 Truncated normal distributions of accepted bad loans ($y = 0$) and accepted good loans ($y = 1$).

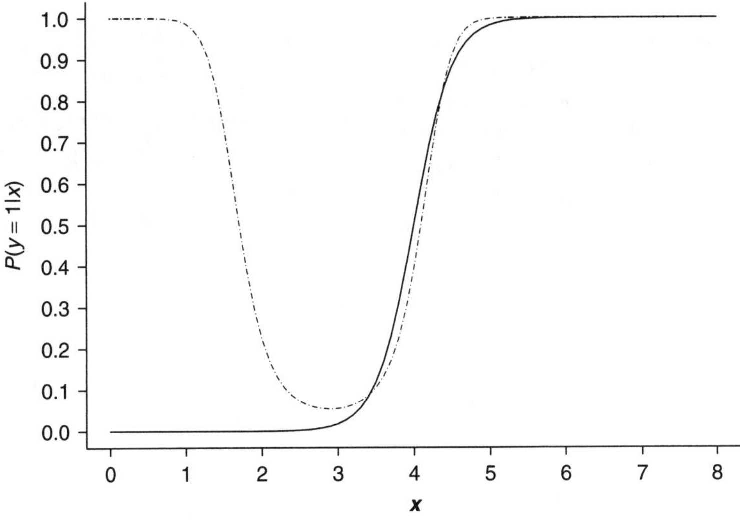

Figure 21.6 $P(y = 1|x)$ for true distribution (solid line) and truncated distribution (dashed line).

the probability of a good loan at $x = 4$ (using Bayes's theorem) to be 0.5; using a normal model but based on the mean and variance after truncation, we compute a probability of 0.39. In Figure 21.6, we show the computed probability of a good loan at different values of x on the basis of the true distribution (solid line) and the normal distribution with mean and variance after truncation (dashed line). We can see that the truncated version is way off in the reject region ($x < 3$), whereas it is reasonably close in the accept region ($x > 3$). It is, however, very hard to draw any general conclusions concerning the bias caused by truncation since this, of course, critically depends on the parameters of the true distributions as well as the selection rule.

There are, however, ways to avoid this bias, by including the rejected applicants in the estimation process. A straightforward way to do this is by using a mixture distribution formulation of the problem. Mixture distributions (Everitt & Hand, 1981) are distributions that can be expressed as "weighted averages" of a number of component distributions. In general, a finite mixture can be written as

$$p(\mathbf{x}) = \sum_{i=1}^{c} \pi_i p_i(\mathbf{x};\boldsymbol{\theta}_i), \tag{21.11}$$

where c the number of components, π_i is the mixing proportions, and $\boldsymbol{\theta}_i$ the component parameter vectors. Henceforth, we assume that the number of components equals the relevant number of classes, so each component models a class-conditional distribution. For the credit-scoring problem, all observations are assumed to be drawn from the two-component mixture

$$p(\mathbf{x}) = \pi_0 p_0(\mathbf{x};\boldsymbol{\theta}_0) + \pi_1 p_1(\mathbf{x};\boldsymbol{\theta}_1), \tag{21.12}$$

where the component from which an observation was drawn is known for the accepted loans but unknown for the rejected loans. We consider the contribution to the likelihood of cases with y observed (component known) and y missing (component unknown):

$$L_j = \begin{cases} \pi_i p_i(\mathbf{x}_j) & \text{if } y_j = i \ (i = 0,1) \\ p(\mathbf{x}_j) = \sum_{i=0}^{1} \pi_i p_i(\mathbf{x}_j) & \text{if } y_j \text{ is missing.} \end{cases}$$

If there are m rejected loans and n accepted loans, the observed-data likelihood may be written as

$$L_{\text{obs}}(\boldsymbol{\Psi}) = \prod_{j=1}^{m} \left\{ \sum_{i=0}^{1} \pi_i p_i(\mathbf{x}_j;\boldsymbol{\theta}_i) \right\} \prod_{j=m+1}^{m+n} \left\{ \sum_{i=0}^{1} z_{ij} \pi_i p_i(\mathbf{x}_j;\boldsymbol{\theta}_i) \right\},$$

where $\boldsymbol{\Psi} = (\boldsymbol{\pi},\boldsymbol{\theta})$ denotes the vector of all unknown parameters and z_{ij} equals 1 if observation j has class label i and 0 otherwise.

For computational convenience, one often considers the log-likelihood $\mathcal{L}_{\text{obs}} = \log L_{\text{obs}}$.

$$\mathcal{L}_{\text{obs}}(\boldsymbol{\Psi}) = \sum_{j=1}^{m} \log \left\{ \sum_{i=0}^{1} \pi_i p_i(\mathbf{x}_j;\boldsymbol{\theta}_i) \right\} + \sum_{j=m+1}^{m+n} \sum_{i=0}^{1} z_{ij} \log(\pi_i p_i(\mathbf{x}_j;\boldsymbol{\theta}_i)).$$

In general, this tends to be a rather complicated function of $\boldsymbol{\Psi}$, and finding maximum likelihood estimates may require special computational algorithms. One can use the expectation-maximization (EM) algorithm of Dempster, Laird, and Rubin (1977) for this purpose. The general strategy is based on optimizing the complete-data log-likelihood

$$Q(\boldsymbol{\Psi} \mid \boldsymbol{\Psi}^{(t)}) = \sum_{j=1}^{m+n} \sum_{i=1}^{c} z_{ij}^{(t)} \log(\pi_i p_i(\mathbf{x}_j;\boldsymbol{\theta}_i))$$

by repeated application of the E step and M step until convergence of the parameter estimates. In the first E step, one uses some initial estimate $\boldsymbol{\Psi}^{(0)}$, to calculate the expectation of the complete-data log-likelihood. For the problem under consideration, this can be done by calculating the posterior probabilities of group membership for the unclassified cases and entering these as values of $z_{ij}^{(0)}$ in the complete-data log-likelihood. In the M step, the algorithm chooses $\boldsymbol{\Psi}^{(t+1)}$, which maximizes the complete-data log-likelihood that was formed in the last E step. In case of normal components, one can find closed-form solutions for the M step (McLachlan & Basford, 1988). The E and M steps are alternated repeatedly until convergence. It has been shown that under very weak conditions, this algorithm will yield a local maximum of the likelihood $\mathcal{L}_{\text{obs}}$ of the observed data. For a more detailed and rigorous account of the application of EM to this problem, the reader is referred to McLachlan (1992, pp. 39–43).

Function Estimation or Density Estimation?

We have discussed two methods that are applicable in the case of ignorable missing data. Which, if any, is to be preferred?

The attractive property of the function estimation approach is that we can use a standard method of analysis—for example, logistic regression—using just the accepted cases. The downside is that this is not fully efficient, since not all information can be used: The information on the rejected applicants is ignored.

A density-based approach allows the use of information available in the rejects but requires more complicated computational techniques. Furthermore, one has to specify an appropriate probability model for the component distributions. As remarked by Hand and Henley (1993), credit-scoring problems tend to contain many discrete variables and nonnormal marginal distributions (see, e.g., the German Credit data set discussed in the section The Data). An interesting alternative might be to use the general location model (Schafer, 1997), which allows for the occurrence of discrete variables but is still based on normality for the continuous part. Feelders, Chang, and McLachlan (1998) discuss a method for modeling nonnormal distributions, based on modeling the *class-conditional* distributions as mixtures as well. They show how the evidently nonnormal distributions of a number of financial ratios can be modeled as mixtures of two normal components. Unfortunately, this resulted in only a marginal improvement in classification accuracy.

Feelders (1999) performs a small simulation study to compare the function estimation and density estimation approach with reject inference. The data were drawn from two normal distributions, one for each class, with different means and covariance matrices. Hence, the optimal classification rule is a quadratic function of the input variables. Then, selection was performed by taking a linear combination of the variables and rejecting all cases with a score below a certain cutoff level for this linear combination. Subsequently, models were fitted using a density estimation approach (quadratic discriminant analysis) and using a function estimation approach (quadratic logistic regression). To estimate the quadratic discriminant function with the EM algorithm, the attribute values of the rejected applicants (but not their class labels) were included in the training sample. In estimating the quadratic logistic regression model, the rejects were excluded from the training sample, since it has no use for them anyway. The experiments indicate that for moderate sample size, the classification accuracy on an independent test sample of the density-based approach is better, especially in the reject region. As the sample size gets larger, the bias component of prediction error becomes dominant over the variance component. Since the correct specification was used for both models, the difference in predictive performance disappeared as the sample size increased. If we analyze real credit data, the correct model specification is obviously not known, and the behavior could be quite different from the behavior observed in this simulation study.

Nonignorable Selection

Recall that the distribution of the outcome can be written as

$$\Pr(y \mid \mathbf{x}) = \Pr(y \mid \mathbf{x}, a=1)\Pr(a=1 \mid \mathbf{x}) + \Pr(y \mid \mathbf{x}, a=0)\Pr(a=0 \mid \mathbf{x}).$$

In some cases, the ignorability assumption $y \perp\!\!\!\perp a \mid \mathbf{x}$ is not warranted. This typically occurs when acceptance is partly based on characteristics that are not recorded in $\mathbf{x}$—for example, the "general impression" that the loan officer has of the applicant. It may also occur when a formal selection model is used but is sometimes overruled by a loan officer on the basis of characteristics that are not recorded in $\mathbf{x}$. If these other (unobserved) characteristics have an additional influence on y, then

$$\Pr(y=1 \mid \mathbf{x}, a=1) \neq \Pr(y=1 \mid \mathbf{x}, a=0). \tag{21.13}$$

That is, at any particular $\mathbf{x}$, the distribution of the observed y differs from the distribution of the missing y. What can we do in this case?

Without making any assumptions, we can compute bounds on $\Pr(y=1 \mid \mathbf{x})$ as follows:

$$\Pr(y=1 \mid \mathbf{x}, a=1)\Pr(a=1 \mid \mathbf{x}) \quad (21.14)$$
$$\leqslant \Pr(y=1 \mid \mathbf{x}) \quad (21.15)$$
$$\leqslant \Pr(y=1 \mid \mathbf{x}, a=1)\Pr(a=1 \mid \mathbf{x}) + \Pr(a=0 \mid \mathbf{x}). \quad (21.16)$$

The expression in (21.14) is equivalent to $\Pr(y=1, a=1|\mathbf{x})$, which is obviously not larger than $\Pr(y=1|\mathbf{x})$. Expression (21.15) can be written as $\Pr(y=1,a=1|\mathbf{x})+\Pr(y=1,a=0|\mathbf{x})$, which can clearly not have a larger value than (21.16).

The reader should note that in discussing these bounds, we reason as if we knew the true probabilities. Of course, these have to be estimated from data, and any additional uncertainty due to sampling and model specification uncertainty should be taken into account. The lower bound (21.14) corresponds to the case that all rejected loans at $\mathbf{x}$ are bad and the upper bound (21.16) to the case that they are all good. The width of the interval is equal to the rejection probability at $\mathbf{x}$. Suppose for example that the current scoring model has a "gray zone," where an override of the rejection is allowed. Suppose such an override at some point $\mathbf{x}$ occurs in 60% of the cases; that is, $\Pr(a=1 \mid \mathbf{x}) = 0.6$. Suppose, furthermore, that 80% of the accepted loans turn out to be good loans; that is, $\Pr(y=1 \mid \mathbf{x}, a=1) = 0.8$. Then, all we can say is that $\Pr(y=1 \mid \mathbf{x}) \in [0.48, 0.88]$. This interval is too wide to be helpful. We could tighten the upper bound somewhat by assuming that

$$\Pr(y=1 \mid \mathbf{x}, a=0) \leqslant \Pr(y=1 \mid \mathbf{x}, a=1).$$

This seems like a reasonable assumption if the loan officers have any idea what they are doing. Then, the upper bound on $\Pr(y=1|\mathbf{x})$ becomes

$$\begin{aligned}
&\Pr(y=1|\mathbf{x}) \\
&= \Pr(y=1,a=1|\mathbf{x}) + \Pr(y=1,a=0|\mathbf{x}) \\
&= \Pr(y=1|\mathbf{x},a=1)\Pr(a=1|\mathbf{x}) \\
&\quad + \Pr(y=1|\mathbf{x},a=0)\Pr(a=0|\mathbf{x}) \\
&\leqslant \Pr(y=1|\mathbf{x},a=1)\Pr(a=1|\mathbf{x}) \\
&\quad + \Pr(y=1|\mathbf{x},a=1)\Pr(a=0|\mathbf{x}) \\
&= \Pr(y=1|\mathbf{x},a=1),
\end{aligned}$$

since $\Pr(a=1|\mathbf{x}) + \Pr(a=0|\mathbf{x}) = 1$. So $\Pr(y=1 \mid \mathbf{x}) \in [0.48, 0.80]$. This still doesn't help very much. Unless we have some additional information to tighten the bounds, this approach to the problem doesn't seem very fruitful.

Another approach is to make some "heroic" assumptions to get the model identified. The most popular model from this group is the bivariate probit model with sample selection. This model consists of two probit equations (see the section Latent Variable Formulation), one for the selection mechanism (i.e., the accept/reject decision) and one for the outcome (good/bad loan):

$$a_i^* = \mathbf{x}_i\alpha + \varepsilon_i \quad (21.17)$$

$$y_i^* = \mathbf{x}_i\beta + \upsilon_i \quad \text{for } i = 1,2,\ldots,n. \quad (21.18)$$

In these equations, a_i^* and y_i^* are unobserved numeric variables, as discussed in the section Latent Variable Formulation. The binary variable a_i takes the value 1 if the loan was accepted and 0 if the application was rejected:

$$a_i = \begin{cases} 0 & \text{if loan rejected } (a_i^* < 0) \\ 1 & \text{if loan accepted } (a_i^* \geqslant 0). \end{cases}$$

Likewise, the binary variable y_i takes the value 0 if the loan is classified as bad and the value 1 otherwise:

$$y_i = \begin{cases} 0 & \text{if bad loan } (y_i^* < 0) \\ 1 & \text{if good loan } (y_i^* \geqslant 0). \end{cases}$$

Furthermore, y_i is only observed if $a_i = 1$.

The disturbances are assumed to be bivariate normally distributed:

$$\begin{pmatrix} \varepsilon_i \\ \upsilon_i \end{pmatrix} \sim N(\mu, \Sigma),\ \mu = \begin{pmatrix} 0 \\ 0 \end{pmatrix},\ \Sigma = \begin{pmatrix} 1 & \rho \\ \rho & 1 \end{pmatrix}.$$

According to this model, there are three types of observations, rejected loans, accepted bad loans, and accepted good loans, with respective probabilities:

$$\begin{aligned}
a=0 &: \Pr(a=0) = 1 - \Phi(\mathbf{x}\alpha), \\
a=1, y=0 &: \Pr(a=1, y=0) \\
&\qquad = \Phi(\mathbf{x}\alpha) - \Phi_2(\mathbf{x}\alpha, \mathbf{x}\beta; \rho), \\
a=1, y=1 &: \Pr(a=1, y=1) \\
&\qquad = \Phi_2(\mathbf{x}\alpha, \mathbf{x}\beta; \rho), \quad (21.19)
\end{aligned}$$

where $\Phi(\cdot)$ represents the univariate standard normal cdf and $\Phi_2(\cdot,\cdot;\rho)$ the bivariate standard normal cdf with correlation coefficient ρ.

The appropriate log-likelihood function is readily derived from (21.19):

$$\begin{aligned}\mathcal{L}(\alpha,\beta,\rho) \\ &= \sum_{i=1}^{n}\{(1-a_i)\ln(1-\Phi(\mathbf{x}_i\alpha)) \\ &\quad + a_i(1-y_i)\ln(\Phi(\mathbf{x}_i\alpha)-\Phi_2(\mathbf{x}_i\alpha,\mathbf{x}_i\beta;\rho)) \\ &\quad + a_iy_i\ln\Phi_2(\mathbf{x}_i\alpha,\mathbf{x}_i\beta;\rho)\}.\end{aligned}$$

As shown by Meng and Schmidt (1985), this model is identified, except for some pathological cases, and can be estimated with maximum likelihood.

The correlation coefficient of the disturbances provides the link between the two equations. If this is the correct specification (a big if), and $\rho = 0$, then we are back to

$$\Pr(y=1 \mid \mathbf{x}, a=1) = \Pr(y=1 \mid \mathbf{x}, a=0),$$

and the selection mechanism is ignorable after all. On the other hand, if $\rho > 0$, then

$$\Pr(y=1 \mid \mathbf{x}, a=1) > \Pr(y=1 \mid \mathbf{x}, a=0).$$

That is, at a fixed point $\mathbf{x}$, the probability of a good loan is *higher* among the accepts than among the rejects. This is what you would expect when the decision of the model is overruled by loan officers for "good reasons" that are, however, not recorded in $\mathbf{x}$. Finally, if $\rho < 0$, then

$$\Pr(y=1 \mid \mathbf{x}, a=1) < \Pr(y=1 \mid \mathbf{x}, a=0).$$

That is, at a fixed point $\mathbf{x}$, the probability of a good loan is *lower* among the accepts than among the rejects.

Somewhat surprisingly perhaps, Jacobson and Roszbach (1998), Boyes, Hoffman, and Low (1989), and Greene (1998) found *negative* values for ρ of -0.9234, -0.353, and -0.1178, respectively.[1] Jacobson and Roszbach (1998) conclude that the bank involved does not appear to be minimizing the default risk. This follows not only from the negative correlation found but also from the fact that many of the variables that make the bank approve loans are not among those that reduce the probability of default (i.e., these are significant in the selection equation but not in the default equation, or they appear with opposite signs). Boyes et al. (1989) make similar observations and explain these findings by the hypothesis that the bank follows a lending policy where they pick out loans with higher default risk because they have higher returns due to the size of the loan. The findings of Jacobson and Roszbach (1998) contradict this hypothesis because they find that the size of the loan does not affect default risk. They come to the conclusion that the results bear evidence of a lending institution that has *attempted* to minimize default risk or maximize a simple return function but without success.

The ultimate question from a practical viewpoint is whether modeling the selection mechanism leads to a better default equation in terms of predictive accuracy. Unfortunately, this question is hard to answer with real credit data because the true class label of the rejected applicants is unknown. Neither of the studies by Jacobson and Roszbach (1998), Boyes et al. (1989), and Greene (1998) attempted to answer this question. Thomas, Banasik, and Crook (2003) report on a study that did compare the predictive performance of the single equation model and the bivariate probit model. They conclude that the adoption of a bivariate probit model only marginally improves predictive performance. Apart from this lack of empirical success, the bivariate probit model has serious theoretical shortcomings. The model outcomes are highly sensitive to an unverifiable normality assumption (see Little & Rubin, 2002, sec. 15.4).

Summary

We have provided an introduction to the use of probabilistic and statistical methods for the construction of credit-scoring models from data. Such models attempt to estimate the default probabilities of loan applicants using information on the applicant such as income, occupation, and other relevant characteristics. We have briefly

[1] The correlations reported in Boyes et al. (1989) and Greene (1998) are in fact positive, but the value of y was defined the other way around—that is, 1 for a bad loan and 0 for a good loan.

discussed the problems of estimating a given model from data, selecting a model from a large set of possibilities, and evaluation of the selected model. In the second part of the chapter, we have given an overview of the problem of reject inference in credit scoring. The conclusion must be that it is fundamentally a data problem: The sampling mechanism does not yield the appropriate data for the question we wish to answer. Researchers have attempted to compensate for this data inadequacy by introducing largely unverifiable assumptions. The empirical success of these approaches has been negligible. We are convinced that the only way to solve the reject inference problem is to make it go away by collecting data from the reject region in a controlled manner.

REFERENCES

Avery, R. B. (1981). *Credit scoring models with discriminant analysis and truncated samples* (Research Papers in Banking and Financial Economics No. 54). Washington, DC: Board of Governors of the Federal Reserve System.

Boyes, W. J., Hoffman, D. L., & Low, S. A. (1989). An econometric analysis of the bank credit scoring problem. *Journal of Econometrics, 40*, 3–14.

Dempster, A. P., Laird, N. M., & Rubin, D. B. (1977). Maximum likelihood from incomplete data via the EM algorithm. *Journal of the Royal Statistical Society Series B, 39*, 1–38.

Everitt, B. S., & Hand, D. J. (1981). *Finite mixture distributions*. London: Chapman & Hall.

Feelders, A. J. (1999). Credit scoring and reject inference with mixture models. *International Journal of Intelligent Systems in Accounting, Finance and Management, 8*, 271–279.

Feelders, A. J., Chang, S., & McLachlan, G. J. (1998). Mining in the presence of selectivity bias and its application to reject inference. In R. Agrawal, P. Stolorz, & G. Piatetsky Shapiro (Eds.), *Proceedings of the fourth international conference on knowledge discovery and data mining (KDD-98)* (pp. 199–203). Menlo Park, CA: AAAI Press.

Feelders, A. J., le Loux, A. J. F., & van't Zand, J. W. (1995). Data mining for loan evaluation at ABN AMRO: A case study. In U. M. Fayyad & R. Uthurusamy (Eds.), *Proceedings of the first international conference on knowledge discovery and data mining (KDD-95)* (pp. 106–111). Menlo Park, CA: AAAI Press.

Friedman, J. H. (1997). On bias, variance, 0/1-loss, and the curse-of-dimensionality. *Data Mining and Knowledge Discovery, 1*(1), 55–77.

Greene, W. H. (1993). *Econometric analysis* (2nd ed.). New York: Macmillan.

Greene, W. H. (1998). Sample selection in credit-scoring models. *Japan and the World Economy, 10*, 299–316.

Hand, D. J., & Henley, W. E. (1993). Can reject inference ever work? *IMA Journal of Mathematics Applied in Business and Industry, 5*(4), 45–55.

Hand, D. J., & Henley, W. E. (1994). Inference about rejected cases in discriminant analysis. In E. Diday, Y. Lechevallier, M. Schader, P. Bertrand, & B. Burtschy (Eds.), *New approaches in classification and data analysis* (pp. 292–299). New York: Springer.

Jacobson, T., & Roszbach, K. (1998). *Bank lending policy, credit scoring and value at risk* (SSE/EFI Working Paper Series in Economics and Finance No. 260). Stockholm: Stockholm School of Economics.

Little, R. J. A., & Rubin, D. B. (2002). *Statistical analysis with missing data* (2nd ed.). Hoboken, NJ: Wiley.

Manski, C. F. (1995). *Identification problems in the social sciences*. Cambridge, MA: Harvard University Press.

McLachlan, G. J. (1992). *Discriminant analysis and statistical pattern recognition*. New York: Wiley.

McLachlan, G. J., & Basford, K. E. (1988). *Mixture models, inference and applications to clustering*. New York: Marcel Dekker.

Meng, C. L., & Schmidt, P. (1985). On the cost of partial observability in the bivariate probit model. *International Economic Review, 26*(1), 71–85.

Newman, D. J., Hettich, S., Blake, C. L., & Merz, C. J. (1998). *UCI repository of machine learning databases*. Retrieved March 14, 2006, from http://www.ics.uci.edu/~mlearn/MLRepository.html.

Schafer, J. L. (1997). *Analysis of incomplete multivariate data*. London: Chapman & Hall.

Thomas, L. C., Banasik, J., & Crook, J. N. (2003). Sample selection bias in credit scoring models. *Journal of the Operational Research Society, 54*, 822–832.

Venables, W. N., & Ripley, B. D. (2002). *Modern applied statistics with S-PLUS* (4th ed.). New York: Springer.

22

INVESTMENT PORTFOLIOS AND STOCK PRICING

CRAIG G. RENNIE

INTRODUCTION

Investment is the process of the deferral of current consumption for expected greater future consumption. To achieve increased wealth and higher levels of future consumption, investors construct and manage baskets, or portfolios, of assets the ultimate realized value of which is not fully known. These risky assets include equities (common and preferred stock, master limited partnerships, equity-based options and futures, and equity-based mutual funds), fixed-income securities (government, agency, corporate, or municipal notes and bonds, asset-backed securities, guaranteed investment contracts, interest rate options and futures, convertible securities, inflation-protected notes and bonds, and fixed-income mutual funds), and alternative assets (private equity, venture capital, commodities, commodity options and futures, real estate, hedge funds, gold or other precious metals, jewels, and collectibles such as art). Most investment portfolios also include cash (physical or electronic cash, bank balances, Treasury bills, agency notes, municipal notes, bankers' acceptances, certificates of deposit, repurchase agreements, money market funds, ultrashort-bond funds, or stable-value funds). However, even the real value of cash assets whose nominal values tomorrow are known with a high degree of precision today is subject to some degree of fluctuation owing to changes in inflation. To estimate the likely future value of wealth invested in risky assets, investors have a battery of portfolio management and risky-asset analysis and selection techniques available that are derived from modern probability theory.

In this chapter, I summarize some of the most important tools based on modern probability theory that are used by sophisticated investors in the management of investment portfolios and the analysis and selection of risky securities to hold in portfolios. The first section describes modern portfolio theory and the theory underlying risky-asset security analysis. I summarize the historical development, classical and current interpretive paradigms, major issues and approaches, research, methodology, theory, and caveats associated with the relevant body of knowledge. The second section demonstrates how portfolio management and risky-security analysis are implemented. I walk the reader through the development of an appropriate statement of investment policy for a hypothetical client, show how top-down asset allocation decisions are made, describe sector and industry analysis, and summarize bottom-up security analysis using fundamental and technical analysis. Additional risk control and investment portfolio performance evaluation issues are addressed. The third section discusses ethics and values, validity, and interpretation and outlines promising areas for future research. The final section offers concluding thoughts on portfolio management and risky-security analysis, two of the most exciting and financially rewarding areas of applied probability theory.

MODERN PORTFOLIO THEORY AN RISKY-SECURITY ANALYSIS

Modern portfolio theory was initially developed as a result of pioneering research by Markowitz (1952, 1959), into the nature of risk, return, and probability. Markowitz suggests that variance in the rate of return is the appropriate measure of portfolio risk for all investors, under certain assumptions. These assumptions include the following: (1) investors view investment alternatives strictly in terms of the probability distributions of their expected returns; (2) investors seek to maximize expected utility, subject to diminishing marginal utility; (3) investors evaluate risk in terms of fluctuations in expected returns; (4) investors make investment decisions exclusively on the basis of risk and expected returns; and (5) investors prefer higher expected returns for a given level of risk or, equivalently, lower risk for a given level of expected returns. Given these assumptions, Markowitz suggests that variance of returns, equal to the square of the standard deviation of returns, is the appropriate statistical measure of the dispersion of returns around the mean. Consequently, variance and standard deviation of returns are appropriate measures of overall investment risk.

In the Markowitz mean-variance model, the expected returns associated with an investment portfolio p consisting of a number n of risky assets i is the weighted average of the expected returns of the risky assets in the portfolio:

$$E(R_{\text{portfolio}}) = \sum_{i=1}^{n} w_i R_i, \qquad (22.1)$$

where w_i is the proportion of risky asset i in the portfolio and R_i is the expected returns associated with risky asset i. The expected returns of individual investments are estimated using the arithmetic average of historic returns, where returns are calculated as the ending value minus the beginning value plus intermediate cash flows (interest, dividends, etc.), all scaled by the beginning value of the investment. Historic returns are often used to estimate future returns, although investors sometimes adjust raw historic returns to reflect their own expectations about the future economy, markets, or interest rates.

The risk of portfolio p is more complex than the expected returns of the portfolio because risk involves not only the variance of returns of individual assets (or, equivalently, the square of standard deviation of these returns) but also the correlation of the returns of different assets with one another. This is because returns on different risky assets are not independent from one another.

Assuming that returns are normally distributed, variance is an estimate of the dispersion in the returns R_i of a given risky asset i from expected (mean) returns $E(R_i)$, measured as

$$\sigma_i^2 = \sum_{i=1}^{n} [R_i - E(R_i)]^2 P_i, \qquad (22.2)$$

where P_i is the probability of R_i occurring for risky asset i. The correlation coefficient r_i, j, where $-1 \geqslant r_{i,,j} \geqslant +1$, is an estimate of the degree to which the returns of two assets i and j move together. The covariance of returns on risky assets i and j is

$$\text{Cov}_{i,j} = E\{[R_i - E(R_i)][R_j - E(R_j)]\}, \qquad (22.3)$$

where the expected returns $E(R_i)$ and $E(R_j)$ are estimated in practice using arithmetic means of returns on risky assets i and j. The correlation coefficient $r_{i,j}$ relates to the covariance and variance of risky assets i and j as follows:

$$r_{i,j} = \frac{\text{Cov}_{i,j}}{\sigma_i \sigma_j}, \qquad (22.4)$$

where σ_i and σ_j are the square roots (standard deviations) of the variance of risky assets i and j.

Combining the concepts of variance, correlation, and covariance, the portfolio risk of a two risky-asset portfolio is

$$\sigma_{\text{portfolio}}^2 = w_i^2 \sigma_i^2 + w_j^2 \sigma_j^2 + 2 w_i w_j \sigma_i \sigma_j \rho_{ij}, \qquad (22.5)$$

where w_i and w_j are the proportions in which risky assets i and j are held in the portfolio. In the more general case of n risky assets, the formula for the risk of a portfolio is

$$\sigma^2_{\text{portfolio}} = \sum_{i=1}^{n} w_i^2 \sigma_i^2 + \sum_{i=1}^{n} \sum_{j=1}^{n} w_i w_j \sigma_i \sigma_j \rho_{ij}, \tag{22.6}$$

where i and j are now defined as risky assets. In addition, weights w_i sum to 1 across all n assets:

$$\sum_{i=1}^{n} w_i = 1, \tag{22.7}$$

where weights can be positive (i.e., assets are held "long," as in the case of buying a share of stock or a bond), negative (i.e., sold "short," as in the case of borrowing and immediately selling a share of stock, which has to be repurchased in the future to replace the debt, or the issue of a bond).

Importantly, (22.1), (22.6), and (22.7) form a quadratic programming problem whereby a set of risky-asset portfolios can be identified to maximize expected returns for any given level of risk or, equivalently, minimize risk for any given level of expected returns. This type of problem can be solved in MS Excel with the Data Analysis and Solver add-ins or with software specifically designed for nonlinear programming, such as LINDO or LINGO.

To visualize the problem, picture a two-dimensional graph with risk, measured as portfolio standard deviation of returns, on the x-axis and expected returns, measured as the mean of historic returns, on the y-axis, as in Figure 22.1. The relation between expected returns and risk could then be graphed for each risky asset under consideration—that is, single-asset portfolios—or for each possible combination of risky assets—that is, multi-asset portfolios. Those assets or portfolios that lie farthest to the northwest are said to be "efficient" because they offer greater expected returns for a given level of risk or lower risk for a given level of expected returns. The curve that connects these points is an upward-sloping concave hull termed the "efficient frontier." Any point to the east or south is "dominated" by any point to the north or west. Specifically, for an asset or portfolio to be dominated, another asset or portfolio must exist that offers a higher level of expected returns for the same or lower level of risk, or a lower level of risk and a higher or at least equal level of expected returns. Dominated or "inefficient" assets or portfolios will not be selected by rational investors, who always prefer more expected returns and less risk. Consequently, dominated assets and portfolios will not form part of the set of mean-variance efficient portfolios that make up the efficient frontier.

If we add comparatively risk-free assets, such as cash or short-duration Treasury bills, to our two-dimensional risk-expected return graph, we can draw a straight line from the point on the y-axis that is equal to the expected return on the risk-free security to the highest possible point on the efficient frontier. This line is tangent to the efficient frontier. We can also extend this line beyond the point of tangency. The line is called the capital market line and consists of all possible efficient combinations of risky and risk-free investments.

The y-axis has a standard deviation equal to 0, so the asset on this axis is necessarily risk-free. If an investor bought nothing but risky assets, he would hold 100% of his portfolio in the market portfolio, which we will somewhat arbitrarily call portfolio M. If he holds risk-free and risky assets, his portfolio would lie between the y-axis and M (such as the portfolio at point A in Figure 22.1) on the capital market line. If he is an aggressive investor, investing over 100% of his portfolio in risky assets by purchasing risky assets on margin, then his portfolio would lie beyond M (such as the portfolio at point B) on the capital market line. This analysis assumes that lending and borrowing rates are the same.

If the rate at which an investor borrows is higher than the rate at which he can loan money, which is likely, then the capital market line would be kinked. Specifically, it would consist of a line segment from the risk-free rate on the y- axis to point M, where the segment is tangent to M. The capital market line would also consist of a line segment with a lower slope starting at some point beyond M on the efficient frontier—say point M′—and reflecting higher rates for borrowing than for lending. In addition, a segment of the capital market line would be coincident with the efficient frontier between points M and M′ between its two line segments.

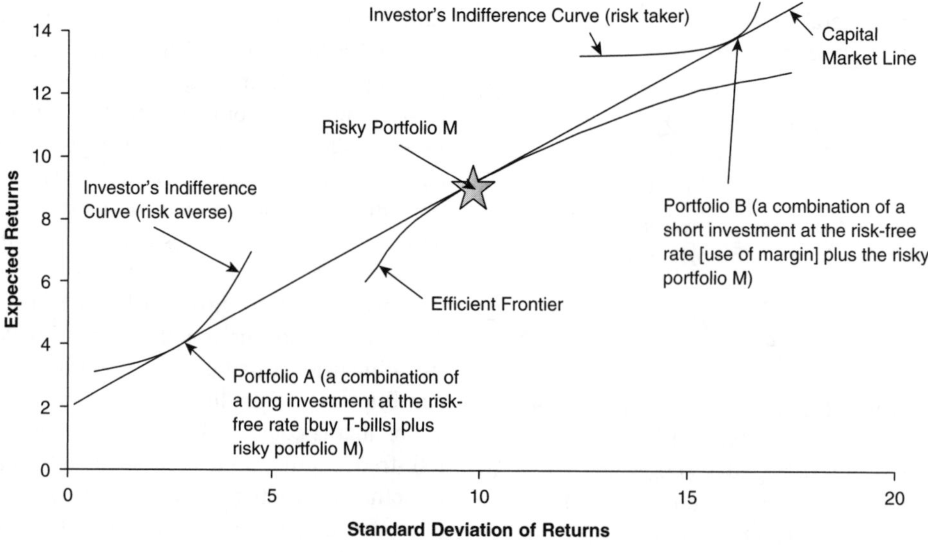

Figure 22.1 The efficient frontier, the capital market line, the risky market portfolio M (the case of identical borrowing and lending rates).

In theory, investors will hold some portion of their portfolio in risk-free securities (they will buy Treasury bills, borrow, or not invest at all in risk-free securities) and the risky portfolio M (or some range of portfolios between M and M′ if borrowing and lending rates are different). This result contributed to the development of the capital asset pricing model (CAPM), which states that

$$ER_i = R_f + \beta_i(ER_m - R_f), \qquad (22.8)$$

where ER_i is the expected returns on risky security i, R_f is the risk-free rate, $ER_m - R_f$ is the expected return on the market less the risk-free rate (i.e., the market risk premium associated with investing in risky assets), and β_i is the degree to which expected returns on security i vary with the risk premium associated with the market (Sharpe, 1964).

According to CAPM, each investor will select one point along the capital market line that combines risk-free securities (held long, short, or not at all) and the same risky portfolio M (or range of portfolios M to M′ in the case of different lending and borrowing rates). Precisely where each investor chooses to invest is determined by the point of tangency of their highest feasible indifference curve and the capital market line (or the curve between segments in the case of different lending and borrowing rates). An indifference curve is a locus of combinations of expected risk and return that connect points where investors are indifferent (obtain the same "utility," or satisfaction) from various combinations of expected returns and risk. Unfortunately, utility is a somewhat abstract concept from economics that does not lend itself to direct measurement and is not defined for comparisons between investors or even comparisons at different points in time for the same investor.

Importantly, if we knew an appropriate risk or expected returns target for the investor, we could solve the quadratic programming problem consisting of (22.1), (22.6), and (22.7). This is done by adding an inequality constraint setting portfolio risk less than or equal to target risk or expected returns greater than or equal to target expected returns. The result is an investor-specific optimized mean-variance solution that can be used to identify the appropriate weights of each risky asset, and the risk-free asset, to hold in a portfolio. This is a top-down investment approach.

One limitation of modern portfolio theory is that variance in rates of returns is probably not the only appropriate measure of portfolio risk for all investors. Most investors are not concerned with deviations above the mean because these are unexpectedly good outcomes and thus hardly a measure of risk. Semivariance is a measure that considers only deviations below the mean. Other investors are concerned about preservation of capital. In this case, a more appropriate measure of risk than variance might be deviation below 0 or perhaps below some benchmark return based on inflation or the relatively risk-free short-term Treasury bill. Alternatively, the range of possible outcomes could matter to some investors. In this scenario, the distance between the maximum and minimum possible returns could be the appropriate measure of portfolio risk. Finally, the maximum potential loss over a given investment horizon might be the appropriate risk measure. For these investors, portfolio value at risk can be calculated to predict, within a certain probability, the maximum potential loss that could occur over a given time period. However, most modern portfolio theory is based on the case where variance or standard deviation is the appropriate measure of portfolio risk.

Another limitation of modern portfolio theory involves the sensitivity of parameter estimates to estimation errors and the nonstationary nature of these parameters over time. Expected returns and standard deviations of returns have to be calculated for each risky asset, and correlation coefficients or covariance terms must be estimated for each possible combination of risky assets included in the analysis. When more than two risky assets are involved in the analysis, the number of correlation coefficients can be substantial. Michaud (1998) and Darst (2003) and also personal experience lead me to caution that mean-variance optimization results tend to be sensitive to choices of parameter estimation periods.

Finally, computation can be a problem because of the exponential growth in the number of correlation coefficients as more and more assets are evaluated. Smaller models can be solved in MS Excel, but larger ones need industrial strength programs such as LINDO or LINGO.

Bottom-up investing seeks to identify individual undervalued (or overvalued) securities to include long (or short) securities in an investment portfolio. Valuation of individual securities is typically done through technical analysis, fundamental analysis, or some combination of both. Underlying both technical and fundamental analysis are certain assumptions about market efficiency.

Three forms of market efficiency are suggested in the finance literature: weak form, semistrong form, and strong form. If markets are weak-form efficient, then all historic price and volume information is already fully reflected in current securities prices. If markets are semistrong-form efficient, then all public information, including public earnings announcements, public filings (such as U.S. Securities and Exchange Commission [SEC] 10-K annual reports), and so on, as well as historic price and volume information, are fully and immediately reflected in current securities prices.[1] If markets are strong-form efficient, then all information, including private insider information as well as public and historic information, is fully reflected in securities prices.

In theory, if markets are weak-form efficient, then technical analysis may not provide usable information for predicting future securities prices because all historic price and volume information has already been analyzed and acted on by market participants, leaving it already fully reflected in current market prices. Similarly, if markets are semistrong-form or strong-form efficient, then fundamental and technical analysis may not provide information helpful for forecasting prices.

The degree to which market efficiency holds is not well established in the empirical finance literature. Some studies show that securities prices follow a random walk with drift, suggesting that technical analysis provides little or no value (Malkiel, 2004). Others suggest that abnormal profits can be earned by pursuing momentum strategies, concluding that some forms of technical analysis may provide value. Empiricists have shown that most investment managers do not perform as well as their benchmarks. However, there are cases of exceptional managers, such as Warren Buffett and Peter Lynch, who have

[1]The theory of semistrong-form market efficiency does not allow for time lags in the digesting of information. Empirical evidence suggests that markets do not respond instantaneously (i.e., see my discussion of "post-earnings announcement drift" below).

long-term track records that appear to consistently outperform their benchmarks. Trading rules, at least those that have been published, rarely seem to generate abnormal risk-adjusted returns. Some evidence suggests that anomalies that are inconsistent with weak-form market efficiency, such as day of the week, time of year, and size effects, persist. The dynamics underlying speculative bubbles and subsequent market corrections (crashes) are also inconsistent with market efficiency.

One problem associated with many of the studies that attempt to prove that markets are efficient is that they make some rather strong assumptions about asset pricing when testing market efficiency. As a consequence of testing a dual hypothesis (i.e., both market efficiency and an asset-pricing model such as CAPM), it is not clear whether they show that markets are efficient or inefficient or that asset-pricing models are correctly or incorrectly specified.

CAPM suggests that security prices are determined by a single factor—the market risk premium. More recently, arbitrage pricing theory was developed as a multifactor asset-pricing model (Roll & Ross, 1995). However, initial research was unable to determine with certainty what these factors are. Most investment practitioners believe that there are three factors that explain security returns and that these factors correspond to the Fama-French three-factor model (Fama & French, 1993). This model suggests that beta, growth opportunities (usually measured by firms' market-to-book ratios), and firm size determine most of the differences in expected returns of risky assets.

Substantial empirical research suggests that weak-form market efficiency holds in the U.S. stock market, with some notable exceptions. Recent research suggests that stock returns exhibit momentum, whereby stocks that have outperformed (or underperformed) over 3 to 12 months in the past continue to outperform (or underperform) the market, although not necessarily after transaction costs and taxes. Similarly, considerable evidence indicates that semistrong-form market efficiency exists, but with important exceptions. One of these exceptions is the phenomenon of postearnings announcement drift, whereby stock prices appear to take time to fully reflect public earnings announcements. One proposition that rationalizes the existence of both technical and fundamental analysts is that there is an efficient amount of inefficiency in the markets (Grossman & Stiglitz, 1980). This view holds that markets are generally efficient because there are sufficient opportunities available for fundamental and technical analysts to entice them to constantly scour the markets for opportunities to make abnormal risk-adjusted returns. This process helps make our financial markets relatively efficient.

Technical analysis typically attempts to forecast future securities prices, thereby identifying over- or undervalued securities and, thus, potentially profitable investment opportunities, based on an analysis of historic price and volume information. Most technical analysts view Charles Dow as the founder of their discipline. The Dow theory, initially published by Charles Dow in *Wall Street Journal* editorials, is the first technical analysis model (Murphy, 1999; Pring, 2002). Current technical analysis models track market consensus/contrarian indicators, follow informed (insider) investors, make use of price momentum, and work with variations of traditional price and volume patterns. Many investment firms employ some technical analysis, sometimes exclusively but more often in combination with fundamental analysis.

Fundamental analysis seeks to identify the underlying economic value of a firm (its "fundamentals") and thus identify over- or undervalued securities. Most fundamental analysts attribute the origins of their discipline to Graham and Dodd's *Security Analysis*, first published in 1940 (see Graham & Dodd, 2002). Current fundamental analysis typically includes an analysis of the overall economy and markets, an economic sector or industry analysis, and individual company analysis. Most investment texts describe how to analyze economies, industries, and companies and suggest valuation models. Models typically suggested in investment texts include some version of a multigrowth rate discounted cash flows model or multiples based on a comparison of similar firms (i.e., usually firms operating in the same industry) using general or industry-specific ratios (such as price-earnings or some form of price/cash flow ratios).

The above description of technical and fundamental analysis applies chiefly to common stocks. Fixed-income securities such as U.S. Treasury notes and bonds are evaluated chiefly in terms of their interest rate risk (i.e., the sensitivity of their price to a change in interest rates). Price sensitivity is measured chiefly in terms of bond duration and convexity. Corporate notes and bonds are priced based on default risk. Default risk is also estimated using a form of fundamental analysis, either by a rating agency such as Standard and Poor's (S&P) or by the investment firm or manager.

From the perspective of applied probability theory, stock options are an especially interesting security because their payoffs are nonlinear. For example, a call option on a stock gives its owner the right but not the obligation to purchase a pre-agreed amount of stock (typically 100 shares) at a pre-agreed exercise price X at any time T up to option expiration (an "American option") or at the time of option expiration (a "European option"). At the time of option expiration, if the stock were trading at a price S below the exercise price, X, rational investors would not exercise their options because they could buy the underlying stock at the lower price, S, in the open market. If the option expired at a time when the current stock price, S, was above the exercise price, X, they would exercise the option (i.e., buy the underlying stock at price X) because they could then sell the underlying stock at the higher price, S, in the stock market. Moreover, if the option has not yet expired, the option has a time value based on the possibility that the option will expire when the stock price is greater than the exercise price. This time value decays over time. Payoffs associated with options are thus nonlinear depending on whether the options expire when stock prices are above or below exercise prices, and also change over time.

Stock options are typically valued using the Black-Scholes option-pricing model (Black & Scholes, 1973). The Black-Scholes option pricing model assumes that stock price changes follow a geometric Brownian motion, wherby stock returns from the present through the future include both expected and unexpected (noise) components. Specifically, the Black-Scholes model states that the value of a call option C_0 on a non-dividend-paying stock is

$$C_0 = SN(d_1) - X(e^{-Rf*T})N(d_2), \qquad (22.9)$$

where

$$d_1 = \left[(\ln(S/X) + (Rf + 0.5\sigma^2)T)/[\sigma T^{0.5}]\right], \qquad (22.10)$$

$$d_2 = \left[d_1 - \sigma[T]^{0.5}\right]. \qquad (22.11)$$

S is the stock price, X is the exercise price, e^{-Rf*T} is the discount factor for continuous compounding at the risk-free rate Rf over the period ending with option expiration at time T, and s is the standard deviation of the underlying stock. Once d_1 and d_2 are calculated, $N(d_1)$ and $N(d_2)$ are estimated from standard normal distribution tables. Importantly, stock option valuation is a function of stock price, exercise price, risk-free rate, option time to maturity, and volatility of the underlying stock price.

A parallel model also exists for put options that give their owners the right but not the obligation to sell a pre-agreed quantity of underlying stock at a pre-agreed price. The Black-Scholes model has been modified for stocks that pay dividends. A binomial option pricing model has also been developed. It is sometimes used as an alternative to the Black-Scholes model. Interest rate option pricing models exist, but they are well beyond the scope of this chapter (for more details, see Reilly & Brown, 2006).

The bottom line: Portfolio management and both fundamental and technical analysis currently remain art as well as science. Cutting-edge research is constantly being performed by proprietary trading desks at leading investment firms, from Goldman Sachs to less-known but fast-growing hedge funds. Some of this research involves the development of sophisticated models for the pricing of complex nonlinear payoff securities, such as options. The ultimate goal of all this research is to construct investment portfolios that consistently outperform the market on a risk-adjusted returns basis.

Portfolio Management and Risky-Security Analysis Implementation

One of the best ways to illustrate precisely how portfolio management and risky-security analysis and selection are done in practice is to describe the manner in which a typical investment portfolio is managed. This is demonstrated through the development of an appropriate investment policy for a hypothetical client, showing how top-down asset allocation decisions are made, describing economy and sector/industry analysis, and summarizing bottom-up security analysis and selection using fundamental and technical analysis. Relevant risk control and investment portfolio performance evaluation considerations are also addressed.

In practice, the portfolio management and risky-security analysis and selection process is similar for a client that is an institution (represented by one or more trustees, a board, etc.) or an individual. However, certain preliminary financial needs must be addressed for individuals before an appropriate investment program can be devised. These preliminaries include provision for income and asset protection and short-term cash reserves. Income and asset protection products include life, health, disability, property, and casualty insurance. For individuals, most practitioners recommend a minimum of 3 months' living expenses to be held in highly liquid low-volatility investments (bank accounts, money market funds, Treasury bills, or short-term-bond funds) to prevent forced liquidation of long-term investments during unfavorable market conditions. Financial protection and cash reserve needs also change over time as individuals age through their asset accumulation (approximately 15–35 years), asset consolidation (35–65), and asset-spending phases (65 to death).

For individuals, investment goals change with age. During their asset accumulation phase, individuals tend to accumulate wealth for specific goals, such as purchasing a car or house or college education for their children. Income and net worth are typically low and debt obligations high (usually too high). However, retirement is distant, so asset accumulators can afford to take higher levels of risk (subject to their risk tolerance) for higher expected returns (e.g., by investing mostly in equities). During their consolidation phase, net worth and income are high, and debt obligations are low (or at least they should be). As retirement approaches, the need for capital conservation increases, and investors gradually reduce risk (e.g., hold a mix of bonds and equities rather than just equities). During the spending phase, individuals typically receive little or no employment income and some social security benefits, and they rely heavily on income from their investments (this trend is strengthening with the gradual replacement of traditional defined benefit pension plans with defined contribution plans, e.g., U.S. 401(k)s).

Like individuals, institutional investors have cash flow needs, and these needs change over time. For example, a university foundation may be required to disburse some percentage of total assets each year to augment other sources of funding (tuition, possible state funding) for the operation of the affiliated university. Similarly, pension funds disburse annuities to pensioners. Consequently, a portion of an institution's portfolio will typically be held in cash or other liquid nonvolatile assets to meet the institution's cash flow needs. Institutional investor needs also change over time, as new funds are raised or as spending requirements change.

The portfolio management process, whether for individuals or institutions, typically consists of five steps. First, the portfolio manager meets with the client and develops a written investment policy statement. Second, the manager examines current and projected economic and market trends. Third, the manager implements the investment policy by constructing a portfolio, using top-down asset allocation, bottom-up security selection, or some mixture of both. Fourth, the manager periodically reviews portfolio performance (usually monthly). Finally, the manager meets with the client to update client needs (at least annually), and the process recycles.

Investment policy statements help investors (and investment managers) identify realistic risk-return goals and map out plans for the achievement of these goals. They also establish benchmarks for the assessment of portfolio (and manager) performance. Investor goals are determined by risk tolerance and, for individuals, the phase of the investor life cycle that the individual is in. Risk tolerance is in turn affected by psychological needs and wants, insurance and liquidity protections that are in place, marital and family status, and also age, wealth, and income (including expectations).

Most investors select some mix of risky and risk-free investments as if they were responding to some multidimensional construct of investment objective considerations. These dimensions include length of investment horizon (i.e., how long the investment will be held until disposal), risk tolerance, liquidity needs, tax considerations, and legal or other regulatory constraints.

In practice, expectations are difficult to quantify, so managers often administer questionnaires to investors with multiple-choice questions on investment scenarios to identify investor risk tolerance levels. The resulting levels are frequently described as conservative, moderate, or aggressive. Alternatively, investors are described as being primarily concerned with capital preservation, current income, total return, or capital appreciation. Poorer older couples with many children are more likely to be classified as conservative investors—that is, investors primarily interested in capital preservation. Young, single investors who are wealthy and highly paid are more likely to be described as aggressive investors chiefly interested in capital appreciation.

In addition to investor risk tolerance, investment constraints such as liquidity needs, applicable time horizons, taxes, laws and regulation, and investor-specific criteria affect the development of an appropriate investment policy statement. Liquid assets are those that are easily liquidated at little cost for cash. Investors have varying needs for cash, and these needs change over time. The longer the period funds can be invested for, the longer the time horizon of the portfolio. Longer time horizons permit greater risk to achieve higher expected returns. Taxation varies between investors and can materially affect the mix of investments to be included in a portfolio.

For example, investors who hold tax-exempt accounts, such as some trusts and Roth IRAs (individual retirement accounts) in the United States, may be unconcerned about the form in which income is paid (interest, dividends, or capital gains). Some instruments, such as U.S. tax-efficient municipal bonds and mutual funds, might be inappropriate for these kinds of accounts. On the other hand, individuals with high employment income, and thus high marginal tax rate, may prefer some portion of their taxable accounts to be invested in tax-efficient mutual funds or municipal bonds because of the lower taxes that these forms of income incur. Taxation, of course, varies between countries and even states, so individuals in different jurisdictions will make different portfolio choices. Legal and regulatory restrictions are particularly relevant for institutional managers. Finally, some investors may have personal biases for or against specific investments. For example, self-described socially conscious investors might elect not to invest in alcohol, defense, pornography, tobacco, or electric utilities that operate nuclear power plants. Relatively inexperienced investors may have limited knowledge of specific investment products such as hedge funds or derivatives. Some investors may already have substantial wealth exposure to specific firms (i.e., the CEO of a company depends on his company for his employment income and probably has a large portion of his wealth tied up in company stock and options).

Once the investor's risk tolerance and investment constraints have been identified and the investment policy statement written, the portfolio manager examines current and projected economic and market trends. This is done because of a well-documented linkage between the overall economy and securities prices. Recall that CAPM states that the expected return on stock *i* is determined by its beta—that is, the sensitivity of the returns on that stock to changes in the market risk premium. Even in the Fama and French (1993) three-factor model, beta is one factor underlying risky-security returns.

One of the most basic models of macroeconomic activity is the business cycle model. Stock market prices tend to do well during periods of economic growth and poorly during recessions or depressions. In the United States, the National Bureau of Economic Research (NBER) identifies leading, coincident, and lagging indicators to help identify where we are going, are, and have been in the business cycle (see http://www.nber.org). A composite index also exists, but, as noted in Reilly and Brown (2006), it is usually the changes in the relationship between leading, coincident, and lagging indicators that help identify potential slowdowns in the economy. The NBER Web site shows that business cycles average between 48 and 67 months, although recent cycles have tended to be longer

(128 months between the July 1990 and March 2001 peaks). Nevertheless, the prediction of precisely where we are going, are, and have been is art as well as science. False signals, data revisions, and missing sectors limit the usefulness of such data. Other key variables, such as those relating to money supply, inflation, and interest rates, also matter. For example, when U.S. interest rates were at historic low levels in 2003, fixed-income securities were at historic highs, with the result that long-duration bonds had unusually high levels of interest rate risk.

Once forecasts of the relevant economy (or economies) have been made, portfolio managers typically identify an optimal top-down asset allocation strategy for their clients. Market trends are considered. Weights are sometimes determined mechanically based on a formula that tries to link investor risk tolerance with investment constraints into some mix of cash, bonds, stocks, and other assets. However, larger portfolios often use mean-variance optimization to determine these weights.

The first step in building a mean-variance optimization model in practice is to identify an appropriate set of investments to consider for the portfolio. In this chapter, I assume we have a highly experienced U.S. institutional investor who has a trust worth approximately $1 million (it could just as easily apply to an individual investor with similar risk tolerance and investment constraints). The portfolio has a theoretically infinite time horizon and is used to fund institutional-related programs at a low rate. The portfolio is tax exempt and can invest in cash, fixed-income securities, and equities. For simplicity, assume that it cannot use margin to borrow to invest or invest in derivatives. The trustees indicate that they are somewhat concerned about capital preservation, but they insist that they do not want to consistently underperform the S&P 500 Index. The trustees have agreed to take on approximately the same level of risk as the S&P 500. The trust only has this one account. A diversified mix of securities, including some cash; fixed-income securities (such as bonds); and stocks of large-, mid-, and small-capitalized firms, including value and growth firms, both domestic and foreign, would therefore be appropriate for consideration in this portfolio.

In theory, one could perform mean-variance optimization using historic returns for all publicly traded securities in these asset categories. In practice, this would be impractical owing to data collection and computation requirements. Instead, real-world investors will typically collect historic returns information on market benchmarks for each asset category. For example, numerous Wall Street asset management firms use the Russell 1000 or 2000 indexes, often with Value or Growth versions of these indexes, foreign indexes, real estate equity indexes, domestic bond indexes, and so on, when using Markowitz mean-variance optimization to estimate optimum mixes of different assets.

For the purposes of this example, I chose to consider returns information for the period January 1980 to January 2005 for the following major indexes: Gold; North American Real Estate Investment Trusts (NAREIT); the Lehman Brothers Aggregate Bond Index; the Russell 1000 Growth Index (including U.S. large- and midcap growth stocks); the Russell 1000 Value Index; the Russell 2000 Growth Index (including the next smallest growth stocks); the Russell 2000 Value Index; and the Morgan Stanley Country Index for Europe, Australia, and the Far East (MSCI EAFE, essentially the developed world outside the United States). I also collected returns information on the U.S. 30-day Treasury bill (the risk-free rate), inflation (as measured by the Consumer Price Index), and the S&P 500 benchmark. Data are from Ibbotson and Associates.

Table 22.1 reports real (inflation adjusted) returns, mean returns (expected returns), and standard deviations of returns (total risk) for the indexes used in my mean-variance optimization. The highest expected real return (12.75%) is associated with the Russell 2000 Value Index, but its risk is substantial (17.84%). The Russell 1000 Value Index also dominates the Russell 1000 Growth Index, reflecting the tendency for value stocks to outperform growth stocks over long periods of time.

Table 22.2 reports correlation coefficients and the variance-covariance matrix of these real returns using the Analysis ToolPak add-in from MS Excel.

Gold is negatively correlated with the Lehman Brothers Aggregate Bond Index, the Russell

Table 22.1 Real Annual Returns on Selected Indexes: January 1980 to January 2005

Year	*Gold*	*NAREIT Equity*	*LB Aggregate Bond*	*Russell 1000 Growth*	*Russell 1000 Value*	*Russell 2000 Growth*	*Russell 2000 Value*	*MSCI EAFE*	*U.S. 30-Day Treasury Bill*
1980	165.50	26.64	−16.90	14.68	5.96	38.83	17.60	−3.30	−3.52
1981	−34.14	6.36	−5.73	8.61	5.21	22.87	8.19	5.35	−0.21
1982	−32.04	−4.99	−1.60	−15.11	−8.23	−19.43	1.40	−8.77	5.99
1983	25.32	23.22	28.26	23.02	24.63	34.60	35.97	−4.80	6.67
1984	−29.30	26.12	6.29	3.13	20.82	1.48	27.71	27.19	4.75
1985	−21.52	18.73	11.82	10.51	12.19	−2.86	9.65	2.01	6.16
1986	10.41	14.69	16.17	18.74	20.80	13.22	14.01	53.23	3.74
1987	12.83	19.07	14.84	29.42	30.62	12.87	16.15	81.94	4.58
1988	10.30	−7.81	0.83	−10.88	−6.95	−23.19	−14.25	10.90	1.29
1989	−18.64	5.31	1.05	13.00	17.45	18.44	22.26	23.88	1.95
1990	0.14	−3.14	6.36	11.63	4.66	−1.85	−5.39	−0.37	3.18
1991	−17.47	−7.68	5.97	8.36	−3.21	−4.91	−14.22	−23.29	2.11
1992	−5.85	25.67	10.42	28.44	16.82	46.46	38.79	4.05	2.81
1993	−9.94	13.02	7.72	3.11	13.67	−2.10	22.23	−13.20	0.14
1994	11.84	13.19	6.61	3.98	16.61	12.43	19.27	41.66	0.39
1995	−3.60	−4.74	−5.12	−0.33	−5.46	−9.70	−8.20	−6.99	1.27
1996	5.45	17.05	14.21	36.09	35.67	29.93	24.47	13.75	2.88
1997	−17.85	31.51	0.21	24.45	20.64	11.95	19.38	−0.82	2.19
1998	−13.34	16.76	9.17	24.01	25.54	7.15	25.87	9.02	3.66
1999	−8.05	−20.48	6.39	40.92	16.56	5.54	−8.56	13.06	3.11
2000	−3.41	−4.94	−4.53	17.20	0.35	32.98	−4.51	16.88	2.07
2001	−10.43	23.46	10.03	−16.78	7.25	−19.16	25.81	−11.97	2.23
2002	5.59	11.84	6.41	−28.02	−7.82	−20.16	11.29	−26.49	2.27
2003	27.58	−2.01	6.88	−30.97	−19.53	−32.25	−17.64	−17.24	−0.99
2004	6.85	45.44	2.92	33.77	33.67	58.79	53.53	45.35	−0.93
2005	2.63	12.56	1.19	−2.27	9.48	0.74	10.62	13.86	−1.67
Mean	2.26	11.34	5.38	9.57	11.05	8.18	12.75	9.42	2.16
σ	37.03	15.09	8.70	18.92	14.17	22.81	17.84	24.86	2.47

Table 22.2 Pearson Correlation Coefficients and Variance-Covariance Matrix for Selected Index Annual Returns, January 1980 to January 2005

	Gold	*NAREIT Equity*	*LB Aggregate Bond*	*Russell 1000 Growth*	*Russell 1000 Value*	*Russell 2000 Growth*	*Russell 2000 Value*	*MSCI EAFE*
Panel A: Correlation coefficients								
Gold	1	0.211018402	−0.2890781	0.0392718	−0.0478177	0.2706772	0.0488468	−0.0001251
NAREIT equity	0.211018402	1	0.1979052	0.271206	0.6233437	0.531986	0.8831686	0.2786982
LB aggregate bond	−0.289078138	0.197905188	1	0.2081456	0.4505345	0.0050504	0.3127448	0.1900182
Russell 1000 Growth	0.039271773	0.271205981	0.2081456	1	0.8033522	0.7808922	0.4191422	0.5035439
Russell 1000 Value	−0.047817687	0.623343656	0.4505345	0.8033522	1	0.6701327	0.760746	0.6287645
Russell 2000 Growth	0.270677227	0.531986039	0.0050504	0.7808922	0.6701327	1	0.6520302	0.4220024
Russell 2000 Value	0.048846751	0.88316856	0.3127448	0.4191422	0.760746	0.6520302	1	0.323951
MSCI EAFE	−0.00012513	0.278698223	0.1900182	0.5035439	0.6287645	0.4220024	0.323951	1
Panel B: Variance-covariance matrix								
Gold	1,371.43767	517.5709638	−455.649779	349.9801	68.0726377	617.816802	186.291924	−0.1108
NAREIT equity	85.91147063	227.6445847	69.42459006	145.332577	178.100381	165.375324	198.433485	100.5115
LB aggregate bond	−25.12744766	23.06477848	75.62985846	36.0171079	48.1517477	9.9717274	30.0747574	39.4998
Russell 1000 Growth	91.36490206	228.5692307	170.5012883	358.02398	269.846031	283.636053	208.253069	227.7437
Russell 1000 Value	9.959887905	156.9876432	127.7546489	151.238327	200.658678	117.338588	160.091393	212.8972
Russell 2000 Growth	234.4554762	378.0855885	68.62049562	412.312078	304.340432	520.447277	391.699409	230.1210
Russell 2000 Value	43.21532595	277.3176267	126.5111153	185.05428	253.82236	239.43962	318.141145	138.1154
MSCI EAFE	4.502075264	207.4783456	185.1710828	240.121819	405.812976	94.2071248	164.33456	594.2090

1000 Value Index, and the MSCI EAFE Index, suggesting that reduced portfolio risk could perhaps be achieved for some investors by combining gold with U.S. bonds, large-cap-value stocks, and stocks of developed foreign markets. Table 22.3 shows mean-variance optimization results calculated in MS Excel with the Solver add-in. Panel A shows that mean-variance estimation for maximum expected portfolio returns with unconstrained short sales (i.e., an unrealistic lack of margin requirements on short sales) generates nonfeasible results with astronomical expected returns and portfolio risk. Panel B shows feasible solutions at different levels of expected return when short sales are prohibited. Panel C summarizes expected returns, risk, and weights for portfolios with risk and return characteristics similar to those of a variety of equity and fixed-income indexes.

Panel C of Table 22.3 shows that a portfolio with risk characteristics similar to those of the S&P 500 (i.e., $\sigma_p = 15.73\%$) would generate an expected return of 12.09% per year (compared with only 10.44% for the S&P 500). A total of 7.77% of the portfolio's assets would be held in real estate (NAREIT), 32.18% in large-cap-value stocks (the Russell 1000 Value Index), and 60.06% in small-cap-value stocks (the Russell 2000 Value Index). Graphically, this portfolio would be represented by point A in Figure 22.2. The portfolio at point A dominates the S&P 500-index-only portfolio shown in Figure 22.2 (portfolio A has a higher expected return with the same level of risk as the S&P 500).[2] If margin were permitted at realistic levels, then some portfolio corresponding to point B could be realized that would achieve an even higher expected return for the same level of risk as the S&P 500 or the point A solution. However, point B depends on real margin rates that vary between providers and investors. Consequently, the point B solution shown in Figure 22.2 is only conceptual. The theoretical investor's indifference curve, efficient frontier, and kinked capital market line, discussed earlier, are also shown for conceptual purposes.

The results described in Table 22.3 suggest that an investor who takes on the same level of risk as the S&P 500 could expect to achieve an extra 1.83% per year in expected returns by holding specific levels of real estate, large-cap-value stocks, and small-cap-value stocks. One low-cost way to implement this resulting top-down asset allocation strategy would be to buy and hold mutual funds or exchange traded funds based on these indexes, with periodic rebalancing as security prices change to approximately maintain the recommended 7.77%, 32.18%, and 60.06% portfolio weights.[3] Alternatively, portfolio managers frequently use bottom-up security analysis techniques to try to identify under- or overvalued securities to further enhance portfolio returns.

Expected rates of return based on historic information are a reasonable but imperfect predictor of future performance. For example, had optimal weights been estimated in January 1995, the portfolio expected return would be 10.37% per year, portfolio standard deviation would be 11.20% (set to the same value of that of the S&P 500 between January 1980 and January 1995), and optimal weights would have been 32.25% NAREIT, 18.98% Russell 1000 Growth, 33.77% Russell 1000 Value, and 15.00% Russell 2000 Value Index. Had this portfolio been held from January 1995 through January 2005 with no rebalancing, total realized holding period returns would have been 11.14% per year (compared with only 9.04% for the S&P 500), and portfolio standard deviation would have been 15.85% (compared with 21.85% for the S&P 500). Such a portfolio would have realized a higher return at lower risk than the S&P 500.

[2]The S&P 500 index portfolio is inefficient. In other words, a portfolio combining assets other than just the S&P 500 can achieve higher expected returns for equivalent risk, or the same level of expected returns for lower risk, or higher expected returns for lower risk.

[3]Precise maintenance of these weights would require continuous rebalancing as relative prices change. Transaction costs would be substantial, so periodic rebalancing, quarterly or monthly, would be a much better approach. This result also suggests a hedging strategy whereby a portfolio manager could short exchange traded funds based on the S&P 500 while buying long funds based on the NAREIT, the Russell 1000 Value Index, and the Russell 2000 Value Index. Interestingly, portfolio expected returns and standard deviations are insensitive to small deviations in optimal portfolio composition. Specifically, portfolio expected returns and standard deviation are identical to two decimal places of precision if the weight of the portfolio held in NAREIT was forced to zero. New optimal weights would be 28.47% Russell 1000 Value Total Return and 71.53% Russell 2000 Value Total Return.

Table 22.3 Mean-Variance-Efficient Portfolios Based on Selected Indexes: January 1980 to January 2005

	ER_p	σ_p	*Gold*	*NAREIT Equity*	*LB Aggregate Bond*	*Russell 1000 Growth*	*Russell 1000 Value*	*Russell 2000 Growth*	*Russell 2000 Value*	*MSCI EAFE*
Panel A: Short sales permitted (in %) (sample solution only)										
	2,144,928K	9,523,471K	−265,494K	46,489K	15,962K	37,395K	45,017K	30,298K	53,687K	36,646K
Panel B: No short sales permitted (in %)										
Maximum ER_p portfolio	12.75	17.84	0	0	0	0	0	0	100.00	0
	12.00	15.48	0	11.23	0	0	34.81	0	53.96	0
	10.00	12.06	0	42.63	20.74	0	36.63	0	0	0
	8.00	9.47	2.39	36.40	51.97	0	9.24	0	0	0
	6.00	6.63	12.20	0	74.23	0	0	0	13.57	0.22
Minimum σ^2 portfolio	5.88	4.88	16.39	0	83.81	0	0	0	0	0.22
Panel C: No short sales permitted (in %); targets set at ER_p and σ_p of major indexes										
ER_p of S&P 500	10.44	12.68	0	42.34	13.05	0	44.61	0	0	0
σ_p of S&P 500	12.09	15.73	0	7.77	0	0	32.18	0	60.06	0
ER_p of Russell 3000	10.31	12.49	0	42.43	15.35	0	42.22	0	0	0
σ_p of Russell 3000	12.21	15.54	0	10.34	0	0	34.19	0	55.47	0
ER_p of Wilshire 5000	10.29	12.46	0	42.44	15.67	0	41.88	0	0	0
σ_p of Wilshire 5000	12.22	15.58	0	9.85	0	0	33.66	0	56.49	0
ER_p of LB aggregate bond	5.38	5.65	13.88	0	80.25	0	0	0	5.87	0
σ_p of LB aggregate bond	8.21	8.70	5.10	27.35	58.38	0	7.83	0	1.35	0

NOTE: This table shows results from mean-variance optimization applied to historic real returns of eight indexes. Panel A shows a nonfeasible solution maximizing expected returns when short sales are unconstrained. Panel B describes maximum expected returns and minimum portfolio standard deviation solutions when no short sales are permitted. Panel C illustrates portfolio expected returns and standard deviations when no short sales are permitted and investor risk tolerance targets are set at the expected return or standard deviation of major market indices (S&P 500, Russell 3000, and Wilshire 5000).

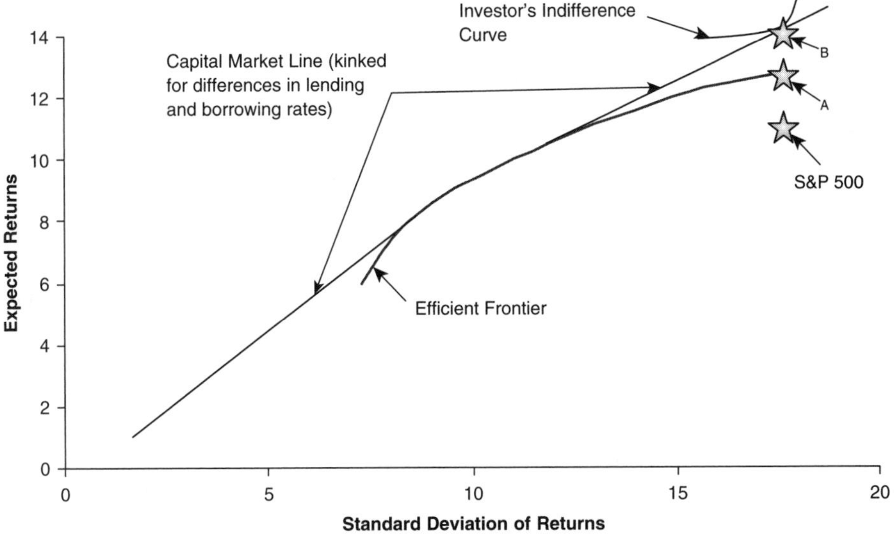

Figure 22.2 The efficient frontier, the capital market line, and sample portfolios based on selected indexes: January 1980 to January 2005.

Interestingly, periodic rebalancing (monthly, quarterly, or annual) will lead to substantial revisions to portfolio composition over time.

To implement bottom-up security analysis, portfolio managers typically analyze (or purchase analytical reports on) the economic sectors and industries that comprise those sectors. Prior empirical research shows that the returns of these sectors and industries vary in cross section and over time, suggesting that this kind of analysis may have value. Next, managers (analysts) screen individual firms in these sectors and industries and use detailed fundamental and/or technical analyses for individual firms. The fact that returns on individual firms vary within economic sectors and industries also suggests that fundamental or technical analysis may be worthwhile.

S&P divide the economy into 10 economic sectors: consumer discretionary, consumer staples, energy, financials, health care, industrials, information technology, materials, telecommunications, and utilities. Each sector is then divided into industries. For example, the largest sector is financials. It consists of commercial banks, insurance, real estate, capital markets, consumer finance, thrifts and mortgage, and diversified financial services industries.

Predictions can be made about over-, equal-, or underweighting specific sectors or industries based on the sensitivity of sectors or industries to current or predicted macroeconomic conditions or by the unique strengths, weaknesses, opportunities, and threats faced by these sectors and industries. For example, firms that tend to perform well during the latter stages of recessions, when interest rates are declining, are financials (fixed-income securities also tend to do well because their value is inversely related to interest rates). As the economy begins to recover, industrials tend to do well. When the economy first goes into recession, consumer staples tend to outperform. During periods of unexpected inflation, financials tend to underperform. Demographics also affect industries. For example, as baby boomers age, health care will likely do well.

One of the most widely used models of sector or industry performance is the industry (or product) life cycle model. This model suggests that industries (and products) tend to experience distinctly different periods of growth rates in sales. In the earliest stages of initial research and first product introduction, sales are small but accelerating. In the mature growth phase of the industry, sales continue to grow, but at decreasing rates. As the market matures, sales cease to grow at rates other than those of inflation. Finally, the market enters a period of decline as the industry (or product) becomes obsolete. The industry (or product) life cycle model helps predict whether the industry (or product) is in its growth or value stage. This determination has potentially important implications when evaluating a company.

In practice, portfolio managers will make over-, equal-, or underweight decisions on economic sectors or industries, but they do so under severe constraints, such as limiting over- or underweight decisions to $\pm 3\%$ of the total portfolio. The selection of Russell 1000 and 2000 Indexes effectively controls for firm size. The selection of Value versus Growth Indexes controls for firm growth opportunities. Constraints on how far over- or underweight a sector can be roughly control for beta. In other words, the top-down asset allocation approach described in this chapter, when combined with limits on industry weights, essentially controls for the three Fama-French factors.

Many institutional portfolio managers at major Wall Street firms apply mean-variance optimization to indices such as the Russell 1000 Barra Value Index, the Russell 1000 Barra Growth Index, the Russell 2000 Barra Value Index, the Russell 2000 Barra Growth Index, the Morgan Stanley Country Index—EAFE (Europe, Australia, Far East), and the Lehman Brothers Aggregate Bond Index to estimate the efficient frontier. Next, they select a model portfolio allocation based on investor risk tolerance, investment objectives, and so on. Finally, they impose restrictions on how far a given portfolio manager can deviate from market weights by industry (typically $\pm 3\%$ of the market value of each of the 10 S&P economic sectors in the applicable S&P index).

For bottom-up security analysis and selection, fundamental screens are applied to individual securities comprising the economic sectors and industries that make up the universe of securities in each of the indexes considered in a mean-variance optimization model. These screens could include the P/E ratio (stock price/net income before extraordinary items), price to cash flow (stock price/earnings before interest, depreciation, and amortization), dividend yield (common dividends/stock price), and rate of growth of dividends. Typically, relevant screens vary between sector and industry, and firms are only compared with similar firms in the same sector or industry.

Once the most promising candidates for analysis have been identified, spreadsheet models based on fundamental financials are constructed. These models typically include income statements, balance sheets, and cash flow statements. Models are generally constructed using quarterly data from publicly available U.S. SEC filings and project *ex ante* earnings, assets, and cash flows for at least eight quarters. *Ex ante* spreadsheet data are usually coded such that manual changes in certain key variables, such as sales revenues, gross profit margin, or inventory or receivables turnover, will automatically update the rest of the model. *Ex ante* earnings forecasts are compared with Wall Street consensus forecasts (to assess what the Street consensus is), assumptions are rechecked, and earnings forecasts are generated. Earnings and other forecast data are used in earnings or cash flow multiples or discounted cash flow models to estimate the economic fundamental value (the "intrinsic value") of a company. This value is then scaled by the number of outstanding shares and compared with the current stock price. If the intrinsic value per share is substantially higher than the stock price, the security is classified a "buy"; if it is approximately the same, it is a "hold"; if it is less, it is a "sell." Alternatively, a large variety of technical analysis models could be employed to estimate imbalances in the supply and demand for a particular security.

At this stage, the portfolio manager typically selects 30 to 40 individual securities to hold within the portfolio and buys (sells) them in amounts consistent with the client's statement of investment policy, asset allocation (if any), and economic sector or industry weighting decisions. Portfolio performance needs to be reviewed, and the manager must meet with the client on a regular basis to ensure that changing client needs are met.

Portfolio performance evaluation is complicated by the need to consider risk as well as actual versus expected portfolio returns. One of the simplest methods of evaluating portfolio risk is to estimate portfolio beta and compare it with the market beta (which by definition equals 1.0). If the portfolio beta is less than 1.0 and the actual return is equal to or higher than the market return, then the portfolio outperformed the market on a risk-adjusted basis. However, if the portfolio beta is greater than 1.0, it is not immediately apparent whether the portfolio over- or underperformed the market on a risk-adjusted basis. Moreover, precisely what constitutes "the market" is uncertain, although in practice the S&P 500 Index is most often used, as it accounts for almost 80% of the U.S. stock market. Alternatively, broader market indexes, such as the Russell 1000 or Wilshire 5000, are sometimes used.

Three relatively sophisticated measures of portfolio risk-adjusted returns are the Sharpe Ratio, the Treynor Ratio, and Jensen's Alpha. The Sharpe Ratio is the difference in the average return of the portfolio less the risk-free rate, all scaled by the standard deviation of returns of the portfolio. This measure is appropriate for investors who only hold one portfolio, as in the example detailed in this chapter, because risk is measured using standard deviation of portfolio returns—a measure of total risk (both diversifiable company specific risk and nondiversifiable systematic market risk). The Treynor Ratio resembles the Sharpe Ratio but uses beta instead of standard deviation of returns in its denominator. This measure is appropriate for a fully diversified investor who has many other investments, as well as the current one under assessment, because beta is a measure of systematic risk (nondiversifiable market risk, i.e., the sensitivity of the asset's returns to changes in the returns of the overall market). Jensen's Alpha is the excess return on the portfolio realized over the predicted return on the portfolio, expressed as

$$\alpha_p = R_p - [R_f + \beta_i(ER_m - R_f)], \qquad (22.12)$$

where α_p is Jensen's Alpha, R_p is the return on portfolio p, and $[R_f + i(ER_m - R_f)]$ is the expected return on the portfolio according to CAPM, as described in (22.8). One of the problems associated with all these measures is that it is not precisely clear over what period the expected returns, standard deviation of returns, or beta should be estimated. In practice, estimates are often made using between 5 and 25 years of data.

Another measure of portfolio risk-adjusted returns is M^2. Conceptually, M^2 (developed by Modigliani and Modigliani, hence Modigliani squared) combines a long or short investment in risk-free Treasury bills with a managed portfolio of risky securities to precisely match the volatility of the S&P 500. A portfolio with 75% of the volatility of the S&P 500 would be converted into a portfolio with 133% invested in the risky portfolio, with 33% financed by borrowing on margin at the risk-free rate. M^2 would then be the difference between the return on this new portfolio and the return on the S&P 500. However, M^2 uses the standard deviation of returns (total risk) both of the S&P 500 and of the managed portfolio as the appropriate measures of risk, with the result that it is only appropriate for an investor with one portfolio (as in the case of the example given in this chapter).

For diversified investors (i.e., those who have many portfolios), a Treynor-squared measure analogous to M^2 exists. For example, if you were trying to assess whether risky portfolio p with beta 1.25 outperformed the market on a diversified risk adjusted basis, you would create virtual portfolio $p*$ with proportion w in the risky portfolio p and proportion $(1 - w)$ in the risk-free security. For the Treynor-squared measure, proportion w is the inverse of the beta of portfolio p—in this case 0.80, so proportion $(1 - w)$ is 0.20. Treynor-squared is the difference between the weighted expected returns of both securities and the expected return on the market. If the expected return on p was 0.15, the expected return on the market was 0.10, and the risk-free rate was 0.05, then Treynor-squared would be $(0.2)(0.05) + (0.8)(0.15) - (0.10) = 0.03$. When Treynor-squared is greater than 0, the investment outperforms the market on a diversified risk-adjusted basis. When it equals 0, it performs as well as the market, and when it is less than 0, it underperforms.

Many larger institutional portfolio managers employ multifactor models such as the Aegis System offered by Barra. These programs seek to decompose portfolio performance into common sources of risk, allowing managers to focus on the areas of their greatest strength (such as individual security selection) while avoiding areas of weakness (such as market or industry timing).

The final step in the portfolio management and risky-security analysis and selection process involves periodic meetings with the client to determine whether client risk tolerance or investment constraints have changed. Client risk tolerance, liquidity needs, time horizons, taxes, and legal and regulatory factors change over time. Consequently, effective portfolio managers normally meet with their client to review their investment policy statements at least once per year. Frequently, this step is combined with quarterly or semi-annual updates and reports to clients on portfolio performance. Following changes in investment policy, the process recycles.

Ethics and Values, Validity, Interpretation, and Areas for Future Research

Portfolio managers act as agents when managing investment portfolios on behalf of clients or principals. When an agent performs a service on behalf of a principal, a potential conflict of interest arises because the agent has incentives to act in his own interests rather than those of his principal. Steps taken to curtail agency conflict between portfolio managers and clients include external monitoring of larger managers by rating agencies such as Morningstar and Lipper, internal alignment of managerial incentives with those of clients through performance-based pay, and especially securities law and regulation. Because portfolio managers are responsible for trillions of dollars belonging to clients, the investments industry is one of the most heavily regulated and policed industries in the world.

In the United States, relevant securities laws include The Securities Act of 1933, The Securities and Exchange Act of 1934, The Investment Advisers Act of 1940, The Investment Company Act of 1940, and The Employee Retirement Income Security Act of 1974. These acts govern public securities offerings (including shares of mutual funds), broker-dealers, mutual fund advisors, investment companies, and pension funds. The SEC is the federal agency chiefly responsible for regulating investments industry activities and sets standards on margin, fund governance, and reporting. Other interested agencies include the Department of Labor (for pension plans), the Commodity and Futures Trading Commission (for futures), and the Internal Revenue Service (for taxes).

States and industry associations are also involved in investment industry regulation and supervision. For example, The Attorney General for the State of New York, The National Association for Securities Dealers, and The New York Stock Exchange are deeply involved in oversight of the U.S. investment industry. Even traditionally loosely regulated hedge funds, which were exempt from much of this regulation, are increasingly becoming subject to regulatory scrutiny. Industry associations, such as The CFA (Chartered Financial Analyst) Institute, have their own codes of ethics and standards of conduct that often go beyond the minimum levels of ethical behavior required by law.

Portfolio management techniques based on mean-variance optimization offer no guarantees for future performance, partly because they rely on historic returns and partly because of problems encountered when implementing the model in practice. The efficient frontier and the individual-client-optimized portfolio are highly sensitive to the indexes and estimation periods chosen. The choice of indexes to include is constrained by the availability of data, which is why most real-world mean-variance optimizers use the longer-running Russell 1000 and 2000 Growth and Value Indexes (available since 1979) than the more recent competing S&P indexes. Michaud (1998) describes the chief drawbacks of mean-variance optimization as a practical tool in terms of instability and ambiguity. He suggests that small estimation errors lead to large optimized portfolio errors and mean-variance optimization overfits the estimated data. Darst (2003) also points out that historic returns may not be appropriate for current market conditions.

Similarly, risky-asset analysis and selection techniques based on fundamental or technical analysis offer no guarantees for future performance, partly because they too rely on historic-based financial accounting data and partly because of a current lack of validation for fundamental and technical analysis.

In the fields of mean-variance optimization and security analysis and selection, there are promising areas for future research. Areas warranting future investigation include a sensitivity analysis of estimators to mean-variance optimization solutions, how sensitivity changes over time, mean-variance optimization over different time horizons, links between estimators and macroeconomic variables such as interest rates, changes in the correlation of market returns associated with the globalization of financial markets, and changes in market volatility. Mean-variance optimization, possibly combined with fundamental and technical analysis, all well-grounded in modern probability theory, has potential for near-universal application in portfolio management and risky-security analysis and selection. Michaud (1998) nevertheless laments that its acceptance is incomplete.

For additional information on modern probability theory applied to portfolio management and risky security analysis and selection, the reader is referred to several sources. First, Reilly and Brown (2006) provide an excellent overview of all aspects of investments. An excellent theoretical discussion of modern portfolio theory is contained in Elton and Gruber (1995). Limitations of portfolio theory and problems encountered in its implementation are summarized in Michaud (1998) and Darst (2003). Fundamental analysis is described in Graham and Dodd (2002) and technical analysis in Murphy (1999) and Pring (2002).

Conclusion

This chapter summarizes some of the techniques available to modern portfolio managers and other sophisticated investors in the management of their investment portfolios and the analysis and selection of risky securities to hold in these portfolios. The second section describes modern portfolio theory and risky-security analysis based on fundamental and technical analysis, dating from the times of Markowitz (1952, 1959), Graham and Dodd (2002), and Charles Dow (the early 20th century). The third section walks the reader through an example of how top-down asset allocation is done in practice. Historic returns data are used to estimate expected returns, standard deviation (or variance), and correlation coefficients. Equations (22.1), (22.6), and (22.7) are solved to estimate the efficient frontier, and investor risk tolerance is estimated to identify an appropriate asset allocation strategy. Bottom-up security selection, typically using fundamental analysis, technical analysis, or both, is then performed, and individual securities are purchased or sold to hold long or short in the portfolio. Performance reassessments are performed, and changes are made to the portfolio as the process recycles. In the fourth section, ethics, values, validity, interpretation, and areas for future research are examined. Some of the most promising areas for future research include the analysis of the sensitivity of estimators to mean-variance-optimized portfolios, how this sensitivity changes over time, and mean-variance optimization over different time horizons.

References

Black, F., & Scholes, M. (1973). The pricing of options and corporate liabilities. *Journal of Political Economy*, *81*(2), 637–654.

Darst, D. M. (2003). *The art of asset allocation: Asset allocation principles and investment strategies for any market.* New York: McGraw-Hill.

Elton, E. J., & Gruber, M. J. (1995). *Modern portfolio theory and investment analysis* (5th ed.). New York: Wiley.

Fama, E. F., & French, K. R. (1993). Common risk factors in the returns on stocks and bonds. *Journal of Financial Economics*, *33*(1), 3–56.

Graham, B., & Dodd, D. (2002). *Security analysis* (2nd ed.). New York: McGraw-Hill.

Grossman, S. J., & Stiglitz, J. E. (1980). Impossibility of informationally efficient markets. *American Economic Review*, *70*(3), 393–408.

Malkiel, B. G. (2004). *A random walk down Wall Street.* New York: W. W. Norton.

Markowitz, H. (1952). Portfolio selection. *Journal of Finance*, *7*(1), 77–91.

Markowitz, H. (1959). *Portfolio selection: Efficient diversification of investments.* New York: Wiley.

Michaud, R. O. (1998). *Efficient asset management: A practical guide to stock portfolio optimization and asset allocation.* Boston: Harvard Business School Press.

Murphy, J. J. (1999). *Technical analysis of the financial markets: A comprehensive guide to trading methods and applications.* New York: New York Institute of Finance.

Pring, M. J. (2002). *Technical analysis explained* (4th ed.). New York: McGraw-Hill.

Reilly, F. K., & Brown, K. C. (2006). *Investment analysis and portfolio management* (8th ed.). Mason, OH: Thomson South-Western.

Roll, R., & Ross, S. A. (1995). The arbitrage pricing theory approach to strategic portfolio planning. *Financial Analysts Journal*, *51*(1), 44–53.

Sharpe, W. F. (1964). Capital asset prices: A theory of market equilibrium under conditions of risk. *Journal of Finance*, *19*(3), 425–442.

23

EXPERT SYSTEMS

GEORGE LUGER AND CHAYAN CHAKRABARTI

INTRODUCTION

An important research enterprise for the Artificial Intelligence (AI) community since the 1970s has been the design of expert or "knowledge-based" systems. These programs used explicitly encoded human knowledge, often in the form of a production rule system, to solve problems in the areas of diagnostics and prognostics. The earliest research on, and development of, expert systems was by Professor Edward Feigenbaum at Stanford University (Buchanan & Shortliffe, 1984). Because the expert system often addresses problems that are imprecise and not fully specified, with data sets that are often inexact and unclear, the role of various forms of probabilistic support for reasoning is important.

The 1990s saw radical new approaches to the design of automated reasoning and diagnostic systems. With the creation of graphical models, the explicit pieces of human knowledge (of the expert system) were encoded into causal networks, sometimes referred to as Bayesian belief networks (BBNs). The reasoning supporting these networks, based on two simplifying assumptions (that reasoning could not be cyclic and that the causality supporting a child state would be expressed in the links between it and its parent states) made BBN reasoning more computationally manageable. In recent years, the use of graphical models has replaced the traditional expert system, especially in situations where reasoning was diagnostic and prognostic—that is, extending from concrete situations to the best explanations for their occurrence. This type of reasoning is often termed *abductive*.

In this chapter, we first present the technology supporting the traditional knowledge-based expert system, including the production system for reasoning with rules. In the second section, we discuss Bayesian inference and the adoption of simplifying techniques such as the Stanford certainty factor algebra. In the third section, we introduce graphical models, including the assumptions supporting the use of BBNs, and present an example of BBN reasoning. We conclude with a brief introduction of a next-generation system for diagnostic reasoning using more expressive forms of the BBN.

EXPERT SYSTEMS

We begin with the presentation of some of the traditional application areas of the rule-based technology. We then describe the software architecture supporting its development.

Introduction of the Traditional Expert System

The rationale behind building knowledge-based problem solvers was that human experts know a lot about their area of expertise. Expert systems designers acquire this knowledge from skilled human practitioners and then program the system to emulate the human expert's methodology. These human experts also augment the system's knowledge with shortcuts and heuristics that they have gained from experience. These heuristics can also be encoded using probabilistic methods. Expert systems are built to solve a wide range of problems in domains such as medicine, mathematics, engineering, chemistry, geology, computer science, business, law, defense, and education. The range of problem categories can be summarized as follows (Waterman, 1986):

- *Interpretation:* Forming high-level conclusions from collections of raw data
- *Prediction:* Projecting the probable consequences of given situations
- *Diagnosis:* Determining the cause of malfunctions in complex situations based on observable symptoms
- *Design:* Finding a configuration of system components that meets performance goals while satisfying a set of design constraints
- *Planning:* Devising a sequence of actions that will achieve a set of goals given certain starting conditions and run-time constraints
- *Monitoring:* Comparing a system's observed behavior with its expected behavior
- *Instruction:* Assisting in the education process in technical domains
- *Control:* Governing the behavior of a complex environment

Generally, the programs implementing expert systems are built using the iterative development software methodology. This requires that programs be easily prototyped, tested, and changed. Easy modification of the knowledge base is vital for successful expert system design. Also, it is important that the expert system be able to display all the intermediate problem-solving steps and justify its choices and decisions. These explanations are important for a human expert, such as a doctor or an engineer, if he or she is to accept the system's recommendations.

The Design of Rule-Based Expert Systems

Figure 23.1 shows the modules that make up a typical expert system. The user interface, often graphical, hides much of the complexity of the system. All the knowledge of a problem domain is encoded in the knowledge base, which is the heart of the system. Most often, this consists of *if... then ...* rules. The inference engine applies the knowledge to the solution of actual problems. This can be done using a production system (see the next subsection). The knowledge base and inference engine are separated for several reasons:

1. *If... then ...* rules are a very natural way to represent human problem-solving skills.
2. System designers can focus on capturing problem-solving knowledge without worrying about implementation details.
3. Changes can be made in one part of the knowledge base without affecting others.
4. The same inference engine can be plugged into different expert systems and work with different knowledge bases.

The knowledge base is augmented with case-specific data, which contain information relevant to the case under consideration and are often acquired as the program runs. The explanation subsystem allows the system to explain its reasoning to the user.

The Production System in Expert System Problem Solving

The *production system* is a model of computation that has proved particularly important in AI, both for implementing search algorithms and for modeling human problem-solving behavior. A production system provides pattern-directed control of the problem-solving process and consists of

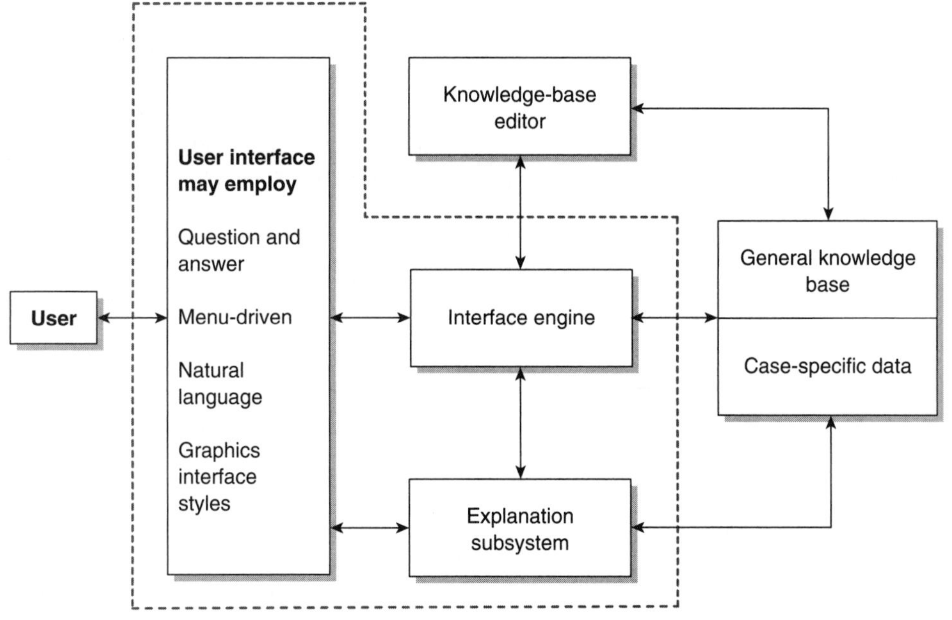

Figure 23.1 Architecture of a typical expert system for a particular problem domain.

SOURCE: Adapted from Luger, G. F. (2005). *Artificial intelligence: Structures and strategies for complex problem solving* (5th ed.). London: Addision-Wesley/Pearson.

a set of *production rules*, a *working memory*, and a *recognize-act* control cycle, as detailed below:

- *Set of production rules:* These are often simply called *productions*. A production is a *condition* → *action* pair and defines a single chunk of problem-solving knowledge. Both the condition part and the action or goal part of a rule are formed of patterns that determine when that rule may be applied to a problem instance.

- *Working memory:* Working memory contains a description of the *current state of the world* in a reasoning process. This description is a pattern that in *data-driven reasoning* is matched against the condition part of the set of productions to select appropriate problem-solving actions and in *goal-driven reasoning* is matched against the current goal or subgoal being explored.

- *Recognize-act cycle:* The control structure for a production system is simple: *Working memory* is initialized with the beginning and goal problem descriptions. The current state of problem solving is maintained as a set of patterns in working memory. These patterns are matched against the conditions or actions of the production rules; this produces a subset of the production rules, called the *conflict set*, whose conditions (or goals) match the patterns in working memory. After a selected production rule is fired, the control cycle repeats with the modified working memory. The process terminates when the contents of working memory do not match any rules or the problem is solved.

- *Conflict resolution:* Conflict resolution is a set of heuristics that is used to choose a rule from the conflict set for firing. Conflict resolution strategies may be simple, such as selecting the first rule whose condition or action matches the state of the world, or may involve complex rule selection heuristics (Forgy, 1982; Luger, 2005, chap. 6).

The architecture of rule-based expert systems may be best understood in terms of the production system model for problem solving. The

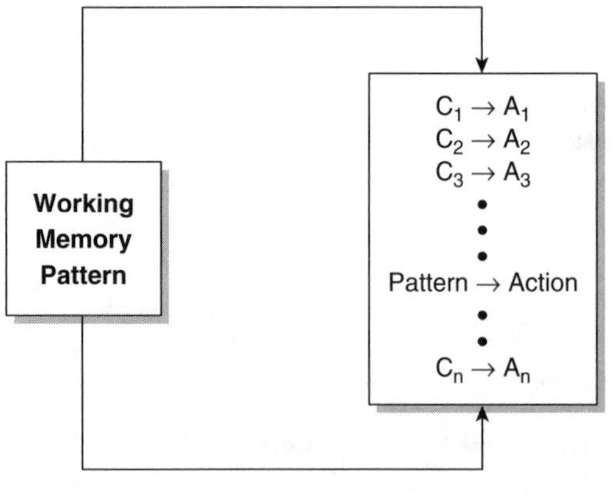

Figure 23.2 A production system: Control loops until working memory pattern no longer matches the conditions of any productions.

SOURCE: Adapted from Luger, G. F. (2005). *Artificial intelligence: Structures and strategies for complex problem solving* (5th ed.). London: Addison-Wesley/Pearson.

parallel between the two is more than an analogy: The production system was the intellectual precursor of modern expert system architectures, where application of production rules leads to refinements of understanding of a particular problem situation. When Newell and Simon (1976) first developed the production system, their goal was to model human performance in problem solving.

If we regard the expert system architecture in Figure 23.1 as a production system, the domain-specific knowledge base is the set of production rules (Figure 23.2). In a rule-based system, these condition-action pairs are represented as *if*... *then* ... rules, with the premises of the rules—the *if* portion—corresponding to the condition, and the conclusion—the *then* portion—corresponding to the action. In data-driven reasoning, when the condition is satisfied, the expert system takes the action of asserting that the conclusion as true. In goal-driven reasoning, the *then* portion of the rule is matched to see what conditions (subgoals) must be supported for the goal to be true. Case-specific data can be kept in the working memory. The inference engine implements the recognize-act cycle of the production system, which may be either data driven or goal driven.

Many problem domains seem to lend themselves more naturally to forward search. In an interpretation problem, for example, most of the data for the problem are initially given, and it is often difficult to formulate a hypothesis or a goal. This suggests a forward-reasoning process, in which the facts are placed in working memory, the conditions of rules matching those facts are matched, and the system searches for an interpretation.

In a goal-driven expert system, the goal expression is initially placed in working memory. The system matches the conclusions of the rules with that goal, selecting one rule and placing its premises in the working memory. This corresponds to a decomposition of the problem's goal into simpler subgoals. The process continues in the next iteration of the production system, with these subgoals becoming the new goals to match against rule conclusions. The system thus works back from the original goal until all the subgoals in working memory are known to be true, indicating that the hypothesis has been verified. Thus, backward search in an expert system corresponds roughly to the process of hypothesis testing in human problem solving. In an expert system, subgoals can be solved (when the production rules offer no matches) by asking the system's user for information. Furthermore, some expert systems allow the designer to specify which subgoals are to be solved by asking the user. Others simply ask the user about any subgoals that fail to match rules in the knowledge base; that is, if the program cannot infer the truth of a subgoal, it asks the user.

Knowledge-Based Reasoning in Conditions of Uncertainty

We next present the technology supporting uncertain reasoning in expert systems. Although a few early systems used Bayesian approaches, these by and large proved unsuitable to the task. We discuss these issues and then present a popular alternative, the Stanford certainty factor algebra.

A Brief Introduction to the Bayesian Approach

Up to this point in our presentation, we have ignored an important component of expert system work. That is, in many applications, the *if*... *then* ... rules of the system are *not* always certain "if and only if" or cause-effect relationships. That is, many of the rules express "usually," "it is likely that," "often," or "sometimes" relations between their conditions and the actions.

This is not always the case, of course. The rules in many expert systems express direct cause and effect; for example, in software to configure a computer hardware system, there will be no uncertainty as to whether a certain disk and bus can be linked. Furthermore, in working with algebraic expert systems, there is no uncertainty involved in relationships, for example, between a function and its derivative.

Most expert systems, however, especially those reasoning from effects back to causes, do have some uncertainty in their condition-action relationships. Medical systems—and MYCIN is certainly the prototype (Buchanan & Shortliffe, 1984) of this genre—reason from patient's symptoms back to possible causes (explanations) for these symptoms. In fact, most diagnostic expert systems reason back from the facts of situations to their probable causes. The vast majority of these relationships are inherently uncertain!

A further issue that affects uncertain reasoning is the vagueness and lack of clarity that is often found in data sets. When a rule asks if a patient's temperature is "high," what precisely does that mean? Even if the rule is rewritten using a range of explicit temperatures, certainly some will be "higher" than others. There will also be some variation within the testing devices that are used to obtain patient's temperatures. Finally, in many diagnostic situations, key pieces of data may in fact be missing. In all these situations, the expert system must still track what information it has and attempt to come up with the best possible explanation.

Bayes's theorem (1763) is a mathematically sound methodology for interpreting uncertain relationships, such as those just mentioned. Furthermore, Bayes's equation relates the a priori (what we know about and/or have been trained to "see") with the a posteriori (what we are currently observing). We will not describe Bayes's work in detail here—this has been done adequately in other places in this *Handbook*. Although Bayes's theorem is often seen as natural for expert system work, and several systems have used it, most famously PROSPECTOR (Duda, Gaschnig, & Hart, 1979), we make the larger point that Bayes's theorem is not used in the development of the vast majority of expert systems. We then describe the most common alternative for uncertain reasoning in expert systems, the Stanford certainty factor algebra.

There are several major reasons for not using Bayes's theorem to address the uncertainty requirements in rule-based expert systems. The first reason is the task of collecting all the necessary probability measures. This is especially difficult because most expert systems are dynamic: If the designer wants to add new "knowledge" to the system, he or she simply adds one or more new production rules. This, of course, requires the strict Bayesian to readjust many of the probability measures already in the system to accommodate this new rule relationship. Second, many of the uncertainties of the knowledge-based system are not, in fact, probabilistic, and it is difficult to assign an appropriate probability measure to them. Finally, we must assume in our application domain that the pieces of evidence for a particular hypothesis are independent. In many important problem domains, this assumption of independence cannot be justified.

It is interesting to note, however, that many situations that violate this assumption (that the individual pieces of evidence partition the evidence set) behave quite well! Using this partition assumption, even in situations where it is not justified, is called using *naive Bayes* or a *Bayes classifier* (Luger, 2005, chap. 5).

In general, we use Bayes's theorem to determine the probability of some hypothesis h_i given a set of evidence E, or $p(h_i \mid E)$. In this situation, Bayes requires that we obtain the values of $p(E \mid h_i)$ and $p(h_i)$. These numbers are often much more easily obtainable, compared with obtaining the values for $p(h_i \mid E)$ directly. For example, because the population is smaller, it is much easier to determine the number of meningitis patients who have headaches than it is to determine the percentage of headache sufferers that have meningitis. Even more important, for the simple case of a single disease and a single symptom, not very many numbers are needed. The trouble begins, however, when we consider multiple hypothesized diseases h_i from the domain of diseases H and multiple symptoms e_n from the set E of possible symptoms. When we consider each disease from m hypotheses from H and each symptom from n pieces of evidence from E singly, we have mn measures to collect and integrate (actually mn posterior probabilities plus $m+n$ prior probabilities).

Unfortunately, our analysis is about to get much more complex. Up to this point, we considered each symptom e_i individually. In actual situations, single symptoms are rarely the case. When a doctor is considering a patient, for instance, there are often many combinations of symptoms he or she must consider. We require a form of Bayes's theorem to consider any single hypothesis h_i in the context of the union of multiple symptoms e_i:

$$p(h_i|(e_1 \cup e_2 \cup \cdots \cup e_n)) = \frac{p(h_i)p((e_1 \cup e_2 \cup \cdots \cup e_n)|h_i)}{p(e_1 \cup e_2 \cup \cdots \cup e_n)}.$$

The term $p(e_1 \cup e_2 \cup \cdots \cup e_n)$ does not affect the conditional probability on the left-hand side of the above equation. It is simply a normalizing constant, and we can eliminate it from our calculations. With one disease and a single symptom, we needed only mn measurements. Now, for every pair of symptoms e_i and e_j and a particular disease hypothesis h_i, we need to know $p(e_i \cup e_j \mid h_i)$. There will be n such observations when there are n symptoms in E. Now, if we want to use Bayes's theorem, there will be about mn(conditional probabilities) + n (symptom probabilities) + m(disease probabilities) or about $mn+n+m$ pieces of information to collect. This number can become very large in realistic medical systems.

In many diagnostic situations, we must also deal with negative information—for example, when a patient does not have a symptom such as bad blood pressure. We require both

$$\text{not}(p(e_i)) = 1 - p(e_i)$$

and

$$\text{not}(p(h_i \mid e_i)) = 1 - p(h_i \mid e_i)$$

We also note that $p(e_i \mid h_i)$ and $p(h_i \mid e_i)$ are not the same and will almost always have different values. These relationships, and the avoidance of circular reasoning, is important in the design of BBNs.

A final problem, noted briefly earlier, is the need to rebuild probability measures when new relationships between hypotheses and evidence sets are discovered. In many active research areas, such as medicine, new discoveries happen continuously. Bayesian reasoning requires complete and up-to-date probabilities, including joint probabilities, if its conclusions are to be correct. Such extensive data collection and verification can be prohibitively expensive.

Where these assumptions are met, however, Bayesian approaches offer the benefit of a mathematically well-founded handling of uncertainty. Most expert system domains do not meet these requirements and must rely on heuristic approaches, such as Stanford certainty theory (presented next). Furthermore, due to complexity issues, we know that even fairly powerful computers cannot use full Bayesian techniques for successful real-time problem solving.

An Alternative to Bayes: The Stanford Certainty Factor Algebra

Stanford certainty theory, a calculus for subjective probability measures, is based on a number of observations. The first is that in traditional probability theory, the sum of the probability for a relationship and the probability against the same relationship must add to 1. However, it is often the case that a human expert might have "confidence" 0.7 (say) that some relationship is true and have no feeling at all of it being not true. A further assumption that underpins certainty theory is that the knowledge content of the rules is much more important than the algebra for computing the confidences. Confidence measures correspond to the informal evaluations that human experts attach to their conclusions, such as "it is probably true," "it is almost certainly true," or "it is highly unlikely." Furthermore, they make absolutely no claims about a statistics-based relationship between the condition of a rule and its corresponding action!

The Stanford certainty theory makes some simple assumptions for creating confidence measures and has some equally simple rules for combining these confidences as the program moves toward its conclusion. The first assumption is to split "confidence for" from "confidence against" relationship:

> Call MB($H \mid E$) the measure of belief of a hypothesis H given evidence E.
>
> Call MD($H \mid E$) the measure of disbelief of a hypothesis H given evidence E.

Now, either

$$1 > \text{MB}\ (H \mid E) > 0 \quad \text{while MD}\ (H \mid E) = 0$$

or

$$1 > \text{MD}\ (H \mid E) > 0 \quad \text{while MB}(H \mid E) = 0.$$

These two measures constrain each other in that a given piece of evidence is either for or against a particular hypothesis, an important difference between certainty theory and probability theory. Once the link between measures of belief and disbelief has been established, they may be tied together again, by

$$\text{CF}(H \mid E) = \text{MB}(H \mid E) - \text{MD}(H \mid E).$$

As the certainty factor (CF) approaches 1, the evidence is stronger for a hypothesis; as CF approaches -1, the confidence against the hypothesis gets stronger; and a CF around 0 indicates that either little evidence exists for or against the hypothesis or the evidence for and against the hypothesis is balanced.

When experts put together a rule base, they must agree on a CF to go with each rule. This CF reflects their confidence in the rule's reliability. Certainty measures may be adjusted to tune the system's performance, although slight variations in the confidence measure tend to have little effect on the overall running of the system. This second role of certainty measures confirms the belief that "the knowledge gives the power"; that is, the integrity of the knowledge itself best supports the production of correct diagnoses.

Because the architecture for expert systems is a production system, the premises for each rule are formed of *and*s and *or*s of a number of facts. When a production rule is used, the CFs associated with each condition of the premise are combined to produce a certainty measure for the overall premise as follows. For $P1$ and $P2$ premises of the rule,

$$\text{CF}(P1 \text{ and } P2) = \min(\text{CF}(P1), \text{CF}(P2))$$

and

$$\text{CF}(P1 \text{ or } P2) = \max(\text{CF}(P1), \text{CF}(P)).$$

The combined CF of the premises, using the above rules, is then multiplied by the CF of the rule itself to get the CF for the conclusions of the rule. For example, consider the rule in a knowledge base

$$(P1 \text{ and } P2) \text{ or } P3 \rightarrow R1\ (0.7) \text{ and } R2\ (0.3)$$

where $P1$, $P2$, and $P3$ are premises and $R1$ and $R2$ are the conclusions of the rule, having CFs 0.7 and 0.3, respectively. These numbers are attached to the rule when it is designed and represent the expert's confidence in the conclusion if all the premises are known with complete certainty. If the running program has produced $P1$, $P2$, and $P3$ with CFs of 0.6, 0.4, and 0.2, respectively, then $R1$ and $R2$ may be added to the collected case-specific results with CFs 0.28 and 0.12, respectively. Here are the calculations for this example:

$$\text{CF}(P1\,(0.6) \text{ and } P2\,(0.4)) = \min(0.6, 0.4) = 0.4.$$
$$\text{CF}(P2\ (0.4) \text{ or } P3\ (0.2)) = \max(0.4, 0.2) = 0.4.$$

The CF for $R1$ is 0.7 in the rule, so $R1$ is added to the set of case-specific knowledge with the associated CF of $(0.7) \times (0.4) = 0.28$. The CF for $R2$ is 0.3 in the rule, so $R2$ is added to the set of case-specific knowledge with the associated CF of $(0.3) \times (0.4) = 0.12$.

One further measure is required: how to combine multiple CFs when two or more rules support the same result R. This rule reflects the certainty theory analog of the probability theory procedure of multiplying probability measures to combine independent evidence. By using this rule repeatedly, one can combine the results of any number of rules that are used for determining a result R. Suppose CF($R1$) is the present CF associated with result R and a previously unused rule produces result R (again) with CF($R2$); then, the new CF of R is calculated by

$$\mathrm{CF}(R1) + \mathrm{CF}(R2) - (\mathrm{CF}(R1) \times \mathrm{CF}(R2))$$
$$\text{when } \mathrm{CF}(R1) \text{and } \mathrm{CF}(R2) \text{ are positive,}$$
$$\mathrm{CF}(R1) + \mathrm{CF}(R2) + (\mathrm{CF}(R1) \times \mathrm{CF}(R2))$$
$$\text{when } \mathrm{CF}(R1) \text{ and } \mathrm{CF}(R2) \text{are negative,}$$

and

$$\frac{(\mathrm{CF}(R1) + \mathrm{CF}(R2))}{(1 - \mathrm{MIN}(|\mathrm{CF}(R1)|), |\mathrm{CF}(R2)|)}, \text{ otherwise,}$$

where $|X|$ is the absolute value of X and $\mathrm{MIN}(a,b)$ means the minimum value of a or b.

Besides being easy to compute, these combination equations have other desirable properties. First, the CFs that result from applying this rule are always between 1 and -1. Second, the result of combining contradictory CFs is that they cancel each other, as is desired. Finally, the combined CF measure is a monotonically increasing (decreasing) function in the manner one would expect for combining evidence.

Finally, the confidence measures of the Stanford certainty factor tradition are a human (subjective) estimate of symptom/cause probability measures. As noted in the earlier subsection, A Brief Introduction to the Bayesian Approach, in the Bayesian tradition if A, B, and C all influence D, we need to isolate and appropriately combine all the prior and posterior probabilities, including $p(D)$, $p(D \mid A)$, $p(D \mid B)$, $p(D \mid C)$, $p(A \mid D)$, when we want to reason about D. The Stanford certainty factor tradition allows the knowledge engineer to wrap all these relationships together into one confidence factor, CF, attached to the rule; that is, if A and B and C, then D (CF). It is felt that this simple algebra better reflects how human experts combine and propagate multiple sets of beliefs.

Certainty theory may be criticized as being excessively ad hoc. Although it is defined in a formal algebra, the meaning of the certainty measures is not as rigorously founded as is formal probability theory. However, certainty theory does not attempt to produce an algebra for "correct" reasoning. Rather, it is the "lubrication" that lets the expert system combine confidences as it moves along through the problem at hand. Its measures are ad hoc in the same sense that a human expert's confidence in his or her results is approximate, heuristic, and informal. When MYCIN is run, for example, the CFs are used in the heuristic search to give a priority for goals to be attempted and a cutoff point when a goal need not be considered further. But even though the CF is used to keep the program running and collecting information, the power of the program remains invested in the quality of the rules.

Graphical Models for Uncertain Reasoning

In most of AI, the primary inference mechanism in stochastic domains is some form of Bayes's rule. As we noted in the subsection A Brief Introduction to the Bayesian Approach, however, the full use of Bayesian inference in complex domains quickly becomes intractable. In the following sections, we present several inference techniques specifically designed to address this complexity; these include BBNs, Markov models, and hidden Markov models (HMMs).

The Bayesian Belief Network

The two preceding sections describe the origins of and software architecture for the rule-based expert system. It is not the purpose of this present chapter to critique the "expert system experiment" in the context of software applications. It is sufficient to mention that in many situations, especially where the problem domain was well understood, the expert system technology proved successful. In many of these situations, once a solution was achieved, the expert system technology simply morphed into the larger suite of successful software systems. Where problems were imprecise, ill defined, and ambiguous, however, the expert system approach could prove both brittle and cumbersome. This is because the semantics (basic meaning entailed) through the use of expert systems technology is rather weak, if it exists at all. For example, the expert system designed to help sick people simply does not *understand* sick people. In summary, where the technology fit, it worked well; in other contexts, it was often unsuccessful.

Although Bayesian probability theory, as discussed earlier, offers a mathematical foundation for reasoning under uncertain conditions, the complexity encountered in applying it to realistic problem domains is often prohibitive. Fortunately, we can often prune this complexity by focusing the search on a smaller set of more highly relevant events and evidence. One approach—BBNs (Pearl, 1988)—offers a computational model for reasoning to the best explanation of a set of data in the context of the expected causal relationships of a problem domain.

BBNs can dramatically reduce the number of parameters of the full Bayesian model and show how the data of a domain (or even the absence of data) can partition and focus reasoning. Furthermore, the modularity of a problem domain often allows the program designer to make many independence assumptions not allowed in a full Bayesian treatment. In most reasoning situations, it is not necessary to build a large joint-probability table in which the probabilities for all possible combinations of events and evidence are listed. Rather, human experts seem to select the local phenomena that they know will interact and obtain probability or influence measures that reflect only these clusters of events. Experts assume that all other events are either conditionally independent or that their correlations are so small that they may be ignored.

As an example of BBN, consider the traffic problem presented in Figure 23.3. Suppose you are driving an automobile in rural New Mexico. Suddenly you begin to slow down with the traffic. You begin to wonder what the traffic problem might be. Because you have driven quite a bit in rural New Mexico, you have a set of prior expectations for bad traffic, related mainly to highway construction and traffic accidents. Thus, our Bayesian belief net representation of these prior expectations is reflected in Figure 23.3, where road construction is C, an accident is A, the presence of orange barrels is B, bad traffic is T, and flashing lights is L. To calculate the joint probability of all the parameters of the example required knowledge of or measurements for all parameters being in particular states. Thus, the joint probability is

$$p(C,A,B,T,L) = p(C) \times p(A|C) \times p(B|C,A) \times p(T|C,A,B) \times p(L|C,A,B,T).$$

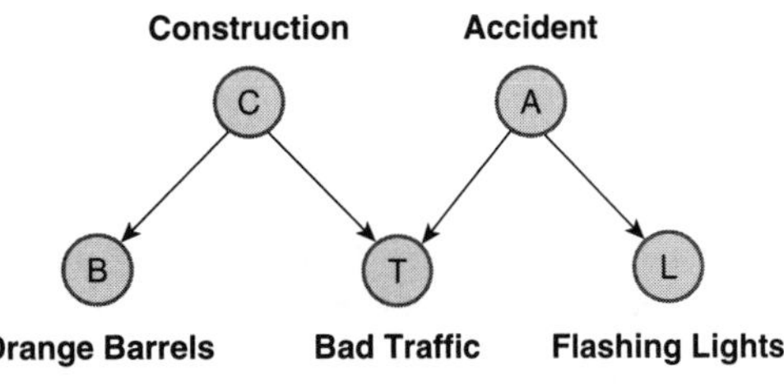

Figure 23.3 The graphical model for the traffic problem.

SOURCE: Adapted from Luger, G. F. (2005). *Artificial intelligence: Structures and strategies for complex problem solving* (5th ed.). London: Addison-Wesley/Pearson.

The number of parameters in this joint probability is 31. This table is exponential in the number of variables involved. For a problem of any complexity, say with 30 or more variables, the joint distribution table would have more than 1 billion elements (see the discussion in the subsection A Brief Introduction to the Bayesian Approach).

Note, however, that if we can support the assumption that the parameters of this problem are only dependent on the probabilities of their parents—that is, if we can assume that nodes are independent of all nondescendents, given knowledge of their parents, the calculation of $p(C,A,B,T,L)$ becomes

$$p(C,A,B,T,L) = p(C) \times p(A) \times p(B \mid C) \times p(T \mid C,A) \times p(L \mid A).$$

To better see the simplifications we have made, consider $p(B \mid C,A)$ from the previous equation. We have reduced this to $p(B \mid C)$ in our most recent equation. This is based on the assumption that road construction is not a causal effect of there being an accident. Similarly, the presence of orange barrels is not a cause of bad traffic, but construction and accident are, giving as a result $p(T \mid C,A)$ rather than $p(T \mid C,A,B)$. Finally, $p(L \mid C,A,B,T)$ is reduced to $p(L \mid A)$! The probability distribution for $p(C,A,B,T,L)$ now has only 20 (rather than 32) parameters. And if we move to a more realistic problem, with 30 variables say, and if each state has at most two parents, there will be at most 240 elements in the distribution. If each state has three parents, the maximum is 490 elements in the distribution—considerably less than the exponentially large number required for the full Bayesian approach!

We need to justify this dependence of a node in a belief network on its parents alone. Links between the nodes of a belief network represent the conditioned probabilities for causal influence. Implicit in expert reasoning using causal inference is the assumption that these influences are directed, that is, the presence of some event somehow causes other events in the network. Furthermore, causal influence reasoning is not circular in that some effect cannot circle back to cause itself. For these reasons, BBNs will have a natural representation as a directed acyclic graph, or DAG (Luger, 2005, sec. 3.1), where coherent patterns of reasoning are reflected as paths through cause-effect relationships. BBNs are one instance of what are often called graphical models.

In the case of our traffic example, we have an even stronger situation that allows us to calculate very simply the probability distribution at every node. The distributions of nodes having no parents are directly looked up. The values of child nodes are computed using only the probability distributions of each child's parents by doing the appropriate computations on the child's conditional probability table and the parent's distributions. This is possible because we don't have to worry about the relationship between the parents of any node (since the network is given as a DAG). This produces a natural abductive separation where accident has no correlation at all with the presence of orange barrels, as is seen in Figure 23.3. We summarize our discussion of BBNs and the traffic example with the following definition:

- A graphical model is called a BBN if its graph, annotated with conditional probabilities, is directed and acyclic. Furthermore, BBNs assume that nodes are independent of all their nondescendents, given knowledge of their parents.

- A *dynamic Bayesian network* (DBN) is a sequence of identical Bayesian networks whose nodes are linked in the (directed) dimension of time. We consider the general DBN briefly in the subsection Diagnostic and Prognostic Reasoning With Graphical Models; for further details, see Friedman (1998) or Ghahramani and Jordan (1997).

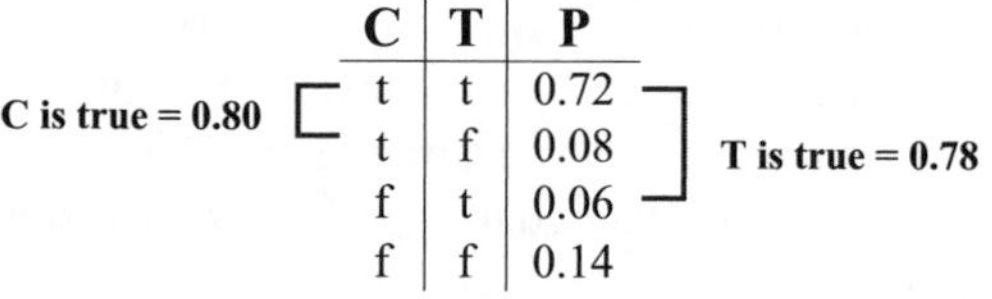

C	T	P
t	t	0.72
t	f	0.08
f	t	0.06
f	f	0.14

Figure 23.4 The joint-probability distribution for the traffic and the construction variables of Figure 23.3.

Inference With a Bayesian Belief Network

We now extend our belief net example. Again, suppose you are driving the interstate highway system and realize you are gradually slowing down because of increased traffic congestion. You begin to search for possible explanations of the slowdown. Could it be road construction? Has there been an accident? Perhaps there are other possible explanations. After a few minutes' driving, you come across orange barrels at the side of the road that begin to cut off the outside lane of traffic. At this point, you determine that the best explanation of the traffic congestion is road construction. At the same time, the alternative hypothesis of an accident is explained away. Similarly, if you would have seen flashing lights in the distance ahead, such as from a police vehicle or an ambulance, the best explanation for your current traffic slowdown, given this new evidence, would be a traffic accident, and road construction would have been explained away. When a hypothesis is explained away, it does not mean that it is no longer possible. Rather, in the context of new evidence, it is simply less likely.

Figure 23.3 presented a Bayesian network account of what we have just seen. *Road construction* is correlated with *orange barrels* and *bad traffic*. Similarly, accident correlates with *flashing lights* and *bad traffic*. We next examine Figure 23.3 and build a joint-probability distribution for the *road construction* and *bad traffic* relationship. We simplify both of these variables to be either true (t) or false (f) and re-present the probability distribution in Figure 23.4. Note that if *construction* is f, there is not likely to be *bad traffic*, and if it is t, then *bad traffic* is likely. Note also that the probability of *road construction* on the interstate, $C =$ t, is 0.8 and the probability of having *bad traffic*, $T =$ t, is 0.78.

C	T	B	P
t	t	t	0.576
t	t	f	0.144
t	f	t	0.064
t	f	f	0.016
f	t	t	0.012
f	t	f	0.048
f	f	t	0.028
f	f	f	0.112

Figure 23.5 The probability measure for construction, traffic, and barrels. (Note the result on construction from marginalizing across the situations where $T = \text{t}$ and $B = \text{t}$).

We next consider the change in the probability of *road construction* given the fact that we have experienced *bad traffic*, or $p(C \mid T)$ or $p(C = \text{t} \mid T = \text{t})$. The following equation reflects the new probability, where the numerator is the outcome we have ($C = \text{t}$ and $T = \text{t}$) and the denominator reflects all possible outcomes for this situation (the sum of $C = \text{t}$ and $T = \text{t}$ plus $C = \text{f}$ and $T = \text{t}$):

$$p(C \mid T) = \frac{p(C=\text{t}, T=\text{t})}{p(C=\text{t}, T=\text{t}) + p(C=\text{f}, T=\text{t})}$$
$$= 0.72/(0.72 + 0.06) = 0.923.$$

So now, with the normal probability of *road construction* being 0.8, given that there actually is *bad traffic*, the probability for *road construction* goes up to 0.923!

Consider the expanded probability distribution table of Figure 23.5. This is an extension of Figure 23.4 as the probabilities of Figure 23.4 remain the same for all values of C and T in Figure 23.5. We now want to determine the new probability for construction C given that we are experiencing bad traffic T and see yellow barrels B:

$$p(C \mid T, B)$$
$$= \frac{p(C=\text{t}, T=\text{t}, B=\text{t})}{(p(C=\text{t}, T=\text{t}, B=\text{t}) + p(C=\text{f}, T=\text{t}, B=\text{t})}$$
$$= 0.576/(0.576 + 0.012)$$
$$= 0.98.$$

This new calculation of $p(C \mid T, B)$ shows that the traffic slowdown plus the presence of yellow traffic control barrels makes the new probability of construction even higher! This is the insight supporting the Bayesian belief net technology. The priors of the situation represent our ongoing expectations of the "state of the world." When new information appears, such as the yellow traffic control barrels, then our current expectations for the state of the world change. Bayesian inference captures these changing expectations quite naturally.

The next example, adapted from Pearl (1988), shows a more complex Bayesian network. In Figure 23.6, the season of the year determines the probability of rain as well as the probability of water from a sprinkler system. The wet sidewalk will be correlated with rain or water from the sprinkler. Finally, the sidewalk will be slick depending on whether or not it is a wet sidewalk. In the figure, we have expressed the probability relationship that each of these parameters has with its parents. Note also that, as compared with the traffic example, the slippery sidewalk example has an undirected cycle (a cycle in the underlying undirected graph).

We can now ask the question "How can the probability of wet sidewalk, $p(\text{WS})$, be described?" It can't be done as previously, where $p(\text{W})$ is equal to $p(W \mid S)p(S)$ or $p(R)$ is equal to $p(R \mid S)p(S)$. The two causes of WS are not independent given *S*; for example, if *S* is summer, then $p(W)$ and $p(R)$ could both go up. Thus, the complete conditional probabilities of the two variables, along with their further relation to *S*, must be calculated. In this situation, we can do it, but as we will see, this calculation is exponential in the number of possible causes of WS. The calculation is represented in Figure 23.7, where we calculate one entry in that table, $p(\text{WS})$, where *R* and *W* are both true. To make life simpler, we assume that the season *S* is either hot or cold:

$$p(WS)$$
$$= p(R = \text{t}, W = \text{t}), \text{ for all condition of } S, \text{ season}$$
$$= p(S = \text{ hot}) \times p(R = \text{ t} \mid S = \text{ hot})$$
$$\times\, p(W = \text{ t} \mid S = \text{ hot})$$
$$+\, p(S = \text{ cold}) \times p(R = \text{ t} \mid S = \text{ cold})$$
$$\times\, p(W = \text{ t} \mid S = \text{ cold}).$$

In a similar fashion, the remainder of Figure 23.7 can be completed. This makes up the joint probability for rain and water from the

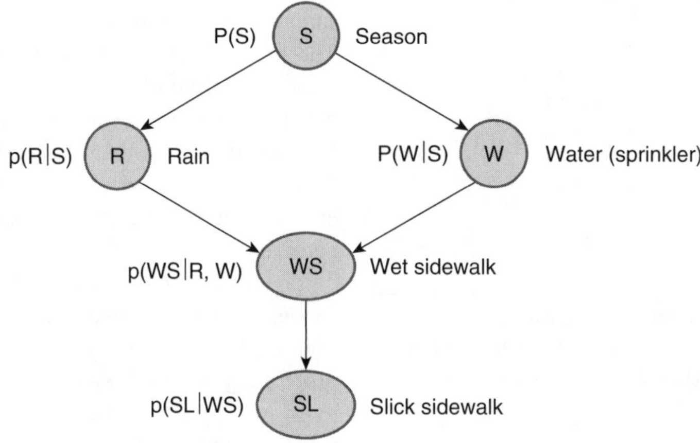

Figure 23.6 An example of a Bayesian probabilistic network where the probability dependencies are located next to each node.

SOURCE: This example is from Pearl (1988).

R	**W**	**WS** p(WS)	{ S = hot; S = cold }
t	t		
t	f		
f	t		
f	f		

Figure 23.7 The probability distribution for $p(\text{WS})$, a function of $p(W)$ and $p(R)$, given the effect of S. (We calculate the effect when $R =$ t and $W =$ t.)

sprinkler. This larger "macro element" represents $p(\text{WS}) = p(\text{WS} \mid R, W)p(R, W)$. We have gotten away with a rather reasonable calculation; the problem is that this calculation is exponential in the number of parents of the state.

We call this macro element the *combined variable*, or *clique*, for the calculation of $p(\text{WS})$. We employ this concept of a clique to replace the constraint propagation of the DAG of Figure 23.6 with an acyclic clique tree, as seen in Figure 23.8. The rectangular boxes of Figure 23.8a reflect the variables that the cliques above and below it share. The table that passes the relevant parameters through to the next clique is exponential in the number of these parameters. It should also be noted that a linking variable along with all its parents must be present in the clique. Thus, in setting up a belief network or other graphical model (the knowledge engineering process), we ought to be careful how many variables are parents of any state. The cliques will also overlap, as seen in Figure 23.8b, to pass information through the full tree of cliques, called the junction tree. We next present an algorithm developed by Lauritzen and Spiegelhalter (1988) that creates a junction tree from any BBN:

1. For all nodes in the belief network, make all directed links undirected.

2. For any node, draw links between all its parents (the dashed line between R and W in Figure 23.8b).

3. Look for any cycle in the resulting graph of length more than 3 and add further links that reduce that cycle to 3. This process is called triangulation and is not necessary in the example of Figure 23.8b.

4. Create the junction tree from the triangulated structure of Step 3 by finding the maximal cliques (cliques that are complete subgraphs and not subgraphs of a larger clique). The variables in these cliques are put into junctions, and the junction tree is created by connecting any two junctions that share at least one variable, as in Figure 23.8a.

The triangulation process described in Step 3 above is critical, as we want the resulting junction

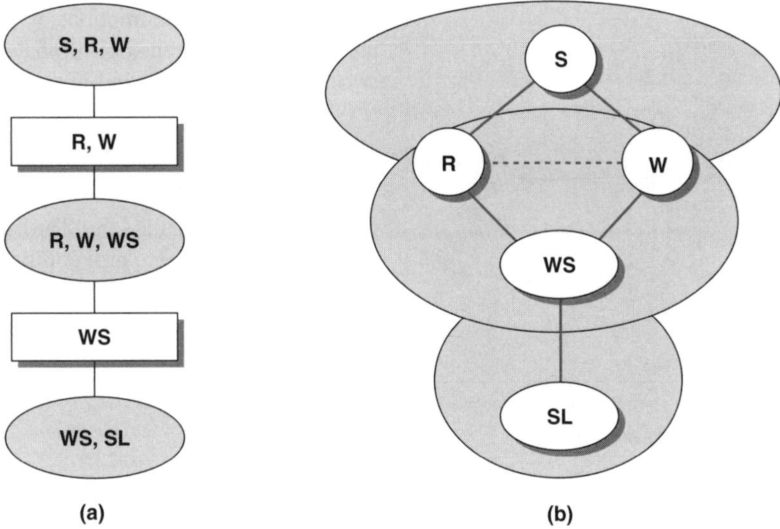

Figure 23.8 A junction tree (a) for the Bayesian probabilistic network of (b). Note that we started to construct the transition table for the rectangle R, W.

SOURCE: Adapted from Luger, G. F. (2005). *Artificial intelligence: Structures and strategies for complex problem solving* (5th ed.). London: Addison-Wesley/Pearson.

tree to have minimal computational cost when propagating information. Unfortunately, this decision of designing optimal cost junction trees is NP-hard (informally, solutions for nondeterministic polynomial time hard problems cannot be found within a useful time when the problem is large, in this case if the belief net has 50 or more nodes, say). Often, fortunately, a simple greedy algorithm can be sufficient for producing useful results. Note that the sizes of the tables required to convey information across the junction tree of Figure 23.8 are $2 \times 2 \times 2$, $2 \times 2 \times 2$ and 2×2.

A final comment: BBNs seem to reflect how humans reason in complex domains where some factors are known and related a priori to others. As reasoning proceeds by the progressive instantiation of information, search is further restricted and, as a result, more efficient. This search efficiency stands in strong contrast to the approach supported by using a full joint distribution, where more information requires an exponentially greater need for statistical relations and a resulting broader search.

Many algorithms exist for building belief networks and propagating arguments as new evidence is acquired. We recommend especially Pearl's (1988) message-passing approach and the *clique tree triangulation* method (just described) proposed by Lauritzen and Spiegelhalter (1988). Druzdel and Henrion (1993) have also proposed algorithms for propagating influence in a network. Dechter (1996) presents the bucket elimination algorithm as a unifying framework for probabilistic inference.

Expert Systems and Graphical Models: The Continuing Story

This chapter has summarized the evolution of expert systems and graphical models over the past several decades. Our goal has been to give a top-down description of this technology and to describe, without overwhelming detail, the key features of both its evolution and its use. We conclude our presentation by giving short introductions to several other technologies that have come to extend and sometimes replace the traditional expert system. These include Markov models, HMMs, and DBNs.

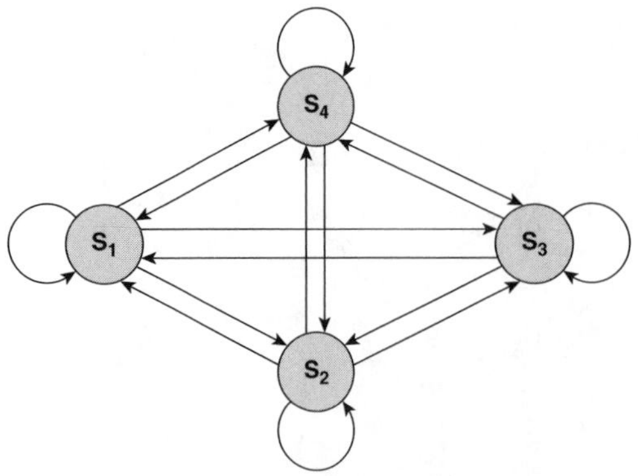

Figure 23.9 A Markov state machine or Markov chain with four states, s_1, s_2, s_3, and s_4.

Diagnostic and Prognostic Reasoning With Graphical Models

Figure 23.9 presents a Markov state machine (sometimes called a Markov chain) with four distinct states. This general class of systems may be described at any time as being in one of a set of n distinct states, $s_1, s_2, s_3, \ldots, s_n$. The system undergoes changes of state, with the possibility of it remaining in the same state, at regular discrete time intervals. We describe the ordered set of times t that are associated with the discrete intervals as $t_1, t_2, t_3, \ldots, t_n$. The system changes state according to the distribution of probabilities associated with each state. We denote the actual state of the machine at time t as s_t.

A full probabilistic description of this system requires, in the general case, the specification of the present state s_t in terms of all its predecessor states. Thus, the probability of the system being in any particular state s_t is

$$p(s_t) = p(s_t \mid s_{t-1}, s_{t-2}, s_{t-3}, \ldots),$$

where the s_{t-i} are the predecessor states of s_t. In a *first-order Markov chain*, the probability of the present state is a function only of its direct predecessor state:

$$p(s_t) = p(s_t \mid s_{t-1}),$$

where s_{t-1} is the predecessor of s_t. We next assume that the right side of this equation is time invariant; that is, we hypothesize that across all time periods of the system, the transitions between specific states retain the same probabilistic relationships.

Based on these assumptions, we now can create a set of state transition probabilities a_{ij} between any two states s_i and s_j as follows:

$$a_{ij} = p(s_t = s_i \mid s_{t-1} = s_j), \quad 1 \geqslant i, j \geqslant N.$$

Note that i can equal j, in which case the system remains in the same state. The traditional constraints remain on these probability distributions; for each state s_i,

$$a_{ij} \geqslant 0,$$

and for all j,

$$\sum_{i=1}^{N} a_{ij} = 1.$$

The system we have just described is called a first-order observable Markov model since the output of the system is the set of states at each discrete time interval and each state of the system corresponds to a physical (observable) event. We make the observable Markov model more formal with the following definition and then give an example.

An (observable) Markov model may be defined thus:

- A graphical model is called an (observable) Markov model if its graph is directed and the probability of arriving at any state s_t from the set of states S at a discrete time t is a function of the probability distributions of its being in previous states of S at previous times. Each state s_t of S corresponds to a physically observable situation.
- An observable Markov model is *first order* if the probability of its being in the present state s_t at any time t is a function only of its being in the previous state s_{t-1} at time $t-1$, where s_t and s_{t-1} belong to the set of observable states S.

As an example of an observable first-order Markov model, consider the weather at noon, say, for a particular location. We assume that this location has four different discrete states for the variable *weather*: $s_1 =$ sun, $s_2 =$ cloudy, $s_3 =$ fog, $s_4 =$ precipitation. We assume that the time intervals for the Markov model will be noon each consecutive day. We also assume that the transition probabilities between the states of the weather remain constant across time (not true for most locations!) and that the observable, *weather*, can remain in the same state over multiple days. This situation is represented by Figure 23.9 and is supported by the matrix of state transitions a_{ij}:

$$a_{ij} = \begin{array}{c|cccc} & s_1 & s_2 & s_3 & s_4 \\ s_1 & 0.4 & 0.3 & 0.2 & 0.1 \\ s_2 & 0.2 & 0.3 & 0.2 & 0.3 \\ s_3 & 0.1 & 0.3 & 0.3 & 0.3 \\ s_4 & 0.2 & 0.3 & 0.3 & 0.2 \end{array}.$$

In this a_{ij} transition matrix, the first row represents the transition probabilities from s_1 to each of the states, including staying in the same state; the second row represents the transition probabilities from s_2 to each of the states, and so on. Note that the properties required for the transition probabilities to be probability distributions from each state are met (they sum to 1.0).

We now can ask questions of our model. Suppose that the state of the weather today, s_1, is sun; what is the probability of the next 5 days remaining sun? Or again, what is the probability of the next 5 days being sun, sun, cloudy, cloudy, precipitation? We solve this second problem. We wish to determine the probability of observing, given our model, the set of states where the first day, s_1, is today's observed sunshine:

$$O = s_1, s_1, s_1, s_2, s_2, s_4.$$

The probability of this sequence of observed states, given the first-order Markov model M is

$$\begin{aligned} p(O \mid M) &= p(s_1, s_1, s_1, s_2, s_2, s_4 \mid M) \\ &= p(s_1) \times p(s_1 \mid s_1) \times p(s_1 \mid s_1) \\ &\quad \times p(s_2 \mid s_1) \times p(s_2 \mid s_2) \times p(s_4 \mid s_2) \\ &= 1 \times a_{11} \times a_{11} \times a_{12} \times a_{22} \times a_{24} \\ &= 1 \times (0.4) \times (0.4) \times (0.3) \\ &\quad \times (0.3) \times (0.3) \\ &= 0.00432. \end{aligned}$$

This equation follows from the assumptions of the first-order Markov model. Thus, the state of the weather for each day is a function (only) of the weather the day before, and we observed the fact that today is sunshine.

We can extend this example to determine, given that we know today's weather, the probability that the weather will be the same for exactly the next t days—that is, that the weather remains the same until Day $t+1$, at which time it is different. For any weather state s_i and Markov model M, we have the observation O:

$$O = s_i, s_i, s_i, \ldots, s_i, s_j,$$

where there are exactly (t) s_i and where s_i does not equal s_j, then

$$p(O|M) = 1 \times a_{ii}^{t} \times (1 - a_{ii}),$$

where a_{ii} is the transition probability of taking state s_i to itself. This value is called the *discrete probability density function* for the duration of t time periods in state s_i of model M. This duration density function is indicative of the state duration in a Markov model. Based on this value, we can calculate, within model M, the expected number of observations, or duration d_i within any state s_i, given that the first observation is in that state:

$$d_j = \sum_{d=1}^{n} d \times a_{ij}^{(d-1)} \times (1 - a_{ij}),$$

where n approaches infinity, or

$$= \frac{1}{1 - a_{ij}}.$$

For example, the expected number of consecutive precipitation days, given this model M, is $1/(1-0.3)$ or 1.43. Similarly, the number of consecutive sunny days one might expect is 1.67.

We next consider Markov models whose states are not observable events; that is, they are themselves probabilistic functions of the state. In the Markov models we have seen up to this point, each state corresponded to a discrete physical—or observable—event, such as the value of weather at a certain time of day. This class of models is really fairly limited, and we now generalize it to a wider class of problems. In this section, we extend Markov models to the situations where the observations are themselves probabilistic functions of a current hidden state. This resulting model, called an HMM, is a doubly embedded stochastic process.

The HMM is an observable stochastic process masking a further nonobservable, or hidden, stochastic process. An example of an HMM would be to determine a phoneme (an atomic unit of voiced speech) through the interpretation of noisy acoustic signals. The *phone patterns* themselves—that is, which phonemes or units of basic sound that the speaker is intending to articulate—make up the hidden level of the Markov model. The *observations*—that is, the noisy acoustic signals—are a stochastic function of these phonemes. The phoneme level of the model cannot be "seen," except though the top-level stream of acoustic signals.

An HMM may be defined as follows:

- A graphical model is called an HMM if it is a Markov model whose states are not directly observable but are "hidden" by a further stochastic system interpreting their output. More formally, given a set of states $S = s_1, s_2, \ldots, s_n$ and given a set of state transition probabilities $A = a_{11}, a_{12}, \ldots, a_{1n}, a_{21}, a_{22}, \ldots, a_{nn}$, there is a set of observation likelihoods, $O = p_i(o_t)$, each expressing the probability of an observation o_t (at time t) being from a state i.

For example, consider the problem of N urns, each urn containing a collection of M differently colored balls. The physical process of obtaining observations is, according to some random process, to pick one of the N urns. Once an urn is selected, a ball is removed, and its color is recorded in the observable output stream. The ball is then replaced, and the random process associated with the current urn selects the next (which might be the same) urn to continue the process. This process generates an observable sequence consisting of a number of colors (of the balls).

It is obvious that the simplest HMM corresponding to this ball selection process is the model in which each state corresponds to a specific urn—the values of the transition matrix for that state produce the next state choice—and in which the ball color probability is defined for the urn at each state.

In a second example, an HMM is used to monitor the running "health" of helicopter rotor systems (Chakrabarti, 2005). Suppose that we have three hidden states intended to describe the current condition of the transmission of a helicopter. The three states of the transmission are *safe*, *unsafe*, and *faulty*. These states are hidden in the sense that they are not directly observable by the human diagnostician—except, of course, when the helicopter is a pile of rubble on the ground! We would like to make a probabilistic estimate of the state of the helicopter transmission without being able to directly observe it. We do have a lot of observable data for this system, however, including the current temperatures of certain components and the vibration measurements for others. Figure 23.10 presents raw time-series data for this application. We first use a number of data-processing tools (from Mathlab), especially the fast Fourier transform, to change the data to a time-frequency domain. Correlation plots across time periods were then used to note radical changes in the sampled data. These changes were used to determine the hidden states of the model described and presented in Figure 23.11.

Finally, the HMM model, monitoring changes of a system across time periods, can also be seen as an instance of a dynamic Bayesian network (or DBN). The DBN approach to diagnosis is represented by a sequence of Bayesian networks each of whose states is mapped to itself across time periods. That is, the changes of a system are described through the changes of the particular states of the Bayesian network across time intervals. Thus, the diagnosis of the state of the helicopter rotor system just described (Figure 23.11) may be seen as the changes in the states of the network across time—for example, going from *safe* to *unsafe* to *faulted*. For further details, see Chakrabarti (2005).

Graphical Models: Some Thoughts About the Future

Finally, we mention some current research that is expanding the expressive flexibility of Bayesian networks. Although there are many research institutions involved in this work worldwide, our primary reference will be to our own work, especially Luger (2005) and Pless, Chakrabarti, Rammohan, and Luger (2006).

First, it should be noted that the nodes of the traditional BBNs are *propositional* in nature. Being propositional, they can only represent the likelihood that two concrete individuals or situations can be related to each other according to some distribution. We saw this with the

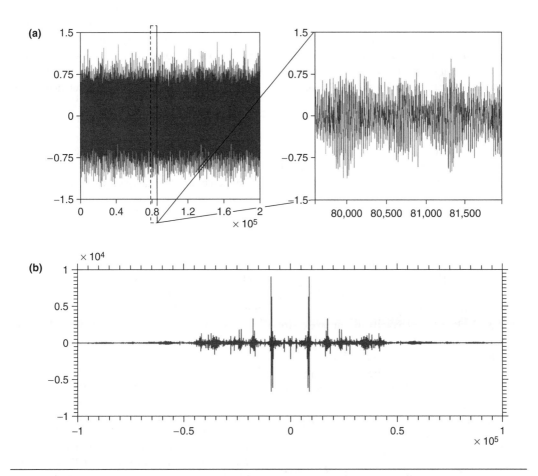

Figure 23.10 (a) Raw time-series data obtained from the sensors monitoring the helicopter rotor system; (b) a time slice projected to the frequency domain using a fast Fourier transform.

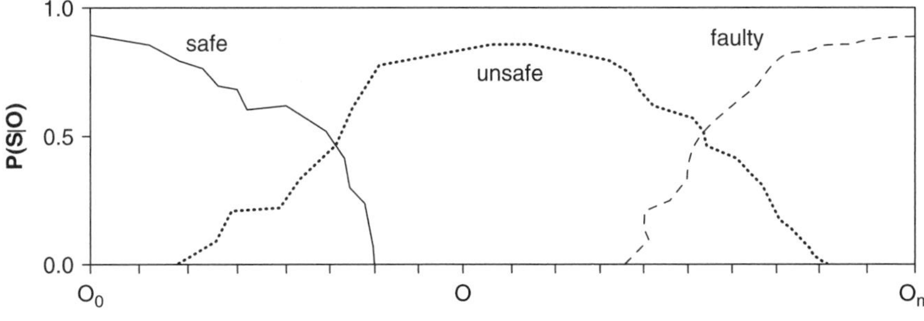

Figure 23.11 The probability distribution of hidden state *S* given sensor observations *O*.

road/traffic example in the section Graphical Models for Uncertain Reasoning. It is often desired to extend the Bayesian representation to *prepositional* or variable-based relationships. For example, we might wish to represent the fact that "all automobile transmissions" have specific failures (with a distribution, of course). This requires a predicate-calculus-based representational scheme. A number of research groups, including Pless et al. (2006) and Koller and Pfeffer (1998), are currently building these (so called) first-order representations for graphical models.

A second extension to the traditional Bayesian graphical model is to make it fully recursive and "Turing complete"—powerful enough to compute any function that is computable. This means that its inference scheme will be able to compute a broader range of probabilistic outcomes. It also greatly broadens the types of models that may be computed—for example, DBNs. The authors (Pless et al., 2006) used exactly this approach for diagnosing faults in helicopter transmission systems, as presented in the previous section.

Finally, many research groups are attempting to do structured probabilistic model induction. What this means is that component facts and rules that will make up possible models of a problem domain can be stated in a declarative fashion ("This fact is true with distribution P_1," "This rule relationship is true with distribution P_2," etc.). Then, the interpreter *will automatically construct the models most consistent* with this set of current (a priori) expectations and the current set of observable (a posteriori) facts. The general form of this model induction task still remains outside our current technology and inference schemes. However, several research groups are addressing this challenge, including Getoor, Friedman, Koller, and Pfeffer (2001), Segel, Koller, and Ormoneit (2001), Cussens (2001), and Pless et al. (2006).

ACKNOWLEDGMENTS

The research group at the University of New Mexico led by Professor George F. Luger has been investigating models for diagnostic and prognostic reasoning for the past two decades. This research includes developing various forms of expert systems and Bayesian belief networks, as well as other forms of stochastic models. We are grateful to the National Science Foundation, the Department of Energy (through Sandia and Los Alamos National Laboratories), and the Department of Defense (through the U.S. Air Force, the U.S. Navy, and Management Sciences, Inc.) for their support over these years. We are also in debt to the various graduate students who have developed their research as part of our Artificial Intelligence (AI) group at the University of New Mexico. Finally, several of the ideas and figures of this chapter were adapted from the book *Artificial Intelligence: Structures and Strategies for Complex Problem Solving* (fifth edition; Luger, 2005), whose author is George Luger. We thank our publisher Addison-Wesley and Pearson Education for their permission to use this material and figures. More complete detail on much of the information presented in this chapter may be found in this AI book.

REFERENCES

Bayes, T. (1763). Essay towards solving a problem in the doctrine of chances. *Philosophical Transactions of the Royal Society of London, 53*, 370–418.

Buchanan, B. H., & Shortliffe, E. H. (Eds.). (1984). *Rule based expert systems: The MYCIN experiments of the Stanford heuristic programming project.* Reading, MA: Addison-Wesley.

Chakrabarti, C. (2005). *First order stochastic systems for diagnosis and prognosis.* Unpublished master's thesis, Department of Computer Science, University of New Mexico.

Cussens, J. (2001). Parameter estimation in stochastic logic programs. *Machine Learning, 44*, 245–271.

Dechter, R. (1996). Bucket elimination: A unifying framework for probabilistic inference. In *Proceedings of the conference on uncertainty in AI (UAI-96)* (pp. 211–219). Menlo Park, CA: AAAI Press.

Druzdel, M. J., & Henrion, M. (1993). Efficient reasoning in qualitative probabilistic networks. In *Proceedings of the Eleventh National Conference on Artificial intelligence (AAI-93)* (pp. 548–553). Cambridge: MIT Press.

Duda, R. O., Gaschnig, J., & Hart, P. E. (1979). Model design in the PROSPECTOR consultant system for mineral exploration. In D. Michie (Ed.), *Expert systems in a micro-electronic age* (pp. 153–167). Edinburgh, UK: Edinburgh University Press.

Forgy, C. L. (1982). Rete: A fast algorithm for the many pattern/many object pattern match problem. *Artificial Intelligence*, *19*(1), 17–37.

Friedman, N. (1998). The Bayesian structural EM algorithm. In G. F. Cooper & S. Moral (Eds.), *Proceedings of the Fourteenth Conference of Uncertainty in Artificial Intelligence* (pp. 129–138). San Francisco: Morgan Kaufmann.

Getoor, L., Friedman, N., Koller, D., & Pfeffer, A. (2001). Learning probabilistic relational models. In S. Dzeroski & N. Lavorac (Eds.), *Relational data mining* (pp. 307–335). New York: Springer.

Ghahramani, Z., & Jordan, M. I. (1997). Factorial hidden Markov models. *Machine Learning*, *29*, 245–274.

Koller, D., & Pfeffer, A. (1998). Probabilistic frame-based systems. In C. Rich & J. Mostow (Eds.), *Proceedings of the Fifteenth National Conference on Artificial Intelligence* (pp. 580–587). Cambridge: MIT Press.

Lauritzen, S. L., & Spiegelhalter, D. J. (1988). Local computations with probabilities on graphical structures and their application to expert systems. *Journal of the Royal Statistical Society Series B*, *50*(2), 157–224.

Luger, G. F. (2005). *Artificial intelligence: Structures and strategies for complex problem solving* (5th ed.). London: Addison-Wesley/Pearson. (Sixth edition is in press)

Newell, A., & Simon, H. A. (1976). Computer science as empirical inquiry: Symbols and search. *Communications of the ACM*, *19*(3), 113–126.

Pearl, J. (1988). *Probabilistic reasoning in intelligent systems: Networks of plausible inference*. Los Altos, CA: Morgan Kaufmann.

Pless, D. J., Chakrabarti, C., Rammohan, R., & Luger, G. F. (2006). The design and testing of a first-order stochastic modeling language. In I. Russell, Z. Markov, & L. B. Holder (Eds.), *Proceedings of the International Journal on Artificial Intelligence Tools* (pp. 979–1005). Singapore: World Scientific.

Segel, E., Koller, D., & Ormoneit, D. (2001). Probabilistic abstraction hierarchies. In *Neural information processing systems (NIPS)*. Cambridge: MIT Press.

Waterman, D. A. (1986). *A guide to expert systems*. Reading, MA: Addison-Wesley.

24

PROBABILITY AND EVIDENCE

JULIA MORTERA AND PHILIP DAWID

INTRODUCTION

Legal applications of probabilistic and statistical reasoning have a long history, having exercised pioneers such as Nicolas Bernoulli, Condorcet, Laplace, Poisson, and Cournot (Zabell, 1988). After a period of neglect, interest has resurfaced in recent years, and the topic has given rise to many challenging problems.

Evidence presented in a case at law can be regarded as data and the issue to be decided by the court as a hypothesis under test. The relationship between these may be immediate, or else indirect, involving a long chain or tangled web of intermediate propositions. In any case, there will almost always be some uncertainty about the ultimate issue, the evidence, and the way in which these are related. Such uncertainty can, in principle at least, be described probabilistically. In a legal setting, where it is understood that different "reasonable men" (and women) can reasonably hold a range of opinions, it is natural to take a subjective interpretation of probability, regarding it as a measure of a specific individual's uncertainty about a specific (not necessarily repeatable) event in the light of specified information. This interpretation should be borne in mind in the sequel. In particular, under it there is no obstacle to assigning a noncategorical probability to the guilt of the suspect in the light of evidence presented while at the same time believing that it has a definite, though currently unknown, truth value that might even be revealed if only enough evidence were available.

We do not suggest that judges and juries are likely to have (or should be expected to acquire) a sophisticated understanding of probability or facility in manipulating probabilities or that explicit probability arguments should become routine in courts of law. There are, however, increasing numbers of cases—such as DNA identification or the Sally Clark case (see the section The Prosecutor's Fallacy)—where evidence about probabilities is clearly relevant, and the court would stand to benefit from advice about how to handle them. This does not, of course, imply that it will appreciate this need or be ready to accept such advice: For example, at the first appeal of Sally Clark, the expert statistical evidence of Philip Dawid and Ian Evett was essentially dismissed by the court on the grounds that statistics is "hardly rocket science."

Sometimes—but all too rarely—there will be extensive relevant frequency data in the light of which all reasonable subjective probabilities for some event should essentially agree with its observed relative frequency. In other cases, all parties may be willing to accept an expert witness's assessments of some probabilities. Yet other probabilities, relevant for the juror or other judicial decision maker, will be subject to subjective vagueness, although we will usually be able to distinguish between "reasonable" and "unreasonable" probability assessments. But even where probability values can be agreed on, their correct handling is far from obvious or intuitive, and fallacious intuitions, arguments, and inferences abound.

Probability Logic

In a case at law, let $\mathcal{E}$ denote one or more items of evidence (perhaps its totality). We need to consider how this evidence affects the comparison of the hypotheses, H_0 and H_1 say, offered by either side. Thus, in a criminal case with a single charge against a single defendant, the evidence might be that the defendant's DNA profile matches the one found at the crime scene. Hypothesis H_0, offered by the defence, is that the defendant is innocent ($\overline{G}$); the prosecution hypothesis, H_1, is that of guilt (G).

The adjudicator needs to assess his or her conditional probability for either hypothesis, *given* the evidence: $\Pr(H_0|\mathcal{E})$ and $\Pr(H_1|\mathcal{E})$. However, it will not usually be possible to assess these directly, and they will have to be constructed out of other, more basic, ingredients. In particular, it will often be reasonable to assess directly $\Pr(\mathcal{E}|H_0)$ and $\Pr(\mathcal{E}|H_1)$: the probability that the evidence would have arisen in each of the competing scenarios.

Bayes's theorem—a trivial consequence of the definition of conditional probability—tells us that

$$\frac{\Pr(H_1|\mathcal{E})}{\Pr(H_0|\mathcal{E})} = \frac{\Pr(H_1)}{\Pr(H_0)} \times \frac{\Pr(\mathcal{E}|H_1)}{\Pr(\mathcal{E}|H_1)}. \qquad (24.1)$$

The left-hand side of (24.1) is the *posterior odds* for comparing H_1 and H_0 given the evidence $\mathcal{E}$: This is a simple transformation of $\Pr(H_1|\mathcal{E})$, the desired *posterior probability* of H_1.

The second term on the right-hand side of (24.1) is constructed out of the directly assessed terms $\Pr(\mathcal{E}|H_0)$ and $\Pr(\mathcal{E}|H_1)$: It is the *likelihood ratio* (for H_1, as against H_0) engendered by the evidence $\mathcal{E}$. It is noteworthy that only the ratio of these terms enters, their absolute values being otherwise irrelevant.

To complete (24.1), we need the term $\Pr(H_1)/\Pr(H_0)$, the *prior odds* for comparing H_1 and H_0 (i.e., before evidence $\mathcal{E}$ is incorporated). This might reasonably vary from one individual juror to another, so that it would not be appropriate to treat it as a subject for direct evidence. For this reason, forensic experts are often instructed to give their evidence in the form of a likelihood ratio, it being left to the adjudicator to combine this appropriately with the prior assessment, using (24.1).

We can express (24.1) in words as

POSTERIOR ODDS
= PRIOR ODDS × LIKELIHOOD RATIO.

When $\mathcal{E}$ denotes all the evidence in the case, all the probabilities in (24.1) are unconditional; in particular, the prior odds should be assessed on the basis that there is no evidence to distinguish the suspect from any other potential suspect—this can be regarded as one way of formalizing the legal doctrine of "presumption of innocence" (which, of course, is not the same as an *assumption* of innocence). When $\mathcal{E}$ denotes a piece of evidence presented in midprocess, all the probabilities in (24.1) must be conditioned on the evidence previously presented: In particular, the "prior" probabilities could themselves have been calculated using (24.1), as posterior probabilities based on earlier evidence.

Notwithstanding the unarguable correctness of (24.1), it is often replaced by other, more "intuitive" probabilistic arguments that can be very misleading.

The Prosecutor's Fallacy

In a criminal trial, an item of evidence $\mathcal{E}$ may be offered in proof of the guilt, G, of a defendant S, on the basis that the probability of $\mathcal{E}$ would be very low if S were not guilty ($\overline{G}$). For example, in the trial of Sally Clark for double infanticide (Dawid, 2005, 2007), an expert medical witness testified that the probability that both her babies would have died from natural causes was one in 73 million.[1] If, as appears very natural, we describe this figure as "the probability that the babies died by innocent means," it is all too easy to misinterpret

[1] This figure has itself been widely and properly criticized, but that is not the issue here.

this as the probability (on the basis of the evidence of the deaths) that Sally is innocent—such a tiny figure seeming to provide incontrovertible proof of her guilt. Mathematically, this is equivalent to misinterpreting $\Pr(\mathcal{E}|\overline{G})$ as $\Pr(\overline{G}|\mathcal{E})$. For obvious reasons, this error is known as "transposing the conditional" or, because it typically produces seemingly convincing evidence of guilt, "the prosecutor's fallacy."

The prosecutor's fallacy is a seductive and widespread mode of reasoning, affecting the general public, the media, lawyers, jurors, and judges alike. Although we do not have access to the deliberations of Sally Clark's jury, it has generally been considered that their "guilty" verdict was strongly influenced by such mistaken reasoning.

Forensic Identification

A particularly fertile field where the prosecutor's fallacy flourishes is that of *identification evidence*. Here, unlike the case of Sally Clark, it is undisputed that a crime has been committed: The issue before the court is whether or not the suspect, S, is indeed the culprit C. Thus, the hypothesis G of guilt is equivalent to that of identity, $C = S$. Evidence $\mathcal{E}$ is presented that bears on this. This may be, for example, eyewitness evidence (as in the celebrated "Collins case" [Fairley & Mosteller, 1977], which kick-started modern interest in the interpretation of probabilities in the law) or forensic evidence of a *match* between some characteristic of the crime scene (the "crime trace") and a similar characteristic measured on the suspect. Examples include handwriting, rifling marks on bullets, glass fragments, fibers, footprints, fingerprints, bite marks, and, of especial importance and power, DNA profiles. It is common in such a case for the jury to be told something like "The probability of this DNA match arising from an innocent man is only one in one billion" and for all parties to misinterpret this number, in line with the prosecutor's fallacy, as the probability of S's innocence (Balding & Donnelly, 1995).

The Island Problem

The "island problem" (Eggleston, 1983, Appendix 3) is a toy example that well illustrates the uses and misuses of statistical logic in forensic identification.

A murder has been committed on an island, cut off from the outside world, on which $N+1$ inhabitants remain. Forensic evidence at the scene consists of a measurement, $I_C = x$, on a "crime trace" characteristic I_C, which can be assumed to come from the criminal C. The initial probability of any given islander having the characteristic x is assessed as P, independently for different islanders. Moreover, before observing any evidence, all inhabitants of the island are considered to have the same probability of being the culprit. The mainland police arrive and arrest a random islander, S. It is found that S matches the crime trace: $I_S = x$. There is no further relevant evidence. How should this match evidence be used to assess the claim that S is the murderer?

We shall consider a number of arguments that have been used to address this question. Those in the sections Defence Counterargument, Bayesian Argument, and Supreme Court Variation 3 below yield the correct answer, the remainder being fallacious: We leave it to the reader to identify the reasons. For illustration, following Eggleston, we take $N = 100$, $P = 0.004$.

Prosecutor's Fallacy

Prosecuting counsel, arguing according to his favorite fallacy, asserts that the probability that S is guilty is $1 - P$, or 0.996, and that this proves guilt "beyond a reasonable doubt."

Defence Counterargument

Counsel for the defence points out that while the guilty party must have characteristic x, the expected further number having this characteristic among the remaining N innocent islanders is NP. Hence, the set of islanders having this characteristic can be taken to have size $1 + NP$. The match evidence places S in this set but does not otherwise distinguish him from any of the other members of it. Since just one of these is guilty, the probability that this is S is thus $1/(1 + NP)$, or 0.714—indicative, perhaps, but *not* "beyond a reasonable doubt."

Bayesian Argument

Conditioning all the time on the evidence $I_C = x$ from the crime scene (which, we assume, of itself has no bearing on the issue of guilt) and taking $\mathcal{E}$ to be the additional "match evidence" $I_S = x$, the probability of this evidence would be $\Pr(\mathcal{E}|G) = 1$ if S were guilty ($S = C$) and $\Pr(\mathcal{E}|\overline{G}) = P$ if S were innocent. Hence, the *likelihood ratio* in favor of guilt, on the basis of the match evidence, is

$$\mathrm{LR} := \frac{\Pr(\mathcal{E}|G)}{\Pr(\mathcal{E}|\overline{G})} = \frac{1}{P},$$

or $\mathrm{LR} = 250$.

While this seems strong evidence in favor of guilt, a complete probabilistic argument must also incorporate the prior odds on guilt before taking account of the match evidence. We can argue that in the absence of any other evidence, S is no more or less likely to be the culprit than any other islander, so that the prior probability of guilt is $1/(N+1)$, corresponding to prior odds on guilt of $1/N$.

We can now apply Bayes's theorem (24.1) to obtain the posterior odds on guilt

$$(1/N) \times (1/P) = 1/NP. \tag{24.2}$$

The corresponding posterior probability of guilt is

$$\Pr(G|\mathcal{E}) = \frac{1}{1+NP}, \tag{24.3}$$

or 0.714.

Note that this Bayesian argument could be readily modified to incorporate additional evidence if available—it is merely necessary to adjust the prior odds appropriately (either informally or formally by means of yet another application of Bayes's theorem) to take that into account.

We see that in the absence of additional evidence, this result accords with that of the defence argument above.

Supreme Court Argument

In its appeal judgment on the "Collins case," the Supreme Court of California argued on the following lines. Denote by M the unknown number of islanders possessing characteristic x. Before obtaining any evidence, we can take M to have the binomial distribution $\mathrm{Bin}(N+1;P)$. Now, we have observed that S has characteristic x and so have learned that $M \geqslant 1$. If $M = 1$, there is no other matching individual and S must be guilty; however, if there is a nonnegligible probability that $M > 1$, so that S is not the only matching individual, this would be a source of doubt as to S's guilt. Hence, the Supreme Court calculated

$$\Pr(M > 1|M \geqslant 1) = \frac{1-(1-P)^{N+1}-(N+1)P(1-P)^N}{1-(1-P)^{N+1}},$$

which, for our illustrative figures, yields 0.19. An approximately 20% chance of there being another islander having the matching characteristic could be considered enough to raise reasonable doubt as to S's guilt.

Supreme Court: Variation 1

The above line of argument can be developed further, as follows. With no other evidence, we can take $\Pr(G|M = m) = m^{-1}$. As above, we condition the initial $\mathrm{Bin}(N+1;P)$ for M on the known fact that $M \geqslant 1$, to obtain

$$\Pr(G|\mathcal{E}) = \mathrm{E}\left(M^{-1}|M \geqslant 1\right).$$

This is not simply expressible algebraically but can be calculated numerically: For our illustrative figures, it yields $\Pr(G|\mathcal{E}) = 0.902$.

Supreme Court: Variation 2

An alternative argument is that given the evidence, we know that there is one guilty match, and out of the remaining N innocent individuals, each has, independently, a probability P of supplying a match. So the conditional distribution of M is $1+\mathrm{Bin}(N;P)$. Using this to take the expectation of M^{-1} yields

$$\Pr(G|\mathcal{E}) = \frac{1-(1-P)^{N+1}}{(N+1)P}, \tag{24.4}$$

which, for our values, gives 0.824.

Supreme Court: Variation 3

We can consider the total evidence ($I_C = x$, $I_S = x$) as the results, both successes, of two draws, *with replacement* (since C and S could be the same individual), from the population. The probability of this, given $M = m$, is $\{m/(N+1)\}^2$, and using Bayes's theorem, the resulting conditional distribution of M is

$$\Pr(M = m | I_C = x, I_S = x)$$
$$= cm \binom{N}{m-1} P^{m-1} (1-P)^{N-m+1}$$
$$(m = 1, \ldots, N+1),$$

where the normalizing constant is $c = 1/(1 + NP)$. Taking the expectation of M^{-1} with respect to this distribution then yields

$$\Pr(G|\mathcal{E}) = 1/(1+NP),$$

or 0.714—in agreement with the Bayesian and defence arguments.

THE EFFECT OF SEARCH

We have so far supposed that the suspect S was selected at random from the island population and, quite fortuitously, was found to match the crime trace. More realistically, the police might trawl through the population until they discover an individual who provides a match. Because this will yield further information beyond the mere fact of a match, we can expect the resulting inference to differ from that appropriate to the "lucky match" case previously considered.

If the search delivers a (first) match for the $(q+1)$th individual examined, then q necessarily innocent parties have been eliminated, thereby reducing the size of the remaining suspect population from N to $N-q$. Intuitively, it would seem that formulas (24.2) and (24.3) given above must therefore be adjusted by making this substitution, so yielding

$$\Pr(G|q) = \frac{1}{1+(N-q)P}. \quad (24.5)$$

This is correct, although the full analysis is more subtle since it must account for the probabilistic nature of the outcome q of the search (Dawid & Mortera, 1995).

Formula (24.5) can only be applied when we know q, the number of nonmatching individuals examined before the matching suspect S is found. But whatever the value of q, (24.5) will yield a value at least as large as (24.3). It follows that if we know that a search has been conducted to identify a suspect but are not told q, the answer given by Formula (24.3) must be too small. In fact, in this case of a known search of unknown size, the appropriate answer is now given by Formula (24.4).

Database Search

Search scenarios are common in cases where a DNA trace is found at the crime scene and, in the absence of any obvious suspect, a search for a match is made through a police database of DNA profiles. Such databases can be very large—by December 2005, the U.K. database comprised around 3 million profiles, with about 3,000 "matches" being made per month.

Computerized search typically allows us to identify every individual in the database whose DNA profile matches the crime trace. Suppose that there is exactly one such individual, S. If the initial suspect population is of size $N+1$ and the database is of size $n+1$, then the search has eliminated n individuals from the suspect population, and so, if there is no other evidence to distinguish among those remaining, the odds on S being guilty are increased from $1/NP$, as in (24.2), to $1/(N-n)P$. (If there is other evidence for or against S, this could be expressed as a likelihood ratio and combined with the above odds using Bayes's theorem. It is also possible to account for evidence pointing the finger toward or away from other individuals.)

When n is small in relation to N, the effect of the database search is only a small increase in the probability that S is guilty. This is fortunate, since evidence that a search was conducted to identify the suspect is usually inadmissible in court. Ignoring it will typically make little difference, and to the extent that it does, it will be to the advantage of the defendant.

However, at the other extreme, where the whole population is searched ($n = N$) and S is the only individual found to match, we obtain infinite odds, corresponding to certainty, that S is guilty—as is obviously appropriate in this case.

Alternative Arguments

Other arguments, with very different implications, have also been brought to bear on this problem.

One *frequentist* view, recommended by the U.S. National Research Council (1996), treats the problem as analogous to that of multiple statistical hypothesis testing, where the strength of the evidence has to be adjusted to account for the very fact that a search has been conducted. It is argued that since *any* match found in the database would have resulted in a prosecution, the relevant "match probability" is no longer the probability, P, that S would match the crime trace (if innocent) but the probability, approximately $(n+1)P$, that *some* match would be found in the database (if all its members were innocent). The impact of the evidence, as measured by the match probability, is thus attenuated by a factor of $n+1$, the size of the database. Even if this is only a very small fraction of the total population, it can be very large in absolute size, which would appear to render the match evidence essentially worthless.

A closely related *likelihood* viewpoint is taken by Stockmarr (1999). He claims that it is not appropriate to assess a likelihood for the hypothesis H_S that S is guilty, since that hypothesis could not even have been formulated before the search was conducted. Hence, he claims, we should instead focus on the hypothesis H_D—which *can* be formulated before the search—that the database D contains the culprit. When the search then turns up a single match, the corresponding likelihood ratio in favor of H_D (as against its negation) is about $1/(n+1)P$ (as compared with $1/P$ in favor of the "data-dependent" hypothesis H_S). Moreover, whoever the (unique) matching individual turns out to be, the hypothesis H_D becomes logically equivalent to the hypothesis that this matcher is the culprit, which is the proposition that will be put before the court. Consequently, the strength of the evidence is more appropriately measured by a likelihood ratio of $1/(n+1)P$ than one of $1/P$.

We can reconcile this view with the analysis given in the section Database Search if we remember that a likelihood ratio is only one of the ingredients in Bayes's theorem (Dawid, 2001). If we replace H_S by H_D, not only will the likelihood ratio change, but so too will the prior odds: Because the database contains $(n+1)$ individuals, a priori, the odds on the culprit being one of these will be about $(n+1)$ times greater than the odds on his or her being the specific individual S. It turns out that on performing this replacement of the hypothesis, the change to the prior odds exactly cancels with that to the likelihood ratio. There is thus no net effect on the posterior odds: Both approaches deliver the same ultimate verdict.

Which Likelihood Ratio?

The above analysis does, however, lead to problems for the forensic scientist, who is, quite properly, trained to testify as to "the likelihood ratio" generated by the evidence and not directly as to the posterior probability. When, as above, we have a choice as to how to frame the hypotheses, there is no unique likelihood ratio (although the posterior probability will be unaffected by this indeterminacy). In that case, it would seem more helpful to the court to present the likelihood ratio for the hypotheses of direct interest: that S is, or is not, the culprit.

A related issue arises when it can be assumed that the crime was committed by two persons, each of whom has left a DNA trace at the scene (say one on a pillow and one on a sheet). S is arrested and it is found that his DNA matches the trace from the pillow, which has population frequency P. Under reasonable assumptions, it can be shown (Dawid, 2004) that the likelihood ratio in favor of the hypothesis that S was one of the culprits, as against his innocence, is $1/(2P)$. But (given the evidence) S is guilty if and only if he left the stain on the pillow and taking this as the hypothesis at issue leads to a likelihood ratio (as against S's innocence) of $1/P$. Other ways of framing the hypotheses yield yet other results (Meester & Sjerps, 2004).

Once again these different answers can be reconciled by taking proper account of the differing prior probabilities. But if one value is to be given to the court as "the likelihood ratio," what should it be? The first value quoted above, $1/(2P)$, does directly address the question at issue: Is S guilty or not? On the other hand, the very existence of two culprits makes it a priori about twice as probable that S is guilty as would hold for the case of a single-culprit crime. If the court is used to thinking about this latter case, and is not attuned to the need to double the prior probability, one might argue, as a pragmatic solution, that the "correct" likelihood ratio, $1/(2P)$, should be doubled, so as to build this correction in automatically—which would bring us back to the value $1/P$.

COMPLEX PATTERNS OF EVIDENCE

The difficulties of assessing a single item of evidence are compounded when we want to account for the complex interrelationships between the many items of evidence in a case. To organize the evidence it is then helpful to construct a diagrammatic representation of all the evidence and hypotheses in the problem and the relationships between them. This idea was first suggested by Wigmore (1937) (see Anderson, Schum, & Twining, 2005, for an introduction to the "Wigmore chart" method). More recently, the methods of graphical modeling and Bayesian networks—also known as probabilistic expert systems (Cowell, Dawid, Lauritzen, & Spiegelhalter, 1999)—have been applied. Such a network contains a node for each variable in the problem, with arrows between nodes to denote probabilistic dependence of a "child" node on all its "parents." To complete the description, we need the numerical or algebraic specification of the associated conditional probabilities.

Example

Dawid and Evett (1997) consider a fictitious burglary case, described as follows:

> An unknown number of offenders entered a commercial premises late at night through a hole, which they cut in a metal grille. Inside, they were confronted by a security guard who was able to set off an alarm before one of the intruders punched him in the face, causing his nose to bleed.
>
> The intruders left from the front of the building just as a police patrol car was arriving and they dispersed on foot, their getaway car having made off at the first sound of the alarm. The security guard said that there were four men, but the light was too poor for him to describe them, and he was confused because of the blow he had received. The police in the patrol car saw the offenders only from a considerable distance away. They searched the surrounding area and, about 10 min later, one of them found the suspect trying to "hot wire" a car in an alley about a quarter of a mile from the incident.
>
> At the scene, a tuft of red fibers was found on the jagged end of one of the cut edges of the grille. Blood samples were taken from the guard and the suspect. The suspect denied having anything to do with the offence. He was wearing a jumper and jeans, which were taken for examination.
>
> A spray pattern of blood was found on the front and right sleeve of the suspect's jumper. The blood type was different from that of the suspect but the same as that from the security guard. The tuft from the scene was found to be red acrylic. The suspect's jumper was red acrylic. The tuft was indistinguishable from the fibers of the jumper by eye, microspectrofluorimetry and thin layer chromatography (TLC). The jumper was well worn and had several holes, though none could clearly be said to be a possible origin for the tuft.

In this example, there are three general kinds of evidence: eyewitness, blood, and fiber; and for each kind a variety of individual evidential items. We can summarize the salient features of the evidence against the suspect as follows:

- *Eyewitness*

  G: The evidence of the security guard

  W: The evidence of the police officer who arrested the suspect

- *Blood*

  R: The bloodstain in the form of a spray on the suspect's jumper

  X_1: Suspect's blood type

  X_2: Guard's blood type

  Y_2: Blood type of blood spray on jumper

- *Fibers*

  X_3: Properties of the suspect's jumper

  Y_1: Properties of fiber tuft

The uncertain hypotheses and variables that enter are

- *Hypotheses*

  C: Whether the suspect was or was not one of the offenders

  A: The identity of the person who left the fibers on the grille

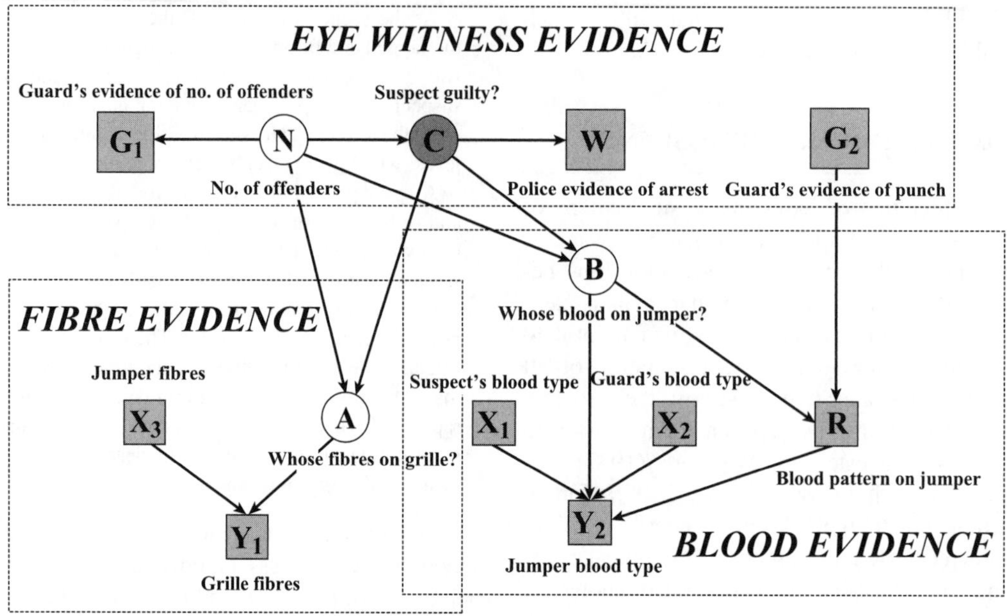

Figure 24.1 Bayesian network for burglary example.

B: The identity of the person who punched the guard

N: The number of offenders

Of these, the specific charge before the court is $C = \text{TRUE}$; the others are included to provide a complete account of the problem.

Figure 24.1 shows a graphical representation of the problem as a Bayesian network. The evidence items are shown as squares and the hypotheses as circles. Variable Y_2, the measurement of the blood type of the spray on the jumper, is dependent on X_1, the suspect's blood type (because it might be a self-stain) and the guard's blood type X_2. But information is also provided by R, the variable that describes the shape of the stain, because that sheds light on whether or not it might be a self-stain. In turn, the shape of the stain is influenced by the way in which the guard was punched, G_2, and B, the identity of the person who did it; while B is, in turn, influenced by whether or not the suspect was one of the offenders, variable C, and also the number of offenders, N.

Dawid and Evett (1997) describe how the graph can be used to read off implicit properties of independence: For example, to show that conditionally on knowing A and N, the pair of variables (B,R) is independent of the pair (G_1,Y_1). These properties can then be used to simplify the algebraic and numerical identification of the overall likelihood ratio for comparing the hypotheses $C = \text{TRUE}$ or $C = \text{FALSE}$, based on the evidence.

Taroni, Aitken, Garbolino, and Biedermann (2006) give a detailed account of theory and applications of Bayesian networks in problems of forensic inference. See Baio and Corradi (2006) and Cavallini and Corradi (2005) for further interesting examples.

Forensic Genetics

Most of the logic so far presented applies in principle to any kind of identification evidence. But forensic DNA evidence has some additional special features, principally owing to its pattern of inheritance from parent to child. These make it possible to use it to address queries such as the following:

Disputed paternity:
Is individual A the father of individual B?

Disputed inheritance:
Is A the daughter of deceased B?

Immigration:
Is A the mother of B? How is A related to B?

Criminal case—mixed trace:
Did A and B both contribute to a stain found at the scene of the crime? Who contributed to the stain?

Disasters:
Was A among the individuals involved in a disaster? Who were those involved?

In a simple disputed paternity case, the evidence $\mathcal{E}$ will comprise DNA profiles from mother, child, and putative father. Hypothesis H_1 is that the putative father is the true father, while hypothesis H_0 might be that the true father is some other individual, whose DNA profile can be regarded as randomly drawn from the population. We can also entertain other hypotheses, such as that one of one or more other identified individuals is the father or that the true father is the putative father's brother.

In a complex criminal case, we might find a stain at the scene of the crime having the form of a *mixed trace*, containing DNA from more than one individual. DNA profiles are also taken from the victim and a suspect. We can entertain various hypotheses as to just who—victim, suspect, person or persons unknown—contributed to the mixed stain.

When we are only comparing two hypotheses H_0 and H_1, the impact of the totality of the DNA evidence $\mathcal{E}$ available, from all sources, is once again crystallized in the *likelihood ratio*, $\mathrm{LR} = P(\mathcal{E}|H_1)/P(\mathcal{E}|H_0)$. If we wish to compare more than two hypotheses, we require the full *likelihood function*, a function of the various hypotheses H being entertained (and, of course, the evidence $\mathcal{E}$):

$$\mathrm{LR}(H) \propto \Pr(\mathcal{E}|H). \qquad (24.6)$$

The proportionality sign in (24.6) indicates that we have omitted a factor that does not depend on H, although it can depend on $\mathcal{E}$. Such a factor is of no consequence and need not be specified, since it disappears on forming ratios of likelihoods for different hypotheses on the same evidence. Only such relative likelihoods are required, not absolute values.

We also now need to specify the prior probabilities, $\Pr(H)$, for the full range of hypotheses H. Then, posterior probabilities in the light of the evidence are again obtained from Bayes's theorem, which can now be expressed as

$$\Pr(H|\mathcal{E}) \propto \Pr(H) \times \mathrm{LR}(H). \qquad (24.7)$$

Again, the omitted proportionality factor in (24.7) does not depend on H, although it might depend on $\mathcal{E}$. It can be recovered, if desired, as the unique such factor for which the law of total probability, $\sum_H \Pr(H|\mathcal{E}) = 1$, is satisfied.

Genetic Background

To proceed further, we need some basic genetic facts about DNA profiles, which we summarize very briefly below: See, for example, Buckleton, Triggs, and Walsh (2005) for more details.

A gene is a particular sequence of the four *bases*, represented by the letters A, C, G, and T, that carry the genetic information in DNA. A specific position on a chromosome is called a *locus*; since chromosomes come in pairs, there are two genes at any locus. A *DNA profile* consists of measurements on a number of *forensic markers*, which are specially selected loci, on different chromosomes. Current technology uses around 12–20 *short tandem repeat* (STR) markers. Each such marker has a finite number (up to around 20) of possible values, or *alleles*, generally positive integers. For example, an allele value of 5 indicates that a certain word (e.g., CAGGTG) in the four-letter alphabet of the genetic code is repeated exactly five times in the DNA sequence at that locus on a chromosome.

An individual's *DNA profile* comprises a collection of *genotypes*, one for each marker. Each genotype consists of an unordered pair of alleles, one inherited from the father and one from the mother (though one cannot distinguish which is which). When both alleles are identical, the individual is *homozygous* at that marker, and only a single allele value is observed; else the individual is *heterozygous*. In most cases, a DNA profile can be measured without error, even from a single cell.

Assuming *Mendelian segregation*, at each marker a parent passes a copy of just one of his two alleles, randomly chosen, to his or her child, independently of the other parent and independently for each child. Distinct forensic markers are located on different chromosomes, so segregate independently. It is often reasonable to assume *random mating* within an appropriate population, which then implies independence of alleles both within markers (*Hardy-Weinberg equilibrium*) and across markers (*linkage equilibrium*). Databases have been gathered from which allele frequency distributions, for various populations, can be estimated for each forensic marker. On the basis of these values and the independence assumptions, a *profile probability* can be assigned to any DNA profile, measuring its rarity in the population.[2]

Simple Disputed Paternity

A man is alleged to be the father of a child, but disputes this. DNA profiles are obtained from the mother `m`, the child `c`, and the putative father `pf`. On the basis of these data, we wish to assess the likelihood ratio for the hypothesis of *paternity*: H_1: `tf=pf`, the true father is the putative father; as against that of *nonpaternity*: H_0: `tf = af`—where `af` denotes an unspecified alternative father, treated as unrelated to `pf` and randomly drawn from the population.

The disputed pedigree can be represented as in Figure 24.2.

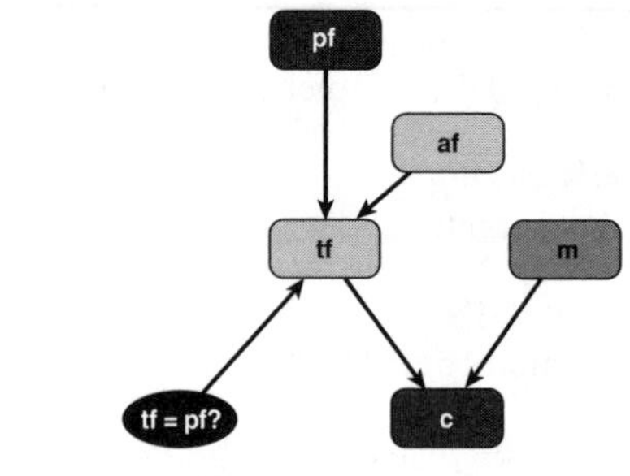

Figure 24.2 Pedigree for simple disputed paternity.

Because of our independence assumptions, we can analyze the markers one at a time, finally multiplying their associated likelihood ratio values together to obtain the overall likelihood ratio based on the full collection of markers.

Consider now the measured genotypes, from all three parties, for some fixed marker. Under paternity, H_0, we just apply Mendel's laws of segregation; under nonpaternity, H_1, we require (estimates of) the frequencies of relevant marker alleles among the population. Using (24.1), this can then be combined with the prior odds of paternity, based on external background evidence B, to obtain the posterior odds for paternity. As an illustrative example, suppose that the data, for marker D7, are child's genotype `cgt`= $\{12, 12\}$, mother's genotype `mgt`= $\{10, 12\}$, putative father's genotype and `pfgt`= $\{10, 12\}$. The estimated population frequencies of alleles 10 and 12 are, respectively, 0.284 and 0.260. In this case, by conditioning on the genotypes of mother and putative father, we see that the child's genotype will be as observed if and only if both the mother and the true father contributed allele 12 to the child. This event has probability 0.5×0.5 if the true father is the putative father, and probability 0.5×0.260 if the true father is, instead, some unrelated individual from the population. Thus, the likelihood ratio in favor of paternity, based on marker *D*7 alone, is 1.93.

DNA Mixtures

A *mixed DNA profile* is typically obtained from an unidentified biological stain or other trace thought to be associated with a crime. This commonly occurs in rape cases, in robberies where an object might have been handled by more than one individual, and also in a scuffle or brawl. For a mixed DNA trace, there is no constraint on the number of distinct alleles observed for each marker, since the trace might have been formed as a mixture of biological material from more than one person.

[2] Although we do not develop this here, one should really allow for the fact that allele frequency estimates based on finite databases remain uncertain. This raises some subtle new issues (Balding & Nichols, 1994; Dawid & Mortera, 1996).

In simple cases of DNA mixtures when using only the qualitative allele information, algebraic formulae for calculating the likelihoods of all hypotheses involving a specified set of known and unknown contributors to the mixture can be computed (assuming Hardy-Weinberg equilibrium and known allele frequencies).

To illustrate, suppose that for a single DNA marker, we have a three-allele crime trace $\{A,B,C\}$, and individual profiles from a victim, $v = \{B,C\}$ and a suspect, $s = \{A\}$. These together with the allele frequencies constitute the evidence $\mathcal{E}$ for the case. Suppose we wish to compute the likelihood ratio in favor of the hypothesis that the victim and suspect contributed to the mixture, H_0: $v\,\&\,s$, as against the hypothesis that the victim and an unknown individual u contributed to the mixture, H_1: $v\,\&\,u$. It is not difficult to show that in this case

$$\text{LR} = \frac{1}{p_A^2 + 2p_A p_B + 2p_A p_C}, \qquad (24.8)$$

where p_i is the frequency of allele i in the population.

Bayesian Networks for Forensic DNA Identification

In more complex scenarios than those described above, it can become difficult or impossible to obtain the required probabilistic formulas.

In cases of disputed paternity, it commonly occurs that the DNA profiles of one or more of the "principal actors" in the pedigree are not available; but there is indirect evidence, in the form of DNA profiles of various known relatives. In the section Complex Disputed Paternity below, we consider such a case, where the putative father is unavailable for testing, but we have DNA from two of his brothers and an undisputed child of his by another woman. The analysis of all the data is clearly now much more complex. Likewise the appropriate extensions of (24.8) become relatively complex when the number of potential contributors to the mixture becomes large; if we want to use quantitative data (peak areas), which contain important additional information about the composition of the mixture, and to allow for uncertainty in allele frequencies and/or population substructure.

To handle such cases, sophisticated probabilistic modeling tools are required. Again, Bayesian networks, together with their associated computational methodology and technology, have been found valuable for this, particularly in their "object-oriented" Bayesian networks (OOBN) form, as implemented in commercial software such as HUGIN 6.[3] Bayesian networks for evaluating DNA evidence were introduced by Dawid, Mortera, Pascali, and van Boxel (2002). Further description and developments can be found in Mortera (2003, chap. 1B); Mortera, Dawid, and Lauritzen (2003); Vicard, Dawid, Mortera, and Lauritzen (2008); Cowell, Lauritzen, and Mortera (2007); Dawid, Mortera, and Vicard (2006); Dawid, Mortera, and Vicard (2007); and Taroni et al. (2006).

For some illustrative cases, we describe below how we can construct a suitable OOBN representation of a complex DNA identification problem incorporating all the individuals involved and the relationships between them.

Simple Disputed Paternity

We use the example of simple disputed paternity given in the section Forensic Genetics to introduce some basic ingredients of forensic OOBNs.

In fact, Figure 24.2 is just the relevant "top-level" network, constructed using the graphical interface to HUGIN 6. Each node (except the hypothesis node `tf=pf?`) in Figure 24.2 is itself an "instance" of another generic ("class") network, with further internal structure. In what follows, **bold face** will indicate a network class, and `teletype face` will indicate a node or instance. We describe only selected features here. A fuller description of OOBN networks for paternity casework can be found in Dawid et al. (2007) and Dawid et al. (2006).

Each of `m`, `pf`, and `af` is an instance of a class **founder**, while `c` is an instance of class **child** and `tf` is an instance of class **query**.

Within **founder** (not shown) we have two instances (maternal and paternal genes) of a class **gene**, which embodies the relevant repertory of

[3]Obtainable from http://www.hugin.com.

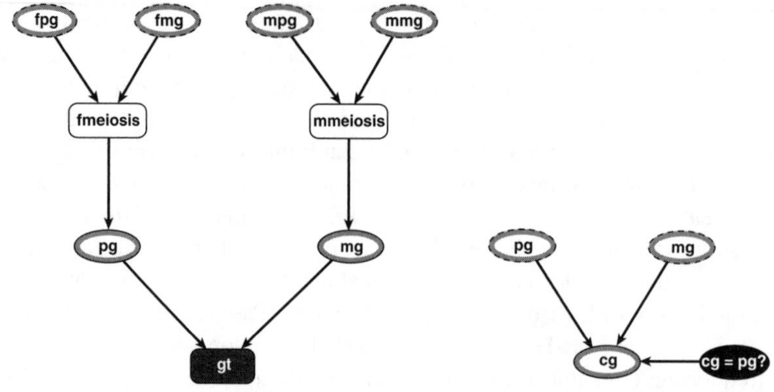

Figure 24.3 Networks **child** and **meiosis**.

alleles and their associated frequencies in the relevant population.

The internal structure of **child** is displayed in Figure 24.3.

On the paternal (left hand) side of **child**, the input nodes fpg and fmg represent the child's father's paternal and maternal genes. These are then copied into nodes pg and mg of an instance fmeiosis of a class network **meiosis**, whose output node cg is obtained by flipping a fair coin (node cg=pg?) to choose between pg and mg; this is then copied to pg (child's paternal gene) in network **child**. A similar structure holds for the maternal (right hand) side of **child**. Finally, pg and mg are copied into an instance gt of a network class **genotype**, which forgets the information on parental origin (this is also a feature of **founder**). Any DNA evidence on the individual is entered here.

The hypothesis node tf=pf? embodies H_0 (tf = pf) when it takes the value *true* and H_1 (tf = af) when *false*; it feeds into the instance tf of class **query** to implement this selection. We initially, and purely nominally, set both hypotheses as equally probable, so that, after propagation of evidence, the ratio of their posterior probabilities yields the paternity ratio based on this marker. By entering the data for each marker into the appropriate Bayesian network, we can thus easily calculate the associated likelihood ratio for paternity.

We build a separate such network for each STR marker, incorporating the appropriate repertoire of alleles and their frequencies. On entering the available DNA data, we can compute the associated likelihood ratio. Finally, we multiply these together across all markers to obtain the overall likelihood ratio.

Once supplied with the basic building blocks **founder**, **child**, and **query**, we can connect them together in different ways, much like a child's construction set, to represent a wide range of similar problems. An illustration is given in the next section.

Complex Disputed Paternity

Figure 24.4 is a OOBN representation of a disputed paternity case, where we have DNA profiles from a disputed child c1 and from its mother m1 but not from the putative father pf. We do, however, have DNA from c2, an undisputed child of pf by a different, observed, mother m2, as well as from two undisputed full brothers b1 and b2 of pf. The sibling relationship is made explicit by the incorporation of the unobserved grandfather gf and grandmother gm, parents of pf, b1 and b2. The "hypothesis node" tf=pf? again indicates whether the true father tf is pf or is an alternative father af, treated as randomly drawn from the population.

Nodes gf, gm, m1, m2, and af are all instances of class **founder**; pf, b1, b2, c1, and c2 are instances of class **child**; tf is an instance of class **query**.

The DNA evidence $\mathcal{E}$ consisted of the 6 DNA profiles, each comprising 10 STR markers, from m1, m2, c1, c2, b1, and b2. By entering the data for each marker into the Bayesian network (incorporating the appropriate alleles for that marker and their frequencies), we can thus easily

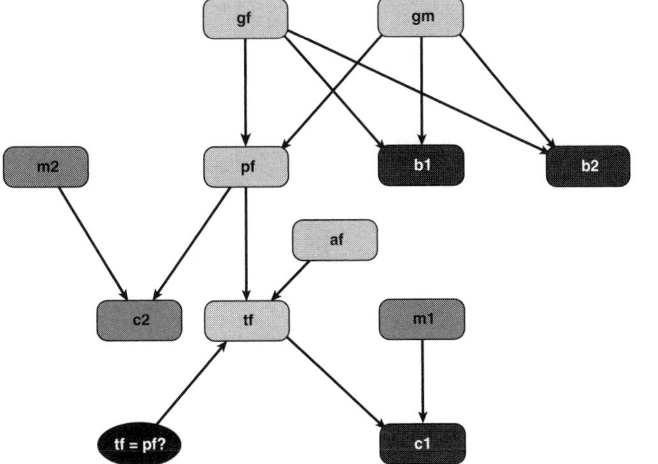

Figure 24.4 Pedigree for incomplete paternity case.

calculate the associated likelihood ratio for paternity. The overall paternity ratio is then given by their product.

For this particular case, this overall paternity ratio evaluates to around 1,300, meaning that the observed DNA evidence is 1,300 times more probable on the hypothesis of paternity than it would be were we to assume nonpaternity. According to Evett and Weir (1998, chap. 9), such a value might be considered as offering "very strong support" to the hypothesis of paternity (although paternity applications such as this will never produce the kind of likelihood ratio value, sometimes in the billions, that can occur when DNA profiling evidence is used to match a suspect to a crime). However, it is important to remember, in all cases, that the likelihood ratio derived from the DNA evidence is only one element of the whole story, which also involves prior probabilities, and perhaps further likelihood ratios based on other evidence in the case. All these ingredients need to be combined appropriately, using Bayes's theorem, to produce the final probability of paternity.

Mutation

It is easy to modify these networks to incorporate a variety of additional complications. One such is the possibility of *mutation* of genes in transmission from parent to child, which could lead to a true father appearing to be excluded (Dawid, Mortera, & Pascali, 2001; Dawid, Mortera, Dobosz, & Pascali, 2003; Dawid, 2003; Vicard & Dawid, 2004; Vicard et al., 2008). We must now distinguish between a child's *original gene* cog, identical with one of the parent's own genes, and the *actual gene* cag available to the child, which may differ from cog because of mutation. We elaborate the class network **meiosis** of Figure 24.3, as shown in Figure 24.5 by passing its original output cog ("child's original gene") through an instance cag ("child's actual gene") of a new network **mut**, constructed to implement whatever model is used to describe how the value of cog is stochastically altered by mutation. The output of cag is then copied to cg. Thus, **meiosis** now represents the result of mutation acting on top of Mendelian segregation.

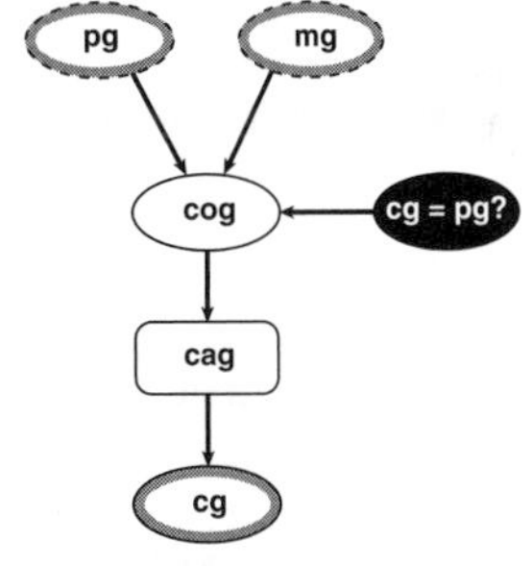

Figure 24.5 Revised network **meiosis**, incorporating mutation.

Table 24.1 Disputed paternity with brother too. mgt = {12, 15}, pfgt = {14, 14}, cgt = {12, 12}.

pr(silent)	L_D	L_B *with* bgt =						
		{16,20}	*{12,17}*	*{12,14}*	*{14,17}*	*{14,14}*	*{16,16}*	*{12,12}*
0	0	1	1	0.546	0.546	1	6.13	3,334
0.000015	0.472	1	1	0.546	0.546	1.0000	6.12	1,595
0.0001	2.473	1	1	0.546	0.546	0.9999	6.07	403.7
0.001	7.485	1	1	0.551	0.551	0.9992	5.54	46.07
0.01	8.100	1	1	0.590	0.590	0.9932	3.19	5.45

NOTE: Likelihood ratio in favor of paternity allowing for silent alleles: L_D, without brother's genotype. L_B, further (multiplicative) effect of brother's genotype.

Once an appropriate network **mut** has been built, and **meiosis** modified as described above, pedigree networks constructed as in the section Silent Allelles will now automatically incorporate the additional possibility of mutation.

Silent Alleles

Yet another complication that is easily handled by simple modifications to lower-level networks is the possibility that some alleles may not be recorded by the equipment, so that a truly heterozygous genotype appears homozygous (Dawid et al., 2007, 2006). This may be due to sporadic equipment failure, in which case it is not inherited and we talk of a *missed* allele; or to an inherited biological feature, in which case we refer to the allele as *silent*.

In some cases, making proper allowance for these possibilities can have a dramatic effect. Table 24.1 shows results for a particular case where, in addition to the genotypes mgt, pfgt, and cgt of mother, putative father, and child, we also have the genotype bgt of the putative father's brother. These refer to the single STR marker vWA.

If we had complete data on the genotypes mgt, pfgt, and cgt, the additional data bgt would have no effect whatsoever on the paternity ratio, since the child's genotype is conditionally independent of information on the putative father's brother given the mother and putative father's genotypes. In the case shown, in the absence of silence we would have an exclusion. Allowing for silence at various rates, but using only the data on the basic family triplet, gives the paternity ratios in the column labeled L_D, from which we already see that a small probability of silence can, in fact, lead to a paternity ratio greater than 1—now constituting evidence in favor of paternity. The remaining columns show the *additional* (multiplicative) effect of using the information on the brother's genotype bgt for various cases. The first row shows that even as the probability of silence tends to 0, its disturbing effect can be very substantial. In fact, when bgt $= \{12, 12\}$, the overall paternity ratio LR $= L_D \times L_B$ achieves a maximum value of $1,027.3$, at pr(silent) $= 0.0000642$, even though it vanishes for pr(silent) $= 0$.

Bayesian Networks for Analyzing Mixed DNA Profiles

Bayesian networks have also been constructed to address the challenging problems that arise in the interpretation of mixed trace evidence, as described in the section DNA Mixtures. Typically, one would be interested in testing whether the victim and suspect contributed to the mixture, H_0: $v\,\&\,s$, against the hypothesis that the victim and an unknown individual contributed to the mixture, H_1: $v\,\&\,u$. One might alternatively consider an additional unknown individual u_2 instead of the victim, with hypotheses H_0: $u_2\,\&\,s$ versus H_1: $u_2\,\&\,u_1$.

Figure 24.6 shows a top-level network that can be used for analyzing a mixture with two contributors, $p1$ and $p2$. Nodes sgt, vgt, u1gt, and u2gt are all instances of a network class **genotype** and represent the suspect's, the victim's, and two unknown individuals' genotypes.

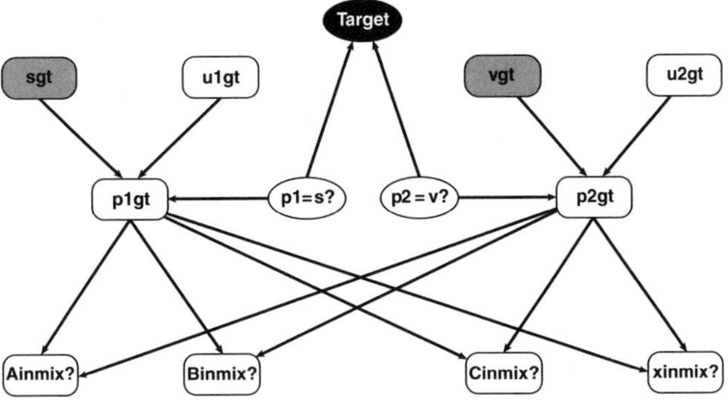

Figure 24.6 Bayesian network for DNA mixture from two contributors.

Boolean node `p1=s?` represents the hypothesis that contributor $p1$ is the suspect s. Node `p1gt`, the genotype of $p1$, is an instance of a network **query** that selects between the two genotypes `sgt` or `u1gt` according to the true/false state of the Boolean node `p1=s?`. A similar relationship holds between nodes `p2gt`, `vgt`, `u1gt`, and `p1=v?`. Possible genotype information on the suspect and/or the victim is entered and propagated from nodes `sgt` and `vgt`. The `target` node is the logical combination of the two Boolean nodes `p1=s?` and `p2=v?` and represents the four different hypotheses described above. `Ainmix?` determines whether allele A is in the mixture: This will be so if at least one A allele is present in either `p1gt` or `p2gt`. Similarly, for `Binmix?`, `Cinmix?`, `Dinmix?`, and `xinmix?` (where `x` refers to all the alleles that are not observed). Information on the alleles seen in the mixture is entered and propagated from these nodes.

The modular structure of Bayesian networks supports easy extension to mixtures with more contributors, as in cases where a rape victim declares that she has had one consensual partner in addition to the unidentified rapist or that she has been victim of multiple rape. Simple modification of the network handles such scenarios, so long as the total number of contributors can be assumed known.

In general, however, although the evidence of the trace itself will determine a lower bound to this total, there is in principle no upper bound. Thus, if in a trace we see that the maximum number of alleles in any marker is three, we know that the minimum number of contributors that could have produced this trace is two, but we cannot be sure that there were only two. However, it is often possible to set a relatively low-upper limit to the number it is reasonable to consider. We allow, as contributors to the mixture, persons with known DNA profiles, such as the victim and suspect and possibly also unknown individuals. Each of the various hypotheses H we might consider will involve a specification, x, for the number of unknown contributors. Although not strictly necessary, for extra clarity we write $\Pr_x(\mathcal{E}|H)$ for the probability of the evidence under this hypothesis. Thus, the likelihood ratio (LR) needed to evaluate the DNA evidence $\mathcal{E}$—comprising the DNA profiles of the victim, the suspect, and the mixed trace—in favor of a hypothesis H_0 against an alternative hypothesis H_1 is

$$\mathrm{LR} = \frac{\Pr_{x_0}(\mathcal{E}|H_0)}{\Pr_{x_1}(\mathcal{E}|H_1)},$$

where x_i denotes the number of unknown individuals involved in the hypothesis H_i.

When computing the weight of evidence, one should give the defendant the benefit of any doubt or uncertainty and so present the most favorable reasonable scenario for the defence. This implies that we should seek and use a lower bound for the value of the LR as we vary our assumptions within reasonable limits. And this, in turn, requires that we use an upper limit for the number of unknown contributors it is reasonable to consider. If the evidence is incriminating even in this most favorable case, it will be even more so for a larger number of unknown contributors.

To aid in setting such an upper limit, we can use the fact that $\Pr_x(\mathcal{E}|H)$ can be no larger than the probability that all the alleles of the x unknown contributors are in the mixed trace. This implies (Lauritzen & Mortera, 2002)

$$\Pr_x(\mathcal{E}|H) \leq \prod_{m=1}^{M} \kappa_m^{2x},$$

where, for each marker m, κ_m is the total probability that a randomly chosen allele will be one of those seen in the mixed trace. From this, it follows that if H_1 is any alternative hypothesis, yielding likelihood L_1, we need not consider an alternative hypothesis H with more than $b(L_1)$ unknown contributors, where

$$b(y) = \frac{\ln y}{2\sum_{m=1}^{M} \ln \kappa_m},$$

since that would yield a likelihood smaller than L_1.

Once it has been agreed to limit attention to some maximum total number of potential contributors, cases where the number of unknown contributors is itself uncertain can again be addressed using a Bayesian network, now including nodes for the number of unknown contributors and the total number of contributors (Mortera et al., 2003). This can be used for computing the posterior distribution of the total number of contributors to the mixture, as well as likelihood ratios for comparing all plausible hypotheses.

The modular structure of the Bayesian networks can be used to handle still further complex mixture problems. For example, we can consider together missing individuals, silent alleles, and a mixed crime trace simply by piecing together the appropriate modules.

The issue of silent alleles in a mixed trace arose in the celebrated case of *People v. O. J. Simpson* (Los Angeles County Case BA097211). At VNTR marker D2S44, the crime trace showed a three-band profile *ABC*, the victim had profile *AC* and the suspect had profile *AB*. The population allele frequencies are taken as $p_A = 0.0316$, $p_B = 0.0842$, and $p_C = 0.0926$ and the frequency of a silent allele as $p_n = 0.05$. For this marker, Table 24.2 gives the likelihoods (arbitrarily normalized to sum to 1) based on a network that handles silent alleles and allows for up to two unknown contributors. Results are shown both ignoring and allowing for silent alleles, and also for a "simplified" rough rule for accounting for silence, recommended in the report of the National Research Council (1996), which replaces the frequency p^2 by the much larger quantity $2p$.

Table 24.2 O. J. Simpson case: Likelihoods for hypotheses as to constitution of mixed trace, for suspect s, victim v, and varying number of contributors u (allowing for silent alleles).

Hypothesis	*Without Silent*	*With Silent Allele*	
		Exact	*2p Rule*
s & v & $2u$	0.0017	0.0039	0.0836
s & $2u$	0.0015	0.0032	0.0598
v & $2u$	0.0015	0.0031	0.0719
$2u$	0.0006	0.0008	0.0027
s & v & u	0.0392	0.0578	0.1886
s & u	0.0271	0.0340	0.0878
v & u	0.0253	0.0315	0.0805
s & v	0.9031	0.8657	0.4251

Note that the likelihood ratio in favor of H_0: $s\&v$ against H_1: $v\&u$, when correctly accounting for a silent allele, is 27.5, as compared with 5.3 based on the $2p$ rule. This clearly shows that in this case the rule recommended by the National Research Council is over conservative. Without accounting for the possibility of a silent allele, the likelihood ratio is 35.7.

So far we have only used qualitative information, namely which allele values are present in the mixture and the other profiles. A more sensitive analysis additionally uses measured "peak areas," which give quantitative information on the amounts of DNA involved. This requires much more detailed modeling, but again this can be effected by means of a Bayesian network (Cowell et al., 2007). Because the mixture proportion `frac` of DNA contributed by one of the parties is a common quantity across markers, we must now handle them all simultaneously within one "super network." Figure 24.7 shows the top-level network for two contributors, involving six markers, each an instance of a lower-level network **marker** as shown in Figure 24.8. This network is an extended version of the one shown in Figure 24.6, incorporating additional structure to model the quantitative peak area information. In particular, the nodes `Aweight` etc. in **marker** are instances

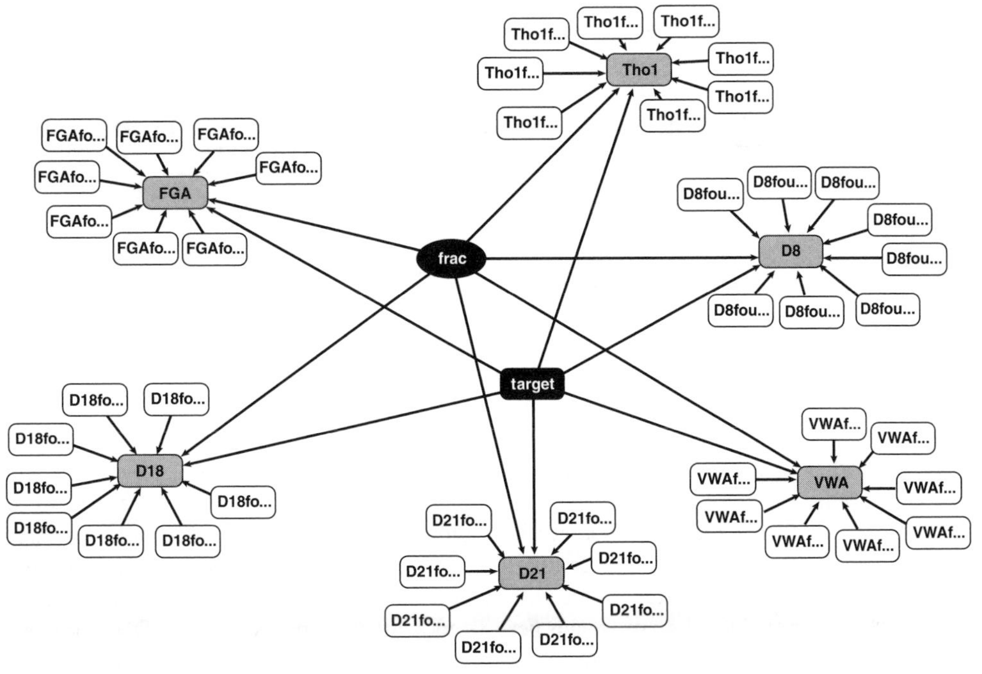

Figure 24.7 Six-marker OOBN for mixture using peak areas, two contributors.

SOURCE: Cowell, R. G., Lauritzen, S. L., & Mortera, J. (2007). Identification and separation of DNA mixtures using peak area information. *Forensic Science International, 166*, 28–34.

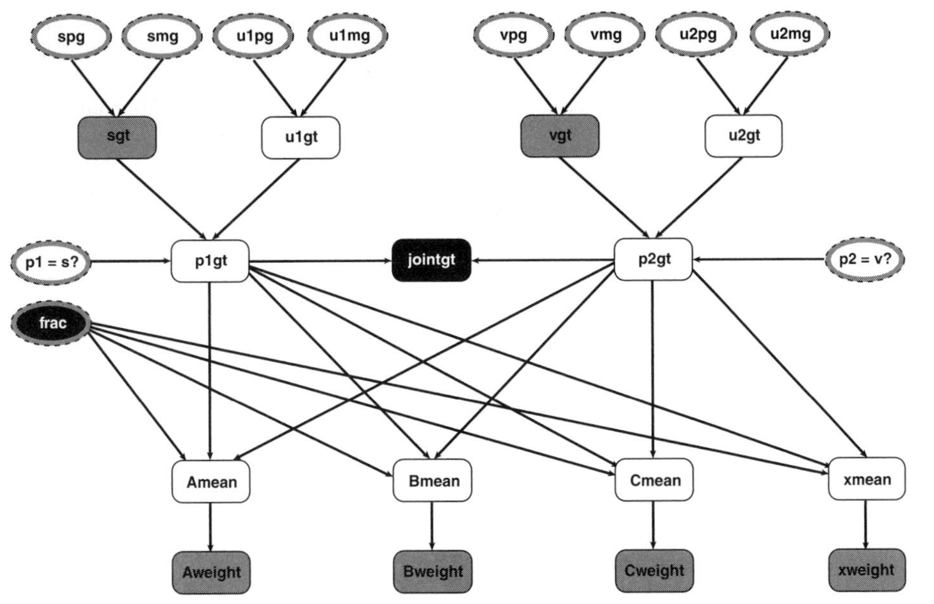

Figure 24.8 Network **marker** with three observed allele peaks.

Table 24.3 Data for mixed trace with two contributors.

Marker	*D8*			*D18*			*D21*			
Alleles	10*	11	14*	13*	16	17	59	65	67*	70*
Peak area	6,416	383	5,659	38,985	1,914	1,991	1,226	1,434	8,816	8,894

Marker	*FGA*			*THO1*		*vWA*			
Alleles	21*	22*	23	8*	9.3*	16*	17	18*	19
Peak area	16,099	10,538	1,014	17,441	22,368	4,669	931	4,724	188

NOTE: The starred values are the suspect's alleles.

of a class network that models the quantitative information on the peak weight.

Cowell et al. (2007) analyze the data shown in Table 24.3, taken from Evett, Gill, and Lambert (1998), involving a six-marker mixed profile with between two and four distinct observed bands per marker and a suspect whose profile is contained in these. It is assumed that this profile is a mixture either of the suspect and one other unobserved contributor or of two unknowns. Using only the allele values as data, the likelihood ratio for the suspect being a contributor to the mixture is calculated to be around 25,000. On taking account of the peak areas also, this rises to about 170,000,000.

Conclusion

We hope we have stimulated the reader's interest in the application of probability and statistical reasoning to forensic science. There are many challenging logical subtleties, ambiguities, and probabilistic pitfalls in legal reasoning, some of which we have illustrated. Some of the issues arising in this context have valuable lessons for other applications of statistics, such as confidentiality of census data (Skinner, 2007).

We have also aimed to show the usefulness of Bayesian networks for representing and solving a wide variety of complex forensic problems. Both genetic and nongenetic information can be represented in the same network. A particularly valuable feature is the modular structure of Bayesian networks, which allows a complex problem to be broken down into simpler structures that can then be pieced back together in many ways, so allowing us to address a wide range of forensic queries. In particular, using OOBN we have constructed a flexible computational toolkit and used it to analyze complex cases of DNA profile evidence, accounting appropriately for such features as missing individuals, mutation, silent alleles, and mixed DNA traces.

References

Anderson, T. J., Schum, D. A., & Twining, W. L. (2005). *Analysis of evidence* (2nd ed.). Cambridge, UK: Cambridge University Press.

Baio, G., & Corradi, F. (2006). Handling manipulated evidence. *Forensic Science International, 169*, 181–187.

Balding, D. J., & Donnelly, P. J. (1995). Inference in forensic identification (with discussion). *Journal of the Royal Statistical Society Series A, 158*, 21–53.

Balding, D. J., & Nichols, R. A. (1994). DNA profile match probability calculation: How to allow for population stratification, relatedness, database selection and single bands. *Forensic Science International, 64*, 125–140.

Buckleton, J. S., Triggs, C. M., & Walsh, S. J. (Eds.). (2005). *Forensic DNA evidence interpretation*. Boca Raton, FL: CRC Press.

Cavallini, D., & Corradi, F. (2005). OOBN for forensic identification through searching a DNA profiles database. In R. G. Cowell & Z. Ghahramani (Eds.), *Proceedings of the workshop on artificial intelligence and statistics 2005* (pp. 41–48). Key West, FL: Society for Artificial Intelligence and Statistics. (Retrieved from http://www.gatsby.ucl.uk/aistats)

Cowell, R. G., Dawid, A. P., Lauritzen, S. L., & Spiegelhalter, D. J. (1999). *Probabilistic networks and expert systems.* New York: Springer.

Cowell, R. G., Lauritzen, S. L., & Mortera, J. (2007). Identification and separation of DNA mixtures using peak area information. *Forensic Science International, 166*, 28–34.

Dawid, A. P. (2001). Comment on Stockmarr's "Likelihood Ratios for Evaluating DNA Evidence, When the Suspect Is Found Through a Database Search" (with response by Stockmarr). *Biometrics, 57*, 976–980.

Dawid, A. P. (2003). An object-oriented Bayesian network for estimating mutation rates. In C. M. Bishop & B. J. Frey (Eds.), *Proceedings of the ninth international workshop on artificial intelligence and statistics* (pp. 41–48). Key West, FL: Society for Artificial Intelliegence and Statistics. (Retrieved from http://www.tinyurl.com/39bmh)

Dawid, A. P. (2004). Which likelihood ratio? In discussion of Meester and Sjerps (2004). *Law, Probability and Risk, 3*, 65–71.

Dawid, A. P. (2005). *Probability and proof.* (Online appendix to Anderson et al. (2005). Retrieved from http://www.tinyurl.com/7g3bd)

Dawid, A. P. (2007). Statistics and the law. In K. Tybjerg, J. Swenson-Wright, & A. Bell (Eds.), *Evidence.* Cambridge, UK: Cambridge University Press.

Dawid, A. P., & Evett, I. W. (1997). Using a graphical method to assist the evaluation of complicated patterns of evidence. *Journal of Forensic Sciences, 42*, 226–231.

Dawid, A. P., & Mortera, J. (1995). In discussion of Balding and Donnelly (1995). *Journal of the Royal Statistical Society Series A, 158*, 46.

Dawid, A. P., & Mortera, J. (1996). Coherent analysis of forensic identification evidence. *Journal of the Royal Statistical Society Series B, 58*, 425–443.

Dawid, A. P., Mortera, J., Dobosz, M., & Pascali, V. L. (2003). Mutations and the probabilistic approach to incompatible paternity tests. In B. Brinkmann & A. Carracedo (Eds.), *International Congress series: Vol. 1239. Progress in forensic genetics 9.* Amsterdam: Elsevier Science.

Dawid, A. P., Mortera, J., & Pascali, V. L. (2001). Non-fatherhood or mutation? A probabilistic approach to parental exclusion in paternity testing. *Forensic Science International, 124*, 55–61.

Dawid, A. P., Mortera, J., Pascali, V. L., & van Boxel, D. W. (2002). Probabilistic expert systems for forensic inference from genetic markers. *Scandinavian Journal of Statistics, 29*, 577–595.

Dawid, A. P., Mortera, J., & Vicard, P. (2006). Representing and solving complex DNA identification cases using Bayesian networks. In A. Amorim, F. Corte-Real, & N. Morling (Eds.), *International Congress Series: Vol. 1288. Progress in forensic genetics 11* (pp. 484–491). Amsterdam: Elsevier.

Dawid, A. P., Mortera, J., & Vicard, P. (2007). Object-oriented Bayesian networks for complex forensic DNA profiling problems. *Forensic Science International, 169*, 195–205.

Eggleston, R. (1983). *Evidence, proof and probability* (2nd ed.). London: Weidenfeld & Nicolson.

Evett, I. W., Gill, P. D., & Lambert, J. A. (1998). Taking account of peak areas when interpreting mixed DNA profiles. *Journal of Forensic Sciences.*

Evett, I. W., & Weir, B. S. (1998). *Interpreting DNA evidence.* Sunderland, MA: Sinauer.

Fairley, W. B., & Mosteller, F. (1977). A conversation about Collins. In W. B. Fairley & F. Mosteller (Eds.), *Statistics in public policy* (pp. 369–379). Reading, MA: Addison-Wesley.

Lauritzen, S. L., & Mortera, J. (2002). Bounding the number of contributors to mixed DNA stains. *Forensic Science International, 130*, 125–126.

Meester, R. W. J., & Sjerps, M. (2004). Why the effect of prior odds should accompany the likelihood ratio when reporting DNA evidence (with discussion by A. P. Dawid, D. J. Balding, J. S. Buckleton, and C. M. Triggs). *Law, Probability and Risk, 3*, 51–86.

Mortera, J. (2003). Analysis of DNA mixtures using Bayesian networks. In P. J. Green, N. L. Hjort, & S. Richardson (Eds.), *Highly structured stochastic systems* (pp. 39–44). Oxford, UK: Oxford University Press.

Mortera, J., Dawid, A. P., & Lauritzen, S. L. (2003). Probabilistic expert systems for DNA mixture profiling. *Theoretical Population Biology, 63*, 191–205.

National Research Council. (1996). *The evaluation of forensic DNA evidence.* Washington, DC: National Academy Press.

Skinner, C. J. (2007). The probability of identification: Applying ideas from forensic statistics to disclosure risk assessment. *Journal of the Royal Statistical Society Series A, 170*, 195–212.

Stockmarr, A. (1999). Likelihood ratios for evaluating DNA evidence when the suspect is found through a database search. *Biometrics, 55*, 671–677.

Taroni, F., Aitken, C., Garbolino, P., & Biedermann, A. (2006). *Bayesian networks and probabilistic inference in forensic science.* Chichester, UK: Wiley.

Vicard, P., & Dawid, A. P. (2004). A statistical treatment of biases affecting the estimation of mutation rates. *Mutation Research, 547*, 19–33.

Vicard, P., Dawid, A. P., Mortera, J., & Lauritzen, S. L. (2008). Estimating mutation rates from paternity casework. *Forensic Science International: Genetics*, 2, 9–18.

Wigmore, J. H. (1937). *The science of judicial proof* (3rd ed.). Boston: Little, Brown.

Zabell, S. L. (1988). The probabilistic analysis of testimony. *Journal of Statistical Planning and Inference*, *20*, 327–354.

25

PROBABILITY IN THE COURTROOM

BASIL C. BITAS

INTRODUCTION

The use of statistics and probabilistic concepts in the courtroom, particularly in the United States, has gained increasing currency over the past quarter century with the growing complexity and interdependence of the economy, the heightened penetration of science and scientific doctrine into virtually all aspects of daily life, and, conversely, the expansion of legal doctrine and related approaches to address and mediate among all forms of human interaction.

The collision, or, more positively, the integration, of science with the law, or vice versa, has placed increasing importance on the need to delineate between the two spheres, so as to better promote the synergistic effects that can lead to balanced and informed decision making. If scientific concepts are imported into the courtroom, they should ideally retain their scientific integrity while, at the same time, facilitating the resolution of the legal question at issue. However, the needs of the courtroom, or at least the parameters thereof, may not be those that are classically associated with scientific inquiry, in terms of both form and substance. It is this issue that lies at the heart of the use (and abuse) of scientific testimony in the courtroom.

As a practical matter, for scientific evidence, including statistical and probabilistic analysis, to be admissible in the U.S. federal courts, it must be relevant, valid, and reliable. These basic parameters are reflected in the codification set forth in the U.S. Federal Rules of Evidence (originally adopted 1972), particularly Rule 702—"Testimony by Experts,"[1] as subsequently clarified by the ruling in *Daubert v. Merrell Dow Pharmaceuticals* (1993). State courts in the United States have adopted these general criteria to varying degrees, but their interpretation can vary depending on the jurisdiction (Bernstein & Jackson, 2004). This is due to the fact that the parallel system of state courts is not bound by either the Federal Rules of Evidence or the related clarification set forth in the *Daubert* ruling, though both have exerted a certain effect on the direction of the law. These issues will be dealt

[1] Rule 702:

> If scientific, technical, or other specialized knowledge will assist the trier of fact to understand the evidence or to determine a fact in issue, a witness qualified as an expert by knowledge, skill, experience, training, or education, may testify thereto in the form of an opinion or otherwise, if (1) the testimony is based upon sufficient facts or data, (2) the testimony is the product of reliable principles and methods, and (3) the witness has applied the principles and methods reliably to the facts of the case.

with in greater detail in the first and second sections of this chapter.

In addition to the legal conditions for admissibility, statistical and probabilistic evidence, particularly in the United States, must further meet certain practical criteria. To begin with, such evidence must be transparent to the maximum extent possible and accessible to lay juries and judges. When scientific analysis is put at the service of the courts, let alone the lawyers, there is a risk that the analysis will be diluted to the point where its basic scientific integrity may be lost. It may, indeed, be testimony, but no longer expert testimony per se, as the lawyers seek to conform—some might say, contort—scientific concepts to meet the needs of their legal argumentation.

The complexity of modern society and the related difficulty in distilling and analyzing discrete phenomena and situations militate in favor of putting expert testimony at the service of the courts, but such testimony should not become a "slave" to the legal process. In adversarial systems, whereby the parties' experts often become technical advocates for the positions being espoused by the lawyers, the dilution of the underlying scientific analysis constitutes a distinct risk. Just as Von Clausewitz (1982) talked of war being "the continuation of politics by other means," expert analysis often becomes an alternative means for carrying out the legal debate. The so-called battle of the experts can distort the legal issues at hand, obfuscate rather than illuminate the scientific analysis, and undermine the credibility of the particular specialty at issue (Eder & Garg, 2006, p. 13). One need only look at the skeptical light in which psychiatric testimony is often viewed (Gutheil, 1999) to appreciate the pitfalls of contorting expert testimony to fit the legal box.

This chapter will examine the use of scientific analysis in greater detail, highlighting the practical considerations and constraints in relying on expert, and particularly statistical, testimony in the courtroom and proposing ways in which the most egregious pitfalls can be avoided. The first section of this chapter will focus on the context in which science meets the law. The next three sections will then examine three specific applications of statistics and probability to the law in the fields of toxic torts and epidemiology, employment discrimination cases, and the use of DNA evidence in criminal cases, respectively. Finally, the last two sections will offer some practical observations on using scientific evidence and experts in the courtroom, both in U.S. and non-U.S. jurisdictions, as well as some additional reflections and recommendations concerning future trends and perspectives.

There are "lies, damned lies, and statistics," so they say. With an enlightened approach to the use of statistical and probabilistic analysis in the courtroom, there may be ways to ensure that such testimony contributes to both the legal and the adversarial process without losing its essential scientific integrity. By surveying this area from both a practical and a theoretical perspective, it is hoped that this chapter may shed some light on the appropriate courtroom dynamic and the prospects for bringing statistical and probabilistic evidence to bear in a meaningful and constructive manner.

Context: Science and Law—An Intersection of Disciplines

The interaction between scientific inquiry and legal analysis offers great potential for both enriching and distorting the debate, depending on the manner in which such issues are handled. The expert's testimony will necessarily be "conditioned" by the legal environment. In assessing the nature and impact of this interaction, it is perhaps useful to visualize a Venn diagram. If the expert testimony is irrelevant, there will be no point of intersection between the scientific and legal inquiries, and indeed, the analysis will be deemed to be inadmissible in the U.S. federal and state courts in light of the aforementioned *Daubert* test, the Federal Rules of Evidence, and the related state doctrines governing these issues.

At the point of entry into the legal sphere of apparently relevant testimony, there is perhaps a necessary "bending" of the concepts to allow the layman to grasp the overriding ideas. If, however, the testimony is wholly adapted to the legal sphere, it may cease to be expert testimony and become mere advocacy. Many trial lawyers would take this circumstance for granted. Indeed, it may be this type of cynicism, or smug omniscience, among lawyers that has contributed to the devaluation of certain forms of scientific testimony. Moreover, the melding—some might say, muddling—of scientific concepts into the legal debate is facilitated to the extent that both science and law lay claim to a certain precision and related technical vocabulary.

We are, to some extent, confronted with a similar vocabulary but a conflict of visions. Seemingly similar statements made in either the scientific or the legal field may have vastly different meanings or implications when transplanted from one context to the other. For instance, the notion of "causation," an issue that lies at the heart of the legal debate, can take on a vastly different meaning when examined through either a "scientific" or a "legal" lens (Eder & Garg, 2006, pp. 15–16). This circumstance will be examined more closely in the discussion of epidemiologic statistics (in the fourth section) and the associated risk assessments. For now, the overriding point is that the cross-fertilization between science and the law, without adequate qualification, can lead to legalized notions of scientific concepts that become increasingly divorced from their original scientific foundation due to overzealous advocacy and/or the absence of adequate judicial vigilance.

The Impact of Methodology on Meaning

The scientific method seeks to process all relevant material in order to understand the underlying mechanism and determine the root of a given problem or phenomenon. All sources of information are examined, regardless of provenance, once they are deemed to be broadly conducive to understanding the context and question at study. The nature of the scientific inquiry can therefore be described as being process—rather than result—oriented. It is this openness to inquiry that leads to "blind alleys," qualified conclusions, and the stimulus for further study. While no single piece of research may embody the answer, there is a belief that through scientific inquiry and the process of accretion, a more accurate rendering of the truth can be established. Science seeks answers, but there is no formal time frame or route for getting to the appointed destination.

If scientific inquiry for the purposes of this analysis can be categorized as "process oriented," then the legal inquiry can perhaps be described as "result oriented." Certainly, we are all familiar with notions of legal process, but the exercise in the courtroom is essentially aimed at resolving disputes and at reaching a result. While both scientific and legal inquiries are formulated to provide answers, the scientific inquiry seeks to explore systematically every aspect of a particular issue, whereas the scope of the legal inquiry is limited to evidence directly related to resolving the case at hand. The evidence that is admitted to the courtroom for consideration by the judge and jury is therefore deemed conducive to settling the dispute. It is evaluated and assessed in that light and is sometimes transformed in the process. Accordingly, the "meaning" of a given epidemiologic study can vary widely depending on whether it is being parsed by a group of scientists or presented to, and evaluated by, a jury, subject to the judge's instructions regarding legal liability.

Mindful of the implications of scientific evidence for influencing—indeed, determining—a given result, courts have elaborated procedural rules governing admissibility. In contrast to the scientific inquiry where "everything" is considered to promote a fuller understanding of a given question or phenomenon, the judicial process admits scientific evidence selectively, with a view to reaching a "firm" legal conclusion (or result) in a specific case and within a specific time frame. The evidence-gathering process is thus volitionally less inclusive, to the extent that the overall exercise and related decision making are intended to be "final" with regard to the underlying dispute.

This has implications for judicial proceedings, where the data and analyses admitted enjoy a certain judicial imprimatur and attendant presumption of validity. This circumstance, in turn, explains the bitter battles over the admissibility of scientific evidence as a threshold matter and the subsequent efforts of opposing counsel to provide contradictory testimony, leading to the aforementioned "battle of the experts." In most continental legal systems, where expert testimony is adduced through court-appointed experts, the threshold inquiry of admissibility is combined with the interpretation of the scientific analysis, thereby rationalizing the process by providing one scientific channel to the court. The adversarial element is lost, thereby raising the risk that the evidence will be interpreted as an indisputable scientific truth, but the "science," as such, is preserved as a separate dimension of the inquiry, to be measured against, but not subsumed by, the legal argumentation.

Diverse non-U.S. systems, whether in Europe, Latin America, or Asia, treat the court-appointed expert with varying degrees of deference (Barkacs, Browne, & Williamson, 2002), sometimes allowing the parties to pose questions framing the inquiry or, alternatively, constituting a panel, including the parties' experts, to ensure that all scientific points of view are represented. Regardless of the precise procedures adopted, the overriding goal is to provide the court with a unified or at least a synthesized voice concerning the scientific analysis to be brought to bear on the legal questions at issue. Such an approach may be worth considering in more adversarial systems, such as those in the United States, Australia, and, to some extent, Japan, where expert testimony proffered by the respective parties is increasingly viewed as a mere extension of the legal argumentation (Guzelian, 2006).

A Closer Look: "Meaning" in the Legal and Scientific Context—Epidemiology

Within the field of statistics and expert testimony, epidemiological evidence has become increasingly important. With the advent of mass toxic torts, particularly in the product liability field, recourse is often had to epidemiologic evidence to "prove" that exposure to a given product "caused" a particular injury. When we enter into this realm of proof and causation, we begin, as alluded to above, to mix and match the legal and scientific worlds.

As a practical matter, medical science is often at a loss to identify the specific source or cause of a condition, particularly when it relates to a multifactorial disease, such as cancer. Epidemiologic studies are therefore used to assess the disease incidence in a given population and to identify associations between a given factor and the onset of disease in the population at study. Drawing a causal inference from the strength of the association requires an additional logical leap. The point at which such an inference will be drawn can vary among epidemiologists and therefore constitutes fertile ground for scientific debate and interaction. Moreover, since the nature of scientific inquiry is to explore all plausible angles, attorneys will have a number of studies and approaches from which to choose, subject to certain criteria regarding admissibility.

To meet the criteria for admissibility, epidemiologic studies must conform essentially to a type of best practices, involving an accepted methodology and design, a detailed protocol, and a scientifically credible conclusion. There is some dispute in the U.S. courts as to whether epidemiologic evidence on causation must be "well founded" or "generally accepted." The former test widens the scope of admissible evidence, allowing it to come in if the findings are novel but well founded. This formulation represents the more liberal approach reflected in the U.S. federal courts following the adoption of the aforementioned Federal Rules of Evidence and the subsequent *Daubert* ruling of the U.S. Supreme Court in 1993. The "generally accepted" test derives from an earlier 1924 ruling, *Frye v. United States* (1924), and requires that the findings and related analysis be more mainstream or settled.

The more stringent *Frye* standard continues to influence jurisprudence in the parallel system of state courts, which, as noted in the second section, is not formally bound by either *Daubert* or the Federal Rules of Evidence and is therefore free to strike a different balance among the competing standards on a state-by-state basis. At the present time, 27 state court systems have adopted *Daubert*, 14 have retained the *Frye* standard, 6 other states have adopted *Daubert* while not explicitly disavowing *Frye*, and 4 states have opted to develop and apply their own tests (Collie, 2006, p. 72). However, even in jurisdictions applying the more stringent general acceptance standard derived from *Frye*, attorneys will generally not have any lack of contradictory data or opposing experts from which to choose.

Statistical Techniques: Interaction With Legal Standards of Proof

Scientific evidence, specifically statistical and probabilistic analysis, is used to clarify otherwise opaque phenomena. It is thought that by breaking down various situations through "sampling," one can isolate and better understand the underlying process at issue, whether it be related to disease or social issues, such as employment discrimination. It is important here to examine the statistical methodology and its subsequent application to the legal context. Moreover, different types of legal procedures will apply disparate standards of proof depending on whether the proceeding involves criminal or civil liability. Though there are various gradations in between, the two standards that represent the opposite ends of the spectrum are "beyond a reasonable doubt" in criminal proceedings and a "preponderance of the evidence" in civil trials. Each of these standards, and those in between, will have serious implications for the interpretation of the statistical evidence presented in the courtroom. Moreover, translating these descriptive standards into numerical parameters has proven to be an elusive target.

EPIDEMIOLOGY: OBSERVATIONAL DATA— LEGAL ADMISSIBILITY AND UTILITY

To the extent that epidemiology deals with associations—that is, probabilities within populations—it is difficult to extrapolate from a general conclusion (i.e., that a given exposure causes disease in a study population), which itself may require an inferential leap, to a conclusion that said exposure caused the specific plaintiff's condition. This juxtaposition between so-called general and specific causation lies at the heart of many cases involving product liability and toxic torts. Moreover, while the demonstration of general causation is a necessary precondition for proceeding to the inquiry concerning specific causation, it is not sufficient to demonstrate the latter.

U.S. courts have expressed diverse views on the necessity of using epidemiological evidence in exposure cases to demonstrate general causation, particularly where the science is evolving and where there may be no conclusive biological evidence.[2] Courts seem to be gravitating toward a standard holding that the best available evidence should be used to demonstrate causation.[3] This will involve a heavy reliance on epidemiologic studies in situations where there is no biological evidence concerning the alleged "causal" mechanism and perhaps less where the former exists.

A recent case, *Norris v. Baxter Healthcare Corporation* (2005), may be instructive in this regard. The plaintiff in *Norris* claimed that she had suffered various immune disorders following her breast augmentation surgery using silicone implants. The related expert testimony consisted essentially of a series of case studies generated by the plaintiff's own experts, suggesting that the implants could cause the alleged medical condition. In disallowing the plaintiff's expert testimony, the court noted that such analysis could not be deemed reliable or valid, to the extent that it ignored a vast body of epidemiologic evidence supporting the proposition that there was no link between silicone implants and immune disorders. The court noted that "in cases where there is no epidemiology challenging causation available, epidemiological evidence would not necessarily be required" (p. 878).[4] However, where there is a vast body of epidemiology that finds no association between silicone implants and immune diseases, such findings must be addressed in connection with the plaintiff's own counter arguments on general and specific causation. Putting the point into overall context, the court stated,

> We are not holding that epidemiological studies are always necessary in a toxic tort case. We are simply holding that where there is a large body of contrary epidemiological evidence, it is necessary to at least

---

[2]Compare *Glastetter v. Novartis Pharmaceutical Corporation* (2001) (noting "the absence of epidemiological evidence did not doom [plaintiff's] case") and *Siharath v. Sandoz Pharmaceutical Corporation* (2001) (stating that the Court looks not only at epidemiology but also at the totality of other evidence) with *Daubert v. Merrell Dow Pharmaceuticals* (1993) (stating that in the absence of scientific understanding of cause of injury or disease, causation may only be shown through epidemiological evidence).

[3]For example, *Globetti v. Sandoz Pharmaceutical Corporation* (2000) (noting that while epidemiological evidence is best, it is not required by *Daubert*, finding nonepidemiologic evidence admissible, and concluding that the plaintiff's experts offered the best practically available scientific evidence).

[4]*Norris v. Baxter Healthcare Corporation* (2005, p. 882).

> address it with evidence that is based on medically reliable and scientifically valid methodology.[5]

The plaintiff's expert evidence was essentially anecdotal and in direct contradiction to the prevailing body of mainstream epidemiology. The evidence presented by the plaintiff's expert was biological but not mainstream, having been more or less compiled for—some might say "tailored" to—the litigation at hand. As such, it could not be considered consistent with the courts' evolving standard of requiring the best available evidence in evaluating the necessity of using epidemiology to establish a suitable foundation for issues of general causation.

Use of Epidemiological Evidence: Legal Sufficiency

To the extent that epidemiologic evidence is adduced, the studies submitted must meet certain scientific standards. They must, for instance, be carried out pursuant to a written protocol designed to either "validate" or "disprove" a written hypothesis developed by the researchers. Moreover, the data must be drawn from a definable population and analyzed pursuant to identifiable statistical techniques. Inferences drawn from the data should be qualified, as appropriate, particularly as to the strength of the association and the extent to which the findings can be generalized.

Numerous factors affect the use and presentation of epidemiologic evidence in the courtroom, including the issue of bias. Biases can arise from the selection of the population, the sample subjects' recall of the level of their exposure, and the reporting of disease incidence in a given population, with such reporting sometimes being overestimated in exposed populations (Gordis, 1999).[6] In addition to biases stemming from the design and execution of the study, there may also be biases arising from publication, with studies finding statistically significant associations between a given exposure and disease gaining currency within the literature (Gordis, 1999).

[5] *Norris v. Baxter Healthcare Corporation* (2005, p. 882).

[6] See also (Green, Freedman, & Gordis, 2000, pp. 363–369).

Key Concepts: Statistical Significance

Epidemiologic studies seek to establish or draw statistically significant results, despite the limitations that can arise from relatively limited samples or from samples that are inappropriately selected or replete with the biases mentioned above. The demonstration of scientifically credible statistical significance, as described below, is therefore a key to the admissibility of epidemiologic evidence.

As a practical matter, the use of epidemiologic evidence in the courtroom will always involve a process of education, whereby the nature of what is sought to be admitted is explained and certain statistical terms are elucidated to the satisfaction of the judge and jurors, as the case may be, so that the overall "statistical significance" of the results can be placed in proper context. Among the most important of these terms are the confidence interval and relative risk.

Confidence Interval

To put a given epidemiologic study in context for both the judge and jury, attorneys must be able to explain the relationship of sampling error to the conclusions reported in a given study. While such concepts are the stock and trade of statisticians, they are often being presented to lay judges and jurors possessing little or no statistical background. Accordingly, explaining that a two-tailed study will generate an upper and lower bound to circumscribe a given relative risk is important to establish context. It should be further emphasized that a relative risk of ≤ 1 is not statistically significant, to the extent that it suggests that there is no difference in disease incidence between the exposed and unexposed populations. Moreover, it is important to explain that an overall finding of a relative risk > 1 can be questioned, should the confidence interval indicate bounds that go below such a threshold. It may also be useful to explain that the accepted scientific standard for epidemiologic studies requires a confidence interval of 95%, whereby a 5% chance that the results are due to chance is tolerated.[7]

[7] Green et al. (2000) defines *confidence interval* as

> a range of values calculated from the results of a study within which the true value is likely to fall; the width

The point here is that the use of statistics in the courtroom can often involve a blizzard of new concepts for lay juries and judges, thereby placing a premium on the manner in which such data are presented and explained. The risk of confusing concepts is thereby multiplied, influencing certain strategic considerations of the litigator, as will be discussed below.

Relative Risk

Together with the confidence interval, judges and jurors must be educated as to the notion of relative risk[8]—that is, the frequency of disease observed in an exposed versus unexposed population. It must be explained that relative risk is a ratio bounded by its confidence interval, as described above. Because epidemiologic studies seek to establish an association between a given risk factor and a given disease rather than causation per se, this nuance is a key factor in determining how best to use and present such evidence in the courtroom.

Application to the Legal Context

With these technical terms and considerations as a basis, the link to the legal context can then be made. If one takes the civil liability standard of a preponderance of the evidence—that is, "more likely than not," a relative risk of $\geqslant 2$ has come to assume a certain "benchmark" status in legal contexts, suggesting that causation is more likely than not.[9] While this might appear to be a neat fit in a legal context, it is important to recognize that a finding of a relative risk of 2 constitutes, in some respects, the lower bound of what can be considered a meaningful association between a given exposure and the onset of a disease. It is through this type of "mixing and matching" exercise that the application of scientific standards to the legal context can lead to confusion or erroneous conclusions, particularly where the underlying concepts have not been adequately explained.

A case decided in January 2005 by an appellate court in California involving workers exposed to two specific solvents at the manufacturing premises of the Lockheed Martin Corporation is instructive (*Lockheed Litigation Cases*, 2005). The plaintiffs claimed that two particular solvents, acetone and methyl ethyl ketone, manufactured by ExxonMobil Corp. and Union Oil Co. of California, respectively, had caused the medical condition(s) at issue but proffered epidemiologic studies that dealt solely with exposure to multiple solvents and the alleged relationship to the medical conditions in the case. Moreover, the studies offered into evidence dealt with relative risks >1 but <2. The trial court held that studies demonstrating a relative risk of <2 were inadmissible as a matter of California law, to the extent that such studies failed to meet the reliability prong of the aforementioned *Daubert* test.

On appeal, the California Second District Court of Appeal affirmed the lower court ruling, albeit by citing lack of relevancy rather than reliability. The court noted that the multiple exposures examined in the studies were not relevant to establishing that the two specific, individual chemicals cited by the plaintiffs caused the medical conditions at issue and could therefore not provide a rational basis for the related expert opinion. The court went on to state, however, that a relative risk of <2 was not in and of itself a disqualifying criterion for admissibility based on lack of

---

of the interval reflects random error. Thus, if a confidence level of .95 is selected for a study, 95% of similar studies would result in the true relative risk falling within the confidence interval. The width of the confidence interval provides an indication of the precision of the point estimate or relative risk found in the study; the narrower the confidence interval, the greater the confidence in the relative risk estimate found in the study. Where the confidence interval contains a relative risk of 1.0, the results of the study are not statistically significant. (p. 389)

[8]Green et al. (2000) defines *relative risk (RR)* as

> the ratio of the risk of disease or death among people exposed to an agent to the risk among the unexposed. For instance, if 10% of all people exposed to a chemical develop a disease, compared with 5% of people who are not exposed, the disease occurs twice as frequently among the exposed people. The relative risk is $10\%/5\% = 2$. A relative risk of 1 indicates no association between exposure and disease. (p. 395)

[9]For example, *Siharath v. Sandoz Pharmaceutical Corporation* (2001) ("In the world of epidemiology, the threshold for concluding that an agent was more likely than not the cause of a disease is a relative risk greater than 2.0") (p. 1356), Carruth and Goldstein (2000) (examining 31 federal and state toxic tort cases from 1982 to 1999, comparing minimum threshold relative risk for general causation), and Santoro (1995).

reliability. The court explained that where additional evidence and factors support the scientific proposition at issue, epidemiologic studies yielding a relative risk of <2, provided that they are relevant to the claims at issue, may be admissible.

The case demonstrates in microcosm the interplay between scientific and legal concepts in an adjudicative forum and the ongoing elasticity regarding the interpretation and application of relevant legal standards. The appeals court sought to examine the nature of the exposure and the relevance of the epidemiologic studies to that exposure. Concluding that the studies were not relevant to the nature of the exposure claimed by the plaintiffs, the court was able to rule such studies inadmissible. Visualizing the Venn diagram discussed earlier, the court essentially concluded that there was no intersection between the plaintiffs' claims and the statistical proof and related expert testimony adduced in support thereof.

Had the plaintiffs been able to demonstrate the relevance of their proof (i.e., to show an intersection between the scientific data and their legal claim), the court would have been prepared to show greater flexibility regarding the interpretation of the probabilities reflected in the epidemiologic studies proffered by the plaintiffs and the related criteria for admissibility. Numerical targets, such as a relative risk of 2, would not have been viewed as mandatory thresholds for admissibility where the totality of the evidence suggested that there was support for the scientific proposition at issue. Accordingly, the appreciation of scientific evidence, including the statistical and probabilistic elements thereof, involves a qualitative analysis regarding both admissibility and the ultimate relationship of such statistical elements to legal standards of proof such as a "preponderance of the evidence."

Such nuances of interpretation and application are likely to continue to play out on a case-by-case basis as the circumstances relating to new types of exposures surface in the absence of, or pursuant to, epidemiologic support. One immediately thinks of the claims involving the alleged adverse health effects caused by prolonged exposure to cell phones or high-tension power lines and the manner in which this will affect the courts' view of low-risk epidemiology and related issues of causation. It is likely that many of the epidemiologic studies analyzing these phenomena will end up in the so-called statistical no man's land with relative risks between 1 and 2. Moreover, as the *Daubert* analysis gains currency, courts will increasingly be forced into the role of "gatekeeper," evaluating the admissibility of novel but well-founded scientific theories that are at the outer bounds of their expertise. This dynamic differs from the more straightforward general acceptance test of "Frye," and while this expanded role for judicial discretion is probably necessary in light of the ever-increasing velocity in the acquisition of scientific knowledge, it will no doubt lead to a degree of continuing uncertainty in the area.

Legal Standards for Admissibility—The Evolution of Frye and Daubert: Future Perspectives

In many respects, the ongoing evolution of the legal standard for admissibility from *Frye* to *Daubert* was intended to give courts access to developing theories bearing scientific merit that were too new to be considered generally accepted. With the broad criteria of relevance, validity, and reliability as a benchmark, the court in *Daubert* provided guidance in terms of the factors to be considered, particularly with regard to the qualifying conditions of "validity" and, more specifically, "reliability":

1. The testability of the scientific theory or technique (whether the scientific theory or technique is capable of repetition and withstanding falsification)
2. Whether the scientific theory has been peer reviewed and published
3. The technique's known or potential error rate
4. Whether the opinion has been generally accepted in the relevant scientific community (an echo of *Frye*)[10]

The above criteria were intended to provide courts with a road map for assessing the admissibility of scientific evidence, thereby rationalizing the process and providing predictability

[10] *Daubert v. Merrell Dow Pharmaceuticals* (1993, pp. 593–595).

regarding the expectations of the respective parties concerning the use of such proof in the courtroom. As a practical matter, the *Daubert* criteria have not fully clarified the situation. The criteria described above are, for instance, applied in a nonexclusive manner, with substantial deference being given to the judge's appreciation of the proposed expert submission and his or her application of the *Daubert* criteria thereto. In a Supreme Court case interpreting *Daubert*, *General Electric v. Joiner* (1997), the court established the rather high standard of an "abuse of discretion" as the measure of whether a trial judge's decision concerning the admissibility of expert testimony should be overturned on appeal.

The *Daubert* standard has been hailed as an improvement on the more conservative *Frye* test, which some had disdained as a mere "nose-counting" exercise to establish whether a given theory had gained general acceptance in the particular field at issue. While the *Daubert* standard theoretically allows for a more flexible and fulsome approach to scientific evidence, it will remain to be seen whether courts applying this standard will be able to discharge their oversight responsibilities in a consistent and predictable manner, particularly given the pace of scientific advance. Because the *Daubert* criteria define, or at least describe, a minimum hurdle of credibility that must be overcome, some have cast the guidance reflected in these criteria as an "antidote" to the use of "junk" or, indeed, "adversarial" science in the courtroom. A more nuanced appreciation would suggest that while *Daubert* will help frame, rationalize, and focus the debate concerning the use of scientific and statistical proof in the courtroom, the flexibility of the *Daubert* criteria in terms of their scope and application will continue to provide ample room for the aforementioned battle of the experts.

Probabilistic Techniques: From Jury Selection to Employment Discrimination—The Use and Interpretation of Statistical Significance

Paralleling the increased use of epidemiology and related statistical and probabilistic analysis in toxic tort cases has been a similar rise in the use of statistics and probabilistic techniques in assessing discrimination in the employment context. The case law in this area has developed substantially since the 1970s, beginning with the case of *Castaneda v. Partida* (1977). The heart of these cases lies in an assessment of statistical significance, [11] whereby the court tries to assess whether the difference between the expected and observed results with respect to employment, or, in the case of *Castaneda*, jury selection, can be ascribed to random chance or to other circumstances meriting a legal remedy.

Castaneda: U.S. Courts' Adoption and Interpretation of Statistical Significance

In assessing statistical significance in discrimination cases, U.S. courts have increasingly looked to the notion of standard deviation as set forth in the aforementioned *Castaneda* case, wherein the court examined the jury selection process and noted the underrepresentation of Spanish-surnamed panelists, despite the significance of their numbers in the general population. The court noted that within the relevant sample, Spanish-surnamed jurors composed only 39% of the average jury, despite representing 79% of the general population in the relevant county. The court determined that the difference between the expected and the observed number of Spanish-surnamed panelists was 29 standard deviations and concluded,

> As a general rule for such large samples if the difference between the expected value and the observed number is greater than two or three standard deviations,[12] then the hypothesis (of random chance) would be suspect to a social scientist.[13]

In ensuing years, the basic formulation in the *Castaneda* case has been extended and refined by

[11]Miller and Wilson (1984) say that the result of a statistical test is said to be *significant* if it can be shown that a particular value of the statistic computed in the test is unlikely to have occurred by chance. See also DeGroot and Schervish (2002, pp. 527–530).

[12]Miller and Wilson (1984) provide a working definition of *standard deviation* as a measure of the spread or dispersion of a set of scores, also noting that standard deviation is the square root of the variance. See also DeGroot and Schervish (2002, pp. 197–199).

[13]*Castaneda v. Partida* (1977, p. 496, n. 17).

courts to address issues running the full gamut of discrimination issues, ranging from jury selection to employment.

Employment Discrimination: "Disparate Treatment"

Hazelwood School District v. United States (1977), a "disparate treatment" case, explicitly cited the methodology in *Castaneda*, noting, "If the difference exceeds two or three standard deviations, then the hypothesis that teachers were hired without regard to race would be suspect" (p. 496, n. 17). *Hazelwood* dealt with a situation in which the number of African Americans employed as schoolteachers in St. Louis County was 6%, but during the period at issue, only 15 of the 405 teachers (or 4%) in the Hazelwood district were of African-American descent. The court went on to state that such a statistical disparity could be used to demonstrate a prima facie case of discrimination, thereby shifting the burden of proof to the defendants to prove the absence of discrimination.

It is worth noting that *Hazelwood* dealt with an instance of "disparate treatment" under Title VII of the U.S. Civil Rights Act,[14] whereby the allegation involved an intentional discriminatory practice. With regard to statistical proof, such cases require a higher degree of statistical disparity than the line of cases founded on "disparate impact." The latter group of cases relates to employment practices, such as the administration of a written test, that may serve to disproportionately disqualify a given, otherwise qualified group.

Employment Discrimination: "Disparate Impact"

A seminal example of a case involving disparate impact is *Griggs v. Duke Power* (1971), which dealt with the question of whether the requirement of a high school diploma and the passage of a written IQ test for certain unskilled jobs was a legitimate business tool or a subtle means of discriminating unfairly among applicants. It was established on the basis of census data that 34% of white males in the state had a high school diploma compared with 12% of African Americans, resulting in the disproportionate exclusion of African Americans from these positions. Moreover, prior to the adoption of the new educational requirements, a minimum of 10 years of school in total had sufficed for employment in these jobs. In assessing the situation, the court held that unless the new criteria could be demonstrated to be "job related," the statistically demonstrated "adverse impact" of these requirements was sufficient to support a violation of Title VII of the Civil Rights Act even in the absence of clear discriminatory intent. Lower courts have since followed the reasoning in *Griggs*, using statistically demonstrated adverse impact to invalidate or otherwise require modification of diverse employment tests and admissions criteria.[15] The subjective aspects of demonstrating clear "job relatedness" of the employment criteria have put a significant burden on employers, but, as will be seen, there are signs that courts are seeking a more practical balance between the interests of employers and employees in assessing the merits of these cases.

Current and Future Trends in Probabilistic Techniques and Employment Discrimination Cases

As courts have become increasingly familiar with the use of statistical analysis in the employment field, there is a growing trend toward evaluating the results of the statistical evidence against competing economic concerns. The tests for "job relatedness" or "business necessity" mentioned above are increasingly subject to interdisciplinary scrutiny that seeks to measure the observed statistical disparity against the prevailing economic context. This approach holds that the inquiry in the employment area should not be founded solely on the uncovering of statistical significance but also on an analysis of the economic impact or justification (O'Donnell & Steward, 2005). It may be that in a given context, tests for statistical significance suggest a

[14]Title VII of the U.S. Civil Rights Act of 1964 protects individuals against employment discrimination on the bases of race and color, as well as national origin, sex, and religion.

[15]For example, *EEOC v. Atlas Paper Box Co.* (1989) (citing *Griggs* in holding that the employer must show that the cognitive ability test is related to job performance).

disproportionate impact, either in terms of hiring or discharge, among a given group. However, if such impact is evaluated against the broader trend within an industry, prevailing business conditions, and specific factors concerning the nature of the work at issue, there may be objective economic reasons explaining the observed statistical pattern. Tasks involving heavy lifting might, for instance, be skewed toward men rather than women, given the physical attributes required. Similarly, other less obvious, but valid, reasons for employment selection, such as linguistic abilities, might militate in favor of, or against, a given group, depending on the underlying nature of the task.

The greater sensitivity of courts to evaluating economic factors suggests that statistical benchmarks, such as 2 or 3 standard deviations from the expectation under random chance, are viewed in an increasingly flexible manner, allowing employers full scope to rebut claims in situations where discrimination appears statistically to exist. In this regard, there may be a certain convergence between cases involving disparate treatment and disparate impact in terms of the quantum of statistical proof required and the employers' ability to rebut or otherwise question the statistical thresholds at issue. Moreover, the melding of law, statistics, and economics in this area is indicative of a broader trend favoring the use of interdisciplinary approaches to facilitate or otherwise inform legal decision making in complex cases, whether in the fields of labor law, antitrust, tort law, or intellectual property (Balkin, 1998). This trend will only become more pronounced as courts seek to balance the needs of a dynamic and increasingly global economy reliant on flexible labor markets, diverse industry combinations, and the free flow of information with individual rights and "entitlements."

Probabilistic Techniques and the Use of DNA Evidence in the Courtroom

No area of scientific evidence has commanded more attention in the literature or among lawyers and judges of late than the use of DNA evidence in the courtroom. The literature in this area is voluminous and growing, highlighting both the biological and the mathematical bases underlying the use and presentation of this type of evidence (Weir, 1995). While a detailed examination of this area is beyond the scope of this chapter, several core points can be made to provide the reader with a general framework for how DNA evidence is actually used in the courtroom.

DNA evidence, like other forms of expert testimony, is subject to standards of admissibility, including *Daubert* in the federal courts and the analogous rules in the state courts, as discussed above. As the use of DNA testing is now widely accepted for identifying a perpetrator, the *Daubert* and other similar challenges concerning admissibility often focus on the issues of validity and reliability arising from the specific methodology of the laboratory in question. Such challenges are commonplace and concern the manner in which the material was handled, highlighting, for instance, the scope for contamination or degradation of the DNA sample from undue exposure to bacteria or sunlight. These allegations all essentially focus on whether the samples were treated and analyzed in a manner consistent with the notion of "best practices" and handled pursuant to the relevant protocols for managing and preserving crime scene evidence. The power of DNA evidence and related expert testimony for swaying jurors and the potentially prejudicial effect of admitting DNA testimony that may not conform to best practices have resulted in courts heightening the degree of vigilance they exercise over admissibility.

Even in instances where evidence is admitted, defense counsel will often continue to challenge the sufficiency of the DNA evidence based on the practical pitfalls of collecting, handling, and testing such material. In the 1995 California case involving O. J. Simpson, the famous football player in the United States accused of murdering his wife and her friend, defense counsel repeatedly questioned the manner in which the DNA evidence was handled, going so far as to accuse the Los Angeles Police Department of planting the evidence at the crime scene in order to overcome the otherwise overwhelming probabilities derived from the crime scene DNA implicating Mr. Simpson as the likely perpetrator.

Presentation and Experts

The presentation of DNA evidence proffered to identify an individual in a legal context can require multifaceted expertise involving laboratory techniques, statistics, and principles of molecular biology. Accordingly, issues often surface as to whether a given individual is qualified as an expert to testify on each of these diverse areas. The laboratory technician may not have the background necessary to opine on the statistical significance of the data and its relationship to the background population frequency of such genetic patterns. Similarly, academic experts who are generally familiar with statistical analysis may not have a specific background in forensic typing. As a practical matter, judges have great discretion in assessing the sufficiency of the credentials of the proposed expert(s). Moreover, presentation of the DNA evidence can be, and often is, split among several experts. For instance, a laboratory technician, a statistician, and a forensic scientist, all might testify to ensure that the evidence is supported by an adequate expert foundation in each individual specialty.

DNA Evidence: Probabilities and Matching

It may be useful at this juncture to examine a typical situation involving the identification of a suspect through DNA evidence and the manner in which the scientific and probabilistic findings interact with the judicial context. In a typical situation, material bearing DNA is found at a crime scene in the form of hair, saliva, or some other bodily substance or fluid. To proceed with the DNA analysis, a suspect will be asked for a sample, which will be tested and compared with the forensic sample found at the crime scene.[16] There are diverse ways to test for these matches, involving the comparison of specific points (loci) that indicate a genetic sequence that varies among the members of the population (i.e., a polymorphism), as opposed to other sequences (i.e., monomorphisms) that are common to virtually all members of the population (Kaye & Sensabaugh, 2000, p. 493). The science of DNA identification focuses on polymorphisms to distinguish an individual from the general or relevant population.

On receipt of the results, there is a threshold issue as to whether the findings lead to exclusion or inclusion. If the distinctive genetic patterns of the suspect and the forensic samples taken at the crime scene are clearly inconsistent, the suspect can be excluded without further debate. For exclusionary purposes, if even a single polymorphism differs between suspect and evidence, it will be sufficient to exclude the person as a suspect. If, however, the distinctive patterns between the test and the forensic sample are consistent, then the exercise and interpretation now become one of "including" the suspect. The inquiry changes to one involving the likelihood that such a match could have arisen from other factors, such as random chance within the relevant population, laboratory error, or some other "exculpatory" circumstance. It is at this point that arguments concerning the statistical methodology and the manner in which a statistical "match" can be best described become paramount for the legal process.

In expressing the nature and magnitude of the match, experts and their lawyers will have recourse to various statistical approaches, including those based on likelihood ratios and posterior probabilities. The former compares two alternative hypotheses, such as the likelihood of a laboratory finding a match between two samples containing the defendant's DNA and the same laboratory finding a match based on coincidence from two randomly selected individuals from the population. The posterior ratio puts the likelihood ratio into context by including prior odds. The use of posterior ratios rests on Bayesian analysis intended to demonstrate that the likelihood ratio itself rests on a number of antecedent premises, including, *inter alia*, that the genotype at issue has been correctly identified. Other issues that could be brought in under this type of analysis would involve the nature of the population and subpopulations being

[16]See Bureau of National Affairs (2006) for the proposition that in addition to the scenario described above, DNA found at the crime scene is sometimes matched through comparison with existing DNA databases maintained by the authorities and including samples from known criminals. Such "cold hits" are proving to be an increasingly powerful tool for law enforcement, triggering on the legal side the issues relating to the appropriate statistical characterization of a "match" as described in this section.

compared and the source of the DNA, including whether it could have come from a relative.

The posterior analysis essentially seeks to give a fuller rendering of the context, and, indeed, of the qualifying factors from which the probabilities have been derived. In criminal cases, there tends to be far less reliance on likelihood ratios, and, conversely, more on the posterior approach, particularly since the latter focuses not on the relative strength of the hypothesis but on the probability of the hypothesis itself. As such, it more closely parallels the legal inquiry as to whether in a given context, taking into account all relevant circumstances, suspect X can be deemed to be the perpetrator with the requisite degree of legal "certainty."

DNA Evidence: Probabilities and Presentation

Given the established techniques for DNA analysis and statistical computation, such testimony will, if based on best practices, generally meet the *Daubert* requirements of validity and reliability. Courts will, however, also examine the testimony from the standpoint of whether the probabilities as expressed by a given expert are unduly prejudicial.[17] Such appreciation goes to statements such as "There is only a 1 in 300,000,000 chance that this could have been someone other than the suspect." The hyperbole in this area can sway jurors by blinding them with astronomical odds. Moreover, the presentation of DNA findings sometimes involves use of the "transposition fallacy,"[18] whereby prosecutors equate (a) the "random match probability" of, for instance, finding the genotype in the sample from the individual tested if said individual is selected at random with (b) "the probability that the match is random"—that is, the probability that the individual has been selected at random, given that he or she has the alleged genotype. The former exercise, which essentially starts with the sample result and works backward to the suspect in a type of "transposition" of the conditional probability at issue, will yield a much more favorable result for prosecutors.

As a practical matter, judges will often allow statements based on the transposition fallacy on the assumption that such formulations will be clarified on cross examination. Judges can also issue appropriate clarifying instructions. Some members of the bar have argued that match probabilities should be excluded altogether in favor of a discussion of the frequency with which a specific genotype is present in the relevant population and a related examination of the relative rarity thereof. However, in the present circumstances, the presentation of random match probabilities will continue to be a foundation of expert testimony in this area, with lawyers and their experts seeking to make these concepts as powerful and accessible as possible to their audiences.

Scientific Evidence: Practical Considerations—Attitudes of Judges/Jurors

Regardless of the legal sufficiency and scientific validity of the scientific evidence proffered, such argumentation is destined to collide with the preexisting attitudes of judges and jurors. For instance, lawyers using statistical proof, including epidemiology, to demonstrate causation must assess the extent to which such studies can be used in a compelling manner. Even if the studies cannot generally be used as a legal matter to demonstrate individualized or specific causation as such, there are nevertheless threshold questions as to whether the plaintiff in the case can be perceived to have undergone the type of exposure identified in the populations that are the subject of the epidemiologic studies at issue and whether such exposure is generally considered to be a "cause" of such a disease.

Often it will be the jurors' preconceived notions concerning these threshold issues rather than the scientific argumentation per se that will

---

[17]For example, *Spencer v. Murray* (1994) (appellant claiming "prejudicial injection of astronomical probability ratios").

[18]Browne (1998) says,

> This is not to suggest that criminal courts do not commit the transposition fallacy, for they do, probably most commonly in their interpretation of DNA evidence. In fact, in the criminal literature, the fallacy goes by the name of the "prosecutor's fallacy" because of the recognition that it gives the prosecutor an undue advantage. (p. 451)

See generally Balding and Donnelly (1994).

carry the day. This is particularly true in cases involving risks to which jurors can relate, such as cigarette smoking. In cases involving more esoteric or less well-known risks, there may be enhanced scope to use statistical testimony, provided that it is presented in an accessible and credible manner, to promote understanding or to otherwise affect initial juror perceptions. As a corollary to this last point, it is not always the most rigorous scientific presentation that jurors will find to be the most persuasive. Sometimes, a second-best argument will prove to be more convincing, to the extent that it can be presented in an accessible manner that appeals to what the "receiver of information" feels he or she already knows or senses on some commonsense level. It is, for instance, conceivable that a juror will relate more to the random match probability derived from, or "enhanced" by, the transposition fallacy than to a detailed discussion of Bayesian analysis, with the former conjuring up such colloquial notions as a "needle in a haystack."

Statistics and Probabilistic Evidence: Strategic Considerations

Assuming that lawyers must ideally appeal to the common sense of juries puts a premium on the presentation of evidence, and, indeed, in U.S. courts where witnesses appear, on the presenter himself (or herself). There will be distinct limits concerning the extent to which juries can be educated on complex issues of statistics and probability during the course of a trial. The goal therefore should be to render such concepts relevant to the jury's decision-making process without necessarily convincing the jury that this should be the sole basis of the decision. As a practical matter, it will be difficult for plaintiffs' lawyers to convince jurors to decide issues of medical causation based solely on statistical evidence, whether epidemiological or other. Conversely, it will be difficult for defense lawyers to win complex medical or toxic tort cases on the strength of statistical argumentation alone. It is, however, possible to ensure that such concepts are duly factored into the jury's deliberations in a meaningful and constructive manner.

The selection of the expert is of utmost importance. As mentioned in the discussion of DNA evidence, his (or her) credentials must qualify him as an expert, and, ideally, his appearance and demeanor should inspire confidence. In a manner analogous to using second-best arguments that are sometimes more accessible to the jury, there are times when using a slightly less well-qualified expert may be desirable, to the extent that his demeanor and talent for pedagogical explanation may be more highly developed (Pager, 2005).

U.S. Considerations Versus International Context

It may be useful to compare here the use of experts in the U.S. context against prevailing practices in international jurisdictions, particularly Europe. With regard to the selection of experts in the United States, the points made above are relevant. Expert testimony is highly developed and regulated. Moreover, experts appear and make their points in oral (vive voce) testimony and are subjected to oral cross-examination by the adverse party. This oral presentation of their testimony is in addition to any written submissions that the expert may have made to the court, either in the form of a disclosure statement (i.e., the short synopsis of the testimony) or in the form of a full written expert opinion that is entered into evidence as a trial exhibit. Accordingly, the jury's assessment of the expert as a person assumes an importance commensurate with that of the testimony itself.

This dynamic differs significantly from that found in most European jurisdictions, where expert testimony, at least in civil cases, is adduced only through documentary submissions. The expert need not appear, nor will he or she be subjected to cross-examination. Accordingly, priority is given to finding the most eminent individuals in a given field regardless of their demeanor and ability to explain their views orally in court. The idea of finding a slightly less qualified expert with an attractive demeanor and highly developed pedagogical skills and allowing him to express his views in open court is, for the most part, moot.

There are, however, exceptions to which the international practitioner needs to be alert. For instance, in Spain, a change to the procedural code[19] in 2001 now requires that expert witnesses appear in court to present their views and to defend them under cross-examination from the adverse party. In this regard, then, the Spanish system necessitates due consideration of the expert witness's temperament and demeanor in a manner that is broadly analogous to the U.S. context. Jurisdictions, such as Ireland and the United Kingdom, including its subdivisions, that are rooted in the common-law tradition place a similar emphasis on oral testimony and the related appearance and demeanor of expert witnesses. The international practitioner must therefore be alert to the context in which the evidence is to be presented and to the evolving procedural rules that may apply.

Finally, with regard to the presentation of complex statistical and probabilistic arguments in non-U.S. jurisdictions, it is useful to bear in mind that civil tort cases are generally heard before professional judges rather than juries. This may allow for a heightened degree of sophistication in putting forth the statistical argumentation because the concepts contained therein will be parsed in a systematic manner by a trained jurist. It is, however, worth remembering that judges as well as legal systems differ greatly in their ability, willingness, and overall receptivity to grappling with complex statistical argumentation.

CONCLUSION

Scientific expertise will continue to influence the legal process with ever-growing frequency and scope. As has been seen, statistical and probabilistic proof will have a direct impact on many aspects of legal reasoning and standards of proof whether in the field of employment, toxic torts, or criminal proceedings. The fields of antitrust, environmental law, and intellectual property, not touched on in this chapter due to their vastness, will also provide fertile ground for such analysis. Mindful of the implications of expert testimony, including statistical and probabilistic analysis, for shaping the legal proceedings and, where applicable, the views of jurors, diverse judicial systems, and U.S. courts in particular, have sought to gain control over the integrity of the expert process. In the United States, this has most recently taken the form of the Federal Rules of Evidence and the aforementioned *Daubert* test, which can be viewed as "filtering devices" designed to give courts general benchmarks for evaluating the admissibility of scientific evidence and thereby maintaining control over the process.

Still, the problem of overly "adversarial" science in the courtroom remains. In two post-*Daubert* surveys of the Federal Judicial Center taken among judges and lawyers in 1998 and 1999, respectively, the problem most often cited was that experts abandon objectivity and become advocates for their clients' positions (Krafka, Dunn, Johnson, Cecil, & Miletich, 2002). The problem appears to be well-known and is perhaps endemic to a system founded on the "adversarial process" as a means of "discovering" the truth. As noted, many continental systems have opted for the court-appointed expert to provide the judge with a clear channel for receiving scientific evidence. Certain systems, such as those in France and Brazil, provide for the court-appointed expert to interact with the parties' technical experts, such that all points of view are taken into account but are ultimately synthesized and assessed by the court-appointed expert's final report.

Common-law systems and judges have seen the merits of using a court-appointed expert, but, in practice, have availed themselves of this prerogative with less frequency than their continental-law brethren for fear of upsetting the adversarial dynamic. In a case in the United Kingdom, known as *A & Others v. National Blood Authority* (2001), involving contaminated blood and a potentially groundbreaking interpretation of the European Product Liability Directive (Council Directive 85/374EEC, 1985), Judge Burton, the presiding judge, suggested that medical submissions and testimony be funneled to him through a court-appointed technical advisor. This suggestion was roundly criticized and rejected by counsel for both sides, who saw this proposal as potentially diluting their argumentation and related access to the judge on technical points critical to the case (Brooke & Forester, 2005).

[19]Spanish Code of Civil Procedure (2000) (gives the adverse party, plaintiff or defendant, as the case may be, the right to compel the expert witness to appear and to undergo cross examination).

In the United States, judges have inherent authority to use technical advisors, and, under Federal Rule of Evidence 706, explicit authority to appoint experts on their own motion. Both in *Daubert* and in the aforementioned related case, *General Electric v. Joiner*, members of the U.S. Supreme Court have cited the use of court-appointed experts approvingly and have urged judges to make greater use of this authority. In 1998, the American Association for the Advancement of Science, working under the auspices of the National Conference of Lawyers and Scientists, founded a project known as CASE (Court-Appointed Scientific Experts) to facilitate the identification and selection of court-appointed experts in diverse scientific and technical fields.[20] To date, however, recourse to using court-appointed experts in U.S. courts remains underdeveloped (Runkle, 2005).

Faced with this circumstance, the responsibility for maintaining the integrity of scientific testimony in general, and statistical testimony in particular, is likely to remain with the experts themselves. The expert will be subjected to diverse pressures, stemming from the nature of the court procedure, the attitudes and expectations of the lawyers, and a general desire to "do well." The objectivity to which scientific and statistical data lay claim and their related capacity to influence the legal decision-making process will raise the stakes to an even higher level. Probably the surest safeguard for ensuring the integrity of the testimony in this context is for the expert to understand clearly the nature of the question at issue and the precise manner in which he or she can contribute to its resolution or clarification.

Scope for abuse or undue advocacy often surfaces when the expert is asked to go beyond or to "stretch" not just his or her own expertise but also what the field itself can address. In a series of tobacco cases in the United States during the mid to late 1990s, known generically as medical cost recoupment litigation, whereby the states sought to recover past and projected future costs related to the treatment of "smoking-attributable diseases," statisticians were called on to generate astronomical damages figures amounting to billions of dollars from diverse epidemiological and smoking survey data (Zeger, Wyant, Miller, & Samet, 2000, pp. 309–318). Estimates that were inherently based on conjecture and imputation (i.e., the filling in of missing data), and subject, at a minimum, to the limitations of statistical and probabilistic calculations arising from the biases inherent to the generation of epidemiological studies were offered as precise measures of damage (Rubin, 2000).

It is in such a situation that a type of self-policing is required, whereby statistical experts explain the nature of their expertise and the limits of their findings. Such qualifications are often drowned out in the "heat of battle." However, if the use of probabilistic and statistical analysis in the courtroom is to develop in a manner that (a) reinforces the specialty, (b) fulfills its promise as an analytical tool, (c) maintains its credibility, and (d) contributes to informed judicial decision making without excess, it will doubtless require this type of strong self-awareness on the part of statistical experts regarding the scope, nature, and execution of their mission.

[20]CASE Web site: http://www.aaas.org/spp/case/case.htm

ACKNOWLEDGMENTS

The author wishes to acknowledge the valuable research and editing assistance of Mr. Christopher S. Duncan, Juris Doctor candidate, Washington University School of Law, Saint Louis, Missouri.

REFERENCES

Balding, D. J., & Donnelly, P. (1994, October). The prosecutor's fallacy and DNA evidence. *Criminal Law Review*, 711–721.

Balkin, J. M. (1998). The canons of constitutional law. *Harvard Law Review*, 968–969.

Barkacs, L. L., Browne, M. N., & Williamson, C. L. (2002). The perspectival nature of expert testimony in the United States, England, Korea, and France. *Connecticut Journal of International Law*, *18*, 55–102.

Bernstein, D., & Jackson, J. (2004). The Daubert trilogy in the states. *Jurimetrics Journal*, *44*, 351–366.

Brooke, M., & Forester, I. (2005). The use of comparative law in A & others v. National Blood Authority. In D. Fairgrieve (Ed.), *Product liability in comparative perspective* (pp. 13–41). Cambridge, UK: Cambridge University Press.

Browne, K. (1998). The strangely persistent "transposition fallacy": Why statistically significant evidence of discrimination may not be significant. *Labor Lawyer*, *14*, 451.

Bureau of National Affairs. (2006). *Expert Evidence Report, 6*(2), 47.

Carruth, R., & Goldstein, B. (2000). Relative risk greater than two in proof of causation in toxic tort litigation. *Jurimetrics Journal*, *41*, 195.

Collie, F. J. (2006). A tale of two standards: Regulatory standards and general causation in toxic torts litigation. In C. Cwik & J. L. North (Eds.), *Scientific evidence review, Monograph 7* (pp. 71–85). Chicago: American Bar Association.

Council Directive 85/374EEC, on the approximation of the laws, regulations, and administrative provisions of the Member States concerning liability for defective products. (1985, 25 July).

DeGroot, M. H., & Schervish, M. J. (2002). *Probability & statistics* (3rd ed.). Reading, MA: Addison-Wesley.

Eder, E., & Garg, S. (2006). Selecting and working with scientific and technical experts. In C. Cwik & J. L. North (Eds.), *Scientific evidence review, Monograph 7* (p. 13). Chicago: American Bar Association.

Gordis, L. (1999). Scientific methodology and epidemiology. *Kansas Journal of Law and Public Policy*, *9*, 89, 94–96.

Green, M. D., Freedman, D. M., & Gordis, L. (2000). Reference guide on epidemiology. In J. Cecil (Ed.), *reference manual on scientific evidence* (2nd ed., pp. 363–369, 389, 395). Washington, DC: Federal Judicial Center.

Gutheil, T. (1999). A confusion of tongues: Competence, insanity, psychiatry, and the law. *Psychiatric Services*, *50*, 767.

Guzelian, C. (2006). Did Daubert rid courtroom of advocacy science? In C. Cwik & J. L. North (Eds.), *Scientific evidence review, Monograph 7* (pp. 38, 44). Chicago: American Bar Association.

Kaye, D. H., & Sensabaugh, G. F., Jr.. (2000). Reference guide on DNA evidence. In J. Cecil (Ed.), *Reference manual on scientific evidence* (2nd ed., p. 493). Washington, DC: Federal Judicial Center.

Krafka, C., Dunn, M. A., Johnson, M. T., Cecil, J. S., & Miletich, D. (2002). Judge and attorney experiences, practices, and concerns regarding expert testimony in federal civil trials. *Psychology, Public Policy, and Law*, *8*(3), 309–332.

Miller, P., & Wilson, M. (1984). *A dictionary of social science methods*. Hoboken, NJ: Wiley.

O'Donnell, S. W., & Steward, D. (2005). Evaluating the statistical and economic significance of statistical evidence in employment discrimination. *Expert Evidence Report*, *5*(5), 117–119.

Pager, C. (2005). Blind justice, colored truths, and the veil of ignorance. *Willamette Law Review*, *41*, 413.

Rubin, D. (2000). Statistical issues in the estimation of the causal effects of smoking due to the conduct of the tobacco industry. In J. Gastwirth (Ed.), *Statistical science in the courtroom* (pp. 321–351). New York: Springer.

Runkle, D. (2005). Court-appointed scientific experts: Providing objective scientific evidence to the judiciary [Monograph]. *Scientific Evidence Review*, *7*, 19–38.

Santoro, F. H. (1995). Courts must scrutinize use of epidemiology in proving causation. *Legal Backgrounder*, *10*, 9–12.

Spanish Code of Civil Procedure. (2000).

Von Clausewitz, C. (1982). *On war*. Penguin Books.

Weir, B. (1995). A bibliography for the use of DNA in human identification. In B. Weir (Ed.), *Human identification: The use of DNA markers* (pp. 179–213). New York: Springer.

Zeger, S. L., Wyant, T., Miller, L. S., & Samet, J. (2000). Statistical testimony on damages in Minnesota v. Tobacco Industry. In J. Gastwirth (Ed.), *Statistical science in the courtroom* (pp. 303, 309–318). New York: Springer.

A & Others v. National Blood Authority, No. 1998 A458 (2001).

Castaneda v. Partida, 430 U.S. 482, 496 (1977).

Daubert v. Merrell Dow Pharmaceuticals, 727 F. Supp. 570, 572 (S.D. Cal. 1989), affŠd, 951 F.2d 1128 (9th Cir. 1991), vacated on other grounds, 509 U.S. 579 (1993).

EEOC v. Atlas Paper Box Co., 868 F.2d 1487, 1490 (6th Cir. 1989).

Frye v. United States, 293 F. 1013 (D.C. Cir. 1924).

General Electric v. Joiner, 522 U.S. 136 (1997).

Glastetter v. Novartis Pharmaceutical Corporation, 252 F.3d 986, 992 (8th Cir. 2001).

Globetti v. Sandoz Pharmaceutical Corporation, 111 F. Supp.2d 1174, 1179 (N.D. Ala. 2000).

Griggs v. Duke Power, 401 U.S. 424 (1971).

Hazelwood School District v. United States, 433 U.S. 299 (1977).

Lockheed Litigation Cases, 23 Cal. Rptr. 3d 762 (Cal. Ct. App. 2005).

Norris v. Baxter Healthcare Corporation, 397 F.3d 878, 882 (10th Cir. 2005).

Siharath v. Sandoz Pharmaceutical Corporation, 131 F. Supp.2d 1347, 1356 (N.D. Ga. 2001).

Spencer v. Murray, 18 F.3d 229, 232 (4th Cir. 1994).

About the Editor

Tamás Rudas is Professor of Statistics and Head of the Department of Statistics of the Faculty of Social Sciences, Eötvös Loránd University (ELTE) in Budapest and Director of the Program in Survey Statistics. Currently, he also serves as Dean of the Faculty. He is also Academic Director of the TARKI Social Research Institute. He has held several visiting appointments in the United States, Germany, Austria, Slovenia, and Poland. He is General Secretary of the European Association of Methodology. His main research area is statistics and its applications in the social sciences, especially the analysis of categorical data. Among other topics, he has contributed to the development of methods of measuring model fit and to the theory of marginal models. He has published in many theoretical and methodological journals, including *The Annals of Statistics, Journal of the Royal Statistical Society, Sociological Methodology, Communications in Statistics, Journal of Educational and Behavioral Statistics,* and *Quality and Quantity*. He is also the author of *Odds Ratios in the Analysis of Contingency Tables* (Sage, 1998) and *Probability Theory: A Primer* (Sage, 2004) and of books in Hungarian, including one (now in its second edition) on opinion polls. Professor Rudas holds a PhD in mathematics (probability theory and mathematical statistics) from the Eötvös Loránd University and a Doctor of Science degree from the Hungarian Academy of Science.

About the Editor

ABOUT THE CONTRIBUTORS

Basil C. Bitas has substantial experience in international legal and business matters, having been both in-house counsel to the Philip Morris Group of Companies in Lausanne, Switzerland, and Managing Partner of the law offices of the U.S. firm Shook, Hardy, & Bacon LLP in Geneva. The nature of his practice has involved intensive interaction with the legal systems, commercial practices, cultures, customs, and citizens of North America, Europe, the Middle East, and Asia. The latter region became a subspecialty of his practice, with particular emphasis on Korea, Japan, and China. His practice background encompasses extensive experience with complex litigation, particularly product liability issues, where he developed a specialty in the use and interpretation of medical and economic statistics in the development and presentation of legal argumentation. More recently, he has been a visiting professor at the Business School of Lausanne and the law faculty of the University of Fribourg in Switzerland as well as a guest speaker at the law faculties of the Catholic University and the Fundação Getulio Vargas in Rio de Janeiro and the Federal University in Porto Alegre, Brazil. He holds bachelor's degrees in history and economics from Brown University in Providence, Rhode Island, having graduated Magna Cum Laude and Phi Beta Kappa in 1981. He also holds a Juris Doctor degree (1987) Cum Laude from Georgetown University Law Center in Washington, D.C., and maintains active bar memberships in the State of New York and Washington, D.C.

Chayan Chakrabarti is at the University of New Mexico. His research interests include artificial intelligence, machine learning, and emergent computing. He was a staff research assistant in the Space Data Systems (ISR-3) group at Los Alamos National Laboratory, where he designed machine-learning algorithms for object recognition in satellite images. He holds a master's degree in computer science from the University of New Mexico and a bachelor's degree in computer engineering from the University of Mumbai (Bombay), India.

Philip Dawid is Professor of Statistics at Cambridge University. From 1989 to 2007, he was Pearson Professor of Statistics at University College London. He is a fellow of the Royal Statistical Society, which has awarded him the Guy Medal in bronze and in silver; elected fellow of the Institute of Mathematical Statistics; elected member of the International Statistical Institute; and member of the Organising Committee for the Valencia International Meetings on Bayesian Statistics. He has served as editor of *Journal of the Royal Statistical Society Series B, Biometrika,* and *Bayesian Analysis* and as president of the International Society for Bayesian Analysis. His research focuses on the foundations of statistics, with emphasis on the Bayesian approach. His coauthored book *Probabilistic Networks and Expert Systems* (1999) won the 2002 DeGroot Prize. He is interested in the logical problems of structuring legal evidence and led an international research project applying Bayesian networks to complex cases of forensic identification from DNA profiles. He recently directed a multidisciplinary research program, Evidence, Inference and Enquiry, at University College London.

Richard A. Derrig, PhD, is President of OPAL Consulting LLC of Providence, Rhode Island, providing research and regulatory support to the property/casualty insurance industry. Prior to forming OPAL in 2004, he held various positions with the Automobile Insurers Bureau (AIB) and the Insurance Fraud Bureau (IFB) of Massachusetts for over 27 years, retiring as senior Vice President of AIB and Vice President, Research of IFB. He was a visiting scholar during 2004–2007 in the Department of Insurance and Risk Management at the Wharton School, University of Pennsylvania and was an adjunct professor for spring 2006. He has had a career-long affinity with probability theory, beginning with his doctoral thesis in mathematics at Brown University, on ergodic theory and operator algebras, and continuing with papers on insurance finance and economics, applications of fuzzy set theory, and, currently, predictive modeling or data mining, published in *The Journal of Risk and Insurance, North American Actuarial Journal, Proceedings of the Casualty Actuarial Society, Risk Management and Insurance Review*, and others.

Wilco H. M. Emons is an assistant professor at the Department of Methodology and Statistics, Faculty of Social Sciences, Tilburg University, the Netherlands. His main scientific interests cover psychometric and measurement issues in psychological assessment, including test development, (non)parametric item response theory models, person-fit analysis, detection and diagnosis of aberrant response behavior, and measurement in medical and health psychology. His work has appeared in *Applied Psychological Measurement, Journal of Psychosomatic Research, Multivariate Behavioral Research*, and *Psychological Methods*. He holds a PhD from the University of Tilburg, The Netherlands.

Ad Feelders is an assistant professor at the Department of Information and Computing Sciences of Utrecht University in The Netherlands. He has worked as a consultant for a data-mining company, where he was in charge of projects for banks and insurance companies. Before coming to Utrecht, he was an assistant professor at the Department of Economics of Tilburg University. He has published several articles on data mining and credit scoring in international conference proceedings and journals. He is a member of the editorial board of the *International Journal of Intelligent Systems in Accounting, Finance and Management*.

Edward W. Frees is a professor of business and statistics at the University of Wisconsin–Madison and is holder of the Assurant Health Insurance Professorship of Actuarial Science. He is a fellow of both the Society of Actuaries and the American Statistical Association. He has published two books, *Data Analysis Using Regression Models* (1996) and *Longitudinal and Panel Data: Analysis and Applications for the Social Sciences* (2004). He has served as editor of the *North American Actuarial Journal* and is currently an associate editor for *Insurance: Mathematics and Economics*. His research interests include actuarial science, regression, and modeling of complex data sets.

Herwig Friedl is a professor of statistics at the Graz University of Technology, Austria. Since 2004 he has been the editor of *Austrian Journal of Statistics*, and since 2006 he additionally serves as coeditor of *Statistical Modelling: An International Journal*. Currently, he is also the secretary of the Statistical Modelling Society. His recent research interest is in generalized linear models with random effects, and he has published his work in *Biometrics, Computational Statistics, Applied Statistics*, and *Environmetrics*, among others.

Chas Friedman was a professor of mathematics at the University of Texas–Austin. His early interests included mandolin building, tuba playing, and mathematics. He decided on the latter, attending the Graduate School at Princeton, which resulted in a PhD in 1971. He spent two years as an instructor at the Massachusetts Institute of Technology, and then went to the University of Texas–Austin in 1973. His professional interests included mathematical physics, differential equations, and probability, and he published articles on these subjects and others (e.g., number theory). He resided in the Texas Hill

Country near San Marcos and Wimberley with his wife, five dogs, six cats, two miniature goats, and a pot-bellied pig. In his spare time, he played various instruments, did woodworking and made jewelry, played poker with the local gamblers, and thought about mathematics and its applications. Professor Friedman passed away before this book went to press.

Mauro Gasparini is a professor of statistics at Politecnico di Torino, and he has been teaching engineers since 1999. From 1996 to 1999, he was a senior statistician at Novartis Pharma, Basel, working in PK/PD modeling, Phase I and Phase II trials, and pharmacoepidemiology and offering statistical consulting to production. From 1992 to 1996, he taught statistics at Purdue University as a visiting assistant professor. He has been consulting with Novartis Pharma in Basel and in Milan, Schering Berlin, RAI (the Italian public television), San Raffaele in Milan, and the Istituto Tumori Toscano in Florence. He has received grants from the Italian Ministry of Research and the European Commission. His main publications include papers in *The Annals of Statistics, Biometrics*, and *Journal of Statistical Planning and Inference*, among others. He received his PhD in statistics in 1992 at The University of Michigan, where his advisor was Michael Woodroofe.

Oded Goldreich is a professor of mathematics and computer science at the Weizmann Institute of Science (Israel), where he is the incumbent of the Meyer W. Weisgal Professorial Chair. He is a corresponding fellow of the Bavarian Academy of Sciences and Humanities. He was a postdoctoral fellow at the Massachusetts Institute of Techonology's Laboratory for Computer Science from 1983 to 1986. He is the author of the book *Modern Cryptography, Probabilistic Proofs and Pseudorandomness* (1999) and the two-volume work *Foundations of Cryptography* (2001 and 2004). He is the editor of *Journal of Cryptology, Computational Complexity*, and *SIAM Journal on Computing* and was an invited speaker at various conferences, including the International Congress of Mathematicians (ICM), 1994, and the Crypto97 conference. He received BA, MSc, and DSc degrees in computer science at the Technion–Israel Institute of Technology in 1980, 1982, and 1983, respectively.

Siegfried Hörmann is a scientific assistant at the Institute of Statistics, Graz University of Technology. In the near future, he will hold an appointment as an assistant professor at the University of Utah. His main research interests are probability theory, time-series analysis, and applied statistics. He is especially interested in the asymptotic theory of dependent random processes. He has published in *Journal of Theoretical Probability, Probability and Mathematical Statistics, Statistics and Probability Letters*, among others. He finished his PhD under the supervision of Prof. István Berkes in November 2006.

Jee-Seon Kim is Associate Professor of Quantitative Methods in the Department of Educational Psychology at the University of Wisconsin–Madison. Her research interests concern the development and application of quantitative methods in education and the social sciences, especially focusing on multilevel models and other latent variable models; methods for modeling change, learning, and human development using longitudinal data; categorical data analysis; and issues related to omitted variables, test equating, and school effectiveness. Her scholarly work has been published in *Psychometrika, Multivariate Behavioral Research, Journal of Educational Measurement, British Journal of Mathematical and Statistical Psychology, Educational Measurement: Issues and Practice, Applied Psychological Measurement*, and *Psychological Methods*. She received the Outstanding Dissertation Award for Quantitative Methods from the American Education Research Association in 2002 and was selected as a fellow by the National Academy of Education and Spencer Foundation in 2004.

Igor Kopylov is an assistant professor at the Department of Economics, University of California, Irvine. He is also affiliated with the Institute of Mathematical Behavioral Sciences. He has done research mainly in decision theory. In his doctoral thesis, he studied the extent to which subjective probabilities are used under Knightian ambiguity. More recently, he has focused on modeling choice in the presence of costly emotions, such as temptation and guilt. He has published in *Journal of Economic Theory*. He received his PhD in Economics at the University of Rochester in 2003 under the supervision of Larry Epstein.

Peter M. Lee has recently retired from the Department of Mathematics in the University of York, United Kingdom, after 33 years (but is still there from time to time). Before that, he was a fellow of Peterhouse, Cambridge. His main interests are in Bayesian statistics and the history of statistics. He is the author of *Bayesian Statistics: An Introduction* (now in its third edition).

Michael Anthony Lewis is an associate professor at the Stony Brook University School of Social Welfare and visiting professor at the Hunter College School of Social Work. His main areas of interest are poverty/inequality, civic participation, and (recently) the environment. He is the coauthor of *Economics for Social Workers* and the coeditor of *The Ethics and Economics of the Basic Income Guarantee*. His work has also appeared in *The Journal of Sociology and Social Welfare, The Journal of Socio-Economics, Review of Social Economy, The Journal of Poverty, Social Work in Health Care, Rutgers School of Law Journal of Law and Urban Policy*, and *International Journal of Environment, Workplace, and Employment.*

Nicholas T. Longford is the Director of SNTL, a statistical research and consulting company in Reading, England. Previously, until 2004, he was a senior research fellow in statistics at De Montfort University, Leicester, England. His areas of specialization are multilevel analysis, missing data, small-area estimation, and model uncertainty. He has several publications in *Journal of the Royal Statistical Society, Survey Methodology, Statistics in Medicine, Computational Statistics and Data Analysis*, and *Psychometrika.* He is the author of three monographs, *Random Coefficient Models* (1993), *Models for Uncertainty in Educational Testing* (1995), and *Missing Data and Small-Area Estimation* (2005). He was the first Campion Fellow, an award received for collaboration between academic and official statistics (2000–2002). He is a former president of the Princeton-Trenton Chapter of the American Statistical Association.

George Luger has been a professor in the University of New Mexico Computer Science Department since 1979. George Luger had a five-year postdoctoral research appointment at the Department of Artificial Intelligence of the University of Edinburgh in Scotland, where he worked on several early expert systems, participated in development and testing of the Prolog computer language, and carried out research on the computational modeling of human problem-solving performance. At the University of New Mexico, George Luger has also been made a professor in the Psychology and Linguistics Departments, reflecting his interdisciplinary research and teaching in these areas. His most recent research, supported by the National Science Foundation, is in diagnostic reasoning, where he has developed stochastic models, mostly in an extended form of Bayesian belief networks. His book *Cognitive Science* was published in 1994. His other book, *Artificial Intelligence: Structures and Strategies for Complex Problem Solving* (2005), is now in its fifth edition. His two master's degrees are in pure and applied mathematics. He received his PhD from the University of Pennsylvania in 1973, with a dissertation focusing on the computational modeling of human problem-solving performance in the tradition of Allen Newell and Herbert Simon.

Julia Mortera is a professor of statistics at Università Roma Tre and director of the PhD program in "Statistical Methodology for Economics and Business." Her current research interests are in probabilistic expert systems for analyzing complex forensic DNA identification cases, including paternity testing and DNA mixtures, and in object-oriented Bayesian networks and their applications. Her publications have appeared in *Biometrika, Forensic Science International, Theoretical Population*

Biology, Journal of the Royal Statistical Society Series B, Journal of the American Statistical Association, Scandinavian Journal of Statistics, Journal of Statistical Planning and Inference, Management Science, Bayesian Analysis, International Statistical Review, TEST, and *Uncertainty in Artificial Intelligence*. She is an associate editor of *Bayesian Analysis*. She was the principal scientific organizer of the 5th International Conference on Forensic Statistics and is a member of the Organising Committee for the International Conference on Forensic Inference and Statistics. She has coordinated research grants from EU, MIUR, and CNR and was local coordinator for the DNA Forensic Research Interchange Grant of the Leverhume Trust.

Anthony O'Hagan is a professor of statistics at the University of Sheffield, United Kingdom. He is a fellow of the Royal Statistical Society and has served on the Society's Council and Research Section. His research is on the methodology and applications of Bayesian statistics. On the methodological side, his principal areas of active research are in the elicitation of expert judgments and in characterizing the uncertainty in mechanistic process models (such as models of climate, aero-engines, proteins, or hydrology). His applied work is wide-ranging, including water supply systems, auditing, and archaeology, but most recently, it has focused on health economics. Tony has published in most of the leading statistics journals, as well as journals in other fields. He has also written or cowritten six books. *Bayesian Inference* (Volume 2b in Kendall's *Advanced Theory of Statistics*, 2006; coauthor Jonathan Forster) is one of the leading graduate texts in the field. His latest book, *Uncertain Judgements* (2007; seven coauthors), is the most systematic and comprehensive text on elicitation of expert probability judgments to date.

Krzysztof Ostaszewski is Actuarial Program Director and a professor of mathematics at Illinois State University in Normal, Illinois. His main areas of research are asset-liability management for insurance enterprises and other financial intermediaries, and connections between microeconomics, especially price theory, and actuarial science, insurance, and investments. He is a chartered financial analyst, a member of the American Academy of Actuaries, and a fellow of the Society of Actuaries. He was a Fulbright Research Fellow in 1995 and a Fulbright Senior Specialist in 2003–2004. He received, jointly with Richard Derrig, the 2005 Mehr Award of the American Risk and Insurance Association. He also won the Hardigree Award of the Western Risk and Insurance Association for the best research paper published in 2003 in *Journal of Insurance Issues*. He has authored six research monographs published by the American Mathematical Society, Society of Actuaries, Elsevier, and Wydawnictwa Naukowo-Techniczne in Poland; as well as several other books, including five volumes of poetry. His research works in mathematics have appeared in journals such as the *Proceedings of the American Mathematical Society, Forum Mathematicum*, and *Journal of Mathematical Analysis and Applications*. His works in economics appeared in *American Economic Review* and *Journal of Business*. His research in actuarial science has been published in *The Journal of Risk and Insurance, North American Actuarial Journal, Proceedings of the Casualty Actuarial Society, Journal of Insurance Issues*, and other journals. He has worked in asset-liability management and modeling, as well as investment management, at Hartford Life, Providian Capital Management, and his private consulting practice. He holds a PhD in mathematics from the University of Washington in Seattle.

Philippa Pattison is a professor in the Department of Psychology and President of the Academic Board at the University of Melbourne. Her research is focused on the development of statistical models for networks and on network-based social processes and on applications of these models to a diverse range of phenomena. Recent publications have appeared in journals such as *Sociological Methodology, American Journal of Sociology, Social Networks, and Organization Science*. She is also a contributor to *Models and Methods in Social Network Analysis* and to *Dictionary of Economics*. Philippa was elected a fellow of the Academy of Social Sciences in Australia in 1994.

Craig G. Rennie is an associate professor of finance in the Sam M. Walton College of Business, University of Arkansas, where he holds the appointment of Brewer Professor of Business/Financial Markets. He has authored numerous scholarly articles in finance and has published or has forthcoming papers in *The Journal of Business, Journal of Financial Research, The Financial Review, European Financial Management*, and *Southern Business and Economic Journal*. He has served as reviewer for three peer-reviewed journals and presented cutting-edge finance research at international, national, and regional conferences. He currently teaches applied portfolio management at the graduate and undergraduate levels, consults in the investments industry, and is faculty advisor for the third oldest and one of the largest student-managed investment funds in the world. His students regularly outperform the S&P 500 while managing a large portfolio of stocks, bonds, funds, and derivatives. He holds a PhD in finance from the University of Oregon.

Garry Robins is an associate professor in the Department of Psychology, School of Behavioural Science at the University of Melbourne, Australia. His research concentrates on the development of social network methodologies and their application in a wide number of empirical projects. His research has won awards from the Psychometric Association and the American Psychological Association. He is a Linton Freeman Award winner for significant contributions to the scientific study of social structure. He is the editor of *Journal of Social Structure* and a member of the Board of the International Network for Social Network Analysis. Recent publications have appeared in journals such as *Sociological Methodology, American Journal of Sociology*, and *Social Networks*.

Maria Piera Rogantin is currently Associate Professor of Statistics in the Department of Mathematics at the University of Genoa, where she has major responsibilities for the Mathematical Statistics and Information Processing program. She has taught a vast range of statistics and probability courses for undergraduate degrees, master's degrees, and training courses. Her research interest concerns the investigation of theoretical problems and the construction of statistical and probabilistic models. She has worked in design of experiments, survival analysis, time series, multivariate analysis, and survey analysis. Various consulting projects allowed the applications of her results in industry, psychometrics, medicine, meteorology, and e-consulting. Her methodological research uses mathematical theory developed in nonstatistical research framework for statistical modeling, in particular differential geometry for information geometry and commutative algebra for algebraic statistics. She has a degree in mathematics, summa cum laude, from the University of Genoa.

Rudi Seljak works as Head of the Department for Sampling and Survey Methodology at the Statistical Office of the Republic of Slovenia. His background is mathematics, and he has theoretical and practical experience in the field of survey sampling. He has actively taken part in many international conferences and published in this area. He was also a member of the program committee of the European Conference on Quality in Survey Statistics, Cardiff, 2006. He has a BSc in mathematics from the Faculty of Mathematics, University Ljubljana.

Nicholas Shackel is James Martin Research Fellow in Theoretical Ethics at the Future of Humanity Institute, Faculty of Philosophy and James Martin 21st Century School, University of Oxford. Dr. Shackel is a philosopher. His interests include ethics, epistemology, philosophy of mind, philosophy of mathematics, and logic. He has conducted research on the relations between practical and theoretical reason, and paradoxes, including paradoxes of rational decision, philosophy of probability, intentionality, and deontic logic. His publications include papers in *Analysis*, *British Journal for the Philosophy of Science*, *Erkenntnis*, *Metaphilosophy*, and *Philosophy of Science and Mind*.

Klaas Sijtsma is Professor of Methodology of Psychological Research at Tilburg University, Tilburg, The Netherlands. He is Head of the Department of Methodology and Statistics, Faculty of Social

Sciences, Tilburg University, and also Chair of the Committee on Psychological Testing in The Netherlands (COTAN) of the NIP, the Dutch professional association of psychologists. Dr. Sijtsma's scientific interest concentrates on the measurement of individual differences with respect to psychological constructs. His research covers topics such as reliability of measurement and scalability of items, theoretical properties and goodness-of-fit investigation of item response models, person-fit analysis, item selection, models for cognitive processes underlying item responses, analysis of missing item scores, and detection of outliers. Dr. Sijtsma is a member of the editorial boards of *Applied Psychological Measurement* and *Psychometrika.* He has published in *Applied Psychological Measurement, British Journal of Mathematical and Statistical Psychology, Multivariate Behavioral Research, Psychological Methods,* and *Psychometrika.* He is the coauthor of two textbooks, one on psychological test theory and the other on nonparametric item response theory. He has a PhD from the University of Groningen, The Netherlands.

Michael Sobel is a professor at Columbia University. He has published extensively in the social sciences and statistics and is a past editor of *Sociological Methodology.* His current interests include causal inference, especially when interference is present, as in neighborhood effects, and methods of election forecasting.

Klaus G. Troitzsch has been a professor of computer applications in the social sciences at the University of Koblenz-Landau since 1986. His main interests in teaching and research are social science methodology and, especially, modeling and simulation in the social sciences. He was among the signatories of the European Social Simulation Association (ESSA) and acts as its treasurer and webmaster. He has been involved in several international projects, for example, those devoted to curriculum development in social science methodology, during which he organized summer schools, particularly in social simulation, which continue to be offered in close cooperation with Nigel Gilbert, University of Surrey, United Kingdom. Current projects are devoted to analyzing traffic route decisions, to microsimulation analysis of the marriage between different ethnic groups in New Zealand, and to the simulation of emerging norms in social systems. He is author, coauthor, and coeditor of a number of books on simulation, has authored several articles on social simulation, and organized or co-organized many national and international conferences on social simulation.

Nancy Brandon Tuma is a professor of sociology at Stanford University and was the 2003–2005 Director of Stanford's Program on Urban Studies. She is a leading sociological methodologist who has focused primarily on models and methods for studying change. In 1994, she was awarded the Lazarsfeld award for her contributions to sociological methodology. She has served as editor of *Sociological Methodology* and also as associate editor of *Journal of the American Statistical Association.* Best known as the coauthor of *Social Dynamics: Models and Methods* (1984), a pioneering book on event history analysis, she has also developed models for diffusion processes that are extensions of event history models. In addition, she has published studies of life careers and social inequalities in the United States, Germany, China, Poland, the Soviet Union, and various countries formerly part of the Soviet Union. Her primary research interest currently is the impact of the transition from socialism on people's life careers. She recently coauthored an article on household power and decision making of married women in Tajikistan. She has a BA with distinction in mathematics and chemistry from Cornell University, an MA in biochemistry from the University of California at Berkeley, and a PhD in sociology from Michigan State University.

Vasja Vehovar is a professor of statistics at the Faculty of Social Sciences, University of Ljubljana, Slovenia. He teaches courses on Sampling, Survey Methodology, and Information Society. He has been a survey sampling consultant for various academic, commercial, and official surveys and also serves as a member of the Methods Group of the European Social Survey (ESS). He has published chapters in monographs of leading publishers and also published scholarly articles in leading journals such as *Journal of Official Statistics* and *Journal of the American Statistical Association.* In addition, he is developing the WebSM portal (http://www.websm.org) that is devoted to Web survey methodology and was the coordinator of the corresponding EU framework project. Since 1996, he has been the principal investigator of the Research on the Internet in Slovenia project (http://www.ris.org), which is today the leading source for information society research in Slovenia.

Jeffrey M. Wooldridge is University Distinguished Professor of Economics at Michigan State University, where he has taught since 1991. He previously taught at the Massachusetts Institute of Technology. He is a fellow of the Econometric Society and of *Journal of Econometrics.* His other awards include the Plura Scripset award from Econometric Theory and the Sir Richard Stone prize from *Journal of Applied Econometrics.* He has also served on several editorial boards, including as editor of *Journal of Business and Economic Statistics.* He has written chapters for the *Handbook of Econometrics* and the *Handbook of Applied Econometrics.* He is the author of *Introductory Econometrics: A Modern Approach* (third edition, 2006) and *Econometric Analysis of Cross Section and Panel Data* (2002). He received his bachelor of arts, with majors in computer science and economics, from the University of California, Berkeley, and his doctorate in economics from the University of California, San Diego.

Matka Zaletel works as Director of the Section for General Methodology and Standards at the Statistical Office of the Republic of Slovenia. She has a long theoretical and practical experience in sampling surveys and in the field of quality of statistical data. She has also been involved in many infrastructural projects at the Statistical Office of the Republic of Slovenia. She has actively participated in many international conferences related to official statistics and published in these areas. Her background is mathematics (she has a BSc from the Faculty of Mathematics, University of Ljubljana), and she received a postgraduate diploma in Social Science Data Analysis at the University of Essex, United Kingdom.

INDEX